Charles R. McFeeters
Credit Manager

DUFFERIN CONCRETE PRODUCTS GROUP
304 The East Mall
Islington, Ontario   M9B 6C8

Office 239-2961
Residence 827-5920

MECHANICS'
LIENS
IN CANADA

FOURTH EDITION

by

DOUGLAS N. MACKLEM, Q.C.

and

DAVID I. BRISTOW, Q.C.

of the Ontario Bar

Chapter 14 on the Law of Construction Privileges
in Quebec
by

LEONARD W. FLANZ

of the Quebec Bar

1978
THE CARSWELL COMPANY LIMITED
Toronto, Canada

1st Edition, 1951 by R.W. Macaulay and H.M. Bruce
2nd Edition, 1962 by D.N. Macklem and D.I. Bristow
3rd Edition, 1972 by D.N. Macklem and D.I. Bristow
4th Edition, 1978 by D.N. Macklem and D.I. Bristow

Canadian Cataloguing in Publication Data

Macklem, Douglas N., 1927-
    Mechanics' liens in Canada

First ed. by R.W. Macaulay and H.M. Bruce,
published in 1951 under title: Handbook on
Canadian mechanics' liens.

Includes indexes.
ISBN 0-459-32170-6

1. Mechanics' liens — Canada. 2. Mechanics' liens
— Canada — Forms. I. Bristow, David I., 1931 —
II. Macaulay, Robert W., 1921 — Handbook on
Canadian mechanics' liens. III. Title.

KE930.M32 1978   346'.71'024   C78-001540-1

Dedicated
to
Roma and Suzanne

PREFACE

The time span between previous editions of our text was approximately 10 years but this fourth edition appears only six years after the third edition as a result of the number of important cases decided in this period and a great number of amendments to the various provincial acts.

Part of the case law concerns the growing tendency in the Courts of every jurisdiction to no longer accept all contracts at face value or to enforce those contracts without due regard to the surrounding circumstances. Principles such as unreasonableness and unconscionability are beginning to challenge those of precedent and predictability, and some of the most firmly established rules are now being questioned.

We are seeing the now familiar reminder of the Honourable Mr. Justice Laskin, in the recent *Northern Electric Company* decision in the Supreme Court of Canada, that the form of the transaction will not be allowed to mask the substance being heeded consciously or subconsciously by more and more jurists.

Nowhere is this trend becoming more evident than in the field of law relating to building contracts and mechanics' liens, and we will watch with great interest the developments of the next decade.

Our thanks to Mr. Leonard W. Flanz of Montreal for his revision to Chapter 14 on the law of construction privileges in the province of Quebec.

Finally, we would like to acknowledge the kind assistance and support of Mr. R. B. Moldaver, Mr. J. E. G. Gilgan and Mr. B. L. Rochester, P.Eng.

Toronto, September 1978.   D. N. Macklem
                                                 D. I. Bristow

TABLE OF CONTENTS

CHAPTER 3

THE LIEN CLAIMANT

CHAPTER 4

RIGHTS AND DUTIES OF THE OWNER

CHAPTER 5

THE MORTGAGEE

CHAPTER 6

OBTAINING A LIEN

CHAPTER 7

LOSS OR DISCHARGE OF LIEN

CHAPTER 8

PRIORITIES

CHAPTER 9

THE TRUST FUND

CHAPTER 10

JURISDICTION

CHAPTER 11

PRACTICE BEFORE TRIAL

CHAPTER 12

PRACTICE AFTER TRIAL

CHAPTER 13

LIENS ON CHATTELS

CHAPTER 14

THE LAW OF CONSTRUCTION PRIVILEGES IN QUEBEC

TABLE OF CASES

A

B

C

F

G

TABLE OF CASES

Mc

N

O

P

S

T

W

1

Introduction

§1 History and Purpose of The Mechanics' Lien Act.

The mechanics' lien was unknown to English common law and comes to us, by way of the United States, out of early Roman law. The protection of a lien against the land benefited by labour and materials supplied, given to the supplier of such labour and material, is found in the law of all European countries governed by the civil code. In North America, the Civil Codes of the State of Louisiana and the Province of Quebec which are based on Roman law also contain provisions for workmen's liens against land. The law of England contained no such provision and does not to this date. However, the common law jurisdictions of North America, commencing with Maryland in 1791, have progressively enacted mechanics' lien legislation and today there are Mechanics' Lien Acts in every common law province of Canada. The first of these Acts to come into force in Canada were enacted in Ontario and Manitoba in 1873. While their provisions vary somewhat from province to province, the general scope and effect of all of the Acts are similar. Over the past few years, a number of provinces have amended their Statutes to incorporate new provisions with respect to trust funds, to make provincial public works subject to some of the rights given by The Mechanics' Lien Act, and to permit lessors of rented equipment to avail themselves of this remedy. Further amendments can be expected as changes occur in the construction industry.

Because there was no right to a lien upon land in favour of workmen performing work or services or of suppliers of material, either at common law or in equity, the lien is clearly a creature of statute: *Shuttleworth v. Seymour* (1914), 7 Sask. L.R. 74; *Johnson v. Crew* (1836), 5 O.S. 200 (C.A.); *Fitzgerald v. Apperley,* [1926] 2 W.W.R. 689 (Sask. C.A.); *Clarke v. Williams,* [1939] 3 W.W.R. 481 (B.C.); *Cross and Grant v. Brooks* (1958), 26 W.W.R. 15 (B.C. C.A.); *Granby Const. & Equipment Ltd. v. Player* (1964), 49 D.L.R. (2d) 658 (B.C.). In *Read v. Whitney* (1919), 45 O.L.R. 377 (C.A.), Meredith C.J.C.P. stated: "At common law there was no such lien, and the fact that in the civil law there was, should only accentuate the point that the common law was against it ... by statute-imposed injunction we are bound to give effect to the Act as a remedial enactment."

In *Clarkson Co. v. Ace Lbr. Ltd.*, [1963] S.C.R. 110; reversing [1962] O.R. 748, Ritchie J. stated that in his opinion the proper approach to the interpretation of The Mechanics' Lien Act had been expressed in the dissenting judgment of Kelly J.A. in the Court below where he said that "The lien commonly known as the mechanics' lien was unknown to the common law and owes its existence in Ontario to a series of statutes, the latest of which is R.S.O. 1960, c. 233 [see now R.S.O. 1970, c. 267]. It constitutes an abrogation of the common law to the extent that it creates, in the specified circumstances, a charge upon the owner's lands which would not exist but for the Act, and grants to one class of creditors a security or preference not enjoyed by all creditors of the same debtor; accordingly, while the statute may merit a liberal interpretation with respect to the rights it confers upon those to whom it applies, it must be given a strict interpretation in determining whether any lien-claimant is a person to whom a lien is given by it." See also *Hett v. Samoth Realty Projects Ltd.* (1977), 76 D.L.R. (3d) 362 (Alta. C.A.).

At common law, as in equity, the workmen or material suppliers could only rely on the credit of the persons from whom they had their contracts: *Johnson v. Crew* (1836), 5 O.S. 200 (C.A.). The Mechanics' Lien Act gives to persons who perform services or supply materials, security on the lands on which those services are performed or to which those materials are delivered provided that they comply with the provisions of the Act. The Act provides the machinery by which the workman or material supplier can realize on that security: *Travis Lbr. Co. v. Cousineau; Beaver Lbr. Co. v. Cousineau,* [1956] O.W.N. 585 (C.A.); *Read v. Whitney* (1919), 45 O.L.R. 377 (C.A.).

It was stated in *Hickey v. Stalker* (1923), 53 O.L.R. 414 (C.A.), by Meredith C.J.C.P. that "Speaking generally the object of The Mechanics' Lien Act is to prevent owners of land getting the benefit of buildings erected and work done at their instance on their land without paying for them." The same general proposition is stated in *Earl F. Wakefield Co. v. Oil City Petroleums (Leduc) Ltd.,* [1958] S.C.R. 361; reversing 22 W.W.R. 267 (*sub nom. Oil City Petroleums Ltd. v. Earl F. Wakefield Co.*); *Brooks-Sanford Co. v. Theodore Telier Const. Co.* (1910), 22 O.L.R. 176; *Bunting v. Bell* (1876), 23 Gr. 584; and *Re Shields and Winnipeg* (1964), 47 D.L.R. (2d) 346 (Man.). In *Scratch v. Anderson,* [1917] 1 W.W.R. 1340 (Alta.), the purpose of the enactment was expressed by Harvey J. to be to ensure that "the land which receives the benefit shall bear the burden".

In Ontario, New Brunswick, Manitoba, Saskatchewan and British Columbia, in addition to the lien given on the land, the workman or supplier of materials is given a right in the nature of a lien on the moneys paid by the owner of the land to the contractor from whom he has his contract. He is accordingly given two securities, the land and the money paid to the contractor, which are completely independent of one another: see *Can.*

Bank of Commerce v. T. McAvity & Sons Ltd., [1959] S.C.R. 478; *Bank of Nova Scotia v. O. & O. Contractors Ltd.* (1965), 55 W.W.R. 103 (B.C. C.A.). The moneys paid to the contractor by the owner or to the subcontractor by the contractor are constituted a trust fund in the hands of the contractor or the subcontractor, as the case may be, for the benefit of workmen and persons who supplied material on account of the contract: Ont., sec. 2(1); N.B., sec. 3(1); B.C., sec. 3(1); Sask., sec. 3(1); and Man., The Builders and Workmen Act, sec. 3(1). In Ontario and Saskatchewan this trust fund concept has been extended to cover moneys borrowed by the owner which are to be used in financing the construction (Ont., sec. 2(4); Sask., sec. 3(4)), and moneys which have been certified for payment under the terms of the contract but which have not yet been paid to the contractor: Ont., sec. 2(3); Sask., sec. 3(3). See also Chapter 9, The Trust Fund.

In all of the provinces, however, the Legislature has sought to ensure payment of the lienholders' claims by requiring the owner to retain out of all payments made under the contract to the contractor a percentage (usually based on the total contract price) of the value of the work done at the time that the payment is made. This percentage, or holdback, forms a fund out of which the claims of the subcontractors and material suppliers may be paid. (See, *e.g.,* N.B., sec. 15; Ont., sec. 11; Sask., sec. 19). All claimants against this fund rank *pari passu* for the amounts due to them. In the event of a deficiency, the fund is distributed *pro rata* among all claimants of the same class (Ont., sec. 14(2)), with the exception of wage earners who are given preferential treatment. It was pointed out in *Dziewa v. Haviland,* [1960] O.W.N. 343, that the owner's obligation to retain this fund is for the benefit of lienholders only and this obligation cannot be affected by the terms of the owner's contract with the contractor. The "owner's" interest in the land is subject to the lien and all of the Acts provide for the sale of the land to satisfy his obligations to the lienholders, if he himself fails to do so.

In addition to the foregoing, The Mechanics' Lien Act seeks to assist mechanics and materialmen in other ways. For the most part the claims of workmen and material suppliers, at least initially, were for small amounts of money and the claims were being made by persons with little business or legal experience. Accordingly, all of the Acts have sought to devise a machinery for enforcing claims for lien as expeditiously, informally and cheaply as possible. Thus, a mechanics' lien action has been made a "class action" in which all claims against a single property or a group of properties owned by one owner are disposed of at the same time: *D. & M. Building Supplies Ltd. v. Stravalis Holdings Ltd.* (1977), 13 O.R. (2d) 443. The Court expressed the opinion in *McPherson v. Gedge* (1883), 4 O.R. 246 (C.A.); *Baines v. Curley* (1916), 38 O.L.R. 301 (C.A.); and *Ryder v. Garner,* [1955] O.W.N. 9 (C.A.), that the purpose of the Act was to prevent multiplicity of proceedings involving small claims which would result in Court costs out of proportion to and perhaps in excess of the amounts claimed. It has also been held on numerous occasions that the Court should not adjudicate on matters in lien proceedings which have nothing to do with the enforcement of the rights given by the Act. In *Simmons Bros. Ltd. v. Lee,* [1948] O.W.N. 737, it was held that the scope of the Act should not be enlarged to permit third party proceedings (following *Neri v. Benham,* [1934] O.W.N. 192). See also *A.P. Green Fire Brick Co. v. Interprov. Steel Corpn.* (1963), 42 W.W.R. 497 (Sask. C.A.) and *Caruso v. Campanile,* [1972] 1 O.R. 437, to the same effect. Third party proceedings were permitted, however, in *Halls Associates (Western) Ltd. v. Trident Const. Ltd.* (1968), 65 W.W.R. 415 (Man. C.A.). The Court distinguished the foregoing cases on the ground that the Manitoba Act made the practice and procedure of the ordinary Courts applicable to any case not satisfactorily provided for in The Mechanics' Lien Act, whereas the Acts of the provinces in which these cases were decided did not. The ordinary rules of procedure permitted third party proceedings and they did so for the purpose of avoiding multiplicity of proceedings. In *Anchor Shoring Ltd. v. Halton Region Conservation Authority; Dufferin Materials Const. Ltd. v. Halton Region Conservation Authority* (1977), 15 O.R. (2d) 599, the Court followed the *Simmons* and *Caruso* decisions, holding that the Act does not provide for or permit third party proceedings, and it distinguished the *Halls* case on the grounds, firstly, that the third party was already a party defendant to the action, and secondly, that the Ontario Act does not contain a provision similar to that section of the Manitoba Act referred to in the *Halls* case (*supra*). The Court went on to express the opinion, however, that if an independent action were commenced against a third party by a defendant in a mechanics' lien action, the desirability of the two actions being tried together would constitute valid grounds for transferring the mechanics' lien action for trial together with that action at the regular sittings of the Supreme Court pursuant to section 31(1) of the Ontario Act.

In *Western Caissons (Man.) Ltd. v. Trident Const. Ltd.* (1975), 54 D.L.R. (3d) 289 (Man.), the Court held that the Manitoba Act did not authorize the joining of a party as a defendant through a counterclaim in order to obtain a personal judgment against that party for what amounted to an allegation of tortious conduct based on negligence or misrepresentation. It distinguished the *Halls* case (*supra*) on the ground that the issue in that case was purely one of determining whether third party proceedings were permissible under the Act. See also *Nor. Elec. Co. v. Frank Warkentin Elec. Ltd.* (1972), 27 D.L.R. (3d) 519 (Man. C.A.). In *Aqua-Pond Indust. Ltd. v. Gould* (1974), 3 O.R. (2d) 439, an application to strike out that part of the defendant's counterclaim relating to its claim for damages for injury to its name, goodwill and reputation, was dismissed on the ground that there was a direct contractual relationship between the plaintiff and the defendant

4

and the matters in issue between them could readily be determined in the one action, thus avoiding a multiplicity of actions. In *Wasylyk v. Metro. Sep. S. Bd.*, [1970] 3 O.R. 391 (C.A.), it was held that the Court had jurisdiction under The Mechanics' Lien Act to deal with the counterclaim or set-off of the defendant even though it was founded upon a tort rather than upon breach of the contract in question, since it arose out of the work or service done by the plaintiff. In *Alros Products Ltd. v. Dalecore Const. Ltd.* (1973), 2 O.R. (2d) 312 (C.A.), it was held that a claim for damages was not the proper subject matter of a mechanics' lien nor could the Court award personal judgment on such a claim under section 40 of the Ontario Act. In *Travis Lbr. Co. v. Cousineau; Beaver Lbr. Co. v. Cousineau,* [1956] O.W.N. 585 (C.A.), it was held that the Act does not provide for a mortgagee obtaining a judgment in a proceeding under the Act against a mortgagor either on the covenant in the mortgage or otherwise. In *Bermingham Const. Ltd. v. Moir Const. Co.,* [1959] O.R. 355 (C.A.), the Court took the position that there was no jurisdiction under the Act for it to entertain a claim by one defendant over against another or to prosecute a claim by one defendant against another that was completely independent of the plaintiff's claim.

Most of the Acts specifically provide that, the object of the Act being to enforce liens at the least expense, the procedure shall be, as far as possible, of a summary character having regard to the amount and nature of the liens in question (see, *e.g.,* Ont., sec. 46(1); N.B., sec. 61(2); Alta., sec. 36(6)), and the Ontario, Newfoundland and Saskatchewan Acts provide that no interlocutory proceedings except such as are provided for by the Act are to be permitted without the consent of the Court (Ont., sec. 46(2); Nfld., sec. 46(2); Sask., sec. 58(2)). An appeal from an Order made by a Local Judge appointing a Receiver and a Trustee under the Ontario Act was dismissed under this section in *Macon Drywall Systems Ltd. v. H.P. Hyatt Const. Ltd.* (1972), 17 C.B.R. (N.S.) 6 (Ont.). See also *Albern Mechanical Ltd. v. Newcon Const. Ltd.,* [1971] 1 O.R. 350, and *Bennett & Wright Contractors Ltd. v. H.E.P.C. of Ont.,* [1972] 1 O.R. 20. The Act further provides that where the least expensive course is not taken by a plaintiff or other claimant, the costs which are allowed to him by the Court are not to exceed what would have been incurred if the least expensive course had been taken (*e.g.,* Ont., sec. 45(4); N.B., sec. 57; Man., sec. 52).

As was pointed out in *Curtis v. Richardson* (1909), 18 Man. R. 519, the Act is remedial in character, its purpose being to secure the parties entitled to its benefits for their work done and materials supplied, provided, however, they have employed the means and adopted the rules laid down in that statute to obtain and secure those rights. The Act being entirely a creature of statute and being in derogation of the common law the provisions creating the lien must be construed strictly by the Court and the Courts have shown a reluctance to extend the relief given: see *Mallett v.*

5

Kovar (1910), 14 W.L.R. 327 (Alta.); *Haggerty v. Grant* (1892), 2 B.C.R. 173; *Ont. Lime Assn. v. Grimwood* (1910), 22 O.L.R. 17; *Rafuse v. Hunter* (1906), 12 B.C.R. 126; *Shuttleworth v. Seymour* (1914), 7 Sask. L.R. 74; *Metro Woodworking v. Phales Invt. Ltd.,* [1960] O.W.N. 132 (C.A.); *Clarkson Co. v. Ace Lbr. Ltd.,* [1963] S.C.R. 110; reversing [1962] O.R. 748; *Granby Const. & Equipment Ltd. v. Player* (1964), 49 D.L.R. (2d) 658 (B.C.); *Otis Elevator Co. v. Commonwealth Holiday Inns of Can. Ltd.,* (1972), 8 O.R. (2d) 297; *Alspan Wrecking Ltd. v. Dineen Const. Ltd.,* [1972] S.C.R. 829; *Cam Cement Contractors Ltd. v. Royal Bank* (1973), 38 D.L.R. (3d) 427 (B.C.C.A.); *Lee v. Lincoln Const. Ltd.* (1973), 4 N. & P.E.I.R. 116 (Nfld.). In *Nobbs v. C.P.R.* (1913), 6 W.W.R. 759 (Sask.), Hannon D.C.J., at p. 761, quoting from Wallace on Mechanics' Liens, 2nd ed., ch. 3, stated the position as follows: "Sections creating the right to a lien are to be strictly construed, while provisions dealing with procedure on the enforcement of the lien are to receive a broad and liberal construction."

Once the right to a lien is established, the Courts have expressed the view that effect should be given to the spirit rather than to the letter of the statute with respect to the provisions dealing with enforcement of that right: see *R. Bickerton & Co. v. Dakin* (1890), 20 O.R. 695 (C.A.); *Curtis v. Richardson* (1909), 18 Man. R. 519; *Robock v. Peters* (1900), 13 Man. R. 124; *Clarke v. Williams,* [1939] 3 W.W.R. 481 (B.C.); *Inglewood Plumbing & Gasfitting Ltd. v. Northgate Dev. Ltd. (No. 1)* (1965), 54 W.W.R. 225 (Alta.). Thus while the Courts oppose a liberal interpretation of the sections of the Act creating the lien, they have shown that they are equally opposed to technical defences and arguments designed to defeat a lien which has already been created. As was held in *Fitzgerald v. Apperley,* [1926] 2 W.W.R. 689 (Sask. C.A.), the provisions of the Act should be construed so as to ensure the attainment of its object, and errors committed by one entitled to a lien ought to be remedied when this can reasonably be done, without prejudicing anyone's rights. In line with this view, all of the Acts contain a curative section providing that a substantial compliance with the provisions of the Act dealing with the registration of a claim for lien and the mode of realizing the lien shall be sufficient and no lien is to be invalidated by reason of failure to comply with any of the requisites of those sections unless, in the opinion of the Court, some person is prejudiced thereby and then only to the extent of such prejudice. This section is more fully dealt with in the Chapter on the procedure to obtain the lien. In this connection see also *Barrington v. Martin* (1908), 16 O.L.R. 635 (C.A.) and *Polson v. Thomson* (1916), 26 Man. R. 410 (C.A.), in which it was held that the duty of the Court was to give effect to the spirit rather than the letter of the Act and it ought not to deprive a *bona fide* lienholder of his lien because of some technical error in prosecuting his claim under an Act manifestly designed to obtain payment in an inexpensive, informal and expeditious manner. The statement made by Rand J. in *Rocky Mountain S.D. v. Atlas Lbr. Co.,* [1954] S.C.R. 589, at p. 593, that the Alberta Mechanics' Lien Act "undoubtedly is to be interpreted to further its purposes which are to provide security for those who contribute work or materials to the construction of an improvement", was quoted with approval by Laskin J. in *Nelson Lbr. Co. v. Integrated Bldg. Corpn.,* [1973] S.C.R. 456. Among the numerous additional cases dealing with the purpose of the Act are *Nor. Lbr. Mills Ltd. v. Rice* (1917), 41 O.L.R. 201 (C.A.); *Johnson & Carey Co. v. Can. Nor. Ry.* (1918), 43 O.L.R. 10; varied 44 O.L.R. 533 (C.A.); *Craig v. Cromwell* (1900), 32 O.R. 27; affirmed 27 O.A.R. 585; *Braden v. Port Arthur Gen. Hospital* (1930), 39 O.W.N. 243; *Simmons Bros. Ltd. v. Lee,* [1948] O.W.N. 737; *Re Northlands Grading Co.,* [1960] O.R. 455 (C.A.); *Merrick v. Campbell* (1914), 24 Man. R. 446; *Pankka v. Butchart,* [1956] O.R. 837 (C.A.); *Warren Gen. Contracting Ltd. v. Robichaud* (1974), 39 D.L.R. (3d) 478.

§2   The General Nature of the Act.

The Mechanics' Lien Act being one concerned with day-to-day business affairs has been particularly subject to amendment as conditions in the construction industry have changed over the years. The law with respect to mechanics' liens is accordingly in a state of flux. The Acts were recently amended in Ontario, Saskatchewan, Newfoundland and Alberta, for example, to permit a person who rents equipment to claim a lien for the price of the rental of such equipment. As will be seen, provisions peculiar to the Act of one province are on occasion inserted in the Act of another province and subsequently removed from the Act of the first province. Because of this continual tinkering with the statute, it has assumed a patchwork form in most jurisdictions. While the general principles set forth in the preceding section of this Chapter have remained fairly constant, attempts are made from time to time to extend or to limit the relief given by the Act. (See *Re Northlands Grading Ltd.,* [1960] O.R. 455 (C.A.), where an attempt was made to create a special lien in favour of materialmen, and *Can. Bank of Commerce v. T. McAvity & Sons Ltd.,* [1959] S.C.R. 478; affirming [1958] O.W.N. 324, where an attempt was made to limit the application of section 3 (see now sec. 2) of the Ontario Act to projects other than highway contracts).

The Acts usually commence by providing for the creation of the lien (*e.g.,* Ont., sec. 5(1); Man., sec. 4(1); N.S., sec. 5). There has been very little change in these provisions over the years. In general, the lien is created as the result of the performance of work or services or the placing or furnishing of materials in the manner described and on the projects enumerated in these sections. The Act proceeds secondly to provide for the protection of the lien. This is done by means of the registration of a claim for lien, sheltering under a certificate of action, or by giving notice of the lien to certain persons. The Act then goes on to provide a means of enforcing the claim for lien (*e.g.,* Ont., secs. 29*ff*).

Once created, the lien continues until payment is made, or until it expires in accordance with the provisions of the Act. The lien, in fact, has a limited existence and will expire unless it is preserved by registration of a claim for lien within the time prescribed. This time limit varies from province to province but in all cases commences to run from the completion of the work or the supply of the last materials under the contract. Because a mechanics' lien action is a class action the lien may also be preserved, in Nova Scotia and Saskatchewan, if an action is commenced by another lien claimant claiming a lien on the same property within the time limited for the filing of the claim for lien: N.S., sec. 24; Sask., sec. 37(1). Even so, the lien can be preserved by registration of a claim for lien for a limited time only. All of the Acts provide that the lien will expire again unless an action is commenced and a certificate of the action is registered within a specified number of days after the completion of the work. For example, in Ontario, the lien must be filed within 37 days after the contract is completed or the last material is supplied, and an action must be commenced and a certificate thereof registered against the title to the property involved within 90 days after the contract is completed or the last material is supplied (or, if the Act so provides, within 90 days after the expiry of the period of credit, where applicable). As the Court stated in *Re J. Gaspari Const. Co.* (1958), 37 C.B.R. 74 (Ont.), the mechanics' lien is a statutory right, and hence it cannot be revived or restored once it has expired because there is no provision in the Act permitting such a revivor.

As was pointed out in *Crawford v. Tilden* (1907), 13 O.L.R. 169; affirmed 14 O.L.R. 572 (C.A.), the substance of the Act is the sale. There would be no point in giving a lien on land if the land could not be sold to satisfy that lien. Almost all of the Acts provide that on filing his claim for lien the lien claimant becomes a purchaser *pro tanto* of the land against which it is registered (*e.g.,* Ont., sec. 20; Man., sec. 19). The final judgment accordingly provides for the payment of the amounts found due to the various lien claimants and in default of payment that the property involved is to be sold and the proceeds distributed amongst the claimants in accordance with the priorities established at trial and pursuant to the Act.

As stated above, the Courts take the position that the Act, being of a remedial nature, should receive a liberal interpretation. This statement is supported by the provisions of the various provincial Interpretation Acts. However, a claimant who fails to follow the elementary and essential requirements for the creation and preservation of his lien will lose it because, as has also been pointed out, the Act, being in derogation of the common law, must be strictly construed in this respect. Once the lien has been created and preserved by registration, however, the enforcement of it is governed by the provisions of the Act designed to bring about such realization in as summary and expeditious a manner as possible. In keeping with this principle, it has been held that the lien will not be invalidated by failure to comply strictly with the rules of procedure laid down in the Act or because of some minor technical slip: *R. Bickerton & Co. v. Dakin* (1890), 20 O.R. 695 (C.A.); *Craig v. Cromwell* (1900), 32 O.R. 27; affirmed 27 O.A.R. 585. As stated in the previous section, interlocutory proceedings are normally forbidden except with leave of the Court. The reluctance of the Courts to permit any interlocutory proceedings, apart from those provided for in the Act, is illustrated by the decisions in *Rowlin v. Rowlin* (1907), 9 O.W.R. 297; *Moyer v. Martin,* [1951] O.W.N. 395 (C.A.); *Mancini v. Giancento,* [1962] O.W.N. 120; *Robertson v. Bullen* (1908), 13 O.W.R. 56; *Macon Drywall Systems Ltd. v. H.P. Hyatt Const. Ltd.* (1973), 17 C.B.R. (N.S.) 6 (Ont.); *Albern Mechanical Ltd. v. Newcon Const. Ltd.,* [1971] 1 O.R. 350, and *Bennett & Wright Contractors Ltd. v. H.E.P.C. of Ontario,* [1972] 1 O.R. 20.

As was pointed out by Meredith C.J.C.P. in *Baines v. Curley* (1916), 38 O.L.R. 301 (C.A.), the person trying the action must not only determine all questions which arise in the action tried under the provisions of the Act, but also "the rights and liabilities of the persons appearing before the Judge or officer who tries the action or upon whom notice of trial has been served are to be adjusted". In *Richvale Ready Mix Co. v. Belle Aire Const. Co.,* [1960] O.W.N. 230, the Court expressed the opinion that it could give personal judgment in favour of a claimant who, through some inadvertence or error, was unable to establish a lien, where in the absence of such error a valid lien could have been established. Section 40 of the Ontario Act provides that where a claimant fails to establish a lien he may nevertheless recover a personal judgment against any party to the action for such sum as may appear to be due to him and which he might recover in an action against such party. This provision is common to all of the Acts. (See *e.g.,* N.B., sec. 46; Alta., sec. 45(1) and *Warren Gen. Contracting Ltd. v. Robichaud* (1973), 39 D.L.R. (3d) 478 (N.B.C.A.); *Stickelmann v. Switzer,* [1972] 2 W.W.R. 203 (Sask.)). In British Columbia, section 39 permits the Judge to give a judgment for the amount found actually due notwithstanding that such amount exceeds the ordinary jurisdiction of the County Court. The same is true in Manitoba. See *Parsons Plumbing & Heating Co. v. Fletcher Invt. Ltd.* (1966), 55 W.W.R. 442 (Man. C.A.); *Halls Associates (Western) Ltd. v. Trident Const. Ltd.* (1968), 65 W.W.R. 415 (Man. C.A.). It has been held in Ontario, that a lien claimant who fails to establish a lien but who is granted a personal judgment is not entitled to costs: *D. Faga Const. Co. v. Havenbrook Const. Co.,* [1968] 2 O.R. 800. However, in (*A.J. (Archie)) Goodale Ltd. v. Risidore Bros. Ltd.* (1975), 8 O.R. (2d) 427, the Ontario

Court of Appeal did award costs to the plaintiff whose lien was held to be invalid but who was given a personal judgment under section 40 of the Ontario Act. It has also been held in Ontario, that a personal judgment cannot be granted in respect of a claim for damages under this section since such a claim cannot be the subject matter of a claim for lien: *Alros Products Ltd. v. Dalecore Const. Ltd.* (1973), 2 O.R. (2d) 312 (C.A.). See also §164 *ante.*

In addition to the provisions of the Act respecting mechanics' liens on property, many of the Acts also deal with liens on chattels (*e.g.,* Ont., sec. 48; B.C., sec. 42). These sections provide for the creation of a lien in favour of a mechanic or other person who has bestowed money or skill and materials upon a chattel in connection with altering or improving its properties or for the purpose of imparting an additional value to it. The sections provide for the retention of the chattel until payment is made and outline a procedure for the sale of the chattel if payment is not made, the lienor reimbursing himself out of the proceeds.

The various provisions of the Act will be dealt with in more detail in the following Chapters. One of the most important of these provisions is that requiring the owner, contractor or other person primarily liable to the lien claimants to retain a percentage of the value of the work, service or materials done, placed or furnished, in his hands as a fund to which the lien claimants may resort if the person primarily liable to them refuses or neglects to pay them. In *Noranda Exploration Co. v. Sigurdson* (1975), 53 D.L.R. (3d) 641 (S.C.C.), the Court expressed the view that mechanics' lien legislation is intended to protect owners as well as labourers and materialmen. In *Clarke v. Williams,* [1939] 3 W.W.R. 481 (B.C.), Swanson Co. Ct. J. approved the statement of Killam C.J. in *Robock v. Peters* (1900), 13 Man. R. 124 at 142 to the effect that in considering the Act all of its provisions should be read together and one clause considered in the light of others. In *Merrick v. Campbell* (1914), 24 Man. R. 446, the Court in dealing with a section of the Act, which had been amended, expressed the opinion that "all the provisions of the Act should be read together and considered in connection with the provisions in former Acts for which they were substituted".

§3   The General Nature of the Lien.

The lien arises and attaches to the land as soon as work is done or materials are furnished and the amount of the lien is subject to be increased or decreased from time to time as more work is done or payments are made on account: *Ross Bros. Ltd. v. Gorman* (1908), 1 Alta. L.R. 516 (C.A.). As was stated by Beck J. in *Ross Bros. Ltd. v. Gorman, supra,* and *Dom. Radiator Co. v. Payne,* [1917] 2 W.W.R. 974 (Alta.); on appeal (*sub nom. Calgary v. Dom. Radiator Co.)* (1918), 56 S.C.R. 141: "A mechanic's lien is a lien which arises partly by virtue of the statute, and partly by virtue of the acts of the parties, and operates as an assignment in whole or in part of the fund represented by the contract price ... ". Once the lien has arisen it attaches to all parts of the property liable to it so that "every cent is a lien on every inch" and the lienholder "may abandon his lien on any part without interfering with his right in respect of the rest or any part of it". See also *Sparks & McKay v. Lord,* [1929] 2 D.L.R. 32 (Ont.); on appeal see [1930] S.C.R. 351, and *Ont. Lime Assn. v. Grimwood* (1910), 22 O.L.R. 17. In *Bradshaw v. Saucerman* (1913), 18 B.C.R. 41 (Y.T. C.A.), the Court quoted Strong J. in *Edmonds v. Tiernan* (1892), 21 S.C.R. 406 as follows: "The statute does not give a lien but only a potential right of creating it". See also *C. Beckett & Co. (Edm.) v. J.H. Ashdown Hdwe. Co.,* [1967] S.C.R. 610; affirming (*sub nom. Custom Glass Ltd. v. Waverlee Holdings Ltd.*) 59 W.W.R. 204. In *Curtis v. Richardson* (1909), 18 Man. R. 519, the proposition was stated by Macdonald J. at p. 520, that "the lien is created as the work is done and not after its completion and the filing of a lien is only a means of preserving and enforcing it." See also *Galvin Lbr. Yards v. Ensor,* [1922] 2 W.W.R. 15 (Sask. C.A.), where it was held that a person who has supplied labour and materials is enabled by the Act to establish a lien and thus acquire authority to sell the property so as to realize his claim therefor.

It was held in *Wake v. Can. Pac. Lbr. Co.* (1901), 8 B.C.R. 358 (C.A.), following *Dillon v. Sinclair* (1900), 7 B.C.R. 328 that the liability of the defendant in a mechanics' lien action is not a debt but a statutory penalty. The action is brought to enforce a penalty by pursuing a statutory remedy. It was held in *George D. McLean & Associates Ltd. v. Leth,* [1949] 4 D.L.R. 282; affirmed [1950] 1 W.W.R. 536 (B.C. C.A.); *Pankka v. Butchart,* [1956] O.R. 837 (C.A.); and *Nobbs v. C.P.R.* (1913), 6 W.W.R. 759 (Sask.), that the enforcement of a mechanics' lien is a proceeding *in rem* rather than *in personam.* There is nothing in the Act to suggest that a lien could attach to a right of a personal nature. Accordingly, where, as in *Pankka v. Butchart, supra,* and *Bain v. Director, Veterans Land Act,* [1955] O.W.N. 993, none of the defendants before the Court has an estate or interest in the land in question to which a lien can attach, the action must fail *in toto,* the provisions of the Act being unavailable for the determination of the plaintiff's contractual rights.

It is apparent from the provisions of the statute, and it has been held many times by the Courts, that the lien created thereby was intended to be an estate or interest in the land which could be sold and vested by the Court's order in a purchaser: see, *e.g., Pankka v. Butchart,* [1956] O.R. 837 (C.A.); *Galvin-Walston Lbr. Co. v. McKinnon* (1911), 4 Sask. L.R. 68 (C.A.); *F.C. Richert Co. v. Registrar of Land Titles,* [1936] 2 W.W.R. 473; affirmed [1937] 3 W.W.R. 632 (Alta. C.A.); *Roy v. Couturier Const. Ltd.* (1965), 51 M.P.R. 360 (N.B. C.A.); *Shields v. Winnipeg* (1964), 49 W.W.R. 530 (Man.); *Alspan Wrecking Ltd. v. Dineen Const. Ltd.,* [1972] S.C.R. 829;

Wells H. Morton & Co. v. Can. Credit Men's Trust Assn. Ltd. (1965), 53
W.W.R. 178 (Man. C.A.). It was held in *Nobbs v. C.P.R.* (1913), 6 W.W.R.
759 (Sask.), that a subcontractor might have a lien on the lien of the head
contractor against the owner; in other words that he might have a lien upon
a lien. The Court in the *Richert* case, *supra,* held that a mechanics' lien was
an equitable interest in land although in the earlier case of *Wortman v. Frid
Lewis Co.* (1915), 9 W.W.R. 812 (Alta.), the Court held that it was not. It
was held in *King v. Alford* (1885), 9 O.R. 643 (C.A.), that a mechanics' lien is
not analogous to a vendor's lien. In *Re Northlands Grading Ltd.,* [1960]
O.R. 455 (C.A.), it was held that the provisions of section 15 of the Ontario
Act (creating a lien on material delivered to the land but not yet
incorporated in the erection on the land) did not create a special or separate
and distinct lien in the nature of an extension of the vendor's lien under The
Sale of Goods Act. The lien mentioned in that section was held to be simply
an extention or particular application of the basic lien created by section 5 of
the Act, approving the decision in *Maltby's Ltd. v. Can. Packers Ltd.,*
[1947] O.W.N. 757. This section has now been removed from the Ontario
Act. The Court came to the opposite conclusion in *John Wood Co. v. Can.
Credit Men's Trust Assn. Ltd.* (1962), 39 W.W.R. 593 (Alta. C.A.) and
Western Caissons (Alta.) Ltd. v. Bower (1969), 71 W:W.R. 604 (Alta. C.A.),
holding that the corresponding section of the Alberta Act did create a
separate and distinct lien for the purchase price of the materials. After
reviewing the Ontario and Alberta decisions at length, the trial Judge in
Marble Center Ltd. v. Kenney Const. Co (1973), 29 D.L.R. (3d) 64 (N.S.),
concluded that the doctrine expressed in *Re Northlands Grading Ltd.,
(supra)* was to be preferred. An appeal from this decision was dismissed
without reasons: (1974) 38 D.L.R. (3d) 319.

§4 Relationship With Other Acts and The Common Law.

The Act gives the power generally to the Courts to try to completely
dispose of the action and all questions arising in the action under the
building contract or out of the work or service done or the materials
furnished to the property in question (*e.g.,* Ont., secs. 32, 38(4); Man., sec.
39; N.S., sec. 34), although, as has been previously pointed out, the Court
will not deal with claims by a person who is not entitled to invoke the Act:
Travis Lbr. Co. v. Cousineau; Beaver Lbr. Co. v. Cousineau, [1956] O.W.N.
585 (C.A.). There are also circumstances where the mechanics' lien claimant
may contemporaneously exercise his rights both at common law and under
the Act. For example the claimant may file a lien and also institute an action
for the recovery of judgment in the ordinary way. As will be seen later, so
long as his claim is not paid in the other action, the defendant is not unfairly
prejudiced, and if he can show that he is justified in taking such action he
may proceed to realize on the security of the lien as well. See *Standard*

Indust. Ltd. v. E-F Wood Specialities Inc. (1977), 16 O.R. (2d) 398, *Rockwall Concrete Forming Ltd. v. Robintide Invts. Ltd.,* (1977), 15 O.R. (2d) 422 and §83 Loss of Lien through Waiver, Estoppel and Merger. It was conceded by the Court in the former case that it would be improper to commence an ordinary action to recover the same debt where, as in the *Rockwall* case, the amount of the plaintiffs' claim had already been paid into Court in the mechanics' lien proceedings.

The lien claimant may also have a right to a lien where there is no contractual liability to him, because there is no necessity for privity of contract in order to create liability under the Act on the part of the owner or the contractor from whom the person primarily liable to him has his contract. The lien claimant may also have extensive rights under another statute. For example, a claimant who holds a conditional sales contract for the materials supplied for which he claims the lien will retain his rights under that contract at least until the trial of the mechanics' lien action. At that time, however, as will be seen in Chapter 3, he must elect which of the two statutes he intends to proceed under: *U.S.Const. Co. v. Rat Portage Lbr. Co.* (1915), 25 Man. R. 793 (C.A.). It was held in *Constable v. Belvedere Holdings (1962) Ltd.* (1966), 58 W.W.R. 96 (Y.T. C.A.), that the Territorial Court of the Yukon Territory had jurisdiction to entertain an action which combined a claim for lien with other causes of action and to grant all appropriate remedies, under the Yukon Act, 1952-53 (Can.), c. 53 [am. 1955, c. 23 and c. 48; 1958, c 9], and section 8(*e*) of The Judicature Ordinance, R.O.Y.T. 1958, ch. 60. See also *Dom. Elec. Protection Co. v. Leopold Beaudoin Const. Co.* (1963), 5 C.B.R. (N.S.) 72 (Ont.).

The most common source of conflict between the common law and The Mechanics' Lien Act arises in connection with the interpretation of building contracts. The parties to the contract may make any sort of arrangement between themselves that they wish and, except for wage earners, can generally speaking contract themselves out of the provisions of The Mechanics' Lien Act entirely. However, as was held in *Russell v. Williams* (1923), 24 O.W.N. 240 (C.A.), the Court would not permit the parties to contract out of the liability to maintain the holdback fund provided by the Act. Some of the Acts specifically provide that every contract will be deemed to be amended insofar as is necessary to make it conform with the provisions of the section of the Act which governs the retention and payment of holdbacks (*e.g.,* Ont., sec. 11(8); B.C., sec. 21(5); N.B., sec. 15(8)). It would also appear that the parties could not circumvent sections of the Act constituting moneys paid to the contractor by the owner a trust fund: See *Re Northwest Elec. Ltd.,* [1973] 3 W.W.R. 156 (B.C.). Furthermore, the provisions of the contract would be in no way binding on persons who were not parties to that contract such as subcontractors or material suppliers, although the common practice is to make the provisions of the main contract part of the provisions of the subcontract. The Acts specifically provide that no agreement shall deprive any person otherwise entitled to a lien under the Act of the benefit of that lien who is not a party to such agreement (*e.g.,* Ont., sec. 4(3); N.S., sec. 4). With respect to workmen, all of the Acts provide that any agreement verbal or written, express or implied, on the part of a workman that he will not be entitled to the remedies provided by the Act shall be null and void (*e.g.,* Ont., sec. 4(1); N.S., sec. 3(1)).

§5   The Effect of Amendments to The Statute.

In *Hayward Lbr. Co. v. McEachern,* [1931] 3 W.W.R. 658 (Alta.), it was held that the presumption is against an Act being retrospective and thereby impairing vested rights. Accordingly, a retrospective effect will not be given unless required by the statute in the most explicit terms. Here the Court was dealing with an amendment to the statute with respect to matters of priority and it was held that such matters being matters of substantive rights rather than matters of procedure the old Act should govern since the priorities already existed prior to the coming into force of the new enactment. In *Westeel-Rosco Ltd. v. South Sask. Hospital Centre Bd. of Governors* (1977), 69 D.L.R. (3d) 334 (S.C.C.), the Court found that a section in The Mechanics' Lien Act, 1973 (Sask.), c. 62, which provided that any lien which arose under The Mechanics' Lien Act, R.S.S. 1965, c. 277, and which was in existence when the later Act came into force, should continue to be as valid and effectual in all respects as it would have been if the new Act had not been passed, entitled the plaintiff to a charge on the owner's holdback which it would not be entitled to under the new Act. In *Alta. Lbr. Co. v. Hines,* [1931] 2 W.W.R. 558 (Alta.), the Court pointed out that where an amendment to the Act is essentially procedural, it is retroactive because it deals with the mode in which a right of action already in existence is to be asserted and creates no new rights of action. In *Irwin v. Beynon* (1886), 4 Man. R. 10 (C.A.), it was held that, in general, where a statute is passed altering the law, it is to be taken as intended to apply to a state of facts coming into existence after the Act unless the language of the Act is expressly to the contrary. The same position is taken in *Walker v. Walton* (1877), 1 O.A.R. 579 and *Mfrs. Life Ins. Co. v. Hauser,* [1945] 3 W.W.R. 740 (Alta.). Thus, if the amendment deals with a matter of procedure, then, upon its coming into force, it will govern all proceedings thereafter coming before the Court whether or not the lien arose prior to that time. If, however, it governs a matter of substance, unless the enactment clearly and specifically says so, it will not have any effect on liens arising prior to the enactment coming into force and the former law will govern the claimant's rights. See also *McKittrick v. Byers,* [1926] 1 D.L.R. 342 (Ont. C.A.); *Lambert v. Anglo-Scottish Gen. Commercial Ins. Co.,* [1930] 1

D.L.R. 284 (Ont.); *Smith v. London* (1909), 20 O.L.R. 133 (C.A.); *Toronto v. Presswood Bros.,* [1944] O.R. 145 (C.A.); *Mitts v. LeClair* (1957), 10 D.L.R. (2d) 662 (Ont.); *Upper Can. College v. Smith* (1921), 61 S.C.R. 413. The view was expressed in *Re Upper Can. Zoological Society* (1975), 8 O.R. (2d) 340 (C.A.), that where a statute has been consistently interpreted in a certain way the Courts will be slow to reverse that interpretation, particularly where the statute has been re-enacted in the same terms after the decisions interpreting it.

§6   The Constitutional Question.

While the Mechanics' Lien Acts themselves clearly fall within the jurisdiction of the provincial legislatures under the British North America Act, being matters of property and civil rights, certain provisions of those Acts with respect to the manner in which actions were to be tried have been declared *ultra vires* of the provinces. In Ontario the Act provided at one time that mechanics' lien actions would be tried by a Judge of the County or District Court except in the County of York where they would be tried by a master of the Supreme Court or an Assistant Master. As was pointed out in *Reference re The Adoption Act,* [1938] S.C.R. 398; *Lab. Rel. Bd. (Sask.) v. John East Iron Works Ltd.,* [1949] A.C. 134, and *Re Supreme Court Act Amendment Act, 1964; A.G. B.C. v. McKenzie,* [1965] S.C.R. 490, the provincial Legislature was denied power under section 96 of the British North America Act to confer jurisdiction similar to that exercised by Superior, District, or County Court Judges, on officers appointed by the province. Masters began to try actions in the County of York under the Ontario Act in 1916, and in *Johnson & Carey Co. v. Can. Nor. Ry.* (1918), 44 O.L.R. 533; varying 43 O.L.R. 10 (C.A.), Riddel J. indicated that it was his own opinion that this was quite proper. However, it was held in *Atty. Gen. for Ont. and Display Services Ltd. v. Victoria Medical Bldg. Ltd.,* [1960] S.C.R. 32; affirming (*sub nom. Display Services Ltd. v. Victoria Medical Bldg. Ltd.*) [1958] O.R. 759, that the former section 31(1) of The Mechanics' Lien Act which purported to confer jurisdiction upon the Master or Assistant Master to try mechanics' lien actions in the County of York was *ultra vires.* The Court ruled that this assignment of the power of final adjudication on mechanics' lien matters went beyond the assignment of mere matters of procedure and amounted to an appointment of a Judge under section 96 of the British North America Act which the province could not do.

This decision is supported in other jurisdictions by the decision in *C. Huebert Ltd. v. Sharman,* [1950] 1 W.W.R. 682 (Man. C.A.), holding that a provision in the Manitoba Mechanics' Lien Act providing for the referral for hearing and disposition of mechanics' lien actions to a referee in Chambers was *ultra vires* of the Manitoba Legislature since the referee was a provincial appointee; by the decision in *Colonial Invt. & Loan Co. v. Grady* (1915), 8 Alta. L.R. 496 (C.A.), to the effect that a statute which conferred upon a Master the extraordinary powers of a Judge in respect of actions for the enforcement of mortgages or agreements for the sale of land was in conflict with the appointive power of section 96 of the British North America Act; and by the decision of Harvey C.J. sitting in Chambers, in *Polson Iron Works v. Munns* (1915), 9 W.W.R. 231 (Alta.), holding that the office of the Master is essentially that of an officer and that while his duties are largely judicial in their character, they do not constitute him a Judge within the meaning of section 96 of the British North America Act. This, however, is not to say that Masters or other officers of the Court may not exercise some judicial functions: *Re Solloway Mills & Co.*, [1935] O.R. 37 at 43 (C.A.). As pointed out in the *Display Services* case, *supra,* by Judson J. at p. 44, there is "distinction between the position of the Master exercising delegated jurisdiction as a referee under ss. 67 and 68 of The Judicature Act and his position when he exercises original jurisdiction under sec. 31(1) of The Mechanics' Lien Act. Anything that he does on a reference depends for its validity on the judge's original order. His findings must be embodied not in a judgment but in a report which is subject to control of the judge on a motion for confirmation, variation or appeal ... On the other hand under the impugned section the Master issues a judgment which is subject to a direct appeal to the Court of Appeal". The Ontario Legislature following the decision in this case has sought to avoid this difficulty by an amendment to section 31 of the Act. Section 31(2) now provides that, in the County of York, the action is to be tried by a Judge of the Supreme Court but that, on motion, a Judge of the Supreme Court may refer the whole action to the Master for trial pursuant to section 72 of The Judicature Act or, at the trial, the Judge may direct a reference to the Master pursuant to section 71 or 72 of The Judicature Act. In view of the decision of the Court in *C. Huebert Ltd. v. Sharman* (1950), 58 Man. R. 1 (C.A.), this provision may also be *ultra vires* since the Master still appears to exercise the power of final adjudication on the matters in question. In actual practice the order referring the matters in question in the action to the Master for trial, gives a judgment to the applicant or applicants for the amounts found due by the Master against the parties found liable by him after confirmation of his report.

A further conflict occasionally arises between provincial and federal jurisdiction when it is sought to enforce a claim for lien against property owned by a Crown agency or by a firm whose works have been declared to be for the general advantage of Canada by Parliament. In *Westeel-Rosco Ltd. v. South Sask. Hospital Centre Bd. of Governors* (1976), 69 D.L.R. (3d) 334 (S.C.C.), the Court stated that whether a particular body is an agent of the Crown, and therefore not subject to the provisions of The

Mechanics' Lien Act, depends on the nature and degree of control which the Crown exercises over it. The body in question must be subject to the control of the Crown at every turn in order to be an agency of it.

Property owned by the Crown is not subject to a mechanics' lien since, of course, the Crown's interest cannot be sold: see *Bain v. Director, Veterans Land Act,* [1947] O.W.N. 917; *Western Can. Hdwe. Co. v. Farrelly Bros. Ltd.,* [1922] 3 W.W.R. 1017 (Alta. C.A.); *R. v. Algoma Dist. Ct. Judge,* [1958] O.W.N. 330; appeal quashed (*sub nom. Perini Ltd. v. Consol. Denison Mines Ltd.*) [1959] O.W.N. 119 (C.A.); *Pankka v. Butchart,* [1956] O.R. 837 (C.A.); *Dom. Bridge Co. v. Sask. Govt. Telephones* (1963), 42 W.W.R. 577 (Sask.); *Wells H. Morton & Co. v. Can. Credit Men's Trust Assn. Ltd.* (1965), 53 W.W.R. 178 (Man. C.A.); *Kitchen Kabinets Ltd. v. Pinsent Const. Co.* (1974), 6 N. & P.E.I.R. 426 (Nfld.); *Engineered Homes Ltd. v. Popil,* [1972] 4 W.W.R. 357 (Alta.); *Pounder v. Carl C. Schaum Const. Ltd.,* [1972] 2 O.R. 616; *B.A.C.M. Ltd. v. Parkland Bldrs. Contracting Ltd.* (1971), 18 D.L.R. (3d) 377 (Sask.). Since there is no lien against such property, no personal judgment can be given either: *Johnson & Carey Co. v. Can. Nor. Ry.* (1918), 43 O.L.R. 10; varied 44 O.L.R. 533 (C.A.). Note, however, that the Ontario Act was recently amended to make the holdback provisions of the Act applicable to work done on the lands of the Crown which are held by the Province, although the right to register a lien against such lands, and the consequent sale of them, is still withheld: (Sec. 5(2)).

In *Campbell-Bennett Ltd. v. Comstock Mid-western Ltd.,* [1954] S.C.R. 207; affirming 8 W.W.R. 683, it was held that the pipe line in question, being a work or undertaking within the exclusive jurisdiction of Parliament, was not subject to a lien under the provisions of the provincial Mechanics' Lien Act. To hold otherwise would permit the sale of the undertaking piecemeal, nullifying the purpose for which the company was incorporated. The principle that a province cannot impose requirements on a Dominion company that would impair its ability to accomplish the purposes for which it was incorporated is founded on the decisions in *John Deere Plow Co. v. Wharton,* [1915] A.C. 330, and *Great West Saddlery Co. v. R.,* [1921] 2 A.C. 91. In *Toronto v. Bell Telephone Co.,* [1905] A.C. 52, provincial legislation requiring the Bell Telephone Company to obtain the city's consent to erect its poles was held *ultra vires* on this ground. It was held in *C.N.R. v. Nor-Min Supplies Ltd.* (1976), 66 D.L.R. (3d) 366 (S.C.C.), however, that while the Canadian National Railways Act, R.S.C. 1970, c. C-10 declares the railway "or other transportation works in Canada" of the railway to be works for the general advantage of Canada, the declaration does not extend to a quarry owned by the railroad and not adjacent to the railway right-of-way, and accordingly such land is not immune from mechanics' liens being filed against it.

In *Fonthill Lbr. Ltd. v. Bank of Montreal,* [1959] O.R. 451 (C.A.), the

Court dealt with the question whether or not the provisions of section 3 (see now sec. 2) of the Ontario Act (constituting moneys paid to a contractor by the owner a trust fund for the benefit of the subcontractors and material suppliers claiming under him) were *ultra vires* of the province insofar as they were applicable to moneys assigned by the contractor to his bank. It had been held in *Minneapolis-Honeywell Regulator Co. v. Empire Brass Co.,* [1955] S.C.R. 694; *Re Walter Davidson Co.,* [1957] O.W.N. 223; and *T. McAvity & Sons Ltd. v. Can. Bank of Commerce,* [1958] O.W.N. 324; affirmed [1959] S.C.R. 478, that an assignee could give his assignor no better title than he had himself. Accordingly, moneys owing to a contractor under the contract which had been paid under an assignment to a bank by an owner were still impressed with the trust created by section 3 (Ont.). (See also B.C., sec. 19). The bank sought to establish that section 3 could not be invoked against the bank on the grounds that section 91(15) of the British North America Act placed banking and the incorporation of banks within the exclusive jurisdiction of the Dominion and section 96 of The Bank Act provides that the bank is not bound to see to the execution of any trust whether express, implied or constructive to which any deposit is subject. The Court of Appeal held that that section did not release a bank from liability if it knew, not only of the existence of the trust, but also of the commission of a breach thereof, or of circumstances which ought to have put the bank on inquiry. The Court quoted with approval the statement of Masten J.A. in *Brantford v. Imperial Bank* (1930), 65 O.L.R. 625 at 632 (C.A.), as follows: "Notwithstanding the fact that the bank is incorporated by Dominion legislation and that the subject of banks and banking is by the British North America Act specifically and exclusively reserved to the Dominion authority, and notwithstanding the fact that it is clear, having regard to decided cases of which *John Deere Plow Co. v. Wharton,* [1915] A.C. 330, is an example, that the Provincial authority cannot limit the capacity or interfere with the operation of the bank in the conduct of its banking business, yet, on the other hand, the bank is bound by all existing laws competently enacted by the Provincial Legislature, examples of which are afforded by the well-known cases of *Colonial Bldg. & Invt. Assn. v. Atty. Gen. for Que.* (1883), 9 App. Cas. 157 at 164; *Citizens Ins. Co. v. Parsons* (1881), 7 App. Cas. 96; and *Bank of Toronto v. Lambe* (1887), 12 App. Cas. 575". The *Fonthill Lbr.* case, *supra,* was cited with approval in *John M. M. Troup Ltd. v. Royal Bank,* [1962] S.C.R. 487, affirming [1961] O.R. 455. See also Chapter 9, The Trust Fund.

In *Modular Products Ltd. v. Aristocratic Plywoods Ltd.* (1974), 42 D.L.R. (3d) 617 (B.C.C.A.), it was held that a beneficiary of the trust created by section 3 of the B.C. Act was entitled to receive the trust moneys in priority to the claim of the Federal Government to them under The Income Tax Act and The Excise Tax Act. The decision in *Shoquist Const. Co. v.*

Norfolk & Retailers Trust & Savings Co., [1974] 5 W.W.R. 513 (Sask.) is to the same effect. Claims for lien were held to have priority over the claim of the Provincial Government against the owner's holdback for income taxes owing to it by the general contractor in *H & H Trucking Ltd. v. Midas Aggregates Ltd.* (1974), 46 D.L.R. (3d) 637 (B.C.). See also: *Ocean Air Conditioning & Refrigeration Contractors Ltd. v. Dan,* [1977] 3 W.W.R. 456 (B.C.C.A.) and *Anden Vinyl Products Ltd. v. Gauss* (1977), 16 O.R. (2d) 225.

2

The Lienable Interest

§7   The Interest in General.

A mechanics' lien is a creature of provincial statute and the lien rights granted against the land upon which the lien claimant has performed work, or service, or supplied material, are limited to the extent of the value of the estate or interest of the person the various provincial mechanics' lien statutes define as "owner." The whole object of The Mechanics' Lien Act is to prevent statutory "owners"of the lands, whatever their interest in them, from getting the labour and capital of the lien claimants without paying for it: Phillips on Mechanics' Liens, sec. 76; *Galvin Lbr. Yards v. Ensor,* [1922] 2 W.W.R. 15 (Sask.); *Hickey v. Stalker,* [1924] 1 D.L.R. 440 (Ont.); *Scratch v. Anderson,* [1917] 1 W.W.R. 1340; affirmed 44 S.C.R. 86 (*sub nom. Limoges v. Scratch*); *Brooks-Sanford Co. v. Theodore Telier Const. Co.* (1910), 22 O.L.R. 176; *Read v. Whitney* (1919), 45 O.L.R. 377; *Pankka v. Butchart,* [1956] O.R. 837; *Earl F. Wakefield Co. v. Oil City Petroleums (Leduc) Ltd.,* [1958] S.C.R. 361; affirmed 29 W.W.R. 638 (P.C.); *Bank of Montreal v. Sidney (Twp.),* [1955] O.W.N. 581; *Minneapolis-Honeywell Regulator Co. v. Empire Brass Co.,* [1955] 3 D.L.R. 561 (Can.); *Re Shields and Winnipeg* (1964), 47 D.L.R. (2d) 346 (Man.). To this end there need be no direct contractual relationship between the statutory "owner" and the lien claimant.

The lien claimant's ultimate remedy is the sale of the statutory "owner's" interest to satisfy the liability created by the various Acts. A valid lien becomes itself an interest or estate in the "owner's" interest or estate however great or small the estate is found to be: *Pankka v. Butchart, supra.* But see *Suss Woodcraft Ltd. v. Abbey Glen Property Corpn.,* [1975] 5 W.W.R. 57 (Alta.). In most of the provinces it is stated that the lien claimant himself is deemed to be a purchaser *pro tanto:* Ont., sec. 20; Sask., sec. 34(2); P.E.I., sec. 27; Nfld., sec. 22; N.S., sec. 22; Man., sec. 19; N.B., sec. 26. See also *Pannill Door Co. v. Stephenson,* [1931] O.R. 594; *Harrell v. Mosier,* [1956] O.R. 152; *Cook v. Koldoffsky* (1916), 35 O.L.R. 555; *Stinson v. Mackendrick,* [1924] 2 D.L.R. 1000 (Ont.).

The estate or interest of the statutory "owner" must be an estate in realty and not in personalty: *Pankka v. Butchart, supra; George D. McLean & Associates Ltd. v. Leth*, [1949] 4 D.L.R. 282; affirmed [1950] 1 W.W.R. 536 (*sub nom. McLean v. Leth*) (B.C. C.A.); *Nobbs and Eastman v. C.P.R.* (1913), 6 W.W.R. 759 (Sask.); *Pollett's Elec. Services Ltd. v. Guar. Co. of N. Amer.* (1974), 5 N. & P.E.I.R. 579 (Nfld. C.A.).

The statutory definition of "owner" should not be confused with the legal or registered owner of the property. The meaning is an artificial, rather than natural, meaning: *Smith v. Port Hood Collieries*, [1923] 1 D.L.R. 1094 (N.S.); *Big Bend Const. Ltd. v. Donald* (1958), 25 W.W.R. 281 (Alta.); *Dalgleish v. Prescott Arena Co.*, [1951] O.R. 121 (C.A.). While in most instances the statutory "owner" is also the registered or legal owner, in many cases this is not so. For example, the statutory "owner" may be found to be merely the tenant of the registered owner and therefore only the estate or interest of the tenant as statutory "owner" could be sold to satisfy lien claims: *Gearing v. Robinson* (1900), 27 O.A.R. 364; *Roy v. Couturier Const. Ltd.* (1965), 51 M.P.R. 360 (N.B. C.A.); *Sandon Const. Ltd. v. Cafik*, [1973] 2 O.R. 553 (C.A.); *Swalm v. Fairway Finance Ltd.* (1965), 52 W.W.R. 626 (Alta.); *Stuart & Sinclair Ltd. v. Builtmore Park Estates Ltd.*, [1931] O.R. 315 (C.A.); *Dalgleish v. Prescott Arena Co., supra*. Again the mortgagee may be found to be the statutory "owner" and his interest sold to satisfy lien claimants: *M & M Floor Co. v. Motek* (1958), 24 W.W.R. 623 (B.C.); *Michaelis v. Ryan Motors*, [1923] 1 W.W.R. 401 (Sask.); *Nor. Elec. Co. v. Mfrs. Life Ins. Co.*, [1977] 2 S.C.R. 762. The Supreme Court of Canada in *Modern Const. Ltd. v. Maritime Rock Products Ltd.*, [1963] S.C.R. 347, rejected the argument that since the defendant's land was mortgaged and it held only an equity of redemption that it had no estate or interest in the land capable of being the subject of a mechanics' lien.

When the "owner's" estate or interest is sold by the Court under The Mechanics' Lien Act to satisfy liens the Court vests in the purchaser the estate and interest of the lienholders and gives the purchaser title free of liens.

The statutory "owner's" interest need not be legal only but may be an equitable one, and an equitable enforceable possessory title will be an estate or interest that will satisfy The Mechanics' Lien Act: *Dorrell v. Campbell*, [1917] 1 W.W.R. 500 (B.C.); *Galvin-Walston Lbr. Co. v. McKinnon* (1911), 16 W.L.R. 310 (Sask.); *MacDonald v. Hartley*, [1918] 3 W.W.R. 910 (B.C.); *F.C. Richert Co. v. Registrar of Land Titles*, [1936] 2 W.W.R. 473 (Alta.); *Christie v. Mead* (1888), 8 C.L.T. 312 (N.W.T.).

To acquire a valid enforceable lien a prospective lien claimant must show the following:

(a) That the person sought to be charged by him as "owner" under The Mechanics' Lien Act has an estate or interest in the land upon which his work, or service, was performed or material supplied that could be sold under the authority of the Act to satisfy the lien claim: *Pankka v. Butchart, supra; Kosobuski v. Extension Mining Co.* (1929), 64 O.L.R. 8; *Litton v. Gunther* (1908), 12 O.W.R. 1122; *Beaver Lbr. Co. v. Sask. Gen. Trust Co.,* [1922] 3 W.W.R. 1061 (Sask.); *Cunningham v. Sigfusson,* [1928] 1 W.W.R. 16 (Sask.); *Hamilton v. Cipriani,* [1977] 1 S.C.R. 169. See also §8 "Definition of Owner", *post.*

(b) That the person sought to be charged as "owner", generally speaking, requested, directly or impliedly, the work, service, or material to be supplied so as to enhance his estate or interest in the property. If the requirements of (a) and (b) are met, a person sought to be charged is by statute deemed the "owner." See also §10, "Definition of Request", *post.*

(c) If an "owner" under The Mechanics' Lien Act is found, the lien claimant must show that his work, or service performed, or material supplied for the statutory "owner" was of such a nature that it would give rise to the right to a lien on the "owner's" estate or interest. Not all the lien claimant's work, service, or materials give rise to lien rights, and The Mechanics' Lien Act must again be referred to to ascertain what work, service or material would create lien rights: Ont., sec. 5(1); Sask. secs. 12(1), 14(1), 17(1); P.E.I., secs. 2, 3(4); Nfld., sec. 7(1); N.S., secs. 5, 7(1); Man., secs. 4(1), 5(1); B.C., sec. 5; N.B., secs. 4(1), (5); Alta., secs. 4(1), 7(1). For example, in *Hubert v. Shinder,* [1952] O.W.N. 146 (C.A.), work done on laundry machinery, as it did not improve the property, was held not to give rise to lien rights, even though a statutory "owner" was found. See also *Pollett's Elec. Services Ltd. v. Guar. Co. of N. Amer.* (1974), 5 N. & P.E.I.R. 579 (Nfld. C.A.) *supra; A. J. (Archie) Goodale Ltd. v. Risidore Bros. Ltd.* (1975), 8 O.R. (2d) 427 (C.A.); *Mor Light Ltd. v. Rikki's Invts. Ltd.,* [1975] W.W.D. 156 (B.C.); *Dobbelsteyn Elec. Ltd. v. Whittaker Textiles (Marysville) Ltd.* (1976), 14 N.B.R. (2d) 584; *Evergreen Irrigation Ltd. v. Belgium Farms Ltd.* (1976), 3 A.R. 248; *Hett v. Samoth Realty Projects Ltd.* (1977), 3 Alta. L.R. (2d) 97 (C.A.).

Except in the provinces of Alberta, Saskatchewan, Ontario and Newfoundland, persons who rent equipment without operators are not entitled to claim a lien for the price of the rental, nor could they do so in these provinces until amendments were made to the Ontario Act in 1970 and the Alberta, Saskatchewan and Newfoundland Acts in 1971, which now provide otherwise: *Clarkson Co. v. Ace Lbr. Ltd.,* [1963] S.C.R. 110. Generally speaking, an architect who prepares plans for a building which is not proceeded with will not be entitled to a lien for his fees in preparing those plans as his work does not enhance the value of the land: *Burgess v. Khoury (Albrechtsen's Claim),* [1948] O.W.N. 789. This subject is however more fully discussed in Chapter 3, "The Lien Claimant".

§8 Definition of "Owner".

Each provincial Act defines the term "owner", and all are similar to the definition found in section 1(1) (d) of the Ontario Act. The owner includes any person, body corporate, or politic, including a municipal corporation and a railway company, having any estate or interest in the land upon which or in respect of which the work or service is done or materials are placed or furnished, at whose request and upon whose credit, or on whose behalf, or with whose privity or consent, or for whose direct benefit, the work or service is performed, or materials are placed or furnished. The definition further includes all persons claiming under the "owner" whose rights are acquired after the work or service in respect of which the lien is claimed is commenced or the materials furnished have been commenced to be furnished: see Sask., sec. 2(1)(h); P.E.I., sec. 1(j); Nfld., sec. 2(1)(i); B.C., sec. 2; N.S., sec. 1(d); Man., sec. 2(d); N.B., sec. 1; Alta., sec. 2(1)(g).

The meaning of "persons claiming under the owner" was put in issue in Ontario in the case of *Andre Knight Ltd. v. Presement,* [1967] 2 O.R. 289 (C.A.). The Court held that "persons claiming under" meant those holding subordinate tenurial interests in the land and did not include a grantee or mortgagee in fee simple as these persons would be claiming through not under the owner. It therefore appears in Ontario at least that a tenant of an owner having registered his lease after the work in respect of which a lien is claimed has commenced will be caught as an owner pursuant to the definition section of the Act and that the lien will have priority over the lease even if the lien is registered after the registration of the lease. See also *George Taylor Hdwe. Ltd. v. Balzer,* [1967] 2 O.R. 306 (C.A.); *Kelly v. Progressive Bldrs. Ltd.* (1970), 1 N. & P.E.I.R. 1 (Nfld.); *Silver v. R.R. Seeton Const. Ltd.* (1977), 74 D.L.R. (3d) 212 (N.S.).

§9 Request, Privity, Consent, Direct Benefit.

In all provinces a statutory "owner" is one who is found to have requested, either directly or by implication, the work, service, or materials. The British Columbia and Alberta Acts, however, contain special provisions concerning the statutory "owner".

In British Columbia, improvements done with the knowledge but not at the request of the owner, his agent or the person claiming any interest therein are deemed to have been done at his instance and request: sec. 14. The onus to show that the owner, his agent or a person claiming an interest had such knowledge rests upon the lien claimant: *Baker v. Williams* (1916), 23 B.C.R. 124 (C.A.). The section further provides that the person who has knowledge of the improvements being done can post on at least two conspicuous places upon the land or the improvements a notice in writing that he will not be responsible for such improvements or he may in the alternative give actual written notice of same to a prospective lien claimant. He is then free from all liability for improvements made from the time of posting or from the time written notice has been received by the lien claimant, as the case may be: see *Hutchinson v. Berridge* (1922), 66 D.L.R. 753 (Alta. C.A.), a decision rendered at the time when the Act of Alberta contained a section similar to the present British Columbia section 14. See also *Limoges v. Scratch* (1910), 44 S.C.R. 86; *Prentice v. Brown; Bowcott, Dean & Roberts v. Brown; Schwarz Bros. v. Brown* (1914), 6 W.W.R. 989 (Alta. C.A.); *Rohl v. Pfaffenroth* (1915), 31 W.L.R. 197 (Alta.).

In Alberta the early exploitation of oil and gas resources required the enactment of special provisions to protect lien claimants in this field. Section 4 of the present Act provides that when work is done or material furnished respecting the recovering of a mineral then notwithstanding that a person holding a particular estate or interest in the mineral concerned has not requested the work done or materials furnished the lien attaches to his interest or estate in the mineral concerned even though the mineral is severed from the land. The fee simple estate in the mine and mineral concerned will not, however, be subjected to the lien unless the person holding the fee simple has expressly requested the work done or materials furnished. See *Earl F. Wakefield Co. v. Oil City Petroleums* (1959), 29 W.W.R. 638 (P.C.), which deals with a previous Alberta section concerning lien rights on minerals. In Saskatchewan see section 12(2) (3) for similar provisions.

Coupled with request, excluding again British Columbia, and the Alberta and Saskatchewan mineral situations, the definition section of "owner", as previously mentioned, requires that the work, service, or materials be furnished upon the owner's credit, or on his behalf, or with his privity or consent, or for his direct benefit, in order to constitute him a statutory "owner".

In Ontario it was stated thus by Mr. Justice Middleton: "The intention of the statute clearly is to prevent anyone who has an estate or interest in land upon which a lien may be claimed ... from having liability imposed upon his estate unless there is on his part, first, a request, and, secondly, one or more of the alternative requirements mentioned", and he proceeded further to say, "This statutory definition is not to be regarded as creating a method of imposing a new kind of liability in favour of the subcontractor without privity of contract": *Sanderson Pearcy & Co. v. Foster* (1923), 53 O.L.R. 519 at 521-2.

The interpretation of the various terms, request, privity, consent, credit, behalf and direct benefit, are very difficult to distinguish. However, there must be something in the nature of direct dealing between the contractor and the person whose interest is sought to be charged in order to bring the latter within the definition of "owner". It was said in *Marshall*

Brick Co. v. Irving (1917), 35 O.L.R. 542; affirmed (*sub nom. John A. Marshall Brick Co. v. York Farmers Colonization Co.*) 54 S.C.R. 569 at 581 by Anglin J.: "While it is difficult if not impossible to assign to each of the three words 'request', 'privity' and 'consent' a meaning which will not to some extent overlap that of either of the others, after carefully reading all the authorities cited I accept as settled law ... that 'privity and consent' involves 'something in the nature of a direct dealing between the contractor and the persons whose interest is sought to be charged ... Mere knowledge of, or mere consent to, the work being done is not sufficient'." In this case the owners of certain lots agreed to sell them and to advance money to the purchaser for building purposes. On completion of the houses the vendors were to execute deeds of the lots, but the contract was not fulfilled and the purchaser forfeited his rights to the deeds, and it was held that there was nothing in the nature of direct dealing between the vendors and the lien claimants which would enable the Court to find that the vendor was a statutory "owner". See also *Nor. Plumbing Co. v. Greene* (1916), 10 W.W.R. 283 (Sask. C.A.); *Thoreson v. Zumwalt,* [1922] 1 W.W.R. 959 (Sask.); *Hayward Lbr. Co. v. Hammond* (1922), 70 D.L.R. 856 (Alta.); *Michaelis v. Ryan Motors,* [1923] 1 D.L.R. 1186 (Sask.); *Andre Knight Ltd. v. Presement,* [1967] 2 O.R. 289 (C.A.); *Cut-Rate Plate Glass Co. v. Solodinski* (1915); 34 O.L.R. 601 (C.A.); *Eddy Co. v. Chamberlain* (1917), 45 N.B.R. 261 (C.A.); *MacDonald-Rowe Woodworking Co. v. MacDonald* (1963), 39 D.L.R. (2d) 63 (P.E.I. C.A.); *W.J. Kent & Co. v. Legere* (1976), 65 D.L.R. (3d) 144 (N.B. C.A.); *Lefneski Const. Ltd. v. Katz* (1976), 1 C.P.C. 177 (Ont. Div.Ct.); *Hillcrest Contractors v. McDonald (No. 2)* (1977), 2 Alta. L.R. (2d) 273; *Suss Woodcraft Ltd. v. Abbey Glen Property Corpn.,* [1975] 5 W.W.R. 57 (Alta.); *Sandon Const. Ltd. v. Cafik,* [1973] 2 O.R. 553 (C.A.); *Nor. Elec. Co. v. Frank Warkentin Elec. Ltd.* (1972), 27 D.L.R. (3d) 519 (Man. C.A.); *Nor. Elec. Co. v. Mfrs. Life Ins. Co.,* [1977] 2 S.C.R. 762; *Swalm v. Fairway Finance Ltd.* (1965), 52 W.W.R. 626 (Alta.); *Hamilton v. Cipriani,* [1977] 1 S.C.R. 169; *Curran & Briggs Ltd. v. Ryder* (1977), 19 N.B.R. (2d) 330; *E.E. McCoy Co. v. Venus Elec. Ltd.* (1977), 19 N.B.R. (2d) 299.

In *Nuspel v. Lem Foo,* [1949] O.W.N. 476 when one trustee of a Chinese Society ordered work done on the property of the society, such work not being authorized by either of the other trustees or by the society itself through its officers, the definition of "owner" was not satisfied. And even if the society or its trustees knew the work was being done and acquiesced therein, in the absence of some direct dealing that alone would not be sufficient to support a lien claim. See also *Isitt v. Merritt Collieries Ltd.,* [1920] 1 W.W.R. 879 (B.C.). Individual members of a cooperative association were found not to be "owners" against whose individual estates or interest a lien may attach for work performed for the association itself, unless the members had contracted or dealt directly with the claimant: *Re East Central Gas Co-Op Ltd. and Henuset Ranches & Const. Ltd.* (1976), 72 D.L.R. (3d) 598, affirmed 6 A.R. 347 (C.A.).

It was held in *Bank of Montreal v. Haffner* (1881), 29 Gr. 319, that a registered mortgagee was not an "owner" within the meaning of the Act, for, although he fell within the first part of the definition in that he had an estate or interest in the premises sufficient to make him an "owner", there was no request on his part that the work be done so that the latter requirement of the definition was lacking. See also *Graham v. Williams* (1885), 9 O.R. 458 (C.A.). But see *Nor. Elec. Co. v. Mfrs. Life Ins. Co. (supra); Whitehead v. Lach Gen. Contractors Ltd.* (1974), 3 O.R. 680 (C.A.); *Curran & Briggs Ltd. v. Ryder* (1977), 19 N.B.R. (2d) 330; *E. E. McCoy Co. v. Venus Elec. Ltd.* (1977), 19 N.B.R. (2d) 299; and §58, *post,* "The Mortgagee as 'Owner'".

A landlord leased property with an option to purchase. Improvements were made by the tenant but the option was not taken up. It was held that the work was not done for the landlord's direct benefit. Although it might result in future benefit if the tenant forfeited his right to take up the option, it was not immediately and directly for the landlord's benefit when the material was being supplied. The materials were, moreover, not furnished on behalf of the landlord nor purchased on the landlord's credit and therefore the landlord was held not to be a statutory "owner": *Gearing v. Robinson* (1900), 27 O.A.R. 364. See also *Dalgleish v. Prescott Arena Co.,* [1951] O.R. 121 (C.A.); *Swalm v. Fairway Finance Ltd.* (1965), 52 W.W.R. 626 (Alta.); *Eddy Co. v. Chamberlain, supra; Hillcrest Contractors Ltd. v. McDonald (No. 2)* (1977), 2 Alta. L.R. (2d) 273, *supra.*

There must therefore be a request either express or by implication from the circumstances in order to give rise to lien rights against the person's interest sought to be charged.

In Freedman v. Guar. Trust Co., [1929] 4 D.L.R. 32 (Ont. C.A.), when owners of vacant land contracted to have a house erected and conveyed the property to the contractor to facilitate financing and agreed to repurchase the completed building, the re-conveyance being registered prior to any claim for lien, the owners were held to be statutory "owners" within the meaning of The Mechanics' Lien Act. But where a mortgagee was also a part owner of the equity in the property, the mere fact that the mortgagee knew that building was going on and was aware that its money, when advanced, would be put into the venture does not make it subject to the liabilities of an "owner": *Andre Knight Ltd. v. Presement,* [1967] 2 O.R. 289 (C.A.).

§10 Definition of Request.

A request may be implied and the onus is on the claimant to establish this: *Marshall Brick Co. v. Irving* (1917), 35 O.L.R. 542; affirmed (*sub nom.*

John A. Marshall Brick Co. v. York Farmers Colonization Co.) 54 S.C.R. 569 at 580; *Orr v. Robertson* (1915), 34 O.L.R. 147; *Stuart & Sinclair Ltd. v. Biltmore Park Estates Ltd.,* [1931] O.R. 315 (C.A.); *Stead Lumber Co. v. Lewis* (1957), 40 M.P.R. 363 (Nfld.); *Ryan v. X. L. Logging Co.* (1923), 33 B.C.R. 410; *Eddy Co. v. Chamberlain* (1917), 45 N.B.R. 261 (C.A.); *Crown Lbr. Co. v. Hickle & O'Connor,* [1925] 1W.W.R. 279 (Alta. C.A.); *Crown Const. Co. v. Cash,* [1940] O.R. 371; *Turner Valley Supply Co. v. Scott,* [1940] 3 W.W.R. 529 (Alta. C.A.); *Morgan v. Sunray Petroleum Corpn.,* [1941] 2 W.W.R. 517 (Alta.); *Partridge v. Dunham,* [1932] 1 W.W.R. 99 (Man.); *Andre Knight Ltd. v. Presement,* [1967] 2 O.R. 289 (C.A.); *Whitehead v. Lach Gen. Contractors Ltd.,* (1974), 3 O.R. 680 (C.A.); *Hillcrest Contractors v. McDonald (No. 2)* (1977), 2 Alta. L.R. (2d) 273; *Swalm v. Fairway Finance Ltd.* (1965), 52 W.W.R. 626 (Alta.); *Hamilton v. Cipriani,* [1977] 1 S.C.R. 169; *Nor. Elec. Co. v. Frank Warkentin Elec. Ltd.* (1972), 27 D.L.R. (3d) 519 (Man. C.A.); *Nor. Elec. Co. v. Mfrs. Life Ins. Co.,* [1977] 2 S.C.R. 762; *Suss Woodcraft Ltd. v. Abbey Glen Property Corpn.,* [1975] 5 W.W.R. 57 (Alta.); *Sandon Const. Ltd. v. Cafik,* [1973] 2 O.R. 553 (C.A.); *Lefneski Const. Ltd. v. Katz* (1976), 1 C.P.C. 177 (Ont. Div.Ct.); *W. J. Kent & Co. v. Legere* (1975), 65 D.L.R. (3d) 144 (N.B. C.A.).

A plaintiff's lien attaches to the land irrespective of whether the plaintiff looked originally for payment to the person with whom he was directly dealing. Where a son ordered work done for premises owned by his mother, in the circumstances of the case the mother's defence that she did not order the work and was therefore not a statutory "owner" failed: *Cope & Sons v. Armstrong* (1926), 31 O.W.N. 61; *Naftolin v. Skene,* [1932] O.R. 97 (C.A.). Where a father's sole motive was to establish one or more of his sons in a business that would belong to them exclusively, on premises owned by the father, it was held in the circumstances of the case that the father was an "owner" although the lien claimants relied on and dealt with the sons respecting the building contract: *Big Bend Const. Ltd. v. Donald* (1958), 25 W.W.R. 281 (Alta. C.A.). See further *Keewatin Elec. and Diesels Ltd. v. Durall Ltd.,* [1976] W.W.D. 119 (Man.). When a boarder ordered work done on premises, but there was no direct request on the part of the landlady nor circumstances from which a request could be implied, there were no lien rights: *Beaver Lbr. Co. v. Korotky,* [1927] 1 W.W.R. 945 (Sask.). Where A. ordered materials to construct a barn on property owned by his brother B., it was held that B. was not a statutory "owner" regardless of the fact that he knew of the construction and would receive direct benefit from it since all dealings were between A. and the supplier and there was no evidence from which to infer that A. was acting as B.'s agent: *MacDonald-Rowe Woodworking Co. v. MacDonald* (1963), 39 D.L.R. (2d) 63 (P.E.I. C.A.).

Where a registered owner authorizes a contractor to erect a building or any other improvement on his land, there is an implied request on the part of the owner to those persons furnishing material or doing work or performing services at the instance of the contractor to furnish such material, work or service for the direct benefit of such owner, so as to entitle such persons to avail themselves of the privileges or benefits conferred by The Mechanics' Lien Act: *Fortin v. Pound* (1905), 1 W.L.R. 333 (B.C.); *Anderson v. Godsal* (1900), 7 B.C.R. 404; *Sanderson Pearcy & Co. v. Foster* (1923), 53 O.L.R. 519; *Wasdell v. White* (1906), 4 W.L.R. 562 (Man.); *Slattery v. Lillis* (1905), 10 O.L.R. 697 (C.A.); *Reggin v. Manes* (1892), 22 O.R. 443; *B.C. Mills etc. Co. v. Horrobin* (1906), 12 B.C.R. 426 (C.A.); *Orr v. Robertson* (1915), 34 O.L.R. 147 (C.A.); *Nor. Elec. Co. v. Mfrs. Life Ins. Co.,* [1977] 2 S.C.R. 762.

Where the evidence establishes that materials were ordered fraudulently by an unnamed person pretending to call on behalf of the owner, the owner will not be liable to the material man as statutory "owner": *W. J. Kent & Co. v. Legere* (1975), 65 D.L.R. (3d) 144 (N.B. C.A.).

It was held in the case of *Watt Milling Co. (Trustee of) v. Jackson,* [1951] O.W.N. 841, that the purchaser of property having also agreed with the vendor-builder to have a house erected on the property pursuant to model or sample, the required request and direct dealing existed to constitute the purchaser an "owner" within the meaning of the Act.

The Court, however, would not imply a "request" by an "owner" to a supplier, who had no communication, direct or indirect, with the purchaser of a house with regard to work or materials, solely on the basis of the purchaser's complaint of poor workmanship to the supplier: *Cut-Rate Plate Glass Co. v. Solodinski* (1915), 34 O.L.R. 604.

In *Kahn v. Wacket,* [1957] O.W.N. 557 (C.A.), a purchaser agreed to purchase an apartment building, and the vendor agreed to erect a penthouse on top of the building proper, as part of the sale price. Respecting the penthouse portion of the contract, the purchaser was held to be an "owner" under the Act.

§11 The Tenant as Statutory Owner.

The statutory definition of "owner" contained in the Acts of each of the provinces has special application to a tenant in that there are two situations wherein he may come within the definition.

In the first situation, if the work is done or materials are furnished at his request and upon his credit or on his behalf or with his privity or consent or for his direct benefit then his estate or interest is lienable and may be sold by the Court to satisfy lien claims: *Gearing v. Robinson* (1900), 27 O.A.R. 364; *High River Trading Co. v. Anderson* (1909), 10 W.L.R. 126 (Alta.); *Prentice v. Brown* (1914), 6 W.W.R. 989 (Alta. C.A.); *Roy v. Couturier Const. Ltd.* (1965), 51 M.P.R. 360 (N.B. C.A.); *Orr v. Robertson* (1915), 34 O.L.R. 147 (C.A.); *Suss Woodcraft Ltd. v. Abbey Glen Property Corpn.,* [1975] 5

W.W.R. 57 (Alta.); *Sandon Const. Ltd. v. Cafik,* [1973] 2 O.R. 553 (C.A.).

In *Ryan v. X.L. Logging Co.* (1923), 33 B.C.R. 410, it was held that a logging lease could be the subject of a mechanics' lien. See also *Vaughan-Rys v. Clary* (1910), 15 B.C.R. 9; but see, *contra, Rafuse v. Hunter* (1906), 3 W.L.R. 381 (B.C.).

In the second situation, where work is done or materials are placed or furnished at the request of and on behalf of a person having an interest in the property superior to that of the tenant, the tenant may nevertheless come within the statutory definition of "owner". In 1967 the Ontario Court of Appeal held that a tenant whose rights are acquired after the work in respect of which the lien is claimed is commenced, or the materials placed or furnished have been commenced to be placed or furnished, will come within the definition of "owner" and that the lien will have priority over the lease even if the lien is registered subsequent to the registration of the lease. It appears that tenants in this situation will be badly exposed as priority of registration does not prevail and there is virtually nothing the tenant can do to protect his interest: *Andre Knight Ltd. v. Presement,* [1967] 2 O.R. 289 (C.A.); *George Taylor Hdwe. Ltd. v. Balzer,* [1967] 2 O.R. 306 (C.A.).

Where the tenant has requested the work done or materials furnished his interest is nonetheless subject to a lien even if the landlord may be exempt from the operation of The Mechanics' Lien Act. For example, the tenant of a Government Railway is still subject to the provisions of the Act. Therefore, where material was supplied to build a grain elevator which was situated on land leased from the C.N.R., it was held that the elevator was lienable only insofar as the leasehold interest was concerned, notwithstanding the C.N.R. was the owner of the land: *Man. Bridge etc. Works Ltd. v. Gillespie* (1914), 7 Sask. L.R. 208 (C.A.).

The ultimate remedy of a lien claimant is to sell the term for which the tenant holds the land and his interest in the building. This remedy would be nugatory if the landlord was allowed to cancel or forfeit the lease and as a result the Acts of Ontario, Prince Edward Island, New Brunswick, Newfoundland and Alberta prohibit the landlord from cancelling or forfeiting the lease, except for non-payment of rent and even in this case the lien holder is given the right to pay rent accruing in default after he became entitled to a lien and then add the amount so paid to the landlord to his lien claim: *High River Trading Co. v. Anderson* (1909), 10 W.L.R. 126 (Alta.); *Sandon Const. Ltd. v. Cafik,* [1973] 2 O.R. 553 (C.A.); P.E.I., sec. 12(2); N.B., sec. 12(2); Alta., sec. 12(2); Nfld., sec. 9(2); Ont., sec. 7(2). The lienholder's remedy of sale and his protection from forfeiture of the lease will be of little use where the tenant's estate is not saleable as for example, a tenancy at will: see *Roy v. Couturier Const. Ltd., supra.*

Where the tenant's interest in the land and the building is sold to a purchaser, the purchaser should be entitled to have possession of the land

and the building for the term of the lease, subject of course to its provisions. If the building is to remain the property of the tenant with the right of removal, the purchaser, in addition to the term of the lease, acquires the tenant's property in the building and the tenant's right to remove the building at the end of the term: *Galvin Lbr. Yards v. Ensor,* [1922] 2 W.W.R. 15 (Sask. C.A.); *Zabriskie v. Greater Amer. Exposition Co.* (1903), 62 L.R.A. 369.

§12 The Landlord's Liability as "Owner".

The relationship of landlord and tenant, or of head tenant and sub-tenant, will not of itself render the former liable as statutory "owner" under the Mechanics' Lien Acts. The definition of "owner" must again be referred to and the landlord or head tenant brought within the definition before any liability is created.

As previously stated in §9 and §10 *ante,* something in the nature of direct dealing between landlord, or head tenant, and the lien claimant is required: *Gearing v. Robinson* (1900), 27 O.A.R. 364; *John A. Marshall Brick Co. v. York Farmers Colonization Co.* (1917), 54 S.C.R. 569, affirming 35 O.L.R. 542 (*sub nom. Marshall Brick Co. v. Irving*).

In Alberta, a tenant engaged an electrician on two occasions to perform certain work on the demised premises and on both occasions the landlord paid the account. Notwithstanding the tenant was advised by the landlord that no further accounts would be paid, she again ordered work done and the landlord paid for part of the account only. The electrician claimed a lien for the balance of the account and the Court held that the landlord was not an "owner" within the definition section of the Alberta Act. There had been no direct dealings between the claimant and the landlord; no express request for the work done and the payment of the previous accounts was not sufficient to imply a request or infer that the tenant was acting as the landlord's agent: *Swalm v. Fairway Finance Ltd.* (1965), 52 W.W.R. 626 (Alta.).

Where a lease is entered into with express provisions that renovations be carried out by the lessee, there is still not sufficient direct dealing between the contractor carrying out the renovations and the head tenant lessor to render the latter liable as "owner", if the lessor takes no further part in the renovations: *Dalgleish v. Prescott Arena Co.,* [1951] O.R. 121 (C.A.). See further *Hillcrest Contractors Ltd. v. McDonald (No. 2)* (1977), 2 Alta. L.R. (2d) 273; *Sandon Const. Ltd. v. Cafik,* [1973] 2 O.R. 553 (C.A.).

This is also true of a leasing agreement obliging the lessee to erect a new building, with plans to be approved, changed, or modified by the lessor, and the right of supervision or alteration of plans, and the use of certain rooms in the structure by the lessor, and the lessor acting as the tenant's agent to sell certain shares and memberships to raise funds for the erection of the building: *Stuart & Sinclair Ltd. v. Biltmore Park Estates Ltd.*, [1931] O.R. 315 (C.A.).

However, in an earlier decision of *Orr v. Robertson* (1915), 34 O.L.R. 147 (C.A.) (explained in *John A. Marshall Brick Co. v. York Farmers Colonization Co., supra*), when the lessee covenanted in the lease to build according to plans approved by the head tenant, the head tenant expending some of his own capital on the structure, and the structure reverting to the head tenant on the expiration of the lease, he taking out the building permit and being consulted on building progress and ordering some of the work to be done, it was held that there was the requisite request and direct dealing to make the head tenant liable as "owner" under the Act. See also *Eddy Co. v. Chamberlain* (1917), 45 N.B.R. 261 (C.A.); *Garing v. Hunt* (1895), 27 O.R. 149; *Pavich v. Tulameen Coal Mines Ltd.*, [1936] 3 W.W.R. 593 (B.C. C.A.); *Limoges v. Scratch* (1910), 44 S.C.R. 86; *Nuspel v. Lem Foo*, [1949] O.W.N. 476; *Partridge v. Dunham*, [1932] 1 W.W.R. 99 (Man. C.A.); *Graham v. Williams* (1885), 9 O.R. 458 (C.A.); *Turner Valley Supply Co. v. Scott*, [1940] 3 W.W.R. 529 (Alta. C.A.); *Morgan v. Sunray Petroleum*, [1941] 3 D.L.R. 747 (Alta.); *Webb v. Gage* (1902), 1 O.W.R. 327 (C.A.); *Johnson & Johnson Ltd. v. Butler* (1914), 7 W.W.R. 385 (Alta.).

In Alberta, where a landlord approved plans, received part of the contractor's construction contract with the tenant, received payment from the contractor for the cost of the building permit, gave instructions directly to the contractor during the course of construction, and the lease stated that all construction improvements became the landlord's property on the expiry of the lease, the Court held the landlord to be an "owner": *Suss Woodcraft Ltd. v. Abbey Glen Property Corpn.*, [1975] 5 W.W.R. 57 (Alta.).

For sale leaseback transactions see *Nor. Elec. Co. v. Mfrs. Life Ins. Co.*, [1977] 2 S.C.R. 762 and §58 "The Mortgagee as 'Owner'", *post*.

The amount to be assessed for holdback against a landlord who has been found to be an "owner" may cause some concern to the Court, since there is no construction contract between the landlord and the tenant upon which to calculate the statutory holdback. The Court was faced with this problem in *Nor. Elec. Co. v. Metro Projects* (1977), 1 R.P.R. 286 (N.S.) as a result of the Supreme Court of Canada decision in *Nor. Elec. Co. v. Mfrs. Life Ins. Co., (supra)*. After finding that the mortgagee had not entered into a construction contract upon which the 15% holdback could be based, it found that the contract price upon which the percentage would apply was the amount the mortgagee agreed to advance to the developer in return for the benefits it derived under the contract between them. See also *Hamilton v. Cipriani*, [1977] 1 S.C.R. 169. It is reasonable to conclude therefore that the statutory holdback would be calculated on the contract price between the tenant and his contractor.

When the estate or interest upon which the lien attaches is leasehold, the Acts of the various provinces provide a means by which the lien claimant may subject the fee simple to the lien. In Ontario, sec. 7(1), and Newfoundland, sec. 9(1), the lien claimant may give written notice, by personal service, to the owner or his agent of the work to be done or material to be furnished and thereafter, in order to avoid liability, the owner or his agent must give written notice, by personal service, within fifteen days, to the lien claimant that he will not be responsible for the work or the material. The Acts of New Brunswick, sec. 12(1) and Prince Edward Island, sec. 12(1) provide the same method except the lien claimant may send the notice by registered mail and the owner has ten days to give his notice of disclaimer which need not be personally served upon the lien claimant. The Alberta Act, sec. 12(1) does not specify that the lien claimant's notice must be served personally or otherwise and the time limited for reply by the owner is within five days. In Saskatchewan, sec. 17(2), Manitoba, sec. 5(2) and Nova Scotia, sec. 7(2), the fee simple may be subjected to the lien with the consent of the owner only; provided that such consent is testified to by the signature of the owner upon the claim for lien at the time of registration thereof and duly verified by affidavit.

Notice must be given with respect to work contemplated and not with respect to work already performed: *Patsis v. 75-89 Gosford Ltd.; Papas v. Patsis,* [1973] 1 O.R. 629. The delivery of the contractor's plans and part of his construction contract with the tenant showing the price of the work to the landlord was held not to be sufficient notice in writing under the Alberta Act: *Suss Woodcraft Ltd. v. Abbey Glen Property Corpn.,* [1975] 5 W.W.R. 57 (Alta.); *Hillcrest Contractors Ltd. v. McDonald* (1976), 1 Alta. L.R. (2d) 221. See also *Beyersbergen Const. Ltd. v. Edmonton Centre Ltd.* (1977), 78 D.L.R. (3d) 122 (Alta. C.A.).

In British Columbia sections pertaining to leasehold interests have been replaced by section 14, previously discussed, which provides that all improvements done with the knowledge, but not at the request, of the owner shall be deemed to have been done at the owner's request unless there has been posted on at least two conspicuous places upon the land or upon the improvements, by the owner, a notice in writing that he will not be responsible for the improvements, or after actual notice in writing to the like effect has reached the person claiming a lien under the Act. If the estate sold under the British Columbia or Saskatchewan Acts is leasehold the purchaser is deemed to be the assignee of the lease: B.C., sec. 37; Sask., sec. 52.

§13 Agreements of Purchase and Sale.

(a) *The Purchaser's Position.*

Unless he comes within the statutory definition of "owner" a *bona fide* purchaser without notice of an unregistered lien will have priority over such lien since he is entitled to rely on the protection of The Registry Act as against any liens of which he has no notice or knowledge: *Morton v. Grant*, [1956] 3 D.L.R. (2d) 478; *Charters v. McCracken* (1916), 36 O.L.R. 260 (C.A.); *Ross v. Hunter* (1882), 7 S.C.R. 289; *Rose v. Peterkin* (1884), 13 S.C.R. 677; *Re Irvine and Main,* [1933] O.W.N. 476; *Re Pridham,* [1934] O.W.N. 560; *Sterling Lbr. Co. v. Jones* (1916), 36 O.L.R. 153; *Cut-Rate Plate Glass Co. v. Solodinski* (1915), 34 O.L.R. 604; *Andre Knight Ltd. v. Presement,* [1967] 2 O.R. 289 (C.A.); *George Taylor Hdwe Ltd. v. Balzer,* [1967] 2 O.R. 306 (C.A.); *Kelly v. Progressive Bldrs. Ltd.* (1970), 1 N. & P.E.I.R. 1 (Nfld.).

In order to come within the statutory definition of "owner" there must be more than mere knowledge that the building is going on before the transaction of purchase and sale is completed: *Sterling Lbr. Co. v. Jones, supra; Andre Knight Ltd. v. Presement, supra; George Taylor Hdwe. Ltd. v. Balzer, supra.*

But if the purchaser engages in any sort of direct dealing with the contractor, materialman, or employee of the vendor he may put himself within the statutory definition of "owner", and therefore become liable. Where a purchaser encouraged and persuaded a builder engaged by the vendor, who was in doubt that he might not be paid by the vendor, to continue the work, the builder thus feeling assured of payment, the purchaser was held to be an "owner": *Blight v. Ray* (1893), 23 O.R. 415.

The purchaser might even go so far in his assurances of payment to the subcontractor that the Court would find a direct contract, and therefore hold the purchaser liable for the entire amount of the subcontract: *John C. Love Lbr. v. Moore,* [1963] 1 O.R. 245 (C.A.); *Conrad v. Kaplan,* [1914] 18 D.L.R. 37 (Man. C.A.). See also Chapter 4, Rights and Duties of Owner.

A purchaser who buys a house built to sample evidences the necessary direct dealing to render him liable as "owner" under the Act: *Watt Milling Co. (Trustee of) v. Jackson,* [1951] O.W.N. 841. See also *Reggin v. Manes* (1892), 22 O.R. 443; *Freedman v. Guar. Trust Co.,* [1929] 4 D.L.R. 32 (Ont. C.A.).

In the case of *Fred H. Blanchard & Son v. Poetz Const. Co.* (1953), 8 W.W.R. 225 (Alta.) the purchasers agreed with the defendant owner to purchase a house already in the course of construction. No agreement of purchase and sale was executed. The plaintiffs performed certain work under a contract with the owner which work was incomplete when the purchasers, without a deed, took occupation. While in occupation of the premises the purchasers had urged the plaintiff to complete but subsequently refused the plaintiff entry. One of the purchasers then registered a *caveat* on title, claiming an interest under the aforesaid agreement. Subsequently, a lien was registered, naming the defendant, only, as owner. Thereafter the deed to the purchasers was registered. The Court held that the lien was valid against the purchasers and the failure to name them in the claim for lien did not vitiate the lien's validity.

Where the relationship of vendor and purchaser of a property was so close that the Court found the transaction to be in the nature of a joint venture in a building project the purchaser was held liable as statutory "owner": *Crown Lbr. Co. v. Hickle* (1925), 21 Alta. L.R. 128 (C.A.). For a further discussion of the joint venture relationship, see *Nor. Elec. Co. v. Mfrs. Life Ins. Co.,* [1977] 2 S.C.R. 762; *C.M.H.C. v. Graham* (1973), 43 D.L.R. (3d) 686 (N.S.); *Grannan Plumbing & Heating Ltd. v. Simpson Const. Ltd.* (1977), 17 N.B.R. (2d) 569; *Dahl v. Phillips* (1960), 33 W.W.R. 238 (B.C.).

(b) Vendor's Position if Purchaser Defaults.

If, after an agreement of purchase and sale is entered into, and work or service is ordered by the purchaser, who subsequently defaults before the transaction is completed, and the lands revert to the vendor, in the absence of anything in the nature of direct dealing between the vendor and the contractor, materialman, or worker engaged by the purchaser, the vendor will incur no liability as "owner": *John A. Marshall Brick Co. v. York Farmers Colonization Co.* (1916), 54 S.C.R. 569; affirming (*sub nom. Marshall Brick Co. v. Irving*) 35 O.L.R. 542; *Nor. Plumbing Co. v. Greene* (1916), 10 W.W.R. 283 (Sask. C.A.); *Thoreson v. Zumwalt,* [1922] 1 W.W.R. 959 (Sask.); *Hayward Lbr. Co. v. Hammond* (1922), 70 D.L.R. 856 (Alta.); *West v. Elkins* (1894), 14 C.L.T. 49 (Ont.); *Flack v. Jeffrey* (1895), 10 Man. R. 514; *B.C. Timber & Trading Co. v. Leberry* (1902), 22 C.L.T. 273 (B.C.); *Michaelis v. Ryan Motors,* [1923] 1 D.L.R. 1186 (Sask.).

Where the agreement for sale between vendor and purchaser provided that the purchaser build upon the property, the Court held the vendor was not an "owner" under the Act: *Rogers Lbr. Yards Ltd. v. Jacobs,* [1924] 2 W.W.R. 1128 (Alta. C.A.). See also *Thoreson v. Zumwalt, supra;* but *cf. B.C. Granitoid etc. Co. v. Dom. Shipbuilding etc. Co.,* [1918] 2 W.W.R. 919 (B.C. C.A.).

In British Columbia however, something short of direct dealing between the vendor and contractor may render the vendor liable as statutory "owner". As previously mentioned, section 14 provides that improvements done with the knowledge of the owner, although not at his request, are deemed to have been done at his request and instance, unless and until he notifies the prospective lien claimant that he will not be responsible. Moreover, section 15 provides that improvements placed upon the premises held under an option or working bond, where the grantor of the option permits the grantee to make such improvements, are deemed to have been constructed at the instance and request of the owner of the premises and the grantor of the option and liens will attach to the interest of the owner of the premises and grantor of the option. There is no provision for notice relieving the owner of the property and the grantor of the option from liability as was the case in section 14.

(c) Lien Claimant's Position if Purchaser Defaults.

(i) *The Purchaser's Interest:* The purchaser under an agreement of purchase and sale has an estate or interest sufficient for a lien to be claimed thereon, and a lien claimant is entitled to any estate or interest which the purchaser had before he forfeited and released to the vendor, but the claim is subordinate to the claim of the vendor: *Flack v. Jeffrey* (1895), 10 Man. R. 514. Before a purchaser's interest may be found the subject of a lien the interest must have been in existence at the time of the arising of the lien, and so where M. obtained materials for building upon lands to which he had no title, of which he was not in possession, and in which he had no interest, no lien could attach: *B.C. Timber & Trading Co. v. Leberry, supra.*

In *Hoffstrom v. Stanley* (1902), 14 Man. R. 227, it was indicated that if the work or service was done while the purchaser still had a valid agreement of purchase and sale with the vendor, and before the purchaser's rights were forfeited, then the estate or interest that the purchaser had could be acquired by the lien claimant. See also *Montjoy v. Heward S. Dist. Corpn.* (1908), 10 W.L.R. 282 (Sask.). Since the lien claimant could acquire the interest of the purchaser, it appears that he would be able to enforce specific performance of the agreement of purchase and sale from the vendor upon paying the purchase price, provided the agreement of purchase and sale was still subsisting in that the purchaser's rights thereunder had not been forfeited.

It was held in the case of *Dorrell v. Campbell,* [1917] 1 W.W.R. 500 (B.C. C.A.), that in order to affect the purchaser's interest, it was not necessary that the agreement of purchase and sale be registered. See also *Clarke v. Williams,* [1939] 3 W.W.R. 481 (B.C.).

(ii) *The Vendor's Interest:* As previously indicated, unless the vendor can be brought within the definition of a statutory "owner" and subject to sections 14 and 15 in the British Columbia Act, the vendor's interest is not lienable. However, the Acts of the various provinces have dealt with the priorities between the vendor and lien claimant. The Acts of Manitoba, sec. 11(2), Nova Scotia, sec. 14(2) and Saskatchewan, sec. 26(2), state that, for the purposes of the Act, where there is an agreement of purchase of land and the purchase money or part thereof is unpaid, and no conveyances made to the purchaser, the purchaser shall be deemed a mortgagor and the vendor a mortgagee. In Ontario, sec. 7(6), British Columbia, sec. 7(3), Alberta, sec. 9(4) and Newfoundland, sec. 9(6), the agreement of purchase and sale must be registered. In Prince Edward Island, sec. 9(5) and New Brunswick, sec.

9(4); it is provided that the unpaid vendor under the purchase and sale agreement has priority over a lien only to the extent of the value of the land at the time the lien arose.

If the unpaid vendor pays off certain liens incurred by the purchaser, he cannot then add these amounts to his prior claim under the sale agreement in priority to other lien claimants: *Fitzpatrick v. Fitzpatrick,* [1923] 1 W.W.R. 1118 (Sask.). However, the Acts of Alberta, sec. 9(3) and British Columbia, sec. 7(2), provide that where a mortgagee pays mortgage money to satisfy a registered statement of lien, the mortgagee is subrogated to the rights of the lien claimant for the amount so paid. The Acts of the two provinces further provide that if an agreement of purchase and sale is registered, the vendor is deemed to be a mortgagee and the purchaser a mortgagor and it would therefore appear that these sections apply equally to a vendor.

If the lien claimant seeks to charge the interest of the vendor, the lien claim must so state, and the vendor must be made a defendant in the action: *Nor. Plumbing Co. v. Greene* (1916), 10 W.W.R. 283 (Sask. C.A.). But see time limit in *Rocca Steel Ltd. v. Tower Hill Apts. Ltd.,* [1968] 2 O.R. 701.

(*iii*) *Unjust Enrichment:* As previously indicated, where work and service is done or materials are supplied on behalf of a purchaser and the purchaser subsequently defaults under the agreement of purchase and sale, the lien claimant can look only to the interest of the purchaser to enforce his remedies provided by the Acts of the various provinces, unless the vendor can be brought within the statutory definition of "owner".

Where a vendor is not within this statutory definition of "owner" the lien claimant's remedies against the purchaser may be of doubtful value. Since the purchaser has defaulted, it is not likely that the lien claimant's personal judgment will be of any great consequence. His right of lien against the purchaser's interest in the property may be of little use for his ultimate recourse is sale, but only of the purchaser's interest. Moreover, in the limited circumstances in which specific performance is available to the lien claimant, it may be that the lien claimant would not have sufficient funds in order to avail himself of the purchaser's rights under the agreement of purchase and sale. On the other hand, the vendor will obtain the benefits of the construction without paying for them and as a result may be unjustly enriched.

The above issue came before the Ontario Court in *Nicholson v. St. Denis* (1975), 8 O.R. (2d) 315 (C.A.). Having bought a building from the vendor the purchaser contracted with the plaintiff for construction improvements. The work was completed without knowledge of the vendor. The purchaser defaulted and the building reverted to the vendor. The Court in holding the plaintiff could not succeed against the vendor under the doctrine of unjust enrichment found that there was no special relationship between the plaintiff and the vendor, no express or implied request by the vendor for the benefit, no encouragement or acquiescence in the work being performed, no mistaken belief by the plaintiff that he held title to the property, and further, that the plaintiff could have at least registered a lien to secure whatever rights he might have had under the Mechanics' Lien Act. See also *Lefneski Const. Ltd. v. Katz* (1976), 1 C.P.C. 177 (Ont. Div.Ct.). In British Columbia see *Ledoux v. Inkman,* [1976] 3 W.W.R. 430 (B.C.).

As to the doctrine of unjust enrichment or restitution generally, see: *Fibrosa Spolka Akcyjna v. Fairbairn etc. Ltd.,* [1943] A.C. 32; *Morrison v. Can. Surety Co. & McMahon* (1954), 12 W.W.R. 57 (Man.); *Estok v. Heguy* (1963), 43 W.W.R. 167 (B.C.); *Deglman v. Guar. Trust Co. & Constantineau,* [1954] S.C.R. 725; *Sinclair v. Brougham,* [1941] A.C. 398 at 431; *Reeve v. Abraham* (1957), 22 W.W.R. 429 (Alta.); *Ings. v. Indust. Accept. Corpn.,* [1962] O.R. 454 (C.A.); *Daniel v. O'Leary* (1976), 14 N.B.R. (2d) 564; *Small v. Stanford,* [1977] 6 W.W.R. 185 (B.C.); *T & E Dev. Ltd. v. Hoornaert* (1977), 78 D.L.R. (3d) 606 (B.C.).

§14 Miscellaneous Estates or Interests.

There are many cases where several persons may be the statutory "owner" at the same time, such as joint tenancy, landlord and tenant, tenancy in common, and life estates, and it would seem, therefore, that the acts of one party might render that party's interest liable as "owner", while the other party might not fall within the statutory definition and therefore incur no liability: see *Sanderson Pearcy & Co. v. Foster* (1923), 53 O.L.R. 519 (C.A.). In *Johnson & Johnson v. Crocker & Crocker,* [1954] O.W.N. 352 (C.A.), it was held that the contract in question was made on behalf of both joint tenants of the property. However, one of several trustees cannot render trust property subject to a lien: *Nuspel v. Lem Foo,* [1949] O.W.N. 476. See also *Crown Lbr. Co. v. Hickle,* [1925] 1 W.W.R. 279 (Alta.); *Isitt v. Merritt Collieries Ltd.,* [1920] 1 W.W.R. 879 (B.C.); *Re East Central Gas Co-op Ltd. and Henuset Ranches & Const. Ltd.* (1976), 72 D.L.R. (3d) 598, affirmed 6 A.R. 347 (C.A.).

In the case of *Beaver Lbr. Co. v. Miller* (1916), 32 D.L.R. 428 (Sask.), a man ordered building material when he did not have his Crown Patent, but was merely a homestead entrant, and he later acquired the patent. The Court held he had an "owner's" interest. It was suggested in this case that a person actually in possession of land had sufficient interest to come within the definition of "owner". See also *Galvin-Walston Lbr. Co. v. McKinnon* (1912), 4 Sask. L.R. 68 (C.A.), where Wetmore C.J. stated at p. 71: "And I am of opinion, too, that a person so actually in possession has a sufficient interest in the land to come within the meaning of "owner" as defined by . . . the Mechanics' Lien Act. . . . But I am of opinion that this possession, so as to create *prima facie* evidence of title, must be an actual possession. And, in order to amount to an interest which would support a lien under the Mechanics' Lien Act, the actual possession or interest would have to exist at the time the materials were ordered." In this case the Court found that there was no evidence that the defendant was in actual possession at the time he ordered the materials and thus no lien. It is difficult, however, to visualize how a Court could vest this sort of title respecting this type of estate or interest. However, in *Pankka v. Butchart,* [1956] O.R. 837 (C.A.), a purchaser under the Veteran's Land Act had no estate or interest until the vendor was fully paid and he got his deed, as his rights were held to be personal until the deed was received, and therefore the interest could not be sold to satisfy lien claims. See also *Cunningham v. Sigfusson,* [1928] 1 W.W.R. 16 (Sask. C.A.) where the Court held that a person in occupation of land under a mere understanding with the owner that he would be given just opportunity to purchase it at a price to be fixed by the owner was not a person with any estate or interest in the land within the meaning of the definition of "owner" in the Saskatchewan Mechanics' Lien Act.

A lien upon an equitable interest of a purchaser under a purchase and sale agreement becomes a charge upon the legal registered estate when the purchaser acquires and registers the deed. So when a prospective purchaser under a purchase agreement did acts that would have rendered a lien valid, and later became the registered owner, the lien attached even though at the time of incurring liability he had no statutory "owner's" interest in the lands: *J.B. Turney & Co. v. Farrelly Bros Ltd.,* [1922] 3 W.W.R. 289; reversed on other grounds [1922] 3 W.W.R. 1017 (Alta. C.A.).

Where a contractor agreed to construct an apartment building on the owner's land, the owner to advance the necessary funds, and thereafter the profit on the sale of the building to be divided between the contractor and the owner, it was held that the contractor had no right of lien against the owner. In this case, the contractor was claiming his share of the estimated profits, or in the alternative, his share on a *quantum meruit* basis. The Court found that this type of profit sharing arrangement was not within the provisions of The Mechanics' Lien Act and that if the contractor had any right to the profits he must sue for same in an action for debt: *Dahl v. Phillips* (1960), 33 W.W.R. 238 (B.C.).

Where a subcontractor supplied material through his partnership to an owner which was in fact himself, it was held that in this situation, the supplier and the owner being different entities, the subcontractor had a right to a valid lien: *Ross Bros Ltd. v. Gorman* (1908), 1 Alta. L.R. 516. Where the owner company and the contractor companies' shares were owned or controlled by one individual the Court held the companies to be separate legal entities: *Nor. Elec. Co. v. Frank Warkentin Elec. Ltd.* (1972), 27 D.L.R. (3d) 519 (Man. C.A.). An owner under the Mechanics' Lien Act cannot contract with himself. The owner and contractor must be distinct and separate persons: *Bore v. Sigurdson,* [1972] 6 W.W.R. 654 (B.C.). But see *Galvin-Walston Lbr. Co. v. McKinnon, supra,* where the Court held that if a lienholder subsequently became the owner of the land, whatever interest he could claim under his lien merged in his title as owner. Respecting joint venture agreements see §13(a) *ante.*

On September 1, 1973 the Saskatchewan Act was amended to clarify the position of lien claimants against condominium property (sec. 13(2).) Where on the request of the owner of a condominium unit, work is done upon or in respect of that unit, or material is furnished to be used in that unit, the lien is upon the estate of the owner of that unit and his share in the common property. The lien is registered against the title to the unit.

Where on the request of the condominium corporation work is done upon or in respect of the common property or any unit or both, or material is furnished to be used in the common property or any unit or both intended for the benefit of the common property generally, the lien is upon the estate of all the owners in all the units and the common property. When the condominium corporation requests work to be done upon or in respect of any unit, or material furnished to be used in any unit intended for the benefit of that unit, the lien is upon the estate of the owner in that unit and his share in the common property. Where the lien is filed respecting requests by the condominium corporation, the lien must be registered against the condominium plan and not against the title to any unit.

§15 Husband and Wife.

Where work, services or materials are furnished to be used upon or in respect of land of a married woman or land in which she has an interest or an inchoate right of dower, with the privity and consent of her husband, the husband will be presumed to be acting as her agent as well as for himself unless before the lien claimant commenced his services he had actual notice to the contrary. The above provisions are found in Ontario, sec. 6, (see *Johnson & Johnson v. Crocker & Crocker, supra*); Saskatchewan, sec. 16; Prince Edward Island, sec. 11; Nova Scotia, sec. 6; New Brunswick, sec. 11; British Columbia, sec. 11. In Alberta, (sec. 11), if either spouse orders work done, he or she shall be presumed to be acting as the agent of the other, unless the person doing the work had actual notice to the contrary. The provision is lacking in Manitoba and Newfoundland and apart from statute there is no presumption that the husband is acting for the wife at common law: *Gillies v. Gibson* (1907), 17 Man. R. 479. In this case the inference was drawn from the circumstances that the husband was authorized to act as agent for his wife to arrange for the erection of a building. The wife entered into building loan arrangements, attended to see the work in progress, was frequently in the building loan company's office and gave directions as to the progress of the building. Where the defendants lived in a common law relationship the Court held the common law husband to be the implied agent of the owner, the common law wife: *Dogwood Drilling Ltd. v. Fitterer,* [1977] 2 W.W.R. 724 (B.C.). See further, *MacDonald-Rowe Woodworking Co. v. MacDonald* (1963), 39 D.L.R. (2d) 63 (P.E.I. C.A.); *Lefneski Const. Ltd. v. Katz* (1976), 1 C.P.C. 177 (Ont. Div.Ct.).

The Manitoba Court in *Bogach v. Huhn,* [1929] 2 W.W.R. 249 held that, since the property in question was the homestead of the husband and wife, both of whom resided on the premises, and the contract was given to the plaintiff in the presence of the defendant wife, the wife was liable as "owner".

§16 Wife's Dower Interest.

Since the lien claimant's ultimate remedy to satisfy his claim is sale of the property, he must have regard to possible dower interests not only so as to be able to obtain an order of the Court vesting the property in the purchaser free of dower, but also to be able to obtain moneys received from a sale in priority to any dower interest. In Ontario on the 31st day of March, 1978, the Family Law Reform Act came into force which by Section 70 abolished dower in that Province. Proceedings are presently under way to repeal the Sections of the Ontario Mechanics' Lien Act dealing with dower which appear to have been left in the Act by oversight. The remainder of this Section should be read in the light of this new Act.

(a) Priority.

In the case of *Re Robinson,* [1938] O.W.N. 361, it was held by Mr. Justice Urquhart following section 6 of the Ontario Act that since the husband is the wife's agent, her dower interest falls within the definition of "owner", and the Act gives the lienholder priority in such cases over the widow's inchoate right to dower. He stated "the liens were quite properly deducted before any consideration of dower took place at all".

In Manitoba and Newfoundland, which do not have a provision similar to that of section 6 of the Ontario Act, in order to claim priority over the wife's dower interest, where there is no direct contract with her, the lien claimant will have to bring her within the definition of "owner" by proving a common law agency relationship between husband and wife. See §15, *ante.*

(b) Sale After Judgment.

The Acts of each province provide that at the trial of a mechanics' lien action the Court may order the estate or interest charged with the lien be sold. The Court is given power to make all necessary orders to complete the sale and vest the property in the purchaser. The proceeds of sale are paid into Court to be distributed according to its direction: Ont., secs. 38(6) and 39; Alta., secs. 45(2), (3) and 46(1), (2); B.C., secs. 30(2) and 40; Man., secs. 40(1) and 41(1); N.B., secs. 44(1) and 45(1); Nfld., secs. 38(6) and 39(1); P.E.I., secs. 46(1) and 47(1); Sask., sec. 51(3) and 51(5); N.B., secs. 43(1) and 44(1).

It is to be noted that what the Court is empowered to sell and therefore what it may vest is the estate or interest charged with the lien. Unless, therefore, the wife's dower interest is so charged it cannot be sold and consequently cannot be extinguished. The wife therefore will have to be an "owner" under the Act whether by direct contract, presumed agency or agency at common law. The claim for lien should then describe her as an owner and she should be made a party defendant in the action.

(c) Sale by Trustee.

The Acts of Ontario, sec. 34, Alberta, sec. 40, Saskatchewan, sec. 50 and Newfoundland, sec. 34 provide for the appointment, at any time before or after judgment, of a trustee with power to manage, mortgage, lease or sell the "property" against which a claim for lien is registered. Any moneys received on the sale are paid into Court pending determination of those entitled to them. The Acts of Ontario and Alberta further provide that any vesting order made in such a sale shall vest the property free of all liens, encumbrances and interests, including dower, unless the order for sale directed otherwise. In Newfoundland and Saskatchewan the section dealing with the vesting order is similar except that there is no specific reference to dower. It is, however, submitted that the words "interests of any kind" found in the Newfoundland and the Saskatchewan Acts are sufficiently broad in scope to include dower.

The vesting order, however, has no effect upon the position of the lien claimants and the wife; the sale moneys taking the place of the land, their rights and priorities in such funds remain to be determined after the sale is completed.

§17 Roads and Streets.

The Acts of the various provinces presently differ in their treatment of lien claims upon public streets and highways or any work or improvement done or caused to be done by a municipal corporation thereon.

The Acts of British Columbia, sec. 4, Alberta, sec. 5(1), New Brunswick, sec. 2, and Nova Scotia, sec. 2, provide that public streets and highways and any work or improvement done or caused to be done by a municipal corporation thereon, are not lienable. The reasoning behind these statutory provisions is obviously that it would be against public policy and public convenience to allow the lien claimant to enforce his ultimate remedy of sale. See: *Can. Bank of Commerce v. T. McAvity & Sons Ltd.,* [1959] S.C.R. 478; *Re Northlands Grading Co.,* [1960] O.R. 455 (C.A.); *Alspan Wrecking Ltd. v. Dineen Const. Ltd.,* [1972] S.C.R. 829; *Westeel-Rosco Ltd. v. South Sask. Hospital Centre Bd. of Governors,* [1977] 2 S.C.R. 238; *Shields v. Winnipeg* (1964), 49 W.W.R. 530, (Man.).

The Acts of Saskatchewan, Prince Edward Island and Manitoba contain no provision exempting from lien claims public streets or highways or any work done thereon by a municipal corporation. Nevertheless, it has been held in *Shields v. Winnipeg, supra,* that despite the Manitoba Act containing no such provision, a registered claim for lien against a public street could not stand because the right of the public to pass and re-pass without obstruction was a higher right than the ultimate right of sale of the lien claimant. See also *Alspan Wrecking Ltd. v. Dineen Const. Ltd., supra,* where the Court adopted the same reasoning with respect to a public bridge; *Van Buren Bridge Co. v. Madawaska* (1957), 15 D.L.R. (2d) 763 (N.B. C.A.), and *Westeel-Rosco Ltd. v. South Sask. Hospital Centre Bd. of Governors, supra.*

The present Acts of Ontario and Newfoundland state that although a lien cannot be registered against a public street or highway, nevertheless, the proper holdback must be maintained by the "person" primarily liable on the contract and instead of registering his claim for lien, the claimant may deliver a notice of claim to holdback, thereby charging the amount directed to be retained under the holdback section: Ont., secs. 5(2), 11(5), 21a, 23a; Nfld., secs. 6(1), 13(5), 23(5), 25(2). These amendments to the Ontario and Newfoundland Acts thereby satisfy the public interest as well as enforce the lien claimant's right.

The interesting question arises as to whether a lien claimant in those provinces which either do not contain any provision with respect to public streets or highways or in those provinces which contain an unqualified exemption of lien, could avail himself of the holdback provisions contained in those Acts. It would appear doubtful upon the reasoning of the decision of *Johnson & Carey Co. v. Can. Nor. Ry. Co.* (1918), 44 O.L.R. 533 (C.A.), which held that the holdback provisions are premised upon the lien claimant being entitled to a lien in the first instance and therefore if there is no lien then the lien claimant would not be entitled to a declaratory judgment for the funds required to be held back. In *Westeel-Rosco. Ltd. v. South Sask. Hospital Centre Bd. of Governors, supra,* the Supreme Court of Canada allowed a charge on the holdback fund even when no lien existed but under sections of the Saskatchewan Mechanics' Lien Act which have now been repealed.

The terms "highways" or "streets" are defined in each of the Acts and are broad in scope, as for example, "highways" in New Brunswick include bridges, subways, piers, ferries, lanes, thoroughfares, squares and public places appropriated to the public use. The definition section of each Act should therefore be reviewed carefully.

Where a plan of subdivision includes construction of streets, the streets not actually having been dedicated by the owners to the use of the public, work done on the streets does not come within the exception and the lien may be enforced thereon: *Vannatta v. Uplands Ltd.* (1913), 4 W.W.R. 1265 (B.C. C.A.). The onus of showing a dedication of road is on the municipality and the burden is by a preponderance of probability: *Reed v. Lincoln* (1974), 6 O.R. (2d) 391 (C.A.), see also *Silliker v. Newcastle* (1974), 10 N.B.R. (2d) 118; *Levesque v. Berube* (1974), 10 N.B.R. (2d) 80.

The date of registration of the plan of subdivision is the date of dedication of the streets on the plan of subdivision for public use: *Niagara Concrete Pipe Ltd. v. Charles R. Stewart Const. Co.,* [1956] O.W.N. 769. Since in this case the first work giving rise to the liens was not done until after registration, there was no lien allowed. See also *Re Plan 69 Dunnville,* [1950] O.R. 350 (C.A.); *Re Westwood Addition, Hamilton,* [1945] O.R. 257 (C.A.).

In *Beseloff v. White Rock Resort Dev. Co.* (1915), 22 B.C.R. 33, it was held that work in clearing a subdivision benefitting the whole subdivision would give rise to a lien on the whole of the subdivision excluding roads if they proved to be public roads. However, if the entire work upon which lien rights were sought was to be done on the roads in the subdivision no lien could be given with respect to lands adjacent to the roads in the subdivision: *Niagara Concrete Pipe Ltd. v. Charles R. Stewart Const. Co., supra.* This decision was questioned in the more recent decision of *Re Ellwood Robinson Ltd. and Ohio Dev. Co.* (1975), 7 O.R. (2d) 556, but see *Canron Ltd. v. Willen Estates Ltd.* (1977), 3 B.C.L.R. 334.

Roads and streets that are vested in the Crown in the right of Canada or declared a work for the general advantage of Canada, are not lienable. Moreover, the lien claimant is not entitled to a personal judgment, nor is he entitled to a declaratory judgment against holdback funds. See: *Queenston Quarries Ltd. v. Bennett & Lovejoy* (1923), 24 O.W.N. 361; *Crawford v. Tilden* (1907), 14 O.L.R. 572, and *Johnson & Carey Co. v. Can. Nor. Ry. Co.* (1918), 44 O.L.R. 533.

§18 Government Property.

(a) *Crown in the Right of Canada.*

The estate or interest in the lands of the Crown in the right of Canada cannot be subjected to a lien or sold under provincial legislation since if provincial legislation purported to provide for such a lien and ultimate sale of the property this would be *ultra vires* of the province: *Bain v. Director,*

Veterans' Land Act, [1947] O.W.N. 917; *Deeks, McBride Ltd. v. Vancouver Associated Contractors Ltd.* (1954), 14 W.W.R. 509 (B.C. C.A.); *B.A.C.M. Ltd. v. Parkland Bldrs. Contracting Ltd.* (1971), 18 D.L.R. (3d) 377 (Sask.); see also: *Gauthier v. R.* (1918), 56 S.C.R. 176; *R. v. Powers,* [1923] Ex. C.R. 131; *Re Director of Soldier Settlement* (1960), 25 D.L.R. (2d) 463 (Alta.); *Ottawa v. Shore & Horwitz Const. Co.* (1960), 22 D.L.R. (2d) 247 (Ont.).

Land acquired subsequent to the enactment of the British North America Act and registered in the name of a Crown Agency stands in the same position as land held in the name of the Crown: BNA Act secs. 108, 109, 117; *B.A.C.M. Ltd. v. Parkland Bldrs. Contracting Ltd., supra.*

The Federal Crown can however subject its property to provincial Mechanics' Lien legislation by specific enactment. For example see the National Energy Board Act, R.S.C. 1970, c. N-6 in respect to pipeline companies.

(b) *Crown in the Right of a Province.*

The interpretation Acts of the various provinces provide that no Act affects Her Majesty unless it is expressly stated therein that she is bound: R.S.O. 1970, ch. 225, sec. 11; R.S.Alta. 1970, ch. 189, sec. 13; R.S.B.C. 1960, ch. 199, sec. 35; R.S.Man. 1970, ch. 180, sec. 15; R.S.N.B. 1952, ch. 114, sec. 32; R.S.Nfld. 1952, ch. 1, sec. 13 [re-en. 1954, ch. 1, sec. 5]; R.S.N.S. 1967, ch. 151, sec. 13; R.S.P.E.I. 1951, ch. 1, sec. 10; R.S.Sask. 1965, ch. 1, sec. 7. As a result the estate or interest in the lands of the Crown in the right of the province cannot be subjected to a lien: *The Pedlar People Ltd. v. McMahon Plastering Co.* (1961), 34 W.W.R. 315 (Alta.); *W.H. Morton & Co. v. Can. Credit Men's Trust Assn. Ltd.* (1965), 53 W.W.R. 178 (Man. C.A.); *Modern Const. Co. v. Maritime Rock Products Ltd.,* [1963] S.C.R. 347; *Dom. Bridge Co. v. Sask. Govt. Telephones* (1963), 42 W.W.R. 577 (Sask.); *Westeel-Rosco Ltd. v. South Sask. Hospital Centre Bd. of Governors,* [1977] 2 S.C.R. 238; *Pounder v. Carl C. Schaum Const. Ltd.,* [1972] 2 O.R. 616; *Kitchen Kabinets Ltd. v. Pinsent Const. Ltd.* (1974), 6 N. & P.E.I.R. 426 (Nfld.).

In *Crane Can. Ltd. v. McBeath Plumbing & Heating Ltd.* (1966), 54 W.W.R. 119 (B.C.), it was held that The Interpretation Act applied to exempt the Crown only where the Crown's rights were affected and therefore the Crown could come within the definition of "owner" to the extent necessary to permit a sub-contractor to apply the trust fund provisions to claim funds in the hands of a general contractor on a government project. See also *Cronkhite Supply Ltd. v. Wrkrs. Comp. Bd.,* (1976), 1 B.C.L.R. 142.

The Supreme Court of Canada recently held that where the Ontario Water Resources Commission was in effect the general contractor for the "owner", the City of Hamilton, its status as an agent of the Crown was irrelevant in Mechanics' Lien proceedings as it was not involved as an "owner": *Hamilton v. Cipriani*, [1977] 1 S.C.R. 169.

In 1975 the Ontario Mechanics' Lien Act was amended to specifically bind the Crown with the exception of work under a contract as defined in The Ministry of Transportation and Communications Creditors Payment Act, 1975, and to which that Act applied; sec. 1(*a*)(1). The Crown is now included in the definition sec. of "owner"; sec. 1(1)(*d*) and includes Crown agencies to which the Crown Agency Act applies; section 1(*ba*). Included in the new provisions of the Ontario Act is what is defined as "public work". Public work is defined as the property of the Crown and includes land in which the Crown has an estate or interest, and also includes all works and properties acquired, constructed, extended, enlarged, repaired, equipped or improved at the expense of the Crown, or for the acquisition, construction, repairing, equipping, extending, enlarging or improving of which any public money is appropriated by the Legislature, but not any work for which money is appropriated as a subsidy only; sec. 1(1)(*da*). While no lien attaches to these lands the Act provides for a charge on amounts directed to be retained under the holdback provisions in favour of the lien claimant without requiring registration or enforcement of the lien against the land; sec. 5(2).

(c) Crown Agencies.

A Crown agency may be created by statute or by contract: *R. v. Montreal & Montreal Locomotive Works Ltd.*, [1945] S.C.R. 621; affirmed [1946] 3 W.W.R. 748 (*sub nom. Montreal v. Montreal Locomotive Works*) (P.C.). In Ontario a "Crown agency" means a board, commission, railway, public utility, university, manufactory, company or agency owned, controlled or operated by Her Majesty in the right of Ontario, or by the Government of Ontario, or under the authority of the Legislature or the Lieutenant Governor in Council: The Crown Agency Act, R.S.O. 1970, c. 100.

Whether or not a particular body is an Agent of the Crown depends upon the nature and degree of control which the Crown exercises over it: *Westeel-Rosco Ltd. v. South Sask. Hospital Centre Bd. of Governors*, [1977] 2 S.C.R. 238; *Halifax v. Halifax Harbour Commrs.*, [1935] S.C.R. 215; *Re Sask. Govt. Ins. Office and Saskatoon*, [1947] 2 W.W.R. 1028 (Sask. C.A.); *R. v. Lab. Rel. Bd. (Ont.); Ex parte Ont. Food Terminal Bd.*, [1963] 2 O.R. 91 (C.A.); *Fairbank Lbr. Co. v. O'Connor* (1974), 4 O.R. (2d) 576; *Re McGruer & Clark Ltd.* (1976), 13 O.R. (2d) 385 (Ont. Dev. Corpn.); *Pike v. Ont. College of Art Council*, [1972] 3 O.R. 808 (Ont. College of Art); *Cronkhite Supply Ltd. v. Wrkrs. Comp. Bd.* (1977), 1 B.C.L.R. 142 (Wrkrs. Comp. Bd. Rehabilitation Centre).

The Ontario Housing Corporation has been held to be an agent of the

Crown, both at common law and under the provisions of The Crown Agency Act, and therefor, not subject to the lien provisions of The Mechanics' Lien Act: *R. v. Lab. Rel. Bd. (Ont.); Ex parte Ont. Housing Corpn.,* [1971] 2 O.R. 723; *Pounder v. Carl C. Schaum Const. Ltd.,* [1972] 2 O.R. 616; *Berardinelli v. Ont. Housing Corpn.* (1977), 15 O.R. (2d) 217. Similarly in Manitoba; see *Bodrug v. Man. Housing and Renewal Corpn.* (1977), 79 D.L.R. (3d) 409 (Man.). But see *Cronkhite Supply Ltd. v. Wrkrs. Comp. Bd.,* (1976), 1 B.C.L.R. 142, where the Court held that the Workers' Compensation Board of British Columbia, a Crown Agency, was lienable.

An agent of the Crown either in the right of a province or in the right of Canada is entitled to the same rights, privileges and prerogatives as the Crown and as a result lands held by such agent are not lienable: *Bain v. Director, Veterans' Land Act, supra; Deeks, McBride Ltd. v. Vancouver Associated Contractors Ltd., supra; Dom. Bridge Co. v. Sask. Govt. Telephones, supra; B.A.C.M. Ltd. v. Parkland Builders Contracting Ltd.* (1971), 18 D.L.R. (3d) 377 (Sask.).

Whether the land is registered in the name of the Crown or in the agent's name does not affect the above principle, because where the land is registered in the agent's name it is deemed to be held in trust for the Crown: *Dom. Bridge Co. v. Sask. Govt. Telephones, supra.* The mere fact that a Crown agency is given the power to contract or sue and be sued in its own name does not change its status nor does it affect the question of whether its lands are subject to a lien; moreover, a Crown agency cannot consent to submit itself or its property to the provisions of a Mechanics' Lien Act: *Dom. Bridge Co. v. Sask. Govt. Telephones, supra.*

(d) *Works and Undertakings, B.N.A. Section 91(29), Section 92(10).*

Pursuant to section 91(29) and section 92(10) of the British North America Act 1867, the Federal Government has jurisdiction over subjects that relate to real property such as railways, canals, telegraphs and other works and undertakings connecting one province with any other or others, or extending beyond the limits of the province, and also such works, although wholly situate within a province, as are before or after their execution declared by the Parliament of Canada to be for the general advantage of Canada or for the advantage of two or more of the provinces.

It was at one time a widely held view that works declared to be for the general advantage of Canada were expressly subject to the exclusive jurisdiction of the Parliament of Canada and therefore exempt from the provisions of the provincial Mechanics' Lien Acts. This was stated in the head note in *Crawford v. Tilden* (1907), 14 O.L.R. 572 (C.A.), although the reasoning in the case did not bear out this interpretation.

In the recent case of *C.N.R. v. Nor-Min Supplies Ltd.,* [1977] 1 S.C.R. 322, the C.N.R. owned land adjacent to its railway line and used that land as a quarry for the supply of rock ballast for its line. The Supreme Court of Canada held that while section 18(1) of the C.N.R. Act declared the railway "or other transportation works in Canada" of the railway to be work for the general advantage of Canada the declaration did not extend to the railway's quarry, nor did the quarry fall within the definition of railway under section 2(1) of the Railway Act and accordingly the land was not immune from provincial Mechanics' Liens.

Mr. Justice Laskin stated in his reasons at 333: "The mere economic tie-up between the C.N.R.'s quarry and the use of the crushed rock for railway line ballast does not make the quarry a part of the transportation enterprise in the same sense as railway sheds or switching stations are part of that enterprise. The exclusive devotion of the output of the quarry to railway uses feeds the convenience of the C.N.R., as would any other economic relationship for supply of fuel or materials or rolling stock, but this does not make the fuel refineries or depots or the factories which produce the materials or the rolling stock parts of the transportation system."

Thus the entire function of the railway or other transportation works of the railway is not exempted by section 92(10) of the British North America Act from the provincial Mechanics' Lien Acts but only those functions that are shown as essential to its day-to-day operations.

In *Crawford v. Tilden* (1907), 14 O.L.R. 572, a lien was registered against a part of railway lands, the railway being incorporated by Federal Charter and declared to be a work for the general advantage of Canada. The Court held the land was not subject to a lien because the ultimate effect of The Mechanics' Lien Act would cause the piecemeal sale of the railway contra the public interest and convenience.

Johnson & Carey Co. v. Can. Nor. Ry. Co. (1918), 44 O.L.R. 533 (C.A.), was to the same effect; however, the Court went further and stated the lien claimant was not entitled to recover personal judgment nor seek a declaratory judgment against holdback funds because his rights in this regard were dependent upon his having a "valid" lien in the first instance. Note that in the present section 40 of the Ontario Act dealing with the power to award personal judgment, the word "valid" has been deleted so that even if the claimant fails to establish any lien he may still obtain personal judgment.

In *Campbell-Bennett v. Comstock Midwestern Ltd.,* [1954] S.C.R. 207, a lien was registered against part of the lands owned by a company incorporated under a Special Act of the Federal Parliament. The Court held that since the pipeline was to extend from Alberta to British Columbia, it was a work within the exclusive jurisdiction of the federal Legislature and since the ultimate remedy of the claimant would cause the piecemeal sale of the line and would destroy the federal undertaking it was not subject to the provincial Mechanics' Lien Act. But presently respecting pipelines see the

National Energy Board Act, R.S.C. 1970, c. N-6 and §18(*a*), *supra.*

In *Western Canada Hdwe. Co. v. Farrelly Bros. Ltd.,* [1922] 3 W.W.R. 1017, reversing [1922] 3 W.W.R. 289 (Alta. C.A.), the Court held that an irrigation ditch or canal being a work constructed under the authority of Dominion legislation for the purpose of using federal property could not be attached by a lien as it would be an interference with the existence of federal property and federal legislation. The work being done for the general benefit of a large number of landowners, it would be against public policy to destroy such an undertaking by the process of execution.

However, in *R. v. Algoma Dist. Ct. Judge,* [1958] O.W.N. 330, it was held that uranium mines declared to be works for the general advantage of Canada were subject to lien rights since the enforcement of the remedies provided under The Mechanics' Lien Act could not be said to impair the companies' function or status. The Court stated at 331: "While sec. 92(10)(c) read with sec. 91(29) gave legislative control of works declared to be for the general advantage of Canada to the Dominion, it did not declare such works should cease to be part of the Province or exempt from provincial legislation. . . ." The learned Judge then examined the Atomic Energy Control Act and said it was regulatory only. It in no way expressly affected the operation of The Mechanics' Lien Act. The decision stands for the proposition that even if the works in question come within the exemptions contained in section 92(10) of the British North America Act and would otherwise be exempt from the provisions of the provincial legislation the work is still subject to provincial laws of general application and it is only those provincial laws which purport to or have the effect of impairing or sterilizing the function of the works which will be held to be invalid. In *Campbell-Bennett Ltd. v. Comstock Midwestern Ltd.,* [1954] S.C.R. 207 at 216, Mr. Justice Rand stated: "The mutilation by a province of a federal undertaking is obviously not to be tolerated in our scheme of federalism, and this from the beginning has been the view taken of provincial legislation of the nature of that before us." Thus the mere fact that provincial legislation may affect such a work is not enough; the question is, does the act purport to, or will it operate to impair the purpose of the undertaking, and the answer to this is to a large degree dependent upon public policy.

On the subject of legislative powers of the provinces in respect of Crown property see generally: *Canadian Constitutional Law,* 4th edition, pp. 526-7; *Constitutional Law of Canada,* 1st edition, c. 22, p. 391; *Interjurisdictional Immunity in Canadian Federalism,* (1969) 47 Can. Bar Rev. 40.

§19 Railway Property.

The right of lien against railway property should be reviewed in the light of the decision in *C.N.R. v. Nor-Min Supplies Ltd.*, [1977] 1 S.C.R. 322, in the Supreme Court of Canada and see §18(*d*), *ante*.

It can also be argued that a railway is a public highway and as such is exempted from lien claims by the provisions of the Acts of the various provinces. See §17 *ante; Crawford v. Tilden* (1907), 14 O.L.R. 572; *Gardner v. London, Chatham & Dover Ry.* (1867), L.R. 2 Ch. 201; *Ottawa v. Can. Atlantic Ry. Co.* (1902), 4 O.L.R. 56 at 75n; affirmed 33 S.C.R. 376; *Strange v. Bd. of Commrs. of Grant County*, 91 N.E. 242 (U.S.); *Sharpless v. Philadelphia*, 59 Am. Dec. 159 at p. 169 (U.S.); *Olcott v. Supervisors*, 83 U.S. 678.

A subway has been held to constitute a railway within the definition section of The Railways Act R.S.O. 1950: *Lofting v. T.T.C.*, [1958] O.W.N. 243.

In *King v. Alford* (1885), 9 O.R. 643 (C.A.) a mechanics' lien did not attach upon an engine house and turn-table built for a railway company, the works being necessary for the proper working of the railway. But see *C.N.R. v. Nor-Min Supplies Ltd., supra*, with respect to railway sheds or switching stations.

§20 Municipal Property.

The definition section of each provincial Act must be reviewed with respect to the position of municipal corporations or the status of property owned by them in a particular province. The Acts of Ontario, sec. 1(*d*), Manitoba, sec. 2(*d*) and Nova Scotia, sec. 1(*d*), include a municipal corporation in the definition of "owner". Municipal corporations are not included in Saskatchewan, Prince Edward Island, Newfoundland, British Columbia, New Brunswick and Alberta.

As previously discussed, municipal streets are subject to exemption from liens by the Acts of Ontario, British Columbia, New Brunswick and Nova Scotia; however, as to Ontario and Newfoundland, see §17, *ante,* respecting enforcement of rights. In provinces not exempting streets by statute it has been held that on grounds of public policy, they would fall within the same class as railways and would therefore be exempt: *Shields v. Winnipeg* (1964), 49 W.W.R. 530 (Man.); *Crawford v. Tilden, supra; Queenston Quarries Ltd. v. Bennett & Lovejoy* (1923), 24 O.W.N. 361; *Alspan Wrecking Ltd. v. Dineen Const. Ltd.*, [1972] S.C.R. 829; *Westeel-Rosco Ltd. v. South Sask. Hospital Centre Bd. of Governors*, [1977] 2 S.C.R. 238.

In *Alberta Lbr. Co. v. Hines*, [1931] 2 W.W.R. 558 (Alta.), a lien attached to a hospital building erected by a hospital district established under The Municipal Hospitals Act of Alberta, on the grounds that the municipal hospital was an entity in itself, and not just an integral part of the whole as were railways and irrigation projects, and that if the hospital were sold another could be erected in its place. This case followed *Lee v. Broley* (1909), 2 Sask. L.R. 288 (C.A.). See also *Groundwater Dev. Corpn. v. Moncton* (1970), 2 N.B.R. (2d) 941.

The Winnipeg City Hall was held to be the subject of mechanics' liens and the defence that the building was for public purposes was not allowed: *McArthur v. Dewar* (1885), 3 Man. R. 72; *Guest v. Hahnan* (1895), 15 C.L.T. 61 (Ont.). These cases should now be carefully reviewed in the light of the recent Supreme Court of Canada decision in *Westeel-Rosco Ltd. v. South Sask. Hospital Centre Bd. of Governors, supra,* wherein the Court held that any sale of the hospital property in the present case would be clearly contrary to the public interest and should not be permitted.

In *Revelstoke Sawmill Co. v. Alberta Bottle Co.* (1915), 9 Alta. L.R. 155; affirmed 9 Alta. L.R. at 162 (C.A.), a municipality agreed to sell industrial property to X. X was to build a bottling plant on the site and was not to have title until 60 days after the plant was in operation. Liens were filed before the transfer was completed and the municipality's defence that the project was for public purposes which would be defeated if the lands were sold, and that such a sale would be contrary to public policy, was not accepted.

In *Anthes Imperial Ltd. v. Earl Grey (Village)* (1970), 75 W.W.R. 566 (Sask. C.A.), it was held that a village was clearly an owner within the meaning of the Act and that the plaintiff in that action was entitled to a lien on a sewage and waterworks installation on land owned by and registered in the name of the village.

§21 Public Corporations.

The Mechanics' Lien Act makes no distinction between private owners and ownership by public corporations or public utilities except the exemptions previously discussed. As was said in *Benson v. Smith & Son* (1916), 37 O.L.R. 257 (C.A.): "It is made very plain in the Act that it was not meant to be applicable to private property only; nor to such property only as is exigible under ordinary writs of execution."

§22 School Property.

It was held in *Benson v. Smith & Son, supra,* that there was no reason why it would be against the public interest to permit a lien on school property, and it was further indicated that court houses, jails, hospitals, churches, and railway stations might be in the same category as schools. See also *Gen. Contracting Co. v. Ottawa* (1910), 16 O.W.R. 479 (C.A.). But see *Westeel-Rosco Ltd. v. South Sask. Hospital Centre Bd. of Governors,*

[1977] 2 S.C.R. 238; *Alspan Wrecking Ltd. v. Dineen Const. Ltd.,* [1972] S.C.R. 829.

The defence that school property should be exempt because of its use for the benefit of the public without profit, and as a general public educational system for the province was not accepted in *Connely v. Havelock School Trustees* (1913), 9 D.L.R. 875 (N.B.). It was held that The Mechanics' Lien Act was passed in the interest of workmen and contractors to afford them security, and this argument was stronger than the public policy defence. See also *Hazel v. Lund* (1915), 22 B.C.R. 264; *Moore v. Bradley Protestant School District* (1887), 5 Man. R. 49; *Cronkhite Supply Ltd. v. Wrkrs. Comp. Bd.* (1977), 1 B.C.L.R. 142.

In *Lee v. Broley* (1909), 2 Sask. L.R. 288 (C.A.), it was stated that if the property of the School Board was taken from them under The Mechanics' Lien Act, then the most that could be said was that they would have to build another school house, and they were in no worse position than any other judgment debtor. See also *Mallett v. Kovar* (1910), 14 W.L.R. 327 (Alta.).

The distinction between the decisions in the above cases and those in *W.H. Morton & Co. v. Can. Credit Men's Trust Assn. Ltd.* (1965), 53 W.W.R. 178 (Man. C.A.), and *Crane Can. Ltd. v. McBeath Plumbing & Heating Ltd.* (1966), 54 W.W.R. 119 (B.C.), where no liens were allowed, is that in the latter cases, the land was held by the Crown in the right of the province. See §18, *ante.*

§23 Payment into Court Standing in the Place and Stead of the Land.

The Acts of the various provinces provide a means of removing liens from the title upon security being posted or payment into Court. The purpose and intent of such provisions was expressed by Mr. Justice Riley in *Pedlar People Ltd. v. McMahon Plastering Co.* (1960), 33 W.W.R. 47 (Alta.), where he stated: "A procedure was laid down to permit liens to be removed from the title pending litigation over the validity of the liens, thus enabling the owner to free the property from the liens upon adequate security being given. To suggest that once the security is given and the liens removed, the parties to the proceedings are to be conclusively held to have admitted the validity of the lien is in direct conflict with the concept of 'security' being the section enabling the court to vacate the lien upon directing security for or payment into court of the amount of the lien." See also *Laguna Holdings Ltd. v. Plempe,* [1972] 1 W.W.R. 211 (B.C.); *Re Tri-Lateral Enterprises Ltd.,* (1977) 74 D.L.R. (3d) 519 (Ont.); *Ocean Air Conditioning & Refrigeration Contractors Ltd. v. Dan; Re A & W Food Services of Can. Ltd. and Vancouver A & W Drive-Ins Ltd.,* [1976] 3 W.W.R. 131, affirmed [1977] 3 W.W.R. 456 (*sub nom. Ocean Air Conditioning & Refrigeration Contractors Ltd. v. Dan*) (B.C.C.A.); *Re Collavino Bros.,* [1977] 1 A.C.W.S. 351 (N.S.).

In Ontario, sec. 25(2)(*a*) and Newfoundland, sec. 27(2)(*a*), an application may be made at any time to allow security for or payment of the amount of the lien claim into Court together with the amount of the claims of any other subsisting lien claimants plus such costs as the Court may fix. Thereupon an order will be made vacating the registered lien and Certificate of Action if any. Both Acts, (Ont., sec. 25(2)(*b*); Newfoundland, sec. 27(2)(*b*)) further state that upon any other proper ground, the registration of a lien or liens and Certificate of Action may be vacated. These latter subsections contemplate situations where, for example, it is plain to the Court that the amount of the claim for lien is inflated, that there is duplication, that part of the lien claim is for work that is nonlienable, or upon land that cannot be the subject of a lien. The Court may therefore allow the posting of security for, or payment into Court of, less than the amount of the lien or liens claimed. Generally, lien claimants are entitled to have paid into Court the highest amount for which the owner could reasonably be foreseen to be liable: *Otis Elevator Co. v. Commonwealth Holiday Inns of Can. Ltd.,* [1972] 2 O.R. 536; *Nation Drywall Contractors Ltd. v. All Round Properties Administration Ltd.* (1975), 10 O.R. 295; Re *Cloverlawn Invts. Ltd.,* [1977] 1 A.C.W.S. 251 (N.S.); *Bristol Const. Co. v. D.K. Invts. Ltd.,* [1972] 4 W.W.R. 119 (B.C.).

If the Court is of the opinion that there is no right of lien or that the lien claimant is owed no money, then the action may be dismissed on this application: Ont. sec. 25(2)(*c*); Nfld., sec. 27(2)(c). See also *Saccary v. Jackson* (1975), 11 N.S.R. (2d) 316 (C.A.). See further §89, §154(b) and §161, *post.*

In British Columbia the Court held that The Mechanics' Lien Act did not permit a reduction in the amount of the security which had already been paid into Court: *E.A. Parker Dev. Ltd. v. Doric Dev. Ltd.,* [1977] 3 W.W.R. 191. See also *Re Pecco Cranes (Can.) Ltd.,* [1973] 3 O.R. 737.

By sections 25(4) Ontario, section 35(2) Alberta, section 51(3) New Brunswick, section 54(3) P.E.I., section 40(3)(a) Saskatchewan and 27(4) Newfoundland, the money paid into Court or the security deposited with the Court takes the place of the property just as if the money or the security had been realized by a sale of the property after an action to enforce a lien. The money or security therefore becomes the lienable interest.

These latter subsections of the Ontario and Newfoundland Acts provide further that such money or security is subject to the claims of every person who has at the time of the application a subsisting claim for lien or given a notice of his claim for lien; provided however, that the amount found to be owing to the person whose lien was vacated by the application is a first charge against the security or the money. On May 1, 1970 the Ontario Act was amended and the word "subsisting" in section 25(4) was substituted for the word "registered". It therefore now appears that valid, although at the time of the application for payment unregistered, lien claimants may share in the money or security. The case of *Financial Bldg. Ltd. v. Bird Const. Ltd., infra* would therefore have no application in Ontario or Newfoundland.

Although section 25(4) of the Ontario Act provides that where money is paid into Court or security posted and the lien vacated, that the amount the Court finds due to the lien claimants is a first charge upon the money or security, this charge is limited to situations in which the sale of the owner's equity in the lands results in the realization of less than the owner's statutory liability. Where an owner paid into Court the statutory holdback amount required to discharge all liens the Court held that all lien claimants should share this fund on a *pro rata* basis: *Bond Structural Steel* (1965) *Ltd. v. Cloverlawn Invts. Ltd.,* [1973] 3 O.R. 856. But see contra *Nor. Elec. Co. Ltd. v. Frank Warkentin Elec. Ltd.* (1972), 27 D.L.R. (3d) 519 (Man. C.A.) and *Re Collavino Bros.,* [1977] 1 A.C.W.S. 351 (N.S.). As to the entitlement to any excess funds paid into Court under section 25(2) after the lien claimants have been satisfied see *Re Tri-Lateral Enterprises Ltd.* (1977), 74 D.L.R. 517 (Ont.).

The Acts of New Brunswick (sec. 51), Prince Edward Island (sec. 54), and Saskatchewan (sec. 40(3)(*b*)) contain provisions similar to Ontario and Newfoundland with the exception that those entitled to share in the security or payment are not "subsisting" lien claimants but "registered" lien claimants whose liens have not expired.

The Acts of British Columbia (sec. 33), Manitoba (sec. 25), and Nova Scotia (sec. 28) provide a similar means of vacating a lien upon the posting of security for, or payment into Court of, the amount of the lien plus costs. It is not stated that the security or payment takes the place of the land; however, see: *Nanaimo Contractors Ltd. v. Patterson* (1964), 48 W.W.R. 600 (B.C. C.A.); *Bank of Montreal v. Sidney,* [1955] O.W.N. 581, *Jenkins v. Wilin Const. Ltd.* (1977), 25 N.S.R. (2d) 19, which indicate that at least insofar as the lien vacated under such an application is concerned, the security or payment stands in the place of the land and becomes the lienable interest. Moreover, none of these Acts makes provision for who is to share in the security or payment.

In Saskatchewan it was recently held that on an application under sec. 40(1) for an order vacating a lien by the payment of money into Court, the applicant must provide "proof" that no other person is entitled to a lien before the order will be made: *Atamanenko v. Terra Cement Service Ltd.,* [1976] 6 W.W.R. 381. See further *Financial Bldg. Ltd. v. Bird Const. Co.* (1960), 32 W.W.R. 189 (Sask.).

In many cases the security allowed is a bond (see form 96) or a letter of credit (see form 97) approved by the Court. In Ontario see the Guarantee Companies Securities Act, R.S.O. 1970, c. 196 and R.R.O. 1970, Regulation 387 for the list of approved Guarantee Companies.

§24 Insurance Money as Security for Estate or Interest in the Land.

In all provinces the various Acts provide generally that where property is wholly or partially destroyed by fire, any proceeds from fire insurance policies received by the owner or prior mortgagee, shall take the place of the property destroyed, and the money is to be dealt with according to the priorities governing lien claimants in each provincial Act, as if the money had been realized by a sale of the property in proceedings to enforce the liens: Ont., sec. 8; Man., sec. 6; B.C., sec. 16; Alta., sec. 13; N.B., sec. 13; P.E.I., sec. 13; N.S., sec. 9 and Nfld., sec. 10. See also the judgment of Laidlaw J.A. in *Pankka v. Butchart,* [1956] O.R. 837, and *G.A. Baert Const. (1960) Ltd. v. Can. Gen. Ins. Co.* (1966), 55 W.W.R. 449 (Man. C.A.).

It is to be noted that in Alberta the section refers only to money received or receivable by the owner; there is no reference to mortgagee. None of the Acts refer to money received by a subsequent mortgagee and these sections might appear to shut out lien priority if fire insurance moneys found their way into the hands of a subsequent mortgagee. But see B.C., sec. 16 which includes money received by "an owner, prior mortgagee or other encumbrancer".

The Saskatchewan Act (sec. 4), which was amended in 1973 states that where an improvement is wholly or partly destroyed or damaged by fire or otherwise, any money received or receivable by reason of insurance thereon by the owner, prior mortgagee or chargee, contractor or subcontractor, takes the place of the property so destroyed or damaged to the extent of the value thereof as part of the contract price. The cause of damage or destruction is not restricted to fires as in the other Acts, the moneys may still be in the hands of the insurer, and the recipients of insurance moneys include contractors and subcontractors. If there is an excess after the claims of the mortgagees or chargees under prior registered instruments are satisfied, the balance forms a trust fund in the hands of the owner, contractor or subcontractor to be distributed in accordance with the trust provisions of the Act and does not go to the lien claimants as provided in the other Acts.

In *Liverpool & London etc. Ins. Co. v. Kadlac* (1918), 13 Alta. L.R. 498 (C.A.), an insurance company insured certain property for $5,000.00, the owner being the assured. Loss was payable to the mortgagee, and the property was destroyed by fire. The owner and the insurance company purported to settle the loss for $2,000.00. The mortgagee objected as he maintained the settlement was unjust, and the Court refused the insurance company's attempt to pay the $2,000.00 into Court in full settlement of their liability. *In obiter* the Court indicated that the mortgagee and lien claimants had a right to dispute the amount of loss. The Court suggested an action be taken, with the mortgagee and lien claimants as parties, to establish the proper amount of insurance moneys payable. Once established, this fund could be paid into Court to the credit of the mechanics' lien action at the outset of the latter action. While definitely deciding that the mortgagee had an enforceable interest in the moneys, the Court did not decide that the lien claimants had any right or interest in the action until the fund was ascertained. The case decided, however, that if the amount of the insurance fund was agreed on at the outset by all interested parties there was no reason why the amount should not be paid into Court in the mechanics' lien action.

It is submitted that, since the relevant sections indicate that insurance money is received in the same manner as money realized by a sale of the property, and since lien claimants have an interest in, and participate in the sale of, the property, by analogy the lien claimants might have an interest in the ascertaining of the amount of the fire insurance fund.

It is also seen that, since the Judge or officer has complete jurisdiction to try and dispose of these actions, the question of the amount of the insurance fund might be made part of the mechanics' lien action, and an order made adding the insurance company as a party to the action. See §126; §135(b); §157, *post*.

A judgment in a mechanics' lien action where liens are proved will provide that the lien be upon the land and also upon the insurance money that the owner or mortgagee has received: *Taylor Hdwe. Co. v. Hunt* (1917), 39 O.L.R. 90 (C.A.). If the insurance money is not sufficient to satisfy all the lien claims proved then the land will be sold by order of the Court in the usual manner for the deficiency.

§25 The Holdback.

The foregoing part of this Chapter has been an explanation of how and when a statutory "owner" is created under the various lien Acts.

When a statutory "owner" is found, whatever interest he may have in the property, then he and all other persons primarily liable upon any contract under which a lien may attach are required to retain a holdback fund from the amounts owing under the primary contracts to protect subcontractors and others claiming through the contractors: Ontario, sec. 11 and equivalent provisions of other Acts.

The holdback fund is a certain percentage of the value of the work, service, or material actually done, placed or furnished, and must be held for a certain period of time after the work or service has been performed or the contract has been completed or abandoned in order to assure payment for those working on the project. If the holdback funds have been paid out before the requisite period has expired, then the person paying out the funds would be liable to pay them over again to the unpaid lien claimants. This liability will not exceed the amount of the holdback except where a written notice of claim for lien from a lien claimant is given under the various Acts, and funds paid out in the face of the notice. The holdback fund and duties and liabilities of the owner are more fully discussed in Chapter 4.

3

The Lien Claimant

§26 The Claim for Lien Generally.

The Acts in all of the provinces recognize several types of claim for lien or lien claimants. In general, they are comprised of the contractor, the subcontractor, the wage earner and the material supplier. The provinces of Ontario, Alberta, Saskatchewan and Newfoundland have added the lessor of equipment to the list. Each class of claimant can be subdivided further as we shall see later. Certain distinctions are made between them with respect to priorities and the point at which the statutory period within which their claims for lien must be filed commences to run. Further, as was said in *Swanson v. Mollison* (1907), 6 W.L.R. 678 (Alta.), "the rights of a lien-holder are given by statute, and the rule is clear that he must establish his rights plainly and beyond a doubt before the lien will attach". See also Chapter I, Introduction.

§27 When the Lien Arises.

The lien arises at the commencement of the work or at the time at which the first materials are furnished, the doing of which work or the furnishing of which materials will give rise to a claim for lien under the provisions of the Acts: see Ont., sec. 7(3), (4) and the corresponding sections of the other Acts. This result follows from an examination of the provisions of the section of the Act which creates the lien (*e.g.,* Ont., sec. 5; N.S., secs. 5, 7(1); Sask., secs. 12(1), 14(1), (17(1))), and is supported by the decisions in many of the cases. For example, in *Swanson v. Mollison, supra,* the Court stated that "the lien attaches upon the doing of the work or the supplying of the materials". In *McCauley v. Powell* (1908), 7 W.L.R. 443 (Alta.), the Court held that it was clear from the Act that the lien comes into existence as soon as the work begins or any materials are delivered. In *Merrick v. Campbell* (1914), 6 W.W.R. 722 (Man.), the Court held that the lien arises and takes effect as against the owner from the commencement of the work. The law is stated in similar terms in *Kalbfleisch v. Hurley* (1915), 34 O.L.R. 268 (C.A.); *Ottawa Steel Castings Co. v. Dom. Supply Co.* (1904), 5 O.W.R. 161; *Robock v. Peters* (1900), 13 Man. R. 124; *Ross Bros. Ltd. v. Gorman* (1908),

1 Alta. L.R. 516 (C.A.); *Baxter Const. Co. v. Reo Invt. Ltd.* (1963), 37 D.L.R. (2d) 751 (Alta.); *Western Caissons (Alta.) Ltd. v. Bower* (1969), 71 W.W.R. 604 (Alta. C.A.).

The time at which the first lien arises is important where priorities are involved as, for example, where it must be determined to what extent a mortgage has priority over liens. The Ontario Act and most of the other Acts provide that the mortgage has priority over the liens to the extent of the actual value of the land at the time that the first lien arose. In Nova Scotia, the lien has priority over a mortgage registered prior to the lien to the extent of the increase in the selling value of the mortgaged premises resulting from the work or improvements put upon the premises by the lienholders, provided that the mortgagee consents to the work being done. (see N.S. sec. 9(3)). The provisions of section 7(3) and (4) of the Ontario Act refer to the time at which the first lien arose as the time at which priorities are fixed, and this time is reckoned from the doing of the first work whether or not the person who did that work happens to be before the Court in the particular action in which the question of priorities arises.

In *Currier & Ferguson Elec. v. Pearce,* [1953] O.W.N. 184, the Court held that the words "the time at which the first lien arose" in section 7(4) of the Ontario Act did not relate solely to still-existing liens or to liens that were involved in the litigation, and thereby overruled the decision in *O'Brien v. McCoig,* [1929] 1 D.L.R. 906 (Ont. C.A.), which indicated that those words meant the first lien of the liens before the Court to arise. The question of priorities is considered more fully in Chapter 5, The Mortgagee, and Chapter 8, Priorities.

§28 What is the Lien Claim.

The lien claim is a right given by statute to any person who, in the words of section 5(1) of the Ontario Act, "does any work upon or in respect of, or places or furnishes any materials to be used" for any of the purposes mentioned in that section to recover the value of the same from the "owner" of the lands on which the work is done or the materials are placed or furnished, thus preventing the "owner" of those lands from having the value of them enhanced without paying for such increase in value. This is a simple statement of a somewhat complex subject but in general this is the purpose of the various Mechanics' Lien Acts. The lien is limited to the amount justly due to the person entitled to the lien and to the amount justly owing, subject to the holdback provision of the Act, by the owner: see *S. I. Guttman Ltd. v. James D. Mokry Ltd.,* [1969] 1 O.R. 7 (C.A.); *Can. Comstock Co. v. Toronto Transit Comm.,* [1970] S.C.R. 204; *Noranda Exploration Co. v. Sigurdson* (1975), 53 D.L.R. (3d) 641 (S.C.C.).

In *Bunting v. Bell* (1876), 23 Gr. 584, the Court, adopting the language used in Phillips on Mechanics' Liens, section 176, stated: "The whole object under the Act is to prevent the owner of lands, whatever his estate in them, from getting the labour and capital of others without compensation." This object is stated in similar terms in the following cases: *Hickey v. Stalker,* [1924] 1 D.L.R. 440 (Ont. C.A.); *Scratch v. Anderson,* [1917] 1 W.W.R. 1340; affirmed (*sub nom. Limoges v. Scratch*) 44 S.C.R. 86; *Brooks-Sanford Co. v. Theodore Telier Const. Co.* (1910), 22 O.L.R. 176; *Read v. Whitney* (1919), 45 O.L.R. 377 (C.A.); *Ace Lbr. Ltd. v. Clarkson Co.,* [1962] O.R. 748; reversed, [1963] S.C.R. 110; *Earl F. Wakefield Co. v. Oil City Petroleums (Leduc) Ltd.,* [1958] S.C.R. 361; *Rideau Aluminum & Steels Ltd. v. McKechnie,* [1964] 1 O.R. 523; affirmed without written reasons 48 D.L.R. (2d) 62, 659 (Can.). In *Galvin Lbr. Yards v. Ensor,* [1922] 2 W.W.R. 15 (Sask. C.A.), it was held that the object of the legislation is to ensure, by a cheap and expeditious method, the payment for work and materials out of property on which the work was done or for which the materials were furnished. The person who has supplied labour and materials is enabled by the Act to establish a lien, thus acquiring authority to sell the property so as to realize his claim therefor. He may, however, only sell the particular interest in the property of the "owner" from whom his contract is derived. In *Roy v. Couturier Const. Ltd.* (1965), 51 M.P.R. 360 (N.B. C.A.), for example, where the "owner" was a tenant at will, it was held that only the tenancy at will could be sold to satisfy the lien, subject to the actual owner's estate in the land and to any prior charges.

The work or the services for which payment is claimed must have been actually performed on, or for the benefit of, the lands against which the claim for lien is sought to be enforced or upon land enjoyed therewith: see *Hubert v. Shinder,* [1952] O.W.N. 146 (C.A.); and materials must be placed or furnished on the land against which it is sought to enforce the claim for lien, lands enjoyed therewith, or a place in the immediate vicinity of that land designated for that purpose by the owner or his agent: see *Ludlam-Ainslee Lbr. Co. v. Fallis* (1909), 19 O.L.R. 419 (C.A.); *Milton Pressed Brick Co. v. Whalley* (1918), 42 O.L.R. 369 (C.A.); *Morgan Smith Co. v. Sissiboo Pulp & Paper Co.* (1904), 35 S.C.R. 93. In *Nelson Lbr. Co. v. Integrated Bldg. Corpn.,* [1973] S.C.R. 456, it was held that it did not matter who brought the material to the building site so long as it was furnished in pursuance of the subcontractor's arrangement with the materialman, was intended for the work in question, and arrived during the performance by the subcontractor of his contract with the general contractor. In *Montjoy v. Heward S. Dist. Corpn.* (1908), 10 W.L.R. 282 (Sask.), it was held that it is not necessary to prove that the material supplied was actually used in the building but that it is sufficient to prove that it was supplied "to be used" in the erection of the building. See also *Robinson v. Estevan Brick Ltd.* (1967), 60 W.W.R. 671 (Sask. C.A.). It was held in *Pankka v. Butchart,* [1956] O.R.

837 (C.A.), where it appeared that none of the defendants had any estate or interest in the lands sought to be charged, that the action must fail in total, the provisions of the Act not being available to enforce the plaintiff's contractual rights. See also *Bain v. Director, Veterans' Land Act,* [1955] O.W.N. 993, and *Wells H. Morton & Co. v. Can. Credit Men's Trust Assn. Ltd.* (1965), 53 W.W.R. 178 (Man. C.A.), where the result was the same.

§29 The Contractor.

(a) Definition.

A contractor is defined by most of the Acts as "a person contracting with or employed directly by the owner or his agent for the doing of work or the placing or furnishing of materials for any of the purposes mentioned" in the Act but does not include a workman. In *Davies v. E. B. Eddy Co.,* [1942] 1 W.W.R. 596 (B.C. C.A.), it was held that this definition should be given a liberal interpretation. In *Bore v. Sigurdson,* [1972] 6 W.W.R. 654 (B.C.) it was held that, on a true interpretation of the definitions of the words "contractor" and "owner" set out in the Act, the intention of the legislature was clearly to regard an owner and a contractor as distinct and separate persons. It follows from these definitions that there can be more than one "contractor" employed on any given project: See *Yale Dev. Corpn. v. A.L.H. Const. Ltd.,* [1973] 2 W.W.R. 477 (Alta. C.A.). Generally speaking the contractor cannot enforce his claim for lien until he has completed his contract, since there must be an obligation on the part of the owner to pay him something before his claim for lien arises: see *Cole v. Smith* (1909), 13 O.W.R. 774 (C.A.); *Kosobuski v. Extension Mining Co.,* [1929] 3 D.L.R. 379 (Ont. C.A.); *Leroy v. Smith* (1900), 8 B.C.R. 293 (C.A.); *NePage v. Pinner* (1915), 8 W.W.R. 322 (B.C. C.A.); *Sherlock v. Powell* (1899), 26 O.A.R. 407; *Simpson v. Rubeck* (1911), 21 O.W.R. 260 (C.A.); *Smith v. Stubbert,* [1942] 1 W.W.R. 601 (B.C. C.A.); *Weathermakers Ltd. v. Wetaskiwin* (1966), 56 W.W.R. 271 (Alta.).

(b) Completion of Contract.

Whether or not the contract has been completed is a question of fact and each case must be determined on its own merits. When considering the cases dealing with the question of whether or not a claimant has filed his claim for lien within the requisite number of days following completion of his contract, it must be remembered that the Acts of all the provinces, with the exception of Manitoba and Nova Scotia, now define completion of the contract as "substantial performance, not necessarily total performance, of the contract". This definition is a relatively recent addition to the Alberta, Newfoundland, Saskatchewan and Ontario Acts. In *Union Elec. Supply Co. v. Joice-Sweanor Elec. Ltd.* (1975), 7 O.R. (2d) 227 (C.A.), the Court held that this concept of substantial completion was applicable to subcontractors as well as to general contractors, approving the reasons of Coulter J. which were subsequently reported in *Otis Elevator Co. v. Commonwealth Holiday Inns of Can. Ltd.* (1972), 8 O.R. (2d) 297. See also: *Glenway Supply (Alta.) Ltd. v. Knobloch,* [1972] 6 W.W.R. 513 (Alta. C.A.); *Western Realty Projects Ltd. v. Superior Grout & Gunite Ltd.; Wells Const. Ltd. v. Edwards Const. Ltd.,* [1975] 6 W.W.R. 366 (Alta.); *Crestile Ltd. v. New Generation Properties Inc.* (1976), 13 O.R. (2d) 670. In the last mentioned case it was held that when determining whether or not a contract had been substantially completed within the definition contained in the Ontario Act the term "contract price" should be interpreted as including the price of the work done by the plaintiff pursuant to its original contract as altered and augmented by the addition of extras pursuant to the agreements between the parties. We are concerned in this section, however, with the question of whether or not the contract has been sufficiently completed to permit the contractor to recover the contract price from the owner. The question of when the time for filing the contractor's claim for lien commences to run, will be dealt with in Chapter 6, Obtaining a Lien.

As a guide to what the Courts may consider an uncompleted contract and a sufficiently completed contract, see the following cases: *Adams v. McGreevy* (1907), 17 Man. R. 115 (where the contract was held to be completed notwithstanding that certain trivial portions of it had not been performed); *Wagg v. Boudreau Sheet Metal Works Ltd.* (1959), 43 M.P.R. 154 (N.B. C.A.) (where it was held that the test is whether the work is "finished" or "done" in the ordinary sense even though part of it is defective or not in accordance with the contract); *Hulshan v. Nickling,* [1957] O.W.N. 587 (C.A.) (where it was held that the provision in the contract that the house should be erected in conformity with N.H.A. requirements and according to plans on file with the contractor and purchaser set the standard by which the work was to be judged and that the further words in the contract that it was to be completed to the satisfaction of the purchaser did not add anything to the contract. Accordingly, the contract was sufficiently completed despite the defendant's dissatisfaction with some of the work); *Bigham v. Brake* (1927), 32 O.W.N. 271 (C.A.) (where the Court held that if the defect in carrying out an entire contract is in some minor detail or in the omission of some unimportant thing, damages might be given as compensation, but in no case would a contract be held to be complete where the substitution of something substantially different from that contracted for took place); *Broley v. Mills* (1908), 1 Sask. L.R. 20 (where it was held that the plaintiff could not recover since he had not completed in accordance with the specifications, and that the taking of possession of the building erected and the using of the same by the purchaser was not in itself a sufficient acceptance of an incomplete or imperfect performance of a contract so as to entitle the contractor to recover); *Can. Western Foundry v. Hoover*, [1917] 3 W.W.R. 594 (Alta. C.A.) (where it was held that the words "guaranteed satisfactory" and "terms cash on satisfactory completion of job," contained in the contract, do not mean that the question of completion or non-completion is to be left to a mere whim of the defendant, but it is a question of fact upon the evidence whether or not there has been a satisfactory performance of the contract); *H. Dakin Co. v. Lee*, [1916] 1 K.B. 566 (C.A.) (where it was held that there could be "performance" of a contract by the builder even though some part of the work had been done negligently or inefficiently); *House Repair & Service Co. v. Miller* (1921), 49 O.L.R. 205 (C.A.) (where it was held that the stipulation in the contract that the work should be done to the entire satisfaction of the owner was subject to the condition that approval should not be unreasonably withheld); *Merriam v. Public Parks Bd. of Portage La Prairie* (1911), 18 W.L.R. 151; affirmed 1 W.W.R. 1082 (Man. C.A.); *McDonald v. Simons* (1910), 15 W.L.R. 218 (B.C.) (where it was held that the doctrine of substantial performance had no place in British Columbia jurisprudence and there being no evidence that the defendants had accepted the work, the plaintiffs were not entitled to recover on the written contract); *Sickler v. Spencer* (1911), 17 B.C.R. 41 (where it was held that upon the evidence there was such a substantial performance of the contract as to entitle the claimant to a lien although a trifling part of the material contracted for had not been supplied by one of the contractors when the architect gave him his final certificate); *Stokes Const. Co. v. A.G. N.S.* (1975), 11 N.S.R. (2d) 495 (C.A.) (where it was held that the contractor could not rely on a clause in the contract providing for payment in full for the work completed even though "there are items of work" which are not completed due to conditions beyond the control of the contractor, where the project is unfit for use by the owner); *Doell v. Lawrence*, [1977] 1 W.W.R. 317 (Sask.) (where it was held that the owner was entitled to recover the contract price from the contractor, together with interest from the date of abandonment of the contract, where the contractor had been paid the full contract price but had abandoned the contract before substantially completing it); *Watts v. McLeay* (1911), 19 W.L.R. 916 (Alta.) (where it was held that the question of completion or non-completion must depend on the terms of the contract and the facts and circumstances of the particular case; that where there is an honest intention to complete there is completion of the contract if it is completed in all essential and material respects and there exist only slight imperfections in workmanship or slight deviations from the specifications which can be easily cured and corrected at an expense trifling as compared to the contract price); *Markland Associates Ltd. v. Lohnes* (1973), 33 D.L.R. (3d) 493 (N.S.) (where it was held that where the contractor performs all of the work specified under the contract, but there are defects in his workmanship which can be remedied, the contractor has substantially performed his obligation and is entitled to the contract price less the cost of making good the defects and omissions); *Yakowchuk v. Crawford,* [1917] 3 W.W.R. 479 (Man.) (where it was held that where an entire contract for work and labour has not been substantially performed, or where the contractor refuses to complete a substantially completed contract, he is not entitled to recover on a *quantum meruit* basis, distinguishing *Adams v. McGreevy, supra*); *B. A. Robinson Plumbing & Heating Ltd. v. Rossiter,* [1955] O.W.N. 29 (where the Court adopted the test laid down in *Day v. Crown Grain Co.* (1907), 39 S.C.R. 258 and the reasoning in *Hurst v. Morris* (1914), 32 O.L.R. 346 (C.A.); *Anderson v. Fort William Commercial Chambers Ltd.* (1915), 34 O.L.R. 567 (C.A.); *Benson v. Smith & Son* (1916), 37 O.L.R. 257 (C.A.); and *Russell v. Ont. Foundation & Engineering Co.,* [1926] 1 D.L.R. 760 (Ont. C.A.), holding that the test as to completion or non-completion of the contract was, "could the subcontractor in law have sued and recovered from the contractor as for a completed contract?"); *Weathermakers Ltd. v. Wetaskiwin* (1966), 56 W.W.R. 271 (Alta.); *Ocean Steel & Const. Ltd. v. Kenney Const. Co.* (1972), 31 D.L.R. (3d) 441 (N.S. C.A.) (which approve the use of the same test); *Downie v. Norman* (1964), 50 M.P.R. 150 (N.S. C.A.) and *Webber v. Havill* (1964), 50 M.P.R. 172 (N.S. C.A.) (where it was held that what amounted to substantial performance was a question of degree in each case, and little guidance could be obtained from the decided cases.) For additional cases on this subject see Goldsmith, *Canadian Building Contracts,* 2nd Edition.

(c) *Abandonment.*

A contractor may lose his right to claim a lien if the contract provides that completion is a condition precedent to payment by the owner and he abandons the work before it is completed. He may also lose his right to claim a lien if the contract provides for the payment of damages to the owner in a stipulated sum on failure to complete and that stipulated sum exceeds the amount owing to him when he abandons the work or fails to complete it for any other reason. Abandonment was defined in *Anderson v. Fort William Commercial Chambers Ltd.* (1915), 34 O.L.R. 567 (C.A.), as "not leaving a work under the belief that the contract is completed, but, knowing or believing that the contract was not completed, declining to go on and complete it." This definition was approved in *Granby Const. & Equipment Ltd. v. Player* (1964), 49 D.L.R. (2d) 658 (B.C.), and *B. A. Robinson Plumbing & Heating Ltd. v. Stewart,* [1961] O.R. 445 (C.A.). It was held in *Dieleman Planer Co. v. Elizabeth Townhouses Ltd.* (1975), 48 D.L.R. (3d) 635, affirming 38 D.L.R. (3d) 595 (S.C.C.), that the mere cessation of work without a co-existing intention not to carry on with the project does not constitute abandonment.

Most Mechanics' Lien Acts provide, as does the Ontario Act in section 21(1), that where a contractor or subcontractor abandons the work he must register his lien within the statutory period following the abandonment. It is to be noted that the section does not refer to the doing of the last work but to abandonment of the contract which may take place at any time up until the completion of the contract. For example, if the contractor had not done any work under his contract on the lands in question for more than 37 days, it would still be open to him to notify the owner that he was abandoning the contract and his right to file a lien would continue for 37 days following such notice of abandonment. It was held, however, in *Hodgson Lbr. Co. v. Wendlend*, [1941] 1 W.W.R. 24 (B.C.), that abandonment of the construction of a building does not amount to a "completion" of the building within the meaning of the Act and therefore the right to file and enforce a lien remains in existence until completion of the building; accordingly, abandonment would not terminate the lien. In *Taylor v. Foran* (1931), 44 B.C.R. 529, the plaintiff had partially completed a plumbing contract in the defendant's house when the defendant stopped work and the plaintiff was unable to continue the plumbing work until the defendant resumed construction. The plaintiff waited one year. The defendant failed to continue construction and the plaintiff then filed his lien. It was held that as long as the contract remained in a state of incompletion due to the owner's default the plaintiff was entitled to file a lien and to have judgment for the balance due up to the time he had ceased work. See also *Levin v. Lukewiecki*, [1933] 4 D.L.R. 604 (Man. C.A.), where, in similar circumstances, the Court concluded that the contractor had in fact abandoned his contract and disallowed the claim for lien of one of his material suppliers on the ground that the supplier's lien had been filed more than 30 days after the supply of the last material prior to the abandonment by the contractor. In Ontario it was held in *Corby v. Perkus* (1915), 9 O.W.N. 318 (C.A.), that the lien rights would cease to exist on the expiration of the statutory number of days after the date of abandonment by the contractor and the contractor could not start the time running again by returning to do some work under the contract.

(*d*) *Non-completion Resulting from Acts of Owner.*

If the owner ceases to make payments under the contract, cancels it or, through some act of his own and without cause, makes it impossible for the contractor to complete, then the contractor is justified in abandoning the work and is entitled at that time to enforce his claim for lien to the extent of the actual value of the work performed and materials supplied up until that time. The onus, of course, will be on the contractor to establish that the performance of the contract was rendered impossible by the owner: see *Cragnoline v. Southwick* (1916), 27 O.W.R. 445, where it was held that if the owner failed to make interim payments to the builder as provided for in the contract, the builder would be entitled to abandon the contract and collect for what he had already done on a *quantum meruit* basis and he might enforce a lien to recover the same, the making of the interim payments being a condition precedent to the continuance by the contractor. In *Fuller v. Beach* (1912), 7 D.L.R. 822; reversed 4 W.W.R. 161 (B.C.), the owner improperly terminated the contract and it was held that he then became liable to the builder on a *quantum meruit* basis and a lien could be enforced. See also *Alkok v. Grymek,* [1966] 2 O.R. 235; varied [1968] S.C.R. 452 and *Gettle Bros. Const. Co. v. Alwinsal Potash of Can. Ltd.* (1969), 5 D.L.R. (3d) 719 (Sask. C.A.); affirmed [1971] S.C.R. 320, to the same effect. In *Gidney (Sidney) v. Morgan* (1910), 16 B.C.R. 18; *Taylor v. Foran* (1931), 44 B.C.R. 529; and *Degagne v. Chave* (1896), 2 Terr. L.R. 210, the contractor in each case was prevented from completing his contract due to the default of the owner in proceeding with the portion of the work which was the owner's responsibility and in each case the Court held that the plaintiff was entitled to file a lien and to recover judgment for the balance owing on a *quantum meruit*. In *Morgan v. Sunray Petroleum Corpn.,* [1941] 2 W.W.R. 603; affirmed [1942] 2 W.W.R. 53 (Alta. C.A.), the plaintiff entered into a contract with the defendant for drilling an oil well, which provided that the contractor should receive $10,000.00 on completion of the first 1,000 feet, $10,000.00 on completion of the second 1,000 feet and $30,000.00 when the well had reached 3,000 feet. The last of the three payments was intended, in part, to enable the contractor to buy new machinery to carry on the remainder of the work and he was to receive $15,000.00 for each subsequent 1,000 feet the well was drilled. The contract was terminated by the defendant after the well had been drilled to 3,000 feet and it was held that while the contractor could recover on a *quantum meruit* basis he could only recover that portion of the whole consideration which was represented by the value of the work done having regard to the apportionment of the whole contract price between the completed and uncompleted work. In view of the fact that the $30,000.00 payment made on completion of the first 3,000 feet was to cover the costs of buying new machinery to complete the work he could not recover all of that sum. It was held in *Nor. Lbr. Mills Ltd. v. Rice* (1971), 41 O.L.R. 201 (C.A.) that, where the contract price was to be paid in three instalments and an action was brought to enforce a lien for materials supplied after the first two had become payable and the third had not, the action was not premature either in whole or in part. It was held in the circumstances of *Kelly v. Tourist Hotel Co.* (1909), 20 O.L.R. 267 (C.A.), that the contractor in that case was not entitled to payment on a *quantum meruit* because of the terms of his contract with the owner. It would seem that the law in Ontario is the same as that outlined in the previous cases. In *Nuspel v. Lem Foo,* [1949] O.W.N. 476, it was held that where no firm price had been given for the doing of the work, the contractor was entitled to be paid on the basis of a *quantum meruit*. See also: *Ivan B. Crouse & Son Ltd. v. Cameron* (1974), 6 N.S.R. (2d) 590 (C.A.). In *Hurst v. Downard* (1921), 50 O.L.R. 35 (C.A.), Meredith C.J.O. outlined the principle behind the cases as being that equity gave to the party who was prevented from carrying out the contract what he would have received from the party in default had he not been prevented from completing the work.

(e) *Effect of Contractor's Acts on Rights of Subcontractors.*

Should the contractor improperly abandon the contract, the owner may, generally speaking, deduct from whatever moneys may be owing to the contractor at that time, damages for breach of contract, for non-completion of the contract, or for defective work, but he may not deduct such damages from the statutory holdback, which must be made available by him to satisfy the claims of persons claiming through the contractor: see Ont., sec. 11(9); Alta., sec. 15(7); P.E.I., sec. 15(6); Sask., sec. 19(5); B.C., sec. 21(6); N.B., sec. 15(9); Nfld., sec. 13(9). See also Man., sec. 12(4) and N.S., sec. 15(4), where the same is prohibited in respect of the claims of wage earners only. In the case of *Vaillancourt Lbr. Co. v. Trustees of Sep. School Section No. 2, Balfour Twp.*, [1964] 1 O.R. 418 (C.A.), the Ontario Court of Appeal, relying on the decisions in *Len Ariss & Co. v. Peloso*, [1958] O.R. 643 (C.A.), and *Freedman v. Guar. Trust Co.*, [1929] 4 D.L.R. 32 (Ont. C.A.), held that where the owner has received notice in writing of a claim for lien by a subcontractor, he must retain the amount claimed in the notice in addition to the statutory holdback and must make both sums available to satisfy the claims of persons claiming through the contractor. The Court also held that even if the owner had a claim for set-off against the sum retained in excess of the holdback for damages against the contractor as a result of his abandonment of the work, the lien claimants were entitled to the amount claimed in the notice as well as the holdback in priority to the owner. In the *Vaillancourt* case the owner had paid all but the holdback to the contractor after it had received notice of the lien. The Ontario Court of Appeal distinguished the *Vaillancourt* case in the later case of *S. I. Guttman Ltd. v. James D. Mokry Ltd.*, [1969] 1 O.R. 7 (C.A.), on the ground that that decision must be confined to its peculiar facts. In the *Guttman* case it appeared that the owner had not paid anything to the contractor after it received notice of the lien. The Court held that in these circumstances the owner was entitled to retain the amount it was holding in excess of the holdback in partial satisfaction of its claims for loss and damages against the contractor arising out of his failure to complete. The result of these two cases appears to be that if the owner pays money to the contractor after he receives notice of a lien, he may be obliged to pay the amount claimed in the notice a second time to persons who claim liens through his contractor. If however, he does not pay the contractor he will be entitled to set off his claims for damages against the contractor against the amounts he has retained in excess of the holdback as a result of his receiving the notice. In either case the lien claimants will be entitled to the holdback in priority to the owner. The decision in *S. I. Guttman Ltd. v. James D. Mokry Ltd., supra,* was approved in *Can. Comstock Co. v. Toronto Transit Commn.,* [1970] S.C.R. 205 and *Noranda Exploration Co. v. Sigurdson* (1975), 53 D.L.R. (3d) 641 (S.C.C.) and was followed in *Scarborough Painting Ltd. v. Buckley* (1974), 4 O.R. (2d) 253 and *Curran & Briggs Ltd. v. Ryder* (1977), 19 N.B.R. (2d) 330.

At one time it was thought that the owner's right to set off his claims for damages against moneys owing to his contractor was further restricted in Ontario and Saskatchewan by the provisions of sections 2(3) of the Ontario Act and 3(3) of the Saskatchewan Act. Those subsections constitute all sums which become payable to the contractor by the owner, on the certificate of a person who is authorized under their contract to make such certificates for payment, trust funds in the hands of the owner until they are paid to the contractor. Thus, once the owner's architect certifies a progress draw for payment, it would appear that the owner is no longer able to use any of the amount so certified as owing to the contractor to satisfy a claim for damages against the contractor. This may still be true in Saskatchewan. In Ontario, however, it was held in *Standard Indust. Ltd. v. Treasury Trails Holdings Ltd.* (1976), 24 C.B.R. (N.S.) 8, affirmed 23 C.B.R. (N.S.) 244 (Ont. C.A.), that the operative words in the section were its opening words, "where a sum becomes payable under a contract to a contractor by an owner. . . ." The Court agreed with the result arrived at by the trial Judge who found that, even though the owner's engineer had certified a progress draw for payment to the contractor, which payment had not been made to him, the owner had the right to use the moneys otherwise owing under that certificate to complete the abandoned contract. The trial Judge concluded that, since the amount of the owner's claim for set-off against the contractor exceeded the amount which it owed the contractor, no sum had become payable to the contractor within the meaning of Section 2(3) of The Mechanics' Lien Act and accordingly no trust was created under that section as a result of the giving of the certificate by the engineer. The result of this decision would appear to be that, at least in Ontario, the provisions of Section 2(3) do not in any way restrict the owner's rights of set-off against the contractor and the only restrictions on those rights are those discussed in the previous paragraph.

The lien rights of persons not parties to the main contract cannot be interfered with by the owner or the contractor except by express agreement with those persons: see Ont. secs. 4(3) and 5, and the corresponding sections of the other Acts. It was held in *Lambton (County) v. Can. Comstock Co.,* [1960] S.C.R. 86, that a waiver of lien must be in an express form and the mere acknowledgement by a subcontractor that the work was done, without more, would not constitute such a waiver of lien. Except in British Columbia, the abandonment of the work by the contractor will not start the time running within which the subcontractor must file his lien, unless he is aware of such abandonment: *Dom. Sheet Metal & Roofing Works v. G.H.I. Const. Co.*, [1968] 2 O.R. 665. While the decision in *G. Farwell Co. v. Coast Homes Ltd.* (1969), 4 D.L.R. (3d) 238 (B.C. C.A.) would appear to be to the contrary it was decided under section 23(1) of the British Columbia statute which provides that the subcontractor must file his lien not later than 31 days after "the contract of the contractor has been completed, abandoned, or otherwise determined". In that case the lien of the subcontractor was held to have been filed too late because, even though the subcontractor had not completed or abandoned his contract, the general contractor's contract had been cancelled by the owner, without the subcontractor's knowledge, more than 31 days before the subcontractor filed his lien. In other words, the contract of the contractor had been determined more than 31 days prior to the filing of the subcontractor's lien. See also: *Woodhaven Devs. Ltd. v. Klitch*, [1976] W.W.D. 58 (B.C.).

As was stated in *Baines v. Harman*, [1927] 2 D.L.R. 743 (Ont. C.A.), and *Russell v. Williams* (1923), 24 O.W.N. 240 (C.A.), if a conflict arises between the provisions of The Mechanics' Lien Act and the terms of the contract between the owner and the contractor, the provisions of the Act must prevail. Accordingly, while the owner may make any provision he wishes as to the terms of payment in his contract with his contractor, he must retain the statutory holdback equal to the proper percentage of the value of the work done and materials supplied at the time he makes a payment to his contractor. See also Ont., sec. 11(8); B.C., sec. 21(5); Man., sec. 9(8); Nfld., sec. 13(8), and N.B., sec. 15(8), which provide that all contracts shall be deemed to be amended to be in conformity with the section of the Act requiring the holdback to be maintained. This does not mean that the owner must deduct 15% or 20%, as the case may be, of the value of the work done from each progress payment, but he must retain the proper percentage from each payment made. In this connection see *Dziewa v. Haviland*, [1960] O.W.N. 343. See also Chapter 4, Rights and Duties of the Owner, with regard to the owner's duty to retain a holdback.

(f) Architects' Certificates.

When the contract is under the supervision of an architect and the contract between the owner and the contractor provides that payments will be made upon architects' certificates, then the contractor is not generally entitled to payment until such a certificate is given. The Acts of Prince Edward Island, Saskatchewan, New Brunswick and Nova Scotia provide that in such cases the contractor may demand a certificate and if he does not receive it, he may register his claim for lien within 7 days thereafter. The Acts of Alberta and Saskatchewan provide that if the architect refuses or neglects to give the contractor a certificate of completion on demand, the Court can make an Order that the contract has been completed and such an Order will have the same force and effect as if the certificate of completion had been issued by the architect. It was held in *Vokes Hdwe. v. G.T.R.* (1906), 12 O.L.R. 344 (C.A.), that under the contract between the parties, the architect was the person to determine when the work had been completed and it was not to be considered completed until he had signified his approval. Accordingly, a lien could not be enforced until that time. The decisions in *Benson v. Smith & Son* (1916), 37 O.L.R. 257 (C.A.), and *Metal Studios v. Kitchener* (1925), 29 O.W.N. 216 (C.A.) are to the same effect. It was held, however, in *Degagne v. Chave* (1896), 2 Terr. L.R. 210, that a provision in the contract providing that payments would be made upon an architect's certificate was inoperative since no architect had in fact been appointed. It was held in *Weathermakers Ltd. v. Wetaskiwin* (1966), 56 W.W.R. 271 (Alta.) that an architect's certificate of completion would not bind the lien claimant or start the time running during which he would have to file his lien, especially where the claimant was not present during the architect's inspection.

While the contractor may file his claim for lien as soon as he commences the work, or within the prescribed time after he completes or abandons the work (or within 7 days after the architect refuses to give a certificate if the Act so provides), he cannot usually enforce the lien until the certificate of the architect is given. Where, however, the architect refuses his certificate for improper motives, as was held in *Alta. Bldg. Co. v. Calgary* (1911), 16 W.L.R. 443 (Alta.), the contractor may nevertheless recover under his contract and is entitled to enforce his lien. It was held in that case that under the terms of the contract, the architect's powers were *quasi* judicial and notwithstanding that the contract constituted him an agent of the owner, he was bound to decide impartially between the parties to the contract and to deal equally with both. (See also: *Burgess v. Khoury (Albrechtsen's Claim)*, [1948] O.W.N. 789; Chapter 4, Rights and Duties of the Owner; and §35, *post.*)

§30 Miscellaneous Contract Provisions.

If the contract provides for the payment of the contract price in instalments, a lien may be enforced for the amount of each partial payment as it falls due: see *Black v. Wiebe* (1905), 15 Man. R. 260; *Braden v. Brown,* [1917] 3 W.W.R. 906 (B.C. C.A.), and *Ne Page v. Pinner* (1915), 21 B.C.R. 81 (C.A.). If the contract requires that the property be free of liens before payment is due, the contractor cannot demand payment until this is so:

Henry Hope & Sons v. Richard Sheehy & Sons (1922), 52 O.L.R. 237. In
Ritchie v. Grundy (1891), 7 Man. R. 532, it was held that if the contractor
enters into a contract which is not consistent with his having a claim for lien,
then he will be unable to enforce it. It is doubtful that this is good law in view
of the decision in *Lambton (County) v. Can. Comstock Co.,* [1960] S.C.R.
86, in which it was held that a waiver of lien must be in express terms and
have regard to the wording of the various Acts themselves. In *Westeel-
Rosco Ltd. v. South Sask. Hospital Centre Bd. of Governors* (1977), 69
D.L.R. (3d) 334 (S.C.C.) the Court found that the particular waiver of lien
in question amounted only to an undertaking not to enforce a lien against
the property on which the work was done and that it was not a waiver or
renunciation of the lien claimant's claim to a charge against the holdback
moneys. It would appear that the mere fact that the date for payment under
the contract was fixed by the contract at a time beyond the expiration of the
statutory period allowed for filing liens would not preclude the contractor
from filing a lien. Most of the Acts contain a provision that if a period of
credit has been agreed upon between the parties, the time for commencing
the action will be extended for a specified number of days after such period
of credit has expired and the better view would appear to be that such a term
in a contract would be merely an extension of the time for payment. (See
also §§82 and 83, *post,* with respect to waivers of lien.)

   If the contract is not proceeded with, then there can be no claim for lien
since there is no actual improvement of the property: *Berridge v. Hawes*
(1903), 2 O.W.R. 619; and there can be no lien in respect of the cost of
preparing for work to be done upon a site even though such work has been
frustrated without fault of the contractor: *B.C. Granitoid etc. Co. v. Dom.
Shipbldg. etc. Co.,* [1918] 2 W.W.R. 919 (B.C. C.A.). In *Haley v. The
Comox,* [1920] 3 W.W.R. 325 (B.C.), it was held that under a contract to
purchase materials, supply labour and do work in connection with the
refitting of a ship, the purchase price to be a percentage of the cost, the
contractors were not allowed to charge as for cost of labour for the time
occupied in purchasing materials. In Ontario and British Columbia it has
been held that an architect who prepares plans which are not proceeded with
or who prepares plans alone without supervising the construction, cannot
be said to improve the property so as to be entitled to a lien: *Burgess v.
Khoury (Albrechtsen's Claim),* [1948] O.W.N. 789; *Scott v. Lindstrom*
(1964), 50 W.W.R. 573 (B.C.). In Alberta, however, it was held in *Inglewood
Plumbing & Gasfitting Ltd. v. Northgate Dev. Ltd. (No. 1)* (1965), 54
W.W.R. 225, that an architect who had prepared plans under an agreement
which expressly excluded any supervision, was entitled to a lien as a
claimant for services. However, the Court refused to allow a lien claim by a
developer who had entered into an agreement with the owner under which
he assembled the land, obtained municipal approvals and agreements,

arranged financing for the project, hired the general contractor, oversaw the construction and was generally in charge of the project from start to finish, in *Hett v. Samoth Realty Projects Ltd.* (1977), 76 D.L.R. (3d) 362 (Alta. C.A.), on the ground that the services provided by him did not directly relate to the process of construction as required by the Act. This decision was approved in *P.R. Collings & Associates Ltd. v. Jolin Holdings Ltd.,* [1978] 3 W.W.R. 602 (Sask.). It was held in *Armbro Materials & Const. Ltd. v. 230056 Invts. Ltd.* (1975), 9 O.R. (2d) 226, that engineers who prepared plans of the sewage system, the watermains and the roads in a subdivision were entitled to a lien on the grounds that these plans were different from the plans of an architect for a building in that the plans in question, unlike those of an architect which could be used on another property, were designed specifically for this particular parcel of land and had increased its value since the subdivision could now be sold, with the approved plans, to a purchaser who could proceed at once with the development of the land.

The general provisions of the common law with respect to arbitration clauses apply, and, in general, if the owner enters a defence in the lien action, he will then be taken to have waived his right to arbitration. The proper procedure is for the defendant to bring a motion to stay the lien proceedings until arbitration has been had: *Art Plastering v. Oliver and Excelsior Const. Co.,* [1945] O.W.N. 41. However, the Court in *Great West Elec. Ltd. v. Housing Guild Ltd.,* [1947] 2 W.W.R. 1023 (B.C.) refused an application by a defendant for a stay of the mechanics' lien proceedings where his contract contained an arbitration clause, holding that such a clause did not amount to a waiver of the plaintiff's right to enforce his mechanics' lien. In *Pigott Const. Co. v. Fathers of Confederation Memorial Citizens Foundation* (1965), 51 D.L.R. (2d) 367 (P.E.I.), where the plaintiff applied for an order staying its own mechanics' lien action until the arbitrators had given their decision, it was held that the plaintiff had not waived its right to arbitration by commencing an action, and a stay of proceedings was granted. See also *Lonmar Plumbing & Heating Ltd. v. Representative Holdings* (1968), 1 D.L.R. (3d) 591 (Sask.); *Parsons & Whittemore Pulp-mills Inc. v. Foundation Co.* (1970), 73 W.W.R. 300 (Sask. C.A.); *Fathers of Confederation Bldgs. Trust v. Pigott Const. Co.* (1974), 44 D.L.R. (3d) 265 (P.E.I.), and §128, *post.*

In *Bermingham Const. Ltd. v. Moir Const. Co.,* [1959] O.R. 355 (C.A.), it was held that where a subcontractor has submitted one tender for a class of work in respect of two different phases of the main contract and the contractor has accepted that tender, the subcontract cannot be treated as two separate contracts simply because the contractor by way of confirmation of the acceptance of the tender has issued two purchase orders, one in respect of each phase, nor is the subcontractor bound by printed conditions on the backs of the purchase orders in respect of non-liability for delay where the tenders specifically agree to a certain delay between the two phases of the contract.

Where completion of the contract is a condition precedent to payment and the building is destroyed by accidental fire, the contractor's claim for lien will cease to exist unless he has completed the contract or unless his failure to do so is caused by the defendant's default (*King v. Low* (1901), 3 O.L.R. 234 (C.A.)), and this is so whether or not the materials used had become the property of the defendant: see *Appleby v. Myers* (1867), L.R. 2 C.P. 651. In *Taylor Hdwe. Co. v. Hunt* (1917), 39 O.L.R. 90 (C.A.), it was held, however, that where the subcontractor had not completed as a result of the act of the owner which rendered it impossible for the subcontractor to complete his work, he was entitled to a lien on the land, and the fire insurance moneys which the board had received, to the extent of what was owing to the principal contractor. This would appear to conform with the result intended by the provisions of section 8 of the Ontario Act and the corresponding sections of many of the other Acts which provide that if the property upon which a lien attaches is wholly or partially destroyed by fire, any insurance moneys received by an owner or prior mortgagee shall take the place of the property destroyed and be subject to the same claims and to the same extent as if the money had been realized by a sale of the property in an action to enforce the lien. In *G.A. Baert Const. (1960) Ltd. v. Can. Gen. Ins. Co.* (1966), 55 W.W.R. 449 (Man.), the owner was held to be entitled to recover the value of materials, which had been delivered to the job site but which had not been incorporated in the building, on a fire insurance policy which included in the coverage "materials to enter into and form part of the finished structure . . . the property of the Insured or for which the Insured is legally responsible". The Court found that the owner would be legally responsible for materials delivered to the site because the subcontractors who had supplied them had a claim under The Mechanics' Lien Act for their value and, in certain circumstances, would be entitled to sell the owner's property to satisfy their claims.

§31 The Subcontractor.

A subcontractor is defined in section 1(1)(*g*) of the Ontario Act, section 2(1)(*m*) of the Newfoundland Act, section 2(1)(*n*) of the Saskatchewan Act and section 2(*h*) of the Manitoba Act as "a person not contracting with or employed directly by the owner or his agent ... but contracting with or employed by a contractor or, under him, by another subcontractor". The other Acts use similar definitions. From this definition it follows that there may be subcontractors of subcontractors in a pyramid so to speak and this is often the case. A material supplier may also be a subcontractor under this definition whether he is required to perform any work under his contract or not: see *Robinson v. Estevan Brick Ltd.* (1967), 60 W.W.R. 671 (Sask. C.A.), and §32(*d*), *post*. However, a person who simply contracts to deliver materials to the building site is not a subcontractor under this definition: *Cam Cement Contractors Ltd. v. Royal Bank* (1973), 38 D.L.R. (3d) 427 (B.C.C.A.).

A subcontractor has no direct dealings with the owner but his work is part of the work to be performed by the general contractor who deals directly with the owner and the owner is responsible, as previously mentioned, for retaining a percentage of payments made to the contractor for the benefit of the subcontractor. The minimum amount of the owner's liability to the subcontractor is the amount of the statutory holdback. However, if for some reason the owner retains more than the statutory holdback the subcontractor is entitled to assert his lien against this excess, subject to the owner's right to reduce this excess by the amount of his counter-claim, if any, against the contractor for defective workmanship, breach of contract, additional cost of completion or for other damages. Accordingly, the maximum amount available to satisfy the subcontractor's claim will be the total amount owing to the contractor or to the subcontractor through whom the subcontractor in question is claiming: see *Briggs v. McInnis* (1920), 53 N.S.R. 417 (C.A.) and *Scarborough Painting Ltd. v. Buckley* (1974), 4 O.R. (2d) 253.

While a subcontractor must show that the work which he performed and the materials which he supplied were necessary for the completion of the contract between the owner and the contractor in order to assert his claim for lien, he is not bound to a strict compliance with the terms of the principal contract. In *Mallett v. Kovar* (1910), 14 W.L.R. 327 (Alta.), the subcontractor was able to show that he had complied strictly with the terms of his contract with the contractor and he was held to be entitled to have a lien even though the owner had rejected the furnace which he installed as not conforming to the provisions of the main contract. See also *Anly v. Holy Trinity Church* (1885), 2 Man. R. 248. The earlier decisions in Ontario appear to correspond to the situation in British Columbia where the provisions of section 6 of the British Columbia Act lead to the result that the subcontractor may not claim a lien if no moneys are owing to the contractor by the owner. However, the provisions of sections 11 and 13 of the Ontario Act, the corresponding provisions of the other Acts, and the case law on the subject would appear to entitle the subcontractor to the statutory holdback notwithstanding the fact that because of non-completion, abandonment, defective workmanship or any other reason the contractor is not entitled to receive payment from the owner: see *Lambton (County) v. Can. Comstock Co.,* [1960] S.C.R. 86; *S. I. Guttman Ltd. v. James D. Mokry Ltd.,* [1969] 1 O.R. 7 (C.A.); *Lonmar Plumbing & Heating*

Ltd. v. Representative Holdings (1968), 1 D.L.R. (3d) 591 (Sask.); *Ground Water Dev. Corpn. v. Moncton* (1972), 5 N.B.R. (2d) 487 (C.A.); *Noranda Exploration Co. v. Sigurdson* (1975), 53 D.L.R. (3d) 641 (S.C.C.); and §42, *post.* It was held in the peculiar circumstances in *Can. Cutting & Coring (Toronto) Ltd. v. Howson,* [1968] 2 O.R. 449, however, that work done by persons hired by a general contractor to remedy defects in its work under its guarantee in the original contract was not lienable because the owner was under no obligation to pay the contractor for such remedial work and there was therefore no sum out of which a holdback could be retained.

In general, the abandonment of the main contract by the contractor or the prevention of completion of the subcontract by the contractor or by the owner himself will not prejudice the claim for lien of the subcontractor: see *Bunting v. Bell* (1876), 23 Gr. 584; *Cragnoline v. Southwick* (1916), 27 O.W.R. 445; *George Taylor Hdwe Ltd. v. Can. Associated Gold Fields Ltd.,* [1929] 3 D.L.R. 709 (Ont.C.A.); *Gidney (Sidney) v. Morgan* (1910), 16 B.C.R. 18; *Morgan v. Sunray Petroleum Corpn.,* [1941] 2 W.W.R. 603; affirmed [1942] 2 W.W.R. 53 (Alta.C.A.); *Taylor Hdwe Co. v. Hunt* (1917), 39 O.L.R. 90 (C.A.); *Freedman v. Guar. Trust Co.,* [1929] 4 D.L.R. 32 (Ont. C.A.). The subcontractor will not be prejudiced by any provisions of the main contract between the owner and the general contractor unless those provisions are specifically made a part of his contract with the general contractor. Accordingly, it has been held that if the architect fails to give a certificate to the general contractor approving the work done, and even though it is required by the owner's contract with him as a condition precedent to payment, the subcontractor will not be precluded from recovering or claiming a lien where the subcontract does not include such a provision: see *Lundy v. Henderson* (1908), 9 W.L.R. 327 (Alta. C.A.); *Petrie v. Hunter; Guest v. Hunter* (1882), 2 O.R. 233. Most of the Mechanics' Lien Acts provide, as does section 4(3) of the Ontario Act and section 4 of the Nova Scotia Act, that no agreement shall deprive any person who is otherwise entitled to a lien of the benefit of the lien if he is not a party to the agreement and that such lien shall attach notwithstanding such agreement. It was held in *Anly v. Holy Trinity Church* (1885), 2 Man. R. 248, that a subcontractor who was a workman would be entitled to assert a lien even though the contract between the owner and the original contractor provided that no workman should be entitled to any lien. It was held in *Gorman v. Henderson* (1908), 8 W.L.R. 422 (Alta.), and *Petrie v. Hunter; Guest v. Hunter, supra,* that a provision in the contract between the owner and the general contractor providing for the payment of damages in a fixed amount to the owner for delay in finishing the contract by the contractor would not permit a deduction by the owner from the amount owing to the contractor so as to prejudice existing liens of subcontractors. In *Rideau Aluminum & Steels Ltd. v. McKechnie,* [1964] 1 O.R. 523 (C.A.), it was held that a waiver of lien given by a subcontractor could not prejudice the lien rights of his subcontractors who were not parties to the waiver.

Where the owner dismisses his contractor or a contractor abandons the work and the owner then agrees with the subcontractors that, if they will finish the work, he will pay them, he cannot avoid his liability by saying that the contractor is liable on the basis that his agreement with the subcontractors was merely a promise to answer for the debt, default or miscarriage of another. It was held in *Petrie v. Hunter; Guest v. Hunter* (1882), 10 O.A.R. 127, affirming 2 O.R. 233 and *Union Lbr. Co. v. Porter* (1908), 8 W.L.R. 423; affirmed 9 W.L.R. 325 (Alta.), that such an agreement amounted to a new and independent contract with the subcontractor and that the subcontractor was entitled to a lien for all work done under such an agreement as a "contractor". In this connection see also *McArthur v. Dewar* (1885), 3 Man. R. 72; *McCauley v. Powell* (1908), 7 W.L.R. 443 (Alta.); *John C. Love Lbr. Co. v. Moore,* [1963] 1 O.R. 245 (C.A.); *Len Ariss & Co. v. Peloso,* [1958] O.R. 643 (C.A.); *Western Air Conditioning Ltd. v. Capri Hotels Ltd.* (1962), 38 W.W.R. 184 (Alta.); §47, "Direct Contracts with Owner".

In *Ringland v. Edwards* (1911), 19 W.L.R. 219 (Alta.), where a receipt for payment had been given by a subcontractor even though final payment had not been made and the owner was thereby led to believe that it had been, it was held that the receipt was binding on the subcontractor and he could not then repudiate it and enforce his lien. However, see *Lambton (County) v. Can. Comstock Co.,* [1960] S.C.R. 86, where acknowledgements were obtained from subcontractors that their work was complete before they had completed and the Court held that their liens, filed more than 37 days after the date of the acknowledgements, were valid for the full amount, having been filed within 37 days after the actual completion of the subcontracts. In the latter case the Court took the position that such an acknowledgement did not operate as a waiver of lien since it was not an "express agreement to the contrary" within the meaning of Ontario section 5(1). In *Weathermakers Ltd. v. Wetaskiwin* (1966), 56 W.W.R. 271 (Alta.), it was held that the fact that the subcontractor had rendered an account for the contract price in July should not necessarily be construed as evidence that the work was completed then so as to make its lien, which was filed in October, out of time.

It was held in *Rice Lewis & Son Ltd. v. George Rathbone Ltd.* (1913), 27 O.L.R. 630 (C.A.), and *Smith v. Bernhart* (1909), 11 W.L.R. 623 (Sask.), and is implicit in the provisions of the various Acts with respect to the holdback, that, while the owner may deduct damages from sums in his hands owing to the contractor in excess of the holdback, he may never on any account deduct damages from the holdback itself. The amount of the statutory holdback is, of course, based on the actual value of the work done and it may well be that if the contractor's work has been improperly done, the value of the work will be less and accordingly the amount of the holdback will be less. Such a situation would never arise where the owner's claim for damages arises out of delay in performance of the contract since this would not affect the quality of the work or its value.

§32 The Materialman.

(a) Definition

Section 1(1)(c) of the Ontario Act defines material or materials as including "every kind of movable property". The Mechanics' Lien Act of each province gives persons supplying materials in accordance with the Act a claim for lien for their purchase price. The materialman must prove either that the materials were delivered to the property to be charged with the lien or alternatively that they were incorporated into the building being erected on those lands: *Milton Pressed Brick Co. v. Whalley* (1918), 42 O.L.R. 369; *Ludlam-Ainslee Lbr. Co. v. Fallis* (1909), 19 O.L.R. 419 (C.A.). *Morgan Smith Co. v. Sissiboo Pulp & Paper Co.* (1904), 35 S.C.R. 93; *Giroday Sawmills Ltd. v. Roberts*, [1953] 2 D.L.R. 737 (B.C. C.A.). Section 5(3) of the Ontario Act provides that the lien attaches to the land where the materials delivered are incorporated into the land, building, structure or works on the land notwithstanding that the materials may not have been delivered in strict accordance with the words of subsection (1) of that section. Subsection (1) speaks of placing or furnishing the materials on the land, each of which appears to be synonymous with delivery to the land to be charged. A lien will not be given merely for "placing" or delivering the material, however: *Cam Cement Contractors Ltd. v. Royal Bank* (1973), 38 D.L.R. (3d) 427 (B.C.C.A.). In *Peterson Truck Co. v. Socony-Vacuum Exploration Co.* (1955), 17 W.W.R. 257 (Alta. C.A.), it was held that the one who furnished the material might have a lien for the cost of "placing" it on the property even if he employed someone else to do this work, but one who merely placed the material on the property does not "furnish" that material within the meaning of the Act.

The materialman's right to a lien will exist even though the materials furnished were not actually used by the contractor: *Kalbfleisch v. Hurley* (1915), 34 O.L.R. 268 (C.A.); *Pavich v. Tulameen Coal Mines Ltd.,* [1936] 3 W.W.R. 593 (B.C.); and *McArthur v. Dewar* (1885), 3 Man. R. 72. While there is no obligation upon him to prove that the material placed by him upon the land sought to be charged was actually used in whole or in part, there is an obligation upon him to prove that the material was so placed by him with his intention and expectation that it was to be used in the construction and erection upon the land upon which the lien is claimed: *McArthur v. Dewar, supra; Giroday Sawmills Ltd. v. Roberts*, [1953] 2

D.L.R. 737 (B.C. C.A.); *Montjoy v. Heward S. Dist.* (1908), 10 W.L.R. 282 (Sask.). The material, if not incorporated in the structure, must have been supplied for one of the purposes mentioned in the Act and it must be supplied in connection with the work which is being undertaken by the person to whom the materials were supplied, as was held in *Rocky Mountain S. Dist. v. Atlas Lbr. Co.,* [1954] S.C.R. 589; and *Sprague v. Besant* (1885), 3 Man. R. 519. Accordingly, it was held in *Brooks-Sanford Co. v. Theodore Telier Const. Co.* (1910), 20 O.L.R. 303; reversed 22 O.L.R. 176 (C.A.), that material supplied for experimental purposes only could not give rise to a lien even though in fact it had been incorporated into the building, since it had not been supplied for the purposes enumerated in section 5(1) of the Ontario Act.

(*b*) *Delivery of the Material.*

The material must actually reach the property which is sought to be charged with the lien or lands in the immediate vicinity of that property which have been designated by the owner or his agent for that purpose: *Larkin v. Larkin* (1900), 32 O.R. 80 (C.A.); *Ludlam-Ainslee Lbr. Co. v. Fallis* (1909), 19 O.L.R. 419 (C.A.); *Milton Pressed Brick Co. v. Whalley* (1918), 42 O.L.R. 369 (C.A.); *Morgan Smith Co. v. Sissiboo Pulp & Paper Co.* (1904), 35 S.C.R. 93; *Can. Equipment & Supply Co. v. Bell* (1913), 11 D.L.R. 820 (Alta.); *Trussed Concrete Steel Co. v. Taylor Engineering Co.,* [1919] 2 W.W.R. 123 (Alta.).

If delivery is not made in this manner then it is encumbent upon the materialman to establish that his materials, however delivered, were actually incorporated in the building or buildings being erected on the land sought to be charged with the lien. For example, where the materialman is supplying to the central warehouse of a general contractor who is building on several properties under contracts with several different owners, the materialman would have to trace his material and be able to identify it in each of the buildings being erected on the several properties: see *Kelly & Cracknell Ltd. v. Armstrong Housing Indust. Ltd.,* [1948] O.W. N. 417. It was stated in *Hall v. Hogg* (1890), 20 O.R. 13, that if the materials were picked up by the contractor at the materialman's place of business the lien arises at the time of sale and the statutory period within which the materialman must file his claim for lien commences to run at the time of purchase and not at the time when the materials actually reach the property to be charged with the lien. In *Nelson Lbr. Co. v. Integrated Bldgs. Corpn. Ltd.,* [1973] S.C.R. 456, however, it was held that the statutory period began to run from the date upon which the last of the material reached the building site where a subcontractor had picked up the material from the materialman's premises, and had taken it to the site some weeks later.

In the *Nelson Lbr. Co.* case Laskin J. approved the statement made by

McDermid J.A. in his dissenting reasons when the case was before the Alberta Court of Appeal that "there is no restriction on who may deliver the materials." He went on to say, at p. 463 of his judgment:

"I do not see any distortion of the Mechanics Lien Act in recognizing a materialman's right to lien upon the delivery to the site by the subcontractor of material ordered from the materialman for the subcontractor's use in carrying out its work on the site. A subcontractor may well have to collect or assemble materials before using them on the site, or the site may be, at a particular time, too limited in size or too congested with equipment to permit direct delivery thereto of supplies by a materialman. So long as the materials are intended for the site in pursuance of the subcontractor's arrangement with the materialman — and that is conceded in the present case — the particular date of arrival there, whether brought directly by the materialman or its agent or carrier, or indirectly by the subcontractor, is not material to the subsistence of the materialman's lien, so long, at least, as they do arrive during the performance by the subcontractor of its contract with the general contractor or, if brought directly by the materialman, are so brought pursuant to its contract with the subcontractor. The time for registration by the materialman will run then from the date that the last of the materials are so brought on to the site."

Where the materialman is unable to identify his material in the building but can prove delivery to the land and can also prove that his material was furnished to be used for one of the purposes set out in the Act, then he is entitled to his claim for lien notwithstanding the fact that the material may have been removed subsequent to delivery by the contractor or some other person. The intention and the expectation of the supplier as to the purpose for which the materials were delivered is the test applied by the Courts: *Can. Lbr. Yards v. Ferguson,* [1920] 1 W.W.R. 266 (Sask.); *Montjoy v. Heward S. Dist.* (1908), 10 W.L.R. 282 (Sask.); *Giroday Sawmills Ltd. v. Roberts,* [1953] 2 D.L.R. 737 (B.C.C.A.). See also: *Marble Center Ltd. v. Kenney Const. Co.* (1972), 29 D.L.R. (3d) 64, affirmed without reasons 38 D.L.R. (3d) 319 (N.S.C.A.). In *George Taylor Hdwe Ltd. v. Can. Associated Gold Fields Ltd.,* [1929] 3 D.L.R. 709 (Ont. C.A.), the Court expressed the view that the words of the section setting out the purposes for which material could be supplied so as to give the materialman a right to a lien should receive a wide construction.

(c) Purpose for Which Materials Supplied.

It should be pointed out, however, that the words "materials to be used" which appear in section 5 of the Ontario Act and the corresponding sections of the Acts of the other provinces contemplate the consumption of the material in and about the work in progress on the property to be charged. Some of the Acts provide that the materials will be deemed to have been furnished within the meaning of the Act if they have been delivered on the land upon which they are to be used or if they have been placed in such other "place in the immediate vicinity thereof as is designated by the owner or his agent": N.B., sec. 4(5); P.E.I., sec. 3(4); Alta., sec. 7(1); Nfld., sec. 7(1); Ont., sec. 5(1). It is not intended, however, that the delivery of the materials to the "designated" land in the immediate vicinity of the lands upon which the work is being done should make such "designated" land subject to the lien. Section 5 of the Ontario Act makes this clear by providing that "delivery on the designated land does not make such land subject to a lien."

Materials that are not actually consumed or do not actually produce some benefit to the land such as scaffolding, machinery or tools which are carried away and used on other contracts cannot be called materials supplied for the purposes set forth in the Act since they are not furnished "to be used" in the making, constructing, erecting, fitting, altering, improving or repairing of any erection, building, railway, etc. Thus, it was held in *Wortman v. Frid Lewis Co.* (1915), 9 W.W.R. 812 (Alta.) that a person who supplied coal to a building contractor for the purpose of generating steam to hoist material and for drying out the unfinished building was entitled to a mechanics' lien as a materialman since the coal, while not becoming a part of the building, was used up in its construction. Conversely, in *Crowell Bros. v. Maritime Minerals Ltd.*, [1940] 2 D.L.R. 472 (N.S. C.A.), it was held that renting a drill sharpener to a mine on a straight rental basis is not supplying a service within the meaning of the Act and no lien exists for the rental therefor. While such machinery is furnished for the purpose of facilitating the work, it remains the property of the contractor and is not consumed in its use, remaining capable of use in some other construction or improvement work. In *Clarkson Co. v. Ace Lbr. Ltd.*, [1963] S.C.R. 110, the Supreme Court of Canada refused to allow a lien for the price of the rental of concrete jacks which were used to hold the form work in place while the concrete hardened, for similar reasons. The claim for lien of a supplier of lumber which was used to construct forms to mould the concrete for a building was disallowed in *R.A. Corbett & Co. v. Phillips* (1972), 5 N.B.R. (2d) 499 (C.A.), since it was not attached to the realty nor intended to become a part thereof, and was subsequently removed from the job site. In *Lumberland Inc. v. Nineteen Hundred Tower Ltd.*, [1977] 1 S.C.R. 581, a privilege claimed under the Quebec Civil Code for such material was held to be valid on the ground that such materials enhance the value of the building and correlatively lose their value, totally or substantially, as a result of their being utilized in this manner.

In *J. B. Turney & Co. v. Farrelly Bros. Ltd.*, [1922] 3 W.W.R. 289; reversed on other grounds [1922] 3 W.W.R. 1017 (Alta. C.A.), it was held that if the nature of the land demands the use of an explosive for the purpose of speed, cheapness and efficiency in the labour of executing that class of work, the explosive is material which is "worked into or made part of the works" within the meaning of the Act, as would be fuses and detonators, since they are used up and forever gone. However, it was further held that the wire connecting the batteries to the detonators or the batteries themselves are not worked into or made part of the works but remain tools which may be used again and accordingly these are not "materials" within the meaning of the Act. In *Re Bodner Road Const. Co.; R. v. Can. Indemnity Co.* (1963), 43 W.W.R. 641 (Man.), it was held that gasoline and oil supplied to and consumed by the machines engaged in the construction operation were lienable items provided the machines were actually in use on the job site. Gasoline and oil used in transporting the men, equipment and materials to the job site were accordingly not lienable items. It was further held in that case that no lien could be had for the cost of repairs to the machines being used on the job site since the repairs did not result in an improvement of the property but rather they enhanced the value of the machines themselves. The decision in *Re Joe Pasut Contractors Ltd.* (1973), 18 C.B.R. (N.S.) 87 (Ont.), is to the same effect. In *Cam Cement Contractors Ltd. v. Royal Bank* (1973), 38 D.L.R. (3d) 427 (B.C.C.A.) it was held that suppliers of trucks and equipment employed in conveying materials to the building site, but which were not otherwise employed thereon, were not entitled to liens. In *Aetna Roofing (1965) Ltd. v. Robinson* (1969), 71 W.W.R. 212, reversed on other grounds (*sub nom. Aetna Roofing (1965) Ltd. v. Westeel-Rosco Ltd.*) 72 W.W.R. 634 (Man. C.A.), it was held that electrical energy which was used as a source of power to drive tools and provide lights in a building under construction was "material" within the meaning of the Mechanics' Lien Act. In *E.E. McCoy Co. v. Venus Elec. Ltd.* (1977), 19 N.B.R. (2d) 299, it was held that the supplier of plastic vapour barrier, which was used in connection with some welding done on the building site and was then thrown away, was not entitled to claim a lien therefor because it was never intended that this material was to be or become an "improvement" within the definition of that word as contained in the New Brunswick Act.

In *Northcoast Forest Products Ltd. v. Eakins Const. Ltd.* (1960), 35 W.W.R. 233 it was held by a British Columbia Court that a lien might be had for the rental of tools and equipment if they were supplied together with men to operate the equipment, and the rental included the cost of the equipment as well as the wages of the men. The Court held, however, that a person who claimed solely as a renter of tools and equipment did not qualify as a lien claimant, nor did a person who supplied equipment together with skilled employees to operate it on terms that the contractor should pay the wages of the operator. See also in this connection, *Peace River Oil Pipe Line Co. v. Dutton-Williams Bros.* (1960), 35 W.W.R. 95 (Alta.); *Vannatta v. Uplands Ltd.* (1913), 4 W.W.R. 1265 (C.A.); *Re Bodner Road Const. Co.;*

R. v. Can. Indemnity Co., supra; Re Arthur J. Lennox Contractors Ltd. (1959), 38 C.B.R. 97 (Ont.); *Clarkson Co. v. Ace Lbr. Ltd.,* [1963] S.C.R. 110; *Re Terra Cotta Contracting Co.,* [1964] 1 O.R. 661. In 1970 a new subsection was added to section 5 of the Ontario Act which gives a person who rents equipment a lien for the rental thereof during the period in which it is in use on the contract site. Subsection (5) provides that "a person who rents equipment to an owner, contractor or subcontractor for use on a contract site shall be deemed for the purposes of this Act to have performed a service for which he has a lien . . .". The Acts of Alberta and Newfoundland contain the same provision: Alta., sec. 4(4); Nfld., sec. 8. Section 2(1)(m) of the Saskatchewan Act is to similar effect.

(*d*) *Materialman as a Subcontractor.*

While it is seldom important to differentiate between materialmen and subcontractors, it should be noted that if a person who supplies material also furnishes labour in connection therewith he will be termed a subcontractor and not a materialman: *Fitzgerald v. Williamson* (1913), 4 W.W.R. 1253 (B.C. C.A.); *Irvin v. Victoria Home Const. Co.* (1913), 4 W.W.R. 1251 (B.C.); *Rosio v. Beech (1913), 18 B.C.R. 73 (C.A.); Hill-Clark-Francis Ltd. v. Lanthier,* [1958] O.W.N. 233; *Silver v. R.R. Seeton Const. Ltd.* (1977), 74 D.L.R. (3d) 212 (N.S.). In *Robinson v. Estevan Brick Ltd.* (1967), 60 W.W.R. 671, the Saskatchewan Court of Appeal held however, that a person who supplied material pursuant to a contract qualified as a subcontractor even though neither the supplier of materials nor the person who purchased them from him did any work on the building.

(*e*) *Liability of Owner to Materialmen.*

In the absence of direct dealings between them, the owner of the property involved is liable to the materialman, as he is to the subcontractor, for the statutory holdback only. However, if the owner himself joins with the contractor in ordering the materials, he will be liable on a contractual basis to the materialman for the entire value of the material: see *Rogers Lbr. Co. v. Gray* (1913), 4 W.W.R. 294 (Sask. C.A.); *Slattery v. Lillis* (1905), 10 O.L.R. 697 (C.A.). See also §47, *post.*

(*f*) *Materials Must be Supplied With Intent to Look to Lien Rights.*

In order for the materialman to have a claim for lien, it must have been intended by the parties that the material sold was to be used for purposes set out in the Act and that it was to be used on some particular lands known to the lien claimant. While it is not necessary for him to have the immediate intention of filing a lien when he sells the material to the contractor, the Act contemplates a contract more specific than the mere sale of materials in the ordinary course of business. If the materialman sells his materials without any regard to the purpose for which they are going to be used, or the land on which they are going to be used, then he will be selling on the credit of the buyer alone and without regard to any security which he might have had under the Act. In *Stephens Paint Co. v. Cottingham* (1916), 10 W.W.R. 627 (Man.), the Court expressed the opinion that the material supplier in such circumstances was selling not for the special purpose named in the Act, namely "construction", but for whatever purpose might seem best to the purchaser. In *Dom. Radiator Co. v. Cann* (1904), 37 N.S.R. 237 (C.A.), it was held that the words "we have secured contract for hotel which requires above goods" in a letter to the materialman sufficiently identified the building for which the goods were required. In *Sprague v. Besant* (1885), 3 Man. R. 519, the Court expressed the opinion that the parties should mutually understand that the materials supplied are to be used, and are furnished to be used, in and about the erection or repair of a building, and the materialman has no lien unless the goods were supplied by him on the understanding that they would be used in the particular building upon which he claims to have a lien. In *Polson v. Thomson* (1916), 26 Man. R. 410 (C.A.), it was held that the main objective of the statute is to secure the lien upon the buildings and land upon which the materials were placed or in which they were incorporated and that it is immaterial if the claim for lien in fact describes more land or if in fact the lands are subsequently divided between different owners. In *Giroday Sawmills Ltd. v. Roberts,* [1953] 2 D.L.R. 737, the British Columbia Court of Appeal, after holding that there was no obligation upon the materialman to prove that the material which was placed by him upon the land sought to be charged was actually used, went on to say that there was an obligation upon him, nevertheless, to prove that the material was so placed by him with the intention and with the expectation that it was to be used in the construction and erection upon the land. In that case, the Court refused to allow the lien on the ground that there was no evidence to indicate that the materialman knew anything about the purpose for which the lumber was ordered other than that the contractor wanted it delivered to a certain street address. The Court admitted that conjecture might solve the problem of why the contractor ordered the lumber sent to that particular address but speculation could not satisfy the Court that the shipper knew when he sent the lumber that it was going to be used in an erection or that it was going to be used for one of the purposes set out in the Act on that particular property. He was not looking to the land against which he sought to enforce his lien when the contract was made but on the contrary was looking to the purchaser as the primary source of his protection.

It was held in *Mallett v. Kovar* (1910), 14 W.L.R. 327 (Alta.), that the materialman was entitled to a lien when he was able to prove that the materials which he had supplied had been supplied in accordance with the contract even though the owner subsequently rejected them. In *Campaigne v. Carver* (1915), 35 O.L.R. 232, the Court solved the problem of how to apportion one account rendered with respect to materials furnished for two houses which did not show how much of the material had been used in each house, by deciding that the materialman should be entitled to claim a lien for exactly one-half of the materials with respect to each of the two properties. The same solution was employed by the Court in *Accurate Kitchens & Woodworking Ltd. v. Coreydale Bldrs. Ltd.,* [1970] 3 O.R. 488, where the lien claimant submitted one account for materials supplied for use in five houses. In *Re Moorehouse and Leak* (1887), 13 O.R. 290 (C.A.), it was held that where materials were supplied under one contract with a contractor building houses for several different owners, the time within which the lien would have to be registered would start to run from the date of the last delivery with respect to each separate property. If the contractor had several different contracts with one owner, however, the situation would be different. It was held in *Enrg. & Plumbing Supplies (Vancouver) Ltd. v. Total Ad Dev. Ltd.; Universal Supply Co. v. Total Ad Devs. Ltd.* (1975), 59 D.L.R. (3d) 316 (B.C.), that individual strata lots established under the Strata Titles Act, 1974 (B.C.), c. 89, s. 66, could not be considered as an improvement for the purposes of S. 23(2) of the B.C. Mechanics' Lien Act where the contract for construction applied to the entire building, and accordingly the claims for lien of material suppliers who had filed their liens after certain of the strata lots had been substantially completed and sold were found to attach to the sold lots.

(g) *Materials Not to be Removed.*

All of the Mechanics' Lien Acts, with the exception of the Newfoundland Act and the Ontario Act, contain a provision similar to that contained in section 13 of the Manitoba Act, section 20 of the British Columbia Act and section 16(1) of the Nova Scotia Act, prohibiting the removal of material from the property against which it is sought to enforce the lien, to the prejudice of that lien. Many of the Acts also contain a provision to the effect that material actually brought upon any land to be used on such land for any of the purposes enumerated in the Act, is not to be subject to execution or other process to enforce any debt other than for the purchase price thereof due to the person who furnished it. This section was recently removed from the Ontario and Newfoundland Acts. The meaning and effect to be given to the section are more fully discussed in §34, *post.*

(h) *The Prevenient Arrangement.*

The supply of material by the materialman may take place under separate contracts between the supplier and the subcontractor, or contractor as the case may be, or alternatively by a prevenient arrangement whereby the supplier agrees with the contractor or subcontractor that he will supply materials as ordered from time to time upon terms then agreed upon or to be fixed later as the material is supplied. Where materials are supplied under a prevenient arrangement, the time limit for filing the claim for lien by the materialman will commence to run from the date of the last delivery of materials and it is of course unnecessary to file a lien within 37 days after each delivery is made. The agreement to supply need not be binding on the owner or subcontractor. It can be terminated by him at any time. However, there must be the preliminary understanding that until the material supplier is notified to the contrary, he is to supply materials as requested: *Boake v. Guild,* [1932] O.R. 617; affirmed (*sub nom. Carrel v. Hart*) [1934] S.C.R. 10; *Morris v. Tharle* (1893), 24 O.R. 159 (C.A.); *Robock v. Peters* (1900), 13 Man. R. 124.

In *Rocky Mountain S. Dist. v. Atlas Lbr. Co.,* [1954] S.C.R. 589, reversing 8 W.W.R. (N.S.) 513, Locke J. expressed the opinion at p. 604 that the following quotation was a correct statement of the law:

"Where labour or materials are furnished under separate contracts, even though such contracts are between the same persons and relate to the same building or improvement, the contracts cannot be tacked together so as to enlarge the time for filing a lien for what was done or furnished under either, but a lien must be filed for what was done or furnished under each contract within the statutory period after its compliance. Where, however, all the work is done or all the materials are furnished under one entire continuing contract, although at different times, a lien claim or statement filed within the statutory period after the last item was done or finished is sufficient as to all the items; and in order that the contract may be a continuing one within this rule it is not necessary that all the work or materials should be ordered at one time, that the amount of work or materials should be determined at the time of the first order, or that the prices should be then agreed upon, or the time of payment fixed; but a mere general arrangement to furnish labour or materials for a particular building or improvement is sufficient, if complied with, even though the original arrangement was not legally binding."

In *Flett v. World Bldg. Ltd.* (1914), 15 D.L.R. 628 (B.C. C.A.), where the materialman had contracted to sell all of a certain class of supplies, namely the hardware required in the construction of a particular building as mentioned in the original specifications, and he supplied not only the goods mentioned in the original specifications but further materials which were contemplated by his contract as extras or additions for the amount of which the fixed price was subject to increase, it was held that the lien for all of the material supplied was not lost by reason of the lapse of the statutory period between the last delivery of the goods shown in the specifications and the later delivery of those which were considered extras. It was held in *Lawrence v. Landsberg* (1910), 14 W.L.R. 477 (B.C.), where the plaintiff sought to preserve a lien by means of the supply of material and work after the completion of the building and after the architect had given the final certificate, that it was incumbent on him to prove clearly that the material was supplied and the work was done in pursuance of and as part of his original contract. The onus is upon the claimant who seeks to establish that the materials were supplied under a prevenient agreement or that work was done under such an agreement to prove that the material was so supplied. If he does not do so, it will be assumed that the materials were supplied or the work was done under separate contracts. The Court stated in *Vanderwell Lbr. Ltd. v. Grant Indust. Ltd.* (1963), 42 W.W.R. 446 (Alta.), that the action of a claimant who delivered goods of comparatively small value some time after the bulk of the material had been delivered was open to suspicion and refused to allow the lien. It was held in *Fulton Hdwe Co. v. Mitchell* (1923), 54 O.L.R. 472 (C.A.), *McColl-Frontenac Oil Co. v. Blakeny Concrete Products* (1960), 27 D.L.R. (2d) 507 (N.B. C.A.) and *Western Air Conditioning Ltd. v. Capri Hotels Ltd.,* (1962), 38 W.W.R. 184 (Alta.), that where the labour or materials were furnished under separate contracts, even though such contracts were between the same persons and related to the same building the contracts could not be tacked together so as to extend the time for registering a lien until the expiration of the statutory period after the last of the two contracts was completed. The *Fulton Hardware* case was cited with approval by the Supreme Court of Canada in *Rocky Mountain S. Dist. v. Atlas Lbr. Co., supra,* and *Hectors Ltd. v. Mfrs. Life Ins. Co.,* [1967] S.C.R. 153, affirming (*sub. nom. Inglewood Plumbing & Gasfitting Ltd. v. Northgate Dev. Ltd. (No. 2))* 56 W.W.R. 449. It was held in *Dunn v. McCallum* (1907), 14 O.L.R. 249 (C.A.) that a materialman was not entitled to register as one individual claim a claim for the amount due for materials supplied by him to a contractor against all the lands jointly of the owners of different parcels of land who had made separate contracts with the contractor. It is a question of fact in each case whether or not the materials have been supplied under a chain of separate contracts or under a prevenient agreement. It was held in *Hurst v. Morris* (1914), 32 O.L.R. 346 (C.A.); *Emco Ltd. v. Starlight Towers-Sask. Drive Ltd.* (1969), 70 W.W.R. 3 (Alta. C.A.); *Emco (Western) Ltd. v. Carillon Invt. Ltd.* (1962), 39 W.W.R. 432 (Man. C.A.) and *Winnipeg Supply & Fuel Co. v. Genevieve Mtge. Corpn.,* [1972] 1 W.W.R. 651 (Man. C.A.), that the validity of the claim for lien is not affected by the fact that the last item is a very small one and is furnished some time after the bulk, if it is established that all of the material was supplied under a prevenient agreement.

In addition to the cases already cited bearing on the problem of the prevenient arrangement, see also the following: *Carroll v. McVicar* (1905), 15 Man. R. 379 (C.A.) (where the plaintiff's claim consisted of charges for different jobs done for the defendant which were all in his line of business but were ordered at different times, it was held that under the circumstances of that case he should not be required, in order to secure payment, to file a claim on completion of each piece of work, and his lien was filed in time if it was filed within the statutory period after he had completed all his work); *Chadwick v. Hunter* (1884), 1 Man. R. 39 (where materials were supplied from time to time as the building progressed, not under a contract but supplied as they were required and ordered, each sale was held to be a separate transaction and the subject of a separate registration of lien); *Dom. Radiator Co. v. Payne,* [1917] 2 W.W.R. 974 (Alta.) (holding that materials furnished or machinery installed at different times may be treated as items in a continuous account for the purpose of filing a lien for them under the Act); *Edmund Hind Lbr. Co. v. Amalgamated Bldg. Co.* (1932), 41 O.W.N. 12 (C.A.) (where it appeared that there had been no binding contract for the supply of all the lumber required and each order as the work progressed was held to constitute a separate contract, distinguishing *George Taylor Hdwe. Ltd. v. Can. Associated Gold Fields Ltd.* (1929), 64 O.L.R. 94 (C.A.)); *Sanderson Pearcy & Co. v. Foster* (1923), 53 O.L.R. 519 (C.A.) (where the claimant, knowing that the contractor was about to abandon the work, prevailed upon him to order some additional material so as to revive his lien, it was held that the claim for a lien should be disallowed, there being no evidence that the material was needed for the building, that it was actually used in it, or that it was part of any original contract); *Sayward v. Dunsmuir & Harrison* (1905), 11 B.C.R. 375 (C.A.) (where it was held that the question of whether or not material is supplied in good faith to complete a contract or as a pretext to revive a lien is a question of fact for the trial Judge and his decision should govern); *Smith v. Bernhart* (1909), 11 W.L.R. 623 (Sask.) (where the plaintiff had at different times supplied hardware and installed plumbing and heating equipment and it was held that the plaintiff's work and materials were supplied with the same object, by one party to another party standing in the same relationship, and were so bound into one as to form an entire contract); *Steinman v. Koscuk* (1906), 4 W.L.R. 514 (Man.) (where it was held that if the work is done in good faith and in order to complete the building, not colorably to revive the lien, the time would begin to run from completion of such work and from delivery of the last of the materials supplied in performing it); *Wilson Gregory Lbr. Co. v. Koman,* [1942] 3 W.W.R. 521 (Man. C.A.) (where the materialman supplied material to a contractor doing certain work on premises pursuant to a written contract with the owner and a month later the owner decided upon further work and made a verbal contract with the contractor covering the work and the materialman supplied further materials to be used in connection with the extra work, it was held that the contract was not a continuing one and a mechanics' lien filed covering all of the materials supplied was out of time as the time for registration had elapsed between the two deliveries of material); *Currier & Ferguson Elec. v. Pearce,* [1953] O.W.N. 184; and *Harper Const. Co. v. Constant Macaroni Ltd.,* [1975] 2 W.W.R. 20 (Man.) (where a prevenient arrangement was established); *Bermingham Const. Ltd. v. Moir Const. Co.,* [1959] O.R. 355 (C.A.) (where it was held that where a subcontractor has submitted one tender for a class of work in respect of two different phases of the main contract and the contractor has accepted that tender, the subcontract cannot be treated as two separate contracts simply because the contractor, by way of confirmation of the acceptance of the tender, has issued two purchase orders, one in respect of each phase of the work); *Western Air Conditioning Ltd. v. Capri Hotels Ltd.* (1962), 38 W.W.R. 184 (Alta.) (where the material supplier failed to file his lien in time and subsequently, under a new and separate contract, delivered additional material which was designed to replace items of the original delivery, it was held that the second delivery did not permit him to file a lien covering both deliveries); *Argus Steel Const. Ltd. v. Burns Tpt. Ltd.,* [1962] O.W.N. 153 (C.A.) (where it was held that the time for registration of the lien ran from the date of the last delivery of material and that the knowledge of the owner that such delivery had been made was not a requisite in law to an extension of time for filing a claim for lien); *Zucchi v. Intervestments Const. Corpn.,* [1970] 2 O.R. 404 (where it was held, on the authority of *Hurst v. Morris* (1914), 32 O.L.R. 346 (C.A.), that it was immaterial whether the material was furnished under one contract or under several contracts; any person who furnished materials to be used in the construction of a building was entitled to a lien for the purchase price thereof whether there was a prevenient arrangement or not); *Conklin Lbr. Co. v. Klymas* (1974), 19 C.B.R. (N.S.) 191, (Ont. C.A.), (where the plaintiff was held to be entitled to a lien for all of the materials supplied to the defendant because they had been supplied pursuant to a continuing agreement between the parties for the supply of material to one particular project).

§33 The Wage Earner.

Section 1(1)(*h*) of the Ontario Act defines "wages" as money earned by a workman for work done by time or as piece work. Most of the other Acts define "wages" in similar terms. The Ontario and Newfoundland Acts go on, however, to provide that "wages" include "all monetary supplementary benefits, whether by statute, contract or collective bargaining agreement". The additional words were added so as to include such benefits as vacation pay credits, welfare plan payments and contributions to pension funds which are in reality part of the workman's wages but which are often paid on his behalf to third persons by his employer. At least in Ontario this definition would appear not to include an assessment made against the owner pursuant to the Workmen's Compensation Act: *Union Elec. Supply Co. v. Gillin Enrg. & Const. Ltd.* [1971] 3 O.R. 125. However, in New Brunswick it has been held that a Workmen's Compensation Board lien for assessments does have priority over the claims of successful lien claimants: see *Dobbelsteyn Elec. Ltd. v. Whittaker Textiles (Marysville) Ltd.* (1976), 14 N.B.R. (2d) 584. By section 15 of the Ontario Act, and by corresponding sections of most of the other provincial Acts, the wage earner is given priority to the extent of 30 days' wages over all other mechanics' lien claims derived through the same contractor or subcontractor to the extent of and on the holdback, as the case may be, to which such contractor or subcontractor is entitled. The wage earner is distinguished from a subcontractor in that he works under the supervision or under the direction of another. In *Rendall, MacKay, Michie Ltd. v. Warren & Dyett* (1915), 8 W.W.R. 113 (Alta.); *Stafford v. McKay,* [1919] 2 W.W.R. 280 (Alta.), the Court drew a distinction between a claimant who worked under supervision and one who made his own decisions as to the manner in which the work which he did was done, the latter being a subcontractor and hence not entitled to the priority given to the wage earner. The wage earner will be entitled to a claim for lien if he fulfills the requirements of the relevant statute with respect to the creation of a lien; for example, under section 5(1) of the Ontario Act, if he performs any work upon or in respect of the making, constructing, erecting, fitting, altering, improving or repairing of any land, building, structure or works or the appurtenances of any of them. While the British Columbia Act does not include the word "improving" it has been held that the relevant section is broad enough to give the same result: see *Beseloff v. White Rock Resort Dev. Co.* (1915), 8 W.W.R. 1338 (B.C. C.A.); *Mylnzyuk v. North West Brass Co.* (1913), 5 W.W.R. 483 (Alta.); and *Vannatta v. Uplands Ltd.* (1913), 4 W.W.R. 1265 (B.C. C.A.).

Most of the Acts contain a provision similar to that contained in section 6(1) of the New Brunswick Act, section 10(1) of the British Columbia Act and section 4(1) of the Ontario Act, to the effect that any agreement on the part of a wage earner that The Mechanics' Lien Act does not apply or that the remedies provided by it are not available for the benefit of such person is void. It is provided in the Acts of Newfoundland, Nova Scotia and Ontario, however, that this provision does not apply to a manager, officer or foreman. The Ontario and Newfoundland Acts also provide that the section does not apply to any person whose wages are more than $50.00 a day. The British Columbia Act provides that the section does not apply to a workman whose wages exceed $15.00 per day. The Alberta and Saskatchewan Acts contain a provision that an agreement by any person to waive his lien rights is void: Alta. sec. 3; Sask. sec. 11. The claim for lien must be made by the wage earner himself, however, and in *Hill-Clark-Francis Ltd. v. Lanthier,* [1958] O.W.N. 233, where a blended claim was made by a claimant for rental of a bulldozer and truck with drivers at a certain sum per hour, the claimant argued that the wages paid by him to his drivers should be allowed as a wage claim and thus enjoy the priority given by the Act. The Court held that the wage earner must be the lien claimant and the subcontractor who pays him his wages cannot be subrogated to claim wages paid out to him. See also *Union Elec. Supply Co. Ltd. v. Gillin Enrg. & Const. Ltd., supra.*

The Acts of most of the provinces provide that the wage earner shall be entitled to enforce a lien in respect of a contract or subcontract which has not been completely fulfilled and accordingly the abandonment or non-completion of his contract by the person who employed him will not have any effect on the wage earner's claim: see Ont., sec. 15(2), N.S., sec. 15(2), Man., sec. 12(2), and the corresponding sections of the other Acts. The Acts of British Columbia and Prince Edward Island do not contain this provision although they do give the wage earner's claim priority over the claims of other lienholders.

The question of priorities is discussed in greater detail in §92, *post.* It should be pointed out that, at least in Ontario, the priority given to the wage earner for 30 days' wages, mentioned in section 15 of the Ontario Act, is taken to mean 30 days' unpaid wages and not the wages earned during the 30 days preceding the filing of the lien. A contrary opinion was expressed in at least two Alberta cases, however. According to the Act of that province a lien for wages of a labourer has, to the extent of 6 weeks' wages, priority over all other liens derived through the same contractor or subcontractor to the extent of the statutory holdback to which the contractor or subcontractor through whom the lien is derived, is entitled. At the time of the decision in *Rendall, MacKay, Michie Ltd. v. Warren & Dyett* (1915), 8 W.W.R. 113 (Alta.), the wage claims of labourers were given priority for "not more than six weeks' wages" and the Court interpreted that wording as giving a wage earner priority for the wages earned within a continuous period of 6 weeks counting backwards from the last day's work, rather than giving priority for the wages earned prior to such period but aggregating in total 6 weeks wages or less. At the time of the decision in *Stafford v. McKay*, [1919] 2 W.W.R. 280 (Alta.), the Act gave priority to the wage earner for wages "not exceeding the wages of six weeks or a balance equal to his wages for six weeks" and the Court held that those words meant wages earned within a continuous period of 6 weeks counting back from the last day worked. It was held in *Cole v. Pearson* (1908), 17 O.L.R. 46 (C.A.), that beyond the statutory holdback the wage earner has no priority over other lienholders.

There are a number of decisions dealing with wage earners' rights and decisions distinguishing wage earners from other classes of lien claimants. It was held in *Bradshaw v. Saucerman* (1913), 3 W.W.R. 761, (Y.T. C.A.), that a wage earner was entitled to assert his lien even though the product of his labour, namely timber which he had cut, had been diverted by the owner to a different purpose. It was held in *Vannatta v. Uplands Ltd.* (1913), 4 W.W.R. 1265 (B.C. C.A.), that even though the wage earner had been employed by someone who had no claim for lien, in the circumstances of that case the wage earner was nevertheless entitled to a lien himself. It was held in *Brown v. Allan* (1913), 4 W.W.R. 1306 (B.C. C.A.), that although the wage earner did not have a lien as a materialman, he could nevertheless have one as a wage earner where he was able to segregate the amount due to him for labour from the amount due to him for material. However, the contrary result was obtained in *Allen v. Harrison* (1908), 9 W.L.R. 198 (B.C.) and *Mylnzyuk v. North West Brass Co.* (1913), 5 W.W.R. 483 (Alta.), where it was held that a labourer who had worked for a materialman in fabricating materials to be installed in the property against which it was sought to assert a lien was not entitled to a lien upon those lands. In the latter case, labourers employed by a subcontractor to dig earth and load it on wagons for transportation to the place where it was used in improving other property were held not to be entitled to a lien on such other property. However, teamsters employed by a subcontractor in conveying material to a building in the course of erection were held to be entitled to a lien thereon for their services. In *Vannatta v. Uplands Ltd.* (1913), 4 W.W.R. 1265 (B.C. C.A.), it was held that a lien could not be acquired for conveying building materials to the land where they are to be used but that one who furnished a contractor with horses, wagons and drivers for use on premises which the subcontractor is improving is entitled to a lien. This decision was approved in *Cam Cement Contractors Ltd. v. Royal Bank* (1973), 38 D.L.R. (3d) 427 (B.C.C.A.). In *Peterson Truck Co. v. Socony-Vacuum Exploration Co.* (1955), 17 W.W.R. 257 (Alta. C.A.), the Court felt that there was no doubt that one who furnishes the material would have a lien for the cost of placing it on the property even if he employed another to do this work. In this connection see also *Stafford v. McKay,* [1919] 2 W.W.R. 280 (Alta.), where the claimant claimed a lien for hauling material to the building site to be paid for in a lump sum, the hauling not being done by himself but by others hired or sent by him and the lump sum price including the services of his horses and equipment. The Court allowed the claim for lien to the claimant as a subcontractor but would not allow it to him as a wage earner. It was held in *Rendall, MacKay, Michie Ltd. v. Warren & Dyett* (1915), 8 W.W.R. 113 (Alta.), that a subcontractor is not a "labourer" under the Act so as to acquire as to labour done as part of the contract the privileges given by the Act to labourers. In *Boker v. Uplands* (1913), 24 W.L.R. 768 (B.C. C.A.), a wage earner was held entitled to a claim for lien for work done by him upon the part of a sewer extending below low water mark into the ocean. It was held in *Davis v. Crown Point Mining Co.* (1901), 3 O.L.R. 69 (C.A.), that a blacksmith employed for sharpening and keeping tools in order for the work of mining was entitled to a lien on the mine for his wages but that a cook who did the cooking for the men employed in the mine was not entitled to a lien for his wages; and in *Hill-Clark-Francis Ltd. v. Lanthier,* [1958] O.W.N. 233, that, in order to obtain the priority given to the wage earners, the claimant must be the wage earner and the subcontractor who pays him his wages cannot be subrogated to his position. In *DeCook v. Pasayten Forest Products Ltd.* (1966), 56 W.W.R. 292; affirmed 58 W.W.R. 561 (B.C. C.A.), the Court discussed the factors which distinguished an independent contractor from a "workman" under the British Columbia Woodsmen's Lien for Wages Act. It held that a person who operates equipment which is owned by him, under the direction of an employer who tells him when and where to work, is a workman within the meaning of the Act, but he is an independent contractor if he operates his equipment in his own way and at times of his own choosing. In *Foley v. Can. Credit Men's Assn. Ltd.,* [1971] 2 W.W.R. 703 (Man.), it was held that the president and major shareholder of a limited company engaged to carry out a contract was not a "workman" within the meaning of the Act even though he was employed by the company, was paid a salary and did in fact work on the project along with other employees. The Court expressed the opinion that a clear distinction had been drawn by the Legislature between workmen on the one hand and employers, proprietors, contractors, subcontractors and builders on the other.

§34 The So-Called Vendor's Lien.

Most of the Acts contain a section similar to section 13(3) of the Manitoba Act which provides that material delivered to be used for any of the purposes mentioned in section 4 of the Act is subject to a lien in favour of the person furnishing it until it is incorporated in the building, erection, or work. (This provision was removed from the Ontario Act in 1969). The result would appear to be that until the material is actually incorporated in the building the materialman has a lien both upon the realty and upon the material itself. Upon incorporation the material is no longer "material" within the meaning of the Act: see *Collis v. Carew Lbr. Co.* (1930), 37 O.W.N. 413; on appeal 65 O.L.R. 520 (C.A.). The material must reach the land to be charged, or lands designated by the owner or his agent for the purpose of delivery, before the section comes into operation: see *Milton Pressed Brick Co. v. Whalley* (1918), 42 O.L.R. 369 (C.A.).

There is a divergence of opinion in various provinces as to the meaning and effect of this section. *Brooks-Sanford Co. v. Theodore Telier Const. Co.* (1910), 2 O.W.N. 138; reversed 22 O.L.R. 176 (C.A.); *Bunting v. Bell* (1876), 23 Gr. 584; *Larkin v. Larkin* (1900), 32 O.R. 80 (C.A.), were overruled in Ontario by the decisions in *Re Northlands Grading Ltd.,* [1960] O.R. 455 (C.A.) and *Maltby's Ltd. v. Can. Packers Ltd.,* [1947] O.W.N. 757, and amendments made to the Act since those cases were decided. When the two latter cases were decided this provision appeared as section 15 of the Ontario Act. It was held in the *Northlands* case that the lien created by this section is not a special or separate and distinct lien in the nature of an extension of the vendor's lien under The Sale of Goods Act but that it is simply an extension or particular application of the basic lien which is created by section 5 of the Ontario Act. It was further held that the rights given by the section must be enforced in the same manner as those given by section 5 and that the regular conditions for the preservation, perfection and enforcement of the materialman's claim for lien must be complied with. It would seem that to hold otherwise would give the supplier of material an unfair advantage over other lien claimants and bring about something different than the fair and equitable distribution among persons who perform work or supply materials for use in connection with the erection of a building which is contemplated by all other provisions of the Act. This was one reason why this section has been deleted from the Ontario Act. The Alberta Court of Appeal, however, came to the opposite conclusion when considering the effect of the corresponding section of the Alberta Act. The Court held in *John Wood Co. v. Can. Credit Men's Trust Assn. Ltd.* (1962), 39 W.W.R. 593, that the section does create a separate and distinct lien on the materials themselves, and that the material supplier was not required to register a lien or commence an action under the Act in order to enforce that lien. This decision was followed in *Western Caissons (Alta.) Ltd. v. Bower* (1969), 71 W.W.R. 604 (Alta. C.A.). The trial Judge in *Marble Center Ltd. v. Kenney Const. Co.* (1972), 29 D.L.R. (3d) 64 (N.S.), after reviewing the Alberta and Ontario decisions, concluded that the doctrine expressed in *Re Northlands Grading Ltd., (supra)* was to be preferred. An appeal from his decision was dismissed without written reasons: (1974), 38 D.L.R. (3d) 319.

In *McFarland v. Trusts & Guar. Co.,* [1938] 3 W.W.R. 333; affirmed (*sub nom. McFarland v. Greenbank*) [1939] 1 W.W.R. 572 (Alta. C.A.), the Court held that there could only be one lien on the land, and not two liens, one on the improvement and another on the estate or interest in the land, nor was there a lien on materials separate from the estate of or the interest of the "owner" after they have been placed in the improvement. In *Metals Ltd. v. Trusts & Guar. Co.* (1914), 7 W.W.R. 605 (Alta.), the trial Judge took the view that, to preserve the unpaid seller's lien given by this section, possession of the materials delivered must be resumed before they were worked into the building. He expressed the opinion that "the lien given by this section is a seller's lien for unpaid purchase price. Such a lien exists independently of this section, until delivery. The section continues the lien notwithstanding delivery until the material is worked into the building. This special lien ceases on that being done." See also *Can. Equipment & Supply Co. v. Bell* (1913), 11 D.L.R. 820 (Alta.). In *Trussed Concrete Steel Co. v. Taylor Enrg. Co.,* [1919] 2 W.W.R. 123 (Alta.), the Court held that the provisions of the corresponding section of the Alberta Act made it unnecessary to file an affidavit in support of a lien in the Land Titles Office as required in enforcing the ordinary lien against the land. The Court took the view that the general lien, arising under section 4 of the Alberta Act, covering not only land and buildings but also materials for the work, was subject to the lien on materials given by section 5 (now sec. 14), to the person supplying the same. All of the Acts, with the exception of those of Ontario and Newfoundland, specifically provide that the trial Judge may direct the sale of materials and authorize the removal thereof: P.E.I. sec. 46(2); Sask. sec. 51(4); B.C. sec. 45(4).

§35 The Architect.

(a) The Architect as a Lien Claimant.

The decisions in *Re Computine Can. Ltd.* (1971), 18 D.L.R. (3d) 127 (B.C.); *Arnoldi v. Gouin* (1875), 22 Gr. 314; *Burgess v. Khoury (Albrechtsen's Claim)*, [1948] O.W.N. 789; *Read v. Whitney* (1919), 45 O.L.R. 377 (C.A.); *Sickler v. Spencer* (1911), 17 B.C.R. 41, clearly indicate that the architect is entitled to maintain a lien for the cost of plans prepared by him if he superintends or directs the erection of the work or building according to such plans, but, at least in most jurisdictions, he is not entitled to a lien for the cost of preparing plans alone where the building is not proceeded with. This statement was approved in *N.S. Sand & Gravel Ltd. v. Kidstone Estates Ltd.* (1973), 13 N.S.R. (2d) 431. He is a person who performs work within the meaning of section 5 of the Ontario Act and the corresponding provisions of the other Acts, and in *Read v. Whitney, supra,* the architect was held to be entitled to a lien as a contractor and the assistant architect as a subcontractor. In *Cowan v. Kitchener Motor Sales Co.* (1924), 27 O.W.N. 38, the plaintiff was engaged to prepare plans and specifications for a garage for the defendant company and to supervise the work. The rear part of the building was completed in November and because of money difficulties the owner suggested that no further work would be done until the following spring. The plaintiff filed his lien in November of the following year and it was held that the plaintiff's lien was filed too late since he was in the same position as a contractor and accordingly was bound to register his lien within 30 days after the completion of his services which had ended when he had superintended the work done on the rear portion of the building.

The basis of the Ontario decisions disallowing a claim for lien for the drawing of plans only is the fact that such work cannot result in a benefit to the lands sought to be charged. Unless the architect also supervises construction there is no work or service in respect of the "making, constructing, erecting, fitting, altering, improving or repairing" of the building or lands. The situation would appear to be different in Alberta, however; in *Inglewood Plumbing & Gasfitting Ltd. v. Northgate Dev. Ltd. (No. 1)* (1965), 54 W.W.R. 225 (Alta.), it was held that an architect who had prepared plans under an agreement which expressly excluded any supervision of the work by him was entitled to a lien as one who had performed a service, even though he had not done any work on the job site itself. It was further held in that case that since his fee was to be a percentage of the total cost of the building, and since 75% of the building had been completed, he was entitled to a lien for 75% of his fee. It was held in *Hett v. Samoth Realty Projects Ltd.* (1977), 76 D.L.R. (3d) 362 (Alta. C.A.), that the *Inglewood* case had extended the right to file a lien for the "performance of services upon the improvement" to its limit, and the claim of a developer was accordingly disallowed in this case on the ground that the services which he had provided were not directly related to the process of construction as required by the Act. The Hett case was cited with approval in *P.R. Collings & Associates Ltd. v. Jolin Holdings Ltd.,* [1978] 3 W.W.R. 602 (Sask.), where the Court refused to allow a lien for construction management services. The situation may also be different in Ontario when the plans in question have been prepared by an engineer for the sewage system, the watermains and the roads in a subdivision, which plans have been approved by the appropriate municipal authorities. In *Ambro Materials & Const. Ltd. v. 230056 Invts. Ltd.* (1975), 9 O.R. (2d) 226, engineers who had prepared such plans were held to be entitled to a lien for their services since their plans were different from the plans prepared by an architect for a building, in that the engineers' plans, unlike those of the architect which could be used to erect a building on another property, were designed specifically for this particular parcel of land and had increased its value, since the subdivision could now be sold along with the approved plans to a purchaser who would be in a position to proceed at once with the development of the property. It should be noted that the plaintiff in this action had also been retained to supervise the construction of the services but had not commenced to do so. In Nova Scotia it has also been held that an engineer who performed services respecting a proposed project, including the preparation of plans and drawings, obtaining the rezoning of the land and the examination and assessment of the site was entitled to a lien, even though the project was never built: *Jenkins v. Wilin Const. Ltd.* (1977), 25 N.S.R. (2d) 19.

In *Tripp (Fripp) v. Clark* (1913), 4 W.W.R. 912 (B.C.), a British Columbia Court disallowed a claim for lien by an architect where the claim was filed for the total fee of the architect in regard to preparing plans and supervising construction. In this case the Court indicated that had the architect been able to separate his charges for drawing the plans from those for supervising construction, the Court would have been prepared to allow his lien for that portion of his fees applicable to supervision. This decision was cited with approval in *Scott v. Lindstrom* (1964), 50 W.W.R. 573 (B.C.), where it was held that an architect who prepared plans alone, without supervising any of the construction, was not entitled to a lien under section 5 of the British Columbia Act, which limits the right to a lien to a "workman, materialman, contractor, or subcontractor". In *Re Erickson/Massey*, [1971] 2 W.W.R. 767 (B.C.), the Court distinguished the *Scott* decision on the ground that it dealt with the claim of an architect for the preparation of plans alone, and held that an architect who drew plans for and supervised the construction of a building was entitled to a lien for his services. It was held in *Turner v. Johnson* (1932), 41 O.W.N. 497 (C.A.) that the architect could enforce his claim for lien in spite of the fact that the contractor himself was not a party to the action. While the architect may not have a claim for lien for work done in preparation of the plans, he is probably entitled to a lien on the plans themselves unless he is paid for his services in preparing them. If he is paid, he must deliver up the plans: *Gibbon v. Pease*, [1905] 1 K.B. 810 (C.A.); *Hughes v. Lenny* (1839), 5 M & W. 183.

(b) Duties of Architect.

The architect is liable for negligence in the performance of his duties and should he fail to exercise a reasonable degree of skill, care and diligence he will be liable to forfeit his right to compensation as well as being liable to the injured party in damages for his failure: *Nelligan v. Brennan & Whale*, [1955] O.R. 783; affirmed [1956] O.W.N. 366; affirmed [1957] S.C.R. 342; *Burgess v. Khoury (Albrechtsen's Claim)*, [1948] O.W.N. 789; *Cauchon v. MacCosham* (1914), 28 W.L.R. 500 (Alta.); *Harries, Hall & Kruce v. South Sarnia Properties Ltd.* (1929), 63 O.L.R. 597 (C.A.); *Doe v. Can. Surety Co.; Blonde v. Doe*, [1937] S.C.R. 1; *Siegel v. Swartz*, [1943] O.W.N. 532; *Brennan Paving Co. v. Oshawa*, [1952] O.R. 540; affirmed [1953] O.R. 578, [1953] 3 D.L.R. 16; affirmed [1955] S.C.R. 76; *Pratt v. St. Albert Protestant Sep. S. Dist.* (1969), 69 W.W.R. 62 (Alta. C.A.); *Sutcliffe v. Thackrah*, [1974] 1 All E.R. 859 (H.L.); *Dom. Chain Co. v. Eastern Const. Co.* (1974), 3 O.R. (2d) 481; (affirmed with respect to the finding of negligence: 12 O.R. (2d) 201 (C.A.)); *Colchester Dev. Ltd. v. Leslie R. Fairn & Associates* (1975), 60 D.L.R. (3d) 681 (N.S.C.A.); *Surrey v. Church* (1977), 76 D.L.R. (3d) 721 (B.C.).

In *Brennan Paving Co. v. Oshawa, supra,* the Court outlined the duties of an engineer or architect under a building contract as follows:

(1) He is bound to act judicially even though he was employed and paid by one of the parties to the knowledge of both parties;

(2) He must act within the power conferred upon him by the contract;

(3) He is not entitled to construe the contract unless it expressly gives him power to do so;

(4) In the absence of express power to do so, he cannot alter the terms of the contract;

(5) If, in granting or refusing a certificate, he goes beyond the powers given to him under the contract and one of the parties seeks to rely on an unwarranted exercise of his powers, the other party is released from the condition of the contract requiring the certificate as a condition precedent to payment. There is an implied condition in the contract, in other words, that neither of the parties will rely on the purported exercise by the architect or engineer of a jurisdiction which he does not in fact possess under the contract.

See also *Kamlee Const. Ltd. v. Oakville* (1960), 26 D.L.R. (2d) 166 (S.C.C.), and *Re Maredo Ltd. and Elfran Invts. Ltd.* (1975), 9 O.R. (2d) 696, as to an engineer's duty to act judicially.

The architect may also be liable in damages to the injured party where he wrongfully withholds a certificate after being requested to furnish the same. Such a claim cannot be prosecuted in the lien action where the architect is not a lien claimant since there is no jurisdiction under the Act to entertain a claim by one defendant against another or to prosecute a claim by one defendant against another that is completely independent of the plaintiff's claim: *Bagshaw v. Johnston* (1901), 3 O.L.R. 58 and *Bermingham Const. Ltd. v. Moir Const. Co.,* [1959] O.R. 355 (C.A.). If the architect is a lien claimant then it is open to the owner or contractor to counterclaim for damages against him either for negligence or for wrongfully withholding a certificate with respect to the building contract which is the subject of the architect's claim for lien: see *Burgess v. Khoury (Albrechtsen's Claim),* [1948] O.W.N. 789.

(c) The Architect's Certificate.

The certificate of the architect or engineer will be binding and final so long as he acts fairly, honestly and impartially and there has been no collusion between him and the contractor or owner who employs him. This will be so even where he has in fact been negligent. In *Walkley v. Victoria* (1900), 7 B.C.R. 481, where the contract made the right of the contractors to receive payment for the construction of certain works dependent on a certificate of an engineer who was also the sole arbitrator of all disputes, the engineer unjustifiably delayed the issue of the certificate for 7 months and acted in a shifting and vacillating manner probably causing heavy loss to the contractors by his mistake. It was held that since he had not acted in a fraudulent manner nor was there any evidence of collusion on the part of the owner with him, the certificate could not be set aside. In *Hamilton v. Vineberg* (1912), 22 O.W.R. 238 (C.A.), it was held that the architect's decision as to the value of the work done and the materials furnished under a contract declaring that his decision should be final was not open to attack if he acted fairly and honestly and there was no collusion between him and the contractor. It was further held that collusion between an architect and a contractor sufficient to invalidate the architect's certificate had not been shown by the fact that the architect did not make any measurements nor obtain any account of quantities of material supplied and that he acquiesced in the amount which the plaintiff claimed therefor. In *Canty v. Clarke* (1879), 44 U.C.Q.B. 505 (C.A.); *Guelph Paving v. Brockville* (1905), 5 O.W.R. 626 (C.A.), it was held that where the plaintiff was to be paid in accordance with the architect's certificate that the work had been fully completed, the plaintiff was bound by the certificate and could not dispute it in the absence of fraud or undue influence proven against the architect. In *Croft Const. Co. v. Terminal Const. Co.* (1959), 20 D.L.R. (2d) 247 (Ont. C.A.), it was held that the architect's certificate was binding on the plaintiff subcontractor where the plaintiff entered into a subcontract with the defendant to do certain common excavation for a stipulated price which contract provided that "quantities compiled by the Department of Transport engineer in charge of the work will be the final figure in making payments" to the plaintiff, there being no suggestion of fraud, bad faith or breach of duty on the part of the engineer. It was held in *Kerr v. Harrington*, [1947] O.W.N. 237 that if an architect was merely negligent, careless or imcompetent, his certificates were not thereby deprived of their binding effect. But in that case, the architect had approved the contractor's charges mechanically, in effect allowing the contractor whatever he charged without considering the rights of the owner and it was held that this was sufficient to incompetent, his certificates were not thereby deprived of their binding upon the owner. The owner was therefore entitled to have the propriety of the charges adjudicated upon by the Court, following *Hickman & Co. v. Roberts*, [1913] A.C. 229. It was held in *Law v. Toronto* (1920), 47 O.L.R. 251; reversed on other grounds 49 O.L.R. 77 (C.A.), that the certificate will not bind the owner himself if the architect or the engineer has not been impartial. See also *Noren Const. (Toronto) Ltd. v. Rosslyn Plaza Ltd.*, [1970] 2 O.R. 292, *Re Maredo Ltd. and Elfran Invts. Ltd.* (1975), 9 O.R. (2d) 696 and *Modern Const. Ltd. v. Moncton* (1972), 27 D.L.R. (3d) 212 (N.B.C.A.) as to the architect's or engineer's duty to act impartially. In *Nelligan v. Brennan & Whale*, [1955] O.R. 783; affirmed [1956] O.W.N. 366; affirmed [1957] S.C.R. 342, it was held that an architect who undertook to design a house and supervise its construction was bound to exercise reasonable skill, care and diligence. Failure to do so rendered him liable to the owner for any loss occasioned by such failure and he was not relieved of this obligation and liability by the fact that the owner had taken a guarantee from a contractor that a particular installation would perform efficiently. In the peculiar circumstances of *Farquhar v. Hamilton* (1892), 20 O.A.R. 86, however, the Court held that the certificate was binding even though the architect had not been completely impartial in giving his certificate. If the contract provides that the architect may exercise his own discretion in giving certificates and he does so, his decision is not open to review by the Court: *Hutchinson v. Rogers* (1909), 1 O.W.N. 89; *McNamara v. Skain* (1892), 23 O.R. 103 (C.A.).

It was held in *Smith v. Bernhart* (1909), 11 W.L.R. 623 (Sask.), that the owner might waive his right to the architect's certificate. The Court considered that he had done so by taking possession of the premises. selling the same and stating accounts with the contractor without obtaining the architect's certificate. See also *Alkok v. Grymek,* [1966] 2 O.R. 235 at 237; on appeal [1968] S.C.R. 452.

It was held in *Lundy v. Henderson* (1908), 9 W.L.R. 327 (Alta. C.A.), that a subcontractor who had completed his contract might enforce his lien notwithstanding the fact that a final certificate had not been given and the contractor himself was accordingly unable to enforce his lien. This decision rests on the ground that the fact that the contract price did not become payable to the contractor until the certificate had been given did not mean that there was no amount payable by the owner upon which a lien could attach. However, where the contract provides that the work must be done to the satisfaction of the architects before the work is to be considered as completed and before payment is to be due, the contractor will not be able to enforce his claim for lien until the architect signifies that he is satisfied. The certificate then becomes a condition precedent to payment as between the parties to the contract: *Vokes Hdwe Co. v. G.T.R.* (1906), 12 O.L.R. 344 (C.A.); *Coatsworth v. Toronto* (1860), 10 U.C.C.P. 73 (C.A.); *Dobson v. Hudson* (1857), 1 C.B. (N.S.) 652; *Kelly v. Tourist Hotel Co.* (1909), 20 O.L.R. 267 (C.A.); *Morgan v. Birnie* (1833), 9 Bing. 672. In *Coatsworth v. Toronto, supra,* the contract provided for payment in instalments. The defendant admitted part performance of the contract but pleaded general non-performance to the satisfaction of their officer named in the contract and that thorough and complete performance was a condition precedent to payment. It was held that by payment in part, the defendants were not barred from insisting on full performance to the satisfaction of their officer as a condition precedent, the contract being in consideration of performance and not in consideration of the covenant to perform. In *Dobson v. Hudson, supra,* where the plaintiffs contracted to install berths in an immigrant ship to the satisfaction of the commissioner's surveyor, to be paid for at a stipulated sum per berth, it was held that the plaintiffs were entitled to be paid for only so many berths as the commissioner actually approved and not for berths which had been erected but removed by order of the surveyor, his approval being a condition precedent to any amount becoming due whatsoever. In *Morgan v. Birnie, supra,* where the defendant was to pay for a building upon receiving an architect's certificate that the work was done to his satisfaction, the architect checked the builder's charges and sent them on to the defendant and it was held that this did not amount to such a certificate of satisfaction as to enable the builder to sue the defendant. If the owner wrongfully dismisses the contractor because of the architect's failure to give his certificate, the contractor may still enforce his lien: *Alta. Bldg. Co. v. Calgary* (1911), 16 W.L.R. 443 (Alta.); *Smith v. Gordon* (1880), 30 U.C.C.P. 553 (C.A.).

The following cases, as well as Goldsmith on Canadian Building Contracts, may also be consulted in connection with certificates of architects and engineers: *Brown Const. Co. v. Bannatyne S. Dist.* (1912), 2 W.W.R. 176 (Man.); *Brown v. Bannatyne School Bd.* (1912), 2 W.W.R. 742 (Man.) (in which the architect's certificate was held to be conclusive); *Lambton v. Can. Comstock Co.,* [1960] S.C.R. 86 (in which the architect's certificate as to completion, based on acknowledgments received from subcontractors, was held not to preclude the subcontractors from filing liens); *Dom. Const. Co. v. Good & Co.* (1899), 30 S.C.R. 114, affirming (*sub nom. Good v. Toronto, Hamilton, etc. Ry.*) 26 O.A.R. 133 (where the contract for construction of a railway provided that the work was to be done to the satisfaction of the chief engineer of a railway company not a party to the contract who was to be the sole and final arbitrator of all disputes between the parties, and it was held that the contractor was not bound by such condition when the party who was named as arbitrator proved to be in fact the engineer of the other party to the contract). See also §46(*b*), *post,* and Chapter 9, The Trust Fund, in connection with architect's certificates, which are specifically mentioned in The Mechanics' Lien Act, permitting reductions in the owner's holdback and creating trusts.

§36 Notice of the Lien.

The Ontario Act, section 11(6), provides that the owner, contractor or subcontractor as the case may be, may make payments to his contractors, materialmen and so forth up to the amount of the statutory holdback so long as he makes such payments in good faith and he has not been notified in writing of a claim for lien. As long as these conditions are met such payments will operate as a discharge *pro tanto* of the lien. If, however, the subcontractor, materialman or wage earner gives notice to the owner, contractor or subcontractor, from whom the person primarily liable to him has his contract, then his lien attaches to all money which may henceforth become due and payable to the person who is primarily liable to him by such owner, contractor or subcontractor. As Osler J.A. said in *Craig v. Cromwell* (1900), 27 O.A.R. 585, the purpose of such notice is "to stay the hand of the paymaster". The owner, contractor or subcontractor must, after receiving such notice, withhold, in addition to the statutory holdback, an amount equivalent to that claimed by the lienholder giving the notice. In Ontario written notice is required (see *Craig v. Cromwell, supra,* and *Henry Hope & Sons v. Richard Sheehy & Sons* (1922), 52 O.L.R. 237), as is the case in most jurisdictions. In *McCauley v. Powell* (1908), 7 W.L.R. 443, the Court held that in Alberta constructive notice was sufficient to prevent further payments being made. However, the wording of the present Alberta Act, supported by the decision in *Calgary v. Dom. Radiator Co.* (1917), 56 S.C.R. 141, would seem to contradict this decision and require written notice to be given. In *Revelstoke Bldg. Materials Ltd. v. Howe; Neumann v. Howe; Royal Bank v. Neumann,* [1972] 2 W.W.R. 395, affirmed 31 D.L.R. (3d) 602 (Alta. C.A.) it was held that the notice must set out the amount for which the lien is claimed and where the claimant gave notice of a lien for $11,000.00 whereas, in fact, the correct amount was $17,990.00, the owner was only obliged to hold back the lesser amount set out in the notice. See also §§50, 51 and 75, *post,* in this connection.

Section 12 of the Ontario Act permits the owner, contractor or subcontractor, who receives notice of a lien for which he is not primarily liable, to pay over to the person giving the notice all or a portion of his claim and if, within 3 days afterwards, he gives written notice of the payment to the person who is primarily liable to the claimant, or his agent, such payment will be deemed to be a payment on his contract generally to the contractor or subcontractor who is primarily liable to such claimant. However, this payment must not affect the amount of the statutory holdback which he is required to retain. The danger the owner runs in making payment under this section was noted by the Court in *Craig v. Cromwell, supra,* wherein it was stated that "section 12 would appear to authorize him to pay the subcontractor, but if he does so he assumes the risk of being able to prove, as between himself and the contractor, that the debt was justly due . . .". In *Len Ariss & Co. v. Peloso,* [1958] O.R. 643 (C.A.), a subcontractor gave notice in writing of his lien to the owner who did not take advantage of the procedure under section 12 but held back the amount of the lien in addition to what he believed to be the proper amount of the holdback. The owner subsequently paid further amounts to the contractor maintaining what he believed to be the proper holdback plus this additional amount owing to the lienholder who had given notice. It was held that the lienholder was only entitled to rank *pari passu* with other lienholders on the fund consisting of the proper amount of the holdback plus the amount held back for his lien and the owners, having after judgment paid this lienholder in full, were only entitled as against the other lienholders to credit for what would have been this lienholder's *pro rata* share.

In *Vaillancourt Lbr. Co. v. Trustees of Sep. S. Section No. 2, Balfour Twp.,* [1964] 1 O.R. 418, the Ontario Court of Appeal, relying on the decisions in *Len Ariss & Co. v. Peloso, supra,* and *Freedman v. Guar. Trust Co.* (1929), 64 O.L.R. 200, concluded that when an owner received notice in writing of a lien he must retain, in addition to the statutory holdback, an amount equivalent to the sum claimed in the notice, until the lien was either paid or discharged. The Court went on to hold that the total of the holdback plus the amount claimed in the notice must be made available to all the lien claimants notwithstanding the fact that the owner had a claim for damages against the contractor exceeding the amount otherwise owing to him as a result of the contractor's abandonment of the work. The evidence showed that at the time of the trial, the owner only had the statutory holdback in his hands and that he had paid the contractor sums in excess of the amount claimed in the notice after he had received the notice. The Court of Appeal ruled that the owner would have to pay into Court for the lien claimants, not only the holdback, but the amount which he had improperly paid to the contractor after receiving the notice. This question came before the Ontario Court of Appeal again in *S. I. Guttman Ltd. v. James D. Mokry Ltd.,* [1969] 1 O.R. 7, in which the Court ruled that the decision in the *Vaillancourt Lumber* case must be confined to its own facts, i.e., to cases where the owner pays the contractor after receiving notice of a lien. The facts in the *Guttman* case were similar to those in the *Vaillancourt Lumber* case, except that the owner had not paid anything to the contractor after he received the notice of lien. The Court held, again relying on *Len Ariss & Co. v. Peloso, supra,* and *Freedman v. Guar. Trust Co., supra,* that in such circumstances the lienholders were only entitled to the holdback. The owner could apply the amount it was holding in excess of the holdback in diminution of its claims for damages against the contractor arising out of his failure to complete the contract. This decision was approved by the Supreme Court of Canada in *Can. Comstock Co. v. Toronto Transit Commn.; Can. Comstock Co. v. Anglin-Norcross Ont. Ltd.,* [1970] S.C.R. 205. It was pointed out in *Scarborough Painting Ltd. v. Buckley* (1974), 4 O.R. (2d) 253 that, while on the authority of these cases the owner does have the right to set off his increased costs of completing an abandoned contract against moneys owing to his contractor in excess of the holdback, it is encumbant upon the owner to show that the cost of completing the contract did in fact exceed the difference between the value of the work completed by the original contractor and the contract price.

At least in Ontario then, if the owner pays money to his contractor after receiving a notice in writing of a claim for lien, he may be obliged to pay it a second time to the lien claimants. If he does not pay the contractor after receiving such a notice he will be able to use any money in his hands in excess of the holdback to satisfy his claims for damages against the contractor. If of course the owner has no claim for set-off against these moneys they would have to be made available to satisfy the claims of the lienholders. The owner's right of set-off would also appear to be restricted to a certain extent in Ontario and Saskatchewan by the provisions of section 2(3) of the Ontario Act and section 3(3) of the Saskatchewan Act. Once the architect or engineer certifies all or a portion of the contract price for payment, the owner is prohibited from using any of the amounts which become payable under the certificate for his own purposes, (or for purposes not authorized by the trust), until the beneficiaries of the trust created by that section have been paid. Thus, even if the owner has not received notice of a claim for lien, he may be prevented from using moneys owing to the contractor in excess of the holdback to complete an abandoned or negligently performed contract. In Ontario, however, it has been held that if the moneys certified for payment do not become payable to the contractor by reason of the owner's right to set-off his claim for damages against him for the cost of completing or correcting the work to be done under the contract, the owner may use those moneys for that purpose and will not be obliged to turn them over to the beneficiaries of the trust created by this section: See *Standard Industries Ltd. v. Treasury Trails Holdings Ltd.* (1976), 24 C.B.R. (N.S.) 8, affirmed 23 C.B.R. (N.S.) 244 (Ont. C.A.). These sections only apply, in any event, to contracts under which payments on account of the contract price are to be made on the certificate of a person named in the contract.

§37 The Conditional Vendor as a Lien Claimant.

The seller of goods under a conditional sales contract may also have rights under The Mechanics' Lien Act but he must eventually elect under which Act he is going to proceed. If he elects to avail himself of the protection given him by The Conditional Sales Act then he cannot enforce a claim for lien under The Mechanics' Lien Act. In *Hill v. Storey* (1915), 34 O.L.R. 489 (C.A.), the conditional vendor sought to establish a claim for lien and it was held that where a lien claimant for materials insisted upon the terms of a conditional sales contract whereby he had a claim upon the materials until payment, he could not rank as a lienholder and compete with others who had no such right as against the materials. In *U. S. Const. Co. v. Rat Portage Lbr. Co.* (1915), 9 W.W.R. 657 (Man.), the Court of Appeal considered American decisions on the subject and concluded that by enforcing a claim for lien the claimant elected to consider the subject matter of the conditional sales contract as part of the building even though by the terms of the conditional sales agreement, title to the material was reserved to him. Once the conditional vendor made this election he should thereafter be estopped from claiming that the materials were his property or that he had a right to remove them.

The former Conditional Sales Act of Ontario distinguished between building material and goods other than building material which had been affixed to realty. It provided that goods, other than building material, which had been affixed to the realty were to remain subject to the rights of the conditional vendor as fully as they were before being so affixed: sec. 10(1). The Act went on to provide that the owner, any purchaser, mortgagee, or other encumbrancer thereof, should have the right as against the conditional vendor or any other person claiming through him to retain those goods upon payment to him of the amount owing on them. See *Primeau Argo Block Co. v. Ludor Const. Ltd.*, [1966] 1 O.R. 245 and *Pape v. Edfield Holdings Ltd.*, [1968] 1 O.R. 369. Building materials accordingly could not be the subject of a conditional sales contract. This Act was repealed on April 1st, 1976 as a result of the coming into force of the provisions of the new Personal Property Security Act, R.S.O. 1970, c. 344 which pertain to this type of transaction. The new Act also provides that a "security interest" does not include building materials which have been affixed to the realty: sec. 1(*y*). Section 36(1) of that Act provides that "a security interest that attached to goods before they became fixtures has priority as to the goods over the claim of any person who has an interest in the real property." Section 36(2) provides that, subject to the provisions of section 36(3), a "security interest" which attached to goods after they became fixtures has priority over the claims of persons who subsequently acquire an interest in the real property, but not over the interest of a person who had a registered interest in the property at the time the security interest attached to the goods and who has not consented to the security interest or disclaimed an interest in the goods as fixtures. Section 36(3) provides, *inter alia,* that the security interest is subordinate to the interest of "a creditor with a lien on the real property subsequently obtained as a result of judicial process", if the lien was obtained without actual notice of the security interest. Section 36(4) permits a secured party who has priority over the claim of a person who has an interest in the real property to remove his goods from the property if he reimburses any encumbrancer or owner of the property, who is not the debtor, for the cost of repairing any physical injury caused by the absence of the goods removed or by the necessity for replacement of the same. Section 36(5) provides that a person who has an interest in real property that is subordinate to a "security interest" may retain the goods upon payment to the secured party of the amount owing under the security interest.

The question of what constitututes building material and what constitutes goods which may be the subject of a conditional sales contract or a security agreement may become important where the supplier of material seeks to obtain priority over the lien claims by reason of the existence of a conditional sales contract or a security interest covering the goods supplied. In *Collis v. Carew Lbr. Co.* (1930), 65 O.L.R. 520 at 525 (C.A.), Middleton J. A. said, "It may not always be easy to draw the line but a furnace seems very clearly outside this description", holding that a furnace was not building material within the meaning of The Conditional Sales Act. The decision in *Warner v. Foster,* [1934] O.R. 519 (C.A.), is to the same effect. However, in *Alexander v. McGillivray* (1932), 41 O.W.N. 406, it was held that because of the manner in which the bathtub was incorporated into the building it should be considered to be building material, and accordingly the conditional vendor was not entitled to priority over the other lien claimants. In *Re Application A3554* (1967), 60 W.W.R. 509 (B.C.), it was held that irrigation pipes which were sold under a conditional sales contract and which had been installed under the ground had become part of the realty. In *La Salle Recreations Ltd. v. Can. Camdex Invts. Ltd.* (1969), 68 W.W.R. 339 (B.C.C.A.), it was held that carpeting in a hotel had been annexed to the building in such a manner and in such circumstances as to make it a fixture. In *Gough v. Wood,* [1894] 1 Q.B. 713 (C.A.), a boiler was held to be the proper subject of a conditional sales contract but it is submitted that this case depends upon its own peculiar circumstances; and in *Ellis v. Glover & Hobson Ltd.,* [1908] 1 K.B. 388, the Court of Appeal expressed this opinion, saying that the case was hardly ever cited except to be distinguished. In *Primeau Argo Block Co. v. Ludor Const. Ltd.,* [1966] 1 O.R. 245, it was held that a conditional vendor of a furnace who had registered notice of his conditional sales agreement on title had priority over the lien claimants who only had the right to retain the furnace upon payment to the vendor of the amount owing on the contract. In *Greater Winnipeg Gas Co. v. Petersen* (1968), 65 W.W.R. 500 (Man. C.A.), a furnace was held to be a fixture, and therefore the mortgagee of the home in which it had been installed was entitled to retain it as against the conditional vendor since the mortgagee had obtained title under a quit claim deed from the owner before receiving any notice of the conditional vendor's interest. In *Montreal Trust Co. v. Goldaire Rentals Ltd.,* [1967] 1 O.R. 40, elevators were held not to be building materials within the meaning of The Conditional Sales Act since they could be entirely removed from the hoistway without causing any damage to the building apart from the leaving of bolt holes in the hoistway masonry and the dividing beams. In *Gen. Steel Wares Ltd. v. Ford,* [1965] 2 O.R. 81 (C.A.), it was held that gas dryers installed in triplex buildings did not become part of the realty so as to make them building materials. See also §102, "The Lien Claimant and The Conditional Vendor".

§38 The Lien Claimant under The Mining Act.

In Ontario, Part XIII of The Mining Act, R.S.O. 1970, c. 274, s. 641(1) provides that save as otherwise provided in that Act, The Mechanics' Lien Act is to apply to mines, mining claims, mining lands and works connected therewith. Section 641(2) provides that if the lands and mining rights have not been patented, the registration provided for in The Mechanics' Lien Act is to be done in the office of the recorder. Subsection (3) provides that when the claim is for wages, a claimant shall have a lien, in addition to the rights and remedies afforded by The Mechanics' Lien Act, upon any other property of the owner in or on such mine, mining claim, mining land or works for a sum not exceeding 30 days' wages and such claim can be enforced under The Mechanics' Lien Act. This section goes on to provide that if he is satisfied that a claim for lien is not made in good faith or is made for an improper purpose, or the owner is unduly embarrassed thereby, the Commissioner under The Mining Act may make an order cancelling the lien upon such terms as to security or otherwise as he may deem proper. It further provides that a lien upon unpatented lands does not affect the rights of the Crown. The Mechanics' Lien Acts of many of the other provinces contain provisions similar to those of the Ontario Mining Act.

It was held in *Re Reeve-Dobie Mines Ltd.* (1921), 50 O.L.R. 499, that under the Ontario Mining Act the lien upon a mine extended to the money derived from the sale of the ore. However, a British Columbia Court in *Law v. Mumford* (1909), 14 B.C.R. 233, arrived at the opposite conclusion following *Power v. Jackson Mines Ltd.* (1907), 13 B.C.R. 202 (C.A.). In *Free Lance Well Service Ltd. v. Ponoka Calmar Oils Ltd.* (1957), 23 W.W.R. 44 (Alta.), lien claimants claiming for the value of their services in the drilling, cementing and servicing of an oil well were held entitled to the proceeds of the sale of the materials "stripped" from the well in priority to the owner's claim for rent against the oil company for whom the lien claimants had done the work. In *McLeod v. Merriman* (1926), 29 O.W.N. 341, a number of questions were raised by both sides in the Court of Appeal arising out of apparent conflicts between the Ontario Mining Act and the Ontario Mechanics' Lien Act but because of the insufficiency of the evidence before the Court, the Court of Appeal ordered a new trial and these questions were not dealt with. In *Anderson v. Kootenay Gold Mines* (1913), 18 B.C.R. 643, the Court drew a distinction between a lien for the work done in developing the mine and that done in taking out ore from it. See also: *Hutchinson v. Berridge,* [1922] 2 W.W.R. 710 (Alta. C.A.). In *Byer's Tpt. Ltd. v. Terra Mining & Exploration Ltd.* (1972), 24 D.L.R. (3d) 447 (N.W.T.) it was held that a claim by a transport company pursuant to a contract for carrying necessary supplies and equipment into, and ore concentrates out of, a mining property may validly be the subject matter of a lien under the Northwest Territories Miners Lien Ordinance.

§39 The General Lien Claim.

In *Ont. Lime Assn. v. Grimwood* (1910), 22 O.L.R. 17, Middleton J. defined a general lien thus: "Where one owner chooses to enter into an entire contract for the supply of material to be used upon several buildings ... the claimant can ask to have his lien follow the form of the contract and that it be for an entire sum upon all the buildings." He went on to say that if the owner wished to confine the lien upon any building to the value of the material going into that building, the onus was on him to show the facts which must be peculiarly within his knowledge in order to establish that the property he seeks to relieve from the general lien is not subject to it. In this connection see also *Carrel v. Hart,* [1934] S.C.R. 10 at 26, affirming with a variation *(sub nom. Boake v. Guild)* [1932] O.R. 617 and *Polson v. Thomson* (1916), 10 W.W.R. 865 (Man. C.A.). Middleton J. further pointed out that when the owner has sold one or more of the several distinct buildings to which the lien has attached, the equities then arising between the owners of the different buildings might be worked out upon the principles which are applied when part of a property subject to a mortgage is sold and the mortgagee then endeavours to enforce his remedy against both parcels. See also Ont., sec. 33, Nfld., sec. 33 and *Accurate Kitchens & Woodworking Ltd. v. Coreydale Bldrs. Ltd.,* [1970] 3 O.R. 488.

Carrel v. Hart, [1934] S.C.R. 10, and the same case *(sub nom. Boake v. Guild)* [1932] O.R. 617, arose out of the same transaction. Both decisions approved the decision in *Ont. Lime Assn. v. Grimwood, supra,* and the former approves the decision in *Polson v. Thomson, supra.* (The Court in *Polson v. Thomson* held that a materialman furnishing materials to be used in the erection of several buildings may have a lien against any one of them without showing that the particular materials in that building were furnished for that one particular building and that the lien may attach against several pieces of property as one individual claim). The claimant Hart was a supplier of labour and materials. The claimant Boake was a supplier of materials alone. The contracts of both claimants were made with a general contractor and the five properties on which the work was done or the materials were supplied were owned by a third party. The contracts of each claimant were held to be entire contracts covering all the buildings, and the materials supplied by Boake were held to have been supplied under a prevenient arrangement. It was held that the lien was chargeable against all the land irrespective of the work and materials which went into each building; that in applying the Act the Court might and should have regard to the contracts under which the work or materials claimed for were provided, and where the parties by their contract had treated several buildings belonging to the same owner as upon one property, the lien claimant was entitled to have the lien applied as a general lien upon all the land. This principle was held by the Supreme Court of Canada to have been so long and so generally recognized that it must be taken to be settled law by that Court. The judgment of the Supreme Court of Canada refers to three United States cases: *Livingston v. Miller* (1863), 6 Abbott's P.R. 371; *Wall v. Robinson* (1874), 115 Mass. 429 and *Lewis v. Saylors* (1887), 73 Iowa 504, in all of which the same principle was applied. The first of these American cases expressly holds that a mechanics' lien for materials furnished for the erection of several houses for a gross sum attaches to all of the buildings.

The general lien can arise out of a prevenient agreement for the supply of materials or labour as requested or can arise out of a specific contract covering work to be done on several properties. It can also arise where the owners of two separate properties enter into a joint contract with one contractor, for example, to have a mutual driveway paved. It is highly unlikely that the Court would uphold a claim to a general lien when there were several parcels of land situated some distance from each other although the writers can find no authority for not doing so. However, in view of the fact that should the Court decide that there is no proper claim to a general lien, the claimant, while being allowed to prove his claim against each of the parcels, must establish that the claim for lien was filed within the prescribed time after the doing of the last work or the supplying of the last material to each of them, it would appear wise, if there is any doubt, to register against each parcel separately. Alternatively, the claimant should file his claim for lien against all of the parcels within the time prescribed by the Act, reckoning that time from the date on which work was completed on the first parcel and not the last.

It was held in two very similar cases, the Ontario decision of *Campaigne v. Carver* (1915), 35 O.L.R. 232 (C.A.), and the Alberta decision of *A. Lee Co. v. Hill* (1909), 2 Alta. L.R. 368, where a general lien was claimed but not proven, that the claimant should nevertheless be permitted to prove the amount claimed with respect to each property, and that whether the separate claims are valid will then depend upon the date for registration of the claim for lien as related to each property. In both of these cases, the lien was held to have been filed too late with respect to one of the two properties since the work on that property had been completed more than the statutory number of days prior to registration, but since the work on the second property had been completed within the requisite number of days prior to registration the claimant was held to be entitled to his lien on that second property only. It was held, however, in *Barr & Anderson v. Percy & Co.* (1912), 21 W.L.R. 236, a British Columbia decision, and *Fairclough v. Smith* (1901), 13 Man. R. 509, a Manitoba decision, that where a general lien was not proved, the Court would not permit the claimant to break down his claim once it had found the general lien invalid so as to establish a lien against one or more of the several properties. In *Barr & Anderson v. Percy & Co., supra,* however, no evidence was adduced to show what was actually owing with respect to each house and in both of these cases, the properties were owned by different owners. *Fairclough v. Smith, supra,* was referred to in *Campaigne v. Carver, supra,* and distinguished by the Ontario Court on the ground of subsequent amendments to the Ontario Act. It is submitted that, insofar as Ontario is concerned at any rate, if the claimant failing to establish a general lien can establish the amount claimed in respect of each property, he can have his lien on the lot or lots against which the claim for lien was registered, provided the last work was done or the last materials were supplied within 37 days prior to the filing of the claim for lien. The lien claimant should be entitled as well to a personal judgment for the value of work or materials supplied to the lots against which no lien is proven. Such a personal judgment was given against the defendants in *Barr & Anderson v. Percy & Co., supra,* since while the plaintiffs were unable to establish the value of the materials and labour supplied to each property they were able to establish the total amount owing under the contract.

Section 33 of both the Ontario and Newfoundland Acts provide that where an owner enters into an entire contract for the supply of materials to be used in several buildings, the person who supplies the material will be entitled to claim a general lien on all of the buildings. However, if the owner has sold one or more of the buildings, this section gives the Court the power to equitably apportion this general lien between all of the buildings. In *Accurate Kitchens & Woodworking Ltd. v. Coreydale Bldrs. Ltd.,* [1970] 3 O.R. 488, the Court apportioned a general lien for materials by dividing the total claim by the number of buildings for which the materials had been supplied and allowing the claimant a lien on each of the unsold buildings for one-fifth of the total amount claimed. There was no evidence before the Court as to how much of the material had gone into each of the buildings.

Whether or not the claimant is entitled to a general lien will depend upon the facts of each individual case as was pointed out in *Carrel v. Hart,* [1934] S.C.R. 10, affirming with a variation (*sub nom. Boake v. Guild*) [1932] O.R. 617. In most circumstances if the Court finds that the two owners made separate and distinct contracts with one contractor, it will not allow a general lien. However, in *Fraser v. O'Brien* (1918), 41 D.L.R. 324 (C.A.), the Court pointed out that while the provisions of the New Brunswick Act do not enable a lienholder to consolidate liens against several different buildings, each individual building having to bear the burden of its own construction, a joint lien might be had on a number of structures built or repaired under a single contract and thus connected in construction and ownership. In *Enrg. & Plumbing Supplies (Vancouver) Ltd. v. Total Ad Devs. Ltd.; Universal Supply Co. v. Total Ad Devs. Ltd.,* (1975), 59 D.L.R. (3d) 316 (B.C.) it was held that individual strata lots established under the Strata Titles Act could not be considered as separate "improvements" at least for the purpose of establishing time limits for the filing of mechanics' liens, where the contract for construction of the "improvement" related to the entire building. The Court of Appeal in *Dunn v. McCallum* (1907), 14 O.L.R. 249 (C.A.), took the position that the provisions of section 17(1) and (2) of the present Ontario Act, which provide for the joining of claims for lien upon more than one property and for the apportionment by the trial Judge against the respective properties of the amounts included in the claim for lien, do not permit the setting up of a general lien if in fact such a general lien does not exist. In that case the materialman was held not to be entitled to register as one individual claim, a claim for the amount due for materials supplied by him to a contractor, against all the lands jointly of the owners of different parcels of land who had made separate contracts with the contractor for the erection of houses on their respective parcels. The decisions in *Bldrs. Supply Co. v. Huddlestone* (1915), 25 Man. R. 718; *Security Lbr. Co. v. Plested* (1916), 9 Sask. L.R. 183 (C.A.); *Oldfield v. Barbour* (1888), 12 P.R. 554, and *Currier v. Friedrick* (1875), 22 Gr. 243, are to the same effect. However, in the following cases the Court permitted the claim to be apportioned between the separate properties: *Booth v. Booth* (1902), 1 O.W.R. 49 (C.A.), and *Re Moorehouse and Leak* (1877), 13 O.R. 290 (C.A.). Where the contract is to do work or supply material or services to one contractor owning all the lands in question or who has one contract with the owner of all the lots in question there will be no difficulty in establishing a right to a general lien. The difficulty arises where either the contractor has more than one contract with the owner of the various parcels or where the various parcels of land are owned by different owners. The nature and extent of the lien will then be determined by the terms of the contract or contracts, the date of registration of the lien and whether or not the value of materials or services can be apportioned between the various parcels of land.

§40 Miscellaneous Claims for Lien.

Claims for lien made by specific tradesmen have been dealt with by the Courts in the following cases which are perhaps useful in a limited way. In *Davis v. Crown Point Mining Co.* (1901), 3 O.L.R. 69, it was held that a blacksmith employed for sharpening and keeping tools in order for the working of a mine was entitled to a lien for his wages on the mining location but that a cook who did the cooking for the men was not. However, in *Hutchinson v. Berridge,* [1922] 2 W.W.R. 710 (Alta. C.A.), a "bull cook" who took care of the bunk houses, wash houses, hauled coal to the buildings and kept the premises warm and clean was held to be entitled to a lien just as if he had been a labourer handling a pick and spade, on the basis that both devote their time and strength for the benefit of the undertaking as a whole.

The claims for lien of teamsters were considered in the following cases: in *Mylnzyuk v. North West Brass Co.* (1913), 5 W.W.R. 483 (Alta.), teamsters employed by a subcontractor in conveying material to a building in the course of erection were held to be entitled to a lien for their services. This decision was approved in *Stafford v. McKay,* [1919] 2 W.W.R. 280

(Alta.). However, in *Vannatta v. Uplands Ltd.* (1913), 4 W.W.R. 1265 (B.C. C.A.), it was held that a lien for conveying building materials to the land where they are to be used could not be acquired under what was then section 6 of the British Columbia Act, although one who furnished a contractor with horses, wagons and drivers for his use on premises which the contractor was improving would be entitled to a lien for their hire. This decision was approved in *Cam Cement Const. Ltd. v. Royal Bank* (1973), 38 D.L.R. (3d) 427 (B.C.C.A.). In *Re Bodner Road Const. Co.; R. v. Can. Indemnity Co.* (1963), 43 W.W.R. 641 (Man.), it was held that one could have a lien for gas and oil supplied to and consumed by machines which were actually engaged in the construction work, but no lien could be had for the gasoline and oil consumed by machines used in bringing workmen, equipment or materials to the job site. It was also held that one could not have a lien for the cost of repairs to the equipment used on the site. This case was cited with approval in *Re Malvern Const. Co.* (1964), 6 C.B.R. (N.S.) 241 (Ont.). The decision in *Re Joe Pasut Contractors Ltd.* (1973), 18 C.B.R. (N.S.) 87 (Ont.) is to the same effect. See also: *Cigas Products Ltd. v. Tamarisk Devs. Ltd.,* [1976] 6 W.W.R. 733 (B.C.).

In *Jones v. Jarvis,* [1923] 1 W.W.R. 1164 (Sask.), the Court allowed the claim for lien of a well digger and where one of the holes dug by the plaintiff proved to be a dry hole, it was held that the work must be treated as a whole and that his lien should apply in respect of the entire work done and not just to the portion of it which proved successful. This case was distinguished in *Sloan v. Wasson,* [1923] 2 W.W.R. 506 (Alta.), on the ground that the Alberta section differed from the Saskatchewan section in that the latter spoke of work done in improving land generally. Hence the Court in construing the Alberta Act arrived at the conclusion that the doing of work or causing of work to be done in drilling a well on a farm to obtain a supply of water to be used for the purposes of the farm did not entitle the well digger to a lien upon the land. The Court also refused to allow a claim for lien for digging a well in *Stiffel v. Corwin* (1911), 1 W.W.R. 339, another Alberta decision. In *Farr v. Groat* (1913), 4 W.W.R. 1097 (Alta.), it was held that one who digs an excavation for the foundation of a building is entitled to a lien for his services under the Alberta Act. In *Stuckey v. George,* [1924] 1 W.W.R. 1193 (Sask. C.A.), it was held that one who pursuant to an agreement plows another's land and clears stone from it may have a lien under the Saskatchewan Act for the value of the work done. While *Black v. Hughes* (1902), 22 C.L.T. 220 (B.C.), appears to support these two cases, *Mylnzyuk v. North West Brass Co., supra,* would appear to cast doubt upon the possibility of their general application. However, if the object of the statute is to require the owner to pay for improvements made to his premises, it is difficult to see why one should not have a lien for breaking ground and clearing stones from farm land or for excavating a basement when, without such excavation, the building operations could not proceed.

In *Garing v. Hunt* (1895), 27 O.R. 149, the Court held that a scenic painter was not entitled to claim a lien for his services. In *Lee v. Lincoln Const. Ltd.* (1973), 4 N. & P.E.I.R. 116 (Nfld.) the Court disallowed a claim for lien for landscape work done on a shopping mall on the ground that such work was not being done "upon the construction, alteration or repair" of a building within the meaning of the Newfoundland Act. This decision was distinguished in *Star Landscaping & Excavating Ltd. v. Phillips* (1976), 10 N. & P.E.I.R. 296 (Nfld.), on the ground that it had been decided under sections 4 and 5(1) of The Mechanics' Lien Act, R.S.Nfld. 1952, c. 263, which restricted the creation of the lien to the situation where the work and materials were used in the construction, alteration or repair of a building or similar erection, whereas, the present Newfoundland Act provides that such a lien arises or can be created in respect to work upon, or materials supplied and used in, the improving of the land itself. The Court accordingly allowed the plaintiff's claim for lien for landscaping services. It is submitted that under the wording of the corresponding section of the Ontario Act and of the Acts of most of the other provinces a claim for lien for landscaping services would be allowed.

It was held in *Hubert v. Shinder,* [1952] O.W.N. 146 (C.A.), that a claimant whose work consisted of rehabilitating laundry machinery which had been damaged by fire, the work being in the main completed off the premises in question, was not entitled to a lien. It was held further that another claimant who attached the laundry machinery to the water and sewage systems already installed in the building on the premises was also not entitled to a lien since this was not a part of, or an improvement of, the building within the meaning of the Act. But see *Mor Light Ltd. v. Rikki's Invts. Ltd.,* [1975] W.W.D. 156 (B.C.), where the claimant relied on the date of the wiring and installation of a dishwasher and food mixer to support the validity of his claim for lien and the Court held that the lien was valid on the ground that what occurred was a hybrid situation, the wiring and switch installation being relative, in part, to the realty itself by incorporating the work and materials into the building as a permanent installation, although this work also related, in part, to the dishwasher as a chattel. In *Dobbelsteyn Elec. Ltd. v. Whittaker Textiles (Marysville) Ltd.,* (1976), 14 N.B.R. (2d) 584, it was held that a wholesaler who had supplied hardware for use in installing heavy machinery in a textile plant was not entitled to a lien since the machinery was not an "improvement" within the meaning of The Mechanics' Lien Act. See also: *A.J. (Archie) Goodale Ltd. v. Risidore Bros. Ltd.* (1975), 8 O.R. (2d) 427 (C.A.). In *Evergreen Irrigation Ltd. v. Belgium Farms Ltd.* (1976), 3 A.R. 248, it was held that the plaintiff, who had supplied and installed a movable irrigation system, was not entitled to a lien since such a system was not an "improvement" within the meaning of the

Alberta Builders' Lien Act, but rather the equipment in question was more in the nature of a farm implement.

In *Hett v. Samoth Realty Projects Ltd.* (1977), 76 D.L.R. (3d) 362 (Alta. C.A.), a lien was claimed by a developer who, pursuant to a contract with the owners, had conceived and initiated a development, assembled the necessary land, obtained municipal approvals and agreements, arranged financing, hired a general contractor, overseen the construction, and generally had been in charge of the project from start to finish. The Court held that sec. 2(1)(*l*) of the Builders' Lien Act which defines "work" as including the performance of services upon an improvement for which a person is entitled to a lien under sec. 4(1)(*a*) of the Act, covers only such services as are directly related to the process of construction. It found that the claimant's services did not meet this test and his claim was dismissed. The Court expressed the view that: "Unless some limit is put upon the meaning of 'services' in the Act it would be open to any person, such as a lawyer, an accountant, a sociologist or a statistician, whose work contributed in any way to the total project to file a lien under the Act." This case was cited with approval in *P.R. Collings & Associates Ltd. v. Jolin Holdings Ltd.,* [1978] 3 W.W.R. 602 (Sask.), where the Court refused to allow the claim for lien of a construction manager for services rendered prior to the time at which actual construction of the building commenced. In *Jenkins v. Wilin Const.* (1977), 25 N.S.R. (2d) 19, however, the Court refused to vacate the claim for lien of an engineer who performed services respecting a proposed project, including the preparation of plans and drawings, the obtaining of rezoning of the land and the examination and assessment of the site, although the project was never built, on the ground that the wording of section 5 of the Nova Scotia Act, creating the lien, clearly applied to preparatory work even though no actual improvement to the land had been effected.

The question of whether or not persons who rent equipment to contractors are entitled to claim a lien for the rental of the same creates special problems. The view expressed in *Northcoast Forest Products Ltd. v. Eakins Const. Ltd.* (1960), 35 W.W.R. 233 (B.C.), appears to be the correct one. In that case the question arose as to the right of persons renting tools or equipment to share in a trust fund under the trust provisions of the British Columbia Mechanics' Lien Act. It was held firstly, that one who claimed solely for the rental of tools or equipment did not qualify as a lien claimant under the general provisions of the Act and accordingly was not entitled to rank as a lien claimant under the trust provisions. The Court held, secondly, that persons who rented equipment with men to operate that equipment all as part of a single contract were in the position of subcontractors furnishing a service and were entitled to claim a lien. The Court held, thirdly, that persons who supplied equipment together with operators but on terms that the contractor should pay the wages of the operator were in the same position as lessors of equipment alone and had no claim for lien. The decision in *Peace River Oil Pipe Line Co. v. Dutton-Williams Bros.* (1960), 35 W.W.R. 95 (Alta.), agrees with the second conclusion above. See also in this connection, *Re Bodner Road Const. Co.; R. v. Can. Indemnity Co.* (1963), 43 W.W.R. 641 (Man.); *Re Malvern Const. Co.* (1964), 6 C.B.R. (N.S.) 241 (Ont.); *Re Terra Cotta Contracting Co.,* [1964] 1 O.R. 661. In *Clarkson Co. v. Ace Lbr. Ltd.,* [1963] S.C.R. 110, it was held that one who leased concrete jacks to a forming contractor to be used by him to hold his forms in place while the concrete hardened was not entitled to a lien for the price of the rental, either as a material supplier or as one who had performed a service. In *Crowell Bros. Ltd. v. Maritime Minerals Ltd.* (1940), 15 M.P.R. 39 (N.S. C.A.) (approved in *Re Northlands Grading Co.,* [1960] O.R. 455 (C.A.)), it was held that no lien existed for the rental of a drill sharpener to a mine since the equipment remained the property of the contractor, was not consumed in its use, and remained capable of use in some other construction or improvement work. In *R.A. Corbett & Co. v. Phillips* (1972), 5 N.B.R. (2d) 499, it was held that there could be no lien for the price of plywood which had been used to make forms for pouring concrete where it was subsequently removed from the job site. A claim for the loss of, and damage to certain tarpaulins which had been rented to the defendant by the plaintiff at the construction site was disallowed in *Alros Products Ltd. v. Dalecore Const. Ltd.* (1973), 2 O.R. (2d) 312 (C.A.). The Act has now been amended in Alberta, Saskatchewan, Newfoundland and Ontario, however, to provide that a person who rents equipment for use on a contract site will be deemed for the purposes of the Act to have performed a service for which he is entitled to a lien for the price of the rental: Ont., sec. 5(5); Alta., sec. 4(4); Nfld., sec. 8; Sask., sec. 2(1)(m).

In *Hill-Clark-Francis Ltd. v. Lanthier,* [1958] O.W.N. 233, the Court allowed the claim for lien of a subcontractor who rented a bull-dozer and a truck complete with driver as a subcontractor, but refused to allow the claimant the priority given to wage earners to the extent of the wages paid by the subcontractor to his drivers. It should be pointed out that while the subcontractor renting the equipment to the head contractor without an operator would not be entitled to a lien, except in the above mentioned provinces where the Act has been amended, the general contractor can include the cost of renting such equipment in his contract price and in effect claim a lien against the owner therefor. It would also appear that the operator of the equipment would be entitled to claim a lien and be entitled to the priority given to workmen under the Acts for his wages in operating the equipment despite the fact that the lessor of the equipment might not have a lien for the rental of the same. See also §106, *post.*

4

Rights and Duties of the Owner

§41 The Holdback Fund Generally.

A construction project has a pyramidal structure, the owner at the top with the contractors, subcontractors and those claiming under them radiating down to the base. In most cases payments are made as the work progresses and these payments follow the form of the pyramidal structure from the top down to the base. To provide some measure of protection to lien claimants the Acts of all the provinces make provision for a certain percentage of the value of the work done and materials supplied to be held back as the work progresses and retained as a separate fund available to them for the period of time limited in each Act: Ont., sec. 11; Nfld., sec. 13; Sask., sec. 19; P.E.I., secs. 15, 17; N.S., sec. 12; N.B., secs. 15, 17; Man., sec. 9; Alta., secs. 15, 16, 18; B.C., sec. 21.

In the case of *Len Ariss & Co. v. Peloso*, [1958] O.R. 643 (C.A.), McGillivray J. A., referring to the Ontario Act stated at page 653: "The Act was developed primarily with the intention of safeguarding the labourer and materialman. At the same time it was designed, while giving such security, to allow the owner to pay over money to the contractor and to allow the latter to get on with his job." See also *Torrance v. Cratchley* (1900), 31 O.R. 546 (C.A.), as to the purpose of the holdback fund.

Using the Ontario Act as an example, section 11(1) provides that "the person primarily liable" under any type of contract under which liens may arise must, as the work progresses, retain for a period of 37 days after the completion or abandonment of such work, 15% of the value of the work, service or materials actually done, placed or furnished. Therefore, the holdback must be retained by the person primarily liable on each contract that that person makes, whether he is an "owner", contractor or subcontractor, for the benefit of those below him on the pyramid. See: *Rideau Aluminum & Steels Ltd. v. McKechnie,* [1964] 1 O.R. 523, affirmed without written reasons 48 D.L.R. (2d) 62, 659 (S.C.C.); *R.A. Corbett & Co. Ltd. v. Phillips* (1972), 32 D.L.R. (3d) 78 (N.B.C.A.); *Yale Dev. Corpn. Ltd. v. A.L.H. Const. Ltd.,* [1973] 2 W.W.R. 477 (Alta. C.A.).

117

In Prince Edward Island, sec. 15(1), Alberta, sec. 15(2) and New Brunswick, sec. 15(1), the duty to retain a holdback is restricted to the statutory "owner". The Acts of the remaining provinces, however, are similar to the Ontario Act except for the percentage required to be held back and the time limit for which the funds must be retained. See: Nfld., sec. 13(1); Sask., sec. 19(1), (6); N.S., sec. 12(1); Man., sec. 9(1), and B.C., sec. 21(1). These sections create an absolute duty to hold back and it is therefore not material that the "owner" does not know there are subcontractors on the job; he must still keep the holdback: *Dom. Radiator Co. v. Cann* (1904), 37 N.S.R. 237 (C.A.).

The fund retained by the "owner" or the person primarily liable is only available to the lien claimants for the period of time limited in each provincial Act and at the expiration of this time the lien rights against the holdback fund expire and are completely lost, unless proceedings are commenced to realise on the amount of the holdback fund: *Lacroix v. Carriss*, [1923] 3 W.W.R. 1319 (Sask. C.A.). In calculating the period of time limited by each Act the first day is excluded and the last day included: *McLennan v. Winnipeg* (1882), 3 Man. R. 474 (C.A.). See further Chapter 6, Obtaining a Lien, §71(*g*).

Where the "owner" has complied with the Act as to the holdback and payments made, then insofar as the claims of the persons with whom the "owner" has no direct contract are concerned, the holdback fund takes the place of the land and the liens are a charge on the fund in their favour: Ont., sec. 11(5); Nfld., sec. 13(5); Sask., sec. 19(2), (4); P.E.I., sec. 15(4); N.S., sec. 12(3); N.B., sec. 15(6); Man., sec. 9(5); Alta., sec. 15(4) and B.C., sec. 21(2). See also, *Bond Structural Steel (1965) Ltd. v. Cloverlawn Invts. Ltd.,* [1973] 3 O.R. 856.

§42 Nothing Owing to Contractor by Owner.

Earlier decisions of the Courts had indicated that if nothing was ever owing to the contractor by the "owner", then the "owner" was not liable to retain any holdback. Thus, under a lump sum contract which was not to be paid until completion, the contractor abandoned his contract, and since nothing ever became due and owing to the contractor it was held there could be no lien rights against the owner and the owner was not required to hold back: *Burton v. Hookwith* (1919), 45 O.L.R. 348 (C.A.). See also *Farrell v. Gallagher* (1911), 23 O.L.R. 130; *McManus v. Rothschild* (1911), 25 O.L.R. 138 (C.A.); *Rice Lewis & Son Ltd. v. George Rathbone Ltd.* (1913), 27 O.L.R. 630 (C.A.); *Travis v. Breckenridge-Lund Lbr. & Coal Co.* (1910), 43 S.C.R. 59, reversing 10 W.L.R. 392; *Ne Page v. Pinner* (1915), 8 W.W.R. 322 (B.C. C.A.); *Wilks v. Leduc,* [1917] 1 W.W.R. 4 (Man. C.A.). The basis of these earlier decisions appeared to be the provision contained in the various Acts limiting the "owner's" liability to the sum payable by him to the contractor. Thus if there was no sum payable this ended the "owner's" responsibilities.

This inequity was remedied by the provincial Legislatures. Firstly, the limitation upon the "owner's" liability (to the amount owing to the contractor) was made subject to the holdback provisions: Ont., sec. 9; Alta., sec. 15(5.1), (5); B.C., sec. 6,21(1); Man., sec. 7; N.B., sec. 4(2); Nfld., sec. 11; N.S., sec. 10; P.E.I., sec. 3(1) and Sask., sec. 18(1). Secondly, the subcontractor became entitled to enforce his lien rights notwithstanding the abandonment of the contract by the general contractor: Ont., sec. 13; P.E.I., sec. 19; N.B., sec. 19; Nfld., sec. 15. Thirdly, the holdback provisions were made to apply irrespective of whether the contract called for partial or lump sum payments: Ont., sec. 11(1); Alta., sec. 15(2); B.C., sec. 21(1); N.B., sec. 15(1); Nfld., sec. 13(1); P.E.I., sec. 15(1); Sask., sec. 19(1).

The result of the amendments was to make the holdback provisions an absolute duty upon the "owner", even if there was nothing owing to the contractor by reason of default or abandonment. See *Freedman v. Guar. Trust Co.* (1929), 64 O.L.R. 200 (C.A.); *Dziewa v. Haviland,* [1960] O.W.N. 343; *Vaillancourt Lbr. Co. v. Trustees of Sep. School Section No. 2, Balfour Twp.,* [1964] 1 O.R. 418 (C.A.); *S. I. Guttman Ltd. v. James D. Mokry Ltd.,* [1969] 1 O.R. 7 (C.A.); *Can. Comstock Co. v. Toronto Transit Commn.,* [1970] S.C.R. 205; *Lonmar Plumbing and Heating Ltd. v. Representative Holdings* (1968), 1 D.L.R. (3d) 591 (Sask.); *Noranda Exploration Co. v. Sigurdson,* [1976] 1 S.C.R. 296.

There is, however, a distinction between the situation above (where nothing is owing due to the default or abandonment by the contractor) and the situation where no payment was ever contemplated for the work, service or material. In the latter situation, it appears that no holdback need be retained. It was held in *Kosobuski v. Extension Mining Co.* (1929), 64 O.L.R. 8 (C.A.), that the holdback provisions of the Act contemplate an obligation to pay either presently or at a future date money or money's worth from which the holdback may be retained by the person primarily liable. See also *Turner Valley Supply Co. v. Scott,* [1940] 3 W.W.R. 529, reversing [1940] 2 W.W.R. 478 (Alta. C.A.). The Court in *Can. Cutting and Coring (Toronto) Ltd. v. Howson,* [1968] 2 O.R. 449, held that work done by the sub-trades of a general contractor, pursuant to a 5 year guarantee clause contained in the main contract, which work was done after the contract had been completed and all moneys payable in respect of it had been paid by the owner, was not lienable. As no moneys were ever to be paid by the owner for this work, it followed that there was nothing to which the lien could attach. See, however, in this regard, *River Valley Store Fixtures Ltd. v. Camper-Villa-Inn Ltd.,* [1977] 1 W.W.R. 659 (Man.), where the Court appeared to allow a lien for work done during the guarantee period set out in the contract, under somewhat different circumstances.

Provided, therefore, that there was an obligation between the "owner" and contractor to pay for the work, service and materials in money or money's worth, the "owner" will be duty bound to comply with the holdback provisions of the particular provincial Act.

§43 Government Property and the Holdback Fund.

The holdback provisions contained in the Acts of the various provinces are for the benefit of "lien claimants". If there is no lienable interest then no lien rights can arise and consequently the holdback provisions are inapplicable. As a result the holdback provisions do not apply to buildings constructed on Federal Government property or, (except in Ontario), on Provincial Government property or, with three exceptions, to improvements or works on public streets and highways: see Chapter 2, The Lienable Interest, §§17, 18 and 19, *ante*.

The provinces of Ontario and Newfoundland have enacted exceptions to the above rule as it pertains to work done or improvements made to a public street or highway. Although the street or highway is not lienable and thus subject to sale, nevertheless, the holdback provisons apply: Ont., sec. 5(2); Nfld., sec. 6(1). In Ontario the exception is limited to a public street or highway which is owned by a municipality. Also, the Ontario Act provides that, although no lien is to attach to Provincial Crown lands, the holdback provisions of the Act apply to work done on them, except for work which is done under a contract as defined in The Ministry of Transportation and Communications Creditors Payment Act, 1975 and to which that Act applies. See also Chapter 6, Obtaining a Lien, §78, *post*.

§44 Calculation of the Holdback.

As previously indicated the holdback fund is composed of a percentage of the value of the work, service or materials done, placed or furnished and must be retained as the work progresses. This value is to be calculated on the basis of the contract price, or if there is no contract price, on the basis of the actual value of the work, service or materials done, placed or furnished. The amount of the holdback thus increases as the work progresses: Ont., sec. 11(1); Nfld., sec. 13(1); P.E.I., sec. 15(2); N.S., sec. 12(1); N.B., sec. 15(2); B.C., sec. 21(1); Alta., sec. 15(3); Man., sec. 9(1); Sask., sec. 19(3).

The distinction between a holdback based on actual value and one based on the contract price is an important one.

Where there is no contract price set, the holdback required at any given moment as the work progresses is a percentage (e.g. Ontario, 15%) of the actual value of the work, service or materials done, placed or furnished. The actual value is readily ascertainable by producing evidence of the value of the materials supplied or the number of hours worked with corresponding costs per hour, or cost of service rendered.

The Court was faced with a novel situation in *Nor. Elec. Co. v. Metro. Projects* (1977), 1 R.P.R. 286 (N.S.), as a result of the Supreme Court of Canada decision in *Nor. Elec. Co. v. Mfrs. Life Ins. Co.* [1977] 2 S.C.R. 762. The Supreme Court had held that where a developer entered into an arrangement whereby he sold his property to a mortgage company which then leased it back to him, giving him a mortgage on his leasehold interest for the purpose of financing the construction of a building on the lands, the mortgage company was an "owner", primarily liable on the building contract, and the original owner (now the lessee of the property) was a "contractor", within the meaning of The Mechanics' Lien Act. It then remitted the case to the trial Judge to determine the amount of the holdback which the lien claimants could recover from the mortgage company. The trial Judge held that, since the contract was substantially completed before the developer went bankrupt the holdback was 15% of the total contract price. He held, further, that, in the circumstances of this case, the contract price was the amount which the mortgage lender agreed to advance to the developer in return for the benefits it derived under the contract between them.

Where there is a specific contract price set, the value of the work, service or materials done, placed or furnished can only be ascertained after regarding the contract price as a whole, using it as a yardstick or basis of calculation.

The judicially approved method of calculating the amount of holdback under the contract was expressed in the case of *Batts v. Poyntz* (1916), 11 O.W.N. 204 at 205, as follows: "The proper method of finding the value of work done prior to default by a defaulting contractor, is not to deduct the cost of completion from the contract price and take the difference as the work done prior to default. Evidence of the cost of completion is relevant, and may help in arriving at a proportionate valuation of the previous work. But the cost of completion is generally, and often materially, out of proportion to its value compared with the value of the previous work, or calculated on the basis of the original contract price. To be a true guide, the value of the subsequent work must be calculated on the same basis as the previous work; that is, on the basis of the original contract price, and not on a higher basis of cost, whether done by day-labour or by reletting the work to a new contractor. .... To arrive at the 20 per cent. [now 15% in Ontario] due to the lienholders, it must be calculated on the value of the work in proportion to the contract price without any deduction for damages or extra cost of completion. We must get down to the basis of the original contract as far as we can, even when the cost of completion is the only evidence we have to go by."

In *Len Ariss & Co. v. Peloso*, [1958] O.R. 643 at 649 (C.A.), the method of computation was thusly stated: "There being a contract price in the present case the holdback is not to be calculated on the actual value of the work, service and materials furnished but upon a value for such work arrived at 'on the basis of the contract price'. This does not mean that a percentage of the contract price is to be taken but that the value of the work done or materials furnished is to be calculated with the contract price as a basis of value." See also *Hill-Clark-Francis Ltd. v. Lanthier*, [1958] O.W.N. 233; *Lacroix v. Yoos* (1952), 5 W.W.R. 79 (Sask. C.A.); *Horwitz v. Rigaux Bldg. Enterprises Ltd.* (1960), 32 W.W.R. 540, reversing 30 W.W.R. 599 (Alta. C.A.); *Russell v. French* (1897), 28 O.R. 215 (C.A.); *Deldo v. Gough Sellers Invts. Ltd.* (1915), 34 O.L.R. 274 (C.A.); *Rice Lewis & Son Ltd. v. George Rathbone Ltd.* (1913), 27 O.L.R. 630 (C.A.); *Baines v. Harman* (1927), 60 O.L.R. 223 (C.A.); *Sanderson Pearcy & Co. v. Foster* (1923), 53 O.L.R. 519 (C.A.); *C. J. Oliver Ltd. v. Foothills Lighting & Elec. Ltd.* (1965), 54 W.W.R. 37 (Alta. C.A.); *Billinkoff's Ltd. v. R.C. Archiepiscopal Corpn. of Winnipeg* (1959), 67 Man. R. 175; *Aurald Enterprises Ltd. v. Mumford* (1977), 25 C.B.R. (N.S.) 276 (Ont.).

The Court in *Dziewa v. Haviland*, [1960] O.W.N. 343, held that it was improper to calculate holdback by deleting the required percentage from each progress payment as it falls due under the contract. Further, the practice of deducting the cost of completion from the contract price in order to arrive at the value of the work done, service performed or material placed or furnished, has not been judicially approved since the case of *Freedman v. Guar. Trust Co.* (1929), 64 O.L.R. 200 (C.A.). See also in this regard *Milton Pressed Brick Co. v. Whalley* (1918), 42 O.L.R. 369 (C.A.); *Smith v. Bernhart* (1909), 11 W.L.R. 623 (Sask.) and *C. J. Oliver Ltd. v. Foothills Lighting & Elec. Ltd., supra*.

An "owner" may not reduce the amount of the holdback by deducting damages for which he might have a claim against the contractor, and no such damages may be taken into consideration when arriving at the value of the work done: *Russell v. French* (1897), 28 O.R. 215 (C.A.); *Baines v. Harman* (1927), 60 O.L.R. 223 (C.A.); *Batts v. Poyntz* (1916), 11 O.W.N. 204; *Lundy v. Henderson* (1908), 9 W.L.R. 327 (Alta. C.A.); *Milton Pressed Brick Co. v. Whalley, supra; Peart Bros. Hdwe. Co. v. Phillips* (1915), 8 W.W.R. 1159 (Sask C.A.); *Smith v. Bernhart, supra; Cusson v. Myrtle S. Dist.*, [1921] 3 W.W.R. 479 (Man. C.A.); *Coast Lighting Ltd. v. Trend Bldg. Ltd.* (1970), 11 D.L.R. (3d) 735.

In *Denston Co. v. Bd. of Trustees, S. Dist. No. 37 (Delta)* (1958), 27 W.W.R. 141 (B.C. C.A.), the owner maintained that all it needed to hold back was 15% of the subcontractor's (lien claimant's) claim. It was held that the 15% meant 15% of the main contract between the owner and general contractor and as this sum was more than the lien claimant's claim he was awarded full payment out of the "owner's" holdback.

In *Yale Dev. Corpn. Ltd. v. A.L.H. Const. Ltd.,* [1973] 2 W.W.R. 477 (Alta. C.A.), the owner did not employ a general contractor for the entire project, but instead he let contracts to several firms in each of the main areas of construction. A number of liens were filed and the owner sought to pay the lien fund into Court as required by the Alberta Act. The issue before the Court was whether, in these circumstances, there should be a single lien fund for the entire project or several separate lien funds. It was held that the Act contemplated a separate lien fund for each contract entered into by the owner. As a result the owner was required to maintain a separate lien fund for each contract let by him, and each lienholder's claim had to be confined to his appropriate lien fund.

As to when actual value is used even where there is a contract price set see *C.J. Oliver Ltd. v. Foothills Lighting & Elec. Ltd., supra,* where the Alberta Court of Appeal held that when a subcontract had been abandoned, there was then no specific contract price as contemplated by the Act and the amount of holdback to be retained for lienholders was calculated on the value of the work actually done by the subcontractor. See also: *Guglietta v. Oldach* (1977), 3 Alta. L.R. (2d) 347.

In *Aurald Enterprises Ltd. v. Mumford* (1977), 25 C.B.R. (N.S.) 276 (Ont.), the Court found that it had to determine what the actual contract price was before it could ascertain the value of the contractor's work and hence the amount of the owner's holdback. The contractor had agreed to demolish and remove certain buildings from the owner's lands for the sum of $14,000.00. The Court determined that the materials in the buildings belonged to the wrecking company and held that the value of the salvage-able material was part of the contractor's contract price. It found the value of the salvageable material plus the $14,000.00 contract price amounted to $100,750.00 and that the contractor had completed approximately 55% of the work when he abandoned the contract. It therefore held that the owner's holdback was 15% of $55,500.00.

(a) *Holdback on Several Projects.*

The question often arises when the same "owner", contractor and subcontractors are engaged on more than one project at one time, whether there were several separate contracts or but one entire contract, and consequently whether there should be one holdback, or several separate holdbacks. In *Sanderson Pearcy & Co. v. Foster* (1923), 53 O.L.R. 519 (C.A.), four houses were ordered by an owner to be built for a lump sum, but a separate price was named for each house. It was held that, the material being supplied and used for the whole purpose of the general contract, the holdback required was only that to be retained on the general contract.

An "owner" requested a contractor to build an addition to his store and construct a house on another property. Since this work proceeded concurrently on both properties, and since there were no separate sums shown for each project in the contract, the contract was treated as an entire one, and the holdback calculated on the entire contract price. The Court, however, was apparently of the opinion that if separate contract prices had been stipulated in the main contract, in the circumstances of the case, each project would be treated as a separate contract: *Len Ariss & Co. v. Peloso,* [1958] O.R. 643 (C.A.).

Where a subcontractor had submitted one tender for a class of work with respect to two different phases of the main contract, and the main contractor accepted that tender, the subcontract could not be treated as two separate contracts simply because the contractor, in confirming acceptance of the tender, had issued two purchase orders, one in respect of each trade: *Bermingham Const. Ltd. v. Moir Const. Co.,* [1959] O.R. 355 (C.A.).

(*b*) *Extras to and Deletions from Contract.*

Almost invariably in present day building contracts, extras to the original contract will be ordered, or deletions from the original contract will be agreed upon. Extras to a contract increasing the original contract price must be considered when calculating the holdback percentage, thereby increasing the amount to be retained: *Baines v. Harman* (1927), 60 O.L.R. 223 (C.A.); *Smith v. Bernhart* (1909), 11 W.L.R. 623 (Sask.). Conversely, it would seem to follow that deletions from the original contract would reduce the amount of the contract thus reducing the amount of the holdback to be retained at any given time.

(*c*) *Non-Lienable Matter.*

When a contract is made to perform work, service or material on a project and included in the contract price is work, service or material that is not the subject of a lien, then the value of the non-lienable items of the contract would have to be deducted from the contract price in considering the correct holdback amount. It is submitted that the correct method of calculating the non-lienable deductions should be based on the contract price as a whole following the principles set out in *Batts v. Poyntz* (1916), 11 O.W.N. 204.

On various occasions, as in *Turner Valley Supply Co. v. Scott,* [1940] 3 W.W.R. 529 (Alta. C.A.), a contract price is agreed to which is not in terms of money. In the *Turner Valley* case the contract was to drill oil wells, for which the drillers were to receive shares in a company and a percentage of oil royalties. It is submitted that in cases of this nature the value of the work done could not be based on the contract price unless a cash value could be put on the shares and royalties, and actual value would have to be the basis of computation.

Where a contractor agreed to perform work on an owner's property at a stated price, and the contract contained a proviso that all of the contractor's machinery and plant used to carry out the contract were to be the property of the owner until the contract was completed, and the contractor did not complete the contract, it was held that the value of the machinery and plant could not be added to the original contract price in calculating or arriving at the amount of the holdback: *Birkett v. Brewder* (1902), 1 O.W.R. 62.

§45 Set-Off and the Holdback.

The retention of the holdback by the "owner" or person primarily liable is mandatory and it cannot be reduced by the costs of completion, damages for non-completion, payment of any lienholder's claim or for any other purpose: Ont., sec. 11(9); Nfld., sec. 13(9); P.E.I. sec. 15(6); N.B., sec. 15(9); Sask., sec. 19(5); B.C., sec. 21(6), and Alta., sec. 15(7). See also *Eddy Hdwe. (1971) Ltd. v. Keystone Dev. Co.* (1975), 13 N.B.R. (2d) 451 and *Curran & Briggs Ltd. v. Ryder* (1977), 19 N.B.R. (2d) 330. The provision against set-off in Manitoba and Nova Scotia is restricted to wage earners: N.S., sec. 15(4); Man., sec. 12(4). Nevertheless, it would appear that the same prohibition applies in these latter provinces as well: *Len Ariss & Co. v. Peloso,* [1958] O.R. 643 (C.A.); *Billinkoff's Ltd. v. R.C. Archiepiscopal Corpn. of Winnipeg* (1959), 67 Man. R. 175; *Freedman v. Guar. Trust Co.* (1929), 64 O.L.R. 200 (C.A.); *Ross Bros. Ltd. v. Gorman* (1908), 1 Alta. L.R. 516, affirming 1 Alta. L.R. 109 (C.A.); *Rice Lewis & Son v. George Rathbone Ltd.* (1913), 27 O.L.R. 630 (C.A.); *Smith v. Bernhart* (1909), 11 W.L.R. 623 (Sask.).

In *Union Elec. Supply Co. v. Gillin Enrg. & Const. Ltd.,* [1971] 3 O.R. 125, the owner sought to reduce the holdback by the amount of an assessment made against him under The Workmen's Compensation Act of Ontario. The Court refused to allow such a deduction on the grounds that, of itself, the assessment was not the proper subject matter of a lien, nor could such an assessment subrogate the Workmen's Compensation Board to the rights of the workmen for whose benefit the assessment was made.

If the "owner" or person primarily liable has retained more than the statutory holdback, at any time, then this sum is also subject to lien claims: *Piggott v. Drake,* [1933] O.W.N. 197 (C.A.); *Western Tractor and Equipment Co. v. Milestone School Unit No. 12* (1960), 33 W.W.R. 249 (Sask. C.A.); *Horwitz v. Rigaux Bldg. Enterprises Ltd.* (1960), 32 W.W.R. 540, reversing 30 W.W.R. 599 (Alta. C.A.). However, the "owner" or person primarily liable may, generally speaking, set off against such sum retained in excess of the required holdback, damages for delay, faulty work, cost of completion or other claims against the person he contracted with: see:

Noranda Exploration Co. v. Sigurdson, [1976] 1 S.C.R. 296; *Scarborough Painting Ltd. v. Buckley* (1974), 4 O.R. (2d) 253; *Edwards v. Banjo Holdings Ltd.,* [1975] W.W.D. 140 (B.C.C.A.); *Curran & Briggs Ltd. v. Ryder* (1977), 19 N.B.R. (2d) 330. See further Chapter 3, The Lien Claimant, §29(*e*), *ante*, and Chapter 9, The Trust Fund, §109, *post*.

It was stated in *Lundy v. Henderson* (1908), 9 W.L.R. 327 (Alta. C.A.), that, when an owner attempts to set off damages for delay in completion against his contractor, the onus is on the owner to show that the contractor was not entitled to an extension of time to complete. It was held in *Scarborough Painting Ltd. v. Buckley, (supra),* that where the owner seeks to set off damages against the contractor for abandonment of the contract against amounts owing over and above the statutory holdback, the onus is on the owner to establish that the cost of completing the contract exceeds the difference between the value of the work done by the contractor and the original contract price. Where the work undertaken is not completed, the cost of completion to the "owner" or person primarily liable may also be set off up to the amount of the holdback. The "owner" or person primarily liable must, however, complete the contract in as economical a manner as is reasonably possible and in accordance with the original contract provisions: *Union Lbr. Co. v. Porter* (1908), 8 W.L.R. 423; affirmed 9 W.L.R. 325 (Alta.); *Billinkoff's Ltd. v. R.C. Archiepiscopal Corpn. of Winnipeg, supra.* In *Can. Indemnity Co. v. B.C. Hydro and Power Authority,* [1975] 2 W.W.R. 582 (B.C.), it was held that the accounts which the contractor owed at the time it abandoned the contract, for motel accommodation for the workmen and for helicopter services, and which the owner's bonding company had to pay in order to be in a position to utilize the workmen and the helicopter service in completing the contract as cheaply as possible and with the least delay, were not properly part of the "cost of completion" of the contract, although arrears of wages which it paid to the workmen were.

While the "owner" or person primarily liable can set off amounts found due to him for damages, the lien claimant can claim lien rights for nothing more than the value of the work done, materials supplied or services performed, and cannot claim a lien for damages: *Bermingham Const. Ltd. v. Moir Const. Co.,* [1959] O.R. 355 (C.A.); *Earl F. Wakefield Co. v. Oil City Petroleums (Leduc) Ltd.,* [1958] S.C.R. 361, reversing 22 W.W.R. 267; affirmed 29 W.W.R. 638 (P.C.); *Alkok v. Grymek,* [1968] S.C.R. 452; *H.G. Winton Ltd. v. One Medical Place Ltd.,* [1968] 2 O.R. 384 (C.A.); *Alros Products Ltd. v. Dalecore Const. Ltd.* (1973), 2 O.R. (2d) 312 (C.A.); *A.J. (Archie) Goodale Ltd. v. Risidore Bros. Ltd.,* (1975), 8 O.R. (2d) 427 (C.A.). See also Chapter 10, Jurisdiction, §§125 and 127, *post*.

However, a personal judgment for damages may be awarded in the lien action against the person primarily liable to the lien claimant: *Earl F. Wakefield Co. v. Oil City Petroleums (Leduc) Ltd., supra; Bermingham*

Const. Ltd. v. Moir Const. Co., supra; Swansea Const. Co. v. The Royal Trust Co., [1956] O.R. 911; *Andre Knight Ltd. v. Presement,* [1967] 2 O.R. 289 (C.A.); *H.G. Winton Ltd. v. One Medical Place Ltd., supra; Grannan Plumbing & Heating Ltd. v. Simpson Const. Ltd.* (1977), 17 N.B.R. (2d) 569. The Court refused to grant such a judgment, however, in *Alros Products Ltd. v. Dalecore Const. Ltd., supra.*

The person with whom the lien claimant contracts directly is at liberty to set off or counterclaim against the lien claimant in the mechanics' lien action, to reduce the amount owing by him to the lien claimant. In *Henry Hope & Sons of Can. Ltd. v. Richard Sheehy & Sons* (1922), 52 O.L.R. 237, the Court approved a counterclaim by a contractor against a lien claimant for damages for delay, loss of use of moneys that would have been payable by an owner to the contractor but for the lien claimant's delay, and travelling expenses incurred by the contractor to hire new workers. See further in this respect, *Wasylyk v. Metro. Sep. S. Bd.,* [1970] 3 O.R. 391 (C.A.); *Aqua Pond Indust. Ltd. v. Gould* (1974), 3 O.R. (2d) 439; and Chapter 3, The Lien Claimant, §29(b), *ante*; Chapter 10, Jurisdiction, §§125 and 127, *post*.

The owner may also have a cause of action against a lien claimant who improperly registers a Claim for Lien against his land. In *Guilford Indust. Ltd. v. Hankinson Management Services Ltd.,* [1974] 1 W.W.R. 141 (B.C.), the Court found that the defendant had filed liens for outrageous sums for which there was no legal foundation, tying up the plaintiff's lands for a long time so that the plaintiff could not sell them, for the sole purpose of forcing the plaintiff to a settlement of an alleged claim for money due and owing. The Court held that the action was an abuse of the Court's process and awarded the plaintiff $50,000. for damages together with the further sum of $10,000. by way of exemplary damages.

§46 Payments by Owner and the Holdback Fund.

The Acts of the various provinces contain detailed provisions governing payments which can and cannot be made by the "owner" or person primarily liable as they relate to the holdback fund and may be categorized as follows:

(a) payments up to the required holdback fund;

(b) payments in reduction of the holdback fund; and

(c) payment of the balance of the holdback fund.

(a) Payments Up to the Required Holdback Fund.

As previously indicated the holdback fund must be retained for the period of time limited by each Act. The "owner" or the person primarily liable may make payments under the contract up to the amount of the required holdback percentage provided that he does so in good faith and has not received written notice of a lien, and such payments will operate as a discharge *pro tanto* of the lien to the extent of such payments: Ont., sec. 11(6); Nfld., sec. 13(6); Sask., sec. 20(7); P.E.I., sec. 15(5); N.S., sec. 12(4); N.B., sec. 15(7); Man., sec. 9(6). In Alberta and British Columbia such payments must be made in good faith and before registration of a lien: Alta., sec. 15(6); B.C., secs. 13, 21(3). See also *Henry Hope and Sons of Can. Ltd. v. Richard Sheehy & Sons,* (1922), 52 O.L.R. 237; *Merrick v. Campbell* (1914), 6 W.W.R. 722 (Man.); *Vaillancourt Lbr. Co. v. Trustees of Sep. School Section No. 2, Balfour Twp.,* [1964] 1 O.R. 418 (C.A.); *Len Ariss & Co. v. Peloso,* [1958] O.R. 643 (C.A.); *S. I. Guttman Ltd. v. James D. Mokry Ltd.,* [1969] 1 O.R. 7 (C.A.); *Can. Comstock Co. v. Toronto Transit Commn.,* [1970] S.C.R. 205; *Noranda Exploration Co. v. Sigurdson,* [1976] 1 S.C.R. 296; *Bond Structural Steel (1965) Ltd. v. Cloverlawn Invts. Ltd.,* [1973] 3 O.R. 856; *B. & T. Masonry Inc. v. Mirandas Dev. & Bldg. Services Ltd.; Neufeld v. Mirandas Dev. & Bldg. Services Ltd.; Newton Ready Mix Ltd. v. DeGraaf; Ben Deck Elec. Ltd. v. DeGraaf; Cerniuk v. DeGraaf; Ventaire of B.C. Ltd. v. DeGraaf; Central Glass Products Ltd. v. DeGraaf* (1977), 3 B.C.L.R. 357; §§50, 51, 52, 53, and 54, *post.*

With the exception of Alberta and British Columbia, the registration of a claim for lien is not notice to the owner, contractor or subcontractor, as the case may be, and, therefore, with respect to payments up to the required holdback, a search in the appropriate Registry or Land Titles Office is not required before payment of same. Where, however, a payment involves holdback funds, a search is necessary. If a claimant wishes to assert a claim extending beyond the amount of the required holdback, he must give written notice of his lien as set out in the various Acts: see Form 6 and §50, *post.*

The above sections therefore allow payments up to the required holdback, but do not entitle encroachment upon the holdback so that where an "owner" or person primarily liable, as the case may be, pays over amounts exceeding the statutory holdback a double liability may be incurred to the extent of the holdback moneys paid out, as these moneys may have to be paid out again to the lien claimants: *Vaillancourt Lbr. Co. v. Trustees of Sep. School Section No. 2, Balfour Twp., supra; Len Ariss & Co. v. Peloso, supra; S. I. Guttman Ltd. v. James D. Mokry Ltd., supra; Can. Comstock Co. v. Toronto Transit Commn., supra; Eddy Hdwe. (1971) Ltd. v. Keystone Dev. Co.* (1975), 13 N.B.R. (2d) 451.

An owner who pays a contractor or a lien claimant out of holdback moneys before the expiration of the period of lien rights may nevertheless validly apply such payments in reduction of the holdback if he can show that other lien claimants were not prejudiced by such payment. If proceedings are not taken by lien claimants as set out in the various Acts to enforce their liens within the prescribed time and lien rights are thereby lost, there can be no prejudice to the lien claimants. The premature payment of holdback moneys gives lien claimants no greater right than they would have had if the owner had retained the holdback moneys for the required period and then made payment: *Brooks v. Mundy* (1914), 5 O.W.N. 795; *Doig v. Stehn.,* [1924] 1 W.W.R. 1169 (Sask. C.A.); *Rasmussens' Ltd. v. Melville Country Club.,* [1977] 4 W.W.R. 382 (Sask.); *Smithson v. M.L. Plumbing & Heating Ltd.,* [1977] 3 W.W.R. 422 (Sask. C.A.).

Where payments have been made encroaching on the holdback, and liens have been filed within the proper time, payments made may still be applied to reduce the holdback if these valid liens are not prejudiced. Absence of prejudice is established, for example, when the claims paid are those of wage earners who have statutory priority according to the various Acts. In *Metals Ltd. v. Trusts and Guar. Co.* (1914), 7 W.W.R. 605 (Alta.), the owner was entitled to pay liens for 6 weeks' wages of labourers even though the result was to reduce the holdback fund which would otherwise be available for other lien claimants. See also *Torrance v. Cratchley* (1900), 31 O.R. 546 (C.A.). There is a duty on the owner to show that the wage earners he has paid had valid liens, and therefore, that the other lien claimants could not be prejudiced by such payments: *Torrance v. Cratchley, supra.* If wage earners' claims total more than the statutory holdback and a payment is made out of this holdback to one wage earner, then the other wage earners will be prejudiced, and the owner will thus be liable to pay over again the amount by which the wage earners were so prejudiced.

The purpose of the provisions allowing payments under the contract to be made up to the statutory holdback are twofold: to protect the sub-trades, labourers and suppliers and also to allow the "owner" or person primarily liable under a contract to carry out the terms of payment; for if the "owner" or person primarily liable under a contract fails to make payments, he may be liable in damages for breach of his contract. In *Dziewa v. Haviland,* [1960] O.W.N. 343, the owner held back 15% of the progress payments as they fell due under the contract. At the time the progress payments were due the value of the work done justified the releasing of the progress payments in full under the holdback provisions of the Ontario Act. It was, therefore, held that, since payments had been improperly withheld, the owner was in breach of his contract.

If the two duties of an "owner" or person primarily liable, namely to hold back and to comply with the terms of payment under the contract, are in conflict, then The Mechanics' Lien Act prevails over the provisions of the contract since the Acts of several of the provinces provide that all contracts are by statute amended to conform to the holdback requirements: Ont., sec. 11(8); Nfld., sec. 13(8); N.B., sec. 15(8); Man., sec. 9(8); B.C., sec. 21(5); and as to those provinces which do not have this provision see: *Russell v.*

Williams (1923), 24 O.W.N. 240 (C.A.); *Dziewa v. Haviland, supra* and *Russell v. French* (1897), 28 O.R. 215 (C.A.).

All of the Acts, with the exception of the British Columbia Act, permit the owner, contractor or subcontractor to make a payment to a lien claimant for or on account of any debt justly due to him for work, service or materials, done, performed or furnished for which the person making the payment is not primarily liable and provided the proper notice is given to the person who is primarily liable, the person making the payment may deduct the amount of such payment from the amount which he owes to the person who was primarily liable to make payment to the lien claimant. For example, if a subcontractor gives a notice in writing of his lien to an owner, the owner, after satisfying himself that it is a proper lien may pay the subcontractor's claim and deduct the amount of that payment from his next progress payment to the general contractor. However, this provision merely provides a method of preventing the registration of a lien or removing a lien already registered; in no case can such "direct payments" be used to reduce the holdback fund: Ont., sec. 12; Nfld., sec. 14; P.E.I., sec. 18; N.S., sec. 13; N.B., sec. 18; Man., sec. 10; Alta., sec. 20. See further §50, *post*.

(b) *Payments in Reduction of the Holdback Fund.*

The Acts of Ontario, Newfoundland, New Brunswick, Saskatchewan, Manitoba and Alberta allow the owner or person primarily liable, to reduce the holdback fund in limited circumstances; namely, where the contract is under the supervision of an architect, engineer or other person upon whose certificate payments are to be made and a subcontract by his certificate is declared to have been completed to his satisfaction. In these circumstances, once the certificate has been given to the person primarily liable on that contract and also to the person who became a subcontractor by a subcontract made directly under that contract, and when the statutory holdback period has elapsed, then the holdback in the hands of the person primarily liable on the contract may be reduced by an amount equivalent to the holdback being retained on the subcontract. For example, if the owner's architect certifies that a particular subcontract has been completed to his satisfaction, a certificate to that effect has been delivered to the subcontractor and the owner, and the statutory holdback period dating from the date on which the notice was given has elapsed, the owner may pay over to the general contractor, out of the overall holdback which he is maintaining out of payments made to the general contractor, an amount equivalent to the holdback which the general contractor is now obliged to pay to the subcontractor who has completed his work. However, this right to reduce or release part of the holdback is not operative if and so long as any lien derived under the subcontract is preserved by anything done under the Act: Ont., sec. 11(2); Nfld., sec. 13(2); N.B., sec. 15(4); Man., sec. 9(3); Alta., sec. 16(1), (2); Sask., sec. 20(1).

As the owner in most cases knows nothing of the subcontracts, the payment out of the holdback under this section as far as the owner is concerned would, in most cases, be a hazardous course of action; however, when the required certificate is given to the subcontractor or to persons supplying material or service, to the effect that the subcontract has been completed, then that subcontract and any materials furnished or placed, or to be furnished or placed thereunder, and any work or service performed or to be performed thereunder, shall, as far as any lien thereunder of that subcontractor is concerned, be deemed to have been completed or furnished or placed not later than the time at which the certificate was so given: Ont., sec. 11(3); Nfld., sec. 13(3); N.B., sec. 15(5); Man., sec. 9(4); Alta., sec. 16(5); Sask., sec. 20(6). It was held in *Western Realty Projects Ltd. v. Superior Grout & Gunite Ltd; Wells Const. Ltd. v. Edwards Const. Ltd.,* [1975] 6 W.W.R. 366 (Alta.), that the time for filing the subcontractor's lien runs from the date of the certificate even though more work remains to be done under the subcontract and it is done at a later date.

The Ontario and Newfoundland Mechanics' Lien Acts provide that where an architect, engineer or other person neglects or refuses to issue and deliver a certificate upon which payments are to be made under a contract or subcontract, the Court upon being satisfied that the certificate should have been issued, may upon such terms as it deems just, make an order that the work or materials to which the certificate would have related had been completed, and any such order has the same force and effect as if the certificate had been issued and delivered by the architect, engineer or other person: Ont., sec. 11(4); Nfld., sec. 13(4). A similar provision is contained in the Acts of Alberta, sec. 16(3), (4), and Saskatchewan, sec. 20(2), (5). The Acts of Alberta, sec. 16(3) and (4) and Saskatchewan, sec. 20(2) and (5), require a demand in writing to have been made and failure to deliver up the certificate as a condition precedent to an application to the Court for an order of completion.

It is to be noted that by section 16(6) of the Alberta Act, the Court may make an order of completion even though the contract is not under the supervision of a "supervisor" as defined by that Act, if the Court is satisfied that the contract or subcontract has been completed and such order has the same force and effect as a certificate of completion issued by a "supervisor".

(c) Payment of the Balance of the Holdback Fund.

At the expiration of the holdback period the "owner" or person primarily liable should make a search in the appropriate Registry or Land Titles Office to ascertain if any lien has been registered. In this regard it should be noted that the Acts of most of the provinces define completion as substantial completion and not necessarily total completion: Ont., sec. 1(1)(*a*); B.C., sec. 2; Alta., sec. 2(1)(*a*), (2); N.B. sec. 1; P.E.I. sec. 1(*a*); Nfld., sec. 2(1)(*a*); Sask., sec. 2(1)(*a*). See also Chapter 6, Obtaining a Lien, §71(*b*).

Upon effecting the necessary search of title and finding no lien registered and having no notice of lien in writing, the "owner" or person primarily liable is then free to pay out the entire holdback fund. However, if a lien is registered then he should withhold payment. In Ontario, if a lien has been registered but no certificate of action has been registered, or proceedings commenced as required by the Act, then an *ex parte* application can be made to discharge the lien: sec. 25(5). Thereupon the holdback may be paid out. If a lien has been registered and an action commenced within the proper time, then the holdback should be paid into Court, and the person so paying it in assumes the role of a stake holder: Ont., sec. 11(7); see also §161 *post*. A person making payment into Court will in practice be relieved of any costs of the action if the amount of holdback paid in is sufficient: see §167(d), *post*. Similar provisions with respect to the effect of payment into Court of the holdback are found in the Acts of Alberta, (sec. 18), Newfoundland, (sec. 13(7)), Saskatchewan, (sec. 20(9)) and British Columbia, (sec. 21(4)), but there is no such provision in the Acts of the remaining provinces. The person paying the holdback into Court will not be entitled to an order vacating the registration of the mechanics' lien as a result, except in Alberta where the Act provides that such an order may be made but it also requires that the lien claimant must be given notice of the application for payment into Court of the lien fund: Alta. sec. 18. The purpose and effect of the payment into Court of the holdback was discussed in *Cross and Grant v. Brooks* (1958), 13 D.L.R. (2d) 491 (B.C.C.A.) and *Curran & Briggs Ltd. v. Ryder (No. 2)* (1977), 19 N.B.R. (2d) 337.

§47 Direct Contracts With Owner.

A claimant who contracts directly with the "owner" is not limited to the holdback moneys only, but his claim extends to the entire amount found due: *Western Air Conditioning Ltd. v. Capri Hotels Ltd.* (1962), 38 W.W.R. 184 (Alta.). A lien claimant originally contracting directly with the "owner" is entitled to a lien for the full amount of his claim. A problem may arise where a subcontract, originally with a contractor, is subsequently assumed or taken over by the "owner". The question then arises as to whether the amounts found due to the lien claimant by the owner, in excess of the holdback on the lien claimant's original contract with the contractor, give rise to a right of lien, or whether only a personal judgment may be given against the "owner" for any excess over the original holdback. In *Rogers Lbr. Co. v. Gray* (1913), 4 W.W.R. 294 (Sask. C.A.), where lumber was ordered by the owner and the contractor and charged to their joint accounts, both owner and contractor were held liable in a lien action for the full amount and a lien was given against the owner for the full amount of the claim. See also *Western Air Conditioning Ltd. v. Capri Hotels Ltd., supra.*

When an owner took over a contract abandoned by his contractor, and agreed to pay the sub-trades, the owner was held liable for the full amount of the sub-trades' liens: *Union Lbr. Co. v. Porter* (1908), 8 W.L.R. 423; affirmed 9 W.L.R. 325 (Alta.); *Petrie v. Hunter; Guest v. Hunter* (1882), 2 O.R. 233; affirmed 10 O.A.R. 127; *Smith v. Bernhart* (1909), 11 W.L.R. 623 (Sask.); *McCauley v. Powell* (1908), 7 W.L.R. 443 (Alta.). See also *McPherson v. McColl* (1941), 16 M.P.R. 87 (N.S. C.A.).

Where a general contractor defaulted and the subcontractors that he engaged threatened to abandon the work unless they received some assurance of payment and thereupon the owner told them orally that he was financially able to assure payment and would pay if the general contractor did not, it was held that the owner's promise was in the nature of a guarantee and the owner was found liable to pay the claims of the sub-trades: *John C. Love Lbr. Co. v. Moore,* [1963] 1 O.R. 245 (C.A.). See also *Len Ariss & Co. v. Peloso,* [1958] O.R. 643 (C.A.) and *Sanderson Pearcy & Co. v. Foster* (1923), 53 O.L.R. 519 at 524 (C.A.), where the Court in both instances found the facts insufficient to support a direct contract with the owner or a guarantee of payment by the owner.

In the Ontario decision of *Hill v. Pozzeti,* [1936] O.W.N. 632 (C.A.), where an owner assumed direct contractual liability to a subcontractor originally engaged by the contractor, the Court held that the subcontractor could exercise lien rights on the holdback moneys required to be retained under the original contract with the contractor. For the balance of the subcontractor's claim a personal judgment was given against the owner. The decision seems to turn on the fact that the owner had already paid out approximately three-quarters of the purchase price to the contractor who then abandoned the project. If the subcontractor, in this case, was allowed lien rights for the full amount of his lien claim against the owner, then section 9 of the Ontario Act would be contravened and the liens would attach to make the owner liable for a greater sum than that remaining due and owing to the contractor.

§48 Division of the Various Holdbacks.

Where the holdback fund is not sufficient to satisfy all the claims, difficulty may arise as to who is to share, in what proportion, and for what priority. Take as an example a typical construction project in Ontario with an owner, a general contractor, two subcontractors to the general contractor and a sub-subcontractor and material supplier to each of the subcontractors where liens are registered and proceedings to enforce same are commenced:

(*a*) *The Position of the Owner.*

(*i*) *As to the Subcontractors:* If the owner has complied with the Act as to payments and holdback, he can pay the holdback into Court and obtain, after trial, a discharge of the liens of the subcontractors and materialmen; the holdback money paid into Court is then available to them. Aside from the holdback he is not liable to those claiming under the general contractor for any greater sum than that which he owes the general contractor; thus if he retains a sum greater than the required holdback, although the excess is subject to the liens of those claiming under the general contractor, the owner may set off damages for faulty workmanship or costs of completion: see §45, *ante.* If no such set-off is claimed, then the balance of the contract price will be paid into Court and become subject to the lien claims.

(*ii*) *As to the General Contractor:* There being privity of contract between the owner and general contractor, the latter is not limited to the holdback funds, but may enforce his lien for the full balance of the contract price due him. Any such funds received by the general contractor in the action are subject to the unpaid claims of the subcontractors. Since there is privity of contract, the owner may set off costs of completion or damages for faulty workmanship, provided he does not encroach upon the holdback in so doing.

(*b*) *The Position of the General Contractor.*

A contractor is not liable to lienholders claiming under a subcontractor for any amount in excess of that owing by him to the subcontractor, other than the amount of his statutory holdback: *Kilcup v. Lloydminster* (1961), 36 W.W.R. 558 (Sask. C.A.); *R.A. Corbett & Co. v. Phillips* (1972), 32 D.L.R. (3d) 78 (N.B.C.A.). In *Kilcup v. Lloydminister,* an owner O. engaged a general contractor G., who in turn engaged a sub-trade ST., who engaged a sub-sub-trade SS. O. owed G. certain moneys under the contract, and G. owed ST. certain sums that were in excess of the statutory holdback that G. was required to maintain. The lien claimant SS. alleged that he had lien rights on both the sum owed to ST. by the contractor G., and the sum the owner O. owed to the contractor G. The Court held that the lien rights of SS. could not attach to the amount owed to the contractor G. by the owner. The facts were the same in the *R.A. Corbett* case, where the Court held that the lien of SS. constituted a charge on the amount retained by O. only to the extent of the balance owing by G. to ST. and not to the extent of the balance owed by O. to G. under the general contract. See further *Horwitz v. Rigaux Bldg. Enterprises Ltd.* (1960), 32 W.W.R. 540, reversing 30 W.W.R. 599 (Alta. C.A.); §47, *ante.*

In Ontario an owner paid the balance owing under its contract with its general contractor into Court in the amount of approximately $200,000.00.

The general contractor owed its sub-trades the sum of approximately $158,000.00 and one sub-trade, H., went bankrupt leaving part of its subcontract incomplete and owing its sub-sub-trades on the job approximately $47,800.00. Nothing was owing at this time by the general contractor to H. The statutory holdback the general contractor was required to maintain, that is, 15% of the completed work of H., was $26,800.00. Therefore, the Court held that the general contractor was liable to pay $158,000.00 to its unpaid sub-trades that it had contracted directly with, and also the statutory holdback on H.'s contract of $26,800.00. The argument put by the general contractor that since it owed H. nothing, the sub-sub-trades could get nothing was rejected. The argument of the general contractor that its lien and all of the other lien claimants' liens should rank on an equal basis respecting the funds paid into Court by the owner was also rejected, the Court holding that the sub-sub-trades and the general contractor's subcontractors had first priority and the general contractor was only entitled to any amount left over: *Rideau Aluminum & Steels Ltd. v. McKechnie*, [1964] 1 O.R. 523; affirmed 48 D.L.R. (2d) 62, 659 (Can.).

(*c*) *Position of Subcontractors.*

The amount which the owner must make available to satisfy subcontractors' claims for lien is limited to the amount owing by the owner to the general contractor, but in no case can that amount be less than the statutory holdback which must be retained by the owner: Alta., sec. 15(1), (2), (5.1), (5.2); B.C., secs. 6, 21(1); Man., secs. 8, 9(1); N.B., secs. 4(3), 15(1); Nfld., secs., 12, 13(1); N.S., secs. 11, 12(1); Ont., secs. 10, 11(1); P.E.I., secs. 3(2), 15(1); Sask., secs. 18(2), 19(1). To put it another way, the subcontractors are entitled to receive the amount which the owner owes to the general contractor, or the statutory holdback, whichever of those two amounts is the greater. See also *Kilcup v. Lloydminster, supra; Vaillancourt Lbr. Co. v. Trustees of Sep. School Section No. 2, Balfour Twp.,* [1964] 1 O.R. 418 (C.A.); *S. I. Guttman Ltd. v. James D. Mokry Ltd.,* [1969] 1 O.R. 7 (C.A.); *Can. Comstock Co. v. Toronto Transit Commn.,* [1970] S.C.R. 205; *Lonmar Plumbing and Heating Ltd. v. Representative Holdings* (1968), 1 D.L.R. (3d) 591 (Sask.); *Noranda Exploration Co. v. Sigurdson,* [1976] 1 S.C.R. 296; *Eddy Hdwe. (1971) Ltd. v. Keystone Dev. Co.* (1975), 13 N.B.R. (2d) 451; *Rasmussens' Ltd. v. Melville Country Club,* [1977] 4 W.W.R. 382 (Sask.); *Curran & Briggs Ltd. v. Ryder* (1977), 19 N.B.R. (2d) 330.

If there is any deficiency as to the subcontractors' claims they will be given personal judgment against the general contractor.

(*d*) *Position of Materialmen and Sub-subcontractors.*

The amount which must be made available by the general contractor to satisfy their claims is limited to the amount owing by the general contractor to the subcontractor for whom the materials were supplied, but again, in no case is that amount to be less than the statutory holdback which is required to be retained by the general contractor: see sections and cases in part (c), *supra,* and *R.A. Corbett & Co. v. Phillips* (1972), 32 D.L.R. (3d) 78 (N.B.C.A.). See also *C.J. Oliver Ltd. v. Foothills Lighting & Elec. Ltd.,* (1965), 54 W.W.R. 37 (Alta. C.A.). If there is a deficiency after payment of holdback they will be given personal judgment against the subcontractor with whom they contracted directly for the balance still owing.

Using the example as previously set out, the result is that the owner retains the required holdback for the benefit of the subcontractors and the general contractor retains the required holdback for the benefit of persons who supply labour, materials and services to his subcontractors. The protection is thus for those parties two levels below in the construction pyramid. All persons on the same level of the pyramid share *pari passu* except workmen who have a limited priority.

§49 The Alberta "Lien Fund".

The Alberta Act (sec. 15), defines the "lien fund" as the percentage to be retained by the owner as holdback plus any amount payable by the owner under the contract which has not been paid by him in good faith prior to the registration of a lien, (sec. 15(6)), less any amount permitted to be paid pursuant to a "supervisor's" certificate: sec. 16. Thus not only must the owner comply with the holdback provisions, but also he cannot safely make further payments under the contract once a lien is registered. When a lien is registered the holdback and any amount payable under the contract become a "lien fund" and every lien is a charge on this fund: sec. 15(4). The owner's liability is restricted to the lien fund, (sec. 15(5)), and thus if he fails to comply with the Act, he will be required to pay over again. He cannot set off the costs of completion if the contractor or a subcontractor defaults in completing his contract: sec. 15(7).

If no lien is registered and the owner has made proper payments up to the holdback or in reduction of the holdback, then the only remaining component of the "lien fund" will be the holdback or the balance of the holdback and. he can, after the time limited by the Act, pay same with impunity.

If a lien is registered the owner has two choices. Firstly, he may pay the lienholder's claim, obtain a discharge and within 3 days after payment give written notice of such payment pursuant to section 20, provided of course, he does not encroach upon the holdback in so doing. Such payment if properly made will be deemed to be a payment on his contract generally. In adopting this method the owner runs the risk of the Court subsequently finding that the amount paid was not justly due to the lienholder: see §50, *post*. Secondly, he may, pursuant to section 18(2), pay the "lien fund" into Court whether or not an action to enforce the lien is commenced. The Court may receive or hear evidence by affidavit or *viva voce* so as to determine the proper amount of the "lien fund": sec. 18(5). The owner adopted the second course of action in *Guglietta v. Oldach* (1977), 3 Alta. L.R. (2d) 347, in which the Court held that since the contract between the owner and the contractor made it clear that they intended the value of the work done under the contract at any given time to be the contract price plus extras, less the cost of correcting deficiencies, the lien fund available to lien claimants under that contract was limited to 15 per cent of that "value of work done". In *Schlumberger Can. Ltd. v. Superior Contracting Gen. & Mechanical Ltd.* (1977), 4 Alta. L.R. (2d) 191, it was held that the term "lien fund" as it is defined in section 15(2) of the Alberta Act means the total of two separate amounts: (a) 15% of the value of the contract price, minus the cost of work which remains to be done under the contract; and, (b) any amount which is owing to the contractor under the contract but which has not yet been paid by the owner.

In *Yale Dev. Corpn. v. A.L.H. Const. Ltd.,* [1973] 2 W.W.R. 477 (Alta. C.A.), it was held that the Alberta lien fund provisions contemplate a separate fund for each contract entered into by the owner. As a result, where the owner, rather than engaging one general contractor for all the work, let separate contracts for different aspects of the work, he was required to maintain a separate lien fund for each contract. The payment in of the "lien fund" will take the place of the land and entitle the owner to a discharge of all liens registered.

§50 Notice in Writing by Lien Claimants.

A subcontractor or other claimant may give notice in writing of his lien rights (Form 6) to the owner, contractor or subcontractor as the case may be: Ont., sec. 11(5*a*), (6). After receipt of a written notice of lien, the owner, contractor or subcontractor, as the case may be, must in addition to the statutory holdback retain an amount equal to that claimed in the written notice: Ont., sec. 5(*a*); *Henry Hope & Sons of Can. Ltd. v. Richard Sheehy & Sons* (1922), 52 O.L.R. 237; *Craig v. Cromwell* (1900), 27 O.A.R. 585, affirming 32 O.R. 27; *Len Ariss & Co. v. Peloso,* [1958] O.R. 643 at 653 (C.A.); *Vaillancourt Lbr. Co. v. Trustees of Sep. School Section No. 2, Balfour Twp.,* [1964] 1 O.R. 418 (C.A.); *S. I. Guttman Ltd. v. James D. Mokry Ltd.,* [1969] 1 O.R. 7 (C.A.); *Can. Comstock Co. v. Toronto Transit Commn.,* [1970] S.C.R. 205.

If the owner, contractor, or subcontractor, having received such notice makes any payments to the person with whom he contracted directly, he does so at the peril of being required to pay all or some of the moneys again to the lien claimants up to the amount of holdback plus the amount contained in the notice. McGillivray J.A. stated: "the hardship imposed upon an owner called upon to pay twice for the same work was pointed out to the Court but no hardship need occur if the owner proceeds in a proper fashion. He can and would I think in the usual practice, upon receiving notice and before paying further moneys, either demand that the contractor pay the lien forthwith or pay it himself as provided by section 12(1). In the present instance the owner did neither and by paying the contractor some $16,744.00 after receipt of notice of the lien it enabled the contractor to deprive lien claimants of money to which they were entitled. Someone under these circumstances must suffer the loss and the owner at least could cause it to be avoided had it not proceeded at its peril to make the payments mentioned": *Vaillancourt Lbr. Co. v. Trustees of Sep. School Section No. 2, Balfour Twp., supra.*

"The object of the notice is to warn the owner that he cannot safely make payments on account of the contract price, even within the 80% margin, because of the existence of liens of which he was not otherwise bound to inform himself or to look for. The notice does not compel him to pay the lien. It does not prove the existence of the lien. Its sole purpose is to stay the hand of the paymaster until he shall be satisfied — either by the direction of the debtor or of the Court, in case proceedings to realize the lien are taken — that there is a lien, and that some amount is really due and owing to the lienholder": per Osler J.A. in *Craig v. Cromwell* (1900), 27 O.A.R. 585, affirming 32 O.R. 27. See also *Len Ariss & Co. v. Peloso, supra; Can. Comstock Co. v. Toronto Transit Commn., supra; S. I. Guttman Ltd. v. James D. Mokry Ltd., supra; Vaillancourt Lbr. Co. v. Trustees of Sep. School Section No. 2, Balfour Twp., supra.* See also Chapter 3, The Lien Claimant, §36, *ante;* Chapter 6, Obtaining a Lien, §75, *post* and also Article "Notice in writing under The Mechanics' Lien Act and the Vaillancourt decision", Chitty's Law Journal, 1963-64, Vol. 12, p. 313.

Once the amount of money set out in the notice of lien is properly held back, then it awaits the disposition of the Court at the trial of the action. It has now been conclusively held that the owner or person receiving the notice of lien may set off any extra costs incurred on the project against any sums over and above the statutory holdback notwithstanding the notice in writing of lien, provided he does not pay any amounts to his contractor after he receives notice in writing of the lien, except amounts owing over and above the holdback plus the amount claimed in the notice: *Can. Comstock Co. v. Toronto Transit Commn., supra; S. I. Guttman Ltd. v. James D. Mokry Ltd., supra.* See further Chapter 3, The Lien Claimant, §29(e), *ante,* Chapter 6, Obtaining A Lien, §75 *post* and Chapter 9, The Trust Fund, §109, *post.*

However, if an owner or other person not primarily liable receives this notice and satisfies himself that the lien claimant is entitled to payment, he may pay the claim and, within 3 days thereafter, give written notice of the payment to the person primarily liable or his agent. But he must not, by making such a payment, encroach on the amount of the holdback that he is required to retain: Ont., sec. 12. If he chooses, on receiving the notice, to withhold the money from the claimant and pay it into Court, then this sum is not solely for the benefit of the person who gave the notice in writing, but must be added to the holdback and distributed *pro rata* amongst lien claimants according to their respective classes and rights: *Len Ariss & Co. v. Peloso, supra.* A warning note was struck in the case of *Craig v. Cromwell* (1900), 27 O.A.R. 585, affirming 32 O.R. 27, respecting this section when the Court observed "section 12 would appear to authorize him to pay the subcontractor but if he does he assumes the risk of being able to prove, as between himself and the contractor, that the debt was justly due, and his right or power to pay the subcontractor does not depend upon notice having been given to him under section 11(2) [now 11(6)]."

Similar provisions to those in the Ontario Act are found in the Acts of Newfoundland, secs. 13(6), 14; Nova Scotia, secs. 12(4), 13; Saskatchewan, secs., 20(7), 22 and Manitoba, secs. 9(6), 10. The Acts of the provinces of New Brunswick and Prince Edward Island also have similar provisions, except that, in making such a payment, the owner can encroach on neither the holdback nor the special fund created in their Acts respecting amounts claimed in notices of lien: N.B., secs. 15(7), 16, 18; P.E.I., secs. 15(5), 16, 18. See below for a general discussion of this special fund.

The Act of Alberta, sec. 15(6), entitles an owner to make *bona fide* payments to a contractor before a lien is registered. Once a lien is registered, any amount payable by the owner under his contract in excess of the holdback is constituted part of the "lien fund". See §49, ante, respecting the "lien fund". The Act of British Columbia provides, in sec. 13, that the filing of an affidavit of claim of lien shall be deemed to be notice of the claim of lien to all persons. Under sec. 21(3) of that Act an owner is entitled to make *bona fide* payments before registration of a lien. Even though the Alberta and British Columbia Acts require registration to stop the hand of the paymaster, it is submitted that the owner should not disregard a notice in writing of a lien because if he receives such written notice prior to the lien's registration, any payment made by him in disregard of it may not be made in good faith.

The provinces of New Brunswick, sec. 16, and Prince Edward Island, sec. 16, have enacted special provisions to deal with the retention of the amount claimed in the notice of lien. In New Brunswick and Prince Edward Island the lienholder may give the owner notice in writing of his lien, stating under oath the amount claimed, and thereafter the owner must retain, from the amount payable to the contractor under whom the lien is derived, the amount so claimed. Any such amounts so retained constitute a fund, separate from the holdback fund, for the benefit of the lienholders who give notice of their claim. The lien of each lienholder who has given the required notice is a charge on this fund, and each of such lienholders are entitled to rank *pari passu* on the amount to be retained for such sum for which his lien may be enforced. The amount so retained is to be distributed among such lienholders *pro rata*. Any such distribution he receives pursuant to these special provisions does not disentitle him to claim for any balance remaining payable to him from the holdback fund.

In New Brunswick and Prince Edward Island the owner cannot make any payments under the contract which will reduce the amount he is required to retain upon receiving notice: N.B., sec. 18; P.E.I., sec. 18, and he may safely pay over such amount upon expiration of the time limited by the Act applicable to the holdback fund: N.B., sec. 17; P.E.I., sec. 17. Essentially,therefore, although separate from the holdback, the fund created by these sections has the same qualities and characteristics, and the consequences of a breach of these special provisions respecting the retention of the amount claimed in the notice of lien are also similar to those of the holdback fund.

§51 Form of Notice of Lien.

The notice of lien must be in writing, (Ont., sec. 11(6)), but no statutory form is required where the claimant is entitled to a lien on the land. If the claim relates to work on a public street or highway owned by a municipality or a "public work", the contents of the notice are prescribed by section 21(a)(7) of the Act. O. Reg. 849/75 prescribes the form of the notice and provides that it will only be effective as a notice in writing of the claim for lien within the provisions of section 11(5a) of the Act if it is served upon the owner, contractor or subcontractor whom it is intended to bind. Note, however, that Sec. 27(d) of The Interpretation Act, R.S.O. 1970, c. 225, provides that, "where a form is prescribed, deviations therefrom not affecting the substance or calculated to mislead do not vitiate it." Section 11(5a) of the Ontario Act provides that, where the lien does not attach to the land by virtue of section 5(2) of the Act, an owner, contractor or subcontractor who receives written notice of a lien must retain the amount claimed in the notice, in addition to the holdback, out of amounts payable to the contractor or subcontractor under whom the lien is derived.

In Alberta it was held that, at the very minimum, notice in writing of lien in order to satisfy the provisions of that province's Mechanics' Lien Act, must indicate:

(a) that the subcontractor is supplying material to the contractor;

(b) that there is an account owed thereby;

(c) that the subcontractor is claiming a lien (and perhaps will register it unless payment is made to him); and

(d) the amount of the claim.

Bird Const. Co. v. Mountview Const. Ltd. (1969), 67 W.W.R. 515 (Alta.). See also *Revelstoke Bldg. Materials Ltd. v. Howe; Neumann v. Howe; Royal Bank v. Neumann,* [1973] 1 W.W.R. 249 (Alta. C.A.).

In *Craig v. Cromwell* (1900), 27 O.A.R. 585, affirming 32 O.R. 27, the Court found sufficient notice in writing when a letter was sent to the owners naming an overdue account, and informing them that a lien would be filed if payment was not made. The notice must be such as would cause the owner to know that the claimant was claiming a lien under the Act: *Anglin & Co. v. Simmons,* [1933] O.W.N. 136 (C.A.).

A direction by a contractor to the owner to pay directly to a subcontractor the amount of the contractor's indebtedness for materials supplied to the job was held not to be a sufficient notice in writing to the owner: *Anglin & Co. v. Simmons, supra; Sanderson Pearcy & Co. v. Foster* (1923), 53 O.L.R. 519 (C.A.).

Statements sent to the architect on the job merely in response to his request for details of amounts owing to the sub-trades, were held to be for the purpose of showing the progress of the work and its cost to date, and not for the purpose of asserting rights against the "owner" under the notice section: *Dziadus v. Sloan,* [1943] 3 W.W.R. 449 (Man. C.A.).

The delivery to an owner of a bill of materials supplied to the contractor, containing no reference whatever to the supplier's intention of claiming a lien on the land does not constitute the written notice claiming a lien contemplated by the Act: *Direct Lbr. Co. v. Meda* (1957), 23 W.W.R. 126 (Alta.). The delivery of a copy of the construction contract to a company loaning money to the owner to finance the work was held not to be a sufficient notice in writing of the contractor's lien in *River Valley Store Fixtures Ltd. v. Camper-Villa-Inn Ltd.,* [1977] 1 W.W.R. 659 (Man.).

The sending of copies of invoices to the owner, as materials were delivered to the job for the contractor, were held not to be sufficient notice of lien: *Menzies and Herbert Ltd. v. Rocky Mountain S.D.; Rocky Mountain S.D. v. Atlas Lbr. Co.,* [1954] S.C.R. 589, reversing (*sub nom. Atlas Lbr. Co. v. Rocky Mountain S.D.*) 8 W.W.R. 513. See also the following cases and refer to §§36 and 75; *Crown Lbr. Co. v. Hickle,* [1925] 1 W.W.R. 279, reversing [1924] 1 W.W.R. 399 (Alta. C.A.); *Robock v. Peters* (1900), 13 Man. R. 124; *Dom. Radiator Co. v. Payne,* [1917] 2 W.W.R. 974; reversed in part (*sub nom. Calgary v. Dom. Radiator Co.*) 56 S.C.R. 141; *Ross Bros. Ltd. v. Gorman* (1908), 1 Alta. L.R. 516, affirming 1 Alta. L.R. 109 (C.A.).

In most jurisdictions, if no notice in writing as previously discussed has been given to the owner, contractor or subcontractor, as the case may be, all payments, up to the required holdback amount, made in good faith operate to discharge the liens *pro tanto:* Ont., sec. 11(6); Man., sec. 9(6); N.B., sec. 15(7); Sask., sec. 20(7).

§52 The Meaning of Good Faith.

The requirement of good faith is included to protect the lienholder where the owner sets up a contractor who is little more than a man of straw with the intention of securing improvements to his land without paying for them. Whether or not the owner has made payments in good faith is a question of fact to be determined from all the circumstances and the onus in most cases rests upon the person alleging *mala fides: Len Ariss & Co. v. Peloso*, [1958] O.R. 643 at 650 (C.A.). In this case a lien claimant gave written notice of his claim to the owner and thereafter the owners held back an amount sufficient to satisfy the notice plus the holdback (improperly calculated), and proceeded to make further payments. The lien claimants alleged that the subsequent payments were not made in good faith because the owner failed to maintain the holdback properly calculated, he had knowledge of the contractor's financial difficulties and the owner and contractor were close friends. The Court rejected each of the arguments finding that mere knowledge of the financial difficulties was not sufficient to impute *mala fides,* that the owner was not required to make inquiries as to the financial position of the contractor and that mere evidence of friendship was not sufficient to impute *mala fides.* See also *Western Tractor & Equipment Co. v. Milestone School Unit No. 12* (1960), 33 W.W.R. 249 (Sask. C.A.). However, in the case of *Dunlop Can. Ltd. v. Kennedy* (1962), 41 W.W.R. 638 (Sask.), the Court held that transactions between relatives or close friends raise an onus on these parties to prove they acted in good faith.

In *B & T Masonry Inc. v. Mirandas Dev. & Bldg. Services Ltd.; Neufeld v. Mirandas Dev. & Bldg. Services Ltd.; Newton Ready Mix Ltd. v. DeGraaf; Ben Deck Elec. Ltd. v. DeGraaf; Cerniuk v. DeGraaf; Ventaire of B.C. Ltd. v. DeGraaf; Central Glass Products Ltd. v. DeGraaf* (1977), 3 B.C.L.R. 357, the Court followed the decision in the *Len Ariss* case, *supra,* holding that mere knowledge by the owner that liens exist or that the contractor is in difficulties cannot in itself establish that the owner did not make payments in good faith. It held however that the onus of proving that payments were made in good faith rested upon the owner.

§53 What Constitutes a Payment.

In the case of *Jennings v. Willis* (1892), 22 O.R. 439, Boyd C. stated at page 441: "'Payments', as used in section 9 of the Lien Act, R.S.O. ch. 126

[now Ont., sec. 11(6)], is not a technical word but one in popular use. It should not be limited to the case of actual payments in cash by the owner into the hands of the contractor. It may well cover payments made by the owner at the instance or by the direction of the contractor to those who supply materials to him; it may well cover tri-partite arrangements by which an order is given by the contractor on the owner for payment of the materialman out of the fund, and this when accepted, fixing the owner with direct liability to pay for the materials."

In the above case, the owner executed a promissory note to a materialman payable 42 days later. After executing the note, the owner received notice of lien. The Court held that the owner was entitled to deduct the amount of the note from the contract price; it, being executed prior to the notice of lien, constituted a valid "payment". This was so even though at trial the note was still unpaid, since the owner was now fixed with direct liability for it.

In *Don Walker Co. v. Andrews*, [1963] 1 O.R. 358 (C.A.), the facts were similar to the *Jennings* case, *supra*, except that the note was given to the contractor as security for the resumption of delivery of materials. The contractor promptly endorsed the note to the materialman and upon presentation it was dishonoured. The Court held that although at the outset the note was given as conditional payment, once it was negotiated it became an unconditional payment and was validly made since the contractor, after negotiating the note, would be estopped from denying it was payment to him.

In *Western Tractor & Equipment Co. v. Milestone School Unit No. 12* (1960), 33 W.W.R. 249 (Sask. C.A.), an owner guaranteed payment to a sub-trade of a contractor and executed the agreement before a notice of lien to the owner was delivered. The owner later paid the sub-trade on the guarantee. It was held that payment was made in "good faith" since it was deemed that payment was made at the date of the guarantee and was therefore prior to notice.

§54 Preferences by the Owner.

Provisions are found in most of the Acts that prohibit the owner of land giving preferences to certain lienholders by way of conveyance, mortgage or charge on his land. In Ontario, for example, any such conveyance, mortgage or charge given to a lien claimant, in payment of or as security for his lien claim, whether given before or after the lien claim has arisen, is fraudulent and void as against all lienholders who are able to prove their claims: sec. 14(3). See *Don Walker Co. v. Andrews, supra* at 360.

The mortgage, conveyance or charge is, however, valid against all other persons. Similar provisions are found in B.C., sec. 10(3); N.B., sec. 7(2);

P.E.I., sec. 7(2); Nfld., sec. 16(3).; Sask., sec. 26(4). The Acts of Nova Scotia, sec., 15(5), Prince Edward Island, sec., 7(1), New Brunswick, sec., 7(1), and Saskatchewan, sec. 27, provide that payments made to defeat or impair liens are null and void.

In *Ont. Hardwood Flooring Co. v. Dowbenko; Smusiak v. Dowbenko,* [1957] O.W.N. 177 (C.A.), a supplier of material requested a mortgage with a bonus on the lands of the owner before he would supply material. It was held that the mortgage fell within section 14(3) and so was invalid against other lien claimants. The bonus portion was considered as part of the price charged by the material supplier for furnishing the materials on credit, and so was also found to be void as against the other lien claimants. However, a plumber agreed with the owner to perform the plumbing contract, and further agreed to lend the owner $6,500.00. He was given a mortgage for his contract price, plus the amount of the loan, plus a $2,000.00 bonus. It was held that the mortgage to the extent of the contract price was void as against other lien claimants. The amount of the mortgage covering what was actually loaned the owner, namely $6,500.00, was held valid and hence took priority over the lien claimants. As it was not on the facts of the case possible to ascertain what percentage of the $2,000.00 bonus represented the cost of the loan, and what percentage of it represented the price of performing the plumbing contract on credit, the entire bonus was also held void as against the lien claimants. See also *Godden Lbr. Co. v. Morrow,* [1962] O.W.N. 17, and §57, *post.*

An owner must pay particular attention to wage earners, as they are given special protection under the various Mechanic's Lien Acts. Every device by an owner, contractor or subcontractor to defeat the priority given to a wage earner for wages as well as any payment to defeat or impair his lien rights, is null and void: Ont., sec. 15(4); Sask., secs. 27, 28(4); P.E.I., sec. 6; Nfld., sec. 17(4); N.S., sec. 15(5); Man., sec. 12(5); N.B., secs. 6(2), 7(1); B.C., sec. 10(2); Alta., sec. 10(2).

In Ontario the Judge or Officer trying the action, having full power to dispose of the action and questions arising thereunder, would further be entitled to inquire into any alleged fraudulent procedures respecting any parties to the action: secs. 32, 38(4). See also, Alta., sec. 44; Man., sec. 39; N.B., sec. 43; Nfld., sec. 38(4); N.S., sec. 34; P.E.I., sec. 45; Sask., secs. 46, 51.

§55 Removal of Materials.

Formerly in Ontario, material delivered to be used for any purpose giving rise to a right of lien was subject to a lien for the purchase price in favour of the supplier until it was incorporated in the structure. It was not subject to execution or any other process to enforce the owner's, contractor's or any other person's debts: former sec. 15(1). During the continuance of a lien no part of the material could be removed from the project except with leave of the Judge having jurisdiction: former sec. 15(2). The above section has now been removed from the Ontario Act. The Act of Newfoundland is the same as the present Ontario Act. See further §§32(g) and 34, *ante*. The remaining provinces have similar legislation to the former Act of Ontario: Alta., sec. 14; B.C., sec. 20; Man., sec. 13; N.S., sec. 16; N.B., sec. 14; P.E.I., sec. 14; Sask., sec. 14(3), (4). The Acts of Manitoba and Saskatchewan provide that any attempt to remove such material may be restrained on application to a Judge: Man., sec. 13(1); Sask., sec. 14(3). The Acts of all of the provinces except Ontario and Newfoundland provide that the Court may direct the sale of any materials and authorize the removal of them: Alta., sec. 45(4); B.C., sec. 30(2); Man., sec. 40(2); N.B., sec. 44(2); N.S., sec. 34(3); P.E.I., sec. 46(2); Sask., sec. 51(4).

"The creation of this special right in favour of the materialman who supplied the goods, and its continuance up to the point when the goods were incorporated into the building or structure would give the materialman some special interest which could be enforced against a contractor, owner, creditors or others who attempted to remove the goods and prevent them from being used for a purpose foreign to that for which they were furnished and delivered": Schroeder J.A. in *Re Northlands Grading Co.,* [1960] O.R. 455 (C.A.); *Maltby's Ltd. v. Can. Packers Ltd.,* [1947] O.W.N. 757. However it was held in these Ontario cases that the lien created by this section of the Act was not a special or separate and distinct lien, in the nature of an extension of the vendor's lien created by The Sale of Goods Act but that it was simply an extension, or a particular application of, the basic lien created by Section 5 of the Ontario Act.

In Alberta, the situation is entirely different. The Alberta Court of Appeal in *Re Brown-Plotke Enrg. & Const.; J. Wood Co. v. C.C.M.T.A.* (1962), 39 W.W.R. 593, reversing 38 W.W.R. 34 (Alta. C.A.), held that the section of the Alberta Act which corresponds to the former section 15 of the Ontario Act did in fact create a lien which existed independently of the ordinary mechanics' lien, that this lien was in the nature of an unpaid seller's lien for the purchase price of the material supplied and that the material supplier did not have to register a claim for lien in order to enforce his lien on the materials. The Court of Appeal in that case cited with approval the previous Alberta decision in *Trussed Concrete Steel Co. v. Taylor Enrg. Co.,* [1919] 2 W.W.R. 123 (Alta.) and *Metals Ltd. v. Trusts & Guar. Co.* (1914), 7 W.W.R. 605 (Alta.). It refused to follow the decision in *Re Northlands Grading Co., supra.* The same result was obtained in *Western Caissons (Alta.) Ltd. v. Bower* (1969), 71 W.W.R. 604 (Alta. C.A.).

In Nova Scotia it has been held that the doctrine expressed in *Re Northlands Grading Co., supra,* is to be preferred over the reasoning in the

Alberta cases cited in the preceding paragraph: See *Marble Centre Ltd. v. Kenney Const. Co.* (1973), 29 D.L.R. (3d) 64, affirmed without written reasons 38 D.L.R. (3d) 319 (N.S. C.A.).

§56 Lienholder's, Contractor's and Owner's Rights to Information.

In many building projects the subcontractor has little or no knowledge of the contract arrangements between the contractor and the "owner", or of the state of accounts between these parties; nor does he have any knowledge of the arrangements or state of accounts between the "owner" and mortgagee or the "owner" and the unpaid vendor. As a further protection to the lien claimant, the Acts of the various provinces provide for rights to obtain, and duties to disclose, information respecting such arrangements and accounts, however each provincial Act must be regarded separately with respect to these rights and duties: Ont., sec. 28; Alta., sec. 24; B.C., secs. 17, 18; Man., sec. 27; N.B., sec. 32; Nfld., sec. 30; N.S., sec. 31; P.E.I., sec. 33; Sask., sec., 44.

(a) *The Contract and State of Accounts between the Owner and the Contractor.*

The Acts of all provinces except Newfoundland provide that any lienholder may in writing at any time demand from the owner or his agent, inspection of, or information as to, the contract with the contractor under which his lien rights arise and the state of accounts between the owner and contractor. If this information is not given by the owner or his agent within a reasonable time or if he knowingly gives false information and if by reason of the delay or false information the lienholder sustains any loss, the owner is liable to him for the amount of such loss.

In addition the Acts of Alberta, sec. 24(1), New Brunswick, sec. 32(5), Saskatchewan, sec. 44(1) and Prince Edward Island, sec. 33(5), entitle the lienholder to make the above demand upon the contractor. The Acts of Ontario, sec. 28(1), Saskatchewan, sec. 44(4) and Alberta, sec. 24(2), give the lien claimant an option to claim his loss against the owner in the action to enforce his lien or to proceed in an ordinary action. In New Brunswick, sec. 32(2), (6), and Prince Edward Island, sec. 33(2), (6), it appears that the option applies against the contractor only and that the lien claimant must claim his loss against the "owner" in the lien action.

(b) *The Contract and State of Accounts between the Contractor and Subcontractor.*

The Acts of Alberta, sec. 24(1), New Brunswick, sec. 32(5), Saskatchewan, sec. 44(1) and Prince Edward Island, sec. 33(5), entitle the lienholder to make demand upon the contractor or subcontractor for production of the subcontract through which his claim is derived and the statement of accounts between the contractor and subcontractor, and the consequences of delay or default in giving such information are the same as previously indicated. Again the claimant has an option to pursue his claim for any loss suffered by him, as a result of a delay in the giving of the information or the furnishing of false information by the contractor or the subcontractor, in the lien action or in an ordinary action.

(c) *The Mortgagee and the Unpaid Vendor.*

With the exception of British Columbia, Manitoba and Nova Scotia, the Acts of the remaining provinces impose the same duties and penalties on the mortgagee and unpaid vendor respecting the production of information and statements of accounts pertaining to the mortgage or agreement of purchase and sale: Ont., sec. 28(2); Sask., sec. 44(1); Alta., sec. 24(3), (4); N.B., sec. 32(3), (4); Nfld., sec. 30(1); P.E.I., sec. 33(3), (4).

The claimant has the option to pursue his claim for any loss sustained by him, due to delay or default by the mortgagee or vendor in furnishing the information requested, either in the lien action or in an ordinary action.

(d) *The Owner's Right to Information.*

The Acts of Saskatchewan, sec. 44(2), and British Columbia, sec. 18, are singular in providing the owner with the right to demand of the contractor, subcontractor or lien claimant the terms of any contract under which he is performing work or supplying materials, and a statement of account respecting such contract. Such person is liable to the owner for any loss sustained by refusal of such information, neglect or false statement, and in any event, in British Columbia the lien of such person is limited by the statement given.

The Saskatchewan Act requires the owner to make the demand in writing and the contractor or subcontractor to set forth the facts in a written statement which must be verified by statutory declaration: Sask., sec. 44(2). The person of whom the demand is made must reply within 10 days after it is served on him: Sask., sec. 44(3). If the contractor or the subcontractor does not deliver or mail the required written statement to the owner within this 10 day period the owner may, if the demand is made on the contractor, withhold further payments to the contractor, or, if it is made upon a subcontractor, instruct the contractor, or another subcontractor, to withhold further payments from the subcontractor who is in default, until the demand has been complied with.

(e) *Court Order.*

The Acts of Ontario, sec. 28(3); Alberta, sec. 24(5); Manitoba, sec.

27(2); Newfoundland, sec. 30(2); Nova Scotia, sec. 31(2); Saskatchewan, sec. 44(6); New Brunswick, sec. 52 and Prince Edward Island, sec. 55, give the lienholder a right upon summary application at any time, either before or after any action is commenced to enforce his lien, to apply for an order of the Court requiring the owner or his agent, contractor, subcontractor, mortgagee or his agent, or unpaid vendor or his agent, as the case may be, to produce for inspection the contract, agreement, mortgage, agreement of sale, accounts and other relevant documentation. Sec. 44(7) of The Saskatchewan Act provides that no appeal lies from such an Order.

5

The Mortgagee

§57 In General.

Under most of The Mechanics' Lien Acts the mortgagee will hold either a prior mortgage or a subsequent mortgage on the lands subject to the lien. A prior mortgage is described in the Acts of some provinces as one that was registered before any lien arose under the Act: see Ont., sec. 7(3); Nfld., sec. 9(3); P.E.I., sec. 9(4). The requirement that the prior mortgage be registered does not appear in the Manitoba and Nova Scotia Acts: Man., sec. 5(3); N.S., sec. 7(3). Some of the Acts provide that the time at which the first lien arises shall be deemed to be the time at which the first work or service is performed or the first materials are furnished: e.g., Ont., sec. 7(4); P.E.I., sec. 8; Nfld., sec. 9(4). Most of the other Acts contain a provision similar to section 8 of The Alberta Act to the effect that "the lien created by this Act arises when the work is begun or the first material is furnished": see Alta., sec. 8; Man., sec. 4(2); N.B., sec. 8; Sask., sec. 15. The Ontario and Newfoundland Acts further provide that this time is fixed irrespective of whether a claim for lien in respect thereof is registered or enforced, or whether it is before the Court: see Ont., sec. 7(4); Nfld., sec. 9(4); *Smith & Sons Ltd. v. May* (1923), 54 O.L.R. 21 (C.A.); *Currier & Ferguson Elec. v. Pearce,* [1953] O.W.N. 184; *Baxter Const. Co. v. Reo Invt. Ltd.* (1963), 37 D.L.R. (2d) 751 (Alta.); *Winnipeg Supply & Fuel Co. v. Genevieve Mtge. Corpn.; Wiebe v. Dom. Bronze Ltd.,* [1972] 1 W.W.R. 651 (Man. C.A.). All other mortgagees hold subsequent mortgages which, in general, will have priority over the liens for advances made under them prior to the registration of a lien or the receipt by the mortgagee of a written notice from a lien claimant that he claims a lien on the subject property: see Ont., sec. 14(1); Nfld., sec. 16(1); N.S., sec. 14(1). Section 7(5) of the Ontario Act provides that "any mortgage existing as a valid security, notwithstanding that it is a prior mortgage within the meaning of subsection 3, may also secure future advances, subject to subsection 1 of Section 14". The Newfoundland Act contains the same provision: see Nfld., sec. 9(5). In Alberta and British Columbia, a registered mortgage has priority over a lien to the extent of the mortgage money *bona fide* secured or advanced in money prior to the registration of the lien: Alta., sec. 9(2); B.C., sec. 7(1). See also *Bank of Montreal v. Ehattesaht Co-Op. Enterprises Assn.* (1976), 71 D.L.R. (3d) 757 (B.C.).

In addition, most of the Acts provide that a registered agreement for the sale and purchase of land and any moneys *bona fide* secured or payable thereunder has the same priority over a lien as a mortgage has and for the purposes of The Mechanics' Lien Act the seller of the land will be deemed to be a mortgagee of the lands: Ont., sec. 7(6); B.C., sec. 9(4); Alta., sec. 9(4); Nfld., sec. 9(6). The Ontario, Alberta, British Columbia and Newfoundland sections deem any moneys *bona fide* secured and payable under such an agreement to be mortgage moneys *bona fide* secured or advanced. Such a "mortgagee" may be a prior mortgagee or a subsequent mortgagee depending on the date of the agreement for sale. Such a "mortgage" may also secure future advances if the purchase price is payable in instalments.

Some of the Acts specifically require the mortgagee or unpaid vendor to divulge to the lienholder the terms of his mortgage or agreement for sale of the land, as well as furnish him with a mortgage statement showing the amounts of advances made and the times at which they were made: P.E.I., sec., 33(3), (4); N.B., sec. 32(3), (4); Ont., sec. 28(2). These sections also provide that the mortgagee or unpaid vendor will be liable to the lien claimant for the amount of any loss sustained by him as a result of the former's refusal or neglect to furnish such information, or as the result of the furnishing of a false statement. These Acts further provide that a Judge may make an order requiring the mortgagee or his agent to produce the mortgage or agreement for sale and allow the lien claimant to inspect them: N.B., sec. 52; P.E.I., sec. 55; Ont., sec. 28(3). See also Chapter 4, Rights and Duties of the Owner, §56, *ante.*

Most of the Acts provide that any conveyance, mortgage or charge given to a lien claimant in payment of, or as security for, a lien which he might have had on the property, whether such conveyance, mortgage or charge is given before or after the lien has arisen, shall be deemed to be fraudulent and void as against other parties entitled to liens on the same land: Ont., sec. 14(3); P.E.I., sec. 7(2); B.C., sec. 10(3). In *Ont. Hardwood Flooring Co. v. Dowbenko,* [1957] O.W.N. 177 (C.A.), mortgages given by a builder to secure the payment for building materials supplied by the mortgagees were held fraudulent and void, although, in the case of one of the mortgages, where the supplier had actually loaned some money to the defendant builder, that portion of the mortgage applicable to the loan was held to have priority over the lien claims filed subsequent to the advances being made. See also *Don Walker Co. v. Andrews,* [1963] 1 O.R. 358 (C.A.), and Chapter 4, Rights and Duties of the Owner.

§58 The Mortgagee as "Owner".

The mortgagee's interest in the property may itself be subject to a lien if the mortgagee can be brought within the definition of an "owner", as set out in the Act. In order to make the mortgagee an "owner" within the meaning of the Act, it must be shown that the work or service was done or that the materials were placed or furnished at his request and (1) upon his credit, or (2) on his behalf, or (3) with his privity and consent, or (4) for his direct benefit: Ont., sec. 1(1)(d); *Curran & Briggs Ltd. v. Ryder* (1977), 19 N.B.R. (2d) 330; *E.E. McCoy Co. v. Venus Elec. Ltd.* (1977), 19 N.B.R. (2d) 299. This definition is contained in all of the Acts with little variation, but in British Columbia, section 14 provides that improvements made with the knowledge although not at the request of the owner, shall be held to have been made at his instance and request.

In *Baker & Ellicott v. Williams* (1916), 23 B.C.R. 124 (C.A.), it was held that in order to make the owner liable under section 10 (now sec. 14), it was necessary to show that the owner had knowledge of the works or improvements, otherwise it could not be inferred that the work was done at his "instance and request". The Court went on to say that, since the first mortgage on the property was on the owner's interest which, in the circumstances of that case, could not be attacked, the interest of the mortgagee could also not be attacked. This case would appear to depend upon the peculiar wording of the British Columbia Act, and accordingly in the other provinces the mortgagee's interest might well be the subject of a lien even though the registered owner had no interest in the property which could be the subject of a lien. For example, in Ontario, if a mortgagee were to order repairs to a building damaged by fire without the concurrence of the owner, the mortgagee would become liable to the repairer of the building as an "owner" under the Act, although the owner of the equity of redemption would not be so liable.

It was held in *Rogers Lbr. Yards Ltd. v. Jacobs,* [1924] 2 W.W.R. 1128 (Alta. C.A.), that the fact that the agreement of sale authorized the purchaser to erect a building on the property at his own expense did not amount to the work being "done at the request of the mortgagee (vendor) in writing" within the meaning of the Saskatchewan Act so as to constitute the vendor, who was deemed to be a mortgagee with respect to the unpaid purchase price, an "owner". It was held in *Marshall Brick Co. v. Irving* (1916), 35 O.L.R. 542; affirmed (*sub nom. John A. Marshall Brick Co. v. York Farmers Colonization Co.*) 54 S.C.R. 569, where the vendors of the property sold it to the purchaser under an agreement containing the express provision that the purchaser should build upon the land in accordance with plans and specifications prepared by the purchaser, the vendor advancing the cost of the building to the purchaser, that the vendor was a mortgagee of the lands but that these circumstances alone were not sufficient to bring him within the definition of an "owner" under the Act. It would also appear that the mere fact that the mortgagee or vendor has the right under its mortgage, or under the agreement of sale, to inspect materials used, or the method of construction, or to require the building being erected by the mortgagor or purchaser to conform to specifications laid down by the vendor or mortgagee, will not constitute the vendor or mortgagee an "owner". As was stated in the last mentioned case, there must be something in the nature of a direct dealing between the person seeking to establish the lien and the mortgagee in order to bring him within the definition of an "owner". This view was cited with approval in *Nor. Elec. Co. v. Frank Warkentin Elec. Ltd.* (1972), 27 D.L.R. (3d) 519 (Man. C.A.) and *Nor. Elec. Co. v. Mfrs. Life Ins. Co.* (1974), 53 D.L.R. (3d) 303 (N.S. C.A.). In both of these cases the owners had entered into arrangements whereby the property was sold to a mortgage company which leased it back to the vendor and which gave the vendor a mortgage on his leasehold interest for the purpose of financing the construction of buildings on the property. In each case the owner-mortgagee had certain rights under the lease-back agreement to share in the gross rentals received by the lessee from its sub-tenants. The two Courts of Appeal in each case found that such an arrangement did not make the lessee and the mortgagee joint venturers or partners in the project so as to constitute the mortgagee an "owner" within the meaning of The Mechanics' Lien Act.

The decision in the last mentioned Nova Scotia case was appealed to the Supreme Court of Canada which reached a contrary conclusion: See *Nor. Elec. Co. v. Mfrs. Life Ins. Co.,* [1977] 2 S.C.R. 762. That Court found that the mortgagee was an owner for the purposes of The Mechanics' Lien Act, because the work on the building was done at its request and on its behalf, for its direct benefit and with its privity and consent, and accordingly that it was required to maintain a holdback for the benefit of lien claimants such as the plaintiff. It found further that the developer and lessee, Metropolitan Projects Ltd., was a contractor within the meaning of the Act. Laskin C.J.C., at p. 774, stated: "I cannot agree with the submission that Metropolitan was merely borrowing money to enable it to put up a building of its own, and that the respondent was not advancing money for the construction of a building for it by Metropolitan. The title position and the rent payment provisions are against any such submission. Whose building was it if not the respondent's, subject to possession and use by Metropolitan for a limited period, by way of being able to realize some pecuniary advantage from its original ownership of the land and from its exertions as contractor? The letters of commitment are clear enough on this point since they associate the obligation to construct the building with the transfer to the respondent of the land upon which the building is to be constructed, and they provide that the construction will be paid for by the respondent. This is the substance of the overall arrangement, and the security aspect of the transaction, involving a mortgage of the leasehold, cannot be allowed to mask that substance." The type of sale, lease-back and mortgage of lease arrangement which was considered in this case, and in the *Warkentin* case (*supra*) has been a very common method employed by developers to finance construction projects. In the light of this decision it would now appear to be a much less attractive device than it was hitherto thought to be since the lessor-mortgagee must now withhold the statutory holdback, required to be maintained by an "owner" under the Act, out of the mortgage advances which it makes to the developer.

The Supreme Court of Canada remitted the last mentioned case to the trial Judge to determine the amount of the holdback which the lien claimants could recover from the mortgagee. He found that, since the work was substantially complete before the developer went bankrupt and construction stopped, the holdback was 15% of the total contract price. He also found that the contract price in this case was the amount which the mortgagee had agreed to advance to the developer in return for the benefits it derived under their contract. See: *Nor. Elec. Co. v. Metro. Projects* (1977), 1 R.P.R. 268 (N.S.).

Some further examples of what will make the interest of a mortgagee, or owner of the equity of redemption, subject to a lien may be found in Chapter 2, The Lienable Interest. See also *Andre Knight Ltd. v. Presement,* [1967] 2 O.R. 289 (C.A.); *Whitehead v. Lach Gen. Contractors Ltd.* (1974), 3 O.R. (2d) 680 (C.A.).

§59 The Mortgagee as a Party to the Action to Enforce the Lien.

A subsequent mortgagee who has no priority over the lien claims is not properly made a party to the action in either the claim for lien or the statement of claim, although he must be served with the notice of trial as a subsequent encumbrancer in the same way that execution creditors are served. Nor is a prior mortgagee a proper party to the action unless the plaintiff seeks to attack his priority. A prior mortgagee improperly named as a party defendant may, at the trial, have the action dismissed against him with costs.

It was held in *Hubert v. Shinder,* [1952] O.W.N. 146 (C.A.), where a prior mortgagee had not been formally added as a party defendant or served with the statement of claim, although he had been served with the notice of trial and appeared at the trial, that he had by his conduct and intervention as a party in the proceedings precluded himself from arguing in the Court of Appeal that the trial Judge had had no jurisdiction to make any finding affecting his interest. The Court indicated that, if so desired, it would have made an order making the necessary amendments to the pleadings *nunc pro tunc.* In that case, however, the mortgagee had been served with notice of trial within the time limited by the Act for commencing the plaintiff's action. He had received the notice of trial while the plaintiff's claim for lien was still alive and during the time within which the plaintiff was still at liberty to take action against him. In *Arnold Lbr. Ltd. v. Vodouris*, [1968] 2 O.R. 478, the Court, after referring to *Hubert v. Shinder, supra,* refused to make an order adding defendants after the 90 day limitation for bringing action against them had expired. This decision was followed in *Rocca Steel Ltd. v. Tower Hill Apts. Ltd.,* [1968] 2 O.R. 701. It appears, then, that at least in Ontario if the mortgagee is not named as a party defendant in the statement of claim, the Court may grant an amendment adding him as a party where a claim is subsequently made against him, but only if the application is brought within the time limited for commencing the action or if the notice of trial has been served on the mortgagee during this time. In *Saltzman v. Eastside Holding & Brokerage Co.* (1970), 2 N.S.R. (2d) 265 (C.A.), where the mortgagee was already a party to the action, the Court refused to allow an amendment to the statement of claim to include an allegation that the mortgagees were "owners" within the meaning of The Mechanics' Lien Act on the ground that the proposed amendment raised a cause of action which was barred by the expiration of the time limited by the Act for commencing the action. In *N.S. Sand and Gravel Ltd. v. Kidstone Estates Ltd.* (1973), 13 N.S.R. (2d) 431, the Court approved this decision and refused to add a mortgagee as a party defendant after the expiration of the 90 days limited for commencement of the action. The mortgagee had been served with a notice of trial but not within this ninety day period. The Court held, however, that since the mortgagee had been served with notice of trial it was empowered under the Act to make a finding as to the priority of the liens over its mortgage and held that, since the last advance under the mortgage had been made after the liens were registered, the lien claimants had priority over it. In *E.E. McCoy Co. v. Venus Elec. Ltd.* (1977), 19 N.B.R. (2d) 299, the Court approved the decision in the *Saltzman* case and expressed the opinion (at 307) that the failure to name a mortgagee in the claim for lien and in the statement of claim " . . . could only be corrected by amendment upon an application made within the time limited by the Act for the commencement of the lien claimant's action." However the *Saltzman* case was subsequently distinguished by the Nova Scotia Court of Appeal in *E.S. Martin Const. Ltd. v. Penhorn Mall Ltd.* (1976), 62 D.L.R. (3d) 498 (C.A.), on the ground that it had been decided before certain amendments to Rule 15 of the Nova Scotia Civil Procedure Rules came into force. That Court, in the second case, allowed the same amendment which it had denied in the *Saltzman* case because of the additional discretion conferred upon it by the amendment to the Rules and expressed the opinion that even if the amendment resulted in a new cause of action, that cause of action arose out of the same, or substantially the same facts as the original cause of action against the mortgagee. See also in this connection, *Dom. Lbr. & Fuel Co. v. Paskov,* [1919] 1 W.W.R. 657 (Man.); *Robock v. Peters* (1900), 13 Man. R. 124, and

Chapter 11, Practice Before Trial, §141, *post*. The Court in *Robock v. Peters* expressed the opinion that the claims of subsequent encumbrancers and of other lienholders might be disposed of at trial without their having been made parties to the action since the same mortgage may be a prior mortgage with respect to part of its value and a subsequent mortgage with respect to the balance (*e.g.,* where the mortgage is advanced in instalments, some of the instalments being advanced prior to the lien being filed and the balance subsequent to that date). In such a case it would appear to be in order to simply serve the mortgagee with notice of trial as a subsequent mortgagee if there is no intention to attack his position with respect to the part of the mortgage alleged to be prior to the lien. But see Chapter 11 Practice Before Trial.

A prior mortgagee should always be made a party to the action where it appears that the value of the mortgage exceeded the actual value of the property at the time that the first lien arose, since the lienholder has priority over the mortgage to the extent of such excess: *Dufton v. Horning* (1895), 26 O.R. 252; Ont., sec. 7(3). A prior mortgagee should also be made a party defendant where it is sought to set aside the mortgage as a fraudulent attempt to defeat the lien: *Cooke v. Mocroft,* [1926] 1 W.W.R. 827 (B.C. C.A.). Most of the Acts provide that the lien has priority over all advances made on account of a mortgage after a notice in writing of the lien has been given to the mortgagee or after a claim for lien has been registered: Ont., sec. 14(1); Nfld., sec. 16(1); Man., sec. 11(1). Thus, if the mortgagee has continued to advance after receiving such notice of lien or after the registration of the lien, he should be added as a party defendant in order that the claimant may establish his priority over the subsequent advances. It was held in *Beaver Lbr. Co. v. Curry,* [1926] 3 W.W.R. 404 (Sask. C.A.), and in *Security Lbr. Co. v. Johnson,* [1924] 3 W.W.R. 399 (Sask. C.A.), that where a mortgagee had been made a defendant in a lien action but did not appear or file a statement of defence or in any way oppose the lien claimant's claim to priority over his mortgage, he must be taken to have abandoned any rights he might have had to priority over the lien. But see *D. & M. Bldg. Supplies Ltd. v. Stravalis Holdings Ltd.* (1976), 13 O.R. (2d) 443, in which it was held that the failure of a defendant to file a statement of defence in a mechanics' lien action does not entitle the plaintiff to sign default judgment against him, even where the plaintiff is the only lien claimant in the action.

It was held in *Bradshaw v. Saucerman* (1913), 3 W.W.R. 761, affirming 21 W.L.R. 65 (Y.T. C.A.), and *Whaley v. Linnenbank* (1915), 36 O.L.R. 361 (C.A.), that it is not necessary to name a mortgagee, as such, in the claim for lien, even though the claimant intends to claim priority over the interest of such mortgagee at trial or in the statement of claim. However, if it is sought to establish that the mortgagee is an "owner" within the meaning of the Act then, of course, he should be named in both the claim for lien as an "owner" and as a party defendant in the statement of claim: *E.E. McCoy Co.v. Venus Elec. Ltd.* (1977), 19 N.B.R. (2d) 299.

§60 The Rights and Liabilities of the Prior Mortgagee.

It was formerly the law in Ontario, as pointed out in *Cook v. Belshaw* (1893), 23 O.R. 545, that a prior mortgage under the Act was one which existed in fact before the first lien arose although it might not necessarily be prior to the lien in point of registration. This is still true in Manitoba and Nova Scotia, since the Acts of these provinces do not require that the prior mortgage be a registered mortgage: see Man., sec. 5(3); N.S., sec. 7(3). See further *Winnipeg Supply & Fuel Co. v. Genevieve Mtge. Corpn.; Wiebe v. Dom. Bronze Ltd.* [1972] 1 W.W.R. 651 (Man. C.A.). Under the Acts of most of the other provinces, however, including the present Ontario Act, the prior mortgage must be registered: Ont., sec. 7(3); N.B., sec. 9(2); P.E.I., sec. 9(4). Section 7(4) of the Ontario Act specifically provides that the first lien shall be deemed to have arisen when the first work is performed or the first materials are furnished irrespective of whether a claim for lien in respect thereof is ever registered or is before the Court. See also in this connection *Stinson v. Mackendrick* (1924), 55 O.L.R. 358 (C.A.); *Smith & Sons Ltd. v. May* (1923), 54 O.L.R. 21 (C.A.); *Cook v. Koldoffsky* (1916), 35 O.L.R. 555 (C.A.); *Gooding v. Crocker* (1927), 60 O.L.R. 60 (C.A.); *Currier & Ferguson Elec. v. Pearce,* [1953] O.W.N. 184. These provisions with respect to priority of mortgages apply whether or not the mortgage in question is a second or a first mortgage: *Manners v. Cain* (1927), 60 O.L.R. 644 (C.A.).

The priority given to such a mortgagee is of a limited nature and will extend, in Ontario, Prince Edward Island, New Brunswick, Newfoundland and Manitoba, only to the actual value of the lands and premises at the time that the first lien arose. All liens arising out of work done on the property or materials supplied will have priority over the mortgage to the extent to which the amounts advanced by the mortgagee exceed the actual value of the lands when the work is commenced: Ont., sec. 7(3); Man., sec. 5(3); P.E.I., sec. 9(4); also *Manners v. Cain, supra; Martello v. Barnet* (1925), 57 O.L.R. 670 (C.A.); *Winnipeg Supply & Fuel Co. v. Genevieve Mtge. Corpn.; Wiebe v. Dom. Bronze Ltd., supra.* The Nova Scotia Act attempts a similar result by providing that a lien has priority over a prior registered mortgage to the extent of the increase in value of the mortgaged premises resulting from the works or improvements put upon the premises by the lienholders: N.S., sec. 7(3). In British Columbia and Alberta a registered mortgage has priority over a lien to the extent of the mortgage moneys *bona fide* secured or advanced in money prior to the registration of the lien: Alta., sec. 9(2); B.C., sec. 7(1).

It should be noted that the Acts use the word "mortgage" in its popular sense and the Courts have refused to give it its technical meaning:

see *Casson v. Westmorland Invt. Ltd.,* (1961), 35 W.W.R. 521 (B.C. C.A.); *Stinson v. Mackendrick, supra.* In the former case, the trial Court had decided that "mortgage moneys", as used in the Act, meant money advanced under a mortgage and secured thereby and did not extend to past debts subsequently secured by a mortgage. The Court of Appeal, however, took the position that the words meant moneys owning under a mortgage irrespective of how those moneys came to be owing and gave priority over the liens to the defendant mortgagee who was the holder of a mortgage assigned to him by a bank which had taken the mortgage as security for a past due indebtedness of the owner to the bank. In *Toronto-Dom. Bank v. Setter-Donaldson Mechanical Ltd.* (1977), 2 B.C.L.R. 67 (C.A.), where the corporate owner had placed a second mortgage with the plaintiff bank which secured money which the owner had guaranteed to one of its related companies, it was contended that the owner was not liable under the mortgage until default and until it was liable there were no "mortgage moneys" secured within the meaning of section 7(1) of the British Columbia Act. It was also argued that it was the guarantee and not "mortgage moneys" which were secured. The Court disagreed, holding that the mortgage had priority since section 7(1) did not limit the term "mortgage moneys" to amounts due; they need only to have been secured. It held, further, that the term "mortgage moneys" included any sums secured by a mortgage and it therefore included the gurantee. In *Dorbern Invts. Ltd. v. Prov. Bank of Can.,* (as yet unreported), the Ontario Court of Appeal upheld the decision of the Divisional Court, which had distinguished the *Casson v. Westmoreland* case on the ground that the wording of section 7(1) of The British Columbia Act is different from that of section 14(1) of The Ontario Act. In the *Dorbern* case the bank had made advances totalling $245,000 from April to June, as security for which they subsequently obtained a mortgage which they registered on July 31st, the day before the lien claimant registered its claim for lien. The Divisional Court found that the advances made by the bank were not made "on account of any ... mortgage" within the meaning of section 14(1) of the Ontario Act since they were made before the mortgage had even been executed. It found, however, that the bank's mortgage had priority over the lien by virtue of sections 69(1) and 70 of The Registry Act R.S.O. 1970, c. 409 because it had been registered before the lien, at a time at which the mortgagee had no actual notice of the lien, and had been given for valuable consideration.

It should be noted that the Nova Scotia Act provides that the lien may only gain priority over a prior mortgage if the mortgagee consents to the performance of the work or service or the supply of the materials: N.S., sec. 7(3)(b). The Court expressed the opinion in *Saccary v. Jackson* (1977), 2 R.P.R. 175 (C.A.), that the postponement of his mortgage by a second mortgagee to a first mortgage did not amount to the requisite "consent" so as to render his mortgage subsequent in priority to mechanics' liens which had been registered subsequent to the registration of his mortgage.

As previously stated, the Acts provide that an unpaid vendor, under an agreement for the sale of the lands against which the liens had been filed, is deemed to be a mortgagee of the lands and premises. In British Columbia, Newfoundland and Ontario the agreement of purchase and sale must be registered: Ont., sec. 7(6); Nfld., sec. 9(6); B.C., sec. 7(3). In Alberta a *caveat* must have been filed with respect to the agreement for sale: Alta., sec. 9(4). The unpaid vendor will have priority over the liens for the unpaid sale price, as if he were a prior mortgagee, with respect to all liens which arise after the date of the agreement of sale: *Blight v. Ray* (1893), 23 O.R. 415; *Gooding v. Crocker* (1927), 60 O.L.R. 60 (C.A.); *Michaelis v. Ryan Motors,* [1923] 1 W.W.R. 401 (Sask.); *Hayward Lbr. Co. v. Hammond,* [1922] 3 W.W.R. 1176 (Alta.); *John A. Marshall Brick Co. v. York Farmers Coloniza- tion Co.* (1916), 54 S.C.R. 569, affirming (*sub nom. Marshall Brick Co. v. Irving*) 35 O.L.R. 542. An unpaid vendor who takes back a mortgage for part of the sale price will also have priority over claims for lien registered subsequent to his mortgage and such priority will date from the date of the agreement of purchase and sale rather than from the date of the giving of the mortgage: *Gooding v. Crocker, supra.* As was held, however, in *Pannill Door Co. v. Stephenson,* [1931] O.R. 594 (C.A.), if the lien is registered first it will have priority over an unregistered mortgage.

While more than one mortgage on the property may be held to have priority over the liens, if the actual value of the lands and premises at the time that the first lien arose is found to be less than the total amount advanced under both mortgages, then the priority of the mortgages will be reduced, and if the increase in actual value equals the amount of the second mortgage then it will be subsequent in priority to the liens. If the increase in actual value exceeds the amount of the second mortgage then the second mortgage will be subsequent in priority to the liens and the priority of the first mortgage will be reduced by the balance of such increase in value. If, for example, the first mortgage amounts to $10,000.00 and the second mortgage to $3,000.00 and the actual value of the land, at the time the first lien arose, is found to have been $7,000.00, then the second mortgage will rank subsequent to the liens in priority, the first mortgage will be prior to the liens to the extent of $7,000.00 and will rank subsubsequent in priority to the liens to the extent of the $3,000.00 balance. If the actual value of the land had been found to have been $12,000.00 then the second mortgage would have had priority over the liens to the extent of $2,000.00 and the first mortgage would have had priority for its full face value: *Boake v. Guild,* [1932] O.R. 617; affirmed (*sub nom. Carrel v. Hart*) [1934] S.C.R. 10. It was held in *Great West Permanent Loan Co. v. Nat. Mtge. Co.,* [1919] 1 W.W.R. 788 (B.C. C.A.) that the first mortgagee could not increase the amount of his priority over a subsequent mortgagee by paying off liens affecting the lands and adding the amount so paid to his mortgage debt where there had been no adjudication establishing the priority of such liens over the subsequent mortgagees. This was held to be so even though the first mortgagee's mortgage contained a clause entitling him to pay "liens, taxes, rates, charges or encumbrances" affecting the lands and to add them to the mortgage debt. The Court expressed the view that such a covenant in a mortgage must be confined to the payment of liens which actually affect the mortgagee's interest in the property, such as a lien filed prior to his mortgage.

It was held in *Dom. Lbr. & Fuel Co. v. Paskov,* [1919] 1 W.W.R. 657 (Man.), that the onus is on the mortgagee to show that the actual value of the lands and premises at the commencement of the improvements exceeded the value of his mortgage, since that is the limit of his priority under the statute. Where he is a party to the action, he will be put to the strict proof of this fact since there is no presumption of priority in his favour. It was held, however, in *Independent Lbr. Co. v. Bocz* (1911), 4 Sask. L.R. 103 (C.A.) and *Kennedy v. Haddow* (1890), 19 O.R. 240, that the onus of proving the amount by which the selling value of the land was increased by the improvements was on the lien claimants. This would no longer appear to be the law in Ontario. The Ontario statute was amended in 1923 so as to give the mortgagee priority to the extent of the actual value of the land at the time the first lien arose. In provinces where the statute provides that the lienholder will have priority over the prior mortgage to the extent that the improvements made on the property increase its selling value, the latter opinion would appear to be correct. In the "increased selling value" situation, the lienholder is given a priority limited to an amount which he must prove in order to establish the extent of his priority. In the "actual value" situation, the mortgagee is given a priority limited to an amount which he must prove in order to establish the extent of his priority.

It was held in *Boake v. Guild,* [1932] O.R. 617; affirmed (*sub nom. Carrel v. Hart*) [1934] S.C.R. 10, that section 13(1) (now sec. 14(1)) of the Ontario Act, which provides that a lien shall have priority over all payments or advances made on account of any mortgage after registration of a claim for such lien, gave the lienholders priority over expenditures made by a mortgagee in possession to complete the buildings, and that that section gave the lienholders priority over such expenditures even though the mortgage contained a clause permitting the mortgagee to complete the buildings and add the cost of completion to the principal debt. It was held in *Baxter Student Housing Ltd. v. College Housing Co-op Ltd.* (1976), 57 D.L.R. (3d) 1 (S.C.C.), that, since section 11(1) of the Manitoba Act provides that a lien has priority over receiving orders made after the lien arises, and over mortgage moneys advanced after the lien is registered or written notice thereof given, the Court cannot make a receiving order after the registration of a lien which provides that all payments made by a mortgagee to the Receiver shall have priority over the lien.

In *Mercantile Bank of Can. v. Sigurdson, Babcock Fisheries Ltd.,* [1978] 3 W.W.R. 523 (B.C.) the owner had issued two debentures to the bank, both of which had been issued after the lien claimant started its work and both of which had been registered prior to the registration of the claimant's claim for lien. The charging clause in the debentures contained a clause to the effect that the mortgages were "subject to permitted encumbrances" which included "undetermined or inchoate liens". The lien claimant sought to establish the priority of its lien over the two debentures on the basis that its lien was a permitted encumbrance within the meaning of this clause. The Court held that the debentures had priority over the lien by virtue of section 7(1) of The British Columbia Act. It found that when the indenture was examined as a whole, it did not intend to give priority to unregistered liens, since to do so would have defeated the whole purpose of the debenture which was to secure the owner's indebtedness to the lender.

Most of the Acts contain a provision similar to section 14(3) of the Ontario Act, rendering fraudulent and void as against lienholders a mortgage given to a person otherwise entitled to a lien in payment of or as security for such lien. Consequently, such a mortgage, even though it appears to be a prior mortgage, will be invalid against lienholders: *Ont. Hardwood Flooring Co. v. Dowbenko,* [1957] O.W.N. 177 (C.A.); *Don Walker Co. v. Andrews,* [1963] 1 O.R. 358 (C.A.). See also Chapter 4, Rights and Duties of the Owner. The Court has jurisdiction under most of the statutes to set aside any prior mortgage which has been fraudulently given to defeat lienholders: Ont., sec. 32; Nfld., sec., 51. See also *Security Lbr. Co. v. Acme Plumbing Shop Ltd.,* [1930] 2 W.W.R. 663, reversing (*sub nom. Security Lbr. Co. v. Lyons*) [1930] 1 W.W.R. 709 (Sask. C.A.); *Union Bank v. Boulter-Waugh Ltd.* (1919), 58 S.C.R. 385. The last two decisions are also authority for the proposition that the mortgagee's priority is not affected by his knowledge that some person has a claim against the property for which he may be entitled to register a lien. It has also been held on numerous occasions that mere knowledge on the part of the mortgagee that building operations are being carried out on the property will not affect his priority nor will it constitute him an "owner" within the meaning of the Act: *John A. Marshall Brick Co. v. York Farmers Colonization Co.* (1916), 54 S.C.R. 569, affirming (*sub nom. Marshall Brick Co. v. Irving*) 35 O.L.R. 542; *Andre Knight Ltd. v. Presement,* [1967] 2 O.R. 289 (C.A.). The Court will not, however permit any attempt by a mortgagee, contrary to the Act, to achieve priority over the liens: *Rose v. Peterkin* (1884), 13 S.C.R. 677. See also: *Nor. Elec. Co. v. Mfrs. Life Ins. Co.* [1977] 2 S.C.R. 762.

§61 Actual Value and Increased Selling Value.

As set out in the preceding articles, the priority over lien claimants of the prior mortgagee is limited in some provinces to the actual value of the lands and premises at the time that the first lien arises. In Nova Scotia priorities are expressed the other way around and the priority of the lien claims over a prior mortgage are limited to the amount by which the selling value of the lands in question is increased by the improvements made thereon. The latter situation existed in Ontario until the Act was amended in 1923, to provide for determination of priorities on the "actual value" basis, and accordingly Ontario cases decided prior to 1923 on this subject no longer apply: *e.g. Martello v. Barnett* (1925), 57 O.L.R. 670 (C.A.); *Hickey v. Stalker* (1924), 53 O.L.R. 414 (C.A.); *Kennedy v. Haddow* (1890), 19 O.R. 240; *Warwick v. Sheppard* (1917), 39 O.L.R. 99 (C.A.); *Patrick v. Walbourne* (1896), 27 O.R. 221 (C.A.); *Smith & Sons Ltd. v. May* (1923), 54 O.L.R. 21 (C.A.); *Stevenson v. Green* (1926), 58 O.L.R. 546 (C.A.), although they may be useful in Nova Scotia which still determines priorities in this manner. The Acts of Alberta and Newfoundland also used the "increased selling value" method of limiting the priority of lien claims over prior mortgages until both provinces enacted substantially changed Mechanics' Lien Acts in 1970. The present Newfoundland Act employs the "actual value" method of fixing the mortgagee's priority. The present Alberta Act (as does the British Columbia Act) gives the mortgagee priority to the extent of all amounts *bona fide* secured or advanced before the lien is registered. Cases decided in these jurisdictions prior to the coming into force of these new Acts are no longer applicable on this question, except in Nova Scotia. The New Brunswick Act uses the "actual value" method of fixing the mortgagee's priority but gives priority to the mortgagee for all advances made prior to the registration of the lien, or receipt by him of notice in writing of the lien, to the extent that the total of such advances does not exceed the actual value of the land at the time an advance is made.

In the provinces where "actual value" was the criterion, the onus was on the mortgagee to prove such value: *Dom. Lbr. & Fuel Co. v. Paskov,* [1919] 1 W.W.R. 657 (Man.). It would appear that this value cannot be arrived at by simply subtracting the value of the materials supplied and work performed on the property from the present value of the property. While the price obtained on a recent sale of the property was held in *Martello v. Barnet* (1925), 57 O.L.R. 670 (C.A.), not to be conclusive evidence of "actual value", it was held to be relevant and proper evidence to adduce. As a matter of practice, expert evidence as to the sale price of surrounding properties and at least two valuations by *bona fide* real estate evaluators of the property itself should be tendered. In *Uren v. Confederation Life Assn.* (1917), 40 O.L.R. 536, the Court, in considering a sale under the power of sale in a mortgage, expressed the opinion that the real value of the property is usually somewhere between the high and low valuations submitted by expert valuators.

Where the lienholder's priority over a prior mortgagee depends on the increased selling value of the property, the onus is on the lien claimant to establish such increase in value: *Independent Lbr. Co. v. Bocz* (1911), 4 Sask. L.R. 103 (C.A.); *Kennedy v. Haddow* (1890), 19 O.R. 240. In *Security Lbr. Co. v. Duplat* (1916), 10 W.W.R. 1270 (Sask. C.A.), and *Broughton v. Smallpiece* (1877), 7 P.R. 270; affirmed 25 Gr. 290, it as held that in calculating the "increase in selling value" of the premises it was not sufficient to merely take into account the value of the labour and materials supplied to the property, although this is a cogent element in determining such increase in selling value. Expert evidence should also be adduced to establish the original sale value, as well as the final value of the land together with the improvements, to a prospective purchaser. As was pointed out in *Broughton v. Smallpiece, supra; Security Lbr. Co. v. Duplat, supra; Bank of Montreal v. Haffner* (1884), 10 O.A.R. 592, reversing 3 O.R. 183, and *Cook v. Koldoffsky* (1916), 35 O.L.R. 555 (C.A.), the priority given to a mechanics' lienholder as against a prior mortgage in respect of the increase in the selling value of the property is only to the extent of his proportionate contribution to such increased value, although when calculating that proportion all of the materials supplied or the work done by the lienholder should be taken into account whether it is included in the claim for lien or not. Some additional cases dealing with determining priorities where they are governed by "increased selling value" are *McRae v. Planta*, [1924] 2 W.W.R. 323 (B.C. C.A.); *Dure v. Roed*, [1917] 1 W.W.R. 1395 (Man.), and *Whitlock v. Loney*, [1917] 3 W.W.R. 971 (Sask. C.A.). In the last of these decisions the Court took the position that in the case of land having a potential value as a future business site, the proper method of determining the increased selling value was to ascertain the value of the land without the building and then ascertain what the property would bring with the building situated on it.

§62 The Rights and Liabilities of the Subsequent Mortgagee.

As previously pointed out, all mortgages which are not prior mortgages under the Act will be subsequent mortgages. It has been held that a mortgagee who has been made a defendant in the lien action but does not appear or file a statement of defence or in any way oppose the plaintiff's claim must be taken to have abandoned any rights he may have to priority over the lien, (*Security Lbr. Co. v. Johnson*, [1924] 3 W.W.R. 399 (Sask. C.A.); *Beaver Lbr. Co. v. Curry*, [1926] 3 W.W.R. 404 (Sask. C.A.)), in which event he will become a subsequent mortgagee. However, as was pointed out in *D. & M. Bldg. Supplies Ltd. v. Stravalis Holdings Ltd.* (1976), 13 O.R. (2d) 443, the mortgagee's rights cannot be disposed of until the trial of the action, there being no provision in the Ontario Mechanics' Lien Act permitting the signing of default judgment against a defendant who fails to file a statement of defence. It was held in *Gooding v. Crocker* (1927), 60 O.L.R. 60 (C.A.), that the priority of a mortgage taken back by a vendor to secure the unpaid price dates from the date of the sale agreement and not from the date on which the mortgage is given.

In *Coupland Accept. Ltd. v. Walsh,* [1954] S.C.R. 90, reversing (*sub nom. Walsh v. R.; Bowser v. Dyer*) [1952] O.W.N. 665, a subsequent mortgagee, over whom the lien claimants had priority, had paid off a prior mortgage and taken an assignment of it and he was held to have priority over the liens to the extent of the moneys advanced to purchase such prior mortgage. The decisions in *Abell v. Morrison* (1890), 19 O.R. 669 (C.A.); *Brown v. McLean* (1889), 18 O.R. 533, and *Locke v. Locke* (1896), 32 C.L.J. 332, also support the right of the subsequent mortgagee to subrogation in such circumstances. In *Gordon v. Snelgrove,* [1932] O.R. 253, it was held that a person who paid off a first mortgage and accepted a new mortgage together with a discharge of the old first mortgage, was entitled to rank as a first mortgagee upon the property, although there was a mortgage registered subsequent to the original mortgage but prior to his new mortgage. It was held in *McRae v. Planta,* [1924] 2 W.W.R. 323 (B.C. C.A.), that a prior mortgagee who registered his mortgage after the commencement of the work, although before registration of the mechanics' liens, was entitled to priority over the lien since he had advanced the mortgage money prior to the lien arising. It was held in *Nat. Mtge. Co. v. Rolston* (1917), 59 S.C.R. 219, that a subsequent mortgagee might apply, as in a foreclosure action, to pay off prior liens so long as he did so before a sale had been made in the mechanics' lien action.

In most of the Acts, priority is given to the lien claimant, as discussed in the following section, over advances made by a mortgagee after he receives notice of the lien or after the lien has been registered: Ont., sec. 14(1); Man., sec. 11(1); N.S., sec. 14(1). This notice is discussed more fully in Chapter 6, Obtaining a Lien. Most of the Acts require that the notice be in writing: Ont., sec. 14(1); Man., sec. 11(1); Sask., sec. 26(1). See also *Andre Knight Ltd. v. Presement,* [1967] 2 O.R. 289 (C.A.) and *Whitehead v. Lach Gen. Contractors Ltd.* (1974), 3 O.R. (2d) 680 (C.A.). It was held in *Revelstoke Bldg. Materials Ltd. v. Howe; Neumann v. Howe; Royal Bank v. Neumann* (1973), 31 D.L.R. (3d) 602 (Alta. C.A.), that a written notice of a claim for lien which had been given to the owner did not bind the mortgagee who was advancing funds directly to the contractor. In *D. Porter & Son v. MacLeod* (1951), 29 M.P.R. 83 (N.S.), the Court expressed the opinion that the lienholders' priority depended on the mortgagee receiving written notice of the lien, actual notice not being sufficient. In *River Valley Store Fixtures Ltd. v. Camper-Villa-Inn Ltd.,* [1977] 1 W.W.R. 659 (Man.), it was held that the delivery to the mortgagee of a copy of the construction contract between the owner and the contractor was not a "notice in writing of the lien" within the meaning of the Act. The Acts of Alberta and British Columbia contain a proviso, however, that any mortgagee who has applied mortgage moneys in payment of a lien which has been registered is subrogated to the rights and priority of the lienholder who has been so paid to the extent of the moneys so applied: Alta., sec. 9(3); B.C., sec. 7(2).

§63 Future Advances under a Mortgage.

Both a prior and subsequent mortgage may secure future advances which will gain priority over mechanics' liens so long as they are made either prior to notice in writing of a claim for lien being received by the mortgagee or prior to the registration of a claim for lien: Ont., secs. 7(5), 14(1); P.E.I. sec. 9(2), (3), (4); Nfld., secs. 9(5), 16(1). See also *D. Porter & Son v. MacLeod, supra; O'Brien v. McCoig* (1929), 63 O.L.R. 351 (C.A.); *Warwick v. Sheppard* (1917), 39 O.L.R. 99 (C.A.); *Kievell v. Murray* (1884), 2 Man. R. 209 (C.A.); *C.M.H.C. v. Wood* (1967), 53 M.P.R. 294 (Nfld.); *Muttart Bldrs.' Supplies Ltd. v. Hutton Const. (Brantford) Ltd.,* [1973] 2 O.R. 238; *Nor. Elec. Co. v. Frank Warkentin Elec. Ltd.* (1972), 27 D.L.R. (3d) 519 (Man. C.A.). These sections may well lead to the result that a mortgage which is advanced in a lump sum prior to the time at which the first lien arises may not be in as favourable a position as to the amount of its priority as a building mortgage which is advanced from time to time as the work progresses. The former will have priority only to the extent of the actual value of the land at the time that the first lien arises or alternatively, the lien will have priority over it to the extent of the increased selling value of the land occasioned by the work done or materials supplied. The latter will have an absolute priority for all advances made by the mortgagee until notice in writing of the lien is received by the mortgagee or until the claim for lien is registered. In the latter case, the mortgagee might well obtain a priority in excess of the actual value of the land at the time that the first lien arose.

It was held in *Casson v. Westmorland Invt. Ltd.* (1961), 35 W.W.R. 521 (B.C. C.A.), that the words "mortgage-moneys *bona fide* secured or advanced" as contained in section 7(1) of the British Columbia Act included moneys owing under a mortgage taken to secure past indebtedness and registered prior to the filing of the plaintiff's lien. It was held in *Bank of Montreal v. Ehattesaht Co-op. Enterprises Assn.* (1976), 71 D.L.R. (3d) 757 (B.C.), where the plaintiff held a debenture which it had registered with the Registrar of Companies prior to the work on the project in question starting, but which it had not registered in the Land Registry Office as a charge against the land until one day after the registration of the contractor's claim for lien, that the lien had priority over the debenture. It was held in *Miller v. Lavoie* (1966), 63 W.W.R. 359 (B.C.), where the principal sum recited in the mortgage also included the interest payable thereon, that the mortgagee was entitled to priority over a lien claimant for both the principal and the interest, even though the interest had not been advanced in money before the lien was registered. The Court held that the interest was part of the mortgage money *"bona fide* secured" by the mortgage within the meaning of the Act. See also *M. Sullivan & Son Ltd. v. Rideau Carleton Raceway Holdings Ltd.* (1970), 12 D.L.R. (3d) 662 (S.C.C.): *Nor. Elec. Co. v. Frank Warkentin Elec. Ltd.* (1972), 27 D.L.R. (2d) 519 (Man. C.A.) and *Whitehead v. Lach Gen. Contractors Ltd.* (1974), 3 O.R. (2d) 680 (C.A.).

It was held in *Smith & Sons Ltd. v. May* (1923), 54 O.L.R. 21 (C.A.), that an advance made by the mortgagee to the owner and applied by the mortgagee to reduce another mortgage made between the same parties on other lands, was an advance under the first mortgage such as is contemplated by section 14(1) of the Ontario Act, although in *Inglis v. Queen's Park Plaza Co.,* [1932] O.R. 110 (C.A.), subsequent issues of debentures under a bond mortgage were held not to be the type of mortgage advance contemplated by that section. These decisions will, of course, not be applicable in jurisdictions where the statute does not contain a provision similar to section 14(1) of the Ontario Act. In Alberta, for example, prior to the enactment of the present Act in 1970, section 9 of the Alberta Act gave priority to mechanics' liens "over any unregistered mortgage and any mortgage that is registered after the date on which the lien arose". Accordingly, in *Colling v. Stimson & Buckley* (1913), 4 W.W.R. 597 (Alta.), it was held that the lien took priority over a mortgage upon which no money had been advanced until after the commencement of the work although it had been registered before that time. By section 57 of the former Alberta Act, N.H.A. mortgages were expressly given priority over a lien for advances made prior to the registration of the lien or prior to the mortgagee receiving notice of the lien. In *Robock v. Peters* (1900), 13 Man. R. 124, the Court took the position that the section of the Manitoba Act corresponding to section 14(1) of the Ontario Act applied only to payments made subsequent to the taking effect of the lien under conveyances or mortgages otherwise having priority over the lien. In *Elmvale Lbr. Co. v. Laurin* (1977), 16 O.R. (2d) 241, it was held that a mortgagee might estop himself, by his actions, from being able to rely on the necessity of the lien claimant giving written notice of his lien in order to gain priority over future advances being made by the mortgagee under his mortgage. It is submitted that what will be considered an advance within the meaning of the section will depend upon the circumstances of each case and, perhaps, the particular wording of the Act under which the claim for priority is asserted. See also *Winnipeg Supply & Fuel Co. v. Genevieve Mtge. Corpn.: Wiebe v. Dom. Bronze Ltd.,*

[1972] 1 W.W.R. 651 (Man. C.A.); *Casson v. Westmorland Invt. Ltd.* (1961), 35 W.W.R. 521 (B.C. C.A.); *Toronto-Dom. Bank v. Setter-Donaldson Mechanical Ltd.* (1977), 2 B.C.L.R. 67 (C.A.); and the unreported decision in *Dorbern Invts. Ltd. v. Prov. Bank of Can.* discussed in §60.

It was held in *Traders Realty Ltd. v. Huron Heights Shopping Plaza Ltd.,* [1967] 2 O.R. 522, that a mortgagee had priority over lien claimants for moneys it advanced to pay municipal taxes but not for moneys it advanced to pay fire insurance premiums on the buildings. The Court ruled that upon the mortgagee making the tax payment it became subrogated to the rights of the municipality which had a lien in priority to the mechanics' lienholders, but since the insurance company had no such priority over lien claimants the payment of the premiums could not confer any priority on the mortgagee. In *Can. Comstock Co. v. 186 King St. (London) Ltd.,* [1964] 2 O.R. 439 (C.A.), it was held that the lien claimants had priority over the final advance made under a mortgage since the advance had been made conditionally. The mortgagee had paid the final advance into a trust account under an agreement that the funds would only be used to pay for labour and materials supplied to complete the building. The funds were still in the trust account when the liens were registered. The Court held that this was not an "advance" within the meaning of section 14(1). In *Godden Lbr. Co. v. Morrow,* [1962] O.W.N. 17, it was held that a bonus stipulated for by the mortgagee in the form of an agreement by the mortgagor to repay more than the amount actually to be advanced under the mortgage was not earned until the whole of the principal less the bonus had been advanced. The lien claimant was accordingly given priority over the mortgage to the extent of the unadvanced principal and the bonus. On the authority of *London Loan & Savings Co. v. Meagher,* [1930] S.C.R. 378, it appears that the mortgagee will be entitled to priority over liens for a bonus in the mortgage provided he has advanced the whole of the principal sum secured by the mortgage prior to the registration of a claim for lien. Where a mortgagee made further advances on its mortgage after certain claims for lien had been vacated upon payment into Court of security therefor, it was held that the mortgagee had priority for such advances over the liens: *Nor. Elec. Co. v. Frank Warkentin Elec. Ltd.* (1972), 27 D.L.R. (3d) 519 (Man. C.A.).

§64 Assigned or Discounted Mortgages.

The assignee of the mortgage, whether it is prior or subsequent, will stand in exactly the same position as his assignor insofar as the lien claimants are concerned and this is so even though he has paid less than the face value of the mortgage for it. If, however, the assignee has purchased a mortgage which has not been fully advanced, he will have priority over the lien claimants only to the extent of the amount actually advanced: *Sparks &*

McKay v. Lord (1929), 63 O.L.R. 393; on appeal, see [1930] S.C.R. 351. This is so whether or not he purchased the mortgage at a discount. The assignee of a subsequent mortgage will, of course, have the protection given to future advances by any provisions of the Act similar to section 14(1) of the Ontario Act, discussed in §63, *ante*.

§65 Foreclosure by the Mortgagee.

The mortgagee may at any time commence foreclosure proceedings under his mortgage. It is unlikely that a subsequent mortgagee over whom the lien claimants have priority would do so, although there is nothing to prevent him. If mechanics' liens appear on the abstract of title the claimants will be made defendants in the writ, unless, in Ontario, Rule 465(2) of the Rules of Practice applies, in which event they will be added as defendants in the Master's Office and served with notice of the reference before the Master. A lien claimant who is served with such a notice before the trial of the mechanics' lien action will be entitled, in Ontario, to a stay of the foreclosure proceedings for 6 months to permit the claimant to obtain a judgment. He will file an affidavit (Form 12, *post*), asserting that he has a valid claim for lien, setting out the particulars and amount of the same and stating that either he or someone else has commenced an action or intends to commence an action which will preserve the lien. Upon obtaining judgment, the lienholders will then be permitted to prove their judgment in the foreclosure proceedings. It was held in *Dure v. Roed,* [1917] 1 W.W.R. 1395 (Man.), that the rights of lien claimants could not be adjudicated upon in a foreclosure action but could only be given effect to in an action brought to enforce their liens. See also: *Williamson v. Loonstra* (1973), 34 D.L.R. (3d) 275 (B.C.). If, at the time of the reference before the Master, the lien claimant has already obtained judgment, he will be entitled to redeem the property or request the usual period within which to redeem. The lien claimant may also, under the Ontario Rules of Practice, pay the usual security for costs into Court and obtain an order for the sale of the property. While the Court may grant a stay of the foreclosure proceedings to permit a sale in the lien action (*Dure v. Roed, supra*), it is doubtful that the Court has any power in a mechanics' lien action to stay foreclosure proceedings pending the trial of the lien action: *Hutson v. Valliers* (1892), 19 O.A.R. 154; *Toronto Gen. Trusts Corpn. v. Tharle* (1932), 41 O.W.N. 216. It was held in *Atlas Lbr. Co. v. Mfrs. Life Ins. Co.,* [1942] 3 W.W.R. 284 (Alta. C.A.), that in a mortgage foreclosure action brought in respect of property subject to a mechanics' lien, where a sale has been ordered in the foreclosure proceedings which proved to be abortive, or where the sale price was insufficient to pay the amount owing on the mortgage, the lienholder could be foreclosed.

As in any foreclosure action, the claim of a subsequent encumbrancer, such as a mechanics' lienholder, will be foreclosed eventually unless the lienholder redeems. The final order of foreclosure will free the title from the lien claims and there is no necessity in such circumstances to register any order vacating the liens or to obtain discharges of the same: see *Re Angus and Solloway Mills* (1932), 41 O.W.N. 36; *Re Irvine and Main,* [1933] O.W.N. 476; *Re Pridham,* [1934] O.W.N. 560; *Re Mtge. Discount Ltd. and Bushell* (1927), 32 O.W.N. 323, 430. In *Henderson v. Morris* (1916), 10 O.W.N. 34, where the lienholder had secured a judgment in the lien action to the effect that he had priority over the mortgage, it was held that his interest might still be foreclosed where he took no steps to obtain a sale of the property and that the statute did not oblige the mortgagee to realize the lienholder's claim by selling the property. In *Centennial Mtge. Corpn. v. Saratoga Travel Inn Ltd.* (1967), 59 W.W.R. 383 (Alta. C.A.), the Court dismissed the appeals of mechanics' lien claimants against a mortgage foreclosure order because the appellants had made no attempt to deal with their rights under The Mechanics' Lien Act. In *Indust. Dev. Bank v. Lees* (1969), 68 W.W.R. 476; reversed 75 W.W.R. 445 (Sask. C.A.), it was held that even after an order for foreclosure had been made, the Court could order a judicial sale under another statute.

In *Can. Permanent Trust Co. v. Welton Ltd.,* [1973] 2 O.R. 245 an injunction was issued restraining the plaintiff mortgagee from selling the property under the power of sale contained in its mortgage where its action for payment on the covenant and for possession of the property was still pending, following *Marshall v. Miles,* [1970] 3 O.R. 394. In the latter case a mortgagee was restrained from selling under the power of sale where he had commenced foreclosure proceedings and the mortgagor had given notice of his intention to redeem the mortgaged premises. In *Petranik v. Dale,* [1973] 2 O.R. 217, the Court of Appeal had ruled that where a mortgagor does not enter an appearance in the foreclosure proceedings or file a notice "desiring an opportunity to redeem" and the judgment *nisi* in the foreclosure action does not contain the usual clause permitting the mortgagor to redeem, the mortgagee can cease to proceed with the foreclosure action and sell the property under the power of sale contained in the mortgage. The Supreme Court of Canada reversed this decision, however, holding that, in such circumstances, the mortgagee could not sell the mortgaged property under the power of sale without the leave of the Court, since the mortgagor retains the right of redemption after a judgment *nisi* at least until final judgment has been signed: see *Petranik v. Dale,* [1977] 2 S.C.R. 959. In *Lee v. Guettler* (1975), 10 O.R. (2d) 257 (C.A.) it was held that a mortgagee who had given notice of her intention to sell the mortgaged premises under the power of sale clause in the mortgage, could not take any steps to recover possession of the premises during the period between the giving of the notice and the date when payment was to be made, and accordingly her action for possession, which had been commenced two days before the date specified in the notice for payment and in which she had obtained a default judgment, was a nullity.

This subject is more fully dealt with in Ontario in Marriott and Dunn, "Practice in Mortgage Actions in Ontario".

§66 Sale by the Mortgagee under the Power of Sale in the Mortgage.

This matter is dealt with in Chapter 7, Loss or Discharge of Lien, §85. As pointed out in that Chapter, there is no question of the right of a prior mortgagee to sell under the power of sale in the mortgage and to thus free the title from the liens, although any surplus realized on such a sale would have to be paid into Court to be distributed amongst lien claimants. In this connection, see *Atlas Lbr. Co. v. Mfrs. Life Ins. Co.,* [1942] 3 W.W.R. 284, varying [1942] 2 W.W.R. 114 (Alta. C.A.); *Finn v. Miller* (1889), 10 C.L.T. 23 (Ont.); *Re Pridham,* [1934] O.W.N. 560; *Hutson v. Valliers* (1892), 19 O.A.R. 154; *Re Mtge. Discount Ltd. and Bushell* (1927), 32 O.W.N. 323, 430. However, in *Biltmore Invts. Ltd. v. Mazur,* [1957] O.W.N. 468, the Court relied on the decision in *Sparks & McKay v. Lord,* 63 O.L.R. 393; on appeal see [1930] S.C.R. 351, in deciding, on a vendor and purchaser application, that a requisition for discharge of liens registered on title had not been satisfactorily answered by the vendor's statement that the liens were registered subsequent to the registration of the mortgage. Where the mechanics' lien trial has been disposed of and priorities fixed, there is no problem. However, the mortgagee might experience some considerable difficulty in finding a purchaser willing to take such title as he could pass on, prior to the trial, since the property might well be subject to a further sale in the mechanics' lien proceedings.

The practice, where the trial has not been had, is for the mortgagee to give notice to the lien claimants in accordance with the provisions of the Mortgages Act of his intention to sell the property under the power of sale clause in the mortgage. It is submitted that this does not in any way solve the problem since the mortgagee is really only advising the claimants that they may, if they wish, purchase the property themselves, and the question of priorities, and whether or not the mortgagee can pass on a good title free of the liens, is still undecided. It would appear that the wisest course for a purchaser from a mortgagee to follow in such circumstances would be for him to await the disposition of the mechanics' lien action, at which time the priorities will be fixed.

It was held in *Cut-Rate Plate Glass Co. v. Solodinski* (1915), 34 O.L.R. 604 (C.A.), that there was no provision in the Ontario Mechanics' Lien Act permitting the Court to order the sale of a mortgage to satisfy a lien having priority over it. It has been held in Ontario that there is no power in the

169

Court to restrain a mortgagee from exercising his right to sell under the power of sale in his mortgage simply because a lien claimant claims to have priority over his mortgage. See: *Re Comrie Lbr. Co. and Tomlinson Const. Services Ltd.* (1977), 15 O.R. (2d) 613.

The mortgagee is obliged to sell the mortgaged property at a reasonable price and, as previously pointed out, he will be liable to account to the lien claimants for any surplus realized on the sale, over and above the amount required to satisfy his claim on his mortgage. He would also be liable to them in damages if he sold the property at a price which was unreasonably low, or if he conducted the sale in a negligent manner. It has been held that a mortgagee was not negligent in conducting a sale under the power of sale where the sale was by auction, subject to a reserve bid, and the auctioneer announced the amount of the reserve bid prior to conducting the sale: see *Indust. Enterprises Inc. v. Schelstraete,* (1975), 54 D.L.R. (3d) 260, affirmed 8 N. & P.E.I.R. 438 (P.E.I. C.A.). See also in this connection, Mariott and Dunn, "Practice in Mortgage Actions in Ontario".

In *Hardy v. Munn* (1977), 18 N.B.R. (2d) 386 (C.A.) the plaintiff claimed a lien and sought personal judgment against both the original owner of the property involved and the party who purchased it under the power of sale in a mortgage. It appeared that the lien claimant had registered his lien subsequent to the registration of the mortgage, that the mortgage was for less than the appraised value of the property at the time it was made, and that the mortgage had been fully advanced prior to the registration of the lien. It was held that the mortgage had priority over the claim for lien under section 9(2) of the New Brunswick Act. The Court also found that the purchaser had acquired the property free of all subsequent interests by reason of section 47(1) of the New Brunswick Property Act which provides that a mortgagee exercising the power of sale conferred by section 44 of that Act may convey the property freed from all estates, interests and rights over which the mortgage has priority. Accordingly, the claim for a lien and the personal action against the new owner were dismissed. Personal judgment against the old owner was granted.

6

Obtaining a Lien

§67 In General.

As has already been pointed out, the lien itself arises by virtue of the doing of work or the furnishing of material or services, but it is kept alive by the registration of a claim for lien pursuant to the provisions of the statute. McDonald J., in *Curtis v. Richardson* (1909), 18 Man. R. 519 at 520, stated the position thus: "The lien is created as the work is done and not after its completion and the filing of a lien is only a means of preserving and enforcing it". Further, as was said by Hannon D.C.J., in *Nobbs and Eastman v. C.P.R.* (1913), 6 W.W.R. 759 at 761 (Sask.): "Sections creating the right to a lien are to be strictly construed, while provisions dealing with procedure on enforcement of the lien are to receive a broad and liberal construction". See also *Clarkson Co. v. Ace Lbr. Ltd.,* [1963] S.C.R. 110 at 114, reversing [1962] O.R. 748; *Granby Const. & Equipment Ltd. v. Player* (1964), 49 D.L.R. (2d) 658 (B.C.); *Inglewood Plumbing & Gasfitting Ltd. v. Northgate Dev. Ltd. (No. 1)* (1965), 54 W.W.R. 225 at 228 (Alta.); *Hett v. Samoth Realty Projects Ltd.* (1977), 76 D.L.R. (3d) 362 (Alta. C.A.). Accordingly, each of the Acts contains a curative section providing, as does section 18 of the Ontario Act, that a substantial compliance with the sections dealing with registration of the claim for lien and its contents is sufficient, and no lien is invalidated by reason of failure to comply with any of the requisites of these sections unless, in the opinion of the Judge trying the action, some person is prejudiced thereby and then only to the extent to which that party is prejudiced. Rimmer D.C.J., in *Montjoy v. Heward S. Dist.* (1908), 10 W.L.R. 282 at 285 (Sask.), expressed the opinion that "the registration and enforcement of the lien is, I consider, a matter of practice and procedure rather than a right". The curative section of the Act further provides that nothing in that section dispenses with registration of the claim for lien. Hence the claimant must register his claim for lien in order to preserve his lien unless he is protected as an unregistered claimant, by the provisions of either the Saskatchewan or Nova Scotia Acts which dispense with the requirement of registration where a certificate of action is registered by another claimant during the statutory period allowed the unregistered lien claimant for registration of his claim for lien: N.S., sec. 24; Sask., sec. 37(1).

§68 The Form of the Claim for Lien.

The form of the claim for lien is prescribed by each Act in much the same terms as are found in section 16(1) of the Ontario Act. In addition, all of the Acts, with the exception of Alberta, Newfoundland, New Brunswick and Ontario, contain statutory forms of the claim for lien. In Alberta, Newfoundland, New Brunswick and Ontario, the forms are prescribed by regulation: Ont., sec. 49; Alta., sec. 55(c); Nfld., sec. 50(1)(a); N.B., sec. 62. Three forms are usually provided: (Form 1), being the general form of claim for lien by one claimant claiming against one property for materials or services; (Form 2), for use by a wage earner claiming a lien for wages; and (Form 3), for use by several wage earners claiming liens for wages. While the form of the claim for lien is prescribed by the statute it is not inflexible and, as was held in *Crerar v. C.P.R.* (1903), 5 O.L.R. 383, the form used will be sufficient if it contains the information required by the statute and is to the same general effect. It was held in *Nobbs and Eastman v. C.P.R.* (1913), 6 W.W.R. 759 (Sask.), that the provisions of the statute relating to enforcement of the lien should receive a broad and liberal construction, and in *Barrington v. Martin* (1908), 16 O.L.R. 635 (C.A.) and *Man. Bridge, etc. Works Ltd. v. Gillespie* (1914), 5 W.W.R. 1210; affirmed 6 W.W.R. 1582 (Sask. C.A.), it was held that as long as the claimant gives the essentials of his claim, he will not be deprived of his lien on the ground of a lack of technical compliance with the directions of the Act. Also, section 27(d) of the Interpretation Act, R.S.O. 1970, c. 225 provides that: "where a form is prescribed, deviations therefrom not affecting the substance or calculated to mislead do not vitiate it".

It was held in three Ontario cases that even if a material omission had been made in the claim for lien, the Court could grant an amendment to rectify the mistake: *Barrington v. Martin, supra; Fairy and Stephenson v. Doner,* [1947] O.W.N. 217; *Simac v. Waltman,* [1947] O.W.N. 264, relying on the provisions of the curative section already mentioned. It was pointed out by the Court in the first of these cases that the claimant might be faced with three situations after registering his claim for lien. Either the claim complied with the statute, substantially complied with the statute, or did not substantially comply with the statute. In the second situation, the curative section corresponding to section 18(1) of the Ontario Act, renders the claim valid. That section will also render the claim valid in the third situation if no prejudice is caused to any other person, and even so, it will be invalid only to the extent of such prejudice. In *Rendall, MacKay, Michie Ltd. v. Warren* (1915), 8 W.W.R. 113 (Alta.), it was held that the word "prejudice" as used in this section should be defined as meaning "unjustly made to suffer". The onus is on the person claiming prejudice to prove it: see *Man. Bridge, etc. Works Ltd. v. Gillespie, supra; Polson v. Thomson* (1916), 10 W.W.R. 865 (Man. C.A.); *Richardson v. Lohn* (1932), 46 B.C.R. 224; *Robock v. Peters*

(1900), 13 Man. R. 124. While it was not necessary to decide the point in that case, Riddell J. in *Barrington v. Martin, supra,* expressed the opinion that the words "other person" used in the curative section should be interpreted according to the *ejusdem generis* rule and accordingly they do not apply to persons other than the claimant, who are themselves, and in competition with him, claiming a lien against the property.

As has been pointed out, while the curative section can relieve the claimant from irregularities in the claim for lien, it cannot relieve him from failure to register his claim for lien within the time limited by the Act or from failure to register against the proper property. In *Rafuse v. Hunter* (1906), 12 B.C.R. 126, the land sought to be charged was mis-described in the claim for lien and the Court refused to amend the claim for lien by correcting the description as that would, in effect, have created a new lien after the time limited for registration against that property had expired. See also *Stickelmann v. Switzer,* [1972] 2 W.W.R. 203 (Sask.). However, in *Walter F. Golding Const. Co. v. Bell* (1975), 13 N.B.R. (2d) 47, where the description in the lien covered part, but not all, of the land upon which the building stood, the Court permitted the plaintiff to amend the description in the statement of claim so as to include the balance of the land on the ground that no one had been seriously prejudiced and that even greater prejudice might result if the Court were to order a sale of only part of the land. It should be noted that the plaintiff in this case could have established a valid lien, since its claim for lien had been registered against the title to at least some of the lands in question. The inclusion in the description of the land of property against which there is no lien, along with lands on which the claimant does have a lien, will not invalidate the lien, however: *Modern Const. Co. v. Maritime Rock Products Ltd.,* [1963] S.C.R. 347. See also *St. Clair Const. Co. v. Farrell* (1921), 49 O.L.R. 201 (C.A.); *McCoubrey v. Carver Const. Co.,* [1942] 3 W.W.R. 648 (B.C.); *Union Drilling & Dev. Co. v. Capital Oil & Natural Gas Co.,* [1931] 1 W.W.R. 786; affirmed [1931] 2 W.W.R. 507 (Alta. C.A.); *McDonald v. McKenzie* (1914), 7 W.W.R. 604 (Alta.); *Cooper & Gibbard Elec. Co. v. Pine Fir Lbr. Co.* (1959), 27 W.W.R. 584 (B.C. C.A.); *Rodewalt v. Plasky* (1959), 30 W.W.R. 457 (Alta.).

In *Curtis v. Richardson* (1909), 18 Man. R. 519, and *Cooper & Gibbard Elec. Co. v. Pine Fir Lbr. Co., supra,* the Court pointed out that the provisions of the curative section of the Act refer only to the preceding sections dealing with the form of the claim for lien and what may be included in it. In *Monarch Lbr. Co. v. Garrison* (1911), 4 Sask. L.R. 514 (C.A.), the claim for lien did not appear to be properly executed under the seal of the plaintiff company, but the Court allowed proof of due execution to be made. However, in *Valley Const. Co. v. Eberle,* [1974] 5 W.W.R. 537 (Man.), a claim for lien by a foreign corporation which had not obtained the requisite licence to carry on business in the province was ordered vacated.

See also: *D-B Service (Western) Ltd. v. Madrid Services Ltd.* (1975), 60 D.L.R. (3d) 299 (B.C.); and *Suss Woodcraft Ltd. v. Abbey Glen Property Corpn.,* [1975] 5 W.W.R. 57 (Alta.). In *Alta. Lbr. Co. v. Yeats,* [1950] 1 W.W.R. 397 (Alta.), where the affidavit verifying the claim was not executed by a person having "personal knowledge" the Court held that there had been a "substantial compliance" within the meaning of the curative section and that such failure did not invalidate the lien. *Crown Lbr. Co. v. McTaggart Motors Ltd.* (1961), 34 W.W.R. 370 (Alta.), is to the same effect. In Ontario, however, it was held in *Bazarin v. Pezim,* [1965] 1 O.R. 606, where the affidavit verifying the claim was sworn by someone who did not have the required personal knowledge of the facts, that, even though there was no evidence that any person had been prejudiced thereby, there had not been a "substantial compliance" with section 16 so as to bring the remedial provisions of section 18 into operation. The Court also refused to grant the plaintiff a personal judgment: see also §70, *post.*

It was suggested in *Can. Sand etc. Co. v. Pool* (1907), 10 O.W.R. 1041, that, if the defendant failed to complain of an irregularity in the claim for lien until after the time limited for commencing the action had expired, he would be deemed to have waived it. There appears to be no authority for such a conclusion in the statute and from a practical point of view the commencement of the action may be the first notice which the defendant receives of the lien. In fact, the defendant may not become aware of the lien until he has been served with the statement of claim, and accordingly the time limited for commencing the action may have elapsed before he has any opportunity of discovering the irregularity. The following are some additional cases dealing with the curative section in the various Acts: *Chick Lbr. & Fuel Co. v. Moorehouse,* [1933] 3 W.W.R. 465, reversing [1933] 3 W.W.R. 168 (Man. C.A.); *Fitzgerald and Powell v. Apperley,* [1926] 2 W.W.R. 689 (Sask. C.A.); *Mallett v. Kovar* (1910), 14 W.L.R. 327 (Alta.); *High River Trading Co. v. Anderson* (1909), 10 W.L.R. 126 (Alta.); *Imperial Lbr. Yards Ltd. v. Saxton,* [1921] 3 W.W.R. 524 (Sask. C.A.); *Waisman, Ross & Associates v. Crown Trust Co.,* [1970] S.C.R. 553, reversing 67 W.W.R. 61; *Constable v. Belvedere Holdings (1962) Ltd.* (1966), 58 W.W.R. 96 (Y.T. C.A.); *Stickelmann v. Switzer,* [1972] 2 W.W.R. 203 (Sask.); *Peter Leitch Const. Ltd. v. Aquativity Ltd.,* [1971] 2 O.R. 666.

§69 Contents of Claim for Lien.

(a) *The Name and Address for Service or Residence of Claimant.*

The person named as the lien claimant in the claim for lien will be the person doing the work or supplying the materials, the assignee of such person, his trustee in bankruptcy or his personal representative. The person signing the claim will usually take the affidavit verifying the same. The sections of the various acts corresponding to section 16(2) of the Ontario Act, provide that the affidavit is to be taken by the claimant, his agent or assignee. It was held in *Triangle Storage Ltd. v. Porter,* [1941] 3 W.W.R. 892 (B.C. C.A.), that the assignment of the claim for lien need not be registered. Section 24 of the Ontario Act specifically provides that the right of a lienholder may be assigned by an instrument in writing and that if the lienholder dies his claim passes to his personal representative or representatives, as the case may be. If there is more than one personal representative of a deceased lien claimant, then all of their names must appear as claimants, although the claim may be signed, and the affidavit verifying the lien may be taken, by one of them.

In the case of an incorporated company, the name of the claimant is the proper name of the company. The lien should be signed by the proper signing officers and the corporate seal affixed. Alternatively, it should be signed by an employee of the company who has the requisite personal knowledge of the facts as agent for the company. In *Rodewalt v. Plasky* (1959), 30 W.W.R. 457 (Alta.), the Court held that a lien claim naming an individual in his personal capacity respecting work performed by his limited company was invalid and the defect was not curable under the curative section of the Act. It was held in *Inter Property Invt. Ltd. v. Trpchich* (1975), 11 O.R. (2d) 568, that a lien filed by a limited company for work which was done by the president of the company in his personal capacity was not a valid lien. In *Valley Const. Co. v. Eberle,* [1974] 5 W.W.R. 537 (Man.), it was held that a foreign corporation which had not obtained a licence to carry on business in Manitoba under The Corporations Act did not have any status to file a mechanics' lien.

In the case of a partnership the claim for lien should name all partners and indicate the style or firm name under which they carry on business. The claim may be signed by all partners or by one on his own behalf and as agent for the other members of the partnership. In the case of *Chick Lbr. & Fuel Co. v. Moorehouse,* [1933] 3 W.W.R. 465, reversing [1933] 3 W.W.R. 168 (Man. C.A.), the Court held that a claim for lien naming two of the three partners and indicating the firm name was a substantial compliance with the Act. The two partners were claiming a lien on behalf of the firm and when they signed same they did so as agents of the firm. The Court relied upon the curative section of the Act. In *Simac v. Waltman* [1947], O.W.N. 264, the claim for lien was neither in the firm name nor in the name of one of the partners on behalf of the firm, but named one individual partner and the action was brought in his name only. The Court held that although this infringed on the general rule in *Vipond v. Furness* (1916), 54 S.C.R. 521, in that all necessary parties were not before the Court, there had been no prejudice to the owner and the Court could overlook the defect upon the authority of the curative section of the Act. As a result, the Court amended the proceedings *nunc pro tunc* by adding the name of the other partner in the statement of claim and all subsequent proceedings. In *R. Bickerton & Co. v. Dakin* (1891), 20 O.R. 695, it was held that a claim for lien in the partnership name was sufficient compliance with the requirements of the Act and also that a lien registered after the dissolution of the partnership (due to the death of one of the partners) was valid: Meredith J. at page 703: "It was never intended that the benefits of the Act should be frittered away by requiring the skill of a special pleader to secure them." The result was similar in *Waisman, Ross & Associates v. Crown Trust Co.,* [1970] S.C.R. 553, reversing 67 W.W.R. 61, where the claim for lien was filed in the firm name employed by a partnership. While agreeing with the Alberta Court of Appeal that a firm as such was not a legal entity, the Supreme Court of Canada pointed out that the use of the firm name was a convenient and usual way of describing the individual members who collectively make up the firm, and its use was equivalent to naming the partners. It concluded that if the claim for lien did not perfectly comply with the requirements of the Act, the use of the firm name was a substantial compliance with them, sufficient to bring it within the curative section of the Alberta Act, with the result that the lien was held to be valid.

It is better practice, in the case of a partnership, to make it clear in the claim for lien that all partners are before the Court and, in Ontario at least, to comply with the provisions of The Partnership Act of Ontario, and Rules 102 and 110 of the Ontario Rules of Practice. The Ontario Rules of Practice govern the procedure to be followed in proving a claim for lien unless The Mechanics' Lien Act specifies some other form of procedure: Ont., sec. 46(4).

In the case of a sole proprietorship, the claim for lien should name the individual and the firm name under which he carries on business. In *Metro Woodworking v. Phales Invt. Ltd.,* [1960] O.W.N. 132 (C.A.), a claim for lien in the name of "Metro Woodworking" was held to be a nullity since the claimant as described was not a legal entity. But see *O.C. Couch Plumbing, Heating and Sheet Metal v. Target Textiles,* [1969] 1 O.R. 735 (C.A.), where the lien claimant was an individual but the words "plumbing, heating and sheet metal" were added after his name in the lien and the style of cause. The Court held that the inclusion of these words was mere surplusage, which had not misled anyone, and that the name should be amended as a matter of course.

In the case of a joint claim for lien by more than one person, the form corresponding to Form 3 contained in most of the Acts should be used and either all of the claimants will sign at the foot of the claim, or one of them will sign for himself and as agent for the others.

All of the Acts, with the exception of the British Columbia and Nova Scotia Acts, require that the claim for lien shall set out an address for service for the person claiming the lien: Ont., sec. 16(1); P.E.I., sec. 20(5); Sask., sec. 30(2). This provision is relatively new in the Ontario and Newfoundland Acts. Section 47 of the Ontario and Newfoundland Acts provides that, except where otherwise directed by the Court, all documents relating to the action other than statements of claim and notices of trial, will be sufficiently served if they are sent by registered mail addressed to the intended recipient at his address for service. It is therefore important to include the proper street or post office address of the lien claimant in the claim for lien. In those provinces where the claimant has to include an address for service, it is submitted that the failure to do so should not invalidate the lien, as the curative section should be available to rectify the defect. Nevertheless it may cause the claimant to lose an opportunity to appeal or object to the granting of an interlocutory order, if the person serving notice of the same is unable to serve the claimant by registered mail. In such circumstances the Court might well find that the claimant was not entitled to notice of the proceedings, or alternatively, might assess the costs of service by other means against the claimant.

In those provinces where the claimant does not have to include an address for service in his claim, the failure to include his street or post office address will not invalidate the lien. In *Barrington v. Martin* (1908), 16 O.L.R. 635 (C.A.), the word "Toronto" and in *Dufton v. Horning* (1895), 26 O.R. 252, the words "Hamilton, in the county of Wentworth" were held to sufficiently set out the residence of the claimant. In *Crerar v. C.P.R.* (1903), 5 O.L.R. 383, the plaintiffs were day labourers who did work for the defendants on a railway in an unorganized district and they described themselves as residing in that district. The Court held that this was sufficient, particularly in view of the fact that the name and address of the plaintiffs' solicitor was also stated in the claim for lien. In *Anderson v. Godsal* (1900), 7 B.C.R. 404 (C.A.), the Court held that the residence of the claimant was sufficiently stated in the case of a person residing in a small town such as Nelson by using the words "residing in Nelson", and in *Irwin v. Beynon* (1886), 4 Man. R. 10 (C.A.), by use of the words "of the Town of Minnedosa". Where the claim for lien is filed by a solicitor, the solicitor's name and address should appear on the claim as well.

(b) *The Name and Residence of the Owner or Person Believed to be the Owner.*

The curative section is available to rectify errors in the claim for lien with respect to the name of the owner. Provided no one is prejudiced, the failure to name anyone as owner in the claim for lien will not be fatal and an amendment may be permitted at a later stage of the proceedings to cure the omission: see *Man. Bridge, etc. Works Ltd. v. Gillespie* (1914), 5 W.W.R.

1210; affirmed 6 W.W.R. 1582 (Sask. C.A.) and *Fairy and Stephenson v. Doner,* [1947] O.W.N. 217. It was held in *Barrington v. Martin* (1908), 16 O.L.R. 635 (C.A.), where the claim for lien was made out on a printed form and was against the contractor for the erection of certain buildings of which the claimant believed him to be the owner, although in fact he was not, that the claim against the contractor was sufficient since the Act merely required it to be made against the owner or person believed to be the owner. This decision was cited with approval in *Fairy and Stephenson v. Doner, supra,* where the Court took the position that registration of a claim for lien on the title to the property involved was good notice to the owners, whoever they might be, that a lien had been claimed against their property. It would seem that so long as the person named as owner is believed to be the owner by the claimant, no problem arises and even if there is not sufficient grounds for believing that the person named is the owner, the curative section is available to rectify the defect in the claim for lien unless some person is prejudiced and even then only to the extent of such prejudice: see *Bradshaw v. Saucerman* (1913), 3 W.W.R. 761, affirming 21 W.L.R. 65 (Y.T. C.A.); *Irwin v. Beynon* (1886), 4 Man. R. 10 (C.A.); *Foster v. Brocklebank* (1915), 8 W.W.R. 464 (Alta.); *Nobbs and Eastman v. C.P.R.* (1913), 6 W.W.R. 759 (Sask.); *Polson v. Thomson* (1916), 10 W.W.R. 865 (Man. C.A.); *Laurentian Bldg. Co-op Ltd. v. Johnnie's Plumbing & Heating Ltd.,* [1976] W.W.D. 148 (Sask.). The claim, or the style of cause, however, cannot be amended so as to include the proper name of the owner after the time limited for bringing the action has expired because to do so would, in effect, revive a cause of action which had expired: see *Metals Recovery Co. v. Molybdenum Products Co.* (1919), 46 O.L.R. 532 (C.A.); *Arnold Lbr. Ltd. v. Vodouris,* [1968] 2 O.R. 478; *Rocca Steel Ltd. v. Tower Hill Apts. Ltd.,* [1968] 2 O.R. 701; *E.E. McCoy Co. v. Venus Elec. Ltd.* (1977), 19 N.B.R. (2d) 299. See further Chapter 11, Practice Before Trial, §135.

It was held in *Bradshaw v. Saucerman, supra* and *Whaley v. Linnenbank* (1915), 36 O.L.R. 361 (C.A.), that it is not necessary to name a mortgagee having an estate or interest in the land to be charged in the claim for lien, even if it is intended to claim priority over the interest of such mortgagee. The mortgagee can be brought into the proceedings subsequently in the statement of claim.

(c) A Short Description of the Work, Service or Materials.

The description of work, services or materials includes work and service which has already been done or which is yet to be done and in the case of materials includes materials already furnished or yet to be furnished. The purpose of including this information in the claim for lien is merely to advise the owner briefly of the nature and scope of the claimant's claim and it is not necessary to give full particulars or furnish a statement of account.

In the western provinces, very little detail is required. In *Bradshaw v. Saucerman, supra,* the words "for wages for work and labour done and performed on and in respect of said mining claims" were held to be a sufficient description of the work. Similar wording was held to be sufficient in *Foster v. Brocklebank, supra* and *Irwin v. Beynon, supra.* It was held in *Bradshaw v. Saucerman, supra,* and in *Brown v. Allan* (1913), 4 W.W.R. 1306 (B.C. C.A.), that a claim for lien should not be rejected merely because the claim for lien described materials for which the claimant did not have a lien, and that in such circumstances the claimant should be permitted to establish that he was entitled to a lien for some lesser part of the claim. In Ontario it would appear that the nature of the work, services or materials supplied should be properly, but briefly, set out in the claim for lien. In *Barrington v. Martin* (1908), 16 O.L.R. 635 (C.A.), the statement "materials supplied" was held not to be a substantial compliance with the Act although the lien was held valid under the curative section, no prejudice having been occasioned thereby.

(d) *The Name and Residence of the Person for Whom the Work or Service was Done or Materials Furnished.*

These words refer to the person with whom the claimant dealt directly and not necessarily to the general contractor or the person who has his contract directly from the owner. For example, in a claim by a material supplier who supplied materials to a subcontractor, the material supplier will name the subcontractor in the claim for lien and it is not necessary for him to name the general contractor even though he is the person who retains the statutory holdback out of which that material supplier's claim will ultimately be satisfied. The claimant's position if he incorrectly names, or omits to name, the person for whom the work was done is governed by the same principles which have already been discussed under sub-heading (b), ante.

(e) *The Time within which the Work was Done or was to be Done, or the Materials were Furnished or were to be Furnished.*

If the work has been completed or the contract has been abandoned then the date of completion or of the doing of the last work will be shown. If all of the materials have been supplied then the date of the last delivery of materials will be shown. However, if the claim for lien is filed at the commencement of, or during the course of the work, or during the course of supplying materials, then the anticipated date of completion or supply of the last materials is the date to be shown in the claim for lien. In any event, as was held in *Imperial Lbr. Yards Ltd. v. Saxton,* [1921] 3 W.W.R. 524 (Sask.

C.A.), if the wrong date is stated in the claim for lien, the lien will not be invalidated where no person has been prejudiced and even if some prejudice can be shown, only to the extent of the same. It was held in *Barrington v. Martin* (1908), 16 O.L.R. 635 (C.A.) and in *McNamara v. Hanley*, [1955] 4 D.L.R. 30 (N.B.), that it is not necessary to give the date of the commencement of the lien and that it was sufficient to state that the work was done or the materials were supplied on or before a named date. This statement is supported by the decisions in *Flack v. Jeffrey* (1895), 10 Man. R. 514; *Truax v. Dixon* (1889), 17 O.R. 366 (C.A.); *Irwin v. Beynon* (1886), 4 Man. R. 10 (C.A.). In *Holden v. Bright Prospects Gold Mining, etc. Co.* (1898), 6 B.C.R. 439 (C.A.), a statement in the claim for lien that the work was finished or discontinued "on or about a certain date" was held to be sufficient.

(*f*) *The Sum Claimed as Due or to Become Due.*

Where the contract is completed or the claimant does not contemplate doing any further work, the amount to be stated is the amount presently due to the claimant. Where the contract is not complete, and the claimant does contemplate doing further work, then the amount to be stated should be the total contract price less any payment received on account. In the latter case, or where materials are being supplied by a prevenient arrangement, the amount actually owing will be subject to increase as the work progresses or the materials are supplied or, alternatively, subject to decrease as the payments are received. Again, the curative section is available to validate the lien where it subsequently appears that the amount stated is incorrect. It is difficult to see how prejudice can result where the amount actually owing is less than the amount claimed in the lien, although prejudice could result where the amount owing subsequently turns out to be more than the amount claimed in the lien. Any error in amount in the claim for lien should be corrected when the action is commenced. It was pointed out in *Bradshaw v. Saucerman* (1913), 3 W.W.R. 761, affirming 21 W.L.R. 65 (Y.T. C.A.); *Brown v. Allan* (1913), 4 W.W.R. 1306 (B.C. C.A.) and *Montjoy v. Heward S. Dist.* (1908), 10 W.L.R. 282 (Sask.), that, even if the claimant was unable to establish a claim for part of the amount mentioned in the claim for lien, he should not be prevented from establishing some part of the claim merely because the amount mentioned was too large. Even assuming that the claiming of too much money was held not to be a substantial compliance with the section governing the contents of the claim for lien then *Fairy and Stephenson v. Doner,* [1947] O.W.N. 217; and *Barrington v. Martin* (1908), 16 O.L.R. 635 (C.A.), are authority for the proposition that the lien would be invalidated only to the extent of any prejudice caused to the persons objecting.

(g) A Description of the Land Sufficient for the Purpose of Registration.

The Ontario Act requires that the claim for lien contain "a description of the land as required by The Land Titles Act or The Registry Act and the regulations thereunder, as the case may be": sec. 16(1)(*d*). Accordingly, where the land to be charged is registered under The Land Titles Act, the claim for lien must contain a reference to the parcel number of the land and to the register in which such land is registered in the Land Titles office. The amount of land to be included in the description will depend upon the facts of each case: see *Wentworth Lbr. Co. v. Coleman* (1904), 3 O.W.R. 618 (C.A.); *Sparks & McKay v. Lord,* 63 O.L.R. 393; affirmed (*sub nom. Steedman v. Sparks & McKay*) [1930] S.C.R. 351. However, apart from the risk of having to defend an action for slander of title, it is far better to describe too much land than too little.

Most of the Acts provide that the land to be charged is that upon which the work is done, the services are performed or on which the materials are placed and, "the land occupied thereby or enjoyed therewith". For example, in *Wray & Sons Ltd. v. Stewart,* [1958] O.W.N. 65 (C.A.), the defendant owned land comprised of two adjoining parcels separated by a ditch, but there was no boundary line fence or other obstruction to prevent the two parcels being used by the owner as though they constituted one parcel. The company had erected on the first parcel buildings constituting the main plant of the company including one used as a dryer. The company employed the plaintiff to erect a new dryer on the second parcel some 235 feet from the boundary line and the plaintiff filed its lien against the first parcel only. It was held that because the new building replaced one used and enjoyed by the company as part of its main plant on the first parcel, and because of the use of each of the two buildings in conjunction with the other, that the new building was used as an integral part of the whole plant. The use of the new building was not separate or severable from the use of the old plant and accordingly the lien was valid although not filed against the parcel upon which the work had actually been done. See also the similar result in *Crown Lbr. Co. v. McTaggart Motors Ltd.* (1961), 34 W.W.R. 370 (Alta.). It was, however, held in *Sparks & McKay v. Lord, supra,* that the fact that an owner has acquired two connected parcels of land by a single conveyance and has included it all in one or more mortgages does not necessarily entitle a lienholder who has done work on part of it to a lien on the whole parcel. It was held in *Beseloff v. White Rock Resort Dev. Co.* (1915), 8 W.W.R. 1338 (B.C. C.A.), that a lien might be had on the whole of a town site, excluding public streets, for work done in clearing the town site. In *Bldrs. Supply Co. v. Huddlestone* (1915), 25 Man. R. 718, it was held that The Mechanics' Lien Act did not permit the registration of one lien against the lands of different owners even though the work might have been done under one contract for the building of houses on a series of lots. In *Clarke v. Moore* (1908), 1 Alta. L.R. 50, it was held that the words "land ... occupied thereby or enjoyed therewith", are not necessarily restricted to the lot upon which the building actually stands, but will include other lots which are intended to be used with the building. In *Security Lbr. Co. v. Anaka*, [1927] 1 W.W.R. 975 (Sask. C.A.), the Court held that the question as to whether the lien will attach to land in addition to that occupied by the building, as land "enjoyed therewith", is a question of fact in each case. It was held, further, that one test to be applied in determining this is do the two parcels, as used by the owner, constitute a single unit, both being "operated together and for a common purpose, and was the building calculated to facilitate that common purpose and intended to benefit the whole?" This test was approved by the Court in *Nor. Elec. Co. v. Frank Warkentin Elec. Ltd.* (1972), 27 D.L.R. (3d) 519 (Man. C.A.). It was held in *McIlrath Lbr. Co. v. Bloor,* [1942] 3 W.W.R. 573 (Sask. C.A.), that the onus is on the lien claimant, seeking to establish that a parcel of farm land owned by a wife contiguous to a parcel owned by her husband is enjoyed with the husband's parcel so as to give him a lien on both, to show by clear and unequivocal evidence that the two parcels were operated as a unit or that they were enjoyed together.

If too much land is described in the claim for lien the claimant will be entitled to a lien upon the land which should have been described and such an error will not invalidate the lien: see *Polson v. Thomson* (1916), 10 W.W.R. 865 (Man. C.A.); *Beseloff v. White Rock Resort Dev. Co.* (1915), 8 W.W.R. 1338 (B.C. C.A.); *Ont. Lime Assn. v. Grimwood* (1910), 22 O.L.R. 17; *Modern Const. Co. v. Maritime Rock Products Ltd.,* [1963] S.C.R. 347. However, if no land is described or if the wrong land is described, the lien will be invalid and the curative section is unavailable to the claimant to cure the defect once the time for registration of the lien has expired: see *McDonald v. McKenzie* (1914), 7 W.W.R. 604 (Alta.); *Stickelmann v. Switzer,* [1972] 2 W.W.R. 203 (Sask.); *Squeo v. Del Bianco,* [1976] W.W.D. 38 (B.C.); *N. S. Sand & Gravel Ltd. v. Kidstone Estates Ltd.* (1973), 13 N.S.R. (2d) 431, and *Rafuse v. Hunter; McDonald v. Hunter* (1906), 12 B.C.R. 126, where it was pointed out that to give leave to amend by correcting the description in such circumstances would result in the creating of a lien which had already expired. However, in *Walter F. Golding Const. Co. v. Bell* (1975), 13 N.B.R. (2d) 47, where it appeared that the description in the lien covered part, but not all, of the lands occupied by the building for which the plaintiff's materials had been supplied, the Court granted a motion to amend the statement of claim by including the description of the balance of the land on the ground that no one had been seriously prejudiced by the plaintiff's failure to include the full description of the property in its claim for lien and that even greater prejudice might result if the Court were to order a sale of only part of the land upon which the building stood.

In *Christie v. Mead* (1888), 8 C.L.T. 312 (N.W.T.), it was held that, where the Act did not otherwise provide, a description in the claim for lien which merely identified the land on which the lien was claimed would be sufficient. In that case the description stated the size of the lot, that it was situated in the Village of Pincher Creek east of K's private residence, being the second house west of the Methodist Church, now occupied by the defendant, and on which the plaintiff had done his work. But regard must now be had to the provisions of the appropriate Registry Act regarding present day requirements as to descriptions in documents which will be accepted for registration.

Section 29 of the Alberta Act provides that a lien claimant who registers his lien against the wrong land, or the wrong estate or interest in the land, will be liable for legal and other costs as well as damages incurred by or resulting to the owner of the land or of the estate or interest in the land by reason of such wrongful registration of the lien. It was also held in *Guilford Indust. Ltd. v. Hankinson Management Services Ltd.* (1974), 40 D.L.R. (3d) 398 (B.C.), that the malicious filing of an unfounded claim to a mechanics' lien in order to extort a settlement of a dispute from the owner was an actionable tort and, in an appropriate case, the Court would award exemplary damages against the lien claimant. Exemplary damages of $10,000.00 were awarded to the owner in this case as well as general damages. See also, in this connection, *MacFarlane v. R.,* [1973] 2 O.R. 325, where damages were awarded to the owner of the property against the title to which the Minister of Highways wrongfully registered a plan of intent. However, since the Court found that the acts of the defendants' servants were well meaning, although misguided, no exemplary damages were awarded.

While it was held in *Beseloff v. White Rock Resort Dev. Co.* (1915), 8 W.W.R. 1338 (B.C. C.A.), that work done on the streets of a subdivision gave rise to a lien upon the whole subdivision, such would not be the case where the streets had been dedicated so as to become "public streets" within the meaning of the Act. Most of the Acts provide that their provisions shall not extend to any public street or highway: Alta., sec. 5(1); B.C., sec. 4; N.B., sec. 2. In *Niagara Concrete Pipe Ltd. v. Charles R. Stewart Const. Co.,* [1956] O.W.N. 769, claimants sought to establish a lien on the lots adjoining the streets on which the work had been done, on the ground that the installation of lateral connections to the sewers under the streets benefited the adjoining lots, and it was held that no lien could exist for the doing of such work because of this section. This decision was followed in *Canron Ltd. v. Willen Estates Ltd.* (1977), 80 D.L.R. (3d) 38 (B.C.). In Ontario and Newfoundland the holdback provisions of the Act are now applicable to contracts for work on streets and highways, although the registration of liens against the title to streets or highways is still prohibited: Ont., sec. 5(2); Nfld., sec. 6(1). See also §17, *ante* and §78, *post.*

Most of the Acts provide that, where the lien is claimed against railway lands, it is sufficient to describe the land to be charged as the land of the railway company without any further description: *e.g.,* Ont., sec. 16(3); P.E.I., sec. 20(7); Alta., sec. 25(4).

(h) *The Date of Expiry of the Period of Credit.*

When a period of credit has been given to the person primarily liable to the lien claimant, then the time for commencing the action to realize the lien is extended, and commences to run from the date of expiry of the period of credit where such period is mentioned in the claim for lien. The time prescribed by the Act for registering the claim for lien itself is not extended, however. The lien claimant will not be entitled to enforce his lien until the period of credit has expired although if an action is commenced by some other person to enforce a lien against the same property he may nevertheless prove and obtain payment of his claim in that action as if the period of credit had expired: see Ont., secs. 16(1)(*e*), 23, 27; N.B., sec. 20(2)(*f*), 27, 31(3); N.S., secs. 18(1)(e), 25(1), 30. The P.E.I. Act contains similar provisions, but requires the claimant to commence his action and take no further steps in the proceedings until the period of credit expires: P.E.I., secs. 20(2)(*f*), 28, 32(3)(4). The Acts of Alberta, British Columbia and Saskatchewan have no such provisions respecting the extension of the time to commence an action.

If the period of credit takes the form of periodic payments on account, the due dates and amounts of these payments should be set forth in the claim for lien since the claimant will be entitled on default of one payment to enforce his lien for the outstanding balance: see *Spears v. Bannerman* (1907), 1 Alta. L.R. 98, where it was held that the words in section 7 of the former Alberta Act, "no further proceedings shall be taken in the action until after such extension of time", were to be construed distributively and accordingly default in the payment of any one of the deferred payments entitled the lienholder to take further proceedings. See also *Nor. Lbr. Mills Ltd. v. Rice* (1917), 41 O.L.R. 201 (C.A.). Where the period of credit took the form of monthly payments, with the condition that in the event of default of any one payment the whole balance would forthwith become payable without notice or demand, it was held that the lien claimant could not overlook the default and, in effect, unilaterally extend the period of credit beyond the time of default: *Armitage v. Beaver Lbr. Co.,* [1973] 1 O.R. 418. See also §72, *post.*

The period of credit must have been mutually agreed upon and an unsolicited extension of time by the lien claimant alone will not give rise to the extension contemplated by the Act: *Koecher v. Hirano,* [1969] 2 O.R. 300.

§70 The Affidavit Verifying the Claim for Lien.

The claim for lien must be verified by the affidavit of the person claiming the lien or his agent or assignee having a personal knowledge of the matters required to be verified. The affidavit of an agent or of an assignee must state specifically that he has such personal knowledge: Ont., sec. 16(2); Nfld., sec. 18(2); N.B., sec. 20(3), (4). In Alberta and British Columbia, the agent may also swear to facts of which he is informed provided he discloses the source of his information and states that he believes the facts to be true: B.C., sec. 22(4); Alta., sec. 25(7). The form of the affidavit verifying the claim for lien is prescribed by the Act or by the regulations made under it. It was held in *Kydd Bros. v. Taylor*, [1932] 3 W.W.R. 109 (B.C.), and *Bazarin v. Pezim*, [1965] 1 O.R. 606 (C.A.), that where an affidavit in support of a claim is made by an agent of the claimant who has no personal knowledge of the facts stated, the affidavit is fatally defective and the curative section is not available to rectify such a defect. It was further held in *Kydd Bros v. Taylor, supra,* that a bookkeeper whose only knowledge is the inferences drawn by him from the invoice slips which he had entered in his employer's books could not be said to have the required "personal knowledge". In *Jaasma v. Registrar of Titles,* [1974] 4 W.W.R. 673 (B.C.) it was held that in the case of proceedings under section 26(2) of the British Columbia Act the notice to the claimant, which that section then required must be "substantially in the Form 2 set out in the Schedule" to the Act, might be signed by an agent of the owner, such as his solicitor, even though the section stated that the owner was to send the notice and Form 2 provided for signature by the owner, with the word "owner" printed below the place of signature. That section and Form 2 have since been amended so as to provide that the notice may be signed by an agent as well as the owner himself. In *McArthur & Co. v. Fagan,* [1928] 2 W.W.R. 6 (B.C. C.A.), it was held that an affidavit made by an agent partly from personal knowledge, but in some essentials from information and belief, was not sufficient. In *Re King Petroleum Ltd.* (1973), 2 O.R. (2d) 192, the Court, ruling on a preliminary objection to the granting of a receiving order under The Bankruptcy Act based on the fact that the person who swore the affidavit of verification of the petition did not have the required personal knowledge of the facts alleged in the petition, held that the affidavit was sufficient even though the person who swore the affidavit relied on reports from other employees of the petitioning company for statements that he swore to in the petition. Houlden J. at p. 195 stated, "One would expect in a company the size of Imperial Oil that various persons would be working on an account. Providing the person who swears the affidavit of verification has knowledge of the account and has taken the time to familiarize himself with what others in the company have done, I think the requirements of s. 25(3) of the *Bankruptcy Act,* R.S.C. 1970, c. B-3, are satisfied". It is submitted that in the case of many large corporations engaged in the construction industry it would be virtually impossible to find one employee in the organization who had personal knowledge of all of the facts contained in the claim for lien and, accordingly, the approach adopted by Houlden J. in the preceding case ought to be adopted in determining whether or not the person swearing the affidavit verifying the claim for lien as agent for the lien claimant has sufficient knowledge of those facts. It was held in *Alta. Lbr. Co. v. Yeats,* [1950] 1 W.W.R. 397 (Alta.) and *Crown Lbr. Co. v. McTaggart Motors Ltd.* (1961), 34 W.W.R. 370 (Alta.), that the failure to have the affidavit verifying the claim executed by a person having "personal knowledge" did not invalidate the lien in view of the provisions of the curative section, there being no evidence that anyone had been prejudiced by such failure. (For a comment on the decision in *Bazarin v. Pezim, supra,* see article by H. G. Bristow, 1964-65 Vol. 13, Chitty's Law Journal, p. 261). In *Crerar v. C.P.R.* (1903), 5 O.L.R. 383, the Court held that the affidavit verifying the statement of claim required by the Act might be made by the plaintiff's solicitor as agent.

While it is only necessary that the affidavit state that the claim for lien is true and in the case of an agent or assignee that he has full knowledge of the facts set out in it, the omission of an affidavit would probably invalidate the lien. The lien was held to be invalid on this ground in *Central and N.S. Trust Co. v. Laurentide Financial Corpn.* (1976), 15 N.B.R. (2d) 122. In *Hirsch Const. Ltd. v. Marzolf; Hirsch Const. Ltd. v. Myshrall,* [1975] W.W.D. 139 (Sask.), where the plaintiff issued and served an originating notice in the form prescribed by the Act but without filing an affidavit in support of the claim, in accordance with the usual practice, the action was dismissed.

While there are conflicting decisions on the point, it would appear that the affidavit verifying the claim for lien may be sworn before the claimant's own solicitor in most jurisdictions. In *Geo. D. McLean & Assoc. Ltd. v. Leth,* [1949] 4 D.L.R. 282; affirmed (*sub nom. McLean v. Leth*) [1950] 2 D.L.R. 238 (B.C. C.A.), a lien was held to be invalid on this ground. However, the British Columbia Act has since been amended and section 22(2) of that Act now provides that "no affidavit of claim of lien shall be held to be defective or void" solely on this ground. Section 49(4) of the Newfoundland Act gives the same result. In *Clarkson Const. Co. v. Shaw,* [1950] O.W.N. 196, the Court held that while such an affidavit might not be capable of being used, the curative section applied to such a situation and the lien was not thereby invalidated. The same decision was reached in Alberta in *Hutchinson v. Berridge,* [1922] 2 W.W.R. 710 and in Manitoba in *Polson v. Thomson* (1916), 10 W.W.R. 865 (C.A.). In New Brunswick, however, in *Burchill v. Marino,* [1951] 2 D.L.R. 518; *Lewis v. Armstrong Bros.* (1957), 18 D.L.R. (2d) 718 (C.A.) and *R. V. Demmings & Co. v. Caldwell Const. Co.* (1955), 4 D.L.R. (2d) 465 (C.A.), the Court held that affidavits verifying the claim for lien and the statement of claim in a lien action should not be sworn before the solicitor for the claimant, and if they were the lien would be invalidated. However, in *R. V. Demmings & Co. v. Caldwell Const. Co., supra,* the New Brunswick Court of Appeal held that it was open to the court, even on appeal, to allow correction of the fault by having the affidavit resworn.

Most of the Acts further provide that any number of persons claiming liens upon the same property may join in one claim for lien. But where more than one lien is included in one claim, each claim for lien must be verified by affidavit: *e.g.* Ont., sec. 17; P.E.I., sec. 21; Sask., sec. 32. However, if one of the several claimants had personal knowledge of the claims of his co-claimants, the affidavit would appear to be sufficient, if taken by that claimant for himself personally and as agent for the other claimants, so long as the affidavit specified that he had personal knowledge of the claims of each of the other claimants. Similarly, in the case of a firm or partnership, any one of the partners may take the affidavit stating that he has personal knowledge of the facts stated in the claim, all of the partners being named in the claim for lien as joint lienors if such is the case: see *Waters v. Goldberg,* 124 App. Div. N.Y. 511. In Ontario, if the claim has been assigned, the affidavit verifying the claim for lien must be taken by the assignee of the claim, according to the decision in *Grant v. Dunn* (1883), 3 O.R. 376. If the assignee lacks personal knowledge of the claim, it is submitted that the assignee should have the affidavit taken by his assignor as agent and rely on the curative section.

Section 38(10) of the Ontario Act and section 38(9) of the Newfoundland Act permit any party to the action, or any other interested person, to obtain an order allowing him to cross-examine the lien claimant or his agent or assignee on the affidavit verifying the claim. The transcript of that examination can be used on a motion to discharge the lien, if the affiant does not have the requisite personal knowledge of the facts. It was held in *Kleenaire Equipment Ltd. v. Dennis Commercial Properties Ltd.,* [1970] 3 O.R. 776, that proper grounds for dismissing a claim might be found on the cross-examination of a lien claimant under this section, although in the circumstances of that case the Court refused to do so because, owing to the inconclusive answers given to some of the questions asked on the cross-examination, it could not be said that there was no triable issue to be dealt with on the trial of the claim. In *Re Pecco Cranes (Can.) Ltd.,* [1973] 3 O.R. 737, the Master held that he had no jurisdiction to make an order for the cross-examination of the deponent of an affidavit verifying the claim for lien before the action had been referred to him, and in any event, such an order cannot be made under section 38(10) until after an action has been commenced to enforce the lien.

§71 Registration of the Claim for Lien.

(a) Place of Registration.

Normally the claim for lien will be registered in the appropriate Registry Office where the title to the lands to be charged is recorded. If the title to the lands affected is recorded in more than one Registry or Land Titles Office then the claim for lien will be registered in each of the offices in which it is recorded. In Ontario, in the case of railways, the lien will be registered in the General Register in the office of the Registry Division within which the lien is claimed to have arisen: sec. 16(3). In Prince Edward Island (sec. 20(7)), New Brunswick (sec. 20(7)), and Nova Scotia (sec. 18(3)), a claim of lien against a railway is registered in the Registry Office of every county within which the lien is claimed to have arisen. It was held in *Peter Leitch Const. Ltd. v. Aquativity Ltd.,* [1971] 2 O.R. 666, that a claim for lien could be registered against unpatented land.

In the western provinces, a different registration procedure applies with respect to liens against mineral bearing lands. In Manitoba such a lien, if no grant of land has been made by the Crown, is registered in the Office of the Recorder of the Mining District in which the land is situated: sec. 14(5). In Saskatchewan such a claim for lien, where it involves property held from or under the Crown, is to be filed with "the Records Officer, Department of Mineral Resources at the City of Regina" instead of with the Registrar of Land Titles: sec. 35(1). In British Columbia, in the case of mining property held under The Mineral Act or The Placer-mining Act other than a Crown-granted mineral claim, the lien is filed in the nearest Court Registry of the County or Counties in which the land or any part thereof is situate. A copy is also filed in the Office of the Mining Recorder in which the mining property or land is recorded and, if the property is registered in a Land Registry Office, a copy is filed there as well: sec. 25(1). In Alberta, section 26(5) provides that where the lien attaches to an estate or interest in minerals held directly from the Crown in right of Alberta, and the estate or interest is less than a fee simple estate, which is not registered under The Land Titles Act, the statement of lien is to be registered with the Minister of Energy and Natural Resources and not with the Registrar. It was held in *Molner v. Stanolind Oil & Gas Co.,* [1959] S.C.R. 592, affirming (*sub nom. Crown Lbr. Co. v. Stanolind Oil & Gas Co.*) 24 W.W.R. 337, which varied 21 W.W.R. 352, that a lien which was not required to be registered with the Minister of Mines and Minerals, (now the Minister of Energy and Natural Resources), under section 48, (now sec. 26), of the Alberta Act, could be validly registered under The Land Titles Act although the lands were unpatented.

It has been held that the acceptance of the claim by the Registrar for registration relieves the claimant of any further responsibility and, if an error is made by the Registrar in recording the claim, it will not prejudice the claimant's rights or invalidate his lien: see *Gorman, Clancy and Grindley v. Archibald* (1908), 1 Alta. L.R. 524; *Lawrie v. Rathbun* (1876), 38 U.C.Q.B. 255 (C.A.). However, see *Summers' Agricultural Services Ltd. v. Vacation Land Properties Ltd.,* [1972] 2 W.W.R. 477 (Alta.), where the claimant presented its statement of lien to the Registrar for registration on the last day allowed under the Act and received a "counterslip" bearing the same date. The statement of lien was not entered in the day book until the next business day. The Court held that the claimant was only entitled to a lien if it complied strictly with the section of the Act concerning registration, and, since the lien was not registered until it was entered, the lien had ceased to exist.

(b) The Time for Filing the Lien by the Contractor.

A claim for lien by a contractor or a subcontractor may be registered before or during the performance of the contract or subcontract or within the prescribed number of days after the completion or abandonment of the contract or subcontract, as the case may be: Ont., sec. 21(1). The contractor's right to file a lien exists up to the time of the completion of the contract and for the prescribed number of days thereafter, and accordingly, if he files his lien before the contract is complete, the defendant cannot object to it on the ground that it has been filed after the prescribed period: *Davies v. E. B. Eddy Co.,* [1942] 1 W.W.R. 596 (B.C. C.A.). If he fails to file his lien within the prescribed times then his lien will absolutely cease to exist. It was held in *Hutchinson v. Berridge,* [1922] 2 W.W.R. 710 (Alta. C.A.), that, in the case of a mine, the time within which the lien must be registered commences to run from the date of completion of the development work and not from the date upon which the mine commences to operate as a mine. In Nova Scotia, Saskatchewan, New Brunswick and Prince Edward Island, although no longer in Ontario, where the contract is under the supervision of an architect, engineer or other person upon whose certificate payments are to be made, the claim of the contractor may be registered within the previously mentioned times or within 7 days after the architect or other person has given his final certificate or has, after application in writing to him by the contractor, refused or neglected to give a final certificate. The abandonment of the project by the owner is not such a "completion" as will start the prescribed time running and the lien will not be lost by the contractor's failure to file his lien within the prescribed time after such an abandonment by the owner: *Hodgson Lbr. Co. v. Wendlend,* [1941] 1 W.W.R. 24 (B.C.).

When calculating the time for filing a lien by a contractor or subcontractor it must be remembered that in all of the provinces except Manitoba and Nova Scotia, the term "completion of the contract" is defined by the

Act as "substantial performance, not necessarily total performance, of the contract": Ont., sec. 1(1)(*a*); N.B., sec. 1. The Ontario, Alberta, Saskatchewan and Newfoundland Acts also define the term "substantial performance". They provide that "a contract shall be deemed to be substantially performed, (*a*) when the work or a substantial part thereof is ready for use or is being used for the purpose intended, and (*b*) when the work to be done under the contract is capable of completion or correction at a cost of not more than, (i) 3 per cent of the first $250,000.00 of the contract price, (ii) 2 per cent of the next $250,000.00 of the contract price, and (iii) 1 per cent of the balance of the contract price": Ont., sec. 1(3); Alta., sec. 2(2); Nfld., sec. 2(2); Sask., sec. 2(2). These Acts also provide that where the work or a substantial part of it is ready for use or is being used for the purpose intended and the balance of the work cannot be completed expeditiously for reasons beyond the contractor's control, the value of the uncompleted work is to be deducted from the contract price in determining whether or not the work has been substantially performed in accordance with the preceding subsection of the Act: Ont., sec. 1(4); Alta., sec. 2(3); Nfld., sec. 2(3); Sask., sec. 2(3). In *Crestile Ltd. v. New Generation Properties Inc.* (1976), 13 O.R. (2d) 670, it was held that the words "contract price", as they are used in this section, are to be interpreted as including the price of the work done under the original contract as altered and augmented by the addition of extras. The evidence in that case disclosed the original contract price to have been $20,000 but that, as a result of numerous alterations and additions to the work having been ordered by the defendant, the plaintiff had ultimately billed the defendant a total of $36,554. The Master found that the contract was substantially complete when the cost of completing the work amounted to less than 3% of $36,554. Se also *Wagg v. Boudreau Sheet Metal Works Ltd.* (1959), 43 M.P.R. 154 (N.B. C.A.), as to substantial performance under the New Brunswick Act, and *Hasler Bros. Ltd. v. Phillips* (1962), 40 W.W.R. 445 (B.C. C.A.), a case decided under the British Columbia Act.

Section 30(5) of the Alberta Act provides that where, in respect of work done on or material furnished for an improvement, either something is improperly done, or something that should have been done is not done at the proper time, and if the thing is corrected or done at a later date, the doing of the thing at that time will not be deemed to be the completion of the work or the furnishing of the last materials so as to enable a person to extend the time limited for registering a lien. In *Vanderwell Lbr. Ltd. v. Grant Indust Ltd.* (1963), 42 W.W.R. 446 (Alta.), where the lien claimant delivered part of his material late due to a mistake, it was held that section 30(5) precluded the extension of the time for registering his lien until the delivery of the last of the material. See also *Weathermakers Ltd. v. Wetaskiwin* (1966), 56 W.W.R. 271 (Alta.), and *J. Mason & Sons Ltd. v. Camrose S. Dist. No. 1315* (1968), 67 W.W.R. 149 (Alta.).

(c) The Time for Filing the Lien by the Subcontractor.

The subcontractor must file his lien, as previously stated, within the same time limits as the contractor, although the provision as to architect's certificates is not applicable to him (except in the province of Saskatchewan). The doctrine of substantial performance is applicable to subcontractors as well as to general contractors: *Otis Elevator Co. v. Commonwealth Holiday Inns of Can. Ltd.* (1972), 57 D.L.R. (3d) 681 (Ont.); *Union Elec. Supply Co. v. Joice-Sweanor Elec. Ltd.* (1975), 7 O.R. (2d) 227 (C.A.). Except in British Columbia, the date of completion or abandonment from which the statutory period commences to run is the date of completion or abandonment by the subcontractor and not by the main contractor, his claim being in no way dependent on the main contractor's claim: see *Merrick v. Campbell* (1914), 6 W.W.R. 722 (Man.); *Deeves v. Coulson Const. Co.,* [1941] 3 W.W.R. 858 (Alta.); *J. R. Stephenson v. Woodward Stores (Edmonton) Ltd.* (1959), 27 W.W.R. 695 (Alta.); *Dom. Sheet Metal & Roofing Works v. G. H. I. Const. Co.,* [1968] 2 O.R. 665; *G. Farwell Co. v. Coast Homes Ltd.* (1969), 4 D.L.R. (3d) 238 (B.C. C.A.); *Granby Const. & Equipment Ltd. v. Player* (1964), 49 D.L.R. (2d) 658 (B.C.). In British Columbia the time for filing the subcontractor's claim is dependant on the main contractor's claim since the subcontractor must file his claim "not later than 31 days after the contract of the contractor has been completed, than 31 days after the conract of the contractor has been completed, abandoned or otherwise determined": B.C. sec., 23(1). See also: *Woodhaven Devs. Ltd. v. Klitch,* [1976] W.W.D. 58 (B.C.); *Mor Light Ltd. v. Rikki's Invts. Ltd.,* [1975] W.W.D. 156 (B.C.).

The Acts of Ontario, Alberta, Newfoundland, Saskatchewan, New Brunswick and Manitoba contain a section which provides for a partial release of the holdback where the contract is under the supervision of an architect, engineer or other person upon whose certificate payments are to be made: Ont., sec. 11(2); N.B., sec. 15(4); Man., sec. 9(3). If the architect, engineer, or other person issues a certificate under this section to the effect that a subcontract has been completed to his satisfaction,the Act deems that subcontract to have been completed, for the purposes of the section which prescribes the time for registering any lien arising out of that subcontract, not later than the date on which the certificate was given: Ont., sec. 11(3); N.B., sec. 15(5); Man., sec. 9(4). The time begins to run at the date of the certificate even though more work remains to be done under the subcontract and it is done at a later date: *Western Realty Projects Ltd. v. Superior Grout & Gunite Ltd.; Wells Const. Ltd. v. Edwards Const. Ltd.,* [1975] 6 W.W.R. 366 (Alta.).

(d) The Time for Filing the Lien by the Materialman.

Except in British Columbia, a claim for lien for materials may be registered before or during the furnishing or placing thereof or within the statutory number of days after the furnishing or placing of the last of the material: Ont., sec. 21(2); Alta., sec. 30(2); Man., sec. 20(2); *Rocky Mountain S.D. v. Atlas Lbr. Co.,* [1954] S.C.R. 589, reversing 8 W.W.R. 513. In British Columbia a material supplier may file his lien at any time after the contract to supply the materials has been made, but not later than 31 days after the improvement to which the material has been supplied has been completed or abandoned, or the contract for the construction or making of the improvement has been otherwise determined: B.C., sec. 23(2). In this connection see *Dieleman Planer Co. v. Elizabeth Townhouses Ltd.* (1974), 48 D.L.R. (3d) 635 (S.C.C.).

It was held in *F. M. O'Leary Ltd. v. Crane* (1958), 40 M.P.R. 378 (Nfld.), that where a lien is wholly for materials supplied, the lien must be registered within the prescribed number of days after the supplying of the materials and the argument of the materialman that he could register a lien within the prescribed number of days after completion of the contract was rejected. In *Currier & Ferguson Elec. v. Pearce,* [1953] O.W.N. 184, it was held that the time of the delivery or furnishing of the last material or services to the premises to which the lien attaches, fixes the time for registering the claim for lien for all materials or services delivered or furnished to those premises. In *Nelson Lbr. Co. v. Integrated Bldg. Corpn.,* [1973] S.C.R. 456, it was held that the time for registration of the materialman's lien runs from the date that the last of the materials are brought on to the building site irrespective of whether they are brought there by the materialman himself or his agent or carrier. In that case it appeared that the material had been picked up at the materialman's premises by the subcontractor, on or before February 14, 1970, and that the subcontractor brought some of this material to the building site between March 16 and March 28, 1970, during which period an employee of the subcontractor was working on the site. The Court found that the time for registering the materialman's lien commenced to run from the date on which the material was brought to the job site by the subcontractor and not from the date upon which the material was picked up at the materialman's premises.

In this connection see also the articles on the general lien, prevenient arrangements and the materialman in Chapter 3, The Lien Claimant. For a discussion of the special situation which exists in Saskatchewan, where the lien may, subject to certain conditions, be filed after the statutory period prescribed by the Act for doing so has expired, see §79, *post.*

(e) *The Time for Filing a Lien for Services.*

A claim for lien for services may be registered at any time during the furnishing of the service or within the prescribed number of days after the completion of the services. A claim for lien for services, or for wages, may not be registered before the commencement of the work or the performance of the services: Ont., sec. 21(3), (4). In Ontario, Saskatchewan, Alberta and Newfoundland, although not in the other provinces, a person who rents equipment to an owner, contractor or subcontractor for use on a contract site is deemed to have performed a service for which he has a lien: Ont., sec. 5(5); Alta., sec. 4(4); Nfld., sec. 8; Sask., sec. 2(1)(m).

(f) *The Time for Filing the Lien by the Wage Earner.*

A claim for lien for wages may be registered at any time during the performance of the work for which the wages are claimed or within the prescribed number of days after the last work is done for which the lien is claimed: Ont., sec. 21(4). In British Columbia, the time for registering a claim for wages is 31 days, except for work done on a mine or quarry in which case the time is 60 days, and no workman is deemed to have ceased work on a project until its completion if he has in the meantime been employed upon any other work by the same contractor: sec. 23(3).

In Alberta the time limited for filing a claim for wages is 35 days: sec. 30(4); in Manitoba, Newfoundland and New Brunswick, the time is 30 days: Man., sec. 20(4); Nfld., sec. 23(4); N.B., sec. 24(1); in Prince Edward Island the time is 60 days: sec. 25(1); in Nova Scotia the time is 45 days: sec. 23(4), and in Saskatchewan and Ontario the time is 37 days: Sask., sec. 36(3); Ont., sec. 21(4).

In the Northwest Territories the lien for wages may be registered at any time within 30 days after the last day's work or 30 days from the completion of the building upon which the labour was bestowed, but the whole time must not exceed 60 days from the last day's work: R.O.N.W.T. 1974, c. M-8. In the Yukon the lien for wages must be filed within 30 days of the completion of the work: R.O.Y.T. 1971, c. M-5.

(g) *Computation of Time for Registration.*

In Ontario, following the decision in *Can. Sand etc. Co. v. Ottaway* (1907), 15 O.L.R. 128, the times limited by the Act for registration of claims for lien and for commencement of actions run during Court vacation. In computing the time within which the claim for lien must be registered or the action commenced, the rule is that the first day is excluded and the last day is included: see *McLennan v. Winnipeg* (1882), 3 Man. R. 474 (C.A.); *Bunting v. Bell* (1876), 23 Gr. 584; *Kalbfleisch v. Hurley* (1915), 34 O.L.R. 268 (C.A.); *Ludlam-Ainslee Lbr. Co. v. Fallis* (1909), 19 O.L.R. 419 (C.A.); *Gordon Sutherland Realty Ltd. v. MacNaughton* (1961), 45 M.P.R. 324 (N.S. C.A.); *Mike's Contracting Ltd. v. Dawson Lands Ltd.* (1977), 1 R.P.R. 353 (B.C.).

It was held in *Revelstoke Sawmill Co. v. Alta. Bottle Co.* (1915), 7 W.W.R. 1002; affirmed 9 Alta. L.R. 162, that, where the last day for commencing an action to enforce the lien fell on a Sunday, the action would be in time if it was brought on the following day pursuant to the provisions of the Alberta Interpretation Act. Most of the provinces have enacted legislation similar to the Alberta and Ontario Interpretation Acts, providing that where the time limited by an Act for taking a proceeding or for the doing of anything under its provisions expires or falls upon a holiday, the time so limited extends to, and the thing may be done on, the day next following that is not a holiday: R.S.O. 1970, c. 225, sec. 27(*h*), (*i*). In *Argus Steel Const. Ltd. v. Burns Tpt. Ltd.*, [1962] O.W.N. 153 (C.A.), the time for registering a lien fell on a Saturday and the Court held that the lien registered the following Monday was properly registered. See also *Re A. H. Murray & Co. and Newland* (1957), 40 M.P.R. 5 (Nfld.). It was held in *Alta. Lbr. Co. v. Yeats,* [1950] 1 W.W.R. 397 (Alta.), that, in computing the time for filing a claim for lien, fractions of a day were not to be considered, following *Clarke v. Moore* (1908), 1 Alta. L.R. 50.

It was held in *Re Continental Explosives Ltd.* (1964), 49 W.W.R. 762 (B.C.), that there was no conflict between the provisions of the British Columbia Mechanics' Lien Act, requiring the registration of a certificate of *lis pendens* in the Land Registry Office within one year from the date of filing the lien, and the provisions of The Land Registry Act which specifies the hours of the Registrar as being from 8:30 a.m. to 5:00 p.m. Accordingly, where the Registrar admitted the solicitor for a lien claimant at 5:15 p.m. on the last day for registering the certificate of *lis pendens* and accepted the certificate for registration, the certificate was held to have been registered in time under The Mechanics' Lien Act since the Registrar properly exercised the discretion to admit the solicitor after hours which is given to him under The Land Registry Act. See also the cases cited at the end of §71(*a*).

§72 Extending the Time for Registering the Claim for Lien.

When considering cases dealing with the question of whether a claim for lien has been filed in time, it must be remembered that in British Columbia, New Brunswick, Prince Edward Island, Saskatchewan, Alberta, Newfoundland and Ontario, completion of the contract is defined as "substantial performance, not necessarily total performance, of the contract": Ont., sec. 1(1)(*a*). In Manitoba and Nova Scotia, until 1970 in Ontario, Alberta and Newfoundland, and until 1973 in Saskatchewan, the term completion of the contract means total completion: see *Lambton v. Can. Comstock Co.,* [1960] S.C.R. 86, affirming 10 D.L.R. (2d) 583, and *Modern Const. Co. v. Maritime Rock Products Ltd.,* [1963] S.C.R. 347 at 353. As pointed out in the previous section, the Acts of Ontario, Alberta, Saskatchewan and Newfoundland go a step further and define the term "substantial performance": Ont., sec. 1(3); Alta., sec. 2(2); Sask., sec. 2(2);

Nfld., sec. 2(2). It will be a question of fact in each case whether a contract has been "completed" or "substantially performed" within the meaning of the Act under which the claimant seeks to enforce his lien. This section is concerned with situations where the claimant's lien rights would have expired before his claim for lien was registered if they had not been extended because of the peculiar facts of the case. Most of the cases cited were decided under statutes which did not define "completion" as substantial performance of the contract.

It was held in *Lacroix v. Yoos* (1952), 5 W.W.R. 79 (Sask. C.A.), that if the contract requires the supply of material or the performance of services, the time for claiming a mechanics' lien will commence to run from the date of furnishing the last material or performing the last of the services, although the materials were furnished or the labour performed sometime after the substantial performance of the contract and was trivial in character. If it appears, however, that such materials are supplied or such services are performed merely to extend the time for filing a lien which had already expired, the lien will be held to be invalid. As was pointed out in *Russell v. Ont. Foundation etc. Co.* (1926), 58 O.L.R. 260 (C.A.), it does not matter how trivial the work was or how small a quantity of materials were supplied, the question is whether or not the work was done or the materials were supplied in good faith to complete the contract. See also *Glenway Supply (Alta.) Ltd. v. Knobloch,* [1972] 6 W.W.R. 513 (Alta. C.A.). It was held in *Sayward v. Dunsmuir* (1905), 11 B.C.R. 375 (C.A.), that the question of whether or not material was supplied in good faith to complete the contract or as a pretext to revive a lien which had lapsed was a question of fact to be decided by the trial Judge. It was further pointed out in *Lambton v. Can. Comstock Co., supra,* and *Modern Const. Co. v. Maritime Rock Products Ltd., supra,* that time only begins to run from the events mentioned in the Act regardless of the triviality of the work done to complete and the lapse of time after the substantial performance of the contract. The time limited for filing the lien commences to run at the time when the subcontractor is able to sue for his contract price in full and he cannot do this until he has performed all that he is bound to do under his contract. The Court in the former case pointed out that the fact that a contractor who had substantially completed his work might sue for the contract price subject to deductions for minor defects or omissions, could not determine when time began to run under the Act and "completion" meant final and actual completion. The result in most of these cases would have been different, however, in provinces whose Acts define completion as substantial performance of the contract. For example, in *Wagg v. Boudreau Sheet Metal Works Ltd.* (1959), 43 M.P.R. 154 (N.B. C.A.), a heating contractor's lien was held to have been filed too late where the work he relied on to support the lien, although essential to complete his contract, had been performed some time after the heating system had been sufficiently installed to permit the owners to move into the premises and live there without complaint. In *Hasler Bros Ltd. v. Phillips* (1962), 40 W.W.R. 445 (B.C. C.A.), the Court held that the definition of the term "completed" as "substantial performance" applied to a materialman.

While the exchange of material for some already delivered, or the supply of material or of work which is outside the original contract will not generally extend the time for registration of the claim for lien, in *Russell v. Ont. Foundation etc. Co., supra,* it was held that a lien filed within the statutory period after the replacement of a piece of cut stone, which had been cut too short, with one of the proper size, was filed in time. See also *Rodewalt v. Plasky* (1959), 30 W.W.R. 457 (Alta.) (filling cracks in plaster to complete contract). In *Rathbone v. Michael* (1909), 19 O.L.R. 428; affirmed 20 O.L.R. 503 (C.A.), it was held that the words "the last material" as used in the Act referred to the last material supplied by the materialman under his contract and, where materials were subsequently supplied outside the contract, the time would not commence running again. However, in the case of prevenient agreements for the supply of material, it may be extremely difficult to differentiate between material which is supplied as part of such arrangement and that which is not. In *Western Air Conditioning Ltd. v. Capri Hotels Ltd.* (1962), 38 W.W.R. 184 (Alta.), where a materialman failed to register in time and then delivered additional material to replace items of the first delivery which were damaged, the Court held that the second delivery was made pursuant to a separate contract and it did not extend the time for registration of a lien for the materials first delivered. For the same result see *Hectors Ltd. v. Mfrs. Life Ins. Co.,* [1967] S.C.R. 153, affirming (*sub nom. Inglewood Plumbing & Gasfitting Ltd. v. Northgate Dev. Ltd. (No. 2))* 56 W.W.R. 449.

It was pointed out in *McLennan v. Winnipeg* (1882), 3 Man. R. 474 (C.A.), *Lawrence v. Landsberg* (1910), 14 W.L.R. 477 (B.C.) and *Piggott Lbr. v. Bersch* (1926), 30 O.W.N. 8 (C.A.), that, where the date of completion is alleged to be a considerable time after the bulk of the work was performed or materials supplied, clear and satisfactory evidence must be given to enable the Court to find that the work was done or the material was supplied in pursuance of, and as part of, the original contract. In *Anderson v. Fort William Commercial Chambers Ltd.* (1915), 34 O.L.R. 567 (C.A.) and *B. A. Robinson Plumbing & Heating Ltd. v. Stewart,* [1961] O.R. 445 (C.A.), the claimant had left the work believing that the contract had been completed, but afterwards, on it appearing that he was wrong, he had gone back and finished the work, filing his lien within the prescribed number of days after the final completion. His lien was held to be in time on the ground that such a cessation of work was not an abandonment within the meaning of the Act. It was held in *Clarke v. Moore* (1908), 1 Alta. L.R. 50, where the claimant had, by agreement with the owner, delayed completion in order to give the owner time to arrange for payment, that a lien was filed in time when filed within the prescribed time after the doing of further work under the contract since the owner had accepted the benefit of the delay and the work done was necessary to complete the contract. In *Weathermakers Ltd. v. Wetaskiwin* (1966), 56 W.W.R. 271 (Alta.), the claimant had substantially installed its work in July, but, through the failure of another contractor, could not test and put its equipment into operation until October. Its lien, filed within the statutory time, calculated from October, was held to be valid since the work done in October had been done in good faith and for the purpose of discharging its commitment. It was further held in that case, that the fact that the claimant had rendered an account for the full contract price in July should not necessarily be construed as evidence that the work had been completed, nor did the fact that neither the architect nor the owner knew of the work being done, have any bearing on the validity of the lien. It was held in *Otis Elevator Co. v. Commonwealth Holiday Inns of Can. Ltd.* (1972), 8 O.R. (2d) 297, that the removal of the subcontractor's own equipment from the job site long after his contract was otherwise complete did not extend the time for registration of his lien, even where the contract called for the removal of rubbish and waste material.

The following are some further decisions on the question of whether or not the work done had been done in good faith to complete the contract or colourably, so as to revive an expired lien: *Carroll v. McVicar* (1905), 15 Man. R. 379 (C.A.); *Dom. Radiator Co. v. Payne,* [1917] 2 W.W.R. 974; reversed (*sub nom. Calgary v. Dom. Radiator Co.*) 56 S.C.R. 141; *Foster v. Brocklebank* (1915), 8 W.W.R. 464 (Alta.); *Fuller v. Beach* (1913), 21 W.L.R. 391; reversed (*sub nom. Fuller v. Turner*) 4 W.W.R. 161 (B.C. C.A.); *Steinman v. Koscuk* (1906), 4 W.L.R. 514 (Man.); *Whimster v. Crow's Nest Pass Coal Co.* (1910), 13 W.L.R. 621 (B.C.); *Brooks-Sanford Co. v. Theodore Telier Const. Co.* (1910), 22 O.L.R. 176, reversing 20 O.L.R. 303 (C.A.); *Brynjolfson v. Oddson,* [1917] 1 W.W.R. 1000 (Man. C.A.); *Colling v. Stimson & Buckley* (1913), 4 W.W.R. 597 (Alta.); *Day v. Crown Grain Co.* (1907), 39 S.C.R. 258, reversing 16 Man. R. 366, which reversed 2 W.L.R. 142; affirmed [1908] A.C. 504; *Robock v. Peters* (1900), 13 Man. R. 124; *Sherritt v. McCallum* (1910), 12 W.L.R. 637 (B.C.); *B. A. Robinson Plumbing & Heating Ltd. v. Rossiter,* [1955] O.W.N. 29; *Chadwick v. Hunter* (1884), 1 Man. R. 39; affirmed 1 Man. R. 363 (C.A.); *Deeves v. Coulson Const. Co.,* [1941] 3 W.W.R. 858 (Alta.); *Hurst v. Morris* (1914), 32 O.L.R. 346 (C.A.); *Merrick v. Campbell* (1914), 6 W.W.R. 722 (Man.); *Sanderson Pearcy & Co. Ltd. v. Foster* (1923), 53 O.L.R. 519 (C.A.); *Edmund Hind Lbr. Co. v. Amalgamated Bldg. Co.* (1932), 41 O.W.N. 12 (C.A.); *Flett v. World Bldg. Ltd.* (1914), 5 W.W.R. 1127 (B.C. C.A.); *Gorman, Clancy & Grindley v. Archibald* (1908), 1 Alta. L.R. 524;

Querengesser v. Stretton (1928), 33 O.W.N. 427; *Renney v. Dempster* (1911), 2 O.W.N. 1303; *Wagg v. Boudreau Sheet Metal Works Ltd.* (1959), 43 M.P.R. 154 (N.B. C.A.); *Western Air Conditioning Ltd. v. Capri Hotels Ltd.* (1962), 38 W.W.R. 184 (Alta.); *Vanderwell Lbr. v. Grant Indust. Ltd.* (1963), 42 W.W.R. 446 (Alta.); *Modern Const. Co. v. Maritime Rock Products Ltd.,* [1963] S.C.R. 347; *J. Mason & Sons Ltd. v. Camrose S. Dist. No. 1315* (1968), 67 W.W.R. 149 (Alta.); *Emco (Western) Ltd. v. Carillon Invt. Ltd.* (1962), 39 W.W.R. 432 (Man. C.A.); *Emco Ltd. v. Starlight Towers-Sask. Drive Ltd.* (1969), 70 W.W.R. 3, 71 W.W.R. 767 (Addendum); affirmed 72 W.W.R. 236n (Can.); *Zucchi v. Intervestments Const. Corpn.,* [1970] 2 O.R. 404; *Winnipeg Supply & Fuel Co. v. Genevieve Mtge. Corpn.; Wiebe v. Dom. Bronze Ltd.* [1972] 1 W.W.R. 651 (Man.C.A.); *Harper Const. Co. v. Constant Macaroni Ltd.,* [1975] 2 W.W.R. 20 (Man.); *Dobbelsteyn Elec. Ltd. v. Whittaker Textiles (Marysville) Ltd.* (1976), 14 N.B.R. (2d) 584; *Ocean Steel & Const. Ltd. v. Kenney Const. Co.* (1972), 31 D.L.R. (3d) 441 (N.S.C.A.). See also Chapter 3, § 29(b).

Where the contract provides that liens may not be enforced until the amounts of the claim have been submitted to arbitration, the lien must be filed within the time prescribed by the Act as if this provision did not exist. See also Chapter 3, The Lien Claimant and Chapter 10, Jurisdiction, §128.

As has been pointed out, the Acts of some of the provinces provide that, in the case of contracts under the supervision of an architect, engineer or other person on whose certificate payments are to be made, the time for filing the lien may be extended to 7 days after the giving of such person's certificate of completion. Where the architect requires some additional work to be done to complete the contract, the time for registering the claim for lien will be extended even though the work required to be done is of a very minor nature: *Benson v. Smith & Son* (1916), 37 O.L.R. 257 (C.A.); *Vokes Hdwe. Co. v. G.T.R.* (1906), 12 O.L.R. 344 (C.A.); *Morgan v. Birnie* (1833), 9 Bing. 672; *Metal Studios Ltd. v. Kitchener* (1925), 29 O.W.N. 216 (C.A.). The doing of work or the supplying of materials to rectify defective or improper workmanship or material, or to satisfy the claimant's obligation under a guarantee will not extend the time for filing the claim for lien: *J. R. Stephenson Ltd. v. Woodward Stores (Edmonton) Ltd.* (1959), 27 W.W.R. 695 (Alta.); *Wagg v. Boudreau Sheet Metal Works Ltd.* (1959), 43 M.P.R. 154 (N.B. C.A.); *Morton v. Grant,* [1956] O.W.N. 523 (C.A.); *B. A. Robinson Plumbing & Heating Ltd. v. Rossiter,* [1955] O.W.N. 29.

The giving of a period of credit to the person primarily liable to the lien claimant will not extend the time for registering the claim for lien, although, in most provinces it does extend the time for commencing the action where the period of credit is set out in the claim for lien. Where the period of credit has been given prior to registration of the claim for lien and is described therein, the action to enforce the lien need not be commenced until the expiry of the period of credit or until, in the case of instalment payments, a default in one of the payments is made: *Nor. Lbr. Mills Ltd. v. Rice* (1917), 41 O.L.R. 201 (C.A.); *Armitage v. Beaver Lbr. Co.,* [1973] 1 O.R. 418. However, where the time for payment has been extended and such extension of time for payment is not mentioned in the claim for lien, the action must be commenced within the prescribed number of days after completion of the work or supply of the last material and the certificate of action registered, although no further proceedings in the action can be taken until the expiration of such extension of time for payment: Ont., sec. 26(4). In Nova Scotia, however, it has been held that where the amount of the contract is payable by instalments in the future, an action to enforce the lien may be begun at once whether any of the instalments are due and payable or not: see *Beaton v. Nedruvan* (1930), 1 M.P.R. 65 (N.S. C.A.), and also §69(*h*), *ante.*

§73 The Unregistered Lien Claimant.

In Nova Scotia and Saskatchewan a lien claimant's lien will be preserved if an action is commenced and a certificate of action is registered by another lien claimant against the same property within the time prescribed by the Act for the registration of his lien. In such circumstances the claimant can "shelter" under the action which has already been commenced and it will not be necessary for him to register a claim for lien of his own: N.S., sec. 24; Sask. sec. 37. This provision was removed from the Ontario Act in 1970. His lien will be preserved by such certificate of action notwithstanding the fact that the claimant who registered it abandons or settles his action or fails to establish a lien at the trial: see *Del Frari v. Wright,* [1960] O.R. 430 and *Crawford v. Hesselink* (1958), 15 D.L.R. (2d) 294 (Nfld.); *N.S. Sand and Gravel Ltd. v. Kidstone Estates Ltd.* (1973), 13 N.S.R. (2d) 431.

It is implicit in the judgment in *Eadie-Douglas v. Hitch & Co.* (1912), 27 O.L.R. 257 (C.A.), that, if a certificate of action is registered, it preserves a subsisting claim for lien which does not expire until after the certificate was registered. If this were not so, such a claimant would have to deliver his own statement of claim and register his own certificate of action, resulting in a multiplicity of proceedings contrary to the purpose of the Act. This decision was approved by the Ontario Court of Appeal in *Brousseau v. Muircrest Invts. Ltd.* (1977), 15 O.R. (2d) 145 at 155 (C.A.), the Court holding that if an action has been commenced to enforce another subsisting claim for lien and a certificate of action registered before the expiration of the 90 day period mentioned in Section 23 of the Act, such action will shelter a claim for lien which was in existence when the certificate of action was registered although the latter claim for lien is not registered until after that time. See also: *Silver v. R.R. Seeton Const. Ltd.* (1977), 74 D.L.R. (3d) 212 (N.S.). It was held in *Del Frari v. Wright, supra,* that while a lien claimant who has registered a lien and who intends to prove his claim in an action commenced by another claimant has the right to deliver a statement of claim in the pending action, it is not necessary that he do so, and even should the claim of the plaintiff in the pending action be settled, he may nevertheless proceed to the trial of his own claim notwithstanding that no certificate of action in respect of his claim has been registered. See also *Crawford v. Hesselink, supra,* to the same effect. See also Chapter 10, §119, *post.*

§74 Parties to be Named in the Claim for Lien.

As has been pointed out in §69 dealing with the contents of the claim for lien, the failure to name any proper party in the claim will not invalidate the lien: *Barrington v. Martin* (1908), 16 O.L.R. 635 (C.A.); *Bradshaw v. Saucerman* (1913), 3 W.W.R. 761, affirming 21 W.L.R. 65 (Y.T. C.A.); *Makins v. Robinson* (1884), 6 O.R. 1; *Polson v. Thomson* (1916), 10 W.W.R. 865 (Man. C.A.); *Simac v. Waltman,* [1947] O.W.N. 264; *Fairy and Stephenson v. Doner,* [1947] O.W.N. 217; *Cole v. Hall* (1889), 13 P.R. 100, affirming 12 P.R. 584 (C.A.). However, if such a failure is not rectified in the statement of claim, the action to enforce the lien against such a party may be jeopardized: see Chapter 11, Practice Before Trial, §§ 134 and 135. In general the claim for lien will name as parties the claimant, the owner (or the person believed to be the owner), and the contractor or person primarily liable to the claimant. It is not necessary, at this stage of the proceedings, to name the owner's wife to gain priority over her dower interest, or to name a mortgagee even though the claimant intends at the trial to claim priority over his mortgage. It also appears to be unnecessary to name the contractor, or the person primarily liable to the claimant, in the claim for lien if the claimant does not intend to seek a personal judgment against him. The lien may still be enforced against the owner and judgment recovered against him for the amount owing by him to the contractor, or for the holdback, whichever is the greater: *Turner v. Johnson* (1932), 41 O.W.N. 497 (C.A.). It is always prudent practice, however, to name all of the parties mentioned in the sections of the various acts governing the contents of the claim for lien, in order to avoid being in the position of having to rely on the curative provisions of the Act to maintain the lien. It was held in *Whaley v. Linnenbank* (1915), 36 O.L.R. 361 (C.A.), that it was unnecessary to name more parties or give more information in the claim for lien than Ontario section 16 required. Any other person against whom it is sought to establish a claim can be named in the statement of claim when the action is commenced.

§75 Notice of the Lien.

While the lien itself can only be preserved by registration of a claim for lien (or in Nova Scotia and Saskatchewan, by the registration of another claimant's certificate of action), notice in writing of the lien may be given prior to registration to "stay the hand of the paymaster" thus preserving the fund out of which the lien will eventually be satisfied. The giving of the written notice will give the lien, as regards the person to whom such notice is given, priority over further advances made by such person under a mortgage or conveyance (Ont., sec. 14(1)), or over payments made under the contract beyond the statutory holdback: Ont., sec. 11(6). In the case of a mortgagee or a purchaser of the property involved, the notice must be given by leaving it at the proper address of the purchaser or the mortgagee: Ont., sec. 14(1). In order to prevent further payments being made under the contract, notice of the lien should be given by the claimant to the owner or contractor, as the case may be, from whom the person primarily liable to him has his contract: see Form 6. The giving of such written notice will protect the claimant's lien just as effectively as registration insofar as the person to whom the notice is given is concerned: *Re Irvine and Main,* [1933] O.W.N. 476; *Richards v. Chamberlain* (1878), 25 Gr. 402; *Cook v. Koldoffsky* (1916), 35 O.L.R. 555 (C.A.); *Gauthier v. Larose* (1901), 38 C.L.J. 156 (Ont.); *Warwick v. Sheppard* (1917), 39 O.L.R. 99 (C.A.). As was stated in *Craig v. Cromwell* (1900), 32 O.R. 27; affirmed 27 O.A.R. 585 at 587 by Osler J.A.: "The object of the notice is to warn the owner that he cannot safely make payments on account of the contract price ... because of the existence of liens of which he was not otherwise bound to inform himself or to look for. The notice does not compel him to pay the lien. It does not prove the existence of the lien. Its sole purpose is to stay the hand of the paymaster until he shall be satisfied — either by the direction of the debtor or of the Court, in case proceedings to realize the lien are taken — that there is a lien, and that some amount is really due and owing to the lienholder". In *Len Ariss & Co. v. Peloso,* [1958] O.R. 643 (C.A.), a claimant had given notice of his lien to the owner and the owner had held back the amount claimed by such claimant in addition to the proper holdback. The Court of Appeal held that the lienholder giving notice was only entitled to rank *pari passu* with the other lienholders on the fund consisting of the total of these two amounts and was not entitled, by reason of giving notice, to payment in full. Accordingly, the giving of notice in such circumstances benefits all lienholders who prove valid liens at the trial. See also in this connection *Vaillancourt Lbr. Co. v. Trustees of Sep. School Section No. 2, Balfour Twp.,* [1964] 1 O.R. 418 (C.A.); *S. I. Guttman Ltd. v. James D. Mokry Ltd.,* [1969] 1 O.R. 7 (C.A.); *Can. Comstock Co. v. Toronto Transit Commn.,* [1970] S.C.R. 205; *Revelstoke Bldg. Materials Ltd. v. Howe; Neumann v. Howe; Royal Bank v. Neumann,* (1972), 31 D.L.R. (3d) 602 (Alta. C.A.).

Section 11(5a) of the Ontario Act provides that, where the lien does not attach to the land by virtue of section 5(2) of that Act, an owner, contractor or subcontractor who receives a notice in writing of a lien must retain an amount equal to the amount claimed in the notice out of amounts payable to the contractor or subcontractor under whom the lien is derived. Section 16 of both the New Brunswick and Prince Edward Island Acts provides that where a lienholder gives the owner notice in writing of his lien, stating under oath the amount claimed, the owner must retain from the amount payable to the contractor the amount stated in the notice, in addition to the statutory holdback. That section further provides that the additional amounts retained by the owner under this section shall constitute a separate fund from the holdback for the benefit of the lienholders who give such notices. The owner was required to pay amounts which it owed to its contractor in excess of the statutory holdback under this section in *Ground Water Dev. Corpn. v. Moncton* (1972), 5 N.B.R. (2d) 487 (C.A.).

There is some conflict of opinion as to the form of the notice. The better opinion would appear to be that expressed in *Dziadus v. Sloan*, [1943] 3 W.W.R. 449 (Man. C.A.), to the effect that it must be such a notice as will cause the owner to know that a lien is being claimed under the Act. This opinion is supported by the decisions in *Direct Lbr. Co. v. Meda* (1957), 23 W.W.R. 126 (Alta.), and *Anglin & Co. v. Simmons,* [1933] O.W.N. 136 (C.A.). In *Dziadus v. Sloan, supra,* it was held that a notice to the contractor reading "Please retain from H M of United Construction Limited ... $ owing to us on excavating at (Street Address)" was not a sufficient notice under the Act. Such a direction was also held not to be a sufficient notice of a lien in *Sanderson Pearcy & Co. v. Foster* (1923), 53 O.L.R. 519 (C.A.). It was held in *Rocky Mountain S.D. v. Atlas Lbr. Co.,* [1954] S.C.R. 589, reversing 8 W.W.R. 513, that the sending of copies of the invoices as materials were delivered was not the giving of a notice in writing of the lien within the meaning of the Act since delivery of goods alone did not necessarily give rise to a lien, nor did the fact that the goods were furnished on credit constitute notice that a lien would be claimed. However, in *Craig v. Cromwell* (1900), 32 O.R. 27; affirmed 27 O.A.R. 585, Osler J.A. expressed the opinion that the notice was intended to be an informal document, no special particulars or detail being prescribed by the Act, and in *Merrick v. Campbell* (1914), 6 W.W.R. 722 (Man.) and *Robock v. Peters* (1900), 13 Man. R. 124, the opinion was expressed that notice in writing of an indebtedness for which a lien might be claimed was *prima facie* notice of the lien itself.

It is submitted that the notice should contain as many particulars as possible. In order to be effective it must convey to the person to whom it is given the fact that a lien is being claimed and that he makes any further payments or advances at his peril. This view was cited with approved in *Bird*

Const. Co. v. Mountview Const. Ltd. (1969), 67 W.W.R. 515 (Alta.), where it was held that the notice in writing of the lien should, at the very minimum, indicate: (a) that the claimant is supplying material or labour to the contractor; (b) that there is an account owed thereby; (c) that the claimant is claiming a lien (and perhaps will register it unless payment is made to him); and (d) the amount of the claim. See also Chapter 3, §36 and Chapter 4, §§ 50 and 51.

§76 Notice of Lien to Owner of Leased Premises.

The statutes of some of the provinces require that, where the estate or interest upon which the lien attaches is leasehold, in order to make the fee simple subject to the lien, the consent of the owner, testified by his signature, must be on the claim for lien at the time of its registration: N.S., sec. 7(2); Sask., sec. 17(2); Man., sec. 5(2). The statutes of other provinces require notice in writing to be given to the owner prior to the doing of the work: Ont., sec. 7(1); P.E.I., sec. 12(1); Alta., sec. 12(1). Such a notice must be delivered personally to the owner or his agent prior to the doing of the work and must specify the work to be done or the materials to be furnished. If the landlord does not give notice to the claimant that he will not be responsible for the work within the number of days specified by the Act, (15 days in Ontario and Newfoundland, 5 in Alberta, 10 in New Brunswick and Prince Edward Island) the fee simple will also be subject to the lien. If no notice is given and the landlord does not otherwise come within the definition of "owner" contained in the Act, the fee simple will not be subject to the lien and the claimants will only be entitled to dispose of the lease to realize their claims. The notice to the landlord must be given before the work is started: *Patsis v. 75-89 Gosford Ltd.; Papas v. Patsis,* [1973] 1 O.R. 629. It was held in *Hillcrest Contractors Ltd. v. McDonald* (1976), 1 Alta. L.R. (2d) 221, that the notice must state, no matter how informally, in some detail the nature of the work to be done or the kind or quality or quantity of the materials to be furnished. The Court also expressed the view that the requirements of the Act might also be satisfied by the delivery of documents but the cumulative effect of those documents must be to put the landlord on notice that he may be liable in the event that the tenant does not pay for the work done or the materials furnished. See also: *Beyersbergen Const. Ltd. v. Edmonton Centre Ltd.* (1977), 78 D.L.R. (3d) 122 (Alta.C.A.). It has been held that mere knowledge on the part of the landlord that work is going on will not constitute him an "owner" within the meaning of the Act so as to render the fee simple subject to the lien: *Cook v. Koldoffsky* (1916), 35 O.L.R. 555 (C.A.); *Cut-Rate Plate Glass Co. v. Solodinski* (1915), 34 O.L.R. 604 (C.A.); *Richards v. Chamberlain* (1878), 25 Gr. 402; *Beyersbergen Const. Ltd. v. Edmonton Centre Ltd., supra; Hillcrest*

Contractors Ltd. v. McDonald (No. 2) (1977), 2 Alta. L.R. (2d) 273. See also Chapter 2, The Lienable Interest, §12, and *Swalm v. Fairway Finance Ltd.* (1965), 52 W.W.R. 626 (Alta.). Section 14 of the British Columbia Act renders the fee simple subject to the lien unless the owner posts a notice upon the land or building stating that he will not be responsible for such work or, alternatively, he gives actual written notice to that effect to the claimant.

§77 Notice of Lien to the Mortgagee.

Most of the Acts make a distinction between mortgages which are registered and fully advanced before and those which are registered but not fully advanced before, the registration of the claim for lien, or the receipt of written notice of a claim for lien. In the case of the former, such mortgages have priority over the liens but only to the extent of the "actual value" of the land and premises at the time the first lien arises or, as it is stated in the Nova Scotia Act, the lien has priority over the mortgage to the extent of the increased selling value of the land as a result of the furnishing of the work, services or materials by the lien claimants: Man., sec. 5(3); P.E.I. sec. 9(4); Ont., sec. 7(3). In the case of the latter mortgage, it will have priority over the liens to the extent of all advances made under the mortgage prior to receipt by the mortgagee of written notice of the claim for lien, and the actual value of the lands at the time of the making of the advances is irrelevant: Ont., sec. 14(1); Nfld., sec. 16(1); N.S., sec. 14(1). Accordingly, the mortgagee would in most circumstances, appear to be in a better position with regard to advances made under a building mortgage in the absence of notice in writing of the lien than the mortgagee who fully advances his mortgage prior to the commencement of the work. See Chapter 5, The Mortgagee. *Cook v. Koldoffsky* (1916), 35 O.L.R. 555 (C.A.); *Cut-Rate Plate Glass Co. v. Solodinski, supra; Richards v. Chamberlain, supra; Andre Knight Ltd. v. Presement,* [1967] 2 O.R. 289 (C.A.), and *C.M.H.C. v. Wood* (1967), 53 M.P.R. 294 (Nfld.), are authority for the propositions that the notice to the mortgagee must be written notice and that mere knowledge on the part of the mortgagee that work is going on, on the property against which he is advancing the mortgage moneys, will not affect the priority of his mortgage. See also in this connection *McVean v. Tiffin* (1885), 13 O.A.R. 1 and *Stinson v. Mackendrick* (1924), 55 O.L.R. 358 (C.A.). It was held in *River Valley Store Fixtures Ltd. v. Camper-Villa-Inn Ltd.,* [1977] 1 W.W.R. 659 (Man.), that the delivery to the mortgagee by the contractor of a copy of his contract with the owner was not sufficient notice of the contractor's lien to deprive the mortgagee of priority for advances made by it to the owner after it received the contract and before the contractor registered his lien. It was held in *Elmvale Lbr. Co. v. Laurin* (1977), 16 O.R. (2d) 241, however, that a mortgagee could, by his conduct toward a material supplier, estop himself from being able to rely on the necessity of the supplier giving notice of his lien in order to gain priority over future advances being made on the mortgage.

Where there is a registered agreement for the purchase of land and the purchase money or part thereof is unpaid, a conveyance not having been made to the purchaser, the purchaser will for the purposes of the Act be deemed a mortgagor and the seller a mortgagee: Ont., sec. 7(6). If the purchase price is being paid in instalments, all instalments paid to the vendor prior to his receiving notice in writing of the lien will take priority over the lien: see *Stinson v. Mackendrick, supra; Harrell v. Mosier,* [1956] O.R. 152 (C.A.); Ont., sec. 14(1). See also Chapters 5, The Mortgagee, and 8, Priorities, with respect to the effect of notice to the mortgagee on priorities between lien claimants and mortgagees.

§78 Notice of Claim to Hold Back on a Contract for Work on a Public Street or Highway or a Provincial Public Work.

Most Mechanics' Lien Acts provide that the Act does not apply to a public street or highway or to any work or improvement done or caused to be done by a Municipal Corporation thereon. Also, as discussed in article 18 *ante,* lands owned by the Crown, either in the right of Canada or of a province, are exempt from the operation of all but the trust provisions of The Mechanics' Lien Act. In Newfoundland, section 6(1) of The Mechanics' Lien Act provides that, while the lien given by subsection (1) of section 7 does not attach to any public street or highway or to any work or improvement done on, in, or to them, the holdback provisions of section 13 do apply to contracts for work or improvements upon public streets or highways. In Ontario, section 5(2) of The Mechanics' Lien Act provides that where the land upon which the work is done is a public street or highway owned by a municipality or a public work, the lien given by subsection (1) of section 5 does not attach to the land but instead constitutes a charge on the amounts which must be retained under the holdback provisions of section 11. Section 1(1)(*da*) of the Ontario Act defines the term "public work" as meaning "the property of the Crown and includes land in which the Crown has an estate or interest, and also includes all works and properties acquired, constructed, extended, enlarged, repaired, equipped or improved at the expense of the Crown, or for the acquisition, construction, repairing, equipping, extending, enlarging or improving of which any public money is appropriated by the Legislature, but not any work for which money is appropriated as a subsidy only". Section 1 (1)(*ba*) provides that the term "Crown" as used in the Act "includes Crown agencies to which *The Crown Agency Act* applies". Section 1*a*(1) provides that The Mechanics' Lien Act does not apply to work under a contract as defined in The Ministry of

Transportation and Communications Creditors Payment Act, 1975 (Ont.), c. 44, and to which that Act applies.

Section 21a(2) of the Ontario Act provides that where there is no lien on the land by virtue of subsection (2) of section 5, any person who is asserting a claim against a holdback for work done and material placed or furnished must give notice in writing of his claim to the owner in the manner provided in Section 21a. This notice must be given within 37 days after the completion or abandonment of the work or the placing or furnishing of the materials: sec. 21a(5). Section 23(5) of the Newfoundland Act contains similar provisions, except that the notice must also be given to "every person in whose hands are sums retained under Section 13 to which his claim may relate and to the municipal authority, if any, in whose area of authority the land is situate within thirty days", instead of 37 days. In Newfoundland, of course, this provision only applies to work or improvements on public streets, roads and highways. The claimant must also commence an action to realize his claim against the holdback within 90 days after the work has been completed or abandoned or the materials have been furnished or placed: Ont. sec. 23a; Nfld., sec. 25(2). In Ontario, where a period of credit has been given, the action is to be commenced within 90 days after the period of credit has expired where such a period of credit has been mentioned in the notice: sec. 23a. This provision was recently removed from the Newfoundland Act. The action to realize the claim is carried on in the same way as any other action to realize a claim under the Act except that no certificate of action is registered against the title to the public street or highway: Ont., sec. 22(2), (4), sec. 5(2); Nfld., sec. 25(3). Section 1a(2) of the Ontario Act provides that section 7 of The Proceedings Against The Crown Act does not apply in respect of proceedings against the Crown under The Mechanics' Lien Act and, accordingly, it is not necessary for the lien claimant to give the notice of his claim to the Crown, which is required under that statute, before commencing his mechanics' lien action.

In Ontario, the notice of the lien may be served personally or it may be sent by registered mail, in which case the date of mailing is deemed to be the date on which the notice was given: sec. 21a(6). Where the claim is in respect of a public street or highway which is owned by a municipality, the notice of the lien is to be given to the clerk of the municipality: sec. 21a(3). Where the claim is in respect of a public work the notice is to be given to the Ministry or Crown agency for whom the work is done or the materials are placed or furnished, or to such office as is prescribed by the regulations made under the Act: sec., 21a(4). By Ont. Reg. 849/75, section 3 was added to Reg. 575 of the Revised Regulations of Ontario 1970, made under The Mechanics' Lien Act. That section provides that the appropriate office of the Crown to which notice of a claim for lien in respect of a public work must be sent is as follows: "1. Where the contract is with a Ministry of the Crown, the office of the Director of Legal Services of that Ministry; 2. Where the contract is with the Ontario Housing Corporation, the office of the Director of Legal Services of the Ministry of Housing; 3. Where the contract is with a college of applied arts and technology, the office of the president of the college; 4. Where the contract is with any other office of the Crown, the chief executive officer of the office." Under section 2 of Ont. Reg. 849/75 every contractor on a public work is required to display and keep displayed in a conspicuous place on the site of the work a notice stating that the project is a public work, that any person who places or furnishes any materials or does any work on or in respect of the project may be protected by The Mechanics' Lien Act, and that notices of claims for lien must be sent to the address set out in the notice. This notice must set out the name and address of the appropriate office of the Crown to which the notice of a claim for lien must be sent. Section 11(5a) of the Act requires an owner or a contractor or a subcontractor who receives notice of a lien which does not attach to the land by virtue of subsection (2) of Section 5 to retain an amount equal to that claimed in the notice out of amounts otherwise payable to the contractor or the subcontractor under whom the lien is derived.

These sections of the Ontario and Newfoundland Acts in effect give a person doing work or supplying materials on highway contracts (and, in Ontario, on provincial public works contracts as well) a lien on the contract moneys in much the same way that a person doing work or supplying materials in connection with ordinary building contracts are given a lien on the land. The notice which the claimant is required to send should contain much the same information as the claim for lien which is ordinarily registered against land. The notice must be in writing and must set out the name and address of the person making the claim, the name and address of the Municipality in which the land is situated, the name and address of the person with whom the claimant had his contract and the names and addresses of any other persons against whose holdback the claimant may be asserting a claim. The notice must also describe the work done or the materials placed or furnished, the amount claimed as due to the claimant and the date upon which the last work was done or the last materials were placed or furnished. It must also contain a short description of the property upon which the work was done or to which the materials were furnished. The description need not be sufficient for Registry Office purposes, but it should be sufficient to permit the recipients of the notice to identify the contract upon which the claim is being made. In Ontario, if a period of credit has been given, and the claimant intends to rely on this period of credit to extend the time for commencing his action to realize the claim, then the period of credit must also be set out in the notice. In Ontario, the contents of the notice are prescribed by section 21a(7) of the Act. The Ontario Act also requires that the matters set out in the notice be verified by the affidavit of the person claiming the lien, or his agent or assignee who has a personal knowledge of those matters: sec. 21*a*(8). Ont. Reg. 849/75 prescribes the form of the notice of claim for lien. In addition, it provides that the affidavit verifying the notice of claim for lien is to be in form 4, which is the same form prescribed by the regulations as the form of affidavit to be used to verify the ordinary claim for lien.

7

Loss or Discharge of Lien

§79 Loss of Lien due to Failure to Register a Claim for Lien.

Most of the Acts provide that every lien for which a claim is not registered will absolutely cease to exist on the expiration of the time limited for its registration: *e.g.* Ont., sec. 22(1); B.C., sec. 23(4); N.B., sec. 25. Also, in Ontario, a lien on a public work or a public street or highway, which does not attach to the land itself, will cease to exist if notice of the lien is not given as required by the Act within the time limited for giving such notice: Ont., sec. 22*a*. The onus is on the lien claimant to prove that his claim for lien was registered within the time limited for doing so in the Act and if he fails to satisfy that onus his lien will be lost, although he may be entitled to recover a personal judgment against the defendant with whom he had privity of contract: see *Warren Gen. Contracting Ltd. v. Robichaud* (1973), 6 N.B.R. (2d) 821 (C.A.). In Nova Scotia and Saskatchewan however, an unregistered lien will be preserved if an action is started by another lien claimant and a certificate of that action is registered in the appropriate Registry Office within the time limited for registration of the unregistered lien claimant's claim: N.S., sec. 24; Sask., sec. 37(1). This was also the law in Ontario until 1970 when the unregistered lien provisions of the Ontario Act were abolished. Presumably if the claimant himself commenced an action and registered a certificate thereof within the time limited for registering his claim for lien, his lien would be preserved without registration of a claim for lien at all in those two provinces. In the other provinces, failure to register the lien will be fatal to any claim under the Act. As was pointed out in *Rocky Mountain S.D. v. Atlas Lbr. Co.,* [1954] S.C.R. 589, reversing 8 W.W.R. 513, the Act, by declaring that the lien shall "absolutely cease to exist on the expiration of the time hereinbefore limited for the registration thereof", leaves no room for judicial indulgence.

It should be noted that in Saskatchewan a claim for lien may be registered and an action may be commenced to enforce the claim even after the time limited by the Act for registering the claim has expired and even if no action has been started by another lien claimant which would preserve the lien. Section 37(2) of the Saskatchewan Act provides that such a lien is valid except as against: (a) intervening parties who become entitled to any interest or estate in the land, or to a lien or charge upon the land, whose claim is registered or protected by the registration of a caveat prior to the registration of the lien; or (b) an owner, mortgagee, contractor, or subcontractor in respect of payments made in good faith to a contractor, subcontractor or lienholder after the expiration of the statutory period for registering liens under the Act and before any claim for lien is registered and notice of the same is given in writing to the owner, mortgagee, contractor or subcontractor, as the case may be. In *M.L. Plumbing & Heating Ltd. v. Smithson* (1977), 73 D.L.R. (3d) 481 (Sask. C.A.), it appeared that the owners had not retained the holdback which they were required to maintain under section 19 of the Act, and had paid their contractor in full for all work which it had completed at the date upon which the contractor abandoned the contract. Two claims for lien were registered by companies which had supplied materials to the contractor for use on the project. Both claims for lien were registered after the statutory period of 37 days from the supply of the last work or material, prescribed by section 36 of the Act, had expired. One of the claims had been registered less than 37 days after the date of abandonment by the contractor, the other had been registered more than 37 days from that date. The Court held, that the premature payment of the holdback by the owner did not affect the rights of the lienholders, and that under the provisions of section 37(2)(*b*), the lien registered before the expiration of 37 days following the contractor's abandonment of the work was a valid lien. The other lien was held to be invalid since it was registered after the owner became entitled to pay over the holdback. See also *Rasmussens' Ltd. v. Melville Country Club,* [1977] 4 W.W.R. 382 (Sask.), where it was held that, under this section, the owner was entitled to set-off his claim against the contractor for deficiencies, against the holdback which was still in his hands, since the lien claimants had not registered their claims for lien until after the expiration of the statutory period during which the owner was required to retain the holdback.

The following cases, many of which were decided under the old Ontario Act, will be of interest only in those provinces where the Act retains the "sheltering principle" of the unregistered lien. In *Baines v. Curley* (1916), 38 O.L.R. 301 (C.A.), it was held that even if the person who commenced the action and registered a certificate of action failed to establish a lien at the trial, those claimants whose claims were protected by the statement of claim and certificate of action of that claimant would still be entitled to have their liens enforced in the action. See also *McPherson v. Gedge* (1883), 4 O.R. 246 (C.A.); *Crawford v. Hesselink* (1958), 15 D.L.R. (2d) 294 (Nfld.); *N.S. Sand & Gravel Ltd. v. Kidstone Estates Ltd.* (1973), 13 N.S.R. (2d) 431; *Silver v. R.R. Seeton Const. Ltd.* (1977), 74 D.L.R. (3d) 212 (N.S.), and *Del Frari v.*

Wright, [1960] O.R. 430. While the Act appears to require the registration of the certificate of the action as well as the commencement of the action, within the time limited for registration of the claim for lien in order that the claimant may gain protection as an unregistered claimant, it was held in *Howard v. Herod Const. Co.* (1932), 41 O.W.N. 198 (C.A.) and *Ogilvie v. Cooke,* [1952] O.R. 862 (C.A.), that the failure of the plaintiff to register a certificate of action did not affect the right of the other claimants to a judgment for the enforcement of their claims.

The unregistered lien claimant is at a distinct disadvantage, however, and runs the risk of losing his right to a lien in the event that the property is sold or the action which has been commenced is settled without his knowledge. It is always prudent to register the claim for lien on title at the earliest possible moment. As was pointed out in *Stinson v. Mackendrick* (1924), 55 O.L.R. 358 (C.A.), the lienholder by virtue of his lien becomes a purchaser *pro tanto* of the property, but, if he fails to register his lien, he leaves the property in such a position that the owner may deal with it, and with the improvements the lienholder has placed upon it, by parting with it to a *bona fide* purchaser for value without notice who, upon the registration of his deed or mortgage, acquires statutory priority over the claimant's lien. The following cases also illustrate the danger of failing to register the claim for lien or to give written notice of it in accordance with the Act: *Charters v. McCracken* (1916), 36 O.L.R. 260 (C.A.); *Cook v. Koldoffsky* (1916), 35 O.L.R. 555 (C.A.); *Richards v. Chamberlain* (1878), 25 Gr. 402; *Sterling Lbr. Co. v. Jones* (1916), 36 O.L.R. 153 (C.A.); *Cut-Rate Plate Glass Co. v. Solodinski* (1915), 34 O.L.R. 604 (C.A.); *Wanty v. Robins* (1888), 15 O.R. 474 (C.A.); *Morton v. Grant,* [1956] O.W.N. 523 (C.A.); *Geo. Taylor Hdwe. Ltd. v. Balzer,* [1967] 2 O.R. 306 (C.A.); *D. Porter & Son v. MacLeod* (1951), 29 M.P.R. 83 (N.S.); *McVean v. Tiffin* (1885), 13 O.A.R. 1. See also Chapter 5, The Mortgagee, §63, *ante;* Chapter 8, Priorities, §94, *post;* Chapter 11, Practice before Trial, §144 and §84, *post.*

§80 Loss of Lien due to Failure to Commence an Action within the Prescribed Time.

Subject to what has been said above and to the exceptions below, a lien for which a claim has been registered will also cease to exist unless an action is commenced to realize the lien and a certificate thereof is registered in the appropriate Registry Office within the time limited for commencing the action by the Act (in Ontario, the action must be commenced within 90 days after the period of credit has expired or after the work or services have been completed or the materials have been furnished or placed): see Ont., sec. 23; Man., sec. 22; N.B., sec. 27. The Act further provides, since these actions are class actions, that if an action is commenced by any other person to enforce a lien against the same property within the time limited for commencing the claimant's action, his lien will be protected by that action and it will be unnecessary for him to commence one of his own: see *Contract Interiors & Design Ltd. v. Vogel,* [1973] 5 W.W.R. 286 (Alta.); *Silver v. R.R. Seeton Const. Ltd.* (1977), 74 D.L.R. (3d) 212 (N.S.); *Brousseau v. Muircrest Invts. Ltd.* (1977), 15 O.R. (2d) 145 at 155 (C.A.), and §73, The Unregistered Lien Claimant, *ante.* The Acts of Ontario and Newfoundland contain similar provisions with respect to the liens created by those Acts which do not attach to the land, except that the requirement that a certificate of action be registered does not apply: Ont., sec. 23a; Nfld. sec. 25(2), (3). It was held in *Del Frari v. Wright,* [1960] O.R. 430, that if the claim of the plaintiff in the other action is settled, a claimant who has registered a claim for lien may nevertheless proceed to the trial of his lien claim notwithstanding that no certificate of action in respect of his claim for lien has been registered, nor is the second action a separate action which ought to be consolidated with the action already commenced.

In Ontario, where the registration of the lien has been vacated by the Court under clause (*a*) or (*b*) of subsection (2) of section 25, prior to commencement of the action, it is not necessary that the claimant register a certificate of his action, although he must still commence his action within the prescribed 90 day period: sec. 25(3). The Newfoundland Act contains the same provision: sec. 27(3). In view of the changes made in the wording of section 25 by the present Ontario Act, the decision in *Friedman v. Stanton,* [1966] 2 O.R. 59, (to the effect that unless the lien had been vacated by an order made under clause (*a*) of this subsection, it would be necessary to register a certificate of action) no longer applies in that province. It would appear that, in Alberta, where the lien has been vacated under section 35 of the Builders Lien Act, R.S.A. 1970, c. 35, the claimant is not obliged to either commence his action or to register a certificate of *lis pendens* within the 180 days prescribed by section 32 of that Act, although the Court should at the time the application for payment into Court is made, direct the procedure to be followed in settling the issues to be decided: see: *Re Driden Indust. Ltd. and Sieber* (1974), 44 D.L.R. (3d) 629 (Alta. C.A.). It has been held that although Section 26(1) of The British Columbia Act requires the commencement of an action to enforce a lien and the registration of a certificate of *lis pendens* within one year following the date of filing the claim for lien, where the amount of the lien is paid into Court under section 33 of that Act the state of the title becomes irrelevant and a certificate of *lis pendens* need not be registered: see *Universal Supply Co. v. S. Radatske Const. Co.* (1972), 29 D.L.R. (3d) 251 (B.C. C.A.), which was followed in *Re Van Horne Elec. Ltd.* (1977), 2 B.C.L.R. 71 (C.A.). In the last mentioned case the Court refused an application to include a clause in the order cancelling the lien upon the applicant paying security therefor into Court, ordering the lien claimant not to file a *lis pendens* against the land if it commenced an action on its claim for lien, on the ground that section 33 did not give the Court authority to make such an order and, in any event, the lien having been cancelled on payment of the security, a *lis pendens* could not be filed against the land because the lien no longer existed.

It was held in *Constable v. Belvedere Holdings (1962) Ltd.* (1966), 58 W.W.R. 96 (Y.T. C.A.), that the failure to register the certificate of action could not be excused on the ground of lack of prejudice nor could it be classed as a mere irregularity or matter of form. The registration of the certificate was a condition precedent to the continued existence of the lien. In *Annett Chemicals Ltd. v. Moncton* (1971), 3 N.B.R. (2d) 698 (C.A.), the defendants appealed a judgment awarded against them in a mechanics' lien action on the ground, *inter alia,* that there was no proof that a certificate of action had been registered, although this issue had not been raised at trial. The Court pointed out that the evidence disclosed that the action had been commenced within the proper time and that if there had in fact been a failure to file the certificate required by the Act the failure to do so was a matter pending the action to be pleaded as a ground of defence under the rules of court applicable in New Brunswick. Alternatively, it was open to the defendants, in this situation, to apply for an order vacating the lien under section 30(4) of the Act. Since neither course was taken by the defendants, and the matter was not raised at the trial, the appeal was dismissed on this ground. In *Resources Enrg. of Can. Ltd. v. Loch Lomond Shopping Centre Ltd.* (1969), 2 N.B.R. (2d) 629, and also *Resources Enrg. of Can. Ltd. v. Bathurst Shopping Centre Ltd.* (1969), 1 N.B.R. (2d) 924, it was held that the Court had no jurisdiction to extend the time limited by the Act for filing the statement of claim. In *Tempo Bldg. Supplies Ltd. v. Western Realty Ltd.* (1972), 32 D.L.R. (3d) 643 (B.C. C.A.), where the lien claimant had commenced the action in the wrong county court, the Court refused to transfer it to the right county court and dismissed the action.

In Ontario, Manitoba, New Brunswick and Nova Scotia, the time for commencing the action is extended where the claimant has given a period of credit provided that the period of credit has been set out in the registered claim for lien. In these circumstances, the time within which the action must be commenced and the certificate of action registered begins to run from the date of expiry of the period of credit: Ont., sec. 23; Man., sec. 22; N.B., sec. 27; N.S., sec. 25(1). Again, if another claimant commences an action and registers a certificate thereof within the time limited for commencing the action following the expiry of the period of credit, it will be unnecessary for the claimant to commence an action of his own. Furthermore, even where the period of credit has not expired, the lienholder may nevertheless, if an action is commenced by any other person to enforce a lien against the same property, prove and obtain payment of his claim in that action as if the period of credit had expired: Ont., sec. 27; N.B., sec. 31(3); Man., sec. 26(4); N.S., sec. 30. It should be noted that, in Nova Scotia, even where the period of credit mentioned in the registered claim for lien has not expired it will cease to have any effect on the expiration of 6 months from the registration or any re-registration of the claim, unless the claim is re-registered within that period or unless an action is commenced within that period in which the claim can be realized: N.S., sec. 25(2). See also Chapter 10, Jurisdiction, §116, *post*.

In Nova Scotia, where the contract is under the supervision of an architect, engineer or other person upon whose certificate payments are to be made, a claimant who is a party to such contract must commence his action and register a certificate thereof within 30 days after registering his claim for lien: secs. 25(1) and 23(5). Many of the Acts provide a procedure for expediting the commencement of the action. For example, the Acts of Manitoba, Prince Edward Island and Saskatchewan permit any person having an interest in the land against which a lien is registered, to send a notice to the lien claimant at any time after 30 days have expired since the registration of his claim requiring him to commence his action within 30 days from the date of the notice. The form of the notice is prescribed by the Act. If an action is not commenced by the lien claimant within the specified time, the lien will cease to exist: Man., sec. 23(1); P.E.I., sec. 29; Sask., sec. 38(1). The Ontario, New Brunswick, Newfoundland and Nova Scotia Acts do not contain this or any similar provision. A similar procedure has been included in the British Columbia Act. Under that Act the notice can be sent by the owner or his agent and the lien claimant must commence his action within 21 days from the date of the mailing of the notice or his lien will cease to exist: B.C., sec. 26(2), 27. It was held in *Mike's Contracting Ltd. v. Dawson Lands Ltd.* (1977), 1 R.P.R. 353 (B.C.), that: the 21 day period commenced to run from the date of the mailing of the notice, not from the date of delivery; in calculating the 21 day period the first day should be excluded and the last day included; and the Court has no discretion to extend the time. In Alberta, any party to the action may serve any lienholder with a notice, in the form prescribed by the Act, requiring him to prove his lien. This notice may be served at any time after the party serving it has been served with the statement of claim. A lienholder who has been served with such a notice loses his lien unless he files an affidavit with the Court, providing detailed particulars of his lien, within 15 days of the service of the notice or within such further period as the Court may order.

In many of the other provinces, where the claimant is a party to a contract which is under the supervision of an architect, the time limited for registration of the claim for lien is extended until after the giving of the architect's certificate or until a certain number of days after the architect's failure to give a certificate when a demand has been made upon him to do so.

In these provinces, the action must be commenced and the certificate filed, if any, within the usual number of days reckoned from the time of the filing of the claim for lien rather than the time of the doing of the last work, and accordingly, the time for filing the certificate may be, in effect, extended. In all of these cases the claimant will be protected in the usual way if an action is commenced and a certificate of action filed by another claimant within the time limited for bringing his own action: see N.S., secs. 23(5) and 25(1); N.B., secs. 24(5) and 27; P.E.I. secs. 25(5) and 28.

§81 Loss of Lien through Failure to Proceed with the Action.

The various Acts provide a means of removing a certificate of action from the title to the property where the action has been commenced and the certificate registered but the action has not been proceeded with. In Ontario, section 22(3) provides that where a certificate of action has been registered for two years or more and no appointment has been taken out for the trial of the action, any interested party may apply *ex parte* to the Court for an order vacating the certificate and discharging all liens depending thereon. The Newfoundland Act contains the same provision except that the application may be brought where a certificate of action has been registered for one year or more: Nfld., sec. 24(4). Section 33(2) of the Alberta Act is similar to Ont. sec. 22(3), but it requires the interested party to apply on notice of motion. The Acts of most of the other provinces provide that where a certificate of action has been registered or filed, any interested party may obtain a certificate from the Clerk of the Court in which the action was begun, to the effect that the action has been discontinued or that the action having proceeded to trial, judgment was given in favour of the defendant and the time limited for an appeal has expired. This certificate may then be registered on title and has the same effect as a discharge signed by the plaintiff or his agent, or a Judge's Order vacating the registration: Sask., sec. 38(2); N.B., sec. 28. Most of the Acts further provide for the obtaining of an *ex parte* order discharging the claims for lien where the action has not been proceeded with and the certificate of action has not been registered. This order is made by the Court on an *ex parte* application supported by the Registrar's Abstract and an affidavit setting out the facts entitling the applicant to such order: Ont., sec. 25(5); N.B., sec. 30(4); Nfld., sec. 27(5). In Ontario and Newfoundland the applicant must also file a certified copy of the registered claim for lien with the Court. In accordance with the provisions of the Ontario Registry Act, R.S.O. 1970, c. 409, s. 65 [re-en. 1972, c.133, s.26], where an order vacating a certificate of action has been registered upon the title for two years, or where no certificate of action has been registered but a discharge of the lien has been registered on the title for more than two years, the Registrar is empowered to delete the entry in the

Abstract Book. The lien is then validly discharged and the certificate of action is duly vacated. This procedure also applies with respect to partial discharges of certificates of action and claims for lien.

§82 Loss of Lien by Agreement.

In *Jorgenson v. Sitar,* [1937] 2 W.W.R. 251 (Man. C.A.), Richards J.A. stated at page 253 that "it has been decided many times that ordinarily any privilege conferred by statute may be waived by agreement of the parties and that the right to enforce a mechanics' lien is no exception". In *Ritchie v. Grundy* (1891), 7 Man. R. 532, the Court expressed the opinion that the statute did not provide absolutely that there was to be a lien, but that there would be a lien in the absence of an agreement to the contrary. The decisions in *Shipway Mfg. v. Loew's Theatres* (1914), 7 O.W.N. 292 (C.A.) and *C. Beckett & Co. (Edm.) v. J. H. Ashdown Hdwe. Co.,* [1967] S.C.R. 610, affirming *(sub nom. Custom Glass Ltd. v. Waverlee Holdings Ltd.)* 59 W.W.R. 204, are to the same effect. The Saskatchewan and Alberta Acts provide that an agreement by anyone that the Act does not apply, or that the remedies or benefits provided by the Act are not to be available to him, is void: Alta., sec. 3; Sask., sec.11. The Acts of all of the other provinces, except Manitoba, provide that any agreement by a workman that the Act shall not apply, or that the remedies provided by the Act shall not be available to him, is null and void: Ont., sec. 4(1); B.C., sec. 10(1). Some of the Acts go on to provide, as do section 4(2) of the Ontario Act and section 4(2) of the Newfoundland Act, that this section does not apply to a manager, officer, foreman, or any person whose wages amount to more than a specified amount per day. In Ontario and Newfoundland this amount is $50.00 per day.

The Acts of those provinces which permit rights under the Act to be waived specifically state that no one who is not a party to the agreement waiving the lien is to be deprived of his lien rights: Ont., sec. 4(3); Nfld., sec. 5; Man., sec. 3. The decision in *Anly v. Holy Trinity Church* (1885), 2 Man. R. 248; reversed on other grounds 3 Man. R. 193 (C.A.), is to the same effect. The decision in *Forhan v. Lalonde* (1880), 27 Gr. 600, is no longer the law in this respect. See also *Emco (Western) Ltd. v. Carillon Invt. Ltd.* (1962), 39 W.W.R. 432 (Man. C.A.), and *Rideau Aluminum & Steels Ltd. v. McKechnie,* [1964] 1 O.R. 523; affirmed 48 D.L.R. (2d) 62, 659 (S.C.C.).

While the general rule is that the enforcement of the mechanics' lien must await the outcome of arbitration, if the contract contains an arbitration clause, it was held in *Great West Elec. Ltd. v. Housing Guild Ltd.,* [1947] 2 W.W.R. 1023, a British Columbia decision, that the claimant might enforce his lien despite the arbitration clause. Similarly, in *Art Plastering Co. v. Oliver,* [1945] O.W.N. 41, the Court took the position that if an action was commenced, the defendant might either waive the right to arbitration by entering a defence in the action or alternatively move for a stay of proceedings pending arbitration or for an outright dismissal of the action. If the defendant does neither but appears at the trial, it would seem that he will be taken to have waived this provision in the contract. See *Can. Sand etc. Co. v. Poole* (1907), 10 O.W.R. 1041; *Pigott Const. Co. v. Fathers of Confederation Memorial Citizens Foundation (No. 2)* (1965), 51 D.L.R. (2d) 367 (P.E.I.), and Chapter 10, Jurisdiction, §128 *post.*

§83 Loss of Lien through Waiver, Estoppel and Merger.

A waiver of lien must be in writing and must constitute the "express agreement to the contrary" contemplated by the section of the Act creating the lien: Ont., sec. 5(1). See *Lambton v. Can. Comstock Co.,* [1960] S.C.R. 86, affirming 10 D.L.R. (2d) 583; and *Anderson v. Fort William Commercial Chambers Ltd.* (1915), 34 O.L.R. 567 (C.A.). The latter case was cited with approval in the former and is authority for the proposition that estoppel cannot do what the section states only a signed express agreement can do. Accordingly, a person cannot, by his conduct, estop himself from claiming a lien. In *Lambton v. Can. Comstock Co., supra,* subcontractors had signed written acknowledgments that they had completed their contracts when in fact they had not, there being a relatively small amount of work to be done by them. They then completed their work and filed their liens within the proper time reckoned from the date the work was completed, although the liens would not have been filed in time if time had commenced to run at the date of the acknowledgements. The Court refused to infer that such an acknowledgement amounted to the express agreement to waive a lien contemplated by the Act. But see *Winnipeg Supply & Fuel Co. v. Genevieve Mtge. Corpn.; Wiebe v. Dom. Bronze Ltd.* [1972] 1 W.W.R. 651 (Man. C.A.). In *Can. Elec. Co. v. Ellsworth* (1932), 41 O.W.N. 112 (C.A.), it was held that a waiver of lien must be signed by a person having the power to do so, there must be no fraud in procuring it, and it must be given for consideration. The Court in that case approved the decision in *Vansickler v. McKnight Const. Co.* (1914), 31 O.L.R. 531; affirmed 51 S.C.R. 374. It was pointed out in *Lambton v. Can. Comstock Co., supra,* in *Jorgenson v. Sitar,* [1937] 2 W.W.R. 251 (Man. C.A.), and in *C. Beckett & Co. (Edm.) Ltd. v. J. H. Ashdown Hdwe. Co.,* [1967] S.C.R. 610, affirming (*sub nom. Custom Glass Ltd. v. Waverlee Holdings Ltd.*) 59 W.W.R. 204, that the waiver of lien must clearly and unmistakably indicate that the party signing it has renounced the application of the Act and the remedy provided by it, in order for it to become effective. The waiver must be an absolute waiver of the lien. In *Cloutier v. Weitzel,* [1950] 1 W.W.R. 385 (Man. C.A.), the Court held that a waiver of specific liens which was preceded by the statement that it was being made for the purpose of allowing the owner to obtain a mortgage loan on the premises did not constitute such an absolute waiver but was limited to the purpose expressed in the document. In *Westeel-Rosco Ltd. v. Bd. of Governors of South Sask. Hospital Centre* (1976), 69 D.L.R. (3d) 334 (S.C.C.), where the claimant gave a waiver of his right to register a lien against the land, which waiver expressly stated that its purpose was "to allow a loan to be obtained on the land and premises", it was held that the waiver had no legal effect since it did not constitute a waiver or renunciation of the claimant's claim against the holdback moneys which was the only claim which the claimant was seeking to enforce in that action, his claim against the land having been barred by statute.

In *Bill Boivin Plumbing & Heating Ltd. v. Flatt*, [1965] 2 O.R. 649 (C.A.), where the contract between the contractor and one of the lien claimants contained a waiver of lien clause, it was held that neither the owner nor any of the other lien claimants had the right to object to the admission of that claimant's lien as a valid lien since they were not parties to the contract which contained the waiver. This decision has now been overruled by the decision in *C. Beckett & Co. (Edm.) Ltd. v. J. H. Ashdown Hdwe. Co., supra*, where the facts were similar but where it was held that the waiver of lien constituted an absolute relinquishment, release and renunciation of any right of lien by the party signing it. The lien ceased to exist upon the execution of the waiver, which constituted the "express agreement to the contrary" contemplated by the opening words of the section creating the lien. The Court pointed out that the Act did not prescribe how or with whom the "express agreement" had to be made. Accordingly, any lien claimant can object to the admission of the claim of any other lien claimant who has waived his lien rights as can any other party to the action. See further *Winnipeg Supply & Fuel Co. v. Genevieve Mtge. Corpn.; Wiebe v. Dom. Bronze Ltd.*, [1972] 1 W.W.R. 651 (Man. C.A.); *Nor. Elec. Co. v. Frank Warkentin Elec. Ltd.* (1972), 27 D.L.R. (3d) 519 (Man. C.A.); *Grannan Plumbing & Heating Ltd. v. Simpson Const. Ltd.* (1977), 17 N.B.R. (2d) 569.

The Act specifically provides that the taking of any security for, or the acceptance of a promissory note or bill of exchange for, or the taking of any acknowledgment of the claim, or the giving of time for the payment of it, or the taking of any proceedings for the recovery, or the recovery of a personal judgment for the claim, does not merge, waive, pay, satisfy, prejudice or destroy the lien unless the claimant agrees in writing that it has that effect: Ont., sec. 26(1); N.S., sec. 29(1); Alta., sec. 22(1). In *Pomerleau v. Thompson* (1914), 5 W.W.R. 1360 (Alta.), it was held that a workman had not waived his right to a lien by reason of his having recovered a judgment in an action of debt against the contractor who employed him. The decision in

Edborg v. Imperial Timber etc. Co. (1914), 6 W.W.R. 180 (B.C.), is to the same effect.

In *Hamilton Bridge Works Co. v. Gen. Contracting Co.* (1909), 1 O.W.N. 34, the plaintiff had commenced a lien action and also an ordinary action to recover the money in respect of which the lien was sought. An application to stay the action was refused under this section of the Ontario Act. In *Rockwall Concrete Forming Ltd. v. Robintide Invt. Ltd.* (1977), 15 O.R. (2d) 422, where the facts were the same except that the defendant had paid the amount of the plaintiff's lien into Court to obtain an order vacating it under section 25(2) of The Mechanics' Lien Act, and the mechanics' lien action had been started first, the Court distinguished the *Hamilton Bridge Works* case on the ground that in that case the ordinary action had been started before the lien action, not after it. It held that in these circumstances the defendant would be greatly prejudiced if the plaintiff obtained a personal judgment against the defendant in the ordinary action which it would be obliged to pay even though the amount of the plaintiff's claim had already been paid into Court to await the outcome of the mechanics' lien action. The Court expressed the view that this was an abuse of the process of the Court and allowed the defendant's motion for an order staying the ordinary action as being frivolous and vexatious. In *Standard Indust. Ltd. v. E-F Wood Specialties Inc.* (1977), 16 O.R. (2d) 398, where the ordinary action was commenced just prior to the mechanics' lien action, the Court, after considering the decisions in the *Hamilton Bridge* and *Rockwall* cases, *supra,* dismissed the defendant's application to stay the ordinary action. In its decision the Court expressed the opinion that Weatherston J. was correct in staying the action on the facts of the *Rockwall* case but that the issue of the prejudice caused to the defendant in that case (as a result of the payment of the amount in dispute into Court) was sufficient grounds for his distinguishing the reasoning in the *Hamilton Bridge* decision. Maloney J., in the *Standard Industries* case, went on to express the view that section 26(1) of the Ontario Act permits a lien claimant, in proper circumstances, to contemporaneously exercise his rights both at common law and under the Mechanics' Lien Act by filing a lien and also instituting an ordinary action for the recovery of the same debt, and that in deciding the question of whether or not the defendant was entitled to have the ordinary action stayed, it was immaterial which of the two actions had been commenced first. He conceded, however, that there may be circumstances where a stay of one or the other of the actions would be justified where, as for example in the *Rockwall* case, there is real prejudice to the defendant which cannot be compensated for by costs. See also in this connection *Foxboro Co. v. Trident Const. Ltd.,* [1975] W.W.D. 167 (Man.C.A.), where the lien claimant, who had commenced a mechanics' lien action in the County Court, applied for an order dismissing an action commenced against it, and others, in the Court of Queen's Bench by the defendant in the lien action, on the ground that the defendant's action was an abuse of process and that it was frivolous and vexatious. The Court dismissed the lien claimant's application, directed that the lien action be merged in the larger action and heard by the Court of Queen's Bench, on the ground that it was not proper to have the same question before two Courts. The Court expressed the view in this case that, although it would be vexatious for the defendant to commence an action in the Court of Queen's Bench to deal with the same subject matter as the mechanics' lien action, it was not vexatious in the circumstances of this case where there were real issues between the plaintiff in the Queen's Bench action and a number of companies, one of which happened to be the plaintiff in the mechanics' lien action.

In *Robertson v. Bullen* (1908), 13 O.W.R. 56, a motion was brought by a claimant in a mechanics' lien action for personal judgment against one of the defendants who had defaulted in delivering a statement of defence and the Master refused judgment until trial on the ground that such an application was an attempt to combine a proceeding under The Mechanics' Lien Act with that given by the ordinary action for goods sold and delivered. Such a motion was also dismissed, and this decision was cited with approval in *D. & M. Bldg. Supplies Ltd. v. Stravalis Holdings Ltd.* (1976), 13 O.R. (2d) 443. In *Wake v. Can. Pacific Lbr. Co.* (1901), 8 B.C.R. 358 (C.A.), the plaintiff and other workmen obtained judgment for a claim for wages in an action under the British Columbia Woodmen's Lien for Wages Act and realized part of their claim upon execution. It was held that the plaintiff was estopped from enforcing his mechanics' lien for the amount of wages for which he had already obtained a judgment of which he had realized a part. In Ontario, however, the situation would appear to be that the claimant could still enforce his lien for the full amount less whatever had been recovered on the judgment obtained in the other action.

In *Makins v. Robinson* (1884), 6 O.R. 1, it was held that the acceptance of a draft did not amount to a waiver of lien in the absence of an express agreement to the contrary. Some of the Acts provide that where such a promissory note or bill of exchange has been negotiated, the lienholder will not thereby lose his lien if, at the time of bringing his action to enforce his lien or at the time of proving his claim in an action brought by another lienholder, he is the holder of such promissory note or bill of exchange: Ont., sec. 26(2); N.S., sec. 29(2); Alta., sec. 22(2); Nfld., sec. 28(2); Sask., sec. 42(2). The decision in *Stulberg & Son v. Linzon,* [1945] O.W.N. 791, is to this effect. Some of the Acts, however, provide that where a promissory note, bill of exchange or other security taken or accepted as mentioned above is discounted or negotiated by the lienholder, the discounting or negotiation will not prejudice or destroy the lien; but the lienholder shall retain the lien for the benefit of the holder of the promissory note, bill of exchange or other security: P.E.I., sec. 32(2); Man., sec. 26(2); N.B., sec. 31(2). See also Chapter 10, Jurisdiction.

In *Wortman v. Frid Lewis Co.* (1915), 9 W.W.R. 812 (Alta.), a materialman had filed a mechanics' lien, but upon the owner's agreeing to accept an order for the amount from the contractor, and at his request, he executed a discharge of the lien. It was held that this transaction amounted to an accord and satisfaction of his claim and that the claim could not be revived by the subsequent delivery of additional material. This case was cited with approval in *Reisman v. Laworand Properties Ltd.* (1966), 10 C.B.R. (N.S.) 190 (Ont.), where the lienholder had discharged his lien upon receiving some cash and a mortgage for the balance of his claim. The lienholder went on to do further work and then filed a lien for an amount equal to that secured by the mortgage plus the value of the work done subsequent to the giving of the discharge. It was held that the previously discharged lien could not be revived and he could only maintain a lien for the work done after the date on which the discharge was given. It was held in *Halstead v. Arick,* 76 Conn. 382, that a waiver of the right to file a mechanics' lien does not result as a matter of law merely from the fact that the owner, when he ordered the materials, agreed to give, and afterwards did give, a mortgage on the land as additional security for the debt. The question of whether the mortgage was intended to be in lieu of a lien was held to be a question of fact for the trial Court to decide.

The Act provides specifically that every device by an owner, contractor or subcontractor to defeat the priority given to a wage earner for his wages, and every payment made for the purpose of defeating or impairing a lien, shall be null and void: Ont., sec. 15(4); Man., sec. 12(5); P.E.I., secs. 6, 7(1). Most of the Acts further provide that any conveyance, mortgage or charge of or on land given to any person entitled to a lien thereon in payment of or as security for such claim, whether given before or after the lien has arisen shall be fraudulent and void as against other parties entitled to liens on such land: Ont., sec. 14(3); P.E.I., sec. 7(2); N.B., sec. 7(2). In *Ont. Hardwood Flooring Co. v. Dowbenko,* [1957] O.W.N. 177 (C.A.), the defendant owners had contracted with one Foley, a lien claimant, to do the plumbing and heating work in a building for $7,500.00. They also obtained a loan from him for $6,500.00 and agreed to give him a mortgage to secure the payment of the $6,500.00 borrowed and a second mortgage to secure the contract price of $7,500.00 plus a bonus of $2,000.00. It was held that, to the extent that the mortgages given to Foley represented security for the payment for work to be done, they were fraudulent and void as against the other lien claimants but that to the extent that the mortgages were given as security for the moneys actually advanced by way of loan they were valid and had priority over the claims of the lien claimants, having been registered before any of the claims for lien were registered or before any notice in writing of such claims had been given. A mortgage had also been given to another claimant for the value of his contract plus a bonus of $1,000.00. This mortgage was held to be fraudulent and void as against the lien claimants and since the bonus could only be considered as part of the price charged by the claimant for furnishing the materials on credit the bonus was also held to be fraudulent and void as against the lien claimants. See also Chapter 4, Rights and Duties of The Owner.

As has been pointed out in Chapter 3, The Lien Claimant, a conditional vendor of materials may have a claim under The Mechanics' Lien Act as well as under The Conditional Sales Act, but must eventually elect which remedy he intends to pursue. It was held in *U.S. Const. Co. v. Rat Portage Lbr. Co.* (1915), 9 W.W.R. 657 (Man. C.A.), that once the conditional vendor asserts and seeks to enforce a claim for lien, he must be taken to have elected to make the subject of the contract a part of the building and the realty against which he claims his lien. He is accordingly thereafter estopped from claiming that the materials are his property under his conditional sales contract or that he has the right to remove them. See also in this connection, *Agricultural Dev. Bd. v. De Laval Co.* (1925), 58 O.L.R. 35; *Hill v. Storey* (1915), 34 O.L.R. 489 (C.A); *Collis v. Carew Lbr. Co.* (1929), 37 O.W.N. 413; reversed 65 O.L.R. 520 (C.A.); *Dom. Lock Joint Pipe Co. v. York* (1929), 36 O.W.N. 2; affirmed 64 O.L.R. 365 (C.A.).

It was held in *Wake v. Can. Pacific Lbr. Co.* (1901), 8 B.C.R. 358 (C.A.), that where a workman had exercised his rights under the British Columbia Woodmen's Lien for Wages Act, he was estopped from exercising substantially the same rights in an action under The Mechanics' Lien Act. In *J. Coughlan & Co. v. Nat. Const. Co.* (1909), 14 B.C.R. 339 (C.A.), the plaintiffs had given a receipt for payments which they had not in fact received and they were held to be estopped from claiming such amount against the owner. It would appear that so long as the alternate remedy has not been proceeded with to a conclusion, the claimant will not be estopped from proceeding to enforce his lien. Accordingly, a claim for lien may be registered and an action commenced pending conclusion of a settlement in the process of negotiation. Most of the Acts provide, as does Ontario section 26(4), that the extension of the time for payment will not extend the times limited for commencing the action to enforce the lien, although no further proceedings are to be taken until the expiration of such extended time. It was held in *Kertscher v. Green,* (1910) 124 N.Y.S. 461, (1911) 127 N.Y.S. 1127 that a covenant in a building contract to the effect that the contractor would not permit a mechanics' lien to be filed or to remain on the property involved did not amount to a waiver of the contractor's right to file a lien on his own behalf. A similar clause was interpreted in the same way in *Davis v. La Crosse,* 121 Wis. 579, the Court holding that such a clause referred only to the claims for lien of those claiming under or through the contractor.

When such a clause appears in a contract, it refers only to the question of payment as between the parties to the contract. The contractor may still file his lien but will be met with the defence that he must pay the amounts of the claims for lien of the persons claiming under him as a condition of his being entitled to payment under his own contract with the owner.

It was held in *Galvin-Walston Lbr. Co. v. McKinnon* (1911), 4 Sask. L.R. 68 (C.A.), where the plaintiffs had a valid lien on a lot and building for materials supplied and subsequently became the owners of the lot on which the building was then standing, the building having been removed in the meantime by a third party, that whatever interest they could claim in the property under their lien had merged in their title as owners. Most of the Acts provide that the lien claimant, on registering his claim for lien, shall be deemed to be a purchaser *pro tanto* of the property: Ont., sec. 20; P.E.I., sec. 27; Sask., sec. 34(2). He would accordingly appear to be in the same position as a mortgagee with respect to his rights if he subsequently obtains a conveyance of the property.

§84 Loss of Lien Through Operation of The Registry Acts.

In Ontario, it is provided in section 20 that when a claim for lien is registered, the person registering the same is to be deemed a purchaser *pro tanto* and within the provisions of The Registry Act and The Land Titles Act, but, except as otherwise provided in The Mechanics' Lien Act, these Acts do not apply to any lien arising under The Mechanics' Lien Act. Section 14(1) requires that in order for a lien to have priority over subsequent advances made on account of any conveyance or mortgage of the property involved, actual notice in writing of the lien must be given by the claimant to the person making such payments, unless the claim for lien has been registered. As was pointed out in *Cook v. Koldoffsky* (1916), 35 O.L.R. 555 (C.A.), the Registry Acts deal only with priority as between registered instruments and the application of The Registry Act is by section 20 of The Mechanics' Lien Act predicated upon registration. Consequently, until registration, the lien is liable to be defeated by a conveyance of the property to a subsequent purchaser who registers his conveyance without actual notice of the claim for lien: *Wanty v. Robins* (1888), 15 O.R. 474 (C.A.); *Geo. Taylor Hdwe. Ltd. v. Balzer,* [1967] 2 O.R. 306 (C.A.). As it was put by Meredith C.J. in *Charters v. McCracken* (1916), 36 O.L.R. 260 at 263 (C.A.): "The effect of these two enactments seems to be, in such a case as this, that, if the lienholder delays registration of his lien, he does so at the risk of being cut out under the provisions of The Registry Act." It was held in *Kelly v. Progressive Bldrs. Ltd.* (1970), 1 N. & P.E.I.R. 1 (Nfld), that a claim for lien which had been registered after the owner's *bona fide* sale of the property was invalid, and that the lien could not attach to the proceeds

223

of the sale since the owner could not be said to have an "estate" or "interest" in the money.

It was held in *Harrell v. Mosier,* [1956] O.R. 152 (C.A.), that mortgages or conveyances must be registered in order to gain the protection of section 14 of The Mechanics' Lien Act. Schroeder J.A. after a thorough review of the authorities in this connection stated at page 162: "The Mechanics' Lien Act, The Registry Act and The Land Titles Act must be read together and it is perhaps unnecessary to say that registration under the latter two statutes cannot confer any rights upon a lien claimant unless he has a valid lien under the provisions of The Mechanics' Lien Act, nor can the provisions of The Registry Act or The Land Titles Act qualify or modify any limitations which The Mechanics' Lien Act places upon liens created and protected by that statute. The effect of section 20 of The Mechanics' Lien Act is to make the holder of a valid mechanics' lien a purchaser of the property *pro tanto* when he places his claim for lien upon the Register and he thus enjoys all the rights, privileges and advantages conferred by section 75 of The Registry Act upon a purchaser of property who, without actual notice of the rights of another purchaser or mortgagee, is the first to register evidence of his title in the appropriate Registry Office". See also *Whitehead v. Lach Gen. Contractors Ltd.* (1974), 3 O.R. (2d) 680 (C.A.). The protection given against unregistered lien claimants by section 14(1) of The Mechanics' Lien Act to mortgagees making advances and to purchasers making payments on account of the purchase price, continues until written notice has been received by them of the unregistered claim for lien or, alternatively, until a claim for lien is registered. See also Chapter 5, The Mortgagee.

As has already been pointed out, there is no right to a mechanics' lien at common law: *Johnson v. Crew* (1836), 5 O.S. 200 (C.A.). The lien is entirely a creature of statute and accordingly, as has been held in the following cases, strict compliance with the requirements of the statute is a condition precedent to the lien's existence: *Clarkson Co. v. Ace Lbr. Ltd.,* [1963] S.C.R. 110 at 114 reversing [1962] O.R. 748; *Edmonds v. Tiernan* (1892), 21 S.C.R. 406, affirming (*sub nom. Edmonds v. Walter*) 2 B.C.R. 82; *Emard v. Gauthier* (1916), 29 D.L.R. 315 (Que. C.A.); *Banque D'Hochelaga v. Stevenson,* [1900] A.C. 600; *Leroy v. Smith* (1900), 8 B.C.R. 293 (C.A.); *Wake v. Can. Pacific Lbr. Co.* (1901), 8 B.C.R. 358 (C.A.); *Calgary v. Dom. Radiator Co.,* 56 S.C.R. 141, reversing (*sub nom. Dom. Radiator Co. v. Payne*) [1917] 2 W.W.R. 974; *Crone v. Struthers* (1875), 22 Gr. 247; *Gearing v. Robinson* (1900), 27 O.A.R. 364; *Haggerty v. Grant* (1892), 2 B.C.R. 173; *Rafuse v. Hunter* (1906), 12 B.C.R. 126; *Robock v. Peters* (1900), 13 Man. R. 124; *Smith v. McIntosh* (1893), 3 B.C.R. 26; *Hulshan v. Nickling* [1957] O.W.N. 587 (C.A.). It follows that the question of priorities amongst unregistered lien claimants, purchasers, owners and mortgagees must be determined in accordance with the provisions of The Mechanics' Lien Act, and The Registry Act or The Land Titles Act cannot be relied upon unless registration of the claim for lien has taken place, bringing the section referring to those Acts into operation. In *Wanty v. Robins* (1888), 15 O.R. 474 (C.A.), Boyd C. seemed to suggest that because it had been held in *Murphy v. Leader* (1841), 4 Ir. L.R. 139, that The Registry Acts must receive an equitable construction, the requirements of The Mechanics' Lien Act must also receive such a construction and consequently a subsequent purchaser could only gain priority over an unregistered lien if such purchaser was an innocent purchaser entitled to the protection of The Registry Act. Since the lien is the creature of statute, the better opinion would appear to be that the only notice which will defeat the subsequent purchaser is a written notice of lien delivered prior to the registration of his deed or the actual registration of a claim for lien on the title to the property. The mere knowledge that work is under way on the property, or knowledge of a contract which requires work to be done on the property, does not constitute a sufficient notice of the existence of a lien on the part of a prospective purchaser or mortgagee: *Richards v. Chamberlain* (1878), 25 Gr. 402; *Sterling Lbr. Co. v. Jones* (1916), 36 O.L.R. 153 (C.A.); *West v. Sinclair* (1892), 12 C.L.T. 44 (Ont.); *Rose v. Peterkin* (1884), 13 S.C.R. 677; *Andre Knight Ltd. v. Presement*, [1967] 2 O.R. 289 (C.A.); *C.M.H.C. v. Wood* (1967), 53 M.P.R. 294 (Nfld.).

The situation is somewhat different when the purchase price is paid by instalments than when it is paid in one lump sum. A purchaser who pays the **purchase price in one lump sum is in much the same position as a mortgagee who has advanced his mortgage in one lump sum. He would have priority** over the unregistered lien or a lien registered subsequent to the payment being made. Under the provisions of Ontario section 14(1), where mortgage moneys are being advanced or payments on account of the purchase price are being made in instalments, the purchaser or the mortgagee, even though they have registered evidence of their interest in the lands prior to the registration of a lien, or prior to receiving the written notice of a lien contemplated by that section, will have priority over the claim for lien to the extent of the moneys advanced prior to receiving written notice or prior to registration of the claim for lien. The lien claimant in such circumstances loses priority over a subsequent purchaser if he fails to register his claim for lien, but only to the extent of the advances made at the time he does register or at the time that he gives notice of his claim for lien in writing.

In addition to the cases already cited, it may be useful to refer to the following cases on this subject: *Hynes v. Smith* (1879), 27 Gr. 150, affirming 8 P.R. 70 (C.A.); *McVean v. Tiffin* (1885), 13 O.A.R. 1; *Pannill Door Co. v. Stephenson*, [1931] O.R. 594 (C.A.); *Richards v. Chamberlain, supra; Sparks & McKay v. Lord, infra; Stinson v. Mackendrick* (1924), 55 O.L.R. 358 (C.A.); *Morton v. Grant*, [1956] O.W.N. 523 (C.A.); *Re Angus &*

Solloway Mills (1932), 41 O.W.N. 36; *Charters v. McCracken* (1916), 36 O.L.R. 260 (C.A.); *Independent Lbr. Co. v. Bocz* (1911), 4 Sask. L.R. 103 (C.A.); *Re Irvine and Main,* [1933] O.W.N. 476; *John A. Marshall Brick Co. v. York Farmers Colonization Co.* (1916), 54 S.C.R. 569, affirming (*sub nom. Marshall Brick Co. v. Irving*) 35 O.L.R. 542; *Re Pridham,* [1934] O.W.N. 560; *Reinhart v. Shutt* (1888), 15 O.R. 325; *Re Wallis and Vokes* (1889), 18 O.R. 8 (C.A.); *West v. Sinclair, supra.*

§85 Loss of Lien Resulting from Sale of the Property Under A Prior Mortgage.

It was held in *Atlas Lbr. Co. v. Mfrs. Life Ins. Co.,* [1942] 3 W.W.R. 284, varying (*sub nom. Mfrs. Life Ins. Co. v. Hauser*) [1942] 2 W.W.R. 114 (Alta. C.A.), that the limited priority of the lien did not defeat the right of the prior mortgagee to exercise his ordinary remedies and it was also indicated that a sale under the power of sale in a prior mortgage would rid the title of the subsequent liens and dispose of all unregistered liens. It was held in *Re Pridham, supra,* that a purchaser from the mortgagee on a sale under the power of sale contained in a mortgage, the lien action having been dismissed against the mortgagee, was entitled to a certificate of ownership in his favour from the Master of Titles showing his title free of the liens registered subsequent to the mortgage. In *Finn v. Miller* (1889), 10 C.L.T. 23 (Ont.), the mortgagees, under the power of sale in their mortgage, notified the lien claimants of the sale, sold the premises, and on their motion obtained an order annulling the registry of all liens and certificates of action, the mortgagees being ordered to pay any balance of the proceeds of the sale of the premises into Court.

It was indicated in *Biltmore Invts. Ltd. v. Mazur,* [1957] O.W.N. 468 (on the authority of the decision in *Sparks & McKay v. Lord,* 63 O.L.R. 393; affirmed (*sub nom. Steedman v. Sparks & McKay*) [1930] S.C.R. 351, that a sale under the power of sale contained in a prior mortgage would not wipe out the claims of subsequent registered liens. Since these cases were decided, however, the Ontario Mortgages Act was amended and the mortgagee now has the power to sell the mortgaged property free and clear of subsequent mechanics' liens provided he complies with the provisions of that Act: see The Mortgages Act, R.S.O. 1970, ch. 279. The mortgagee must give notice of his intention to sell to the lien claimant as a condition precedent to exercising his power of sale. The form of the notice is prescribed by the Act, (Form 1), and it may be given either by personal service or by registered mail. Under section 32(3) the mortgagee can serve the notice on the lien claimant's solicitor who filed the claim for lien. If there is no solicitor and no address for service is shown on the claim for lien and the mortgagee has no actual knowledge of the lien claimant's address, he does not need to give notice to the lien claimant at all.

See further in this connection, Chapter 5, The Mortgagee, § 66, *ante*.

§86 Loss of Lien as a Result of Foreclosure.

As to a lien claimant's rights in an action by a mortgagee for foreclosure see Chapter 5, The Mortgagee, §65, *ante*.

§87 Discharge of Lien.

The various Acts provide that a lien may be discharged by the registration of a receipt acknowledging payment signed by the claimant or his agent duly authorized in writing and verified by affidavit: Ont., sec. 25(1); Man., sec. 25(1); N.B., sec. 30(1). In Ontario, Saskatchewan and Newfoundland a discharge of a lien by a corporation does not need to be verified by affidavit. It is sufficient if the discharge is executed by the proper signing officers and the company's corporate seal is affixed over their signatures. Some of the Acts prescribe the form of discharge which is to be used. It is either contained in the regulations made under the Act or set out in a schedule at the end of the Act: see N.B., sec. 30(1); P.E.I., sec. 31(1); Alta., sec. 34(1). In *Re Petition of Can. Nor. Town Properties Co. and Nat. Trust Co.*, [1918] 1 W.W.R. 411 (Sask.), where a lien had been filed by a partnership trading under the name of what purported to be an incorporated company, it was held that a discharge of the lien would have to be executed by all of the partners or someone duly authorized on their behalf and that the Registrar was entitled to proof of the composition of the partnership. Once discharged, the lien can not be revived: *Reisman v. Laworand Properties Ltd.* (1966), 10 C.B.R. (N.S.) 190 (Ont.).

Once an action has been commenced, it will no longer be sufficient for the claimant who was plaintiff in that action to give a discharge of his lien. He should also consent to the vacation of the certificate of his action and normally an order is taken out which discharges the lien and vacates the certificate of action at the same time. However, there is nothing to prevent that claimant giving a discharge of his claim for lien as well as a consent to the vacation of his certificate of action. There is also nothing to prevent any other lien claimant from giving a discharge of his own lien, without consenting to the dismissal of the action. The giving of a discharge of his mechanics' lien by the plaintiff in the action will not prejudice the rights of other lien claimants sheltering under that certificate of action. The giving and the receiving of a satisfaction piece terminates the right to a lien, but the lien must still be removed from the title by the registration of a discharge of the lien or of an order of the Court discharging liens and certificates of action.

§88 Discharge of Lien following Judgment and Sale.

The judgment given on the final disposition of the action will provide for the discharge of any claims for lien which have not been established and for the payment into Court by the owner of the amount found owing to the lien claimants who have established valid liens at the trial. Upon this amount being paid into Court, the judgment will direct that all liens and certificates of action, or *lis pendens,* are to be discharged and vacated. If no one has proved a valid lien or if nothing is found due by the owner to the contractor, then the judgment will simply dismiss the action against the owner and provide for the discharge of all of the liens and vacation of all certificates of action. A certificate of this order registered on title will operate as a sufficient discharge. Such a judgment would also dispose of all unregistered liens before the Court. The judgment usually provides that the owner has a specified number of days within which to pay into Court the amount of the liens and goes on to provide that if he does not do so, the property may be sold to satisfy the claims of the lienholders. Once a sale has taken place, the interest of the lienholders in the property will be vested, along with the interest of the owner, in the new purchaser. Both registered and unregistered liens will accordingly be discharged as against the land itself although they attach to the proceeds of the sale which are paid into Court to stand in place and stead of the land.

The Ontario, Alberta, Saskatchewan and Newfoundland Acts also provide for the appointment of a trustee to manage and sell the lands for the lienholders: Ont., sec. 34(2), (3), (4), (5), (6); Alta., sec. 40(2), (3), (4), (5), (6), (7); Nfld., sec. 34(2), (3), (4), (5), (6), (7); Sask., sec. 50(3), (4), (5), (6), (7). The proceeds of the sale are paid into Court and are subject to the claims of all lienholders, mortgagees or other parties interested in the property, as their respective rights may be determined by the trial Judge. Upon a sale being made, the interest of the lienholders merges in the purchaser as is the case on a sale after judgment.

As has been pointed out, a sale by the owner to a *bona fide* purchaser for value without written notice of the liens will wipe out all unregistered liens, although if the purchase price is paid in instalments, the purchaser will gain priority over the liens only to the extent of payments made prior to his receiving notice in writing of the unregistered lien or prior to the registration of a claim for lien on the title to the property.

§89 Discharge of Lien by Payment.

The various Acts provide a procedure for the removal of liens from the title pending litigation over the validity of the liens. The owner, contractor, mortgagee, or any other interested party, may apply to the Court for an order allowing security for or payment into Court of the amount of the claim and such costs as the Court may fix, and the Court may then order that the registration of the lien and the registration of the certificate of action, if any, be vacated. The view was expressed in *Re Pecco Cranes*

(Can.) Ltd., [1973] 3 O.R. 737, that the order must provide for the payment into Court of the full amount of the lien claimant's claim, or the posting of security in a like amount, and that the only discretion the Court has with respect to the amount which is to be paid into Court or secured relates to the costs. However, the Master also noted in that judgment that it had been the practice on occasion to fix the security at, or to order payment into Court of, less than the amount claimed. This was in fact done in *Otis Elevator Co. v. Commonwealth Holiday Inns of Can. Ltd.,* [1972] 2 O.R. 536, where it was ordered that some $404,000 in liens be vacated, under this section, upon the owner paying $215,000 into Court, or furnishing security by way of a bond in the same amount. Colter J., at p. 540 of the judgment in this case, expressed the view that: "The lien claimants are entitled to have paid into Court the highest amount for which, at this stage, the owner can be reasonably foreseen to be liable". As was pointed out in *Pedlar People Ltd. v. McMahon Plastering Co.* (1960), 33 W.W.R. 47, (addendum) 34 W.W.R. 315 (Alta.), the mere payment of the security into Court in no way prejudices any of the parties in questioning the validity of the lien. See also *Nanaimo Contractors Ltd. v. Patterson* (1964), 48 W.W.R. 600 (B.C. C.A.).

The Act further provides that the registration of the lien and the registration of the certificate of action can be vacated upon any other proper ground by the Court: see Ont., sec. 25(2) (*b*); Sask., sec. 40(2), (3); Nfld., sec. 27(2). It was held in *Financial Bldg. Ltd. v. Bird Const. Co.* (1960), 32 W.W.R. 189 (Sask.), that the powers conferred by this section should be exercised only in a clear case and where the rights of the lien claimant will not be prejudiced. In that case, the applicant sought to have the lien vacated on the ground that the lien was embarrassing the applicant in its attempts to obtain funds on the security of the property, and the Court refused to vacate the lien. This statement was approved in *Atamanenko v. Terra Cement Service Ltd.,* [1976] 6 W.W.R. 381 (Sask.), in which the Court pointed out that the section had been amended since the decision in the *Financial Building* case had been given so as to require the applicant to provide "proof that no other person is entitled to a lien". Since the applicant had not given the Court satisfactory proof of that fact, the Court dismissed the application. The Court dismissed an application under the second branch of this section in *Saccary v. Jackson* (1975), 11 N.S.R. (2d) 316 (C.A.), on the ground that there were questions of law involved in the application which should be dealt with at the trial when all of the facts were before the Court. The decision in *Re Ellwood Robinson Ltd. and Ohio Dev. Co.* (1975), 7 O.R. (2d) 556, is to similar effect. It was held in *Bristol Const. Co. v. D.K. Invts. Ltd.,* [1972] 4 W.W.R. 119 (B.C.), that a pleading by a defendant of set-off and counterclaim ought not to be considered on such an application or applied in reduction of the amount of the security to be given. It was held in *Re Phillips-Anderson Constructors Ltd. and Tuxedo Co.* (1977), 77 D.L.R.

(3d) 473 (Man. C.A.), that section 11.3 of The Builders and Workers Act, which provides that a lien created under section 11 of that Act may be realized in the same Court and with the same procedures as a mechanics' lien may be realized, does not confer jurisdiction on a County Court Judge sitting in a mechanics' lien action to vacate a lien created under The Builders and Workers Act.

Where liens have been filed by both the contractor and persons who supplied labour and materials to him for use on the construction project, the Court may direct payment into Court, under this section, of an amount which is less than the aggregate value of all of the liens, either on the ground that the maximum amount which the subsidiary lien claimants will be entitled to is the amount owing to the contractor or, conversely, where the aggregate value of the subsidiary claims exceeds the amount claimed by the contractor, on the ground that the maximum amount which can be recovered from the owner is the larger amount owing to the subsidiary claimants. In *Nation Drywall Contractors Ltd. v. All Round Properties Administration Ltd.* (1975), 10 O.R. (2d) 295, the Court vacated the liens of the contractor and its subcontractors, which totalled in excess of $1,600,000, upon the owner paying into Court the amount claimed by the contractor, namely $822,000, together with security for costs in the sum of $82,000 upon it appearing that the maximum liability of the owner to the lien claimants would not exceed that amount. See also *Otis Elevator Co. v. Commonwealth Holiday Inns of Can. Ltd., supra.*

It is now no longer necessary in Ontario to register a certificate of action where an order to vacate the registration of a lien has been made under either clause (*a*) or clause (*b*) of section 25(2): sec. 25(3). Until the Act was amended in 1970 the section only dispensed with the registration of the certificate of action if the order had been made under clause (*a*) of section 25(2), directing payment of the whole amount of the lien into Court. The decision in *Friedman v. Stanton,* [1966] 2 O.R. 59 is accordingly no longer law in Ontario. The lien claimant must still commence his action to enforce the lien within the 90 day period prescribed by the Act, however: *Re Chimo Lbr. Ltd. and Abode Two Ltd.* (1978), 18 O.R. (2d) 691 (Div. Ct.). Section 27(3) of the Newfoundland Act and section 40(3) of the Saskatchewan Act are to the same effect as Ontario section 25(3). Section 35 of the Alberta Act does not dispense with registration of the certificate of action where the registration of the lien has been cancelled upon the giving of security for or the payment into Court of the amount of the lien. However, it was held in *Re Driden Indust. Ltd. and Sieber* (1974), 44 D.L.R. (3d) 629 (Alta.C.A.), that section 32 of the Act, which provides that a lien ceases to exist unless an action is commenced to realize the lien and a certificate of *lis pendens* is registered within 180 days from the date of registration of the lien, has no application when the registration of the lien has been cancelled by the Court pursuant to section 35. In that case the contractor, who had paid the amount of the lien into Court and obtained an order cancelling the registration of the lien pursuant to section 35, applied to have the moneys in Court paid out to him after the expiry of the 180 days mentioned in section 32 because no action to enforce the lien had been commenced by the lien claimant. The Court dismissed his application and directed a reference back to the trial Judge to settle the issues to be decided between the parties. In *Universal Supply Co. v. S. Radatske Const. Co.* (1972), 29 D.L.R. (3d) 251 (B.C. C.A.) it was held that where the lien is cancelled upon payment of security therefor into Court, under the corresponding section of the British Columbia Act, it is not necessary to register the certificate of *lis pendens* required by section 26(1) of that Act since the state of the title is no longer relevant. This decision was approved in *Re Van Horne Elec. Ltd.* (1977), 2 B.C.L.R. 71 (C.A.) where the Court held that once the lien had been cancelled under this section a certificate of *lis pendens* could not be filed against the land because the lien would be non-existent.

Under section 38(10) of the Ontario Act and section 38(9) of the Newfoundland Act, any interested party may obtain an order permitting him to cross-examine a lien claimant, or his agent or assignee on his affidavit verifying the claim. The transcript of such an examination can of course be used in support of an application under this section, either to have the amount to be paid into Court reduced or to demonstrate that the lien is invalid because, for example, it was registered too late, or against the wrong land. The transcript of the cross-examination must clearly indicate that the applicant is entitled to such relief, however: see *Kleenaire Equipment Ltd. v. Dennis Commercial Properties Ltd.,* [1970] 3 O.R. 776. In Ontario, it has been held that the application for the order permitting the cross-examination of the lien claimant cannot be brought until after the action has been commenced, and that in the Judicial District of York the Master has no jurisdiction to make such an order until after the action has been referred to him under section 31(2) of the Act: *Re Pecco Cranes (Can.) Ltd.,* [1973] 3 O.R. 737.

With respect to the discharge or vacation of the lien as the result of payment into Court, see also Chapter 4, Rights and Duties of the Owner, and § 23, *ante.*

All payments made by owners to contractors or by contractors to subcontractors up to the amount of the holdback operate as discharges *pro tanto* of the claims for lien of such contractors or subcontractors if made before notice in writing of a lien has been given to the person making such payment, and if made in good faith: see Ont., sec. 11(6); Nfld., sec. 13(6); N.S., sec. 12(4). The payment over of the holdback after the time limited for registration of liens has expired operates as a discharge of all liens or charges in respect of the holdack, unless, in the meantime, a claim for lien has been registered or proceedings have been commenced to enforce a lien: see Ont., sec. 11(7); Nfld., sec. 13(7); N.S., sec. 12(5). These sections further provide that if a claim for lien has been registered, or proceedings have been commenced to enforce a lien, the owner may pay the holdback into Court in the proceedings and such payment will constitute valid payment in discharge of the owner to the amount thereof. As was pointed out in *Bond Structural Steel (1965) Ltd. v. Cloverlawn Invts. Ltd.,* [1973] 3 O.R. 856, section 11(6) provides for the discharge of the lien to the extent of 85% and section 11(7) provides for its discharge *in toto,* either as a result of the payment of the holdback to the person entitled to receive it, if no liens have been filed in time, or as a result of the payment of the holdback into Court, if liens have been filed within the time prescribed by the Act.

Section 19(2) of The Mechanics' Lien Act, 1960, the Act formerly in force in Alberta, provided that, after the proceedings had been commenced or a lien had been registered, the person responsible for maintaining the holdback might pay it into Court and such a payment into Court constituted a valid payment in discharge of that person on the contract to the amount thereof. In Alberta it has been held under that Act that such a payment by the owner operated as a discharge of the liens since he could not be liable, under that Act, for a greater amount than that owed to the contractor. See *Kay v. Imperial Lbr. (Jasper Place) Ltd.* (1965), 51 W.W.R. 80 (Alta.); *C. J. Oliver Ltd. v. Foothills Lighting & Elec. Ltd.* (1965), 54 W.W.R. 37 (Alta. C.A.); *Hudson's Bay Oil etc. Co. v. Trustee in Bankruptcy of F. P. C. Const. Ltd.* (1969), 67 W.W.R. 665 (Alta.). The Acts of Ontario (sec. 11(7)), Newfoundland (sec. 13(7)), Saskatchewan (sec. 20(9)) and British Columbia (sec. 21(4)), contain a similar provision. This section is not interpreted in Ontario as entitling the owner to have the registration of the liens and certificates of action vacated upon his paying the holdback into Court. See also *Nanaimo Contractors Ltd. v. Patterson* (1964), 48 W.W.R. 600 (B.C. C.A.). The provisions of section 18(2) of the present Alberta Act are similar to those of section 19(2) of the former Act. The present Act, however, specifically provides that payment into Court under this section discharges the owner from any liability in respect of liens, that the money, when paid into Court, stands in the place of the land, and that the order providing for payment into Court of the holdback shall also provide that the liens be removed from the title to the land concerned: sec. 18(4). Section 18(3) provides that notice is to be given of the application to pay the holdback into Court as provided in section 37(1). On the hearing of the application, the Court may, (a) hear affidavit or *viva voce* evidence to determine the proper amount of the holdback to be paid into Court, (b) direct the trial of an issue to determine this question, or (c) refuse the application if it is of the opinion that the amount of the holdback should be determined at the trial of the action: sec. 18(5).

8

Priorities

§90 In General.

The question of priorities as between mortgagees and lien claimants has been discussed in Chapter 5, The Mortgagee. For a full discussion of priorities with respect to costs in mechanics' lien proceedings see §167, "Costs", *post*.

The Acts of all the provinces, except Alberta, provide that the mechanics' lien shall have priority over all judgments, executions, assignments, attachments, garnishments and receiving orders, recovered, issued or made after the lien arises. The Alberta Act contains a similar provision except that the priority of the lien dates from the time at which the statement of lien is registered: Alta., sec. 9(1). Most of the Acts go on to provide that the lien will have priority over all payments or advances made on account of any conveyance or mortgage after notice in writing of the lien has been given to the person making such payments or after registration of a claim for lien: Ont., sec. 14(1); Sask., sec. 26(1); Man. sec. 11(1). It is clearly the intention of the Act to ensure that the lienholders' rights thereunder cannot subsequently be prejudiced by any other person once he has protected those rights in accordance with the provisions of the Act. In this connection, see *Edwards Welding Ltd. v. Howe & Wilson Const. Ltd.* (1959), 27 W.W.R. 689 (B.C.); *John A. Marshall Brick Co. v. York Farmers Colonization Co.* (1916), 54 S.C.R. 569, affirming (*sub nom. Marshall Brick Co. v. Irving*) 35 O.L.R. 542; *High River Trading Co. v. Anderson* (1909), 10 W.L.R. 126 (Alta.); *Robock v. Peters* (1900), 13 Man. R. 124; *Geo. Taylor Hdwe. Ltd. v. Balzer,* [1967] 2 O.R. 306 (C.A.); *Andre Knight Ltd. v. Presement,* [1967] 2 O.R. 289 (C.A.); *Baxter Student Housing Ltd. v. College Housing Co-op. Ltd.* (1975), 57 D.L.R. (3d) 1 (S.C.C.). Most of the Acts further provide that a lienholder, upon registration of his lien, becomes a purchaser *pro tanto* of the property against which the lien is filed within the provisions of The Registry Act or The Land Titles Act: Ont., sec. 20; Man., sec. 19; P.E.I. sec. 27; *Harrell v. Mosier,* [1956] O.R. 152 (C.A.); *C.M.H.C. v. Wood* (1967), 53 M.P.R. 294 (Nfld.). The lienholder accordingly becomes entitled to the protection of the provisions of those

Acts which state that priority of registration will prevail between documents in the absence of actual notice.

While most of the Acts specifically provide that there will be no priority among lienholders of the same class, all claimants of the same class ranking *pari passu* on any funds available for distribution, they also provide that such provisions do not apply to wage earners. The wage earner is given a priority, usually to the extent of 30 days' wages, over all other liens derived through the same contractor or subcontractor: Ont., sec. 15(1); N.S., sec. 15(1); Sask., sec. 28(1). Where the general contractor, subcontractors and sub-subcontractors all establish liens, the sub-subcontractors will have a claim against the distributive share in the holdback of the subcontractor who is primarily liable to them in priority to the claim of that subcontractor. Similarly, the subcontractors are entitled to be paid out of the holdback, which would otherwise be payable to the general contractor, before he receives any payment on his lien. In this situation there are, in effect, three classes of lienholders. See, *Rideau Aluminum & Steels Ltd. v. McKechnie,* [1964] 1 O.R. 523; affirmed 48 D.L.R. (2d) 62, 659 (Can.).

While priority is given to a lien claimant over judgments or executions recovered or issued after his lien arises, priority is not given for all liens over judgments arising after the first lien arises. Thus, one lien may have priority over a particular judgment or execution creditor while another lienholder may not, since one claimant may have commenced his work before the judgment is recovered and another after the judgment is recovered: *Johnson v. Braden* (1887), 1 B.C.R. 265; *Ottawa Steel Castings Co. v. Dom. Supply Co.* (1904), 5 O.W.R. 161. The latter case is also authority for the proposition that the priority given to the lien claimant is not merely for that portion of the price of his work actually earned at the date of the judgment, but for the full amount of his contract if it is completed after the judgment is recovered. As was pointed out in *Cook v. Koldoffsky* (1916), 35 O.L.R. 555 (C.A.), the person seeking priority must prove that he complied with the Act, and if, for example, he seeks to establish that advances were made by a mortgagee or a purchaser after notice of the lien had been received by such mortgagee or purchaser, the onus is on him to establish that fact. The Court will not, however, permit such a purchaser or mortgagee to gain priority over and defeat a lien fraudulently or by unfair means: *Rose v. Peterkin* (1884), 13 S.C.R. 677.

In *Crown Lbr. Co. v. Smythe,* [1923] 2 W.W.R. 1019 (Alta. C.A.), it was held that sureties on a bond for the completion of a school building contract, who had completed the contract, were subrogated to the rights of the owner under the contract with respect to charging the cost of completion against the moneys in its hands, their rights having priority over those of the lien claimants. This decision would appear to be correct under the law of Alberta as it then stood, but it must be remembered that there were no

234

"holdback" provisions in the Alberta Act at the time of that decision requiring the owner to retain and hold inviolate a percentage of the contract price for the benefit of subcontractors, materialmen and wage earners. It is submitted that the sureties on a performance bond cannot now use such holdback moneys to defray the additional cost of completion in priority to the lien claimants even though they are subrogated to the rights of the owner. They would also be subrogated to the owner's liabilities and this fund could only be used by them after registered lienholders had been paid in full. In most jurisdictions the sureties would, as would the owner, be entitled to use any moneys in the owner's hands at the time of the contractor's default, over and above the statutory percentage retained, to defray costs of completion. They would always be able to use any moneys left over after registered lienholders had been paid for this purpose. This would be so even if claims were lodged by suppliers, workmen or subcontractors under the trust provisions of the Acts which contain trust fund provisions similar to Ontario section 2(1), since such a surplus would not constitute a trust fund in the hands of the owner: see *Oil Well Supply Co. v. Bank of N.S.* (1951), 2 W.W.R. 554 (Alta. C.A.); *Edwards Welding Ltd. v. Howe & Wilson Const. Ltd.* (1959), 27 W.W.R. 689 (B.C.); *Re Bishop, Rowe & Spaith Const. Co.* (1961), 35 W.W.R. 20 (Alta.); *Royal Bank v. Wilson* (1963), 42 W.W.R. 1, varying 41 W.W.R. 465 (Man. C.A.); *Re Northwest Elec. Ltd.* (1973), 18 C.B.R. (N.S.) 26 (B.C.). It was pointed out in *Noranda Exploration Co. v. Sigurdson* (1975), 53 D.L.R. (3d) 641 (S.C.C.) that mechanics' lien legislation is intended to protect owners as well as labourers and materialmen as evidenced by the fact that the Act limits the owners' liability to "the sum payable by the owner to the contractor". In that case the Court upheld the owner's right to set off its cost of completing the contractor's abandoned contract against amounts owing to the contractor over and above the holdback amount.

This situation is now somewhat more complicated in Ontario and Saskatchewan as a result of the decisions in *Vaillancourt Lbr. Co. v. Trustees of S. S. Section No. 2, Twp. of Balfour* [1964] 1 O.R. 418 (C.A.); *S. I. Guttman Ltd. v. James D. Mokry Ltd.,* [1969] 1 O.R. 7 (C.A.); *Scarborough Painting Ltd. v. Buckley* (1974), 4 O.R. (2d) 253, and *Can. Comstock Co. v. Toronto Transit Commn.; Can. Comstock Co. v. Anglin-Norcross Ont. Ltd.,* [1970] S.C.R. 205, and the amendments made to the "trust fund" sections of the Ontario Act in 1970 and the Saskatchewan Act in 1973. The net result of the decisions in these cases would appear to be that, if the owner pays his contractor after receiving notice of a lien he will be obliged to turn over to the lien claimants not only the holdback, but in addition, an amount equal to the sum claimed in the notice. In these circumstances, the owner will not be able to use all of the moneys which he owes to the contractor in excess of the holdback to defray the cost of completing an abandoned contract. A surety on a performance bond will be in the same position. Sections 2(3) of the Ontario Act and 3(3) of the Saskatchewan Act constitute any sum which becomes payable under a contract by an owner to a contractor, on the certificate of a person authorized under their contract to make such a certificate, a trust fund in the owner's hands, for the benefit of the contractor, Workmen's Compensation Board and others who have supplied labour and materials on the contract. The owner is apparently prohibited by this section, from using moneys which become payable on such a certificate for any purpose not authorized by the trust until all of the beneficiaries of the trust have been paid. It would appear then that, on a strict reading of this section, such moneys cannot be used by the owner to complete an abandoned contract. However, in *Standard Indust. Ltd. v. Treasury Trails Holdings Ltd.* (1976), 24 C.B.R. (N.S.) 8, affirmed 23 C.B.R. (N.S.) 244 (Ont. C.A.), the Ontario Court of Appeal upheld the trial Judge's decision that the opening words of the section, which read, "Where a sum becomes payable . . .", constitute the first condition of the owner's liability under it and, accordingly, if the moneys certified for payment do not become payable to the contractor, by reason of the owner exercising his right to set off his claim for damages against the contractor for the cost of completing or correcting his work, then the trust does not arise. See also § 36, "Notice of the Lien", *ante* and Chapter 9, The Trust Fund.

§91 Priority of Taxes.

Provincial statutes providing that taxes shall constitute a lien upon the lands of the taxpayer create a lien which has priority over mechanics' liens. For example, the Ontario Municipal Act, R.S.O. 1970, ch. 284, sec. 511, constitutes taxes due to a municipality, together with costs, a special lien on the land and gives such lien priority over every claim, privilege, lien or encumbrance of every person except the Crown. Such municipal taxes accrue from day-to-day. Also, The Ontario Corporations Tax Act, 1972, c. 143, sec. 167, constitutes taxes under the Act, a first lien and charge upon the property in Ontario of the corporation liable to pay such taxes, together with interest, penalties, costs and other amounts. The Ontario Workmen's Compensation Act, R.S.O. 1970, ch. 505, sec. 113, permits the collection of assessments owing under that Act through the Municipal Tax Collectors. When such an assessment is added to realty taxes it has the same priority over mechanics' liens as municipal taxes. The Ontario Public Utilities Act, R.S.O. 1970, ch. 390, sec. 30 provides for a similar procedure with respect to moneys owing to public utilities. It was held in *A. B. Cushing Mills Ltd. v. Barker* (1952), 5 W.W.R. 170 (Alta.), that there was no provision in The Hospitals Act of Alberta (R.S.A. 1942, ch. 184) or any other statute of that province which gave a municipality's claim for hospital expenses priority over mechanics' liens.

While the provisions of various federal and provincial statutes levying taxes provide that such taxes have priority over other debts owing by the person upon whom the tax is levied, this priority cannot, in most instances, take precedence over the lien except to the extent that the amount held by the taxpayer for the benefit of the lien claimants exceeds the statutory holdback under The Mechanics' Lien Act, unless the tax claimed has been constituted a lien upon the land involved. See *Sandberg v. Meurer,* [1949] 1 W.W.R. 117 (Man. C.A.), where it was held that the words "assets of such person" contained in The Income War Tax Act included only such of the person's properties or assets as were available to satisfy his debts. Since moneys which an owner is required to hold back from the contractor are subject to the payment of such liens as are duly found payable by the Court, they are not assets of the contractor except insofar as such moneys exceed the amount of such liens: *Hudson's Bay Oil etc. Co. v. Trustee in Bankruptcy of F.P.C. Const. Ltd.* (1969), 67 W.W.R. 665 (Alta.); *Ocean Air Conditioning & Refrigeration Contractors Ltd. v. Dan; Re A & W Food Services of Can. Ltd. and Vancouver A & W Drive-Ins Ltd.,* [1977] 3 W.W.R. 456 (B.C.C.A.). See also *Shoquist Const. Co. v. Norfolk & Retailers Trust and Savings Co.* (1974), 19 C.B.R. (N.S.) 151 (Sask.); *H. & H. Trucking Ltd. v. Midas Aggregates Ltd.* (1974), 46 D.L.R. (3d) 637 (B.C.); *Rasmussens' Ltd. v. Melville Country Club,* [1977] 4 W.W.R. 382 (Sask.) and *Modular Products Ltd. v. Aristocratic Plywoods Ltd.; Modular Products Ltd. v. R.,* (1974), 42 D.L.R. (3d) 617 (B.C.C.A.) in which it was held that claims under The Mechanics' Lien Act took priority over a demand for income taxes owing by the person primarily liable to the lien claimants which had been served on the person maintaining the holdback. See also: *Anden Vinyl Products Ltd. v. Gauss* (1976), 16 O.R. (2d) 225.

When funds are distributed by the taxpayer, however, the claim of a federal or provincial government for taxes will be paid first out of the funds in priority to lien claimants: *Wesner Drilling Co. v. Tremblay* (1909), 18 O.L.R. 439 (C.A.). In *Traders Realty Ltd. v. Huron Heights Shopping Plaza Ltd.,* [1967] 2 O.R. 522, a mortgagee was given priority over lienholders for the amount it paid out for municipal taxes after the liens were registered, on the ground that on making the tax payment it became subrogated to the rights of the municipality which had a lien in priority to the mechanics' lienholders.

§92 The Claim for Wages.

Wages are defined by most of the Acts as money earned by a workman, mechanic or labourer for work done by time or as piece work: Ont., sec. 1(1) (h); Sask., sec. 2(1)(*o*); N.S., sec. 1(*g*). The definition of "wages" in the

Ontario and Newfoundland Acts has been expanded to include "all monetary supplementary benefits, whether by statute, contract or collective bargaining agreement". This was done to make it clear that such employee benefits as vacation pay credits, welfare plan payments and contributions to pension funds, which are in reality part of the wage earner's wages, were to be included in the amount for which a workman has priority over other lien claimants. The expanded definition does not, however, appear to be broad enough in scope to include within its ambit an assessment under the Ontario Workmen's Compensation Act: *Union Elec. Supply Co. v. Gillin Enrg. & Const. Ltd.,* [1971] 3 O.R. 125. Many of the Acts also define the term "workman" or "labourer" as meaning a person employed for wages in any kind of labour, whether employed under a contract of service or not: Ont., sec. 1(1)(*i*); Alta., sec. 2(2)(*e*); Sask., sec. 2(1)(*e*).

The wage earner is given a priority over other lien claimants, (whose claims are derived through the same contractor or subcontractor), to the extent of and on the holdback, for his wages earned over a specific period of time: Ont., sec. 15(1); N.B., sec. 10(2); Man., sec. 12(1). Thus, section 15(1) of the Ontario Act provides that: "Every workman whose lien is for wages has priority to the extent of 30 days wages over all other liens derived through the same contractor or subcontractor to the extent of and on the 15 per cent directed to be retained by section 11 to which the contractor or subcontractor through whom the lien is derived is entitled and all such workmen rank thereon *pari passu.*"

Most of the Acts go on to provide that the wage earner shall be entitled to enforce his lien despite the fact that any contract or subcontract has not been completely fulfilled. If the contract has not been completed then the holdback is to be calculated on the value of the work done or materials furnished by the contractor or subcontractor by whom the wage earner is employed: Ont., sec. 15(2), (3); Man., sec. 12(2), (3); Sask., sec. 28(2), (3). Most of the Acts provide that every device adopted by an owner, contractor or subcontractor to defeat the priority given to the wage earner for his wages and every payment made for the purpose of defeating or impairing a lien shall be void: Ont., sec. 15(4); Sask., sec. 28(4), 27; N.B., sec. 6(2), 7(1).

Sections 15(2) of the Ontario Act and 17(2) of the Newfoundland Act provide that a wage earner may serve a notice of motion on the proper persons, returnable within 4 days after service thereof before the Judge or officer having jurisdiction to hear mechanics' lien actions, asking for judgment on his claim for lien immediately. The claimant is required by these sections to serve registered particulars of his claim for lien, duly verified by affidavit, along with the notice of motion. In a proper case he will obtain an immediate judgment for all wages due to him at that time. See also Chapter 10, §131, *post.*

The Ontario Master and Servant Act, R.S.O. 1970, Chapter 263 also provides a speedy mode of obtaining payment of wages through the laying of a complaint on oath before a Justice of the Peace or Magistrate. Section 8(1) of that Act extends the jurisdiction of the Magistrate to make an order for payment of wages equal to 30 days' wages, even though such balance exceeds the sum of $200.00, where the wages are claimed in respect of work of the character mentioned in section 5 of the Ontario Mechanics' Lien Act. Section 8 also provides for the issuing of a distress warrant in certain circumstances and for the filing of an order for payment in the appropriate Small Claims Court where it may be enforced as a judgment of that Court. The procedure under The Master and Servant Act is of a summary nature and in most cases will be less expensive than the procedure contemplated by section 15(2) of The Mechanics' Lien Act, since the latter requires the bringing of a Supreme Court motion.

Once the claimant has obtained his priority for 30 days' wages, he has no further priority. If the claimant is entitled to 40 days' wages, he will rank *pari passu* with the other lien claimants with respect to the amount owing for the other 10 days' wages. The priority, in any event, will only extend to holdback moneys owing to the person from whom he had his contract. Thus, if he is employed by a subcontractor, he will be entitled to priority to the extent of 30 days' wages on the amount of the holdback owing by the general contractor to that subcontractor: *Cole v. Pearson* (1908), 17 O.L.R. 46 (C.A.). All wage earners claiming through such a subcontractor rank *pari passu* as between themselves. Accordingly, if in this example, all of the holdback retained by the general contractor was used to satisfy wage claims, materialmen and other subcontractors claiming through the subcontractor will not receive anything on account of their claims for lien. The workman's priority is limited to the amount of the holdback. If there are any moneys owing to the subcontractor by the contractor in excess of the holdback and the total value of the wage claims exceed the amount of the holdback, the holdback would be divided *pro rata* among the wage earners, but they would share *pari passu* with the other lien claimants in the amount owing in excess of the holdback for the balance of their claims. It was held in *Cole v. Pearson, supra,* that the wage earner has no priority over other lienholders, claiming through the same contractor or subcontractor, beyond the moneys held back by the owner or contractor pursuant to the Act. In *Silver v. R. R. Seeton Const. Ltd.* (1977), 74 D.L.R. (3d) 212 (N.S.), where the workmen were employed directly by the owner, who was acting as his own general contractor, it was held that, because there was no holdback to which they could look for the payment of their claims, they did not have priority over others who had supplied labour and materials to the owner, and they were only entitled to share *pari passu* with those others in the proceeds of sale of the owner's land.

The person claiming the priority given to the wage earner must be the wage earner himself and the subcontractor who pays him his wages cannot be subrogated to his right to claim such priority for wages which the subcontractor has paid him: see *Hill-Clark-Francis Ltd. v. Lanthier*, [1958] O.W.N. 233. To the same effect is *Union Elec. Supply Co. v. Gillin Enrg. & Const Ltd.*, [1971] 3 O.R. 125, in respect of a Workmen's Compensation assessment. In *Wortman v. Frid Lewis Co.* (1915), 9 W.W.R. 812 (Alta.) and *Silver v. R. R. Seeton Const. Ltd.* (1977), 74 D.L.R. (3d) 212 (N.S.), it was held that a person who had done work and also supplied materials must be held to be a subcontractor. He was held not to be entitled to divide his claim into materials supplied and labour performed so as to claim a priority as a labourer. The Court will not permit the subdivision of the contract so as to permit a priority for wages being unjustly acquired. Thus, in *Rendall, MacKay, Michie Ltd. v. Warren* (1915), 8 W.W.R. 113 (Alta.), and *Stafford v. McKay*, [1919] 2 W.W.R. 280 (Alta.), the Court drew a distinction between the claimant who worked under supervision and one who made his own decisions as to the manner in which the work which he did was done, holding the latter to be a subcontractor and hence not entitled to the priority given to a wage earner. In order to establish the right to the priority for his claim, the claimant must bring himself within the definition of a wage earner as contained in the appropriate Act. It was held in *Foley v. Can. Credit Men's Assn.*, [1971] 2 W.W.R. 703 (Man.), that the president and major shareholder of a limited company was not a "workman" within the meaning of the Builders and Workmen Act (now The Builders and Workers Act), even though he was employed by the company, was paid a salary, and did in fact work on the project along with other employees.

It is submitted that the 30 days' wages referred to in the Act, at least in Ontario, means wages equal to 30 days' unpaid wages and not the wages which may have been earned during the 30 days immediately preceding the filing of the lien. Because the construction industry is dependent to a large extent on the weather, there may often be instances when wage earners can work no more than 2 or 3 days per week and accordingly the latter view would result in their receiving a very small priority over other lien claimants which could hardly have been the intention of the enactment. It was held, however, in at least two Alberta cases (*Rendall, MacKay, Michie Ltd. v. Warren, supra* and *Stafford v. McKay, supra*), that the provisions of the Alberta Act, giving priority to wage claimants for 6 weeks' wages, gave the claimant priority for the wages earned within a continuous period of 6 weeks counting backwards from the last day's work. The Alberta Act at the time of the decision in the first of these cases gave a priority for "not more than 6 weeks wages" and at the time of the second decision, a priority "not exceeding the wages of 6 weeks or a balance equal to his wages for 6 weeks". It is submitted that this wording is different than the wording of the present Ontario Act, which merely speaks of "priority to the extent of 30 days' wages", and hence, at least in Ontario and provinces whose Acts use similar wording, these decisions ought not to be followed. It was held in an early Ontario case, *Torrance v. Cratchley* (1900), 31 O.R. 546 (C.A.), that while the owner made payments out of the holdback at his own risk to persons entitled to liens before the expiry of the lien period, the making of such payments to wage earners, who were ultimately shown to have a priority over other lien claimants, would be permitted since the other lien claimants had not been prejudiced thereby. See Chapter 4, Rights and Duties of the Owner.

§93 Priorities between Lienholders.

Apart from wage earners, the Act allows no priority between lienholders of the same class. It was held in *McPherson v. Gedge* (1883), 4 O.R. 246 (C.A.), that lienholders of the same class are defined as lienholders who contract directly with, or who are employed by, the same person. This decision was approved in *Rideau Aluminum & Steels Ltd. v. McKechnie,* [1964] 1 O.R. 523; affirmed 48 D.L.R. (2d) 62, 659 (Can.). Most of the statutes specifically provide that no lienholder shall have priority over, or preference to, another lienholder of the same class; that they shall rank *pari passu* upon any funds available for distribution among lienholders of that class, and that each class of lienholders shall be paid *pro rata* according to their several classes and rights: Ont., sec. 14(2); Nfld., sec. 16(2); Man. sec. 11(3).

In *Rideau Aluminum & Steels Ltd. v. McKechnie, supra,* it was argued, that the general contractor was entitled to share *pari passu* with his subcontractors in the distribution of the owner's holdback. In rejecting this argument, McGillivray J.A., after quoting section 14(2) of the Ontario Act stated, "it need hardly be pointed out that the contractor is not of the same class as the subcontractors in this action and that its claim to share on an equal basis with such subcontractors is excluded by the subsection above quoted. The trial Judge ... has assessed the amounts payable and directed payment to the lienholders according to their class, the contractor, in the lowest class, receiving only the balance after other lien payments have been paid. In this he was correct for liens once filed took precedence over any claim by the contractor against the owner and, to the extent to which the liens were allowed, the contractor never had money owing to him by the owner after such filing". Thus, while there is no priority among lien claimants of the same class it may well be that one class of lien claimants will have priority over another class of lien claimants. Subcontractors have a right to payment of their claims out of the holdback in priority to the claim of the general contractor. Similarly, lien claimants who have supplied labour or material to a subcontractor are entitled to have their claims paid out of that subcontractor's distributive share of the owner's holdback in priority to the subcontractor's claim. See also *Mandatori v. Pyrid Const. Ltd.,* [1969] 1 O.R. 431 (C.A.). In *C. J. Oliver Ltd. v. Foothills Lighting & Elec. Ltd.* (1965), 54 W.W.R. 37 (Alta. C.A.), sub-subcontractors employed by a subcontractor sought to attach the larger holdback in the hands of the owner to satisfy their claims for lien after the subcontractor had abandoned his contract with the general contractor. It was held that the amount which they could claim from the owner's holdback was restricted to an amount equal to the amount required to be held back from the subcontractor by the contractor. The decision in *R. A. Corbett & Co. v. Phillips* (1972), 32 D.L.R. (3d) 78 (N.B.C.A.), is to the same effect.

In *Len Ariss & Co. v. Peloso,* [1958] O.R. 643 (C.A.), a subcontractor had given notice in writing of his lien pursuant to section 11(6) of the Ontario Act, but the owner, instead of taking advantage of the procedure under section 12, permitting him to pay the lien claimed and give notice to the contractor of such payment, merely held back the amount of the lien in addition to the proper holdback percentage. At trial, the amount retained by the owner appeared not to be sufficient to satisfy all liens claimed in full and the subcontractor sought, in effect, to obtain a priority over the other lienholders by maintaining that he was entitled to payment in full of his lien. It was held that the lienholder giving notice was only entitled to rank *pari passu* with the other lienholders on the fund consisting of the proper amount of the holdback plus the amount held back for his lien. The owners having paid this lienholder in full after judgment, were only entitled, as against the other lienholders, to credit for what would have been this lienholder's *pro rata* share. In *Re Northlands Grading Co.,* [1960] O.R. 455 (C.A.), a person who had supplied material but who had not filed a lien sought, in effect, to gain priority over other liens by maintaining that what was then section 15 of the Ontario Act, which appeared to give a material supplier a lien on materials which were not yet incorporated in the building, entitled the material supplier to a separate or distinct lien in the nature of an extension of the vendor's lien under The Sale of Goods Act. The Court of Appeal refused to agree with this contention and pointed out that to give effect to it would be contrary to the provisions of section 14(2) of the Ontario Act which makes it clear that all lienholders of the same class are to have the same rights and are to rank *pari passu* for the several amounts of their liens.

In *Bond Structural Steel (1965) Ltd. v. Cloverlawn Invts. Ltd.,* [1973] 3 O.R. 856, it was held that although section 25(4) of the Ontario Act provides that when money is paid into Court to vacate a lien the amount owing to the person whose lien is vacated is "a first charge upon the money", that person is not entitled to the amount in Court to the exclusion of subsequent lien claimants whose liens have not been vacated. The Master expressed the view that the words quoted above should be treated as relating only to the amount recoverable from the owner because if they were to be interpreted as giving priority to the person whose lien is vacated it would defeat the general scheme of distribution under the Act, namely that all lienholders are to share *pro rata* with others of the same class. Accordingly he directed that the moneys which had been paid into Court in this action should be shared *pro rata* among all of the lien claimants including those whose liens had been vacated as a result of the payment into Court and those whose liens had been registered subsequently, whether they were registered before or after the owner had sold the property in question.

Most of the Acts contain a provision to the effect that, "save as herein otherwise provided", the lien shall not attach so as to make the owner liable for a greater amount than the amount payable by the owner to the contractor, and where the lien is claimed by any person other than the contractor, the amount of the lien is to be limited to the amount owing to the contractor, or subcontractor, or other person for whom the work or service has been done or the materials placed or furnished: Ont., secs. 9, 10; Man., secs. 7, 8; Nfld., secs. 11, 12. The words "save as herein otherwise provided" contained in these sections refer most particularly to the holdback provisions and accordingly, since the statutory percentage must be maintained, the holdback requirements override any apparent limit to liability imposed by them. The sections do have the effect, in certain circumstances, of permitting some claimants to obtain a larger percentage on a *pro rata* distribution of the particular holdback on which they rank *pari passu* than other claimants claiming against another holdback, and consequently they may, in the end result, create different classes of lien claimants: *Cole v. Pearson* (1908), 17 O.L.R. 46 (C.A.). The same result can, of course, be obtained where the owner engages two contractors whose contracts are for different amounts. Where he does so he must maintain separate holdbacks on each contract based on the value of the work performed by each contractor: *Yale Dev. Corpn. Ltd. v. A.L.H. Const. Ltd.* (1972), 32 D.L.R. (3d) 301 (Alta.C.A.). The holdback will be a percentage of different contract amounts and accordingly persons who supply materials to each of the contractors will have a different amount available for the satisfaction of their claims upon which to rank *pari passu*. For example, if the first contractor's contract price amounts to $10,000.00, the second contractor's contract price amounts to $20,000.00, and the statutory percentage to be retained by the owner amounts to 15%, the holdback in the case of the first contractor will be $1,500.00 and in the case of the second contractor will be $3,000.00. Assuming that two claims for lien are filed against each contractor by material suppliers in the amount of $1,500.00 each, then material suppliers claiming under the first contractor will receive 50% of their claims, and those claiming under the second contractor will receive payment in full. If no moneys had been paid to either of the contractors by the owner and each of them abandoned the work at a time when they had performed half of the work under their contracts, three claims for lien having been filed against each contractor in the amount of $2,000.00 each, then those claiming through the first contractor (as the value of the work was $5,000.00) would receive less than the total amount of their claims while those claiming under the second contractor (the value of the work being $10,000.00) would be paid in full.

In *Edwards Welding Ltd. v. Howe & Wilson Const. Ltd.* (1959), 27 W.W.R. 689 (B.C.), the general contractor had run into difficulty and one of the subcontractors did not file a lien but secured judgment against the defendant for the amount due under its subcontract. The statutory holdback was paid into Court and the subcontractor applied for a charging order entitling it to have its judgment paid *pari passu* with the registered lienholders. The Court held that the claimant was not entitled to rank *pari passu* with the lienholders who were given priority by section 40 of the British Columbia Act, although it was entitled to a charging order under the provisions of the trust fund section of the Act on any balance remaining after the registered lienholders' and wage earners' claims and costs had been paid in full. It was held in *Rendall, MacKay, Michie Ltd. v. Warren* (1915), 8 W.W.R. 113 (Alta.), that the priority given to wage earners as the result of giving notice under the then section 32 of the 1906 Alberta Act extended only to other lienholders of the same class. Such a notice was held not to affect priorities fixed by the then section 30 of that Act between other classes of lienholders. This would appear to be sound law, and in Ontario the priority given to wage earners under section 15(1) of the Ontario Act should be interpreted to give a wage earner priority, to the extent of 30 days' wages, over lienholders claiming through the same contractor only.

§94 The Lien Claimant and the Unpaid Vendor.

Most of the Acts provide that an unpaid vendor under an agreement of purchase and sale of land is deemed, for the purposes of the Act, to be a mortgagee to the extent of the balance owing to him under such agreement: Ont., sec. 7(6); Alta., sec. 9(4); N.S., sec. 14(2). The British Columbia, Newfoundland and Ontario Acts refer to "a registered agreement for the sale and purchase of land" and provide that for the purposes of the Act, "the seller shall be deemed to be a mortgagee, and any moneys *bona fide* secured and payable under such agreement shall be deemed to be mortgage money *bona fide* secured or advanced": Ont., sec. 7(6); B.C., sec. 7(3); Nfld., sec. 9(6). The Alberta Act contains a similar provision, except that a caveat must have been filed with respect to the agreement for sale: Alta., sec. 9(4). In Saskatchewan the seller under such an agreement is deemed to be a mortgagee whose mortgage was registered on the date of the execution of the agreement: Sask., sec. 26(2). In most jurisdictions the unpaid vendor will have priority over lien claimants for the unpaid purchase price to the same extent as any other mortgagee. For example, in Ontario, he may be a prior mortgagee whose priority over liens is governed by section 7(3) of the Ontario Act, or, if the agreement of purchase and sale provides for payment of the purchase price in instalments, his priority over liens may be governed by the provisions of section 14(1) of that Act. In New Brunswick and Prince Edward Island, however, the unpaid vendor is given priority over a lien only to the extent of the value of the land at the time the lien arose.

In *Travis Lbr. Co. v. Cousineau,* [1956] O.W.N. 585 (C.A.), it was held by the Ontario Court of Appeal that an unpaid vendor is entitled as between himself and the purchaser, to be paid the full amount owing to him at the date of payment, both for principal and for interest computed at the rate set out in the agreement, and as between himself and the lienholders he was entitled to the priority given him by section 7(3) of the Ontario Act. Of course if the unpaid vendor can be brought within the definition of an "owner" contained in the Act, his interest in the property will be subject to lien claims accordingly, although, as was held in *John A. Marshall Brick Co. v. York Farmers Colonization Co.* (1916), 54 S.C.R. 569, affirming (*sub nom. Marshall Brick Co. v. Irving*) 36 O.L.R. 542, and *Michaelis v. Ryan Motors,* [1923] 1 W.W.R. 401 (Sask.), he will not be held to be an "owner" within the meaning of the Act merely because he has advanced funds to the purchaser to build upon the lands. As pointed out in the latter case, there must be something in the nature of direct dealings between the unpaid vendor and the lien claimant. See also §13, "Agreements of Purchase and Sale", *ante,* in this connection.

In *Michaelis v. Ryan Motors, supra,* it was held than an unpaid vendor was a "mortgagee" under the Act whose mortgage was deemed to have been registered at the date of the agreement of purchase and sale. This case, as well as the following cases, is authority for the proposition that whatever priority the unpaid vendor will have as a "mortgagee" dates from the date of the agreement for sale and he will have his priority in respect of all liens which arise after that date: *Blight v. Ray* (1893), 23 O.R. 415; *Gooding v. Crocker* (1926), 60 O.L.R. 60; *Hayward Lbr. Co. v. Hammond,* [1922] 3 W.W.R. 1176 (Alta.); *John A. Marshall Brick Co. v. York Farmers Colonization Co., supra. Query* whether, since the present Ontario, Newfoundland and British Columbia Acts require that the agreement of purchase and sale be registered, the priority of the unpaid vendor in these jurisdictions dates from the date of the registration of the agreement, rather than from the date of its execution.

In *Fraser River Ventures Ltd. v. Yewdall* (1958), 27 W.W.R. 368 (B.C.), the plaintiff had commenced an action for cancellation of an agreement for the sale of land and a certificate of *lis pendens* was filed in the Land Registry Office. Prior to judgment being given for the plaintiff in that action, claims for lien were filed against the same land. The Court held that the plaintiff was entitled to claim priority for his application for registration of title, under section 52 of the British Columbia Land Registry Act, over any title or charge, application for registration of which was made subsequent to the registration of his *lis pendens,* and accordingly the liens claimed never took effect. Section 12 of the British Columbia Mechanics' Lien Act, providing for priority of liens over judgments, executions, attachments and receiving orders recovered or made after the lien took effect, was held not to have any bearing on the issue. It was also held in *Charters v. McCracken* (1916), 36 O.L.R. 260 (C.A.), where the purchaser defaulted and the unpaid vendor had the property reconveyed to him in settlement of his claim for the purchase price, that the reconveyance upon registration had priority over all unregistered lien claims of which he had no actual notice. It would seem that even actual notice would not prevent the registered reconveyance taking priority over unregistered claims for lien.

As was pointed out in *Kennedy v. Haddow* (1890), 19 O.R. 240 and *Cook v. Belshaw* (1893), 23 O.R. 545, the unpaid vendor's priority as a prior "mortgagee" of the premises is the same as that of any other prior mortgagee and is, of course, based on the value of the lands and premises at the time of the agreement for sale in accordance with the provisions of the Act governing priorities as between lienholders and prior mortgagees: Ont., sec. 7(3); N.S., sec. 7(3). The lien claimants will accordingly have priority over the interest of the unpaid vendor to the extent of any increase in value of the premises after the first lien arose or, alternatively, to the extent of any increase in value of the premises as a result of the improvements made thereon by them: *O'Brien v. Clauson,* [1923] 2 W.W.R. 895 (Alta.). It was held in *Hayward Lbr. Co. v. Hammond,* [1922] 3 W.W.R. 1176 (Alta.), that admissions made to a lien claimant by the purchaser of the property, to the effect that materials had been delivered to him, would not bind the unpaid vendor in a contest between the lien claimant and the unpaid vendor.

See also in connection with this and the following article, Chapter 5, The Mortgagee; §13, "Agreements of Purchase and Sale", *ante,* and the article by Hodgson J. at [1932] 1 D.L.R. 240.

§95 Priorities between Lien Claimant and Purchaser.

It has been held on many occasions and is implicit in the provisions of the Acts, that the purchaser who has paid his purchase price and registered his deed or transfer prior to receiving notice in writing of a lien, or prior to the registration on title of a claim for lien, will have priority over all liens subsequently registered: *Cut-Rate Plate Glass Co. v. Solodinski* (1915), 34 O.L.R. 604 (C.A.); *Re Irvine & Main,* [1933] O.W.N. 476; *Re Pridham,* [1934] O.W.N. 560; *Wanty v. Robins* (1888), 15 O.R. 474 (C.A.); *Morton v. Grant,* [1956] O.W.N. 523 (C.A.); *Sterling Lbr. Co. v. Jones* (1916), 36

O.L.R. 153 (C.A.); *Stinson v. Mackendrick* (1924), 55 O.L.R. 358 (C.A.); *Hager v. United Sheet Metal Ltd.,* [1954] S.C.R. 384, reversing 9 W.W.R. 481, which reversed 7 W.W.R. 481; *Charters v. McCracken* (1916), 36 O.L.R. 260 (C.A.); *Geo. Taylor Hdwe. Ltd. v. Balzer* [1967] 2 O.R. 306 (C.A.); *Andre Knight Ltd. v. Presement,* [1967] 2 O.R. 289 (C.A.); *C.M.H.C. v. Wood* (1967), 53 M.P.R. 294 (Nfld.). Thus, if the lien claimant delays registration of his claim for lien, he may lose priority to a purchaser of the property whose deed is registered ahead of the lien. In *Kelly v. Progressive Bldrs. Ltd.* (1970), 1 N. & P.E.I.R. 1 (Nfld.), where the claim for lien was registered after the owner's bona fide sale of the property, it was held that the lien was invalid and further, that it could not attach to the proceeds of the sale since money was not an "estate" or "interest" of the owner.

In view of the decision in *D. Porter & Son v. MacLeod* (1951), 29 M.P.R. 83 (N.S.), holding that a mortgagee has priority over a lien for materials to the extent of the amount advanced prior to the registration of the lien or notice in writing being received, actual notice not being sufficient, it is doubtful if the lien claimant can even maintain his priority by establishing that the purchaser had actual notice of his claim. The sections of the various Acts corresponding to section 14(1) (Ont.) provide that, unless the claimant gives written notice to the purchaser in lieu of registration of his claim for lien, the payments made by the purchaser on account of the purchase price will have priority over his unregistered claim for lien. The following cases would also support this view: *Cook v. Koldoffsky* (1916), 35 O.L.R. 555 (C.A.); *Calgary v. Dom. Radiator Co.,* 56 S.C.R. 141, reversing (*sub nom. Dom. Radiator Co. v. Payne*) [1917] 2 W.W.R. 974; *Hynes v. Smith* (1879), 27 Gr. 150, affirming 8 P.R. 73 (C.A.); and *Whitehead v. Lach Gen. Contractors Ltd.* (1974), 3 O.R. (2d) 680 (C.A.). It has also been held that mere knowledge on the part of the purchaser or on the part of a mortgagee that building operations were proceeding on the property being purchased or mortgaged does not constitute notice of a claim for lien: *Richards v. Chamberlain* (1878), 25 Gr. 402; *Sterling Lbr. Co. v. Jones* (1916), 36 O.L.R. 153 (C.A.); *Andre Knight Ltd. v. Presement, supra; C.M.H.C. v. Wood, supra; Geo. Taylor Hdwe. Ltd. v. Balzer, supra.*

The view was expressed in *Bond Structural Steel (1965) Ltd. v. Cloverlawn Invts. Ltd.,* [1973] 3 O.R. 856, that a claim for lien operates against the estate or interest of the owner in the land and not against the land itself. Accordingly, the owner may make payments to his contractor of up to 85% of the value of the work done and any liens are a charge only upon the remaining 15% which the owner is required to hold back, or upon such greater amount as the owner is required to retain as a result of receiving written notice of a lien. The Court therefore held that a subsequent purchaser is not responsible to lien claimants for any greater amount than that for which the owner is liable, because section 11(6) of the Ontario Act provides that the payments made by the owner operate as a discharge *pro tanto* of the lien. The Court also pointed out that section 11(7) of the Ontario Act provides that the amount directed to be retained by the owner may be paid into Court "so as to discharge all claims in respect of such percentage". Since, in this case, the owner had paid his contractor 85% of the value of the work prior to receiving any notice of a claim for lien and had paid the remaining 15% into Court after receiving such notice, the Court found that the purchaser of the property was in no way liable to the lien claimants whose claims for lien were registered prior to the purchaser's deed.

Many of the Acts provide that the lien claimant himself becomes a purchaser *pro tanto* of the property once he has registered his claim for lien within the provisions of the appropriate Registry or Land Titles Act: Ont., sec. 20; Man., sec. 19; Nfld., sec. 22. Once his claim or conveyance is registered, the lienholder or the purchaser is entitled to rely on the provisions of the relevant Registry or Land Titles Act which state that priority of registration shall prevail in the absence of actual notice: *Pannill Door Co. v. Stephenson,* [1931] O.R. 594 (C.A.); *Re Irvine & Main,* [1933] O.W.N. 476; *Hager v. United Sheet Metal Ltd.,* [1954] S.C.R. 384, reversing 9 W.W.R. 481, which reversed 7 W.W.R. 481. In *Harrell v. Mosier,* [1956] O.R. 152 (C.A.), it was held that a purchaser who made payments on account of the purchase price, after the right to a mechanics' lien had arisen, and who afterwards became entitled to a purchaser's lien on the land for the amount paid by him, was not entitled to priority over the mechanics' lien since he had not registered any instrument, (such as a caution), constituting evidence of his interest in the property before the lien claimant's claim for lien had been registered. In that judgment, Schroeder J.A. expressed the view that: "the effect of section 20 of The Mechanics' Lien Act is to make the holder of a valid mechanics' lien a purchaser of the property *pro tanto* when he places his claim for lien upon the register, and he thus enjoys all the rights, privileges and advantages conferred by section 75 of The Registry Act upon a purchaser of property who, without actual notice of the rights of another purchaser or mortgagee, is the first to register evidence of his title in the appropriate Registry Office." See also *Whitehead v. Lach Gen. Contractors Ltd.* (1974), 3 O.R. (2d) 680 (C.A.) where the facts and result were the same except that the purchasers there endeavoured to protect their interests by registering a form of assignment of their agreements of purchase and sale. The Court held that in order to protect their interests under the Registry Act they must put actual notice of the instrument under which they claimed on the register, and, since the agreements of purchase and sale had not been attached to the registered assignments, they had not done so. The lienholders were accordingly given priority over the interests of the purchasers.

All of the Acts define the term "owner" as including, "all persons claiming under him or it" whose rights are acquired after the commencement of the work: Ont., sec. 1(1) (*d*); Man., sec. 2(*d*); P.E.I., sec. 1(*j*). It was held in *Carr & Son v. Rayward* (1955), 17 W.W.R. 399 (B.C.), that a purchaser from the owner did not obtain a title free of the liens, even though his conveyance was registered prior to the registration of the claims for lien, because of this definition. The validity of this decision is questionable in the light of the decisions reached by the Court of Appeal in *Andre Knight Ltd. v. Presement,* [1967] 2 O.R. 289 (C.A.), and *Geo. Taylor Hdwe. Ltd. v. Balzer,* [1967] 2 O.R. 306 (C.A.). In both of these cases, it was held that the purchaser had obtained priority over the liens which were registered after the purchaser's deed had been registered. In the latter case, McLennan J.A. stated at page 308 of the report, after referring to the decision in the former case: "it was there held that 'persons claiming under' an owner as defined in the first part of the definition were persons who acquired or held some interest subordinate to that of the owner, as for example, where an owner of the fee simple leased the land to another; such lessee would be a person 'claiming under' the owner. Where an owner transferred all his estate or interest in all or part of his lands then such transferee of all or part of such lands claimed 'through' not 'under' the transferor."

As was pointed out in *Cook v. Koldoffsky* (1916), 35 O.L.R. 555 (C.A.), and *Hager v. United Sheet Metal Ltd., supra,* a specific provision in The Mechanics' Lien Act overrides a similar provision in The Registry Act. In any event, most of the Acts provide that, except as otherwise provided in The Mechanics' Lien Act, The Registry Acts and The Land Titles Acts do not apply to any lien arising under The Mechanics' Lien Act: Ont., sec. 20; Nfld., sec. 22; N.S., sec. 22.

It has been held that the purchaser of property under the power of sale contained in a prior mortgage retains the mortgagee's priority over the liens: *Hayward Lbr. Co. v. McEachern,* [1931] 3 W.W.R. 658 (Alta.); *Brown v. McLean* (1889), 18 O.R. 533; *Abell v. Morrison* (1890), 19 O.R. 669 (C.A.); *McCullough v. Elliott,* [1921] 3 W.W.R. 361, affirming 1 W.W.R. 1144 (Alta. C.A.); *Hardy v. Munn* (1977), 18 N.B.R. (2d) 386 (C.A.). It has also been held that if a purchaser, or a subsequent mortgagee, pays off a prior mortgage, he will be subrogated to the priority of that prior mortgagee with respect to mechanics' liens: *Abell v. Morrison, supra; Coupland Acceptance Ltd. v. Walsh,* [1954] S.C.R. 90, reversing (*sub nom. Walsh v. R.; Bowser v. Dyer*) [1952] O.W.N. 665.

The situation in Saskatchewan with respect to registration is somewhat different in view of section 37(2) of the Saskatchewan Act which provides that, despite the fact that the statutory period for registration has expired, the claimant may still proceed to register a claim for lien. Such a lien will be valid except as against intervening parties becoming entitled to any estate or interest in or a lien or charge upon the land whose claims are registered prior to the registration of the lien, or as against an owner, mortgagee, contractor or subcontractor in respect of payments made in good faith to a contractor, subcontractor or lienholder after the expiration of the statutory period for registration has expired and before any claim for lien is registered and notice thereof has been given in writing to the owner, mortgagee, contractor or subcontractor. See *Regina Heating & Elec. Ltd. v. Daku* (1961), 38 W.W.R. 560 (Sask.). In *Dutton-Wall Lbr. Co. v. Freemanson,* [1923] 3 W.W.R. 1317 (Sask. C.A.), and *St. Pierre v. Rekert* (1915), 8 Sask. L.R. 416 (C.A.), it was held that an intervening purchaser will take subject to the claim for lien if he delays in registering his deed or caveat until after the claims for lien are registered, even though they were registered after the conveyance was made.

It was held in *Fred H. Blanchard & Son. v. Poetz Const. Co.* (1953), 8 W.W.R. 225 (Alta.), that the fact that the claim for lien was registered against the interest of the registered owner only, and notwithstanding that the purchasers from the registered owner under an agreement of sale had filed a caveat and were in occupation of the premises at the time of the completion of the work, did not vitiate the lien as against the purchasers where the registration of the lien conformed in all respects to the provisions of the Act.

§96 The Lien Claimant and the Execution Creditor.

Most of the Acts provide that the claim for lien will take priority over all judgments, executions, attachments and garnishments recovered, issued or made after such lien arises: Ont., sec. 14(1); Sask., sec. 25(1); N.B., sec. 9(1). The lien will be deemed to have arisen in the case of a contractor or subcontractor as soon as the contract is entered into: *Taylor v. Taylor,* [1954] O.W.N. 575. In all other cases it will be deemed to have arisen as soon as the first work is done or the first material is supplied: *Ottawa Steel Castings Co. v. Dom. Supply Co.* (1904), 5 O.W.R. 161. While the Court in *Imperial Lumber Yards Ltd. v. Saxton,* [1921] 3 W.W.R. 524 (Sask. C.A.), appears to have held that a lien will gain priority over an execution creditor only if the claim for lien is registered and then only from the date of registration of the lien, this would not appear to be the law in Ontario, or in Nova Scotia: see *Silver v. R. R. Seeton Const. Ltd.* (1977), 74 D.L.R. (3d) 212 (N.S.). A careful reading of section 14(1) of the Ontario Act leads to the conclusion that an unregistered lien claimant has priority over any execution registered after that unregistered lien arose. In Alberta, however, the Act specifically provides that a lien has priority over all judgments, executions, attachments and garnishments recovered issued or made after the statement of lien is registered: Alta., sec. 9(1).

Because of the fact that the liens of subcontractors and materialmen may arise at different times as the main contract progresses, an execution creditor may be subsequent in priority to one lien claimant and yet have priority over another. It was decided in *S. McCord & Co. v. Chatfield,* [1946] O.W.N. 1, that one judgment creditor may have priority over another judgment creditor in certain circumstances. In that case, the judgment in the lien action stated that the plaintiff lien claimant had priority over a judgment creditor who had filed his execution. Subsequently, the property in question was sold and other judgment creditors attempted to have the surplus funds realized on the sale distributed amongst themselves and the execution creditor mentioned in the original judgment on a *pro rata* basis. The Senior Master in that case relied on the decision of the Saskatchewan Court of Appeal in *Beaver Lbr. Co. v. Quebec Bank,* [1918] 2 W.W.R. 1052 (Sask. C.A.), which held that only those execution creditors whose executions attached to the land while it was the property of the execution debtor were entitled to share in the proceeds of the sale of that land. Since the subsequent judgment creditors had not filed execution with the Sheriff prior to the sale, the execution creditor mentioned in the judgment was entitled to be paid first out of the proceeds of the sale. The Senior Master went on to direct that the surplus be paid to the Sheriff to be distributed on a *pro rata* basis amongst the other judgment creditors.

§97 The Claim of the Unemployment Insurance Commission.

Section 71(1) of The Unemployment Insurance Act, 1971, provides that all premiums, interest, penalties and other amounts payable by an employer under that Act are debts due to Her Majesty, and recoverable as such in the Federal Court of Canada, or any other Court of competent jurisdiction, or in any other manner provided by the Act. Accordingly, such a claim would appear to have priority over a personal judgment in a mechanics' lien action.

§98 Claims under The Workmen's Compensation Act.

Section 9 of the Ontario Workmen's Compensation Act, R.S.O. 1970, chapter 505, makes an owner liable to pay any contribution under the Act which his contractor is liable to make under the provisions of that Act. If the contractor fails to do so, that section makes the owner personally liable to the Workmen's Compensation Board for such contributions which the contractor has not made. The Act further provides, in section 113, that if an assessment is not paid within 30 days after it has become payable, the Board may, at its option, collect the assessment through the appropriate municipal tax collectors who will add the amount of the claim to the taxes upon the owner's land. If the Board follows this procedure, then its claim will gain the priority given to municipal taxes over mechanic's liens. The Board may alternatively, under section 112, issue a certificate setting out the amount owing, and file it with the Clerk of the appropriate County, District or Small Claims Court, and when so filed, it becomes an order of that Court and may be enforced as a judgment of that Court. If this procedure is followed, then the priority of that Court's judgment will be determined with respect to liens in the same manner as that of an ordinary execution creditor. This procedure was followed by the Board in *Crown Trust Co. v. Workmen's Comp. Bd.* (1975), 7 O.R. (2d) 466, where it was held that the Board's claim did not have priority over a registered mortgage or certain floating charges, all of which had been registered, or had crystallized, prior to the date on which the Board issued its certificate. The situation may be different in New Brunswick, however. In *Dobbelsteyn Elec. Ltd. v. Whittaker Textiles (Marysville) Ltd.* (1976), 14 N.B.R. (2d) 584, where the Workmen's Compensation Board signed judgment against the owner in respect of the unpaid balance of its assessment against the owner, after claims for lien had been registered, it was held that the combined effect of section 72 of the New Brunswick Workmen's Compensation Act and section 51 of the Property Act was to give the Board a lien upon the owner's property which ranked subsequent to a prior mortgage but ahead of the successful lien claimants.

The Workmen's Compensation Board is also named in section 2 of the Ontario Mechanics' Lien Act, section 3 of the British Columbia, New Brunswick and Saskatchewan Acts, and in section 3 of the Builders and Workers Act of Manitoba as a beneficiary of the various trust funds created by those sections. However, an assessment made against the owner pursuant to The Workmen's Compensation Act is not the subject matter of a lien under section 5 of the Ontario Act: *Union Elec. Supply Co. v. Gillin Enrg. & Const. Ltd.,* [1971] 3 O.R. 125. This case was cited with approval in *Shoquist Const. Co. v. Norfolk & Retailers Trust and Savings Co.* (1974), 19 C.B.R. (N.S.) 151 (Sask.), where the Court was considering the claim of the Saskatchewan Workmen's Compensation Board under a statute which was identical to the Ontario Act.

In *Hudson's Bay Oil etc. Co. v. Trustee in Bankruptcy of F.P.C. Const. Ltd.* (1969), 67 W.W.R. 665 (Alta.), where the owner had paid the holdback into Court, the Workmen's Compensation Board claimed that it was entitled to be paid the amount of its assessment against the bankrupt contractor in priority to lienholders claiming under the contractor, even though the lienholders' claims were prior in time to the board's claim. The board contended that the money in Court was "property of the employer, including moneys payable to, for, or on account of the employer" within the meaning of section 85(4) (*a*) of The Workmen's Compensation Act, R.S.A. 1970 ch. 397. The Court held that the money in Court was money realized under The Mechanics' Lien Act which was to be applied and distributed in the order set out in that Act, and that it never became the property of the contractor within the meaning of section 85 of The Workmen's Compensation Act.

§99 The Effect of Bankruptcy on Priorities.

Most of the Acts provide that the claim for lien takes priority over all assignments, attachments and receiving orders recovered, issued or made after the lien arises: Ont., sec. 14(1); Sask., sec. 25(1); N.B., sec. 9(1). In Alberta, however, the lien's priority over assignments, attachments and receiving orders dates from the time at which the statement of lien is registered: Alta., sec. 9(1). The Bankruptcy Act, R.S.C. 1970, chapter B-3, section 2(r) constitutes the mechanics' lien claimant a secured creditor where the lien has arisen prior to the date of the making of the receiving order or of an assignment for the general benefit of creditors under that Act. This is so whether or not the claim for lien is registered: see *Re Clinton Thresher Co.* (1910), 1 O.W.N. 445; *Re Empire Brewing & Malting Co.* (1891), 8 Man. R. 424; *Re Rockland Cocoa & Chocolate Co.* (1921), 50 O.L.R. 66. In *Re Archibald* (1909), 6 E.L.R. 454 (P.E.I.), where the assignment in bankruptcy had been registered prior to the registration of the claim for lien, the Court expressed the view that the lien claimant must rank as an ordinary unsecured creditor since all of the estate of the owner had been vested by the assignment in the trustee prior to the registration of the claim for lien. It is submitted that this decision is not good law in the light of the wording of the aforementioned section of The Mechanics' Lien Act which gives priority to the lien from the date on which it arises rather than from the date on which a claim for lien is registered.

Lienholders whose claims arose before the date of the bankruptcy are not affected by the stay of proceedings created by section 49 of the Bankruptcy Act upon the filing of a proposal or upon the bankruptcy of either the owner or the contractor, so long as they merely seek to realize upon the security of the property under The Mechanics' Lien Act. Nor is there any necessity for the lienholder to obtain an order from the Bankruptcy Court permitting him to continue the action: *Re Rockland Cocoa & Chocolate Co., supra; Riordan Co. v. John W. Danforth Co.*, [1923] S.C.R. 319; *Dieleman Planer Co. v. Elizabeth Townhouses Ltd.* (1972), 27 D.L.R. (3d) 692 (B.C.).

However, if the claimant wishes to proceed to obtain a personal judgment or the right to claim against the bankrupt estate for any deficiency after realization of his lien, then he must obtain an order from the Bankruptcy Court permitting him to prosecute his mechanics' lien action against the bankrupt: *Re Rockland Cocoa & Chocolate Co., supra.* The claimant will be permitted to prove in the bankruptcy for any deficiency after he has realized his security under The Mechanics' Lien Act as an unsecured creditor. It is usual for the judgment in the mechanics' lien action to make note of this. Should the owner be the bankrupt, the judgment in the action will require that the trustee pay into Court a sufficient sum to satisfy the claims for lien recognized by the Court, and if the trustee fails to do so, then the lien claimants may proceed to sell the bankrupt's property and the leave of the Court is not required by them to do so as long as the bankruptcy took place after the liens arose.

The lien claimant will not ordinarily be permitted to do nothing, however, since under the Bankruptcy Act, section 99(1), the trustee may require a lien claimant to value his security. If he takes no steps to realize upon his security or surrender it for the general benefit of creditors, the trustee can then redeem the security by paying him the amount of the claim, or the amount at which the lien claimant values it if the debt is unliquidated. Alternatively, if the trustee is not satisfied with the valuation of the claim by the lien claimant, he may require a sale of the claim either in accordance with the directions of the Court or upon such terms as he may be able to agree upon with the claimant: see the Bankruptcy Act, R.S.C. 1970, ch. B-3, secs. 100 and 101.

In *Re Bishop, Rowe & Spaith Const. Co.* (1961), 35 W.W.R. 20 (Alta.), the general contractor prior to going into voluntary liquidation had made a general assignment of book debts to the bank as a continuing collateral security and guarantees were also given to the bank. The guarantors paid the bank prior to the liquidation. Claims for lien were filed by subcontractors whose claims had risen prior to the liquidation and the guarantors claimed to be entitled to priority over those liens. The Court refused to uphold their claim on the basis that the purpose of The Mechanics' Lien Act was to prevent persons entitled to the protection of it from being victimized by impecunious builders or contractors. In *Bank of Montreal v. Sidney,* [1955] O.W.N. 581, following the bankruptcy of a contractor, the bank, which held a general assignment of the contractor's receivables, sought to establish that its assignment took priority over the claims for lien since it had been taken without notice of them. It was held that Ontario section 14(1) giving the lien priority over "assignments" made subsequent to the lien arising, did not refer to equitable assignments of money, such as the bank's assignment was, and in any event the section did not say that to secure priority the lien must arise before an assignment, since to hold otherwise would defeat the whole purpose of the Act. In *Re Putherbough Const. Co.* (1958), 37 C.B.R. 6 (Ont.), the Court took the position that under the trust section of The Mechanics' Lien Act the Trustee in Bankruptcy is bound in equity to distribute funds impressed with the trust ratably among all of the creditors whose claims arise out of the supply of work and material on the building in question without regard to any assignment which may have been given to one of the creditors.

Section 47(*a*) of the Bankruptcy Act provides that the property of a bankrupt divisible among his creditors shall not include property which the bankrupt holds in trust for any other person. Under some of The Mechanics' Lien Acts, various trust funds are created with respect to moneys received by owners and contractors to finance the construction or as payment on account of the contract price. If such moneys are received after the bankruptcy of the person who is named the trustee of the fund in The Mechanics' Lien Act, they are not available for the creditors of the bankrupt estate until all of the beneficiaries of the trust fund have been paid in full. See *Minneapolis-Honeywell Regulator Co. v. Empire Brass Co.* [1955], S.C.R. 694, reversing (*sub nom. The Same v. Irvine & Reeves Ltd.*) 13 W.W.R. 449, which reversed 11 W.W.R. 212; *Royal Bank v. Wilson* (1963), 42 W.W.R. 1, varying 41 W.W.R. 465 (Man. C.A.); *Re Bodner Road Const. Co.* (1963), 43 W.W.R. 641 (Man.); *Wells H. Morton & Co. v. Can. Credit Men's Trust Assn. Ltd.* (1965), 53 W.W.R. 178 (Man. C.A.). In *Re Northwest Elec. Ltd.,* (1973), 18 C.B.R. (N.S.) 26 (B.C.) it was held that money owing by an owner to a bankrupt contractor against which there were claims under the trust fund section of the Mechanics' Lien Act, as well as a claim by a bank under an assignment of the contractor's book debts, ought to be paid to the trustee of the bankrupt contractor for distribution and that the owner was not entitled to withhold payment and pay creditors of the bankrupt directly. See also in this connection Chapter 9, The Trust Fund.

§100 The Effect of Winding-Up Proceedings on Priorities.

Liens which arise before the making of a winding-up order are preferred claims and an action to enforce them cannot be stayed: *Re Clinton Thresher Co.* (1910), 1 O.W.N. 445; *Re Empire Brewing & Malting Co.* (1891), 8 Man. R. 424; *Re Ibex Mining & Dev. Co.* (1903), 9 B.C.R. 557 (C.A.). However, once the winding-up order has been made, section 21 of the Winding-Up Act, R.S.C. 1970, chapter W-10, provides that no suit, action or other proceeding shall be proceeded with or commenced against the company except with the leave of the Court and subject to such terms as the Court imposes. Section 17 of the Act provides that the Court, upon the application of the company or of any creditor or contributory, may, at any time after the presentation of a petition for a winding-up order and before making the order, restrain further proceedings in any action, suit or proceeding, against the company upon such terms as it thinks fit. Thus, the action may be continued to obtain a personal judgment unless an application is made by an interested party under this section. It was held in *Re Haileybury Rink Co.* (1908), 12 O.W.R. 197, that once the winding-up order had been made, the registration of a claim for lien was irregular and might be set aside. In *Re Flowers & Co.* (1897), 75 L.T. 306, it was held that a receiver or manager appointed by the Court was not acting by authority of the partners, but by authority of the Court, and accordingly a petition served upon him as "servant or agent of the partnership" was not properly served. In the light of this decision, the liquidator is probably not a necessary party to the lien action. It was pointed out in *Re James United Indust. Ltd.* (1971), 16 C.B.R. (N.S.) 65 (Ont.), that where the lien is registered against the lands owned by a third party, and not the lands of the company being wound up, the claimant's action is against the third party and he does not have to add the liquidator as a party defendant if he is prepared to forego his claim for personal judgment against the company being wound up.

§101 Assignments by the Head Contractor.

Most of the Acts contain a provision similar to Ontario section 14(1) giving the lien priority over all judgments, executions, assignments, attachments, garnishments and receiving orders recovered, issued or made after the lien arises. In *Bank of Montreal v. Sidney,* [1955] O.W.N. 581, Lebel J. expressed the opinion that it was doubtful that "the word 'assignments', included as it is among certain kinds of judicial process, refers to equitable assignments of money", such as an assignment held by a bank of the head-contractor's contract moneys. However, the section does not specifically exclude such assignments and it is submitted that the claims of registered and unregistered lien claimants have priority over the assignee of such contract moneys owing to the person primarily liable to them. This view is supported by the decisions in *Oil Well Supply Co. v. Bank of N.S.* (1951), 2 W.W.R. 554 (Alta. C.A.) and *Shoquist Const. Co. v. Norfolk & Retailers Trust and Savings Co.,* (1974), 19 C.B.R. (N.S.) 151 (Sask.). Certainly there is no longer any question of the priority over such an assignment of claims under the trust fund provisions. In *Gascoigne Ltd. v. South Cramahe School Bd.,* [1962] O.W.N. 81, the contractor had assigned all moneys that might become payable by the owner under the building contract to the bonding company when he took out the performance bond. After the contractor defaulted, the bonding company claimed to be entitled to all moneys owing by the owner in excess of the holdback. The Court held that such moneys belonged to the lien claimants as well as the holdback, in priority to the suretys claim under its assignment.

As was pointed out in *Minneapolis-Honeywell Regulator Co. v. Empire Brass Co., supra,* an assignor can confer upon his assignee no greater title than he possesses himself. Thus if the moneys were impressed with a trust in the hands of the contractor, they continue to be impressed with that trust in the hands of the assignee. There are now a number of cases supporting this proposition and holding that the beneficiaries of the special trust created by The Mechanics' Lien Act are entitled to priority over the assignee of the assigned contract moneys: see *Dom. Bank v. Fassel & Baglier Const. Co.,* [1955] O.W.N. 709; *Bank of Montreal v. Sidney, supra; Re Walter Davidson Ltd.,* [1957] O.W.N. 223; *Fonthill Lbr. Ltd. v. Bank of Montreal,* [1959] O.R. 451, reversing 38 C.B.R. 68 (C.A.); *Evans, Coleman & Evans Ltd. v. R. A. Nelson Const. Ltd.* (1958), 25 W.W.R. 569; varied 27 W.W.R. 38 (B.C. C.A.); *Re Certain Lands in West Vancouver* (1963), 43 W.W.R. 181 (B.C.); *Royal Bank v. Wilson* (1963), 42 W.W.R. 1, varying 41 W.W.R. 465 (Man. C.A.); *Re Northwest Elec. Ltd.* (1973), 18 C.B.R. (N.S.) 26 (B.C.); *Aetna Roofing (1965) Ltd. v. Robinson,* [1971] 4 W.W.R. 191 (Man.). See also in this connection Chapter 9, The Trust Fund, which deals with some additional cases arising out of assignments by the head contractor, as well as the principles which have been developed by the Courts in determining when the assignee may be entitled to keep contract moneys which it has received under the assignment. For example, a bank will usually be permitted to retain building contract moneys which it has received under an assignment if it dealt with such moneys in the ordinary course of business, and without knowledge of any actual or intended breach of trust.

In *Re Walter Davidson Ltd., supra,* the bank argued that it ought to be able to retain moneys received by it under its assignment from the head contractor on the ground that the moneys originally advanced by it to the head contractor had been used to pay workmen and material suppliers and therefore the bank was entitled to be subrogated to the position of a contractor who was relieved from his obligations under the trust by Ontario section 3(3) (now sec. 2(2)). This subsection provides that, to the extent that the moneys received from the owner by the contractor, and paid out by him, were paid to workmen and material suppliers, the contractor is relieved from the obligations of the trust imposed by section 2(1). The Court refused to recognize this argument since the moneys had not been paid directly to the workmen and material suppliers by the bank. See also in this connection *Clarkson Co. v. Can. Bank of Commerce,* [1966] S.C.R. 513, reversing (*sub nom. John Ritchie Ltd. v. Can. Bank of Commerce*) [1965] 1 O.R. 197, which reversed [1963] 2 O.R. 116; *Geo. W. Crothers Ltd. v. Bank of N.S.,* [1967] 1 O.R. 424, affirming [1965] 2 O.R. 17 (C.A.). In *Re Bishop, Rowe & Spaith Const. Co.* (1961), 35 W.W.R. 20 (Alta.), a general contractor had made a general assignment of his book debts to the bank as a continuing collateral security and had also given guarantees to the bank. Just prior to the contractor going into bankruptcy, the guarantors paid the bank and subsequently claimed to be entitled to priority over the lien claims of the subcontractors. The Court held that the mechanics' lien claimants had priority over the guarantors.

As was pointed out in *R. V. Demmings & Co. v. Caldwell Const. Co.,* [1955] 4 D.L.R. (2d) 465 (N.B. C.A.), it is in the interests of the assignee to have himself made a party to the action, for he will be entitled to any funds owing to the contractor after the valid lien claims have been paid. He accordingly has an interest in ensuring that no claims are admitted which should not be. Thus, in jurisdictions where The Mechanics' Lien Act does not contain a trust fund section, he can increase the amount payable to him under his assignment by having liens which have been registered too late dismissed. Where the Act does contain a trust fund section, however, he can only benefit by establishing that a claimant has no claim which is recognized by The Mechanics' Lien Act. He may also wish to take some part in any trial of an issue respecting the amount owing to the contractor by the owner in order to ensure that the holdback will be as large as possible.

Section 19(1) of the British Columbia Act provides that "No assignment by the contractor or sub-contractor of any moneys due in respect of the contract is valid as against any lien or trust created by this Act". This section was referred to by the Court in *Modular Products Ltd. v. Aristocratic Plywoods Ltd.; Modular Products Ltd. v. R.* (1974), 42 D.L.R. (3d) 617 (B.C.C.A.), where the view was expressed that if the purposes of the Mechanics' Lien Act could not be nullified by an assignment of the contract moneys there was no reason why those purposes should be nullified by a claim for unpaid income or excise taxes. It accordingly found that moneys owing to a subcontractor, which had been paid into Court by the contractor, were impressed with a trust pursuant to the Mechanics' Lien Act in favour of one of the suppliers to the subcontractor, and that such moneys were not subject to the claim of the federal government against the subcontractor for such unpaid taxes. Section 25(2) of the Saskatchewan Act provides that "No assignment by a contractor or subcontractor of any moneys that may be or become payable under or in respect of any contract to which this Act applies is valid as against any lien created by this Act".

§102 The Lien Claimant and the Conditional Vendor.

The question of the rights and liabilities of lien claimants and conditional vendors *inter se* becomes important where the property against which their claims are made is sold either before or after judgment. A conditional seller may be entitled to claim a lien on the property under The Mechanics' Lien Act as well as maintain his rights under his conditional sale contract. He must, however, elect which remedy he intends to pursue before the trial of the mechanics' lien action: *Hill v. Storey* (1915), 34 O.L.R. 489 (C.A.); *U.S. Const. Co. v. Rat Portage Lbr. Co.* (1915), 9 W.W.R. 657 (Man. C.A.). Under the provisions of section 10(1) of the former Ontario Conditional Sales Act, R.S.O. 1970, ch. 76, goods other than building materials, which had been affixed to the realty remained subject to the rights of the seller under his conditional sale contract. That Act was repealed on

April 1st, 1976 when the provisions of the Personal Property Security Act, R.S.O. 1970, c. 344, which pertain to this type of transaction, came into force. The new Act also provides that a "security interest" does not include building materials which have been affixed to the realty: sec. 1(y). Section 36(1) of that Act provides that a "security interest that attached to goods before they became fixtures has priority as to the goods over the claim of any person who has an interest in the real property". Section 36(3) provides that the security interest is subordinate to the interest of a creditor with a lien on the property subsequently obtained as a result of judicial process if the lien was obtained without actual notice of the security interest. If the goods claimed by the conditional vendor are held to be building materials, then, unless he proves a valid mechanics' lien, the property can be sold without reference to his claim at all. The lien claimants will, in effect, get priority over his claim.

It was held in *Primeau Argo Block Co. v. Ludor Const. Ltd.,* [1966] 1 O.R. 245, (where all parties had agreed that the goods in question were not "building materials" within the meaning of section 10(1) of The Conditional Sales Act), that although the lien claimants were deemed to be purchasers *pro tanto* of the property by The Mechanics' Lien Act, they were not subsequent purchasers or mortgagees coming within the provisions of section 69 of the Ontario Registry Act and that neither of these statutes deprived a seller who had complied with the requirements of The Conditional Sales Act of his rights in the goods. It was accordingly held that the lien claimants could only retain the goods if they paid the amount owing on them to the vendor. See further §37, "The Conditional Vendor as a Lien Claimant", *ante.*

In *Gen. Steel Wares Ltd. v. Ford,* [1965] 2 O.R. 81 (C.A.), it was held that gas dryers installed in triplex buildings did not become part of the realty. In *Montreal Trust Co. v. Goldaire Rentals Ltd.,* [1967] 1 O.R. 40, elevators were held not to be building materials within the meaning of The Conditional Sales Act since they could be entirely removed from the hoistway without causing any damage to the building apart from the leaving of bolt holes in the hoistway masonry and dividing beams. It was held in *La Salle Recreations Ltd. v. Can. Camdex Invts. Ltd.* (1969), 68 W.W.R. 339 (B.C. C.A.), however, that carpeting in a hotel was annexed to the land in such a manner and under such circumstances as to constitute it a fixture. It has been held that baths, basins, laundry tubs and similar equipment, built into an apartment building are building materials, (*Alexander v. McGillivray* (1932), 41 O.W.N. 406), but that a furnace is not: *Collis v. Carew Lbr. Co.* (1930), 65 O.L.R. 520 (C.A.); *Warner v. Foster,* [1934] O.R. 519 (C.A.). It was held in *Re Application A3554* (1967), 60 W.W.R. 509 (B.C.), that irrigation pipes which had been installed underground were fixtures. It was held in *Re Patterson* (1969), 12 C.B.R. (N.S.) 251 (Ont.), that the material in a steel silo which could be erected in 21 days and removed in 6 days was building material within the meaning of The Conditional Sales Act.

§103 Forced Expenses.

In Manitoba where a subcontractor's steel shoring supports for a building were essential to hold the building in place and avoid serious damage, the Court ruled that the costs of the continuing supply of the supports and the cost of eventually removing them should rank in priority to lien claims and certain mortgages. See *Winnipeg Supply & Fuel Co. v. Genevieve Mtge. Corpn.; Wiebe v. Dom. Bronze Ltd.,* [1972] 1 W.W.R. 651 (Man. C.A.). This case was distinguished by the Supreme Court of Canada in *Baxter Student Housing Ltd. v. College Housing Co-op. Ltd.* (1976), 57 D.L.R. (3d) 1, where the owner sought to have a receiver appointed, after a lien had been registered, who would receive payments from the mortgage company for use in completing the building, such mortgage advances to have priority over the lien. The Court refused the order since it would be contrary to the provisions of the Act which state in unambiguous terms that a claim for lien has priority over such a receiving order (Man. sec. 11(1); Ont., sec. 14(1)). It pointed out that the purpose of the order in the *Winnipeg Supply* case, *supra,* was to preserve the property pending the litigation, whereas here the owner was seeking to obtain money which he could use to effect improvements to the building.

9

The Trust Fund

§104   The Trust Fund Generally.

The Acts of British Columbia (sec. 3(1)), Ontario (sec. 2(1)), New Brunswick (sec. 3(1)), Saskatchewan (sec. 3(1)) and the Manitoba Builders and Workers Act (R.S.M. 1970, c. B90, sec. 3(1)), provide that all sums received by a builder, contractor or subcontractor on account of the contract price constitute trust funds in the hands of the builder, contractor or subcontractor as the case may be, for the benefit of the owner, contractor, subcontractor, Workmen's Compensation Board, workmen and persons who have supplied material on account of the contract. Until all of the specified beneficiaries have been fully paid for the work done or materials supplied under the contract, the trust moneys may not be appropriated or converted to any use save as permitted by the trust provisions of the Act. As will be seen, any payment to any person supplying material, labour or service to the project is not, however, a payment in breach of the said trust.

The unique additional trust provisions contained in the Ontario and Saskatchewan Acts will be dealt with later in this chapter. LeBel J. stated in *Bank of Montreal v. Sidney,* [1955] O.W.N. 581 at 583: "Another object of the Act . . . is to prevent those entitled to protection from being victimized by unscrupulous or impecunious builders or contractors . . . As a further safeguard for the benefit of those the Act is designed to protect, all moneys received by the contractor from the person primarily liable are, by section 3 [now section 2] expressly said to be and to constitute a trust fund in his hands for the benefit of those other persons. Until those persons have been paid, he must not appropriate or convert any part of it to his own use or to any use not authorized by the trust." In *Standard Indust. Ltd. v. Treasury Trails Holdings Ltd.* (1977), 24 C.B.R. (N.S.) 8, affirmed 23 C.B.R. (N.S.) 244 (Ont. C.A.) Lyon Co. Ct. J., after quoting from *S. I. Guttman Ltd. v. James D. Mokry Ltd.,* [1969] 1 O.R. 7 (C.A.) and *Freedman v. Guar. Trust Co.,* (1929) 64 O.L.R. 200, stated at page 12, in commenting on the purpose of the Mechanics' Lien Act and on the trust created by section 2(3) of the Ontario Act: ". . . I take it that the interpretation should be given to the section which results from a strict construction in the sense of protecting the claims of those who supply work and materials so long as the owner is not prejudiced."

However, in commenting on the same provision of the Ontario Act in *Bre-Aar Excavating Ltd. v. D'Angela Const. (Ont.) Ltd.* (1975), 8 O.R. (2d) 598, Killeen, Co. Ct. J. at p. 603 stated: "... on my construction of s. 2(3), it was not its intent to enlarge the unilateral rights of an owner but, rather, to increase the reach of protection available to suppliers and subtrade claimants." See also *Can. Comstock Co. v. Toronto Transit Commn.; Can. Comstock Co. v. Anglin-Norcross Ont. Ltd.,* [1970] S.C.R. 205; *Re Walter Davidson Ltd.,* [1957] O.W.N. 223; *Minneapolis-Honeywell Regulator Co. v. Empire Brass Co.,* [1955] S.C.R. 694, reversing (*sub nom. The Same v. Irvine & Reeves Ltd.*) 13 W.W.R. 449, which reversed 11 W.W.R. 212; *Evans, Coleman and Evans Ltd. v. R. A. Nelson Const. Ltd.* (1958), 25 W.W.R. 569; varied 27 W.W.R. 38 (B.C. C.A.); *Rosemount Tile & Terrazzo Ltd. v. North York Bd. of Education* (1960), 1 C.B.R. (N.S.) 63 (Ont.); *Gascoigne Ltd. v. South Cramahe School Bd.,* [1962] O.W.N. 81; *Clarkson Co. v. Can. Bank of Commerce,* [1966] S.C.R. 513, reversing (*sub nom. John Ritchie Ltd. v. Can. Bank of Commerce*), [1965] 1 O.R. 197, which reversed [1963] 2 O.R. 116.

"The Mechanics' Lien Act of British Columbia has since 1879 afforded to labourers, materialmen, contractors, and others a means of enforcing their claims against the work produced as a result of their efforts, or with the materials they have supplied by filing claims of lien within a defined period and, if default were made, instituting proceedings to realize the amount payable. Section 19 [now section 3] was apparently designed to provide further security for such persons by providing that moneys received as payments on account of the principal contract or of any subcontract should, in the hands of the recipients, constitute a trust fund for their benefit.": per Locke J., in *Minneapolis-Honeywell Regulator Co. v. Empire Brass Co., supra.* See also *Dom. Bank v. Fassel & Baglier Const. Co.,* [1955] O.W.N. 709. Insofar as any particular trustee is concerned, the trust fund and holdback provisions of the Act are alternative, not cumulative, and it would appear that the trustee is liable for the greater of the two types of funds, but not for both. See *Otis Elevator Co. v. Commonwealth Holiday Inns of Can. Ltd.,* [1972] 2 O.R. 536; *Minneapolis-Honeywell Regulator Co. v. Empire Brass Co., supra* per Rand, J., S.C.R. page 696; *Anden Vinyl Products Ltd. v. Gauss* (1976), 16 O.R. (2d) 225. See also §105 *infra.*

The Ontario and Saskatchewan Acts now specifically provide for the imposition of a trust on moneys in the hands of owners in certain circumstances, as well as on payments made to contractors and subcontractors: see Ont., sec. 2(3); Sask., sec. 3(3). These sections provide that where a sum becomes payable to a contractor by an owner on the certificate of a person authorized under the contract to make such a certificate (usually the architect or engineer retained by the owner) then, upon the issuance of such certificate, an amount equal to the sum so certified that is in the owner's hands or is received by him at any time thereafter shall, until paid to the contractor, constitute a trust fund in the owner's hands for the benefit of the contractor, subcontractor, Workmen's Compensation Board, workmen and persons who have supplied material on account of the contract (or who have rented equipment to be used on the contract site; Ont.) (or who have rendered work or services on the contract site; Sask.). Until the beneficiaries of this trust are paid in full, these trust moneys may not be appropriated or converted by the owner to his own use or to any use not authorized by the trust provisions of the Acts.

The Ontario Act, section 2(4), further provides that all sums received by an owner (other than the Crown, a municipality as defined in The Municipal Affairs Act or a metropolitan or regional municipality or local board thereof), which are to be used in the financing, including the purchase price of the land and the payment of prior encumbrances, of a building, structure or work, constitute, subject to the payment of the purchase price of the land and prior encumbrances, a trust fund in the hands of the owner. This fund is for the benefit of all persons above-mentioned (see section 2(1)), and until all these persons have been paid, the owner cannot appropriate or convert any part of this fund to his own use or to any use not authorized by the trust. A similar provision exists in the Saskatchewan Act, section 3(4).

The Saskatchewan Act, section 3(5) further specifically provides for a trust fund where any part of the consideration of a contract between an owner and a contractor does not consist of money. The value of the part of the consideration that does not consist of money is deemed to be money owing to the contractor from the owner and the owner shall be considered to hold that amount of money in trust for the benefit of the beneficiaries therein named until the claims of all such persons have been paid.

As is more fully discussed in §§106, 107, and 113, *infra,* those statutes which do not contain a specific owner's trust have been interpreted in certain circumstances so as to effectively create trust funds in the hands of owners. Additionally, the right of a named beneficiary to share in any trust funds so created, in certain circumstances and in certain jurisdictions, may be an inchoate right which only becomes consummate upon the trust fund actually or constructively coming into the hands of a trustee with whom the named beneficiary has privity of contract. See also the Saskatchewan Act, section 5(1), (2).

A claimant's right to share in a trust fund is assignable. For a discussion on the sufficiency of the assignment, see *Groves-Raffin Const. Ltd. v. Bank of N.S.,* [1975] 2 W.W.R. 97 reversed and varied in part (*sub nom. Groves-Raffin Const. Ltd. v. Can. Imperial Bank of Commerce*) 64 D.L.R. (3d) 78 (B.C. C.A.). The position of the owner as beneficiary was considered in

Drew v. Royal Bank (1963), 42 W.W.R. 166 (B.C.) and *Scott v. Riehl* (1958), 25 W.W.R. 525 (B.C.) and §112, *infra.*

§105 The Trust Applies Even Where No Lien Rights Exist.

In certain circumstances, a person has no right to register a claim for lien, or it may be that lien rights have expired. For example, it has been held that there is no right to claim a lien against the Crown, either in the right of the province, or in the right of the Dominion: see §43, "Government Property and the Holdback Fund", and §18, "Government Property", *ante.* Nor can a person register a claim for lien against a public street or highway: see Ont., sec. 5(2); B.C., sec. 4; N.B., sec. 2 and §17, *ante.* There also exist subtle differences in wording between the trust provisions of the various Acts and the provisions creating the right to a lien. In *Can. Bank of Commerce v. T. McAvity & Sons Ltd.,* [1959] S.C.R. 478, affirming [1958] O.W.N. 324, where material was supplied for the improvement of a public street, the Court stated that the sole object of prohibiting a lien against a public street was to prevent the sale and the consequential deprivation of use thereof to the public. Therefore, the claim pursuant to the trust provisions was held to be properly before the Court.

The Supreme Court of British Columbia came to the same conclusion in *Crane Can. Ltd. v. McBeath Plumbing & Heating Ltd.* (1965), 54 W.W.R. 119 (B.C.). Dryer J. stated that the trust provisions under the Act are quite separate from the lien provisions, and that even where no lien rights exist against the Crown, the trust provisions are nonetheless enforceable. See also *Bank of N.S. v. O & O Contractors Ltd.* (1965), 55 W.W.R. 103 (B.C. C.A.); *Minneapolis-Honeywell Regulator Co. v. Empire Brass Co.,* [1955] S.C.R. 694, reversing (*sub nom. The Same v. Irvine & Reeves Ltd.*) 13 W.W.R. 449, which reversed 11 W.W.R. 212; *Wells H. Morton & Co. v. Can. Credit Men's Trust Assn. Ltd.* (1965), 53 W.W.R. 178 (Man. C.A.); *Bore v. Sigurdson,* [1972] 6 W.W.R. 654 (B.C.); *Cam Cement Contractors Ltd. v. Royal Bank* (1973), 38 D.L.R. (3d) 427 (B.C. C.A.); *Re Northwest Elec. Ltd.,* [1973] 3 W.W.R. 156 (B.C.); *Re Joe Pasut Contractors Ltd.* (1973), 18 C.B.R. (N.S.) 87 (Ont.); *Chipman v. R.,* [1934] Ex. C.R. 152; *Western Supplies Ltd. v. Cana Const. Co.,* [1976] 1 W.W.R. 289 (Sask.); *Aetna Roofing (1965) Ltd. v. Bank of Montreal,* [1973] 1 W.W.R. 589, affirmed [1973] 5 W.W.R. 672 (Man. C.A.); *Cronkhite Supply Ltd. v. Wkrs. Comp. Bd.* (1976), 1 B.C.L.R. 142; *Rasmussens' Ltd. v. Melville Country Člub,* [1977] 4 W.W.R. 382 (Sask.), *Anden Vinyl Products Ltd. v. Gauss* (1976), 16 O.R. (2d) 225.

In *Perfanick Bros. Trucking Supply Ltd. v. Mc-Ke-Si Co.,* [1975] W.W.D. 69 it was held that although the provisions of The Mechanics' Lien Act of Manitoba did not apply to the Crown, since as a policy and pursuant to the contract the Government had, in fact, held back 15% of the contract price for the benefit of subtrades and others, such holdback was trust money in the same sense that money held back under The Mechanics' Lien Act would be trust money. But see *R. v. Flintkote Co.,* [1976] 1 F.C. 249; *Chipman v. R. supra; Ottawa v. Shore and Horwitz Const. Co.* (1960), 22 D.L.R. (2d) 247; and *Anden Vinyl Products Ltd. v. Gauss* (1976), 16 O.R. (2d) 225.

§106 Beneficiaries of the Trust.

Each Act defines the beneficiaries of the trust fund. Generally speaking these are the owner, builder, contractor, subcontractors, Workmen's Compensation Board (for its assessment), workmen and material suppliers: see *Scott v. Riehl* (1958), 25 W.W.R. 525 (B.C.). In spite of the naming of the beneficiaries of the trust fund in the various Acts, certain questions have arisen, and no doubt will continue to arise, as to when a named beneficiary is entitled to share in the corpus of the trust fund and as to whether a person falls within the definition at all.

Although the problem of claims for the price of the rental of equipment to be used on a contract site has been resolved in Ontario and Saskatchewan, by statutory change, so that these persons are now included as beneficiaries of the various trust funds, it still exists in other jurisdictions: see Ont., sec. 5(1); Sask., sec. 2(1)(m). In these other provinces, if the equipment is merely rented, then there is no right to claim as a beneficiary of the trust fund: see *Clarkson Co. v. Ace Lbr. Ltd.,* [1963] S.C.R. 110, reversing [1962] O.R. 748; *Re Malvern Const. Co.* (1964), 6 C.B.R. (N.S.) 241 (Ont.); *Re Bodner Road Const. Co.* (1963), 43 W.W.R. 641 (Man.); *Re Arthur J. Lennox Contractors Ltd.* (1959), 38 C.B.R. 97 (Ont.). In *Northcoast Forest Products Ltd. v. Eakins Const. Ltd.* (1960), 35 W.W.R. 233 (B.C.), Rutton J. expressed the view that a person who made a claim solely for the rental of tools or equipment would not qualify as a lien claimant nor as a person entitled to rank on the trust fund as a creditor. It was further held in that case that a person who rented equipment with men to operate it, all as part of one contract, was in the position of a subcontractor and was entitled to share in the trust fund, although a person who supplied equipment together with operators on terms that the general contractor should pay the wages of the operators, was in the same position as one renting equipment alone and could not share in the trust fund. It was also held in *Peace River Oil Pipe Line Co. v. Dutton-Williams Bros.* (1960), 35 W.W.R. 95 (Alta.), where the claimant had supplied a tractor together with an operator to be used in the construction of a pipe line at a specified hourly rate, all operating expenses and wages being paid by the claimant, that he was entitled to a valid lien as a subcontractor who had performed work or services upon or in respect of an improvement for an owner, contractor or subcontractor upon the relevant land.

A unique situation confronted the Ontario Supreme Court in the *Re Terra Cotta Contracting Co.* decision, [1964] 1 O.R. 661, where trucks and operators and a loader and operator were supplied by the hour. Maintenance and repairs of the equipment as well as the salaries of the operators were paid by the claimant, however, the operations were performed under the supervision of the lessee-contractor. It was held, following the *Peace River Oil Pipe Line Co.* and *Northcoast Forest Products Ltd.* decisions, *supra,* that the claimant was entitled to claim against the trust moneys. The Court further stated that it would not be proper to divide the contract or claim of the claimant into separate parts for rental and for operators. See further §40, *ante.*

In *Cam Cement Contractors Ltd. v. Royal Bank* (1973), 38 D.L.R. (3d) 427 (B.C.C.A.), it was held that a person who supplied trucks and equipment solely to convey and deliver material to the site, but whose equipment was not otherwise employed on the site cannot be said to place or furnish material so as to become a subcontractor within the meaning of the British Columbia Act. In *Re Northwest Elec. Ltd.,* [1973] 3 W.W.R. 156 (B.C.), it was held that those who had supplied board and lodging to work crews of a general contractor had no rights under the trust created by section 3 of the British Columbia Act. In *Re Joe Pasut Contractors Ltd, supra,* it was held that the word "materials" in section 2 of the Ontario Act was wide enough in its meaning to encompass gasoline and oil supplied by a creditor notwithstanding that those materials did not form part of the building. It was held that it was sufficient that the materials be used directly in connection with the construction. It appears that the gasoline and oil were delivered to the construction site and placed directly into a forklift truck used by the contractor. A claim for automotive supplies and repairs was disallowed as these went only to improve the contractor's personal property. In *Aetna Roofing (1965) Ltd. v. Bank of Montreal* [1973] 1 W.W.R. 589, affirmed [1973] 5 W.W.R. 672 (Man. C.A.), it was held that once it was established that a person was a beneficiary of the type described in section 3 of the Builders and Workmen Act (now the Builders and Workers Act), it was of no concern that the claimant had made his first delivery of materials to the site only after the corpus of the trust fund had been established and this was so notwithstanding the fact that the claimant might not have been entitled to a valid mechanics' lien. In *Cronkhite Supply Ltd. v. Wkrs. Comp. Bd.* (1976), 1 B.C.L.R. 142, certain claims by a local union for wages, union dues and union benefits would have been permitted to share in a trust fund under the British Columbia statute had there been privity of contract between the wage earners and the trustee (as to which see *infra*). The question was left open as to whether the union would have had a valid claim against the trust fund for that part of the claim which related to union benefits provided for in the union agreement.

A major shareholder, who was also the president of the limited company concerned, was held not to be a "workman" within the meaning of section 3(1) of the Manitoba Builders and Workmen Act in *Foley v. Can. Credit Men's Assn.,* [1971] 2 W.W.R. 703 (Man.). See also *Horsman Bros. Holdings Ltd. v. Panton,* [1976] 3 W.W.R. 745 (B.C.).

Notwithstanding that a person is a named beneficiary of a particular trust fund, that person's right to share in the corpus of a particular trust created by the Act may be inchoate until the trust fund is either actually or constructively in the hands of the trustee with whom the beneficiary stands in privity of contract, and therefore in privity of trust. Certainly, in jurisdictions where it has been held that privity of contract between the claimant and the trustee is necessary, the question of the receipt by the trustee of the trust funds, where no actual physical receipt has taken place, becomes more important. In the following cases the question of privity has been directly decided. It may be noted that all of the reported decisions squarely dealing with the question of privity have held that privity of contract, and therefore of trust between the beneficiary and the trustee, is required: *Cronkhite Supply Ltd. v. Wkrs. Comp. Bd., supra; Atlas Glass Co. v. Superior Components Ltd.,* [1976] W.W.D. 109 (B.C.); *Western Supplies Ltd. v. Cana Const. Co., supra.* See also *Crane Can. Ltd. v. McBeath Plumbing & Heating Ltd.* (1965), 54 W.W.R. 119 (B.C.); *Cyrus J. Moulton Ltd. v. R.* (1975), 75 D.T.C. 5056 reversed 75 D.T.C. 5440, and *Anden Vinyl Products Ltd. v. Gauss* (1976), 16 O.R. (2d) 225.

While the question of privity was not directly in issue in the cases referred to in this paragraph, none of the judgments raised privity as a problem in either allowing or dismissing the claim to a trust fund. In *Cam Cement Contractors Ltd. v. Royal Bank* (1973), 38 D.L.R. (3d) 427 (B.C.C.A.), the British Columbia Court of Appeal decided that entitlement or nonentitlement to share in the trust fund was to be determined by the definition of 'subcontractor' contained in the British Columbia Act which is the same as that contained in the Ontario Act. In *Groves-Raffin Const. Ltd. v. Bank of N.S.,* [1975] 2 W.W.R. 97, reversed and varied in part (*sub nom. Groves-Raffin Const. Ltd. v. Can. Imperial Bank of Commerce*) 64 D.L.R. (3d) 78 (B.C.C.A.), the successful bonding company plaintiff was the assignee of various trust claims of materialmen and labourers, some of whom apparently had no privity with the defaulting contractor. See also *Perfanik Bros. Trucking Supply Ltd. v. Mc-Ke-Si Co., supra.* In *Bre-Aar Excavating Ltd. v. D'Angela Const. (Ont.) Ltd., supra,* section 2(3) of the Ontario Act was in issue. In that case it was held that subtrades of the general contractor had valid claims against the owner city pursuant to section 2(3) of The Mechanics' Lien Act applying general principles of trust law. See also *Standard Indust. Ltd. v. Treasury Trails Holdings Ltd.* (1976), 24 C.B.R. (N.S.) 8, affirmed 23 C.B.R. (N.S.) 244 (Ont. C.A.); *Anden Vinyl Products Ltd. v. Gauss* (1976), 16 O.R. (2d) 225.

The position of the owner as beneficiary was considered in the following cases: *Minneapolis-Honeywell Regulator Co. v. Empire Brass Co., supra; Drew v. Royal Bank* (1963), 42 W.W.R. 166 (B.C.); *Scott v. Riehl* (1958), 25 W.W.R. 525 (B.C.); and see §112, *infra*.

§107   The Time at which the Trust Arises.

Insofar as the contractor or subcontractor is concerned, the time at which the trust arises is when the contract moneys are "received" by them. Therefore, the definition of the word, "received" is of vital importance. Obviously once the moneys are in the hands of the contractor or subcontractor, they have been "received". The problem arises during that time period before the contractor or subcontractor has physical possession of the moneys.

The earliest reported decision on the word "received" in the various trust fund sections is that of *Castelein v. Boux,* [1934] 1 W.W.R. 772 (Man. C.A.) in which it was held that moneys must be physically received by the contractor in order to create the trust fund and permit a subcontractor to claim against it. Accordingly, where the owner was served with a garnishment order prior to his parting with the funds to the contractor, the garnishment order of a third party was held to prevail. This decision was followed in *Mike's Roofing & Insulation Ltd. v. Harder* (1964), 49 D.L.R. (2d) 595 (B.C.) and *Western Supplies Ltd. v. Cana Const. Co.,* [1976] 1 W.W.R. 289 (Sask.). The strong dissents in the *Castelein* case as well as the *Minneapolis-Honeywell Regulator Co. v. Empire Brass Co.,* [1955] S.C.R. 694, case appear to have influenced the trial Judge in a later case of *Beaver Lbr. Co. v. Sieffert* (1964), 50 W.W.R. 186, affirming 49 W.W.R. 294 (Man. C.A.) wherein the trial Judge held that the trust arises when the moneys are properly owing to the contractor on account of the contract price, notwithstanding the fact that the owner has not yet physically put the moneys into the contractor's hands. However, of the four Judges sitting in appeal, only one agreed with the trial Judge's reasoning, although the appeal was dismissed. The other three Judges were content to rely upon section 11(1) of the Manitoba Mechanics' Lien Act to dispose of the matter. In *Modular Products Ltd. v. Aristocratic Plywoods Ltd.; Modular Products Ltd. v. R.,* [1974] 2 W.W.R. 90 (B.C.C.A.), the British Columbia Court of Appeal dealt with the word 'received' and held that a third party demand by Her Majesty the Queen in the Right of Canada for taxes owing under the Excise Act, R.S.C. 1952, c. 100 (now R.S.C. 1970, c. E-12) and the Income Tax Act, R.S.C. 1952, c. 148 (now 1970-71-72 (Can.), c. 63) served upon a general contractor resulting in a payment into Court by the general contractor rather than to its subtrades would not take precedence over the trust provisions of section 3(1) of the British Columbia Act. The Court adopted the reasoning in *Royal Bank v. Wilson* (1963), 42 W.W.R. 1, (Man. C.A.); and the *Minneapolis-Honeywell* decision, *supra*.. In essence, the Court decided that had the money been received by the Crown, the Crown would have held the moneys in a transmitted fiduciary capacity since receipt by the Crown would have been correlative of receipt by the taxpayer.

See further in *Re Northwest Elec. Ltd.,* [1973] 3 W.W.R. 156 (B.C.); *Cronkhite Supply Ltd. v. Wkrs. Comp. Bd.* (1976), 1 B.C.L.R. 142; *Crane Can. Ltd. v. McBeath Plumbing & Heating Ltd.* (1965), 54 W.W.R. 119 (B.C.) and *Atlas Glass Co. v. Superior Components Ltd.,* [1976] W.W.D. 109 (B.C.); *Western Caissons (Sask.) Ltd. v. Buildall Const. Ltd.* (1978), 81 D.L.R. (3d) 664 (Sask.).

Where the owner paid moneys owing to the contractor into Court and a creditor of the contractor on consent moved for payment out of Court, the moneys were deemed to be impressed with a trust in spite of the fact that they were not physically received by the contractor, and the Court therefore directed that the moneys remain in Court for the benefit of the contractor's subcontractors: *Re Certain Lands in West Vancouver* (1963), 43 W.W.R. 181 (B.C.). The Court held in that case that this was analogous to an assignment of the contract moneys, and that once the contractor's assignee received the money, it was as though the contractor himself had received it. See also *Royal Bank v. Wilson* (1963), 42 W.W.R. 1, varying 41 W.W.R. 465 (Man. C.A.), where it was held that the trust provisions of the Act cannot be nullified by an assignment of book debts and the subsequent payment of the contract moneys directly to the assignee. In that case the Court expressed the view that any money properly owing to a subcontractor on account of the contract price was received by the subcontractor and was impressed with the trust when it was paid to his Trustee in Bankeuptcy or was paid into Court for distribution among competing claimants to the fund.

Provided the *Beaver Lbr.* decision, *supra,* is accepted, then it can be argued that once the owner properly owes the contractor a sum of money on account of the contract price, this amount is trust money in the hands of the owner for the subcontractors until delivered up to the contractor, at which time the trust shifts to him. This argument is supported by the decision in *Re Bodner Road Const. Co.* (1963), 43 W.W.R. 641 (Man.), where the Court found that moneys in the hands of the owner, which were due and owing to the bankrupt contractor, would be a trust fund upon payment being made to the contractor's Trustee in Bankruptcy and that therefore, the owner should be joined as a party to the trust action. Further weight to the argument is applied by the decision in *Dom. Elec. Protection Co. v. Beaudoin Const. Co.* (1963), 5 C.B.R. (N.S.) 72 (Ont.). In that case a supplier of equipment to a subcontractor obtained judgment against the subcontractor when he refused to pay the amount owing to the supplier. The supplier then brought action against the general contractor under section 3, (now section 2), of The Mechanics' Lien Act. The Court held that the supplier was entitled to judgment against the contractor since the trust section created a civil liability and the contractor, having failed to comply with the provisions of the section was liable to the supplier. The Court went on to find that the fact that judgment had already been recovered in a previous action by the material supplier did not preclude him from proceeding with his action against the contractor since he had separate causes of action against the subcontractor and the contractor. In *Pilkington Glass Ltd. v. Burnaby S.D.* (1961), 36 W.W.R. 34 (B.C.), the owners brought an application for an order dismissing the action as against them which had been brought by beneficiaries claiming under the trust fund section of the Act on the ground that the statement of claim did not disclose any reasonable cause of action as against them because the trust provisions of the Act did not apply to moneys in the hands of the owner. It was held that the application should be dismissed since the decision of the Supreme Court of Canada in the *Minneapolis-Honeywell Regulator Co. v. Empire Brass Co.* case, *supra*, upon which the owners relied, did not deal with the particular point and accordingly, the question of whether or not the owner was a proper party to the proceedings should be left to the trial Judge. However, in *Billinkoff's Ltd. v. R. C. Archiepiscopal Corpn. of Winnipeg* (1959), 67 Man. R. 175, the Court expressed the view that there was no provision in The Mechanics' Lien Act for the creation of a trust fund for the lienholders out of moneys in the hands of the owner. But see *Bre-Aar Excavating Ltd. v. D'Angela Const. (Ont.) Ltd.* (1975), 8 O.R. (2d) 598; *Perfanik Bros. Trucking Supply Ltd. v. Mc-Ke-Si Co.,* [1975] W.W.D. 69 (Man.); *Re Northwest Elec. Ltd.,* [1973] 3 W.W.R. 156 (B.C.); *Cyrus J. Moulton Ltd. v. R.,* 75 D.T.C. 5056 reversed 75 D.T.C. 5440; *Standard Indust. Ltd. v. Treasury Trails Holdings Ltd.* (1977), 24 C.B.R. (N.S.) 8 affirmed 23 C.B.R. (N.S.) 244 (Ont. C.A.) and *Anden Vinyl Products Ltd. v. Gauss* (1976), 16 O.R. (2d) 225.

As previously pointed out, the Ontario Act specifically provides for the imposition of a trust on moneys in the hands of the owner in two situations. The first trust fund is comprised of moneys which the owner's representative has certified for payment by the owner to the general contractor. The second is comprised of moneys which the owner has borrowed for the purpose, *inter alia,* of financing the construction: see Ontario sec. 2(3), (4). In Saskatchewan there are similar provisions and additional complimentary provisions: see Sask., sec. 3(3), 3(4), 3(5); 4.

In *Re Certain Lands in West Vancouver* (1963), 43 W.W.R. 181 (B.C.), where an owner paid money owing to the contractor into Court to the credit of the mechanics' lien action and an application by a creditor of the contractor was made to pay the moneys out of Court to satisfy a judgment in a foreclosure action on the subject premises, the opponents of the application, that was otherwise made on consent, successfully argued, (a) that they were entitled to the money as beneficiaries of the trust created by section 3 of the Act, and (b) that the moneys had been received by the contractor within the meaning of the section, since the payment in for the purposes of distribution was a constructive receipt of the money by the contractor. See also *Re Walter Davidson Ltd.,* [1957] O.W.N. 223; *Royal Bank v. Wilson,* (1963), 42 W.W.R. 1 (Man. C.A.); and *Modular Products Ltd. v. Aristocratic Plywoods Ltd; Modular Products Ltd. v. R.,* (1974), 42 D.L.R. (3d) 617 (B.C.C.A.).

To date there appear to be very few reported decisions on the effect of section 2(3) (Ontario) and section 3(3) (Saskatchewan). In *Bre-Aar Excavating Ltd. v. D'Angela Const. (Ont.) Ltd.,* (1975), 8 O.R. (2d) 598 the purpose of the section was considered and was interpreted, with the aid of general trust principles, as having been enacted to give even stronger protection to the named beneficiaries. The Court held that notwithstanding that moneys were certified by the owner's architect as properly payable by the owner to the general contractor, the owner ought not to pay such moneys to his contractor after being appraised of the fact that the contractor owes outstanding accounts to subtrades and materialmen. The Court ruled that in such circumstances the owner ought to stay his hand as paymaster until further investigation or until there has been a judicial determination as to who is entitled to the money, failing which the owner is liable to account to the beneficiaries of the trust to the extent of the payments made to the general contractor after he became aware of their claims. It is submitted that this decision may be legitimately queried because of the emphasis given by the Court in interpreting the section to the protection of the beneficiaries without regard to the prejudice to the owner which such an emphasis creates. It was held that the owner in the circumstances acted honestly but unreasonably. It is common knowledge, and common practice, that until payment is received by the contractor from the owner he will seldom be in a position to pay the amounts owing by him to his subtrades and material suppliers. It is submitted that the owner having been found to have paid the moneys honestly, the Court might well have held that he was absolved from any liability for breach of trust, since the onus of seeing that the moneys which he paid to the contractor were in turn paid to the contractors' creditors then falls upon the general contractor or his trustee in bankruptcy under the trust created pursuant to section 2(1) of the Ontario Act. The same result might well have been achieved from the facts disclosed in the report by applying the provisions of section 11(6) of the Ontario Act. See further on this point §75, *supra.* The *Bre-Aar Excavating Ltd.* decision, *supra,* should now be read in the light of the decision of the Ontario Court of Appeal

affirming the Trial Judge's decision in *Standard Indust. Ltd., v. Treasury
Trails Holdings Ltd, supra* wherein the purpose of the section 2(3) Ontario
trust was considered to be the same as the general object of The Mechanics'
Lien Act; namely, to protect the claims of those who supply work and
materials so long as the owner is not prejudiced. In both of these last-cited
decisions, although the claimants in the first were successful and in the
second unsuccessful, the question of privity did not stand in the way of the
claims. In the *Standard Industries* decision, it was clearly held that
notwithstanding the existence of a certificate pursuant to section 2(3), the
trust fund, if any, was composed only of funds properly payable on the
contract between the owner and the abandoning contractor. See also §108
infra. In *Aetna Roofing (1965) Ltd. v. Bank of Montreal,* [1973] 1 W.W.R.
589, affirmed [1973] 5 W.W.R. 672 (Man. C.A.), it was held that a material
supplier to a bankrupt contractor who supplied materials after the amount
of the trust fund was fixed by receipt and mis-application by a bank was still
entitled to share in the fund and that different considerations applied to the
question of whether one was entitled to share in the trust fund than in the
determination of the validity of a mechanics' lien.

§108 Moneys not Subject to the Trust.

In Ontario when the owner's building was sold by a trustee appointed
pursuant to the provisions of The Mechanics' Lien Act, the proceeds of sale
not having been received "on account of the contract price", this fund was
held not to constitute a trust fund within the provisions of the trust section
of the Act: *Re Burch Const. Ltd.* (1967), 10 C.B.R. (N.S.) 307, affirmed 10
C.B.R. (N.S.) 307n (Ont. C.A.).

It was held in *Re Williams & Williams (Eastern) Ltd.* (1962), 3 C.B.R.
(N.S.) 76 (Ont.) that moneys received by a contractor from a subcontractor
by way of damages for breach of contract were not a trust fund within the
meaning of the trust section of the Act, since the moneys were not "received
on account of the contract price".

Further, in the British Columbia decision of *Cemco Elec. Mfg. Co. v.
A. Anthony Ltd.* (1952), 6 W.W.R. 552 (B.C.), it was held that the trust
section itself does not constitute constructive notice of a trust such that
where a subcontractor who is already indebted to his material supplier
makes payment to the material supplier, the latter, in the absence of clear
notice that the moneys so received are impressed with a trust, may
appropriate them to the prior debt in accordance with the rule in *Clayton's
Case* (1816), 35 E.R. 767 at 781.

See further on trust funds in the hands of banks or other third persons,
§110 *infra.* See also *Alpa Indust. Ltd. v. Carousel Homes* (1973), 1 O.R.
(2d) 710, affirmed December 12, 1973 without written or recorded reasons

1 O.R. (2d) at 710n (C.A.); *Horsman Bros. Holdings Ltd. v. Panton,* [1976] 3 W.W.R. 745 (B.C.). In *Bore v. Sigurdson,* [1972] 6 W.W.R. 654 (B.C.), a contest arose between foreclosing mortgagees, materialmen and subtrades and a bankrupt owner. The mortgagees, prior to foreclosure, had recouped certain moneys from the owner's bank account in reduction of the mortgage debt. The claimants argued that the owner was a "contractor" within the meaning of the definition contained in The British Columbia Act and accordingly that the funds received by him by way of mortgage advances were held in trust pursuant to section 3(1) of the British Columbia statute. There is no specific trust provision in the latter Act with respect to mortgage advances as there is, for example, in the Ontario Act. It was held that these funds were not received on account of the contract price, and in any event it was not possible as a matter of law to be both an "owner" and a "contractor" under the Act so as to make the trust fund provisions applicable to such funds.

The Supreme Court of Canada in *Bank of Montreal v. Metro. Investigation & Security (Can.) Ltd.; Royal Bank v. Metro. Investigation & Security (Can.) Ltd.; C.F.I. Operating Co. v. Metro. Investigation & Security (Can.) Ltd.* (1975), 50 D.L.R. (3d) 76, reversing 31 D.L.R. (3d) 190 (S.C.C.) left open the question as to whether or not section 3 of the Manitoba Builders and Workmens Act can effectively create a trust with respect to moneys that are not paid or received in the Province of Manitoba.

§109 The Right to Set off Against Trust Funds.

Various provisions of the Acts permit the trustee to retain moneys out of the trust fund or to recoup himself from the trust fund. In addition, the Courts have generally interpreted the various trust provisions so as to permit a proper accounting to be had between the trustee and those with whom he has privity of contract so as to determine the correct amount due, owing and payable. The amount so determined then becomes the corpus of the trust fund. See for example, *B.C. Ventilating Ltd. v. Intercontinental Environmental Controls Ltd.* (1977), 3 B.C.L.R. 89.

Accordingly, notwithstanding the creation of the trust, where a builder, contractor, or subcontractor has paid for materials, services or labour (or for rented equipment in Sskatchewan and Ontario), which is used on the project, out of his own pocket, then retention from the trust fund of an amount equal to the sum paid out by him is deemed not to be a breach of the trust: Ont., sec. 2(2); B.C., sec. 3(3); N.B., sec. 3(3); Sask., sec. 3(2). It is important to note that there appear to be no similar statutory exceptions contained in the Manitoba Builders and Workers Act. See also *Clarkson Co. v. Can. Bank of Commerce,* [1966] S.C.R. 513, reversing (*sub nom. John Ritchie Ltd. v. Can. Bank of Commerce*) [1965] 1 O.R. 197, which reversed [1963] 2 O.R. 116; *Horsman Bros. v. Panton,* [1976] 3 W.W.R. 746 (B.C.).

With certain differences not material to the discussion here, the Ontario Act, section 2(4) and the Saskatchewan Act, section 3(4) provide that moneys received by an owner which are to be used in the financing of the project are a trust fund. Only the Ontario Act contains an express right to recoupment by the owner from trust funds to the extent that he has himself paid in full or in part for any of the work done, materials placed or furnished or for any rented equipment: see Ont., sec. 2(5).

In Ontario, section 2(6) and in Saskatchewan, section 3(6), it is provided that where money is lent to a person upon whom a trust is imposed and the money is used by him to pay in whole or in part for any work done, for any materials placed or furnished or for any rented equipment, then trust moneys may be applied to discharge the loan to the extent that the lender's money was so used by the trustee and this shall not constitute a breach of the trust provisions. As well as applying to situations where the contractor has taken a loan for the purpose of paying his trades, these subsections also apply to an owner who has borrowed money to pay his contractor, and therefore at least in Ontario must be read in conjunction with subsections (4) and (5) and the restricted exceptions therein contained.

Frequently the situation arises where the general contractor makes a claim against the owner for a sum in excess of the statutory holdback. The owner, on the other hand, may counterclaim against the excess by virtue of the general contractor's default in certain situations; *e.g.,* where the general contractor has become bankrupt or otherwise has abandoned the project or where the general contractor has failed to perform adequately, thereby increasing the cost of the project. Of course the same principles would apply between a general contractor and his subcontractor or a subcontractor and his sub-subcontractor or material supplier.

There can be no set-off against holdback moneys. See Chapter 4, §45, *ante.* However, it is permissible to set off costs of completion or other damages against sums owing over and above the holdback or against the trust moneys. See *Can. Comstock Co. v. Toronto Transit Commn.; Can. Comstock Co. v. Anglin-Norcross Ont. Ltd.,* [1970] S.C.R. 205; *S. I. Guttman Ltd. v. James D. Mokry Ltd.,* [1969] 1 O.R. 7 (C.A.); *Noranda Exploration Co. v. Sigurdson* (1975), 53 D.L.R. (3d) 641 (S.C.C.) followed in *Scarborough Painting Ltd. v. Buckley* (1974), 4 O.R. (2d) 253; *Royal Bank v. Wilson, supra;* and *Rasmussens' Ltd. v. Melville Country Club,* [1977] 4 W.W.R. 382 (Sask.). In the latter case a contest arose not only *inter se* between lien claimants as such but additionally as trust claimants and also between that group and the Crown. The latter claimed pursuant to a third party demand served upon the owner pursuant to the Income Tax Act. The lien claims were made out of time. All parties agreed that the amount in the owner's hand, which was otherwise the correct amount of the statutory holdback, could be used by the owner, if the lien claims were invalid, to reimburse himself for the additional cost incurred by him to complete the abandoned contract, over and above the original contract price. The time limited by section 8 of the Saskatchewan Act to assert a claim against trust funds had also expired. The Court nevertheless directed that the amount in the owner's hands in excess of the deficiency be paid into Court for distribution among the lien claimants and declared that such amount was a trust fund within the meaning of section 3(1) of the Saskatchewan Act.

As to when an owner, as opposed to a general contractor or subcontractor, is in possession of trust funds, see §107, *ante.*

In Ontario and Saskatchewan, as noted, a trust is imposed on owners where payments are governed by certificates of an authorized person, usually an architect or engineer: see Ont., sec. 2(3) and Sask., sec. 3(3). In Saskatchewan there appear to be no reported decisions dealing with the right to claim setoff or to have a proper accounting as between the owner and the general contractor in order to determine the quantum of the trust fund. However, it is submitted, in light of the Saskatchewan and other western cases already discussed in this chapter, that a similar result could be achieved in Saskatchewan as was achieved in Ontario in *Standard Indust. Ltd. v. Treasury Trails Holdings Ltd.* (1977), 24 C.B.R. (N.S.) 8, affirmed 23 C.B.R. (N.S.) 244 (Ont. C.A.).

Before this last decision it appeared that the owner was not entitled to use any of the amount so certified as owing to the contractor to satisfy a claim for damages against the contractor. It was decided in this case, however, that the operative words in the section were its opening words, *i.e.,* "Where a sum becomes payable under a contract to a contractor by an owner ..." . The Court agreed with the result arrived at by the trial Judge who found that, even though the owner's engineer had certified a progress draw for payment to the contractor, which payment had not been made to him, the owner had the right to use the moneys stated to be owing under the certificate to complete the abandoned contract. The trial Judge concluded that, since the amount of the owner's claim for set-off against the contractor exceeded the amount which it owed the contractor, notwithstanding the certificate, no sum had become payable to the contractor within the meaning of section 2(3) and accordingly no trust could come into existence under that section as a result of the giving of the certificate by the owner's engineer. The result of this decision would appear to be that a trust fund is limited to the amount, if any, remaining after a proper accounting between the owner and the general contractor. An additional consideration may be necessary in a discussion of this problem in the future in the Saskatchewan Courts by virtue of section 5(2) of the Saskatchewan Act which provides *inter alia* for a lien upon a trust fund which takes priority *inter alia* over a right of set-off. The question of whether the owner's claim for damages in matters arising out of the owner's contract with the general contractor is truly classified as set-off will undoubtedly fall for determination. The trial Judge in the *Standard Industries* case, *supra,* at p. 12, commented that one of the uncited authorities indicated that neither of the legal concepts of set-off or counterclaim was entirely adequate to express the position between the owner and contractor in these circumstances.

Where the owner is claiming an accounting by way of set-off or counterclaim, he must bear the burden of proving that he is entitled to the same, since a trust fund will at least be *prima facie* created pursuant to sections 2(3) and 3(3) of the Ontario and Saskatchewan Acts. As indicated, frequently this type of claim arises by virtue of the contractor having failed to complete his contract with the result that the owner seeks to deduct the additional "costs to complete" which he incurs. Additionally, claims often arise for damages for delay in completion either as a result of the abandonment of the work, constructive or actual, or simply the dilatory completion of it by the contractor. There exists some doubt as to what is included in the expression "costs to complete". It has been held in two unreported decisions in Ontario that with the exception of payments to the Workmen's Compensation Board on behalf of the abandoning party (which are required by statute), such costs as legal fees, premiums for bonds paid into Court to vacate liens and other costs extraneous to the contract itself are not proper. However, the Ontario Court of Appeal in the case of *S. I. Guttman Ltd. v. James D. Mokry Ltd.,* [1969] 1 O.R. 7 at 12 (C.A.), quotes with approval the principle stated by Masten J.A., in *Freedman v. Guar. Trust Co.* (1929), 64 O.L.R. 200 (C.A.), to the effect that all damages suffered as a result of a contractor's failure to complete may be set off by the owner or general contractor as the case may be.

Where a trustee in bankrupty of a general contractor, who had received funds from an owner, set-off against that fund a debt due to the bankrupt contractor from a subcontractor, notwithstanding that the debt was one arising from an entirely separate contract, the Ontario Court of Appeal held the set-off against the trust fund was proper. The Court relied on the provisions of the Ontario Judicature Act, which provides for a set-off of mutual debts notwithstanding the fact that the debts are deemed in law to be of a different nature: see *Royal Trust Co. v. Universal Sheet Metals Ltd.,* [1970] 1 O.R. 374 (C.A.); but see Saskatchewan, sec. 5(1).

The scope of set-off available to the owner or contractor, as the case may be, has been defined in relatively broad terms. In *Len Ariss & Co. v. Peloso,* [1958] O.R. 643 (C.A.) at 656, the Ontario Court of Appeal defined the amount owing to the contractor as being the contract price less costs of completion, any outstanding accounts in favour of the owner against the contractor, damages, if any, awarded to the owner for delay in completion, and past payments by the owner to the contractor. Often the owner will demand and receive a performance bond from a surety of the contractor. In the event that the surety is called upon to complete the contract, he is entitled to payment from the moneys owing in excess of the holdback in priority to lien claimants. (See also *Royal Bank v. Wilson* (1963), 42 W.W.R. 1, varying 41 W.W.R. 465 (Man. C.A.). It is now apparent, at least in Ontario, that despite the existence of an architect's certificate under section 2(3), the owner may make similar deductions from the otherwise apparently absolute trust. In the event, that there are no lien claimants or the total value of the claims for lien is something less than the holdback, then despite section 2(3) of the Ontario Act, in the absence of a situation preventing the application of the *Standard Industries* case, *supra,* an owner or his surety would be entitled to retain any moneys owing to the contractor over and above the value of the valid claims for lien to defray any additional costs of completing the contract, and the owner or the surety will be entitled to these moneys in priority to the beneficiaries of the trust fund. With respect to the rights of a surety of a subcontractor: See *Royal Bank v. Wilson, supra; Crown Lbr. Co. v. Smythe,* [1923] 2 W.W.R. 1019 (Alta. C.A.); followed in *Re Bodner Rd. Const. Co.; R. v. Can. Indemnity Co.* (1963), 43 W.W.R. 641 (Man.); *Cronkhite Supply Ltd. v. Wkrs. Comp. Bd.* (1976), 1 B.C.L.R. 142, and with respect to the surety of a general contractor: *Groves-Raffin Const. Ltd. v. Can. Imperial Bank of Commerce* (1975), 64 D.L.R. (3d) 78 (appeal pending S.C.C.), wherein the question of the assignability and sufficiency of an assignment of the trust fund claims to the surety is discussed by the British Columbia Court of Appeal.

For an interesting discussion of the rule in *Clayton's Case* and possible exceptions thereto as affecting the right to set-off and to recoup from trust funds, see *Horsman Bros. v. Panton,* [1976] 3 W.W.R. 745 (B.C.).

§110 Trust Funds in the Hands of Banks or Other Third Parties and Priorities

Moneys which are made subject to the trust by section 2 of the Ontario Act and the corresponding sections of the other Acts in the hands of a contractor, a subcontractor or an owner may, in certain circumstances, remain subject to that trust when they come into the hands of a third party who is not directly involved in the actual building operation. This becomes particularly important when the actual trustee of the fund is insolvent or has become a bankrupt and there are insufficient moneys to satisfy the claims of the beneficiaries of the trust. An example is where the banker of an insolvent contractor has removed the trust moneys from the contractor's bank account to reduce an overdraft, or where the banker has received trust moneys from the owner under an assignment of accounts receivable. Under certain circumstances, the Courts have on several occasions required banks to repay trust moneys so received to the beneficiaries of the trust fund.

In *Can. Bank of Commerce v. T. McAvity and Sons Ltd.,* [1959] S.C.R. 478, affirming [1958] O.W.N. 324, under an assignment of book debts the defendant bank held from a contractor, the bank collected all accounts receivable including a payment by the owner on a building project upon which the plaintiff had supplied material to the contractor. The plaintiff materialman successfully recovered the payment to the bank as it was held to be money impressed with a trust under section 2 of the Ontario Act.

The scope of the trust section in Ontario was widened in 1959 in *Fonthill Lbr. Ltd. v. Bank of Montreal,* [1959] O.R. 451, reversing 38 C.B.R. 68 (C.A.), to include moneys received by a bank from persons for whom the bank's customer, the contractor, was building, when such moneys were applied to reduce or discharge the customer contractor's overdraft with the bank. Before this general proposition can apply the bank must be found to have knowingly participated in the breach of trust. In this case, the manager of the bank was fully advised by the contractor of the character in which the account was opened, and knew that all deposits to the credit of the account comprised moneys paid to the contractor by the owners of property for whom houses were being built, and he was presumed by the Court to know the provisions of the trust section of The Mechanics' Lien Act. From the evidence it was found the manager should have known that at all material times the contractor was financially embarrassed and that there were unpaid accounts due by him to his sub-trades for material, work, and services in connection with his building operations. Further, the deposit in question was not made in the ordinary course of business, as it was accompanied by express instructions to appropriate it to the building contractor's indebtedness on the overdraft. The deposit being accepted by the bank with full knowledge of the essential character of the money in question and the trusts to which it was subject, the bank was held to be a party to the breach of trust, and the plaintiff's claims were ordered paid out of the trust moneys in the hands of the bank.

The trust section in Ontario has been held not to be repugnant to section 96(1) of the Bank Act, R.S.C. 1970, ch. B-1, which states that, "The bank is not bound to see to the execution of any trust, whether express, implied, or constructive, to which any deposit made under the authority of this Act is subject." This section does not release a bank from liability if it knows not merely of the existence of the trust, but also of the commission of a breach of it, or of circumstances which should put the bank on its inquiry: *Fonthill Lbr. Ltd. v. Bank of Montreal,* [1959] O.R. 451; *Ross v. Royal Bank,* [1966] 1 O.R. 90 at 106; *Clarkson Co. v. Can. Bank of Commerce,* [1966] S.C.R. 513, reversing (*sub nom. John Ritchie Ltd. v. Can. Bank of*

Commerce), [1965] 1 O.R. 197, which reversed [1963] 2 O.R. 116; *Aetna Roofing (1965) Ltd. v. Robinson*, [1971] 4 W.W.R. 191 (Man.). See also Chapter 1, §6, "The Constitutional Question", *ante*.

On the question of the constitutionality of the trust provisions of the Ontario Mechanics' Lien Act, the Supreme Court of Canada has held that the provincial legislation in relation to the obligations of a building contractor is clearly within section 92(13) of The British North America Act, See *John M. M. Troup Ltd. v. Royal Bank*, [1962] S.C.R. 487, affirming [1961] O.R. 455, which affirmed [1969] O.W.N. 350.

It was held in this case that section 3 of the Act (now section 2) was competent provincial legislation relating to property and civil rights and that it was not in conflict with federal legislation on banking and bankruptcy. The ordinary principles with respect to trust funds must apply and a bank is in the same position with respect to the trust created under The Mechanics' Lien Act as it is with respect to any other trust.

The third party who is in possession of trust funds in these circumstances is said to hold the funds in a transmitted fiduciary capacity, or he is, in essence, a constructive trustee. See also in this connection *Banque Romande v. Mercantile Bank of Can.*, [1971] 3 O.R. 433 affirmed 45 D.L.R. (3d) 480 (S.C.C.); *Phoenix Assur. Co. v. Bank of Montreal* (1975), 60 D.L.R. (3d) 385; *Bridgman v. Gill* (1857), 24 Beav. 302; *B.A. Elevator Co. v. Bank of B.N.A.*, [1919] A.C. 658 (P.C.); *Andrews v. Bousfield* (1847), 10 Beav. 511; *Cave v. Cave* (1880), 15 Ch. D. 639; *Sinclair v. Brougham*, [1914] A.C. 398 (H.L.); *Thomson v. Clydesdale Bank*, [1893] A.C. 282 (H.L.); *Coleman v. Bucks & Oxon Union Bank*, [1897] 2 Ch. 243 and as to a volunteer, see *Banque Belge Pour L'Etranger v. Hambrouck*, [1921] 1 K.B. 321 (C.A.).

In *John M. M. Troup Ltd. v. Royal Bank*, [1962] S.C.R. 487, affirming [1961] O.R. 455, which affirmed [1960] O.W.N. 350, Porter C.J.O., stated, ([1961] O.R. 455 at 461), the principle as follows: "The test to be applied is whether the bank manager knew that the customer was committing a breach of trust and he knowingly participated therein. In my view it has not been clearly demonstrated on the evidence that to the knowledge of the bank manager there were unpaid accounts of workmen and for supplies or that they would not be paid. The evidence in this case is clear that at all material times he did not know and therefore could not have participated in any breach of trust. I think that the effect would be the same even if the bank manager had been aware of the provisions of The Mechanics' Lien Act." In this case, an ordinary business account had been guaranteed by the president, cheques were honoured after the alleged breach of trust took place, and the manager had no knowledge of the financial difficulty of the contractor. It was held there was no breach of the trust section. This decision was affirmed by the Supreme Court of Canada, Locke J. dissenting. See also

279

Standard Elec. Co. v. Royal Bank, [1960] O.W.N. 367.

Where the bank acts in good faith and in the ordinary course of business, a breach of trust action against it will be dismissed. See *Can. Pittsburgh Indust. Ltd. v. Bank of N.S.* (1962), 5 C.B.R. (N.S.) 266 (B.C.). Here the bank was aware that there were unpaid subcontractors, but it had no reason to believe that the contractor was in financial difficulty or that the ultimate payment of holdback would be insufficient to pay the subcontractors. The five tests as set out in the *Troup* case, *supra,* were applied in relieving the bank from liability. They were as follows:

(1) The bank was not aware of any actual or intended breach of trust by the contractor;

(2) The owner did not pay the trust moneys directly to the bank by reason of the assignment of book debts or at all;

(3) The owner paid the moneys to the contractor who deposited them with the bank in the usual and ordinary course of business;

(4) Although the banker knew that the deposit was a substantial part of the holdback, he did not know that the balance was insufficient to pay the remainder of the sub-trades' and material suppliers' accounts.

(5) The banker received the cheque from the builder for value in the ordinary course of business in pursuance of a banker and customer relationship.

In this connection, see also *Clarkson Co. v. Can. Bank of Commerce,* [1966] S.C.R. 513, reversing (*sub nom. John Ritchie Ltd. v. Can. Bank of Commerce*) [1965] 1 O.R. 197, which reversed [1963] 2 O.R. 116; *George W. Crothers Ltd. v. Bank of N.S.,* [1967] 1 O.R. 424, affirming [1965] 2 O.R. 17 (C.A.); *Ross v. Royal Bank,* [1966] 1 O.R. 90; *Pilkington Glass Ltd. v. Can. Imperial Bank of Commerce* (1964), 46 W.W.R. 345 (B.C.); *Drew v. Royal Bank* (1963), 42 W.W.R. 166 (B.C.); *Re Walter Davidson Ltd.,* [1957] O.W.N. 223; *Dom. Bank v. Fassel & Baglier Const. Co.,* [1955] O.W.N. 709, and *Aetna Roofing (1965) Ltd. v. Robinson,* [1971] 4 W.W.R. 191 (Man.); *Horsman Bros. Holdings Ltd. v. Panton,* [1976] 3 W.W.R. 745 (B.C.); *Groves-Raffin Const. Ltd. v. Can. Imperial Bank of Commerce* (1975), 64 D.L.R. (3d) 78 (B.C. C.A.) (appeal pending S.C.C.); *Phoenix Assur. Co. v. Bank of Montreal* (1975), 60 D.L.R. (3d) 385; *Banque Romande v. Mercantile Bank of Can., supra; Alpa Indust. Ltd. v. Carousel Homes* (1973), 1 O.R. (2d) 710 at 715, affirmed without written or recorded reasons 1 O.R. (2d) at 710n (C.A.).

In the *Clarkson Co.* case, *supra,* the insolvent general contractor received a cheque from the owner and misapplied it by paying it to his general account with the defendant bank. At this time, his account carried a considerable overdraft and the banker applied the deposit to reduce this overdraft. Subsequently, the general contractor abandoned the project. The claimants asserted that the general contractor and the bank were both in breach of the trust provisions of the Ontario Mechanics' Lien Act. On the facts, it was clear that the general contractor had previously paid its subtrades a sum in excess of the deposit in question from its own pocket. Subsequent to the deposit which the bank took to reduce the overdraft, the general contractor issued cheques to its subcontractors which the bank dishonoured. The bank, in defence, took the position that it was protected by section 3(3) (now section 2(2)). In the Supreme Court of Canada, the majority decision was that the defence could not succeed and that the bank, therefore, held the funds in trust for the claimants.

The Court held that the funds came into the possession of the general contractor impressed with the trust, and further that there were unpaid subcontractors who would normally be *prima facie* entitled to the money. The Court then decided, in the circumstances, that the onus of proving the exception to the trust provisions lay upon the bank and that the bank had failed to satisfy this onus. The reason for which the Court placed this onus on the bank was that prior to the institution of the law suit, the bank had exclusive knowledge of the dealings of the general contractor with it. Further, the Court went on to state that if the general contractor at the time of the receipt of the moneys from the owner was in a position to retain the moneys for its own use pursuant to the provisions of the exception subsection, then the decision whether or not to do so would be an exercise of the discretion vested in it as trustee. Because the general contractor drew cheques to its trades, the Court inferred that the trustee had made a decision against keeping the moneys for its own use. It was not proper for the bank to attempt to make this decision for the general contractor. See also *Banque Romande v. Mercantile Bank of Can.,* [1971] 3 O.R. 433 affirmed 45 D.L.R. (3d) 480 (S.C.C.) and *Phoenix Assur. Co. v. Bank of Montreal* (1975), 60 D.L.R. (3d) 385.

In *Groves-Raffin Const. Ltd. v. Bank of N.S.,* [1975] 2 W.W.R. 97, reversed and varied in part (*sub nom. Groves-Raffin Const. Ltd. v. Can. Imperial Bank of Commerce*) 64 D.L.R. (3d) 78 (B.C. C.A.) (appeal pending S.C.C.) a construction company banked and borrowed at a branch of "S" bank. The company was not prosperous and its application to "S" bank for further credit was refused. The company informed bank manager that it was applying to another bank, "C", for credit, but the manager did not know whether the same had been approved. Through its manager, the "S" bank knew that the company was in serious financial difficulty and had been instructed by his superiors to effect repayment of the company's indebtedness. About that time progress draws were deposited to the company's account at "S" bank, as its manager knew. The company president directed that the company's indebtedness along with his personal overdraft be paid out of the company's account. He also drew a substantial cheque on the company's account for the balance and in so doing advised the "S" bank's manager that the company was transferring its account to the "C" bank. Money was deposited in the president's personal account at "C" bank and shortly thereafter was drawn by way of 170 $1,000.00 bills and $5,000.00 in bills of smaller denomination on the premise that the money was needed to close a land transaction. The president absconded. The company subsequently defaulted on its contractual obligations and a bonding company, having satisfied suppliers and labourers and materialmen, took assignments of the latter's claims including trust claims. The company sued "S" bank for breach of contract and both banks for negligence, conversion and participation in the breach of director's trust. The bonding company sued the "S" bank for breach of the Mechanics' Lien Act trust and as well sued both banks for negligence. The British Columbia Court of Appeal in varying the trial judgment limited the bonding company's recovery from "S" bank for breach of the Mechanics' Lien trust to the sum used to repay the company's own debt, since "S" bank did not know that the purpose of the transfer to the "C" bank was to defeat the mechanics' lien trust. On the facts, "C" bank owed no duty of care to the company or the bonding company, and should not have suspected from the circumstances of which its manager was aware, that the president was carrying out a dishonest and fraudulent design. The Court further held that, except in patent circumstances, a banker is not permitted to set up a *jus tertii* against the order of a customer. (On this issue of benefit to the stranger to the trust, see also the *Minneapolis-Honeywell* decision, *supra,* at page 698) Accordingly, except to the extent of the moneys used to repay the bank, the Court held that in spite of the fact that among other things the bank had knowledge of its customer's financial crisis, that there were outstanding accounts payable by the customer in connection with his project, and that the bank was not in a fully secured position, such knowledge could only affect the part of the fund used to repay the bank.

It is well established that the beneficiaries of the trust fund have priority over the claims of assignees of the trustee of the fund. In this regard, see the Saskatchewan Act, section 5(1) and the British Columbia Act, section 19. In *Bank of Montreal v. Sidney,* [1955] O.W.N. 581, the bank held a general assignment of book debts from the bankrupt contractor to secure an overdraft, and it claimed to be entitled to receive the moneys owing to the trustee in bankruptcy of the contractor from the owner, in priority to the claims of all lien claimants. The Court, applying the principle that an assignee cannot be in any higher position than his assignor, denied the bank priority. See also *Re Walter Davidson Co.,* [1957] O.W.N. 223; *Minneapolis-Honeywell Regulator Co. v. Empire Brass Co.,* [1955] S.C.R. 694, reversing (*sub nom. The Same v. Irvine & Reeves Ltd.*) 13 W.W.R. 449, which reversed 11 W.W.R. 212; *Evans, Coleman and Evans Ltd. v. R. A. Nelson Const. Ltd.* (1958), 25 W.W.R. 569; varied 27 W.W.R. 38 (B.C.

C.A.); *Rosemont Tile & Terrazzo Ltd. v. North York Bd. of Education* (1960), 1 C.B.R. (N.S.) 63 (Ont.); *Gascoigne Ltd. v. South Cramahe School Bd.,* [1962] O.W.N. 81; *Royal Bank v. Wilson* (1963), 4 C.B.R. (N.S.) 316, varying 41 W.W.R. 465 (Man. C.A.); *T. McAvity & Sons Ltd. v. Can. Bank of Commerce,* [1958] O.W.N. 324; affirmed [1959] S.C.R. 478; *Re Certain Lands in West Vancouver* (1963), 43 W.W.R. 181 (B.C.); *Rasmussens' Ltd. v. Melville Country Club,* [1977] 74 W.W.R. 382 (Sask.); *Cyrus J. Moulton Ltd. v. R.* (1975), 75 D.T.C. 5440 (Ont.); *Modular Products Ltd. v. Aristocratic Plywoods; Modular Products Ltd. v. R.,* [1974] 2 W.W.R. 90 (B.C.C.A.); *Re Northwest Elec. Ltd.,* [1973] 3 W.W.R. 156 (B.C.) and the cases discussed in §106, *supra,* and §107, *supra,* dealing with the word "received".

Section 2(6) which was added to the Ontario Act in 1970 now has a counterpart in Saskatchewan, section 3(6). These subsections provide that where money is lent to a person upon whom a trust is imposed by section 2 and the borrowed money is used to pay in whole or in part the accounts of persons who would be beneficiaries of the trust, then trust moneys may be applied to discharge the loan to the extent that the lender's money was so used by the trustee. For example, if a bank lends money to a contractor and takes an assignment of the moneys payable to the contractor by the owner as security for the loan, the bank can use the money which it receives from the owner to discharge the loan so long as it can prove that the contractor used the bank's money to pay beneficiaries of the trust fund. To the extent that any of the money which the bank had advanced to the contractor was misappropriated by him, the bank would lose the protection of this subsection. On the reasoning employed in the *Clarkson Co.* case, *supra,* it would seem that the onus of proving the facts that would entitle the lender to the exemption from liability given by this subsection would be upon the lender.

Section 3 of the Ontario Act provides a 9 month limitation period for actions against a lender of money to a person upon whom a trust is imposed by the Act. The limitation period commences running in the case of a claim by a contractor or subcontractor at the completion or abandonment of the contract or subcontract, in the case of a material supplier at the date of placing or furnishing the last material, in the case of a claim for services upon completion of the service, and in the case of a wage earner at the date the last work was done for which the claim is made. It is important to note that this 9 month limitation period enures to the benefit of money lenders only and does not run against any other person who has participated in the breach with the money lender.

Section 8(2) of the Saskatchewan Act provides for a 120-day limitation period within which contractors, subcontractors, material suppliers, wage earners and those rendering services must commence an action to assert a claim to trust moneys. Section 8(3) provides for an extension of this limitation period by up to 60 days, upon the claimant furnishing the Court with satisfactory evidence that it is proper for the time to be so extended. The application for such an extension must be served upon the trustee and the owner before the expiry of the period specified in subsection 2. Section 9 provides that no appeal lies from an order made under section 8(3). Section 10 provides that any proceedings taken pursuant to section 7 shall be considered to be an action for the purposes of section 8. Section 7 provides that where a dispute arises with respect to the claim of a beneficiary of a trust or with respect to the administration of the trust, the person with respect to whose claim the dispute has arisen, or any other beneficiary of the trust or the trustee, may apply to a Judge to settle the dispute and section 41 of the Act applies *mutatis mutandis*. Section 11 provides that every agreement that the Act or any of its provisions are not to apply or that any benefit or remedy given by the Act shall not be available is void. This section would appear to extend to the trust provisions of the Saskatchewan Act.

As earlier indicated, section 2(4) of the Ontario Act and section 3(4) of the Saskatchewan Act are substantially similar, providing for the creation of a trust fund in the owner's hands out of funds received by the owner for financing the project, including funds borrowed by him to pay the purchase price of the land and for the payment of prior encumbrances, in connection with a building, structure or work. The owner is entitled to use such funds, however, to pay the purchase price of the land and to pay off prior encumbrances without committing a breach of trust. Presumably, the statements which have been made above with respect to the position of bankers and other third parties who participate in a breach of the trust created by the other subsections of this section would also apply with respect to trust funds in the hands of the owner. Hence, for example, if the owner's banker used the proceeds of a mortgage advance which was impressed with the trust created by section 2(4) to reduce the owner's overdraft, the beneficiaries of the trust might well be in a position to recover the amount of that advance from the bank. In this situation and others that might arise, one must also consider section 2(6) of the Ontario Act and section 3(6) of the Saskatchewan Act.

§111 Forum and Nature of the Trust Action.

If no lien action has been commenced, the forum is the Supreme, County or District Court of the proper monetary jurisdiction. If there has been a bankruptcy, then the proceeding under the trust section may be heard in the bankruptcy proceedings. See §113, *infra*. Saskatchewan has a statutory code dealing with trust actions. See the Saskatchewan Act sections 7 - 10 inclusive, 41, 46 - 51(2) inclusive, 53 and 55.

In *Niagara Concrete Pipe Ltd. v. Charles R. Stewart Const. Co.*, [1956] O.W.N. 769, it was held that where there are no lien rights, the lien Court cannot give personal judgment for the breach of trust. The Master here distinguished the decision in *Minneapolis-Honeywell Regulator Co. v. Empire Brass Co.*, [1955] S.C.R. 694, reversing (*sub nom. The Same v. Irvine & Reeves Ltd.*) 13 W.W.R. 449, which reversed 11 W.W.R. 212, which did permit such personal judgment, on the basis that there were valid lien rights shown to exist, as well as the claim, under the trust provisions. Therefore, if the sole cause of action is under the provisions of the trust section, the forum will be the Court of the proper monetary jurisdiction. It might be argued, however, that if there is a lien action commenced by another contractor on the project, or where the trust claimant also has lien rights and has commenced his action, then the statutory lien Court would have jurisdiction to hear the trust claimant's case on the basis that the Act's intent is to provide a method of summarily disposing of all claims that are necessary to be tried in order to completely dispose of the action. It is doubtful that the jurisdiction of the Court if otherwise properly competent could be ousted by the lien Court. If a trust action were commenced, in which the defendants were already parties to an existing lien action, an argument might be made that any excess costs incurred by reason of the duplicative proceedings should be paid by the plaintiff. See also *Minneapolis-Honeywell, supra,* at pp. 698 and 704.

It has been held that a statute such as The Mechanics' Lien Act is not an "instrument" within the meaning of Rules 607 and 611 of the Ontario Rules of Practice, and accordingly, the trustee of a fund created by the trust section is unable to apply pursuant to the provisions of the Rules for the opinion, advice, or direction of the Court pursuant to section 61 of The Trustee Act, R.S.O. 1970, ch. 470. Such a trustee can only seek advice or directions respecting the management or administration of the trust fund under section 61 of The Trustee Act. He cannot bring an application to determine legal rights with respect to competing claims to the fund: see *Re Mann Const. Ltd.*, [1965] 2 O.R. 655. But see Sask., sec. 7.

§112   Civil and Criminal Consequences of Breach of Trust.

It has been clearly established that failure to comply with the trust provisions results in civil liability. In *Minneapolis-Honeywell Regulator Co. v. Empire Brass Co., supra,* Rand J. ([1955] S.C.R. 694 at 696) refers to the trust provisions of the British Columbia Act stating: "I am unable to feel difficulty about what this language provides. The Act is designed to give security to persons doing work or furnishing materials in making an improvement on land. Speaking generally, the earlier sections give to such persons a lien on the land, but that is limited to the amount of money owing by the owner to the contractor under the contract ... For obvious reasons this is but a partial security; too often the contract price has been paid in full and the security of the land is gone. It is to meet that situation that ... [the trust section] has been added. The contractor and subcontractor are made trustees of the contract moneys and the trust continues while employees, materialmen or others remain unpaid." See also, *Bre-Aar Excavating Ltd. v. D'Angela Const. (Ont.) Ltd.* (1975), 8 O.R. (2d) 598; *Standard Indust. v. Treasury Trails* (1976), 24 C.B.R. (N.S.) 8, affirmed 23 C.B.R. (N.S.) 244 (Ont. C.A.).

It is noteworthy that the trust section creates a distinct cause of action such that where a supplier obtained a judgment in contract against a subcontractor, he was not barred from suing the contractor under the trust provisions: see *Dom. Elec. Protection Co. v. Beaudoin Const. Co.* (1963), 5 C.B.R. (N.S.) 72 (Ont.). Lien claimants who have failed to avail themselves of the protection of a lien may still rely on the trust section, but any claimant claiming an interest in the trust fund must prove his claim by action against the contractor. Therefore, where there is a trust fund on hand, claimants could not prove their right to participate in it merely by filing affidavits of their accounts: *Fraser Sash & Door Co. v. Bevenco Const. Ltd.* (1961), 35 W.W.R. 124 (B.C.). It is suggested that in Ontario a reference should be taken in order to permit claimants to prove their accounts.

In the event that a contractor breaches the trust provisions by diverting the funds out of the project, the owner who is also a *cestui que trust* is in no better position to claim against the trust fund than are the subcontractors. Thus when a defrauded owner claimed priority to the trust moneys which were insufficient to cover all trust claims, the Court denied success: see *Drew v. Royal Bank* (1963), 42 W.W.R. 166 (B.C.).

Where a limited company, entirely owned and directed by two individuals, deposited funds received from an owner respecting a building project being carried out for the owner, in a general account, into and from which all moneys received by the company were deposited and withdrawn, the directors knowing the moneys so deposited would be used for the general purpose of the company, in abuse of the trust created by section 3 of the Act, the Supreme Court of British Columbia held that the directors were personally liable for the breach of trust. The Court rejected the directors' argument that no personal liability could be incurred by them as directors for acts done by them on behalf of the company. In this case the plaintiff was the owner who had retained no holdback and was forced to pay lien claimants, and thereafter sued the directors of the contractor company personally for the amount of the payments made by him to the lien claimants. The Court held that the plaintiff as owner was within the class of *cestuis que trust* named in section 3 of the Act: *Scott v. Riehl* (1958), 25 W.W.R. 525 (B.C.). This case was followed by the British Columbia

Supreme Court in *Horsman Bros Holdings Ltd. v. Panton,* [1976] 73 W.W.R. 745 (B.C.) where it was argued that the defendants who were officers and directors of a limited company committed an "innocent" breach of trust by what amounted to sloppy bookkeeping. The Court held that there was a *de facto* breach of trust. The Court further held that so long as funds are dealt with in a manner inconsistent with section 3 of the British Columbia Act, there is a breach of trust. See also *Cemco Elec. Mfg. Co. v. A. Anthony Ltd.* (1952), 6 W.W.R. (N.S.) 552 (B.C.); *Groves-Raffin Const. Ltd. v. Can. Imperial Bank of Commerce, supra* (appeal pending S.C.C.); *Jim's Plumbing and Heating Ltd. v. P. H. Wilson Const. Ltd.* [1975] W.W.D. 22 (B.C.) and §110, *supra.* See also *B. C. Ventilating Ltd. v. Intercontinental Environmental Control Ltd.* (1977), 3 B.C.L.R. 89 where the Court, after applying the recoupment provision of the British Columbia Act, held two directors of the corporate defendant jointly and severally liable along with the corporate defendant for diverting trust moneys.

The Ontario, British Columbia, New Brunswick and Saskatchewan Acts provide for quasi-criminal as well as civil consequences for breach of trust. In Ontario, every person upon whom a trust is imposed who knowingly appropriates or converts any part of any trust moneys to his own use or any use not authorized by the trust is guilty of an offence and on summary conviction is liable to a fine of not more than $5,000.00 or to imprisonment for a term of not more than two years or both. As well, every director or officer of a corporation who knowingly assents to or acquiesces in any such offence by the corporation is guilty of such offence in addition to the corporation.

The argument was presented in *Bank of Montreal v. Sidney,* [1955] O.W.N. 581, that since the remedy for the breach of trust is stated in the Act to be of a penal nature, therefore no civil consequences should flow from it. However, LeBel J. rejected this argument and stated: "The abuse it seeks to remedy is made even clearer by the recent addition of the penal subsection." The British Columbia Court of Appeal in *R. v. Brunner* (1960), 32 W.W.R. 478, upheld a conviction for breach of trust under The Mechanics' Lien Act. The Court concluded that the provincial enactment was not *ultra vires* of the province, and was not in conflict with section 282 of the Criminal Code respecting criminal breach of trust. See also "Criminal Prosecutions under the Mechanics' Lien Act", Chitty's Law Journal, 1963-64, Vol. 12, p. 197.

The basic difference between the offence provided for in the Criminal Code and in The Mechanics' Lien Act appears to be that in the latter, there is no need to prove an intent to defraud. Section 3 of The Builders and Workmen Act of Manitoba does not contain a punitive provision. For a decision on an alleged criminal breach of trust by conversion of moneys for a use not authorized by the trust with intent to defraud and, in addition, an alleged theft of the same moneys contrary to sections 196 and 283 of The Criminal Code, R.S.C. 1970, c. C-34, see *R. v. Petricia,* [1974] 4 W.W.R. 425, leave to appeal to S.C.C. dismissed 17 C.C.C. (2d) 27n (B.C. C.A.).

§113   Distribution of the Trust Fund.

There was a suggestion in *Minneapolis-Honeywell Regulator Co. v. Empire Brass Co.,* [1955] S.C.R. 694, reversing (*sub nom. The Same v. Irvine & Reeves Ltd.*) 13 W.W.R. 449, which reversed 11 W.W.R. 212, that the trust section of the British Columbia Act does not require that the trust fund be distributed by the holder thereof on a *pro rata* basis and that "the subcontractor has, in this respect, a discretionary power and his obligation is satisfied when the trust moneys are paid out to persons entitled, whatever the division". It was held however, in *Re Putherbough Const. Co.* (1958), 37 C.B.R. 6 (Ont.), that where the amount of the total claims of the trust section claimants exceeds the amount available for distribution, equity requires that the fund be distributed ratably among the claimants whose claims are for material and work on the construction in question. It was further held in the *Putherbough* case that this distribution had to take place on a *pro rata* basis, regardless of the fact that one of the trust section claimants held a valid assignment of a portion of the fund sufficient to satisfy his claim. Such an assignment was in the same position as an assignment to a bank and as previously pointed out had no priority over the "section 3" claims. Smily J. points out in the *Putherbough* case, that the contractor who holds the fund makes payments to creditors in the ordinary course of business so long as the work is in progress and is not required to pay the subcontractors and material suppliers on a *pro rata* basis during that time, nor could the materialmen or subcontractors, who were entitled to receive payments, be required to return whatever payments they had received while the work was in progress to enable the Court or trustee to make such a *pro rata* distribution. However, once the work has ceased, either through the abandonment of the contract resulting from the contractor's bankruptcy, or because the work has been completed, the trustee of the section 3 fund must distribute the fund ratably among the unpaid materialmen and subcontractors.

In *Crane Can. Ltd. v. McBeath Plumbing & Heating Ltd.* (1965), 54 W.W.R. 119 at 123 (B.C.), Dryer J. stated: "I have considered the statement in *Re Putherbough Const. Co.* (1958), 37 C.B.R. 6 at 9 (Ont.), to the effect that payments should be made ratably when the situation arises that there will be a deficiency. I feel, however, in view of the decisions in the *Minneapolis-Honeywell* and *John Ritchie* [*Clarkson Co.*] cases, *supra,* that the principle so set forth in *Re Putherbough Const. Co.* should be confined to its own facts. In the case at bar, distribution was not made during bankruptcy but before construction had terminated and it cannot be said that a situation had clearly arisen that there would be a deficiency." It is submitted that Dryer J. here directs his remarks, confirming the *Putherbough* decision, only to that part of it which deals with the point in time at which it becomes necessary to distribute *pro ratably* and not to the principle elicited in the case itself. This submission appears to be strengthened by the decision in *Guar. Trust Co. of Can. v. Beaumont,* [1967] 1 O.R. 479 (C.A.). In that case, the Court, while agreeing with the proposition that the trust fund need not be distributed ratably during the course of the construction (nor would this be practicable), held that once the builder had abandoned the project and had assigned the contract proceeds to a trustee for the benefit of creditors, the trust fund should be distributed on a *pro rata* basis because, although he had not been formally declared a bankrupt, he was in fact insolvent. In Saskatchewan, section 5(2) provides with certain exceptions that the trust funds be distributed *pro rata* from time to time.

As already indicated, the problem of distributing the trust fund does not arise unless something unusual occurs such as the default or bankruptcy of the contractor. Usually the contractor simply pays his materialmen and subcontractors in the normal course of business until all of the money which he has received from the owner is gone, at which point they will have been paid in full or will commence action against him. Where there is a bankruptcy, the Trustee in Bankruptcy of the contractor will obtain from the owner or general contractor, as the case may be, the entire balance of the contract moneys which must be held by him in a separate trust fund and eventually distributed by him amongst the creditors who performed work or supplied materials to the particular contract in question. Where a general contractor having a number of jobs in progress goes bankrupt, the trustee must set up a separate trust account for each of the several contracts. In *Re Arthur J. Lennox Contractors Ltd.* (1959), 38 C.B.R. 97 (Ont.), Smily J. approved the practice, which is now quite general in Ontario, of the Trustee in Bankruptcy paying the trust fund into an interest-bearing bank account, and held that the interest which accrued should be added to the fund and distributed amongst the beneficiaries of the trust. It was further held in that case, following the decisions in *Re Walter Davidson Ltd.,* [1957] O.W.N. 233 and in *Re Putherbough Const. Co.* (1958), 37 C.B.R. 6 (Ont.), that the percentage required to be paid to the trustee under the Bankruptcy Act should be a first charge on the trust fund as should the costs of the trustee in administering and distributing the fund. It was held, however, in *Re Walter Davidson Ltd., supra,* that such a trust fund was not subject to the levy payable to the Superintendent of Bankruptcy under section 118 of the Bankruptcy Act, R.S.C. 1970, ch. B-3, since the fund, while it might have been in the legal title of the bankrupt, was really not his property for distribution among the creditors under section 47 of the Bankruptcy Act. See also *Re Joe Pasut Contractors Ltd.* (1973), 18 C.B.R. (N.S.) 87 (Ont.); *Re Northwest Elec. Ltd.,* [1973] 3 W.W.R. 156 (B.C.), and the further reasons for judgment in the latter case dealing with the form of the order and the trustee's entitlement to interest: [1973] 4 W.W.R. 232. As previously pointed out, the Saskatchewan Act contains a complete code governing the procedure for the distribution and administration of trust moneys.

It is the practice of the Ontario Supreme Court in bankruptcy to allow the trustee a fee of 7½% on moneys actually distributed to trust section creditors unless there are special circumstances: see *Re Core Planning Ltd.* (1969), 12 C.B.R. (N.S.) 264 (Ont.).

Once the Trustee in Bankruptcy is in possession of the balance of the moneys due to a bankrupt under a construction contract, he must distribute these funds among the beneficiaries of the trust as set out in the section of The Mechanics' Lien Act creating it. As a general rule, the Trustee in Bankruptcy will want to obtain the approval of the Court as to the method of distributing the fund for his own protection. This procedure may prove costly if the fund is a very small one, and accordingly the trustee may prefer, after ascertaining who the beneficiaries of the trust are, to obtain an indemnity agreement from each of them and distribute the fund to them directly without obtaining such an order. This involves an element of risk, for if the trustee has omitted one of the beneficiaries, he will be liable to that subcontractor or material supplier for the amount which he would have received on a *pro rata* distribution which would have included him in the list of beneficiaries. This is, of course, subject to whatever protection is given to the trustee by the indemnity agreement: cf. *Guar. Trust of Can. v. Beaumont,* [1967] 1 O.R. 479 (C.A.).

Accordingly, the trustee, if it is at all feasible, will want to obtain a Court order. This is usually done in one of two ways: cf. *Re Northwest Elec. Ltd., supra.* The trustee employing the first method will satisfy himself to the best of his ability as to the beneficiaries of the trust and will prepare a report setting out the names of the claimants and the amounts of their claims. He will then propound a scheme for distribution and, upon notice to all known creditors of the bankrupt contractor (including those who, in the trustee's opinion, have no claim against the trust fund), will make application to the Bankruptcy Court for an order approving the scheme. On the return of this motion, any creditor who has been left off the list of beneficiaries of the trust or who appears on the list but objects to the amount shown due to him, may appear to object to the order being made or to request that the scheme be varied to comply with the circumstances of the case. Any claimant who has any objection to the admission of the claim of any other claimant can appear and state his objection as well. The foregoing was the method employed by the trustee in *Re Arthur J. Lennox*

Contractors Ltd. (1959), 38 C.B.R. 97 (Ont.).

The second and more usual method employed by trustees in distributing the trust fund in accordance with an order of the Court was that used by the trustee in *Re Walter Davidson Ltd.,* [1957] O.W.N. 223. The trustee applies to the Bankruptcy Court for the advice and direction of the Court as to what distribution should be made by him of the moneys which he has received from the owner or general contractor on behalf of the bankrupt contractor. The Court will, if it finds that the moneys constitute a trust fund in the hands of the trustee, direct a reference to the Registrar in Bankruptcy to determine the names of the persons entitled to the benefit of the fund and the amounts to which they are respectively entitled. Normally the Court will at this stage appoint a solicitor to represent the interests of all the ordinary creditors of the estate. They will be adverse in interest to the "section 2" claimants because any surplus remaining, after distribution of the trust fund to the beneficiaries of the fund, will fall into the general assets of the bankrupt estate to be distributed among the ordinary creditors. The order directing the reference will also empower the Registrar to appoint such other persons as he sees fit to represent the various parties interested in the fund in the hands of the Trustee in Bankruptcy. For example, counsel is usually appointed to represent the interests of the bankrupt's bank where it holds a general assignment of the bankrupt's accounts receivable: see Forms 13 and 14.

As was pointed out by the Court in *Re Van Der Liek* (1969), 13 C.B.R. (N.S.) 200, extending time to appeal from 13 C.B.R. (N.S.) 28 (Ont.), two forms of order directing the reference are proper. There may be, (a) a reference for inquiry and report, reserving further directions on the question of costs, or otherwise providing for proceedings in the action, or (b) the whole matter may be referred for trial, in which case, on the Registrar's report becoming final, the issue is fully determined and there is no necessity to reserve the power to give further directions in the order directing the issue. It is now the usual practice in Ontario for the Court to direct that the Registrar in Bankruptcy determine all questions arising on the reference and that the trust fund be distributed in accordance with the Registrar's report forthwith after confirmation of that report: see Form 15. The procedure to obtain the order directing the reference and for the subsequent proceedings may vary according to the local Rules of Practice.

After obtaining the order of the Court directing the reference, the trustee applies to the Registrar in Bankruptcy for an order directing the method to be employed by him of ascertaining who the beneficiaries of the trust fund are and the amounts of their claims: see Form 16. The order usually directs the trustee to send notice by prepaid registered mail to all of the creditors of the bankrupt estate who have filed claims with him or of whose claims he has notice advising them that they must file a proof of claim with him within a specified number of days, and that if they do not do so within the time specified in the notice, they will lose any right to participate in a distribution of the fund. The form of notice which the trustee sends to the creditors is approved by the Court and is annexed to this order. The form of the proof of claim is also approved by the Registrar and annexed to his order. If, as sometimes happens, there are a number of separate trust funds being distributed on the same application, the notice will require the claimant to specify in his proof of claim exactly what project he worked on, or supplied materials to. If a claimant has a claim to more than one trust fund, he must allocate his claim amongst the various funds: see Forms 17 and 18.

After the deadline for receipt of the claims has passed, the trustee will review all of the claims received by him and prepare a report to the Court showing which claims are, in the opinion of the trustee, proper claims against the trust fund and which claims are, in the opinion of the trustee, not proper claims against the fund. He will normally give reasons in his Report for his disallowance of a claim: see Form 19.

If the trustee's report indicates that all claims received by him are proper claims, the trustee will attend on the Registrar, on notice to counsel appointed to represent the other interested parties, and request the Registrar to fix the costs of all parties on the reference and make his final report. The Registrar will then make a report directing payment out of the trust fund of the costs of the trustee, his counsel, and counsel appointed to represent the other interested parties. The report will further provide for the distribution of the balance of the trust fund among those shown to be entitled to it in the trustee's report: see Form 22. The Registrar's report is then filed in the Office of the Registrar in Bankruptcy and notice of filing the report is sent to all parties, including all creditors of the estate. It is normal for the trustee to obtain at this time, a further order permitting service of the notice of filing the report by either prepaid registered mail or ordinary post. The Registrar's report will then become final 15 days after service of notice of filing the report, following which time the trustee will make distribution in accordance with the Registrar's report.

If the trustee's report to the Registrar indicates that certain of the claims which have been received by him are not proper claims under section 2, the Registrar will make an order, (Form 20), directing the trustee to send a notice to those claimants whose claims are disputed, advising them of the time and date of an appointment before him to fix a date for the trial of an issue as to whether or not the claim is in fact valid. The form of the notice to the claimant whose claim has been disallowed is approved by the Registrar and forms part of this order. The notice will provide that, if the claimant does not attend on the appointment at the time and place specified in the notice, his claim will be disallowed by the Registrar. Upon the return of this appointment, the Registrar will allow the trustee and the other interested parties to discuss the disputed claim with the claimant, and if the claimant insists on the validity of his claim, he will fix a date to determine whether or not it is a proper claim against the fund. The trial of that issue is conducted in the same manner as any other trial, both parties having the right to adduce evidence as to whether or not the claim is a valid one. After all of the disputed claims have been disposed of, the Registrar will make his final report. It will be in similar terms to the report made where there are no disputed claims, except that it will refer to his disposition of those claims which have been allowed or disallowed at trial. It will deal with the costs of the various parties on the reference, and on the trials of the disputed claims, it will fix the amount of the trustee's remuneration, and it will set out the manner in which the trustee is to distribute the fund. Upon the Registrar's report being filed and confirmed in accordance with the Rules of Practice, the trustee will distribute the trust funds as directed by the Registrar. Again, the trustee will normally obtain an order permitting service of notice of the filing of the Registrar's report by mail, in order to reduce the cost of service.

If the original order of reference which is made by the Bankruptcy Court Judge takes the form of a reference for enquiry and report, reserving further directions, or otherwise providing for future proceedings in the matter, then a somewhat different procedure is followed after the Registrar in Bankruptcy makes his final report. Service of notice of filing the report is still required and, in addition, the trustee must bring a motion before the presiding Judge in Bankruptcy for an order confirming the report of the Registrar and for such further directions as the trustee may require in order to finalize the distribution. Once again, the usual practice is for the trustee to obtain an order permitting service of notice of filing the report and of the notice of the motion to confirm it by either ordinary or registered mail. The order confirming the report will direct that the trustee pay out to the claimants entitled to share in the trust fund, the amounts shown due to them in the Registrar's report and the trustee will then proceed to do so. Both the report of the Registrar and the order confirming it are of course subject to appeal in accordance with the normal Rules of Practice.

10

Jurisdiction

§114 Right to Enforce Lien Claims.

The right to a lien against land being entirely a creature of statute and in derogation of the common law, the statutory provisions creating a right to a lien must be strictly construed, and the lien claimant must show that his lien is clearly within the statute: *Clarkson Co. v. Ace Lbr. Ltd.*, [1963] S.C.R. 110, reversing [1962] O.R. 748; *Hulshan v. Nickling*, [1957] O.W.N. 587 (C.A.); *Fitzgerald and Powell v. Apperley*, [1926] 2 W.W.R. 689 (Sask. C.A.); *Johnson v. Crew* (1836), 5 O.S. 200 (C.A.); *Edmonds v. Tiernan* (1892), 21 S.C.R. 406, affirming *(sub nom. Edmonds v. Walter)* 2 B.C.R. 82; *Emard v. Gauthier* (1916), 29 D.L.R. 315 (Que. C.A.); *Calgary v. Dom. Radiator Co.* (1917), 56 S.C.R. 141, reversing *(sub nom. Dom. Radiator Co. v. Payne)* [1917] 2 W.W.R. 974; *Gearing v. Robinson* (1900), 27 O.A.R. 364; *Haggerty v. Grant* (1892), 2 B.C.R. 173; *Robock v. Peters* (1900), 13 Man. R. 124; *Rafuse v. Hunter* (1906), 12 B.C.R. 126; *Smith v. McIntosh* (1893), 3 B.C.R. 26, and *Leroy v. Smith* (1900), 8 B.C.R. 293 (C.A.). See also Chapter 1, Introduction, §1, and Chapter 3, The Lien Claimant.

The provisions of the Acts specifying a time limit for the commencement of proceedings, and the subject matter of claims for lien, must be strictly construed, and full compliance with such provisions must be shown before the Court may deal with the question of enforcement: *McCoubrey v. Carver Const. Co.*, [1942] 3 W.W.R. 648 (B.C.); *St. Clair Const. Co. v. Farrell* (1921), 49 O.L.R. 201 (C.A.); *Resources Enrg. of Can. Ltd. v. Bathurst Shopping Centre Ltd.* (1969), 1 N.B.R. (2d) 924; *Resources Enrg. of Can. Ltd. v. Loch Lomond Shopping Centre Ltd.* (1969), 2 N.B.R. (2d) 629.

Once the existence of a valid lien is established, the enforcement provisions, being of a remedial nature, should be given as fair and liberal a construction as possible. Technical objections which do not result in prejudice to a party to the action should not be heeded: *Inglewood Plumbing & Gasfitting Ltd. v. Northgate Dev. Ltd. (No. 1)* (1965), 54 W.W.R. 225 (Alta.); *Len Ariss & Co. v. Peloso*, [1958] O.R. 643 (C.A.); *Curtis v. Richardson* (1909), 18 Man. R. 519; *Nobbs and Eastman v. C.P.R.* (1913), 6 W.W.R. 759 (Sask.); *Polson v. Thomson* (1916), 10 W.W.R. 865 (Man. C.A.); *Robock v. Peters, supra; Fitzgerald and Powell v. Apperley, supra; R. Bickerton & Co. v. Dakin* (1890), 20 O.R. 695; *Barrington v. Martin* (1908), 16 O.L.R. 635 (C.A.); *Henrich v. Hall,* [1940] 3 W.W.R. 409 (B.C.).

§115 Valid but Unenforceable Liens.

In Ontario, a person who has extended the time for payment of an account for which he has a claim for lien, must commence his action to enforce the lien and register his certificate of action within the time prescribed by the Act. No further proceedings may then be taken in the action by him until the time for payment falls due: sec. 26(4). Similar provisions are found in: P.E.I., sec. 32(3); N.S., sec. 29(4); Man., sec. 26(3); B.C., sec. 41; Nfld., sec. 28(4), and N.B., sec. 31(3). When a period of credit respecting a lien claim has not expired, or where time for payment of the claim has been extended, the lienholder may, if an action is commenced by any other person to enforce a lien against the same property, prove and obtain a payment of his claim in the action as if the period of credit or the extended time had expired: Ont., sec. 27. See also P.E.I., sec. 32(4); Sask., sec. 43; N.S., sec. 30; Man., sec. 26(4); N.B., sec. 31(3); Alta., sec. 23; B.C., sec. 41 and Nfld., sec. 29. The Acts of Ontario, sec. 41 and Newfoundland, sec. 41 further provide that when property subject to a lien is sold in an action to enforce the lien, all lienholders are entitled to share in the proceeds of the sale for the respective amounts owing to them, although the sums were not payable at the time of the commencement of the action, or at the time the sale proceedings were taken.

The following cases may be studied in the light of these sections and particular reference made to them respecting provinces where the Acts do not contain provisions as set out above. In *Kerr v. Harrington,* [1947] O.W.N. 237, a lien claimant became entitled to payment of his account at a time after he had registered his claim for lien. The Court held that this immature claim, which had matured before trial, could be dealt with at trial. It was held in *Nor. Lbr. Mills Ltd. v. Rice* (1917), 41 O.L.R. 201 (C.A.), that as the lien claimant had become entitled to payment of two instalments of an account before action was commenced, the third instalment not being due, the Court was not prohibited from giving judgment respecting all three instalments. It has been held that where a contract contained a condition precedent to payment, the condition having been fulfilled respecting part of the contract only at the date of commencement of the action, the lien respecting the balance of the contract, could not be enforced until the conditions had been complied with: *Champion v. World Bldg. Ltd.* (1914), 6 W.W.R. 233; affirmed 6 W.W.R. 1469; appeal quashed 50 S.C.R. 382, and *Burritt v. Renihan* (1877), 25 G.R. 183. See also *Spears v. Bannerman* (1907), 1 Alta. L.R. 98.

§116   Security Taken by Lien Claimant.

In all the provinces the taking of any security for, or the acceptance of any promissory note or bill of exchange for, or the taking of any acknowledgment of, the claim or the giving of time for the payment thereof or the taking of any proceedings for the recovery, or the recovery of a personal judgment for the claim, does not satisfy or prejudice the lien unless the claimant agrees in writing that it has that effect: Ont., sec. 26(1); Sask., sec. 42(1); P.E.I., sec. 32(1); N.S., sec. 29(1); Nfld., sec. 28(1); N.B., sec. 31(1); Man., sec. 26(1); B.C. sec. 41 and Alta., sec. 22(1). See *Dom. Elec. Protection Co. v. Beaudoin Const. Co.* (1963), 5 C.B.R. (N.S.) 72 (Ont.).

All of the provinces have enacted provisions to deal with the rights of a lienholder who has negotiated such promissory note or bill of exchange.

In Ontario (sec. 26(2)), Nova Scotia (sec. 29(2)), Newfoundland (sec. 28(2)), Saskatchewan (sec. 42(2)) and Alberta (sec. 22(2)), it is provided that where any such promissory note or bill of exchange has been negotiated, the lienholder does not thereby lose his lien if, at the time of bringing his action to enforce it, or where an action is brought by another lienholder, he is, at the time of proving his claim in the action, the holder of such promissory note or bill of exchange. In *Stulberg & Son v. Linzon,* [1945] O.W.N. 971, a lien was filed and thereafter a promissory note given to the lienholder, which was discounted by a bank. Later the lien claimant commenced his action while the bank held the note. After commencement of the action the note was dishonoured and returned to the lienholder. Since the lien claimant was not the holder of the note at the time the action was commenced, no lien was allowed for the amount represented by the promissory note. "A holder who wishes to retain his righ to a mechanics' lien should not accept a promissory note and discount it when the date of maturity is subsequent to the time the lien action must be commenced, and he should also be careful not to commence his action until the note is in his hands": per Marriott Master, in *Stulberg & Son v. Linzon, supra.* If this procedure is not followed the lien claimant, not being able to enforce his lien claim until the note is dishonoured, may find that his time to commence the action under the Act has expired, and his lien rights lost. This pitfall might be avoided if a claim for lien was registered, an action commenced and the note then negotiated. The lien claimant could not then proceed until the note was dishonoured but his lien rights would be preserved. If another lien claimant brings the action, then the lien claimant who has discounted a note or bill need only have it in his hands at the time he is called on at trial to prove his claim.

In Prince Edward Island (sec. 32(2)), Manitoba (sec. 26(2)) and New Brunswick (sec. 31(2)), the discounting or negotiation of the promissory note or other security does not destroy the lien, but the lienholder must retain his lien for the benefit of the holder of the promissory note or other security.

Formerly the Act of British Columbia gave no protection to a person taking and negotiating a promissory note or bill of exchange and as a result in *Edmonds v. Tiernan* (1892), 21 S.C.R. 406, affirming (*sub nom. Edmonds v. Walter*) 2 B.C.R. 82, the Supreme Court of Canada, on appeal from the British Columbia Court of Appeal, held that once a note was negotiated the right to claim a lien was lost. This case was approved in Manitoba in *Nat. Supply Co. v. Horrobin* (1906), 16 Man. R. 472, and in *Arbuthnot v. Winnipeg Mfg. Co.* (1906), 16 Man. R. 401 (C.A.). Subsequently the Act was amended and section 41 now provides that the acceptance and discounting of any promissory note or cheque (which on presentation is dishonoured) does not prejudice any lien created under the Act. In the later British Columbia case of *J. Coughlan & Co. v. Nat. Const. Co.* (1909), 14 B.C.R. 339 (C.A.), the Court apparently held that once a lien had been claimed, the subsequent taking and negotiating of a note would not waive the right to a lien. See also *Brooks-Sanford Co. v. Theodore Telier Const. Co.* (1910), 22 O.L.R. 176, reversing 20 O.L.R. 303 (C.A.); *Swanson v. Mollison* (1907), 6 W.L.R. 678 (Alta.); *Clarke v. Moore* (1908), 1 Alta. L.R. 50; *Gorman, Clancey and Grindley v. Archibald* (1908), 1 Alta. L.R. 524.

It should be noted that these various provisions merely afford protection to the lienholder who has taken security or dealt with it as set forth in these sections and they do not in any way extend the time for registration of the claim for lien or for the institution of the action. It is only in those circumstances where the lienholder has extended the time for payment by granting a period of credit that the time for bringing the action is extended in some provinces: see §§69(*h*) and 72, *ante*.

§117 Immoral or Illegal Claims.

Where a lien claimant constructed additional rooms to enlarge a bawdy house, knowing the proprietress required the additions to increase her immoral business, the Court held the contract to be against public policy and therefore invalid and refused to allow the claimant's lien: *Miller v. Moore* (1911), 3 Alta. L.R. 297 (C.A.). See also *Perkins v. Jones* (1905), 1 W.L.R. 41 (N.W.T.). In *Farrell v. Sawitski,* [1929] 3 W.W.R. 23 (Sask.), a contract was entered into on a Sunday. The Court held the contract void for illegality and refused the plaintiff's claim on a *quantum meruit* basis. However, the Court found that the special right to a lien created by the Act could not be taken away simply because the contract upon which it was based was invalid. Further, since both subject matter and consideration were legal, the illegality being of form rather than substance, the lien was allowed.

In British Columbia the plaintiff and defendant entered into an agreement to build a model home and to share the revenue raised from the sale of tickets thereon under a lottery scheme whereby the home would be given away to the holder of the winning ticket as selected by a draw. The Court held their contract was void as the agreement was in fact an illegal lottery and violated the provisions of the Criminal Code: *Exhibition Advertising Enterprises v. Victoria Exhibition* (1962), 132 C.C.C. 303 (B.C.). But see *Ranger v. Herbert A. Watts (Que.) Ltd.*, [1971] 3 O.R. 450 (C.A.).

The Court in the Ontario decision of *One Hundred Simcoe Street Ltd. v. Frank Burger Contractors Ltd.*, [1967] 1 O.R. 195, stated that: "considerations of public policy are the foundation for the defence of illegality in relation to contracts." The Court quoted with approval the principles set out in *Waugh v. Morris*, (1873), L.R. 8 Q.B. 202 at 208 where Blackburn J., stated: "We quite agree, that, where a contract is to do a thing which cannot be performed without a violation of the law it is void, whether the parties knew the law or not. But we think, that in order to avoid a contract which can be legally performed, on the ground that there was an intention to perform it in an illegal manner, it is necessary to shew that there was the wicked intention to break the law; and, if this be so, the knowledge of what the law is becomes of great importance." The alleged illegality in the *One Hundred Simcoe Street Ltd.* case, was that a design was prepared by the plaintiff which did not meet the requirements of the city building code. The Court held that this did not make the contract between the plaintiff and the defendant illegal. See also *Letkeman v. Zimmerman* (1977), 17 N.R. 564 (S.C.C.); *Maschinenfabrik Seydelmann K. G. v. Presswood Bros. Ltd.*, [1966] 1 O.R. 316 (C.A.); *Calax Const. Inc. v. Lepofsky* (1974), 5 O.R. (2d) 259 where a building contractor not being a licensed renovator in accordance with a municipal by-law was denied recovery on his contract; *Cie Immobilière Viger Ltée v. Lauréat Giguère Inc.*, [1977] 2 S.C.R. 67 and *Diversified Crops Ltd. v. Patton Farms Ltd.* (1975), 61 D.L.R. (3d) 749. As to illegality generally see *The Pas v. Porky Packers Ltd.* (1976), 65 D.L.R. (3d) 1 (S.C.C.).

For a more modern view of the defence of illegality where no wicked or fraudulent intent is involved and a close analysis of the statute in question is made see *Royal Bank v. Grobman* (1977), 2 R.P.R. 101 (Ont.) and *Fillmore Products Inc. v. Western States Paving Inc.* (1977), 561 P. (2d) 687.

A lien may not be enforceable by reason of non-registration, licensing or some other failure of a prerequisite condition as to legal status of a claimant. For example, a limited or other type of business may have difficulty enforcing a lien even though properly licensed or registered in its home jurisdiction if it attempts to enforce a lien in a foreign Court. For example, local laws might require licensing or registration generally or with respect to the acquisition of an interest or estate in real property as a condition precedent to the commencement or the maintenance of an action or proceeding. Likewise, a business or corporation not properly registered or licensed in its home jurisdiction may be barred there or in a foreign jurisdiction from enforcing a claim for lien. See *Suss Woodcraft Ltd. v. Abbey Glen Property Corpn.,* [1975] 5 W.W.R. 57 (Alta.); *Valley Const. Co. v. Eberle,* [1974] 5 W.W.R. 537 (Man.); *Albert E. Daniels Ltd. v. Sangster* (1976), 12 O.R. (2d) 512 and *N.S. Sand & Gravel Ltd. v. Kidstone Estates Ltd.* (1973), 13 N.S.R. (2d) 431.

§118 Other Proceedings not a Bar to Lien Claim.

The remedy of a lien under the Acts does not exclude other rights the lien claimant may have, and generally the taking of other proceedings is not a bar to the prosecution of a lien action. See *Foxboro Co. v. Trident Const. Ltd.,* [1975] W.W.D. 167 (Man. C.A.) where a lien action in a District Court was merged with a more comprehensive cross-action commenced in the Queen's Bench. As previously mentioned, the Acts of all the provinces specifically provide that the taking of any proceedings for the recovery, or the recovery of a personal judgment for the lien claim, will not prejudice the lien claim unless the claimant agrees in writing that it is to have this effect. The following authorities may also be referred to in this regard. In *Beaver Lbr. Co. v. Burns,* [1922] 3 W.W.R. 383 (Sask.), it was held that the recovery of a personal judgment does not prejudice the lien or the plaintiff's rights to proceed under the Act. See also *Pomerleau v. Thompson* (1914), 5 W.W.R. 1360 (Alta.); *Edborg v. Imperial Timber etc. Co.* (1914), 6 W.W.R. 180 (B.C.); *Hamilton Bridge Works Co. v. Gen. Contracting Co.* (1909), 1 O.W.N. 34; *Robertson v. Bullen* (1908), 13 O.W.R. 56; *Dick & Sons v. Standard Underground Cable Co.* (1912), 4 O.W.N. 57; leave to appeal refused 23 O.W.R. 96. However, in the case of *Wake v. Can. Pacific Lbr. Co.* (1901), 8 B.C.R. 358 (C.A.), where a plaintiff obtained judgment for a claim for wages in an action under the British Columbia Workmen's Lien for Wages Act, and realized part of his claim upon execution, it was held that he was estopped from enforcing a mechanics' lien for the amount of wages for which he had already obtained a judgment. See also Chapter 7, Loss or Discharge of Lien, §83; and compare *Standard Indust. Ltd. v. E-F Wood Specialties Inc.* (1977), 16 O.R. (2d) 398 with *Rockwall Concrete Forming Ltd. v. Robintide Invts. Ltd.* (1977), 15 O.R. (2d) 422 and see Chapter 11, Practice before Trial, §145.

A conditional vendor of materials may claim a lien under The

Mechanics' Lien Act or proceed under The Conditional Sales Act, but he must elect which remedy he intends to pursue. If he elects to avail himself of the protection given him by The Conditional Sales Act then he cannot enforce a claim for lien. In *Hill v. Storey* (1915), 34 O.L.R. 489 (C.A.), it was held that where a lien claimant relied upon the terms of a conditional sales contract whereby he had a claim upon materials until payment, he could not rank as a lienholder and compete with others who had no such right as against the materials. In *U.S. Const. Co. v. Rat Portage Lbr. Co.* (1915), 9 W.W.R. 657 (C.A.), it was held that once a conditional vendor asserts and seeks to enforce a claim for lien he must be taken to have elected to make the subject matter of his contract part of the building and realty against which he claims his lien. He was accordingly thereafter estopped from claiming that the materials were his property under the conditional sales contract, or that he had the right to remove them. See also *Agricultural Dev. Bd. v. DeLaval Co.* (1925), 58 O.L.R. 35; *Collis v. Carew Lbr. Co.* (1930), 37 O.W.N. 413, reversed 38 O.W.N. 237 (C.A.); *Dom. Lock Joint Pipe Co. v. York* (1929), 36 O.W.N. 2; affirmed 37 O.W.N. 66 (C.A.), and Chapter 3, §37, *ante,* and Chapter 8, §102, *ante.*

§119 Failure of Lien Claimant Commencing Action to Proceed to Enforce Lien.

The failure of the claimant commencing the action to prosecute or enforce his lien will not prejudice the rights of other lien claimants to enforce their liens. This is also true when the original claimant prosecuting the action is found not to have a valid claim for lien. In *Baines v. Curley* (1916), 38 O.L.R. 301 (C.A.), it was held that if the person who commenced the action and registered the certificate of action failed to establish a lien at trial, the other lien claimants relying on his claim and certificate of action might still enforce their lien. See also *Ramsay v. Graham* (1912), 3 O.W.N. 972. In *Ogilvie v. Cooke,* [1952] O.R. 862 (C.A.), notwithstanding the fact that the Act clearly requires a lien claimant to register a certificate of action unless another certificate has been registered within sufficient time, the Ontario Court of Appeal held that since the plaintiff had commenced his action within the required time but had failed to register a certificate of action required by section 23, this was fatal to his claim, but his failure to register a certificate of action did not disentitle other lien claimants not plaintiffs in the action to judgment for enforcement of their liens. The Court, however, awarded the plaintiff a personal judgment for his claim. See also *Howard v. Herod Const. Co.* (1932), 41 O.W.N. 198 (C.A.); *Driden Indust. Ltd. v. Sieber,* [1974] 3 W.W.R. 368, reversing [1974] 1 W.W.R. 165 (Alta C.A.); *Universal Supply Co. v. S. Radatske Const. Co.* (1972), 29 D.L.R. (3d)

251 (B.C.C.A.) and Ont., sec. 25(3). It was further held in *Del Frari v. Wright,* [1960] O.R. 430, that a lien claimant who had registered his lien and was relying on an action commenced by another lien claimant, might, if that lien claimant settled his action, nevertheless proceed to the trial of his own claim and need not register a certificate of action, as he had the right to prove his claim in the action already commenced. See also *McPherson v. Gedge* (1883), 4 O.R. 246 (C.A.), to the same effect. But see *N.S. Sand & Gravel Ltd. v. Kidstone Estates Ltd.* (1973), 13 N.S.R. (2d) 431. In *Crawford v. Hesselink* (1958), 15 D.L.R. (2d) 294 (Nfld.), several lienholders took action in a Court which had no jurisdiction and another lien claimant took action in the proper Court, and later discontinued his action. The former lien claimants, on discovering their error, applied to set aside the discontinued action brought by the latter lien claimant in the proper Court, and to proceed to trial under this action. The Court found that the lienholders were not aware of the action taken in the proper Court, that no moneys had been paid out under the discontinued action, that the owner was not prejudiced, and that the lienholders' solicitor in the proper action had notice of the other lienholders' claims. The application was therefore allowed, but on strict terms as to costs. It was indicated in *McPherson v. Gedge, supra,* that any application to intervene in like circumstances to those previously described, by an unregistered lien claimant, would be received with disfavour. Notwithstanding the above, if a lien claimant wishes to rely upon an action commenced by another lien claimant he should ensure that the proper parties have been named as defendants in that action; see §135(*b*), *post, Brousseau v. Muircrest Invts. Ltd.* (1977), 15 O.R. (2d) 145 (C.A.); *Contract Interiors & Design Ltd. v. Vogel,* [1973] 5 W.W.R. 286 (Alta.) and §145, *ante.*

§120 Application of Ordinary Rules of Practice.

As a result of an amendment to the Act of Ontario in 1970, section 46(4) now provides that: "unless otherwise provided in this Act, the Rules of Practice and Procedure of the Supreme Court apply to proceedings under this Act." See also Alta., sec. 50; P.E.I., sec. 34; N.S., sec. 33(1); B.C., sec. 30(1); Man., secs. 28 and 57; N.B., sec. 61(1); Nfld., sec. 46(4); and Sask., sec. 59(2). Where the Acts are silent the ordinary Rules of Practice will apply so long as they are not inconsistent with the provisions of the Act. In *Orr v. Davie* (1892), 22 O.R. 430 at 435 it was stated by Boyd C., that: "All the ordinary rules of procedure in the conduct of contested litigation are to be read into the Act which was intended to simplify, but not to introduce new rules of practice, which would be diversified according to the arbitrary discretion of each individual officer. The 'ordinary procedure' in actions in the High Court is, generally speaking, applicable to cases under The Mechanics' Lien Act." See also *Secord v. Trumm* (1891), 20 O.R. 174; *R. Bickerton & Co. v. Dakin* (1891), 20 O.R. 695; *Mancini v. Giancento,* [1962] O.W.N. 120. In *V.K. Mason Const. Ltd. v. Courtot Invts. Ltd.* (1974), 6 O.R. (2d) 655 it was held that an application for particulars in the Judicial District of York should be made to the Master, notwithstanding that the action had not yet been referred to him, and that the Act provided generally that interlocutory proceedings should be brought only with leave of the Master. It was held in *Pearcy v. Foster* (1921), 51 O.L.R. 354, that the consolidated Rules of Practice were made applicable to mechanics' lien proceedings where the Act contained no other provisions. The Court stated in *MacPherson v. Laurence,* [1956] O.W.N. 79 at 80, that: "A study of statutes dealing with mechanics' liens from their inception in Ontario reveals that the subject has been on the anvil for a long time, with mutations and even permutations. But always the hammer of the legislators has worked to one end, namely, to provide an inexpensive remedy for realizing a lien in the shortest time possible and in a summary manner." This principle has been legislated in some of the provinces: Ont., sec. 46(1); Alta., sec. 36(6); N.B., sec. 61(2); Nfld., sec. 46(1); and Sask., sec. 58(1). See also *D. & M. Bldg. Supplies Ltd. v. Stravalis Holdings Ltd.,* (1976), 13 O.R. (2d) 433; *V. K. Mason Const. Ltd. v. Courtot Invts. Ltd.* (1974), 6 O.R. (2d) 655. In *Caruso v. Campanile,* [1972] 1 O.R. 437, the effect of the recent amendment to the Ontario Act noted above was considered. It was held that the amendment to section 46(4) did not allow third party proceedings in mechanics' lien actions in Ontario in that section 46(4) merely confirmed what was previously recognized — the Rules of Practice apply insofar as they do not conflict with the provisions of the Act. See also §§125 and 126 *post; Macon Drywall Systems Ltd. v. H. P. Hyatt Const. Ltd.,* [1972] 17 C.B.R. (N.S.) 6; *Anchor Shoring Ltd. v. Halton Region Conservation Authority; Dufferin Materials & Const. Ltd. v. Halton Region Conservation Authority* (1977), 15 O.R. (2d) 599. This principle has also been applied to prevent a review of the amount of security paid into Court to vacate a lien. See *Re Pecco Cranes (Can.) Ltd.,* [1973] 3 O.R. 737 and to the same effect *E. A. Parker Devs. v. Doric Devs. Ltd.,* [1977] 3 W.W.R. 191 (B.C.). See also *M.L. Plumbing & Heating Ltd. v. Smithson* (1977), 73 D.L.R. (3d) 481 at 486 (Sask. C.A.).

§121 Powers of Court at Trial Generally.

All the Acts, with the exception of British Columbia (q.v. secs. 30, 39) give to the Judge or Officer trying the mechanics' lien action, the power to try the action and all questions that arise therein or that are necessary to be tried in order to completely dispose of the action, and to adjust the rights and liabilities of the persons appearing before him, or upon whom notice of trial has been served. Further, the Judge or Officer has the power to take all accounts, make all inquiries, give all directions, and do all other things necessary to finally dispose of the action and of all matters, questions, and accounts therein, and to adjust the rights and liabilities of, and give all the necessary relief to all parties to the action and all persons who have been served with notice of trial: Ont., sec. 38(4); Nfld., sec. 38(4); Sask., sec. 51(1), (2), 46(10); P.E.I., sec. 45(1), (2), 48; N.S., sec. 34(1), 42; Man., sec. 39(1), (2), 42, 56(1); N.B., sec. 43(1), (2), 46; Alta., sec. 44. Indeed, care should be taken to have the Court adjudicate upon all matters that could have been the subject matter of the action. See e.g. *Gettle Bros. Const. Co. v. Alwinsal Potash of Can. Ltd.* (1973), 38 D.L.R. (3d) 319n (S.C.C.); *Groundwater Dev. Corpn. v. Moncton* (1971), 3 N.B.R. (2d) 798 (C.A.); *Nelson Lbr. v. Integrated Bldg.,* [1976] 2 W.W.R. 538 (Alta. C.A.). See also *Dixon v. Ross* (1912), 46 N.S.R. 143 (C.A.); *McPherson v. Gedge* (1883), 4 O.R. 246 (C.A.); *A. J. (Archie) Goodale Ltd. v. Risidore Bros. Ltd.* (1975), 8 O.R. (2d) 427 (C.A.); *P.R. Collings and Associates Ltd. v. Jolin Holdings Ltd.,* [1978] 3 W.W.R. 602 (Sask.). In *C.N.R. v. Nor-Min Supplies Ltd.,* (1977) 66 D.L.R. (3d) 366 at 368 (S.C.C.) and *Modern Const. Co. v. Maritime Rock Products Ltd.,* [1963] S.C.R. 347 it was held that the trial Judge or Officer has the power to amend a description where the description includes not only lienable lands but also non-lienable lands. A similar result was obtained in *Walter F. Golding Const. Co. v. Bell* (1975), 13 N.B.R. (2d) 47. See however, the decision of *Orlando Masonry Contractors v. Dinardo,* [1971] 3 O.R. 774. In this lien action, the Master, to whom the action had been referred, made an interim report which did not provide for interest on the established lien claims. Subsequently, the lien claimants applied to a Judge in Chambers for an order granting interest on the amount of the established liens. Although the Judge doubted his jurisdiction to make such an order, he did so on the consent of all parties to his having jurisdiction. In *Inter Property Invt. Ltd. v. Trpchich* (1975), 11 O.R. (2d) 568 it was held that there was no power to substitute a personal plaintiff for a corporate plaintiff or to adjudicate upon a personal action on a contract in a mechanics' lien action.

The Court in Manitoba allowed claims under The Builders and Workmen Act to be dealt with in an action under the Mechanics' Lien Act in order to achieve finality respecting the rights of the competing claimants: see *Winnipeg Supply & Fuel Co. v. Genevieve Mtge. Corpn; Wiebe v. Dom. Bronze Ltd.,* [1972] 1 W.W.R. 651 (Man. C.A.), and Man. Builders and Workmen Act, section 11.3. See *Phillips-Anderson Constructors Ltd. v. Tuxedo Estates Co.,* [1977] 4 W.W.R. 320 (Man. C.A.) where the Manitoba Court of Appeal held that section 11.3 of the

Manitoba Act does not extend jurisdiction to vacate a lien arising under The Builders and Workmen Act by the payment of security into Court and the priority of such liens with respect to mortgages as compared with liens arising under The Mechanics' Lien Act of Manitoba was discussed.

In *N. S. Sand & Gravel Ltd. v. Kidstone Estates Ltd.* (1973), 13 N.S.R. (2d) 431, the Court held that although the mortgagee had not been named as a party defendant in the pleadings and although it was too late to properly commence action against the mortgagee, since the mortgagee had been served with Notice of Trial, pursuant to section 44(1) of the Nova Scotia Act, the issue of priority could be determined by the trial Judge. In British Columbia, by section 30(1), lien claims are enforced according to the practice and procedure of the County Court, including third party practice, except where the practice is varied by The Mechanics' Lien Act. The Ontario Act, in section 32, enlarges section 38(4) above mentioned, and gives the Judge or Officer, in addition to his ordinary powers, all the jurisdiction, powers and authority of the Supreme Court to try and completely dispose of the action and all questions arising therein. See, however, *Caruso v. Campanile,* [1972] 1 O.R. 437, where it was held that the powers contained in section 38(4) of the Ontario Act did not give the Judge or Officer having jurisdiction to try the action the right to decide third party issues. To the same effect see *Anchor Shoring Ltd. v. Halton Region Conservation Authority; Dufferin Materials & Const. Ltd. v. Halton Region Conservation Authority* (1977), 15 O.R. (2d) 599. In Ontario, in the Judicial District of York, if the action has been referred to the Master for trial, the Master may grant leave to amend any pleadings: sec. 31(4). Previously this section had been interpreted to restrict such powers of amendment "to correcting palpable errors or matters of form and not of substance", per Thompson J., *Western Caissons Ltd. v. Toronto Transit Commn.,* [1966] 2 O.R. 528 at 534, affirming [1966] 2 O.R. 528 at 529. However, in *Union Elec. Supply Co. v. Joice Sweanor Elec. Ltd.,* (1973), 2 O.R. (2d) 97, affirmed 5 O.R. (2d) 457 (C.A.), the *Western Caissons* decision was overruled. Further, it appears that after the referral of the action to a Master for trial and the commencement of the trial, the presiding Master is exclusively seized of the action and all matters arising therein. In view of this decision it is questionable whether the decision in *Scarborough Painting Ltd. v. Buckley* (1974), 4 O.R. (2d) 253 can stand. The latter decision may be distinguishable since the amendment therein had added a new cause of action. In *Ron-Dal Contractors v. Ondrey* (1974), 3 O.R. (2d) 290 (C.A.) the Court held that the Master at trial had the power to permit a counterclaim to be filed pursuant to section 38(3) in spite of default of defence up to that time. See also *Grannan Plumbing & Heating Ltd. v. Simpson Const. Ltd.* (1977), 17 N.B.R. (2d) 569 where an amendment at trial to include an additional claim for damages for delay was permitted so that all questions arising in the lien action could be determined in accordance with the requirements of section 45(1) of the New Brunswick Act.

§122   Powers of Sale.

The ultimate remedy given by the Acts to the lienholders is the right to sell the "owner's" estate or interest in the lands upon which their work or service was performed or materials supplied, to satisfy their lien claims: Ont., sec. 38(6); Sask., sec. 51(3); P.E.I., sec. 46(1); Alta., sec. 45(2), (3); B.C., sec. 30(2); Man. sec. 40(1); N.B., sec. 44(1); Nfld., sec. 38(6), and N.S., sec. 34(2). Most of the provinces also give jurisdiction to sell material to satisfy the lien claims: e.g. Sask., sec. 51(4); N.B., sec. 44(2); N.S., sec. 34(3); Alta., sec. 45(4); B.C., sec. 30(2); Man., sec. 40(2), and P.E.I., sec. 46(2). This provision is no longer contained in the Acts of Ontario and Newfoundland. See also §§169 and 170, respecting procedure on sale, *post*.

§123   Court in Which Action is Brought.

In Saskatchewan, British Columbia, Manitoba, Newfoundland, New Brunswick and Nova Scotia, mechanics' lien actions are brought in the County or District Court: see Sask., sec. 2(1)(c), 46(1) - (9); *Western Tractor & Equipment Co. v. Northwestern Iron Works Ltd. (No. 2)* (1958), 25 W.W.R. 696 (Sask.); *Sask. Cement Corpn. v. Northwestern Iron Works Ltd.* (1958), 25 W.W.R. 538 (Sask.); *Westeel Rosco Ltd. v. Bd. of Governors of South Sask. Hospital Centre*, [1973] 1 W.W.R. 577 (Sask.); Man., sec. 28; *Maitre v. Chisvin* (1958), 25 W.W.R. 664 (Man. C.A.); *Halls Associates (Western) Ltd. v. Trident Const. Ltd.* (1968), 65 W.W.R. 415 (Man. C.A.); B.C., secs. 2, 30(1); *Burrard Const. Supplies Ltd. v. Burnaby School Trustees* (1956), 20 W.W.R. 491 (B.C. C.A.); *Andrews v. Pac. Coast Coal Mines Ltd.* (1922), 31 B.C.R. 537 (C.A.); *Tempo Bldg. Supplies Ltd. v. Western Realty Projects Ltd.*, [1973] 1 W.W.R. 574 (B.C. C.A.); Nfld., sec. 31(1); N.B., sec. 33(1), and N.S., sec. 33(1). In Ontario (sec. 29(1)) and Prince Edward Island (secs. 1(c) and 34), the Supreme Court is given jurisdiction. In Alberta (sec. 2(1))(c)) jurisdiction lies with either the District Court or the Supreme Court, depending on the amount claimed.

In Newfoundland, section 32(2) provides that an application may be made for an order directing the action to be tried by a Judge of the Supreme Court where the amount claimed by any lien claimant exceeds $10,000.00 or if, for any reason, the Judge applied to deems it desirable. In New Brunswick, by section 33(2), where the amount claimed by any lienholder exceeds $5,000.00 any necessary party may apply *ex parte* to transfer the action to the Supreme Court. Section 46(2) of the Saskatchewan Act provides for an application to a Judge of the Court of Queen's Bench to transfer the action to the Court of Queen's Bench or to a Court of a judicial centre other than the judicial centre in which the Action has been brought. See also: Man., sec. 29. As prviously stated, in Ontario all actions are in the Supreme Court, but are seldom tried by a Supreme Court Judge. Except in the Judicial District of York, a lien action is tried by the County or District Court Judge sitting as a Local Judge of the Supreme Court: sec. 31(1). However, upon application to a Supreme Court Judge in Chambers by any party to the action or any other interested person, an order may be obtained directing that the action be tried by a Judge of the Supreme Court at the regular sitting of the Court for trial of actions without a jury in the County or District in which the land or part of it is situated: *Metro Woodworking v. Phales Invt. Ltd.*, [1960] O.W.N. 132 (C.A.); *Scarfe & Co. v. Barmike Holdings Ltd.*, [1959] O.W.N. 5. But see *Simioni Bros. Ltd. v. Fitzpatrick*, [1960] O.W.N. 275, indicating that the application is to be made to a Judge in Court. The application must be on notice. Such notice presumably means notice to all parties in the action, registered lien claimants, encumbrancers, and unregistered claimants of whom the applicant has knowledge: see sec. 31(1). It is to be noted that this power is discretionary and affidavit evidence must be presented in order that the Court may ascertain whether the issues and circumstances are such that the case ought to be tried by a Supreme Court Judge. The order is often made upon terms as to costs: Forms 23 and 24.

In Ontario in the Judicial District of York, the action must be tried by a Supreme Court Judge. However, a motion may be made to a Supreme Court Judge in Chambers after the statement of defence, or of defence to counterclaim if any, has been delivered, or the time for the delivery of the same has expired, to refer the whole action to the Master for trial pursuant to section 72 of The Judicature Act: sec. 31(2)(*a*); Form 25. This is the usual practice that is followed in the Judicial District of York. If the case proceeds to trial before the Supreme Court Judge, he has the power at this time to direct a reference to the Master, pursuant to section 71 or 72 of The Judicature Act: sec. 31(2)(*b*); Form 26. See *V. K. Mason Const. Ltd. v. Courtot Invts. Ltd.* (1974), 9 O.R. (2d) 325. This amendment in jurisdiction was brought about as a result of the decision in *A.G. Ont. and Display Service Ltd. v. Victoria Medical Bldg. Ltd.*, [1960] S.C.R. 32, affirming (*sub nom. Display Service Ltd. v. Victoria Medical Bldg. Ltd.*) [1958] O.R. 759, which held that the power conferred on the Master under the provincial Mechanics' Lien Act purporting to vest in him jurisdiction to deal with the lien action from its inception and completely dispose of it by judgment, was power which could only be exercised by a Court in the nature of a Superior, County or District Court, and was therefore *ultra vires* of the province of Ontario, as it encroached upon federal power respecting the administration of justice. See also *Maitre v. Chisvin* (1958), 25 W.W.R. 664 (Man. C.A.); *C. Huebert Ltd. v. Sharman,* [1950] 1 W.W.R. (Man. C.A.); *Re Blackwell,* [1962] O.R. 832 (C.A.), and Chapter 1, §6, "The Constitutional Question", *ante.* In Ontario, in the Judicial District of York, where the whole action is referred to the Master for trial, any person who is subsequently brought into the action and served with a notice of trial, may apply to a Supreme Court Judge in Chambers to set aside the judgment directing a reference, within 7 days after service of a notice of trial: Form 35 and Form 36. Failure to make such application binds any person so served by the judgment in the action as if he were originally a party thereto: sec. 31(3).

§124 Venue.

The trial in the majority of the provinces is held in the County or District in which the property affected by the lien is situated: N.B., secs. 33(1), 1; Nfld., sec. 31(1); Man. secs. 2(b), 28; N.S., sec. 33(1); Sask., sec. 46(1)-(9); B.C., secs. 2, 30(1). A problem may arise if the property is situated in more than one County or District. Ontario, Newfoundland and British Columbia have thus amended their Acts to give jurisdiction in cases where only part of the land in question is situated within the County or District: Ont., secs. 29(3), 31(1); Nfld., secs. 31(1), 32(1), and B.C., secs. 30(1), (2). See also: Sask. sec. 46. In *Pioneer Pipeline Contractors Ltd. v. B. C. Oil Transmission Co.* (1966), 57 W.W.R. 593 (B.C.), a mechanics' lien action respecting a pipeline within County C. was commenced in County C. but was by subsequent order transferred to V. County. It was held that the Court had no jurisdiction to order the transfer. To the same effect see *Tempo Bldg. Supplies Ltd. v. Western Realty Projects Ltd.,* [1973] 1 W.W.R. 574 (B.C. C.A.). Where the claimant registered his lien and certificate in the proper county, but filed his statement of claim in a different county, the Court in *Handley Lbr. Ltd. v. Ples,* [1971] 2 O.R. 628, held that the statement of claim was sufficient to commence an action and vest the Local Judge of that County with jurisdiction to transfer the action to the proper County for trial. In Manitoba an application may be made to transfer the action to any other County Court: sec. 29. In Prince Edward Island, by sections 1(c) and 34, and Alberta by section 2(1)(c), venue is governed by the ordinary procedure in the Supreme Court. In Newfoundland (sec. 32(2)), and New Brunswick (sec. 33(2)), application may be made to transfer the action to the Supreme Court. Section 46 of the Saskatchewan Act provides for an application to transfer the action to the Court of Queen's Bench or to another Judicial Centre in the District Court. The acts of most of the provinces contain specific provisions respecting the application by a party to the action to fix a time and place for the trial: see §158, *post*.

§125   Set-off and Counterclaim.

The Acts of Ontario (secs. 32 and 38(4)), Newfoundland (sec. 38(4)), Manitoba (sec. 39(1) and (2)), British Columbia (sec. 30(3)) and Saskatchewan (sec. 46(10)), specifically provide for set-off and counter-claim in mechanics' lien actions arising under building contracts or out of the work or service done, or material furnished to the property in question. In Ontario the Court in *Wasylyk v. Metro. Sep. S. Bd.*, [1970] 3 O.R. 391 (C.A.), held that a plaintiff lien claimant's unauthorized excavation had interfered with the defendant owner's right of lateral support and therefore allowed a counterclaim against the plaintiff based upon the tort of trespass, since the matter arose out of the work done to the property in question in the action. See also *Aqua-Pond Indust. Ltd. v. Gould* (1974), 3 O.R. (2d) 439; *Anderson v. DuPont of Can. Ltd.* (1975), 11 O.R. (2d) 300; and *Alros Products Ltd. v. Dalecore Const. Ltd.* (1973), 2 O.R. (2d) 312 (C.A.). The provisions of the remaining Acts respecting the trial Judge's power to determine all questions which arise in the action or which are necessary to be tried to dispose of the action completely, would seem to include the power to adjudicate upon claims for set-off and for counterclaim: P.E.I., sec. 43(1), (2); N.S., sec. 34(1); Alta., sec. 44(*a*), (*b*); N.B., sec. 43(1), (2). The New Brunswick Courts have however held that a defendant has no right to a counter-claim in a Mechanics' Lien action: *J. L. Simms & Sons Ltd. v. Vigneron* (1955), 19 N.B.R. (2d) 426; *Atlantic Paving Co. v. Cameron Properties Ltd.*, [1955] 2 D.L.R. 731 (N.B. C.A.). Regard, however, may be had to the following cases decided when the Ontario Act was generally similar to the other provincial Acts. In *Neri v. Benham,* [1934] O.W.N. 192, a counterclaim for damages for faulty workmanship or materials was struck out as it was held to be outside the scope of the mechanics' lien Court to deal with. It was, however, indicated in that case that set-off was proper in a lien action. This case is further discussed in *Simmons Bros. Ltd. v. Lee,* [1948] O.W.N. 737. See also *Bagshaw v. Johnston* (1901), 3 O.L.R. 58. In three older decisions in Ontario, the Court held a counterclaim in a lien action to be a proper procedure: *King v. Georgetown Floral Co.* (1904), 3 O.W.R. 587; *Pilkington v. Browne* (1898), 19 P.R. 337n; *McNamara v. Kirkland* (1891), 18 O.A.R. 271. See also *A. P. Green Fire Brick Co. v. Interprov. Steel Corpn.* (1963), 42 W.W.R. 497 (Sask. C.A.); *Western*

Caissons (Man.) Ltd. v. Trident Const. Ltd., [1975] 5 W.W.R. 74 (Man.); and §127, *post.*

The distinction between set-off and counterclaim is one of substance and therefore care should be taken with pleadings in this regard: e.g. see *Langlais v. Lavoie* (1975), 12 N.B.R. (2d) 426 (C.A.). As to what might be set-off or counterclaimed against the plaintiff, see §127, *post.*

§126 Third Party Proceedings.

Except for British Columbia (sec. 30(1)), none of the Acts of the various provinces specifically allow third party proceedings in a mechanics' lien action. As a result two points of view as to the validity of third party proceedings in such actions have been developed through the years and differing opinions have been expressed by the Courts.

The proponents of third party proceedings in mechanics' lien actions have argued that, since the various Acts give the Judge or Officer trying the action power to adjudicate upon all questions that arise therein, or that are necessary to be tried in order to completely dispose of the action and to adjust the rights and liabilities of the persons appearing before him, or upon whom notice of trial has been served, third party proceedings are therefore proper. See the following decisions of the Courts where this principle was applied generally: *Baines v. Curley* (1916), 38 O.L.R. 301 (C.A.); *Foreman v. McGowan,* [1934] O.R. 584 (C.A.); *Olson & Johnson Co. v. McLeod* (1913), 25 W.L.R. 472 (Alta.); *A. J. (Archie) Goodale Ltd. v. Risidore Bros. Ltd.* (1975), 8 O.R. (2d) 427 (C.A.); and *N. S. Sand and Gravel v. Kidstone Estates Ltd.* (1973), 13 N.S.R. (2d) 431.

The opponents of the validity of such proceedings in a mechanics' lien action take the position that proceedings under the Act are purely statutory and the scope of actions so begun is limited to the realization of the liens created by the Act. Thus, since actions may be tried before a number of judicial officials who have no jurisdiction to try ordinary actions in the High Court, it would be improper to allow causes of action, other than actions to realize upon liens, to be included, as the defendants would then be deprived of their ordinary rights to trial before the ordinary tribunals, including the right to trial by jury. Further, it was not intended that the machinery provided by the Acts for disposing of lien actions in a summary manner should be a vehicle for bringing within the scope of the Lien Acts, claims which have nothing to do with the enforcement of the rights of the person who has performed services or supplied materials in the manner defined by the Act. See the following decisions of the Courts where these principles were applied generally: *Atlantic Paving Co. v. Cameron Properties Ltd.,* [1955] 2 D.L.R. 731

(N.B. C.A.); *Neri v. Benham,* [1934] O.W.N. 192; *Caruso v. Campanile,* [1972] 1 O.R. 437; *Anchor Shoring Ltd. v. Halton Region Conservation Authority; Dufferin Materials & Const. Ltd. v. Halton Region Conservation Authority* (1977), 15 O.R. (2d) 599; but see *W. J. Kent & Co. v. Legere,* (1975), 65 D.L.R. (3d) 144 (N.B. C.A.); *Western Caissons (Man.) Ltd. v. Trident Const. Ltd.,* [1975] 5 W.W.R. 74 (Man.) and §125, *ante.*

The decisions of the Courts throughout the various provinces have differed when the specific question of third party proceedings in mechanics' lien actions was in issue, and to a large measure this divergence is not only due to the differing points of view as previously stated, but also due to the difference in wording among the various Acts.

In Saskatchewan, the Court held that where a lien claimant claimed a lien against an owner, and the owner thereupon issued a third party notice against an insurance company on a bond of indemnity to complete the structure, the Court held that the third party proceedings were proper. The wording of the various sections of the Saskatchewan Act prior to its amendment in 1973 was carefully scrutinized, and since the then section 33(1) indicated that the Court was to proceed to try mechanics' lien actions in the same manner as ordinary actions, third party proceedings were allowed: *Western Tractor & Equipment Co. v. Northwestern Iron Works Ltd. (No. 2)* (1958), 25 W.W.R. 696 (Sask.). However, in 1963 the Saskatchewan Court of Appeal in *A. P. Green Fire Brick Co. v. Interprov. Steel Corpn.* (1963), 42 W.W.R. 497 (Sask. C.A.), refused to allow third party proceedings in a mechanics' lien action and specifically overruled the *Western Tractor & Equipment Co. v. Northwestern Iron Works Ltd.* case, *supra.* But see now Saskatchewan, sections 46(6), (10), 51(1), (2), 59(2).

In Manitoba, the Court held in *Dell v. Callum* (1952), 6 W.W.R. 428 (Man.), that third party proceedings did not lie in mechanics' lien actions. However, this decision was overruled in *Halls Associates (Western) Ltd. v. Trident Const. Ltd.* (1968), 65 W.W.R. 415 (Man. C.A.). The Court of Appeal stressed the fact that the Manitoba Mechanics' Lien Act made applicable the Rules of Practice, and the Rules of Practice provided for third party proceedings. In this case, the third party was already a party defendant in the action and it appeared to be highly desirable for the closely related claims to be tried together.

In Ontario, the Courts in *Bagshaw v. Johnston* (1901), 3 O.L.R. 58; *Simmons Bros. Ltd. v. Lee,* [1948] O.W.N. 737 and *Bermingham Const. Ltd. v. Moir Const. Co.,* [1959] O.R. 355 (C.A.), rejected the application of third party proceedings in mechanics' lien actions. The decisions, however, were rendered prior to the 1970 amendment to the Ontario Act; which now provides, (sec. 46(4)), that the Rules of Practice and Procedure of the Supreme Court apply to proceedings to enforce a lien unless otherwise provided under the Act. The effect of this amendment was considered in *Caruso v. Campanile, supra,* where the Court rejected an application for leave to issue third party notices in a mechanics' lien action. See also *Anchor Shoring Ltd. v. Halton Region Conservation Authority; Dufferin Materials & Const. Ltd. v. Halton Region Conservation Authority* (1977), 15 O.R. (2d) 599; *Macon Drywall Systems Ltd. v. H. P. Hyatt Const. Ltd.* (1972), 17 C.B.R. (N.S.) 6, and Chapter 11, *post,* Practice Before Trial, §135.

§127 Damages.

(a) Against the Plaintiff.

Generally speaking, damages sustained by a defendant in a lien action are a proper subject of inquiry and adjudication at trial. The owner or person primarily liable may in no circumstances, however, reduce the compulsory holdback by setting off damages against the holdback money retained: see *Len Ariss & Co. v. Peloso,* [1958] O.R. 643 (C.A.); *Western Tractor & Equipment Co. v. Milestone School Unit No. 12* (1960), 33 W.W.R. 249 (Sask. C.A.); *Billinkoff's Ltd. v. R.C. Archiepiscopal Corpn. of Winnipeg* (1959), 67 Man. R. 175; *Freedman v. Guar. Trust Co.* (1929), 64 O.L.R. 200 (C.A.); *Ross Bros. Ltd. v. Gorman* (1908), 1 Alta. L.R. 516, affirming 1 Alta. L.R. 109 (C.A.); *Rice-Lewis & Son Ltd. v. George Rathbone Ltd.* (1913), 27 O.L.R. 630 (C.A.); *Smith v. Bernhart* (1909), 2 Sask. L.R. 315; *Batts v. Poyntz* (1916), 11 O.W.N. 204 and Chapter IV, Rights and Duties of the Owner, §45, *ante.* However, an owner or person primarily liable who receives notice of lien is entitled to set off damages against the sum claimed, provided that he does not make any further payments after having received notice. See also *Noranda Exploration Co. v. Sigurdson,* [1975] 5 W.W.R. 83, (S.C.C.). See Chapter 3, The Lien Claimant, §29(e), *ante.* As to set-off against the trust fund created by Ontario section 2(3) and Saskatchewan section 3(3), of amounts that become payable to a contractor from an owner, on the certificate of the person authorized under their contract to make such certificates, see Chapter 3, The Lien Claimant, §29, *ante,* and Chapter 9, The Trust Fund. Apart from these restrictions therefore, the owner or person primarily liable may reduce his liability to the contractor or sub-contractor, as the case may be, by claiming damages.

A claim for damages for delay against the lien claimant was allowed in the following cases: *Bermingham Const. Ltd. v. Moir Const. Co., supra; Len Ariss & Co. v. Peloso, supra; Billinkoff's Ltd. v. R.C. Archiepiscopal Corpn. of Winnipeg, supra; Ross Bros. Ltd. v. Gorman, supra; Smith v. Bernhart, supra; Lundy v. Henderson* (1908), 9 W.L.R. 327 (Alta. C.A.); *Brown v. Bannatyne S.B.* (1912), 21 W.L.R. 827, 2 W.W.R. 742 (Man.);

Freedman v. Guar. Trust Co., supra; Milton Pressed Brick Co. v. Whalley (1918), 42 O.L.R. 369 (C.A.); *McBean v. Kinnear* (1892), 23 O.R. 313; *Seaman v. Can. Stewart Co.* (1911), 2 O.W.N. 576 (C.A.); *Grier v. Georgas* (1923), 25 O.W.N. 125 (C.A.); *McManus v. Rothschild* (1911), 25 O.L.R. 138 (C.A.); *Shore & Horwitz Const. Co. v. Franki of Can. Ltd.,* [1964] S.C.R. 589. In *Lundy v. Henderson, supra,* it was held that when the owner attempts to set off damages for delay in completion against his contractor, the onus is on the owner to show the contractor was not entitled to an extension of time to complete. The terms of the contract in each case must be carefully scrutinized to ascertain whether there has been delay on the part of the lien claimant: *Brown v. Bannatyne S. B.* (1912), 2 W.W.R. 742 (Man.). In *Hutchinson v. Rogers* (1909), 1 O.W.N. 89, the Court held that since it was impossible to complete a contract on time owing to an addition to the original contract and inclement weather, damages for delay in completion could not be allowed, having regard to the terms of the contract in question. In *Henry Hope & Sons of Can. Ltd. v. Richard Sheehy & Sons* (1922), 52 O.L.R. 237, the Court allowed a counterclaim by a contractor against a lien claimant for damages for delay, loss of use of moneys that would have been payable by an owner to the contractor but for the lien claimant's delay, and travelling expenses incurred by the contractor to hire new workers. It was indicated in *Brown Const. Co. v. Bannatyne S. Dist. Corpn., supra,* that a claim for unliquidated damages respecting salaries that had to be paid to teachers and caretakers despite the fact their services could not be employed, as the school in question was not completed on schedule, might, in certain circumstances be allowed.

A claim for damages for non-completion against the lien claimant was allowed in the following cases: *St. Clair Const. Co. v. Farrell* (1921), 49 O.L.R. 201 (C.A.), and *Union Lbr. Co. v. Porter* (1908), 8 W.L.R. 423; affirmed 9 W.L.R. 325 (Alta.). A claim for damages by the owner for the cost of financing the expense of completing the building after the contractor had abandoned his contract was disallowed in *Freedman v. Guar. Trust Co., supra.*

In *Wasylyk v. Metro. Sep. S. Bd.,* [1970] 3 O.R. 391 (C.A.), the Court allowed the owner's counterclaim for damages caused by the lien claimant's unauthorized excavation which interfered with the owner's right of lateral support. The owner's claim here was based not upon the contract, but upon the tort of trespass.

There appears to be no reported decision where damages of the nature awarded in the *Guilford Industries* case discussed in §147, *post,* have been claimed in the lien action. It is arguable that such a claim in the lien action would be premature. See *e.g. Beckingham v. Sparrow; Sparrow v. Beckingham* (1977), 2 C.C.L.T. 214 (Ont.); *Greenwood v. Magee* (1977), 15 O.R. (2d) 685; *Almas v. Spenceley,* [1972] 2 O.R. 429 (C.A.); *Ont. Indust.*

Loan v. Lindsey (1883), 3 O.R. 66; and *MacFarlane v. R.* (1974), 5 O.R. (2d) 665 (C.A.).

(b) Against the Defendant.

As previously indicated, the mechanics' lien was unknown to the common law, but was a statutory creation to protect the interests of those who perform work or service or supply materials in the construction of a building: see Chapter 1, Introduction. The lien, however, is limited to the value of the work done, services performed and materials supplied: Ont., sec. 5(1); Sask., sec. 12(1); P.E.I., sec. 2; Nfld., sec. 7; Alta., sec. 4; B.C., sec. 5; Man., sec. 4; N.B., sec. 4 and N.S., sec. 5. The "lien", therefore, does not include a claim for damages.

Nevertheless, in setting up a form of procedure to enforce the "lien", the Legislatures of each province gave the Judge or Officer trying the "lien action" the right to dispose of all questions between the parties and award personal judgments: see §§121, 125, 126, *supra;* Chapter 12, §164, *post.* See also *Triangle Storage Ltd. v. Porter,* [1941] 3 W.W.R. 892 at 895 (B.C. C.A.), where O'Halloran J. stated: "A personal judgment for the debt may be obtained under sec. 34 of the statute quite distinct from the enforcement of the mechanics' lien." But see *Inter Property Invt. Ltd. v. Trpchich* (1975), 11 O.R. (2d) 568.

In any such "lien action", questions may arise respecting a claim for damages arising out of the construction project, and although such a claim is not the subject of a lien, the Judge or Officer may deal with it and award a personal judgment for damages, but it is submitted that the claim must be connected to the contractual or quasi-contractual relationship of the parties.

In *Earl F. Wakefield Co. v. Oil City Petroleums (Leduc) Ltd.,* [1958] S.C.R. 361, reversing 22 W.W.R. 267; affirmed 29 W.W.R. 638 (P.C.), the plaintiff claimed a lien for $51,670.62 representing the contract price which had not been completed by reason of the defendant's failure to make payment in accordance with the terms thereof. While the Court gave the plaintiff personal judgment for the sum of $51,670.62, a lien was allowed only on $30,000.00 of that sum on the basis of a *quantum meruit.*

In *Bermingham Const. Ltd. v. Moir Const. Co.,* [1959] O.R. 355 (C.A.), the plaintiff subcontractor claimed a lien, which claim was comprised of holdback, damages for delay, cost of replacement materials and cost of a load test. The Court awarded the plaintiff a lien against the owner's estate for the holdback only and gave personal judgment for all sums claimed, against the contractor. See also *Grannan Plumbing & Heating Ltd. v. Simpson Const. Ltd.* (1977), 17 N.B.R. (2d) 569 to the same effect.

In *Alkok v. Grymek,* [1968] S.C.R. 452, the plaintiff was engaged by the defendant husband and wife to construct a residence upon land owned by the husband. The contract was terminated by the defendants before completion. The Court held that the termination was improper and awarded a lien against the husband's estate and personal judgment against the wife's separate property in an amount based on the value of work done at the termination.

Where damages are claimed, they of course must arise from the construction project. In *Hill-Clark-Francis Ltd. v. Lanthier*, [1958] O.W.N. 223 at 235, the Court stated: "It was not intended that the machinery provided by The Mechanics' Lien Act should be a vehicle for bringing within the scope of its summary proceedings a claim which has nothing to do with the enforcement of the rights of the person who has performed the services or supplied the materials in the manner defined by the Act." In this case, the statement of claim alleged conspiracy on the part of the defendants. In *Bagshaw v. Johnston* (1901), 3 O.L.R. 58, a claim against the architect for fraudulently withholding his certificate was dismissed principally because the relevant Act did not recognize third party proceedings. In *Andre Knight Ltd. v. Presement*, [1967] 2 O.R. 289 (C.A.), a claim for damages for reduction of the plaintiff's credit rating and bonding limit was rejected as being too remote. The Ontario Court of Appeal in *Crown Const. Co. v. Cash*, [1940] O.R. 371 (C.A.), while not deciding the point, strongly doubted a lien claimant's right to recover damages for the wrongful destruction of the statutory "owner's" estate or interest upon which a lien could attach. In *Seaman v. Can. Stewart Co., supra*, the Court held that a lien claimant was not entitled to recover damages for loss suffered by reason of being improperly deprived of a contract. To the same effect (loss of prospective profits) is *East Central Gas Co-op Ltd. v. Henuset Ranches & Const. Ltd.* (1976), 1 Alta. L.R. (2d) 345, affirmed 6 A.R. 347 (C.A.). In *Larkin v. Larkin* (1900), 32 O.R. 80 (C.A.), it was held that no relief could be granted a lien claimant respecting his claim for damages for conversion of material. To the same effect is *Maltby's Ltd. v. Can. Packers Ltd.*, [1947] O.W.N. 757, except that the Court in this case refused to award a personal judgment for damages, because the plaintiff failed to prove a valid lien. See also *Berridge v. Hawes* (1903), 2 O.W.R. 619. In *Alros Products Ltd. v. Dalecore Const. Ltd.* (1973), 2 O.R. (2d) 312 (C.A.) both a claim for lien and a personal judgment were denied for loss of, and damage to, tarpaulins used on a construction site. In Ontario no personal judgment will be granted if the damages claimed arise from something which is not the proper subject matter of a claim for lien. In *A. J. (Archie) Goodale v. Risidore Bros. Ltd.* (1973), 8 O.R. (2d) 427 the *Alros* decision was distinguished. The Court held that if the trial Court has to hear evidence to determine that the claimants' services and work do not come within section 5 of the Ontario Act, or if a lien claim is not perfected or continued properly, a personal judgment could

be granted. In the *Western Caissons Ltd. v. Toronto Transit Commn.,*
[1966] 2 O.R. 534, affirming [1966] 2 O.R. 528 decision discussed *ante* in this
chapter and *post* in §147 a claim in tort, unconnected with the contractual
relationship between the parties, was struck out along with a counterclaim
in tort against a Defendant added by counterclaim.

§128   Arbitration Clauses in Contracts.

It is not uncommon for parties to a building contract to provide that
disputes between them are to be settled by arbitration rather than by
proceedings in Court.

An arbitration clause, in an agreement which attempts to oust the
Court's jurisdiction entirely, is contrary to public policy, and void on the
grounds that public policy requires that if a person wishes a dispute be
adjudicated upon by the Courts, he should have that right: *Scott v. Avery,*
post, and the cases cited therein; *Vinette Const. Ltd. v. Dobrinsky,* [1926]
Que. Q.B. 62. However, the recent tendency of the Courts is to uphold
arbitration clauses on the ground that public policy also demands that
parties who agree to have their disputes determined by an independent
adjudicator, be bound by their contract: *Shirley Ford Sales Ltd. v. Franki of*
Can. Ltd., post; Bristol Corpn. v. John Aird & Co., post; Stokes-Stephens
Oil Co. v. McNaught, [1917] 2 W.W.R. 530, affirmed 57 S.C.R. 549;
Niagara South Bd. of Education v. H.G. Acres Ltd., [1972] 3 O.R. 815.
Generally speaking, there are two types of arbitration clauses recognized as
valid by the Courts; those which provide by express words or by implication
that arbitration shall be a condition precedent to the liability of or the right
of action against a party (called *Scott v. Avery* clauses), and those which
merely provide that disputes be settled by arbitration and do not provide
expressly or by implication that arbitration be a condition precedent to
liability or action (called ordinary arbitration clauses). Whether or not the
clause used in the contract is in ordinary form or *Scott v. Avery* form will
depend upon the intention of the parties derived from the language used in
the agreement between them. For examples of the distinction between the
two types of clauses, reference can be made to the following cases: *Scott v.*
Avery (1856), 10 E.R. 1121; *David v. Swift* (1910), 44 S.C.R. 179; *Doleman*
& Sons v. Ossett Corpn., [1912] 3 K.B. 257; *Brand v. Nat. Life Assur. Co.,*
[1918] 3 W.W.R. 858 (Man.); *Great West Elec. v. Housing Guild Ltd.,*
[1947] 2 W.W.R. 1023 (B.C.); *W. Bruce Ltd. v. Strong,* [1951] 2 K.B. 447;
Shirley Ford Sales Ltd. v. Franki of Can. Ltd. (1965), 55 W.W.R. 34 (Alta.);
Deuterium of Can. Ltd. v. Burns & Roe of Can. Ltd., [1975] 2 S.C.R. 124,
affirming (*sub nom. Burns & Roe of Can. Ltd. v. Deuterium of Can. Ltd.;*
Burns & Roe Inc. v. Deuterium of Can. Ltd., 2 N.S.R. (2d) 703, reversing 15
D.L.R. (3d) 568. For an example of where the Court implied a *Scott v.*

Avery clause from the language used by the parties, see *Jack Bradley (Maritimes) Ltd. v. Modern Const. Ltd.* (1967), 59 D.L.R. (2d) 519 (N.B. C.A.). For an example of where an arbitration clause can be in ordinary form as it affects one party and also in *Scott v. Avery* form as it affects another party to the agreement, see *Jack Bradley (Maritimes) Ltd. v. Modern Const. Ltd., supra; Bond v. Sixty-four West St. Clair Ltd.,* [1940] O.W.N. 299. Moreover, an arbitration clause contained in the contract between the "owner" and general contractor may, by appropriate wording, be included as a term of a subcontract: *Nolan v. Ocean, Accident and Guar. Corpn.* (1903), 5 O.L.R. 544; *Contractors Supply Co. v. Hyde* (1912), 3 O.W.N. 723; *W. Bruce Ltd. v. Strong, supra; Jack Bradley (Maritimes) Ltd. v. Modern Const. Ltd., supra; Lonmar Plumbing & Heating Ltd. v. Representative Holdings, post.*

Unless both parties wish to waive the arbitration clause and proceed by Court action, the arbitration clause in the contract should not be disregarded since it will have a direct bearing upon the procedure to be adopted by the parties in case of dispute, for it now appears to be settled that notwithstanding the fact that a lien, and the procedure to realize upon a lien claim are codified by statute, arbitration clauses can affect proceedings under the various Mechanics' Lien Acts: *Champion v. World Bldg. Ltd.* (1914), 20 B.C.R. 156, affirming 6 W.W.R. 233; appeal quashed 50 S.C.R. 382; *Cubbidge v. Public S. Bd., S.S. No. 7, Toronto Twp.* (1929), 37 O.W.N. 118; *Jorgenson v. Sitar,* [1937] 2 W.W.R. 251 (Man. C.A.); *Art Plastering Co. v. Oliver,* [1945] O.W.N. 41; *Re Rootes Motors (Can.) Ltd. and Wm. Halliday Contracting Co.,* [1952] O.W.N. 553; *Pigott Const. Co. v. Fathers of Confederation Memorial Citizens Foundation (No. 2)* (1965), 51 D.L.R. (2d) 367 (P.E.I.); *Shirley Ford Sales Ltd. v. Franki of Can. Ltd., supra.* See, however, the case of *Great West Elec. v. Housing Guild Ltd., supra,* where upon a motion to stay a mechanics' lien proceeding pending arbitration in accordance with the agreement between the parties, the Court refused to grant the stay upon the ground that exclusive jurisdiction to hear such actions is vested in the Court.

The mere fact that the building contract contains an arbitration clause will not of itself constitute a waiver of lien, even though it is in *Scott v. Avery* form. In *Art Plastering Co. v. Oliver, supra,* the Court held that an arbitration clause in the *Scott v. Avery* form, did not preclude the claimant from obtaining the benefits given by the Act. See also *Lonmar Plumbing & Heating Ltd. v. Representative Holdings, post.* Essentially, an arbitration clause is an attempt by the parties to govern the procedure to ultimately realize upon a lien claim, but not the creation of the lien itself. The Acts of most of the provinces specifically provide that a right of lien is not waived unless "express" words to that effect are contained in the agreement between the parties: Alta., sec. 3; B.C., secs. 9, 10; Man., sec. 3; Nfld., secs. 4, 5; N.S., secs. 3, 4; Ont., secs. 4, 5; Sask., sec. 11. See, however, the Acts of New Brunswick (secs. 5 and 6), and Prince Edward Island (secs. 4 and 5), which do not use the words "express agreement to the contrary", but simply state that with the exception of a labourer, no agreement shall deprive a person of his rights under the Act unless he is a party to the agreement. See e.g. *Grannan v. Simpson,* (1977) 17 N.B.R. (2d) 569.

As previously stated, arbitration clauses should not be disregarded, for they will in most cases govern the procedure to be adopted by the parties. The procedure may depend upon what type of clause has been agreed to by the parties, an ordinary arbitration clause or one of the *Scott v. Avery* variety.

(a) Procedure re: The Ordinary Arbitration Clause.

Prior to the enactment of the various provincial Arbitration Acts, there was no procedure whereby a party seeking arbitration could force another party to arbitrate. The other party could simply disregard the arbitration clause and institute Court action and the party wishing to arbitrate was thus left with his remedy of damages for breach of contract: *Scott v. Avery, supra; Nolan v. Ocean, Accident and Guar. Corpn., supra; Doleman & Sons v. Ossett Corpn., supra; Bristol Corpn. v. John Aird & Co.,* [1913] A.C. 241; *Brand v. Nat. Life Assur. Co., supra.* As a result, various Arbitration Acts were passed setting out the procedure respecting arbitration, providing for enforcement of the arbitrator's award and providing a means whereby a party seeking arbitration could force another party to arbitrate.

For example, The Arbitration Act of Ontario, R.S.O. 1970, ch. 25, sec. 7, provides that if a party to an agreement containing an arbitration clause, or any other person claiming through or under him, commences action against any other party to the agreement, or any person claiming through or under him, in respect of any matter agreed to be referred, any party to such legal proceeding may at any time after appearance and before delivering any pleading or taking any other step in the proceeding, apply to that Court to stay the proceeding. The Court, if satisfied that there is no sufficient reason why the matter should not be referred, and that the applicant was at the time when the proceeding was commenced and at the time of the application, and continues to remain ready and willing to do all things necessary for the proper conduct of the arbitration, may make an order staying the proceeding. See also the Arbitration Acts of the following provinces: Alta., sec. 3; B.C., sec. 6; Man., sec. 8; N.B., sec. 7; N.S., sec. 5; P.E.I., secs. 6, 7; Sask., sec. 5. Where the building contract provides for a submission to arbitration (arbitration clause) in ordinary form, the various Arbitration Acts thus provide a means whereby a party seeking arbitration may apply to the Court for an order staying the mechanics' lien proceedings pending an award by the arbitrator.

The application to stay the mechanics' lien proceeding must be brought before the "Court" referred to in the Arbitration Act and not before the Mechanics' Lien Court: see Arbitration Acts, *supra*. Before the Court will consider such an application, it must be shown that the agreement to arbitrate disputes is mandatory, for an agreement simply stating that if a dispute arises, either party may elect to settle same by arbitration, is not a submission to arbitration: *Lonmar Plumbing & Heating Ltd. v. Representative Holdings* (1968), 1 D.L.R. (3d) 591 (Sask.). The application may be brought by the party who instituted the mechanics' lien proceedings: see Arbitration Acts, *supra; Lonmar Plumbing & Heating Ltd. v. Representative Holdings, supra; Pigott Const. Co. v. Fathers of Confederation Memorial Citizens Foundation (No. 2), supra.* On such an application, the Court will consider the following matters: the precise nature of the dispute between the parties; whether the dispute is one which falls within the ambit and scope of the arbitration clause; whether the clause is still in force or has been waived; whether the party seeking arbitration has been and will be ready and willing to do all things necessary for the proper conduct of the arbitration , and whether there is any sufficient reason why the action should not be stayed and the matter proceed to arbitration: Arbitration Acts, *supra; Heyman v. Darwins Ltd.,* [1942] A.C. 356; *Boychuk Const. (Sask.) Ltd. v. St. Paul's R.C. Sep. S. Dist. No. 20* (1966), 56 D.L.R. (2d) 722 (Sask.); *Pigott Const. Co. v. Fathers of Confederation Memorial Citizens Foundation (No. 2), supra; Madorsky v. Zelinka,* [1947] 1 W.W.R. 654 (Alta.); *Stokes-Stephens Oil Co. v. McNaught,* [1917] 2 W.W.R. 530; affirmed 57 S.C.R. 549; *McDougall & Co. v. Penticton* (1914), 7 W.W.R. 486 (B.C. C.A.). Since the Court must consider the precise nature of the dispute between the parties in order to determine whether it falls within the scope of the arbitration clause, affidavit evidence may be tendered on such an application: *Boychuk Const. (Sask.) Ltd. v. St. Paul's R.C. Sep. School Dist. No. 20, supra; Raymond v. Adrema Ltd.,* [1963] 1 O.R. 305; *Lamont v. Wright,* [1943] O.W.N. 11.

Before the Court will grant a stay of proceedings, it must be shown that the arbitration clause is still in force and thus where, prior to the application, the applicant repudiated the contract, the motion was refused: *Hayward v. Traders General Ins. Co.* (1964), 45 D.L.R. (2d) 431 (N.B. C.A.). Moreover, the application will likewise be refused, if the applicant has not made the application before delivering any pleading or taking any other step in the proceeding, such as: — the delivery of a statement of defence to the plaintiff's action, *Aspegren v. Polly* (1909), 13 O.W.R. 442; *Art Plastering Co. v. Oliver, supra; Rosenberg v. Goldberg,* [1960] O.R. 162; *Shirley Ford Sales Ltd. v. Franki of Can. Ltd., supra:* — an application to extend the time to deliver a statement of defence, *Ford's Hotel Co. v. Bartlett,* [1896] A.C. 1: — the delivery of a statement of defence and counterclaim, *Doleman & Sons v. Ossett Corpn., supra, Brand v. Nat. Life Assur. Co., supra; Madorsky v. Zelinka, supra; Sumitomo Shoji Can. Ltd. v. Graham,* [1973] 3 W.W.R. 122 (Alta.): — the issuance and service of an order for security for costs, *Heistein & Sons v. Polson Iron Works Ltd.* (1919), 46 O.L.R. 285: — the demanding of and receiving of particulars of the plaintiff's claim so as to prepare a defence, *Dufferin Paving Co. v. George A. Fuller Co. of Can. Ltd.,* [1935] O.R. 21 (C.A.). But see *Fathers of Confederation Bldgs. Trust v. Pigott Const. Co.* (1974), 44 D.L.R. (3d) 265 (P.E.I.). However, to constitute a waiver, the act or step taken must be in furtherance of the legal proceedings and not an attempt to suppress them, and thus a motion to set aside service of a writ of summons *ex juris* is not a waiver: *Raymond v. Adrema Ltd., supra.* See also *Mill Indust. Inc. v. St. Anne-Nackawic Pulp & Paper Co.* (1972), 5 N.B.R. (2d) 9 and *Fathers of Confederation Bldgs. Trust v. Pigott Const. Co.* (1974), 44 D.L.R. (3d) 265. It also appears that, in a mechanics' lien action where the claimant whose demand for arbitration was refused by the defendant, and who thereupon instituted action to protect his rights against loss due to expiry of the lien period, and then moved to stay his own action, had not thereby waived his right to arbitration: *Pigott Const. Ltd. v. Fathers of Confederation Memorial Citizens Foundation (No. 2), supra; Lonmar Plumbing & Heating Ltd. v. Representative Holdings, supra.* Even though the applicant may not have waived his right of arbitration, where his conduct is such as would indicate that he was not ready and willing to do all things necessary for the proper conduct of arbitration, the motion to stay the action will be refused: *Raymond v. Adrema Ltd., supra.*

Where it has been shown that the dispute between the parties falls within the scope of the arbitration clause, that the clause is still in force and has not been waived, and the applicant was and is ready and willing to do all things necessary for the proper conduct of the arbitration, it is the tendency of the Court to uphold the clause and grant the stay unless satisfied by the party opposing arbitration that there is a sufficient reason why the matter should not be referred: *Boychuk Const. (Sask.) Ltd. v. St. Paul's R.C. Sep. S. Dist. No. 20, supra; Madorsky v. Zelinka, supra; Lamont v. Wright, supra; Bristol Corpn. v. John Aird & Co.,* [1913] A.C. 241; *Doleman & Sons v. Ossett Corpn.,* [1912] 3 K.B. 257; *Altwasser v. Home Ins. Co. of N.Y.,* [1933] 2 W.W.R. 46 (Sask. C.A.); *Can. Motion Picture Productions Ltd. v. Maynard Film Distributing Co.,* [1949] O.R. 736; *Canex Gas Ltd. v. Sask. Power Corpn.* (1962), 33 D.L.R. (2d) 77 (Alta. C.A.); *Re Rootes Motors (Can.) Ltd. and Wm. Halliday Contracting Co.,* [1952] O.W.N. 553. In *Re Pearl & Russell Ltd. and Vanbots Const. Ltd.* (1977), 15 O.R. (2d) 265 (C.A.), it was found not pertinent that a claim for lien had been filed and later abandoned, and that a Writ of Summons had been issued to protect against the running of a limitation period. The Court in this case upheld the arbitration clause in a contract between a contractor and a subcontractor notwithstanding the fact that various issues had arisen between the contractor and the owner, some of which were directly resultant from the issues that had arisen between the general contractor and the subcontractor and that the issues between the owner and the general contractor would have to be decided in another forum, likely a Court rather than another arbitration board.

The following have been held to constitute sufficient reasons for refusing to stay proceedings: — where the arbitrator would be both adjudicator and witness, *Bristol Corpn. v. John Aird & Co., supra:* — where the dispute raises serious questions of law, or mixed questions of law and fact, *Stokes-Stephens Oil Co. v. McNaught, supra; Re Rootes Motors (Can.) Ltd. and Wm. Halliday Contracting Co., supra; Raymond v. Adrema Ltd., supra; M. J. O'Brien Ltd. v. Seaman Kent Co.* (1928), 62 O.L.R. 160; *Jussem v. Nissan Automobile Co.,* [1973] 1 O.R. 697. But see the various arbitrations Acts which provide for the reference on questions of law to the Court and *Re Pearl & Russell Ltd. and Vanbots Const. Ltd. ante* and *Mobil Oil Can. Ltd. v. Pan West Enrg. & Const. Ltd.* [1973] 1 W.W.R. 412 (Alta.): — where the prior conduct of the arbitrator satisfies the Court that an injustice may be done if the matter were arbitrated, *Cubbidge v. P.S. Bd., S.S. No. 7, Toronto Twp.* (1929), 37 O.W.N. 118; *Lamont v. Wright, supra:* — where at least one of three defendants was not a party to an agreement between a third defendant and a plaintiff which contained an arbitration clause, the Court refused to stay the action pending arbitration, especially since difficult questions of law were also involved. See also in this regard, *Niagara South Bd. of Education v. H. G. Acres Ltd.,* [1972] 3 O.R. 815 where despite the fact that there was an agreement to submit disputes to arbitration and an appeal therefrom to the Court, the Court refused to stay the action since there were other proceedings in Court against another party involving the same facts as were in dispute between the parties to the arbitration: — where an agreement provided concurrent remedies to the parties either to select arbitration or resort to the Court, the Court refused to stay proceedings: *Alta. Power Ltd. v. McIntyre Procupine Mines Ltd.,* [1975] 5 W.W.R. 632 (Alta. C.A.).

Where an application to stay proceedings under The Mechanics' Lien Act is granted, the lien claimant, after the award of the arbitrator is made, could prove the award in the lien action and obtain a lien for the amount thereof, with appropriate remedies for enforcement: Arbitration Acts, *supra; Art Plastering Co. v. Oliver,* [1945] O.W.N. 41; *Cubbidge v. P. S. Bd., S.S. No. 7, Toronto Twp., supra; Champion v. World Bldg. Ltd.* (1914), 20 B.C.R. 156, affirming 6 W.W.R. 233; appeal quashed 50 S.C.R. 382.

(*b*) *Procedure re: Scott v. Avery Clauses.*

Where the contract between the parties contains an arbitration clause in the *Scott v. Avery* form, and the plaintiff commences legal proceedings in disregard of the clause, the procedure which may be adopted by the parties is in some doubt.

By reason of the fact that the arbitrator's award is a condition precedent to the plaintiff's right of action or the defendant's liability, it would appear that the defendant need not move to stay the action, but could in his defence, plead the condition precedent as a complete bar to the action: *Scott v. Avery* (1856), 10 E.R. 1121; *W. Bruce Ltd. v. Strong,* [1951] 2 K.B. 447; *Jack Bradley (Maritimes) Ltd. v. Modern Const. Ltd.* (1967), 59 D.L.R. (2d) 519 (N.B. C.A.); *Shirley Ford Sales Ltd. v. Franki of Can. Ltd.* (1965), 55 W.W.R. 34 (Alta.); *Champion v. World Bldg. Ltd., supra.* However, in *Art Plastering Co. v. Oliver, supra* and *Contractors Supply Co. v. Hyde* (1912), 3 O.W.N. 723, the Court held that the question of the Court's jurisdiction to try a dispute covered by an arbitration clause could not be invoked by way of defence, but only by application to stay pursuant to The Arbitration Act. The defence of prematurity was therefore disallowed. In *Nolan v. Ocean, Accident and Guar. Corpn.* (1903), 5 O.L.R. 544, the defendant, after appearing to the plaintiff's action but before pleading, moved to stay the action on the grounds of prematurity. The Court granted the stay and indicated that in doing so, it had no discretion in the matter since the arbitrator's award was a condition precedent to action. The decision in *Deuterium of Can. Ltd. v. Burns & Roe of Can. Ltd.,* [1975] 2 S.C.R. 124, affirming (*sub nom. Burns & Roe of Can. Ltd. v. Deuterium of Can. Ltd.; Burns & Roe Inc. v. Deuterium of Can. Ltd.*) 2 N.S.R. (2d) 703, reversing 15 D.L.R. (3d) 568, is to the same effect. In *MacDougall & Co. v. Penticton* (1914), 7 W.W.R. 486 (B.C. C.A.), the defendant pleaded prematurity by way of defence, and the Court, in dismissing the plaintiff's action, indicated that it had a discretion in the matter and was exercising its discretion in favour of arbitration.

As a result, until such time as the proper method or methods of procedure respecting *Scott v. Avery* clauses have been judicially defined, it would appear that the safest course for any party seeking arbitration would be to immediately move to stay the action pursuant to the relevant Arbitration Act. Further, it would appear from the decision in the *Deuterium* case, *supra,* that the Court has little, if any, jurisdiction to refuse a stay of proceedings on such a motion.

§129 Receiver.

In order to prevent an owner receiving rentals and any other profits derived from the premises, to the detriment of lien claims, machinery has been set up in the provinces of Ontario, Saskatchewan, Newfoundland and Alberta to provide for the appointment, at any time after delivery of process commencing action, of a receiver of the rents and profits of the property against which a claim of lien is registered: Ont., sec. 34(1); Sask., sec. 50(1); Nfld., sec. 34(1) and Alta., sec. 40(1). The application for the appointment of a receiver in Ontario, Saskatchewan and Newfoundland may be made by any lien claimant, a mortgagee or any other interested party, and in Alberta by any party. On the return of the application, terms may be imposed upon the receiver, as the facts of each case require, and security may be ordered to be furnished. Notice of the application must be given to all the parties to the action and to all registered lien claimants who have not commenced an action. The reasons for the appointment of the receiver are set out in a supporting affidavit, and when all parties consent to the appointment, the consents are filed. An abstract of title is also necessary, as well as the consent in writing of the intended receiver: Form 27. The order should specify the duties of the receiver, as well as the duration of his appointment: Form 29. "The rents and profits of the property" must be those received by a statutory "owner" against whom the lien claimants are claiming. For example, if a tenant ordered work done, and he was found to be the statutory "owner", the rent he was paying to the registered owner, or the profit the registered owner was making because of his tenant, could not be taken by a receiver under these sections. As has been previously mentioned, the mechanics' lien, being a creature of statute, is limited in its scope to what is plainly expressed in the Act, and hence there is no power in the receiver to manage the property, and he is restricted solely to receiving rents and profits. In *Pearcy v. Foster* (1921), 51 O.L.R. 354, it was held that no appeal will lie from a decision allowing or refusing a receiver's appointment. See also *Macon Drywall Systems v. H. P. Hyatt Const. Ltd.* (1973), 17 C.B.R. (N.S.) 6 (Ont.) and *Connie Steel Products Ltd. v. Greater Nat. Bldg. Corpn; Interprice Elec. Ltd. v. Bank of N.S.* (1977), 3 C.P.C. 327 (Ont. Div.Ct.) and Chapter 12, Practice After Trial, §172, *post*. As to the duties of a receiver-manager generally, see *Credit Foncier Franco-Can. v. Edmonton Airport Hotel Co.* (1966), 55 W.W.R. 734, affirmed 56 W.W.R. 623n (Alta. C.A.); *Re Edinburgh Mtge. Ltd. and Voyageur Inn Ltd.; Rothberg v. Federal Business Dev. Bank* (1977), 24 C.B.R. (N.S.) 187 (Man.); *Braid Bldrs. Supply & Fuel Ltd. v. Genevieve Mtge. Corpn.* (1972), 29 D.L.R. (3d) 373 (Man. C.A.). A receiver appointed by the Court, notwithstanding the fact that certain creditors or potential creditors move for his appointment, is an officer of the Court and, generally speaking, all of the property is subject to the control of the Court. A receiver at all uncertain of his position on a particular matter or issue should seek the advice and direction of the Court, failing which, if the receiver's decision turns out to be wrong, he may be penalized not only with respect to non-recovery of fees and disbursements, but also with respect to borrowing. This is especially so, it would appear, when a receiver is appointed pursuant to a statute such as a mechanics' lien act. See also

Walter E. Heller (Can.) Ltd. v. Sea Queen of Can. Ltd. (1976), 19 C.B.R. (N.S.) 252 (Ont.). In *Baxter Student Housing Ltd. v. College Housing Co-op Ltd.,* [1976] 1 W.W.R. 1, reversing (*sub nom. College Housing Co-op. Ltd. v. Baxter Student Housing Ltd.*), [1975] 1 W.W.R. 311 the Supreme Court of Canada held that an appointment of a receiver pursuant to the inherent jurisdiction of the Court, which appointment *inter alia* provided that the receiver could receive the balance of the first mortgage proceeds in priority to any registered or unregistered charges or encumbrances, would not stand since it was contrary to the priority sections of the Manitoba Mechanics' Lien Act, section 11(1).

§130   Trustee.

The Act of Ontario (sec. 34(2)), provides that a trustee or trustees may be appointed at any time before or after judgment in much the same manner, on the application of the same parties, upon giving the same notice, and with the same restrictions regarding appeal, as pertain to the appointment of a receiver. The Acts of Newfoundland (sec. 34), Alberta (sec. 40), and Saskatchewan (sec. 50(3)) contain similar provisions. Section 50(7) of the Saskatchewan Act, however, provides that no trustee is to be appointed with respect to property which is the owner's homestead as defined in section 45(1) of that Act.

In Ontario, Newfoundland and Saskatchewan (and presumably in Alberta as well), on the return of the application to appoint a trustee, the Judge may allow *viva voce* evidence to be given, or affidavit evidence, or both. The abstract of title and consent of the trustees must also be filed with the Court. When all parties consent, the required consents are filed as well. The Court has power to appoint as many trustees as it shall decide upon. The trustee or trustees shall be put upon such terms, and may be required to furnish whatever security the Court deems necessary. An order may be made, however, without security. The trustees may be given power to manage, mortgage, lease and sell, or manage, mortgage, lease or sell, the property against which the claim for lien is registered. All powers conferred upon the trustee or trustees must be exercised under the supervision and direction of the Court, and any sale under this section must be specifically approved by the Court. Further, when specifically directed, the trustee may complete or partially complete the building on the property. There would appear to be no right of appeal from a decision refusing or permitting the appointment of a trustee: *Macon Drywall Systems Ltd. v. H. P. Hyatt Const. Ltd.* (1972), 17 C.B.R. (N.S.) 6; *Connie Steel Products Ltd. v. Greater Nat. Bldg. Corpn.; Interprice Elec. Ltd. v. Bank of N.S.* (1977), 3 C.P.C. 327 (Ont. Div.Ct.).

Before the Ontario Act was amended in 1970, the trustee had no power to obtain a new mortgage on the property involved, but was restricted to taking up unadvanced portions of any already existing mortgage. This procedure was subject to the mortgagee's willingness to advance, and in many cases severely restricted the trustee's ability to obtain financing to complete the project. It is submitted that the power to "mortgage" now gives the trustee the right to obtain a new mortgage as well as to receive advances on an existing mortgage. Since mechanics' liens have priority over mortgage advances made after the registration of the lien (*e.g.* Ont. 14(1)), or after the mortgagee has received notice in writing of the lien from the lien claimant (Ont., sec. 14(1)), the existing mortgagee, or a new mortgagee, should not advance under their mortgages if a lien is filed. An order should be obtained pursuant to the equivalent of Ontario section 34(2), which provides that, if the mortgagee makes advances to the trustee or trustees empowered to receive the advances by the section, these advances will take priority over all liens existing at the date of the appointment of the trustee: cf. *Baxter Student Housing Ltd. v. College Housing Co-op. Ltd., ante.* A mortgagee advancing in this manner to a trustee or trustees must be careful to search the title to the premises on each advance to ascertain if any new liens have been registered after the appointment of the trustee. The meaning of the words "all liens existing" has never been the subject of adjudication by the Courts. A reasonable interpretation would seem to be the actual amount of liens registered or unregistered at the date of the trustee's appointment. The difficulty in interpreting these words is but an added reason why care must be taken by a mortgagee advancing under this section. In the Judicial District of York, in Ontario, the application is made to a Judge in Chambers (Form 31), who will appoint the trustee or trustees and set out the terms of the appointment and the trustee's duties and powers, and will then refer the matter to the Master to administer: Form 32. If the order provides for a sale of the property, all of the relevant Acts provide that the land may be sold subject to the existing mortgages or any other charge or encumbrance, upon a specific direction to the trustee being given by the Court. Previous to 1970, in Ontario, if any dispute arose as to the priority of any mortgage, the property could not be sold under this section, but it would now appear that the property can be sold even if the priority of the mortgage were in dispute. The Acts are also silent respecting disputes arising regarding the priority of any other charges or encumbrances and presumably the property under these circumstances could be sold notwithstanding such a dispute.

The Acts contemplate the sale of the property by the trustee or trustees at any time before or after judgment. The proceeds of any such sale must be paid into Court and are subject to the claims of all lienholders, mortgagees, or other parties interested in the property sold, as their respective rights may be determined at the trial of the action. In Ontario, Newfoundland and Saskatchewan, the manner of distributing the fund paid into Court must follow as closely as possible and, in so far as is applicable, the procedure provided in the Act for distributing the proceeds of a sale made after judgment in the action. In Alberta, presumably the same result would follow. The Judge or Officer shall make all necessary orders for the completion of the sale and for the vesting of the property in the purchaser and for possession: Ont., sec. 34(5); Alta., sec. 40(6); Nfld., sec. 34(5)(7); Sask., sec. 50(6). See further Chapter 12, Practice After Trial, §170, *post*. In the Judicial District of York, the Master is the officer referred to in this section. When a vesting order is made respecting property sold under these sections, it releases the property from the claims of all lienholders, mortgagees, encumbrancers and interests of any kind, except when the order is made subject to the rights of any such mortgagee, encumbrancer, or other person having an interest in the property.

There appears to be a dearth of authority with respect to the remuneration of trustees or receivers who are appointed under the various mechanics' lien Acts. Useful reference may be had to the following cases and to other cases in the bankruptcy Court: *Re Mercer-Marshall* (1973), 18 C.B.R. (N.S.) 209 (Ont.); *Re West Toronto Stereo Centre Ltd.* (1974), 20 C.B.R. (N.S.) 133 (Ont.); *Re Cooke* (1975), 20 C.B.R. (N.S.) 263 (Ont.); *Re Mertens Enterprises Ltd.* (1975), 19 C.B.R. (N.S.) 296 (Ont.).

If dower rights exist, then they are specifically released by a vesting order under these sections in Ontario and Alberta. In Ontario, unless the married woman is a party and suffers judgment, her dower right and the right to have the value of her dower interest ascertained and deducted from the proceeds of sale paid into Court are not extinguished. A married woman entitled to dower rights should therefore be served as an interested party in connection with the application to appoint the trustee. See also Chapter 2, The Lienable Interest, §16(c), *ante*.

As with receivers, trustees appointed by the Court are officers of the Court. They have no more power than the Court and the governing statute provide. Their remuneration, including when, in what manner and by whom it is to be paid, is a matter for the Court. See generally *Braid Bldrs. Supply & Fuel Ltd. v. Genevieve Mtge Corpn.* (1972), 29 D.L.R. (3d) 373 (Man. C.A.); *Walter E. Heller (Can.) Ltd. v. Sea Queen of Can. Ltd.* (1976), 19 C.B.R. (N.S.) 252 affirmed 21 C.B.R. (N.S.) 272 (Ont.).

If the property is directed to be sold by the Court, care should be taken to have included in the Order a direction with respect to whether or not the property is to be sold subject to any mortgage or other charge or encumbrance. If the property is more marketable if it is sold subject to existing encumbrances, arrangements should be made with those existing encumbrances or mortgagees to concur in the sale. See Ont., sec. 34(3); Alta., 40(4); Nfld., sec. 34(3); Sask., sec. 50(4).

(a) Order for Preservation of Property

In Ontario (sec. 35), and Newfoundland (sec. 35) (cf. Alta., sec. 48), at any time after delivery of the statement of claim and before judgment, or after judgment and pending the hearing and determination of any appeal, any lien claimant, mortgagee or other interested person may make an application to the Judge or Officer having jurisdiction to try the action for an order for the preservation of any property pending the determination of the action and any appeal. The Court may hear *viva voce* or affidavit evidence or both in support of the application. This section will be used in specific situations where it is not advisable to appoint a trustee or a receiver. In many cases, it is essential that services such as heat, light and power be maintained in a building as well as securing the structure from vandalism. It would appear that liability for payment of any preservation charges would be in the discretion of the Court and should be established on the application for the preservation order. To date, this section in the Acts has yet to receive judicial consideration; however, in these and other jurisdictions, reference can be made to decisions respecting the order for preservation of property in the Rules of Practice of the Courts. In Ontario see Rule 369 and *Armour v. McColl* (1922), 22 O.W.N. 471. See also Form 34.

§131 Speedy Trial.

In Ontario (sec. 29(6)), and Newfoundland (sec. 31(6)), after one lienholder commences an action under the Act, any lienholder or other interested person may move before the Judge having jurisdiction, to speed the trial of the action: Form 37. In actions in Ontario commenced in the Judicial District of York, this motion is made to a Judge in Chambers. In many cases it is imperative that the action be tried without delay, especially in the case of uncompleted structures, when mortgage advances are stopped and subtrades are fearful of proceeding with their work on a property that has already been liened. An owner whose property has been liened or a general contractor having liens filed on the project he is completing, usually finds that his credit becomes restricted, and for those reasons desires that the action be disposed of as quickly as possible. A claimant who has agreed to a period of credit which has not expired may not move for a speedy trial: Ont., sec. 26(4); Nfld., sec. 28(4). Section 39 of the Alberta Act achieves the same effect, and more, by providing for a statutory pretrial with wide powers vested in the Court to summarily dispose of claims and order a sale of the property. Sections 38 and 41 of the Saskatchewan Act provide for a summary method of settling disputes and speeding the action. See also B.C., sec. 26; Man., sec. 23; and P.E.I., sec. 29.

Ontario section 15(2) provides that a wage earner may apply to the Judge or Officer having jurisdiction to try the action for speedy judgment on his claim. This application is made by notice of motion returnable in 4 days after service on the proper parties: Form 38. The application is supported by particulars of the claim for lien, verified by affidavit: Form 39. Such a notice of motion must be served on all proper parties and therefore, all registered lien claimants, mortgagees and other encumbrancers over whom the labourer wishes to claim priority should be served. The section indicates that the motion may be made before any action is commenced, but that the applicant must have registered a lien. The Court on the return of this application has the power to refuse it or to adjourn it to be dealt with at trial. Unless all the parties consent to this form of judgment, the motion is almost invariably adjourned to the trial of the action. If some of the parties dispute the labourer's right to lien, or to a personal judgment, then a full scale trial (regarding these claims), before the actual trial of the action, might have to be taken. The Act further indicates that every wage earner may bring a motion under this section, and the multiplicity of these preliminary proceedings would defeat the intent and purpose of the Act.

It would appear that a judgment under section 15(2) would give the labourer priority for 30 days' wages, as set out in section 15(1), and the right to rank for the remainder of his claim with the ordinary lien claims that were proven at trial. The matter of enforcement of the judgment is left in doubt. It is not stated in the Act whether a wage earner could sell the property, but it would seem unjust that a sale could be taken by the wage earner, who usually has the smallest interest in a mechanics' lien action, before the trial of the main action. See also Nfld., sec. 17(2) which is the same as Ont., sec. 15(2); Sask., sec. 41(1) and Alta., sec. 39; Chapter 8, Priorities, §92, *ante* and Chapter 3, The Lien Claimant, §33, *ante*.

An effective method of obtaining speedy relief by wage earners is found in The Master and Servant Act, R.S.O. 1970, chapter 263, whereby a summons may be issued by a Justice of the Peace and an order may be made that the wage arrears not exceeding the sum of $500.00 are to be paid together with costs. An effective method of enforcement of the order is provided. By section 8(1), in the case of wages due to a mechanic, labourer or other person of the character mentioned by section 5 of The Mechanics' Lien Act, a provincial Court Judge may make an order under the Act for payment of wages not to exceed the balance equal to the wages for 30 days. In addition a provincial Court Judge may calculate a reasonable wage where there has been no specific rate of wages agreed upon. An effective method of enforcement is also provided pursuant to this section. The section only applies to claims against the wage earner's master or employer, and if the wage earner wishes to proceed against an "owner" with whom he had no direct dealings, he could not pursue this remedy under The Master and Servant Act, but could only claim under The Mechanics' Lien Act. Further, the wage earner proceeding under The Master and Servant Act would not benefit by the valuable right of lien given by The Mechanics' Lien Act, and the corresponding right of sale of the property to enforce his lien.

§132 Expert Witnesses.

The Judge or Officer trying the mechanics' lien action in Ontario, Saskatchewan and Newfoundland may obtain the assistance of any merchant, accountant, actuary, building contractor, architect, engineer or person in such a way as he deems fit, to aid him in the determination of any matter of fact in question: Ont., sec. 46(3); Sask., sec. 59(1); Nfld., sec. 46(3). Remuneration is fixed by the Judge or Officer and he may order payment of such remuneration by any of the parties to the action. Payment of these specialists is of course not guaranteed by the Courts, and before specialists are appointed they are apprised of this fact by the appointing Judge or Officer. Frequently the parties to the action will request the Judge or Officer trying the action to appoint a specialist under this section to review certain matters in dispute before trial and report his findings to the Judge or Officer at trial. Appointment of such specialists by the Court should, however, be governed by the amount and nature of the claims in question, and the basic object of the Acts, to enforce the liens at the least expense and in so far as possible in a summary manner, should be kept in mind: *e.g.* Ont., sec. 46(1); Nfld., sec. 46(1); Sask., sec. 58(1).

The Court has wide discretion in its method of engaging and employing these specialists. They may be called to sit in the Courtroom, and listen to evidence presented and assist the Judge or Officer in his findings. The expert may be asked to view the site of the building project which is the subject of the action, and report his observations regarding general or specific problems. He may be engaged to give opinions of the general practice or custom governing certain facets of the building industry. He may be asked merely to file a report of his findings, or he may be requested to appear at the trial and present his opinions or findings in evidence. In the trial Judge's or Officer's discretion, counsel for the various parties may question the expert, but it is not the practice in these cases to allow cross-examination. *Brazeau v. Wilson* (1916), 36 O.L.R. 396 (C.A.). Nor should the Court allow an expert to participate in the examination of a witness: *Phillips v. Ford Motor Co.*, [1971] 2 O.R. 637, reversing [1970] 2 O.R. 714 (C.A.). The evidence tendered by these specialists is not necessarily followed by the trial Judge or Officer and he is free to reject any or all of the evidence as he sees fit: see Ontario Rules of Practice, Rule 267; *Richard v. Grey Coach Lines Ltd.*, [1950] O.W.N. 136; *MacDonald Elec. Ltd. v. Cochrane*, [1955] O.W.N. 255; *House Repair & Service Co. v. Miller* (1921), 49 O.L.R. 205 (C.A.). In the latter case Hodgins J. stated: "It is a pertinent observation that actions relating to the faulty execution of building contracts, where the parties indulge in evidence running over four hundred pages, are an enormous and an unnecessary expense to them and result in a disproportionate length of time being devoted to them by the Court, under conditions which can never be satisfactory owing to the nature of the case", and he therefore suggested the appointment of an expert to reduce the time spent at trial. A personal inspection of the property by the Judge or Officer trying the case was approved in this case. See also *Brazeau v. Wilson, supra.*

"The expert is not a judicial officer charged with the responsibility of determining the matters in issue, nor is he a Court-appointed investigator empowered to advance possible theories, and state, as conclusions of fact, opinions based on matters not advanced in evidence. While Rule 267 permits the Court to obtain the assistance of experts in such way as it thinks fit, such assistance must be restricted to the purpose of better enabling the Court to determine from the evidence adduced the questions of fact in issue." Per Evans J.A., *Phillips v. Ford Motor Co., supra.* See also *Mellin v. Monico* (1878), 3 C.P.D. 142 at 149, and *Badische Anilin und Soda Fabrik v. Levinstein* (1883) 24 Ch. D. 156 at 167.

The Court cannot, after the evidence has been taken in an action, call in experts to confer with it and advise it as to the proper conclusion to be drawn from such evidence and base its judgment on their opinion. Even though the parties have consented to the Judge consulting such experts, they are not to be taken to have consented to such advisors deciding on the weight and credibility of the conflicting testimony of witnesses whom they have not seen or heard: *Wright v. Collier* (1892), 19 O.A.R. 298; *Bennett v. Peattie* (1925), 57 O.L.R. 233 (C.A.); *Phillips v. Ford Motor Co., supra.* Reference may usefully be had to the Rules of the Court in the other jurisdictions and the cases decided thereunder.

§133 Disposition of Lien Claims Before Trial.

(*a*) *Dismissing Claimant's Action.*

Generally, the Courts will not, except in clear cases, dismiss or otherwise adjudicate upon lien claims before a proper trial of the action. If the lien claimant's action could "possibly" succeed then it should not be dismissed on a summary application before trial: *Re Boulay and Seeh* (1970), 2 O.R. 313. See also *Stickelmann v. Switzer*, [1972] 2 W.W.R. 203 (Sask.); *Re Ellwood Robinson v. Ohio Development* (1975), 7 O.R. (2d) 556; *Mancini v. Giancento*, [1962] O.W.N. 120; *Gen. Contracting Co. v. Ottawa* (1910), 1 O.W.N. 911, affirming Div. Ct. (unreported), which reversed 14 O.W.R. 749 (C.A.); *Moyer v. Martin*, [1951] O.W.N. 395 (C.A.); *Re Wallis & Vokes* (1889), 18 O.R. 8 (C.A.); *Clarkson Const. Co. v. Shaw*, [1950] O.W.N. 196; *Robertson v. Bullen* (1908), 13 O.W.R. 56; *Saccary v. Jackson* (1975), 11 N.S.R. (2d) 316 (C.A.). In *R. v. Algoma Dist. Ct. Judge; Ex parte Consol. Denison Mines Ltd.*, [1958] O.W.N. 330, appeal quashed (*sub nom. Pereni Ltd. v. Consol. Denison Mines Ltd.*), [1959] O.W.N. 119 (C.A.) the question of whether the defendants, Federal Crown corporations, were subject to a lien was decided on an interlocutory application. The question of whether a municipal building was subject to a lien was left to the trial Judge; *General Contracting Co. v. Ottawa, supra*. A useful method of placing sufficient evidence before the Court on an application to dismiss is to cross-examine the lien claimant on the affidavit verifying the lien. See *e.g.* Ont., sec. 38(10); Alta., sec. 38(6); Nfld., sec. 38(9). See also Alta., sec. 39; Sask., secs. 38 and 41; and *Re Pecco Cranes (Can.) Ltd.*, [1973] 3 O.R. 737. It was held in *Taylor v. Taylor*, [1954] O.W.N. 575, that unless it was patently demonstrable from the pleadings and the abstract of title that no lien existed, it was the duty of the Court to decide the matter on evidence adduced at trial. An application to dismiss a mechanics' lien action, on the grounds that the statement of claim was not filed in time, was not allowed: *Moyer v. Martin, supra*. In *Clarkson Const. Co. v. Shaw, supra*, an application to strike out a statement of claim for delay was reserved to the trial Judge. In *Pilkington Glass Ltd. v. Burnaby S. Dist.* (1961), 36 W.W.R. 34 (B.C.), a summary motion to dismiss the action against an owner of property on the grounds that he was not a proper party to a section 3 trust fund action, was dismissed as the matter was in doubt, and should be decided at the trial. If specifically empowered by The Mechanics' Lien Act, the Judge or Officer having jurisdiction may dismiss the claim in a summary way without trial. In *McMurray v. Parsons*, [1953] O.W.N. 414, it was plain that the lien had not been filed in time, and it was dismissed on summary motion. In *East-Central Gas Co-op Ltd. v. Henuset Ranches & Const. Ltd.* (1976), 1 Alta. L.R. (2d) 345, affirmed 6 A.R. 347 (C.A.), part of a claim for lien for loss of prospective profits and the whole of the claim against the individual members of a limited co-operative were dismissed upon interlocutory application. See also *Squeo v. Del Bianco*, [1976] W.W.D.

38 (B.C.) and *Patsis v. 75-89 Gosford Ltd; Papas v. Patsis,* [1973] 1 O.R. 629. In *Kleenaire Equipment Ltd. v. Dennis Commercial Properties Ltd.,* [1970] 3 O.R. 776, the Court of Appeal, held that the Master did have jurisdiction to discharge a lien on proper grounds. But see *Brant Transit Mix Ltd. v. Carriage Lane Estates Ltd.,* [1971] 3 O.R. 82, and *Re Boulay and Seeh,* [1970] 2 O.R. 313. A statement of claim not having been served for almost 12 years, an action was dismissed on summary application: *Campbell v. Turner,* [1937] 1 W.W.R. 228 (Man. C.A.). where the owner had filed a security bond with the Court, with the result that the lien had been vacated, his subsequent application to be struck out as a party defendant was dismissed: *Dom. Bridge Co. v. Janin Const. Ltd.* (1973), 3 N. & P.E.I.R. 418 (Nfld. C.A.).

(*b*) *Judgment as Against Defendant.*

In the Acts of Prince Edward Island (sec. 38(2)), New Brunswick (sec. 36(2)), Manitoba (sec. 32(1)), and Alberta (sec. 39(3)), provision is made for the signing of interlocutory judgment in default of defence. See also *Casford v. Murphy* (1952), 29 M.P.R. 141 (P.E.I.), and *MacDonald-Rowe Woodworking Co. v. MacDonald* (1962), 35 D.L.R. (2d) 268; reversed 39 D.L.R. (2d) 63 (P.E.I. C.A.). The Ontario Act contains no such provision, but in section 38(3) it is stated that in default of defence, a defendant must still be served with notice of trial, and is entitled to defend on such terms as the Judge or Officer may deem just, and therefore it would appear that an interlocutory judgment cannot be signed in Ontario. To this effect see: *Elliott v. Rowell* (1916), 11 O.W.N. 203; *Ron-Dal Contractors Ltd. Ondrey* (1974), 3 O.R. (2d) 290 (C.A.); *D. & M. Bldg. Supplies Ltd. v. Stravalis Holdings Ltd.* (1976), 13 O.R. (2d) 443. In *Kennedy Glass Ltd. v. Jeskay Const. Ltd.,* [1973] 3 O.R. 493 (Div. Ct.) where the Master awarded default judgment at a pretrial against a defendant who failed to file a defence, it was held on appeal that since the pretrial procedure, however desirable, was not sanctioned by the statute and no oral evidence was heard, there had been no trial within the meaning of section 38(4) of The Mechanics' Lien Act and the judgment must be set aside. See also Newfoundland, section 38(3) and Nova Scotia, section 34(1). However in *Crawford v. Wojtyna,* [1953] O.W.N. 369, the plaintiff was awarded judgment on summary application where the reasons submitted for the delay in the delivery of the statement of defence were not satisfactory and the plaintiff could not recover adequate costs to compensate him for the delay. Apart from these sections, the Court's reluctance to dismiss a lien claim before trial, applies equally to its awarding interlocutory judgment for default of defence. In the case of *Robertson v. Bullen, supra,* an application for judgment in default of defence was dismissed and it was held that no judgment could be given until trial. In *Kelly v. Progressive Bldrs. Ltd.* (1970) 1 N. & P.E.I.R. 1, the Court was of the opinion that since mechanics' lien actions follow the usual procedure of the Supreme or District Court, default judgment could be obtained. In British Columbia the practice would appear to be the same. See *Major Platt & Co. v. 1401 West Broadway Medical Offices Ltd.* (1976), 1 B.C.L.R. 255. In Alberta, section 39(3)(*a*) provides that if no defence has been filed and no notice to prove a lien has been filed and served, the Court may declare the liens valid and make such further judgment or order as the Court considers appropriate. This includes the power to sell the property pursuant to the Act. In Saskatchewan, section 47(4) provides that a defendant who fails to appear may, upon proof of service on him of the originating notice, lose his claim upon the land or trust fund, as the case may be. It is to be noted that, with the exception of Alberta, the other provinces whose Acts specifically provide for default judgment also give the Court discretion to allow the defendant to file a defence: P.E.I., secs. 38 and 39; N.B., sec. 36; and Man., sec. 32; and *W. J. Kent & Co. v. Legere* (1975), 65 D.L.R. (3d) 144 at 152 (N.B.C.A.). The effect of the default judgment procedure, where it is available, is that the lien claimant is only required to prove the quantum of his claim at trial. See *Brunswick Const. Ltee. v. Michaud* (1977), 17 N.B.R. 86 and the same at page 107 (C.A.).

The tendency of the Courts to grant judgment for a lien only upon *viva voce* evidence is further illustrated by the decision in *M. L. Plumbing & Heating Ltd. v. Smithson* (1977), 73 D.L.R. (3d) 481 (Sask. C.A.), where the only evidence before the Court that the lien was filed regularly was the affidavit verifying the statement in the lien claim. The Court refused to permit this to stand as evidence and would not apply the Queen's Bench Rules which provided for proof of facts by affidavit if an order to that effect were obtained. the same not having been applied for.

11

Practice Before Trial

§134 Parties to the Action Generally.

The persons to be named in the claim for lien have been fully discussed in Chapter 6, Obtaining a Lien, §69 and §74, and as to the practice respecting third parties see Chapter 10, Jurisdiction, §126. This section will, therefore, deal with parties to be named in the statement of claim, certificate of action and subsequent pleadings in the action.

In so far as parties plaintiff are concerned, the Acts of most provinces provide that a mechanics' lien action is a class action; any number of lien claimants respecting the same land may join in an action, and an action brought by one lien claimant is deemed to have been brought on behalf of all other lien claimants: Ont., sec. 30; Nfld., sec. 31(7); Man., sec. 35; N.S., sec. 33(3); P.E.I., sec. 40; N.B., sec. 38 and Sask., sec. 46(13). See *D. & M. Bldg. Supplies Ltd. v. Stravalis Holdings Ltd.* (1976), 13 O.R. 443, and *Major Platt & Co. v. 1401 West Broadway Medical Offices* (1976), 1 B.C.L.R. 255. The Acts of British Columbia and Alberta have no similar provision.

Accordingly, it was recently held by the Court in Ontario that default proceedings for failure to file a statement of defence were not applicable to a Mechanics' Lien action as it is, in effect, a class action. The Court stated that where the fund available was not sufficient to satisfy all claims, one claimant, by means of default judgment, could satisfy his claim to the detriment of other claimants. Other provisions of the Act indicate such an action must be disposed of at trial since that is the first time all parties and proper persons would be before the Court: *D. & M. Bldg. Supplies Ltd. v. Stravalis Holdings Ltd.* (1976), 13 O.R. 443. In British Columbia, an unopposed application for judgment and for declaration of a lien pursuant to the Rules of Practice was dismissed, notwithstanding default of defence to this action, on the ground that by using the words "trial" and "a judge" in section 30(2) the act contemplated a formal hearing by way of trial before entitlement to a lien was decided: *Major Platt & Co. v. 1401 West Broadway Medical Offices* (1976), 1 B.C.L.R. 255.

With respect to parties defendant, most Acts provide that it is unnecessary to name other lien claimants as defendants since these other lien claimants when served with notice of trial are deemed to be parties to the action: Ont., sec. 29(5); Nfld., sec. 31(5); Man., sec. 34; N.S., sec. 33(4); P.E.I., sec. 43; N.B., sec. 41. British Columbia and Saskatchewan have no similar provision. Alberta's Act provides that lienholders shall not be made defendants, and that upon being served with the statement of claim they are deemed to be parties: Alta., secs. 36(2), 37(2). Furthermore, the Alberta Act is singular in specifying who are to be named parties defendant. In the case of the contractor issuing the statement of claim, the owner and the holder of any prior registered encumbrance are to be defendants, (sec. 36(4)), and where some person other than the contractor is issuing the statement of claim, then the parties defendant are to be the owner, the contractor and the holder of any prior registered emcumbrance: sec. 36(3).

Thus, with the exception of Alberta, the various Acts provide little assistance as to designation of parties to the action, and regard, therefore, should be had to the general principles as established by case law. It has been held that subject to appeal, the judgment or report enforcing a mechanics' lien is a final and conclusive determination of the rights of the parties to the action, but not of persons who are not parties: *Haycock v. Sapphire Corundum Co.* (1903), 7 O.L.R. 21; *Bank of Montreal v. Haffner* (1884), 10 O.A.R. 592, reversing 3 O.R. 183; affirmed (*sub nom. Bank of Montreal v. Worswick*) Cass. S.C. 526, and *Cole v. Hall* (1889), 13 P.R. 100, affirming 12 P.R. 584 (C.A.). The Court stated in *Simac v. Waltman,* [1947] O.W.N. 264 that: "It is clear on general principles of procedure that all persons having a direct legal claim to the moneys sought to be recovered in that action must be either before the Court or represented in a manner provided by the rules of practice". All persons whose interest in the property might be prejudicially affected by the lien claim should also be parties to the action: *Bank of Montreal v. Haffner, supra.*

In each case, therefore, care should be taken to ensure that all persons sought to be affected by the judgment are named as parties, especially since the instances where the Courts have been willing to grant leave to add parties not originally named are in some doubt: see §135, "Adding Parties", *post.* As a general guide the following classes of persons should be named where applicable:

(a) The claimant plaintiff who has commenced the action and filed his certificate of action. If the claim was registered as a multiple claim, all the claimants should be named as plaintiffs. Registered lienholders who have not commenced an action are not named in the pleadings as plaintiffs.

(b) The person or persons considered to come within the statutory definition of "owner", as well as the wife or wives where any inchoate right to dower exists.

(c) Any mortgagee over whom priority is claimed.

(d) The contractor, whether or not he is the person primarily liable to the claimant.

(e) All subcontractors under whom the plaintiff's claim is derived, including the person primarily liable to the claimant.

(f) Any other registered encumbrancer such as a conditional vendor over whom priority is claimed.

§135 Adding Parties.

(a) *Parties Plaintiff.*

Situations arise where the lien claimant is misnamed in the claim for lien, and this misnomer is carried through in the style of cause when the action is commenced. If the defect is curable and is not cured before the time limited for commencement of action has expired, the claimant may find his lien gone and his action to realize upon it dismissed.

In the case of an incorporated company, the Court in *Rodewalt v. Plasky* (1959), 30 W.W.R. 457 (Alta.), held that a lien claim and statement of claim naming an individual in his personal capacity respecting work done by his limited company, was incurable and the action unenforceable as styled. Similarly, where a lien claim was filed by a limited company and the work was done by the president of the limited company in his personal capacity, the lien was held to be invalid: *Inter Property Invt. v. Trpchich* (1975), 11 O.R. 568.

In Manitoba, a foreign corporation which had not obtained a licence to carry on business under The Companies Act of Manitoba did not have status to file a Mechanics' Lien. *Valley Const. Co. v. Eberle* [1974] 5 W.W.R. 537 (Man.). See also, *Suss Woodcraft Ltd. v. Abbey Glen Property Corpn.,* [1975] 5 W.W.R. 57 (Alta.).

In the case of a partnership, the Court in *Simac v. Waltman, supra,* held a claim for lien, and an action instituted in the name of one partner only, was curable, and amended the style of cause throughout, *nunc pro tunc,* by adding the name of the other partner. See also *Chick Lbr. & Fuel Co. v. Moorehouse,* [1933] 3 W.W.R. 465, reversing [1933] 3 W.W.R. 168 (Man. C.A.); *R. Bickerton & Co. v. Dakin* (1891), 20 O.R. 695 (C.A.); *Waisman, Ross & Associates v. Crown Trust Co.,* [1970] S.C.R. 553, reversing 67 W.W.R. 61; *Skyline Associates v. Small,* [1976] 3 W.W.R. 477, (B.C. C.A.). See, however, *Kaltenback v. Frolic Indust. Ltd.,* [1948] O.R. 116 (C.A.).

In the case of a sole proprietorship, the Court, in *Metro Woodworking v. Phales Invt. Ltd.,* [1960] O.W.N. 132 (C.A.), held a claim for lien and an action styled in the name of "Metro Woodworking" was a nullity, incapable of being cured or amended. See however, *O. C. Couch Plumbing, Heating & Sheet Metal v. Target Textiles,* [1969] 1 O.R. 735 (C.A.)., where the claimant was one O. C. Couch who was described in the style of cause as O.C. Couch Plumbing, Heating and Sheet Metal. The Court ruled that the inclusion in the style of cause of the words "Plumbing, Heating and Sheet Metal" was mere surplusage, a trifling mistake which had neither misled nor effected anyone, and accordingly the style of cause should be amended as a matter of course by deleting the words after the plaintiff's name. See also *Competition Coffee Systems v. Lee* (1977), 15 O.R. (2d) 665; *Hydro Mississauga v. Clarke* (1976), 2 C.P.C. 334 (Ont.).

Generally speaking, at least in the case of partnerships, the Courts have inclined to the curative section of the various Acts in upholding the claim for lien and allowing amendments to the parties named as plaintiff in the statement of claim, provided of course, there has been no prejudice to any defendant shown.

(b) Parties Defendant.

The Court's attitude respecting adding of parties defendant is in somewhat more doubt than in the case of adding parties plaintiff.

In many of the earlier decisions, the Court's tendency was to allow amendments adding parties defendant if no prejudice was shown to have been suffered. In *Fairy and Stephenson v. Doner,* [1947] O.W.N. 217, the plaintiff, by error, failed to name the registered owner in his claim for lien and statement of claim. In allowing the motion to add the registered owner as a party defendant, the Court stated that the registration of the claim for lien was sufficient notice to the registered owner and that no prejudice had been shown. See also *Barrington v. Martin* (1908), 16 O.L.R. 635 (C.A.); *Nobbs and Eastman v. C.P.R.* (1913), 6 W.W.R. 759 (Sask.), and *Leesona Corpn. v. Consol. Textile Mills Ltd.* (1977), 18 N.R. 29 (S.C.C.). In the case of *Cooke v. Mocroft,* [1926] 1 W.W.R. 827 (B.C. C.A.), it was held that the plaintiff was entitled to have a mortgagee added as a party after the expiration of the statutory time limit for commencing the action, where the purpose of adding him was to have the mortgage set aside as a fraudulent attempt to defeat the lien. In *Bain v. Director, Veterans' Land Act,* [1955] O.W.N. 993, the Court refused to add a party defendant where the motion therefor was brought after a lapse of 8 years; however, it indicated that had the motion been promptly made, such relief could have been given. In *Hubert v. Shinder,* [1952] O.W.N. 146 (C.A.), a mortgagee was not joined as a party defendant or served with a statement of claim. He was, however, served with a notice of trial, as provided by the present section 38(2) of the Ontario Act, within the period of 90 days within which an action must be commenced. The mortgagee did not object to this procedure at trial, and the objection that he was not a proper party to the action was first raised on appeal. The Court of Appeal held that the appellant, by his conduct and intervention as a party in the proceedings, was precluded from raising the point on appeal.

The Court's tendency in recent decisions has been to refuse to allow the plaintiff to add a party defendant where the time limit within which an action must be commenced has expired. The reason for the Court's refusal appears to be, that the various Acts, in stipulating a time limit to begin an action, require that the action be instituted against all parties whose interests are sought to be affected within that time, and if not, the lien ceases to exist as against those persons not so made a defendant. The curative section does not assist the plaintiff. In the Ontario decision of *Larkin v. Larkin* (1900), 32 O.R. 80 (C.A.), the Court of Appeal held that a prior mortgagee against whom relief was sought must be made a party to the action within the time limited by the Act to commence action, namely, 90 days after the last work was completed.

In Manitoba it was held that, unless some action to which the owner is a party has been commenced within the period prescribed by the Act, the plaintiff's lien ceases to exist, and an amendment to pleadings to add the "owner" could not be made: *Abramovitch v. Vrondessi* (1913), 23 Man. R. 383. See also *Metals Recovery Co. v. Molybdenum Products Co.* (1919), 46 O.L.R. 532 (C.A.); *Bank of Montreal v. Haffner, supra.* In *Arnold Lbr. Ltd. v. Vodouris,* [1968] 2 O.R. 478, the plaintiff, believing the defendants were the owners, named them in his claim for lien and statement of claim. After expiry of the limitation period, the plaintiff discovered that the named defendants were only tenants and moved to add the registered owner. The motion was refused on the ground that if added, the owner would be deemed to be a party as of the date of the order adding him, and since the limitation period had expired, no useful purpose could be served in adding him, as the lien against his interest had ceased to exist. The decision in *Rocca Steel Ltd. v. Tower Hill Apts. Ltd.,* [1968] 2 O.R. 701, was the same where the claimant who brought action against the defendant settled before trial, and then one of the other lien claimants moved for an order for carriage of the action and to add certain persons as defendants. In both these decisions the Court expressly adopted the reasoning in *Larkin v. Larkin, supra, Hubert v. Shinder, supra* and *Metals Recovery Co. v. Molybdenum Products Co., supra,* and it refused to follow the reasoning in *Fairy and Stephenson v. Doner, supra.*

In Nova Scotia, even where a mortgagee was already a party to the action the Court refused to allow an amendment to the Statement of Claim to include an allegation that the mortgagees were "owners" within the meaning of the Act on the ground that the proposed amendment raised a cause of action which was barred by the expiration of the time limited by the Act for commencing the action: *Saltzman v. Eastside Holding & Brokerage*

Co. (1970), 2 N.S.R. (2d) 265 (C.A.). See also *E. E. McCoy Co. v. Venus Elec. Ltd.* (1977) 19 N.B.R. (2d) 299.

In *N. S. Sand & Gravel Ltd. v. Kidstone Estates Ltd.* (1973), 13 N.S. R. (2d) 431, the Court approved the decision in *Saltzman v. Eastside, supra,* and refused to add a mortgagee as a party defendant after the expiry of the 90 days limited for commencing the action. However since the mortgagee had been served with notice of trial, the Court dealt with the question of priority of the liens over the mortgage.

Recently, however, *Saltzman v. Eastside, supra,* was distinguished by the Nova Scotia Court of Appeal on the grounds that that case had been decided before certain amendments to Rule 15 of the Nova Scotia Civil Procedure Rules came into force. Additional discretion had been conferred upon the Court by the amendment to the Rules and the Court stated that even if the amendment resulted in a new cause of action, the cause of action arose out of the same or substantially the same facts as the original cause of action against the mortgagee and accordingly allowed the amendment which had been denied in the *Saltzman* case: *E.S. Martin Const. Ltd. v. Penhorn Mall Ltd.* (1975), 62 D.L.R. (3d) 498 (N.S. C. A.).

Where the application to add a person as a defendant is on consent, the Court has granted the application: *Dom. Bridge Co. v. Sask. Govt. Telephones* (1963), 42 W.W.R. 577 at 585 (Sask.). Moreover, where the assignee of the accounts receivable of one of the defendants seeks to be added as a defendant in order to dispute the plaintiff's lien claim, the application has been granted: *R. V. Demmings & Co. v. Caldwell Const. Co.* (1955), 4 D.L.R. (2d) 465 (N.B. C.A.); *Dorrell v. Campbell* (1916), 10 W.W.R. 492 (B.C. C.A.). In *Brunswick Const. Ltée v. Michaud* (1977), 17 N.B.R. (2d) 86 (C.A.) a general contractor was added as a party defendant upon its application in a material supplier's action against a subcontractor and owner, when the owner and subcontractor did not defend, in order to protect its interest in the holdback.

In Manitoba, an application to join a party as a defendant through a counterclaim in order to obtain a personal judgment against that party for what amounted to an allegation of tortious conduct based on negligence or misrepresentation was refused: *Western Caissons (Man.) Ltd. v. Trident Const. Ltd.,* 54 D.L.R. (3d) 289 (Man.).

§136　**Bankruptcy of the Defendant.**

The Bankruptcy Act, R.S.C. 1970, ch. B-3, sec. 2 makes a mechanics' lien claimant a secured creditor where the lien has arisen before the date of the making of the receiving order or of an assignment for the general benefit of creditors under the Act, whether or not the claim for lien is registered: *Re Rockland Chocolate & Cocoa Co.* (1921), 50 O.L.R. 66; *Re Empire Brewing & Malting Co.* (1891), 8 Man. R. 424; *Re Clinton Thresher Co.* (1910), 1

O.W.N. 445. These lienholders are not affected by a stay of proceedings created by the Bankruptcy Act (sec. 49), nor is there any necessity for the lienholder to obtain an order from the Bankruptcy Court permitting him to continue the action, as long as he merely seeks to realize upon the security of the property under The Mechanics' Lien Act: *Re Rockland Chocolate & Cocoa Co., supra; Riordon Co. v. John W. Danforth Co.*, [1923] S.C.R. 319, affirming 4 C.B.R. 247, which reversed 2 C.B.R. 339; *Dieleman Planer Co. v. Elizabeth Townhouses Ltd.* (1972), 27 D.L.R. (3d) 692 (B.C.). If the claimant wishes to proceed to obtain a personal judgment, or seeks the right to claim against the bankrupt estate for any deficiency after the proceeds of the lien action have been distributed, he must obtain an order from the Bankruptcy Court permitting him to prosecute his mechanics' lien action against the bankrupt: *Re Rockland Chocolate & Cocoa Co., supra.* The claimant will thereupon be permitted to prove in the bankruptcy, as an unsecured creditor, for any such deficiency.

If the "owner" is the bankrupt, the judgment in the action will require that the trustee pay into Court a sufficient sum to satisfy the claims for lien allowed by the Court. If the trustee fails to do so, then the lien claimants may proceed to sell the bankrupt's property and the leave of the Court is not required as long as the bankruptcy took place after the lien arose. See further, Chapter 8, Priorities, §99, *ante.*

As previously stated, a lien claimant wishing to proceed against the bankrupt's estate must obtain an order to this effect from the bankruptcy Court: Form 44. The consent of the trustee in bankruptcy is usually obtained and is filed on the return of the motion: Form 43. The former practice of requiring an affidavit of the plaintiff in support of this consent motion has now been discontinued. If the trustee will not consent, the motion is brought upon notice to the trustee, together with a supporting affidavit according to the practice in the Bankruptcy Court. The correct way of describing a trustee acting in a bankruptcy is "The Trustee of the Estate of (name of the bankrupt), a bankrupt": see the Bankruptcy Act, sec. 11. No other parties need be served with notice of this application and supporting affidavit. The granting or refusing of such an application is discretionary: *Re Cohen* (1948), 29 C.B.R. 111 (Ont.). As a result, the supporting affidavit must completely disclose the relevant facts and the reason why it is necessary to commence action. The order, when made, will also provide that the trustee of the bankrupt estate be added as party defendant.

At the opening of the trial of a lien action, the Judge or Officer will require a bankruptcy certificate to be filed showing that no person against whom any personal judgment may be claimed is in bankruptcy. Usually, if a defendant is bankrupt, this fact is well known to the plaintiff. If however, it is only discovered when the bankruptcy certificate is obtained, an order to proceed against the bankrupt estate would, at this stage, have to be obtained, as outlined above.

§137   Winding-up Proceedings.

All liens arising before the making of a winding-up order are secured claims and the action to enforce them cannot be stayed by the procedure of the Winding-Up Act, R.S.C. 1970, chapter W-10. See also *Re Clinton Thresher Co., supra; Re Empire Brewing & Malting Co., supra; Re Ibex Mining and Dev. Co.* (1902), 9 B.C.R. 557. Once a winding-up order has been made, no action or other proceeding shall be proceeded with or commenced against the company except with the leave of the Court. In *Re Haileybury Rink Co.* (1908), 12 O.W.R. 197, the Court held that once the winding-up order had been made, the registration of a claim for lien was irregular and might be set aside.

However, when a lien claimant registers its lien against land owned by a third party and not the company being wound up, it is actually bringing the action against the third party and does not have to add the company being wound up as a party defendant. In an application by a lien claimant to continue proceedings under The Mechanics' Lien Act against the company being wound up, the Court found that since the same evidence would have to be adduced by the lien claimant to prove its lien against the owner as it would have to adduce to prove that the company being wound up owed the money, in order to prevent multiplicity of proceedings and to allow the company to dispute the validity of the claim, the application was allowed: *Re James United Indust. Ltd.* (1971), 16 C.B.R. (N.S.) 65 (Ont.). See further, Chapter 8, Priorities, §100, *ante.*

§138   Assignment of Rights of Parties; Death of Parties.

All of the Acts provide that the rights of a lienholder may be assigned in writing at any time before death, and, if not assigned, all rights pass to the lienholder's personal representative: Ont., sec. 24; Nfld., sec. 26; Man., sec. 24(1), (2); N.S., sec. 27; P.E.I., sec. 30; N.B., sec. 29; Sask., sec. 29; Alta., sec. 21, and B.C., sec. 29. For form of assignment, see Form 7. The Court of Appeal in *Seaman v. Can. Stewart Co.* (1911), 2 O.W.N. 576 (C.A.), cast strong doubts on the right to assign part only of a lien claim. If the death or assignment takes place before registration of the claim for lien, the assignee, or personal representative of the original claimant should be named in the claim for lien: Man., sec. 24(3) and Chapter 6, Obtaining a Lien, §69(*a*), *ante.* Where the assignment occurs after registration of the claim for lien, the assignment need not be registered: *Triangle Storage Ltd. v. Porter,* [1941] 3 W.W.R. 892 (B.C. C.A.). The Manitoba Act, however, allows the assignee to register the assignment if he so wishes: Man., sec. 24(4). See further, §69, *ante.* Nevertheless, it is suggested, that in the case of any assignment, whether before or after registration of the claim for lien, written notice of same should be given to all persons against which the assignee seeks a remedy; for in many jurisdictions failure to do so will affect the assignee's rights of recovery: see *e.g.,* in Ontario, The Conveyancing and Law of Property Act, R.S.O. 1970, ch. 85, sec. 54. If the defendant dies before the claim for lien is registered, the deceased defendant may be named in the claim for lien as if he were still alive.

The naming of parties to an action to realize upon a lien claim will be affected by death or assignment. None of the Acts make specific provisions in such a case, and, therefore, the Rules of Practice in the particular province should be examined: *Orr v. Davie* (1892), 22 O.R. 430 and Chapter 10, Jurisdiction, §120, *ante.* In the following comments respecting parties to the action in case of death or assignment, the procedure set forth in the Ontario Supreme Court Rules of Practice and various Ontario Acts will be used.

In the case of an assignment of the lien claim made before an action is commenced, the style of cause should name as party plaintiff, the assignee: Rule 299. If the assignment was made after registration of the lien, the claim for lien need not be amended to show the name of the assignee as claimant. Where the lienholder did not assign his lien claim and all rights under it, but merely gave his bank a general assignment of book debts, the lienholder was allowed to bring the action to realize upon the lien in his own name, and it was not necessary that the bank be made a party plaintiff: *Sardara Singh v. Indust. Mtge. and Finance Corpn.* (1967), 61 W.W.R. 338 (B.C.). If the defendant contractor (or other person primarily liable to the lien claimant) makes an assignment of moneys due to him under his contract before the action is commenced, both the assignee and assignor should be named as defendants. In Ontario, a contractor assigned an account to a surety company. At the time of the mechanics' lien action, there were moneys due under the contract in excess of the statutory holdback. It was held that such excess had to go to satisfy lien claimants in addition to the amount of the holdback: *Gascoigne Ltd. v. South Cramahe S. Bd.,* [1962] O.W.N. 81. See also section 19 of the British Columbia Act which provides that no assignment by a contractor or subcontractor of moneys due to him under the contract is valid as against any lien or trust created under that province's Act. See further, §135(*b*), *ante,* respecting the adding of assignees as parties defendant.

In the case of death of the lien claimant before an action is commenced, his personal representative should be named as party plaintiff: Rule 74. If the claimant dies after the action is commenced, his personal representative may continue the action upon obtaining an order of revivor: Rules 74 and 299. However, where the action is commenced in the name of a partnership and one partner dies after the claim for lien is registered, his personal representative need not be added as a party, nor is it necessary to obtain an order of revivor: *R. Bickerton & Co. v. Dakin* (1891), 20 O.R. 695; Rule 299.

Where to the knowledge of the plaintiff, a defendant dies before the action is commenced, his personal representative must be named as a party defendant and no order of revivor is necessary: *Kulessa v. Hefford,* [1972] 1 O.R. 740 (C.A.); Rule 299. Since July 9, 1971, however, where a plaintiff *bona fide* and without knowledge commences an action against a deceased person, the action will not be a nullity if he obtains a validating order: The Trustee Act, R.S.O. 1970, ch. 470, sec. 38(2) [am. 1971, ch. 32, sec. 2]. If the deceased defendant has no personal representative, or if his personal representative fails to apply for letters probate or letters of administration, the plaintiff may apply to a Judge of the Supreme Court for the appointment of an administrator *ad litem:* The Trustee Act, *supra,* sec. 38(3). Where the defendant dies after the action is commenced, his personal representative may continue the action upon obtaining a revivor order: Rules 74 and 299.

§139 The Owner.

As previously stated, the statutory "owner" is a proper party to be named as a defendant in the pleadings. Not only is the statutory "owner" a proper party, but the mechanics' lien action itself cannot proceed unless some person having an interest in the land as "owner", within the meaning of The Mechanics' Lien Act, is a party defendant in the action: *Abramovitch v. Vrondessi* (1913), 23 Man. R. 383; *Bain v. Director, Veterans' Land Act,* [1947] O.W.N. 917; *Rocca Steel Ltd. v. Tower Hill Apts. Ltd.,* [1968] 2 O.R. 701. However, a lien will not be invalidated if the owner has not been named in the claim for lien and no prejudice is occasioned by the omission. See further, Chapter 6, Obtaining a Lien, §69(*b*), *ante,* and the following cases: *Man. Bridge, etc. Works Ld. v. Gillespie* (1914), 5 W.W.R. 1210; affirmed with a variation 6 W.W.R. 1582 (Sask. C.A.); *Barrington v. Martin* (1908), 16 O.L.R. 635 (C.A.); *Fairy and Stephenson v. Doner,* [1947] O.W.N. 217; *Bradshaw v. Saucerman* (1913), 3 W.W.R. 761, affirming 4 D.L.R. 476 (Y.T. C.A.); *Nobbs and Eastman v. C.P.R.* (1913), 6 W.W.R. 759 (Sask.); *Polson v. Thomson* (1916), 10 W.W.R. 865 (Man. C.A.); *Foster v. Brocklebank* (1915), 8 W.W.R. 464 (Alta.); *Irwin v. Beynon* (1886), 4 Man. R. 10 (C.A.); *Whaley v. Linnenbank* (1915), 36 O.L.R. 361 (C.A.); *Cole v. Hall* (1889), 13 P.R. 100, affirming 12 P.R. 584 (C.A.); *Makins v. Robinson* (1884), 6 O.R. 1; *Waisman, Ross & Associates v. Crown Trust Co.,* [1970] S.C.R. 553, reversing 67 W.W.R. 61; *O.C. Couch Plumbing, Heating and Sheet Metal v. Target Textiles,* [1969] 1 O.R. 735 (C.A.); *Chick Lbr. & Fuel Co. v. Moorehouse,* [1933] 3 W.W.R. 465, reversing [1933] 3 W.W.R. 168 (Man. C.A.); *R. Bickerton & Co. v. Dakin, supra. Inter Property Invt. v. Trpchich*

(1976), 11 O.R. 568; *Skyline Associates v. Small,* [1976] 3 W.W.R. 477 (B.C. C.A.); *Hydro Mississauga v. Clarke* (1976), 2 C.P.C. 334 (Ont.); *Competition Coffee Systems v. Lee* (1977), 15 O.R. (2d) 665; *Leesona Corpn. v. Consol. Textile Mills Ltd.* (1977), 18 N.R. 29 (S.C.C.).

If the "owner" sells the property before action is commenced, both the vendor and the purchaser should be named in the style of cause in the pleadings. Any woman having an inchoate dower right in the land involved in the action should be made a party in the statement of claim and subsequent pleadings. This interest is frequently overlooked until a requisition on title is received by a prospective purchaser after the trial of the action has been completed and the property is being offered for sale pursuant to the Act.

The propriety of adding the "owner" as a party defendant at or before trial when the incorrect "owner" has been named, or when the owner has been entirely omitted as a party defendant, has been fully discussed in §135, *ante.*

§140 Prior Mortgagee.

In most jurisdictions, a prior mortgagee is one whose mortgage was registered before the first lien arose, and he has priority over lien claims to the extent of the actual value of the land and premises at the time the first lien arose (Ont., sec. 7(3); Nfld., sec. 9(3); P.E.I., sec. 9(4)). The requirement that the prior mortgage be registered does not appear in the Manitoba and Nova Scotia Acts; Man., sec. 5(3); N.S., sec. 7(3). In Alberta and British Columbia a registered mortgage has priority over a lien to the extent of the mortgage money *bona fide* secured or advanced in money prior to the registration of the lien: Alta., sec. 9(2); B.C., sec. 7(1). See also *Bank of Montreal v. Ehattesaht Co-op. Enterprises Assn.* (1976), 71 D.L.R. (3d) 757 (B.C.). See further Chapter 5, The Mortgagee, §§57 and 60 *ante* and *Smith & Sons Ltd. v. May* (1925), 54 O.L.R. 21 (C.A.); *Cook v. Belshaw* (1893), 23 O.R. 545.

A prior mortgagee is not made a party to the action unless some priority is claimed over him, for example, if it is alleged that the face value of the mortgage exceeds the value of the property at the time the first lien arose; *Dufton v. Horning* (1895), 26 O.R. 252, or the mortgage is sought to be set aside as fraudulent attempt to defeat the lien; *Cooke v. Mocroft,* [1926] 1 W.W.R. 827 (B.C. C.A.). In cases where the prior mortgagee is improperly made a party, he may move at the trial to have the action dismissed against him with costs.

As set out in §135(*b*), *supra,* the principles to be applied in adding a mortgagee as a party defendant are in some doubt. Where a prior mortgagee had not been joined as a party defendant in the action, nor been served with a statement of claim, but only with a notice of trial, and such notice had been served within the 90 day period after which lien rights would expire, and he appeared at the trial to defend his position, the Ontario Court of Appeal held that by his conduct and intervention he had precluded himself from denying that he was a party to the action: *Hubert v. Shinder,* [1952] O.W.N. 146 (C.A.). See also *Fairy and Stephenson v. Doner, supra; Barrington v. Martin, supra; Dorrell v. Campbell* (1916), 22 B.C.R. 584 (C.A.); *R. V. Demmings & Co. v. Caldwell Const. Co.* (1955), 4 D.L.R. (2d) 465 (N.B. C.A.); *Roberts v. McDonald* (1887), 15 O.R. 80; *Nobbs and Eastman v. C.P.R., supra; Dom. Lbr. & Fuel Co. v. Paskov,* [1919] 1 W.W.R. 657 (Man.); *Robock v. Peters* (1900), 13 Man. R. 124. The Ontario Court of Appeal, however, in *Larkin v. Larkin* (1900), 32 O.R. 80 (C.A.), held that a prior mortgagee whose priority is questioned must be made a party to the action within the time limited by the Act for commencement of the lien claimant's action. Therefore, the priority of a prior mortgagee who had not been named as a party in the action, but had only been served with notice of trial after the expiration of the 90 days allowed by the Act for commencing action, could not be attacked by lien claimants since the rights of such claimants against him had expired.

See also *Bank of Montreal v. Haffner* (1884), 10 O.A.R. 592, reversing 3 O.R. 183; affirmed *(sub nom. Bank of Montreal v. Worswick)* Cass. S.C. 526; *Metals Recovery Co. v. Molybdenum Products Co.* (1919), 46 O.L.R. 532 (C.A.); *Abramovitch v. Vrondessi* (1913), 23 Man. R. 383. *Saltzman v. Eastside Holding and Brokerage Co.* (1970), 2 N.S.R. (2d) 265 (C.A.); *N. S. Sand & Gravel Ltd. v. Kidstone Estates Ltd.* (1973), 13 N.S.R. (2d) 431; *E. S. Martin Const. Ltd. v. Penhorn Mall Ltd.* (1975), 62 D.L.R. (3d) 498 (N.S. C.A.).

As a result, if the lien claimant wishes to attack the prior mortgage in its entirety or seek priority to the extent of the increased selling value of the land created by the work done and materials furnished, the mortgagee should be named as a party defendant in the statement of claim.

When a mortgagee has been made a defendant in an action but does not defend the action or in any way oppose the lien claimant's claim to priority over his mortgage, he shall be deemed to have abandoned any rights he may have had to priority: *Beaver Lbr. Co. v. Curry,* [1926] 3 W.W.R. 404 (Sask. C.A.); *Security Lbr. Co. v. Johnson,* [1924] 3 W.W.R. 399 (Sask. C.A.).

§141   Subsequent Mortgage.

A subsequent mortgage is a mortgage that does not fall within the definition of a prior mortgage as described in §140, *ante.* This does not mean that the lien claimant can therefore disregard such a mortgagee when he commences his action, for such a mortgage may nevertheless have priority over his lien claim: see Chapter 5, The Mortgagee, §62, *ante.* Most of the Acts provide that the lien has priority over advances made on account of such a mortgage after notice in writing of a lien is given to the mortgagee or after a claim for lien has been registered: Ont., sec. 14(1); Nfld., sec. 16(1); Man., sec. 11(1); N.S., sec. 14(1); Sask. sec. 26(1); N.B., sec. 9(1), (2).

The remaining provincial Acts provide that priority of the lien claimant is gained over advances made after registration of his lien: Alta., sec. 9(2); B.C., sec. 7(2); and P.E.I., sec. 9(2). The British Columbia Act (sec. 7(2)), entitles a mortgagee who has applied mortgage moneys in payment of a registered lien, to be subrogated to the rights and priority of such lienholder. In addition, the Act of Prince Edward Island provides that a lien claimant for materials may gain priority over advances made after notice of his lien is given to the mortgagee: P.E.I., sec. 9(3).

If, therefore, a lien claimant seeks priority over the whole or any part of the mortgage, or he seeks to set aside the mortgage as being fraudulent, the mortgagee should be named as a defendant: see §140, "Prior Mortgagee", *ante*.

Where the lien claimant does not claim priority over the mortgagee, or does not seek to attack the validity of the mortgage, the question arises as to whether the mortgagee should be named as a defendant so as to obtain a judicial determination of the lien claimant's priority, and thus facilitate the ultimate sale of the property. The practice in Ontario has been to serve the mortgagee with notice of trial rather than naming him as a defendant: Ont., sec. 38(2). This practice was adopted initially from the practice in actions for foreclosure where encumbrancers, subsequent in priority to the foreclosing mortgagee, were not named in the writ of foreclosure, but were added as parties in the Master's Office after judgment. As such, these encumbrancers had 14 days in which to set aside the judgment, otherwise their interests were foreclosed: *Haycock v. Sapphire Corundum Co.* (1903), 7 O.L.R. 21; *Cole v. Hall* (1889), 13 P.R. 100, affirming 12 P.R. 584 (C.A.).

The present Ontario Act allows the lien claimant to serve such mortgagees with notice of trial, (section 38(2)) and further, section 38(4) empowers the Judge or Officer trying the action to determine all rights of the parties named as defendants and the persons upon whom notice of trial has been served. The result therefore would appear to be that the Judge or Officer trying the action could, in his judgment or report, set out the priority of such a mortgage in respect of any proceeds of the sale of the property. This procedure should not be adopted where the claimant questions the validity or the state of account of the mortgage, for the term, "subsequent mortgage", as used in foreclosure proceedings, means a subsequently registered mortgage, whereas in mechanics' lien proceedings the term, "subsequent mortgage", means, generally, a mortgage which has been registered after the first lien arises, but before the first lien is registered. The following provincial Acts have similar provisions: Nfld., sec. 38(2), (4); Man., secs. 37(2), 39(1); N.S., secs. 34(1), 35; P.E.I., secs. 42, 45; N.B., secs. 40, 43; and Alta., secs. 39(2), 44.

§142 The Contractor.

Generally, if the lien claimant wishes to claim against the contractor (or other person primarily liable to the lien claimant) for a lien or personal judgment, the contractor should be made a party to the action in the statement of claim and subsequent proceedings. In Alberta, he must be named a defendant: Alta., sec. 36(3). The general principles respecting the adding of party defendants at or before trial, as set out in §§134 and 135(*b*) in this Chapter, are applicable also to the contractor.

The contractor (or other person primarily liable to the lien claimant) will, in many cases, have registered a lien himself against the statutory "owner's" interest. Therefore, in those provinces whose Acts provide that "lien claimants" served with notice of trial are deemed for all purposes to be parties to the action, it should be unnecessary to name the contractor or person primarily liable to the lien claimant as a defendant in the statement of claim: Ont., secs. 29(5), 38(2); Nfld., secs. 31(5), 38(2); Man., secs. 34, 37; N.S., secs. 33(4), 35; P.E.I., secs. 42, 43; N.B., secs. 40, 41. The Act of British Columbia has no similar provision. In Alberta, although sections 36(2) and 37(2) provide that "lien claimants" should not be named as defendants, but served with the statement of claim, section 36(3) makes it mandatory to name the contractor as a defendant. In Saskatchewan an action is commenced by an originating notice in which the owner, the contractor and the persons primarily liable under the contract must be named as defendants: Sask., sec. 47(1)(*a*), (*b*). The practice in Ontario is to also name him as a defendant, and this practice is recommended, since the contractor is then a party defendant respecting all lienholders, and relief may be obtained against him by any party entitled to a lien.

In some cases the lien claimant may know that the contractor is impecunious and may not wish to join him in the action, but only to obtain the amount of holdback the statutory "owner" is liable to retain. It has been held that it is unnecessary for the contractor to be a party to an action in order that liens may be enforced by lien claimants against the "owner": *Turner v. Johnson* (1932), 41 O.W.N. 497 (C.A.).

In many instances a contractor will have assigned the amounts due to him under a contract before the moneys are actually payable. It is therefore in the assignee's interest to become a party to the action, in order that he may appear and defend the action on behalf of the contractor and in this way strengthen his own position. In the Court's discretion the assignee may be added as a party defendant: *R. V. Demmings & Co. v. Caldwell Const. Co.* (1955), 4 D.L.R. (2d) 465 (N.B. C.A.); *Dorrell v. Campbell* (1916), 10 W.W.R. 492 (B.C. C.A.); *Nobbs and Eastman v. C.P.R.* (1913), 6 W.W.R. 759 (Sask.). See also Chapter 8, Priorities, §101, *ante* and §138, *ante*.

§143 Execution Creditors.

The Acts of all provinces except British Columbia provide that a lien has priority over executions issued after the lien arises: Ont., sec. 14(1); Nfld., sec. 16(1); Man., sec. 11(1); N.S., sec. 14(1); P.E.I., sec. 9(1); N.B., sec. 9(1); Sask., sec. 25(1); Alta., sec. 9(1); B.C., sec. 12. As a result execution creditors over which the claimant has priority, are not named as defendants but are served with notice of trial or statement of claim as the case may be within the time limited by the Acts: Ont., sec. 38(2); Nfld., sec. 38(2); Man., sec. 37; N.S., sec. 35; P.E.I., sec. 42; Sask., sec. 46(11); Alta., sec. 39(2); N.B., sec. 40. In Ontario the time limited for service is 10 clear days before trial. As a search for executions is usually made well before the 10 day period mentioned, and notices of trial prepared and served before this period, a sub-search must be made at the end of the eleventh day preceding the trial date, in order to ascertain if any new executions have been filed. If such an execution has been filed, the notice of trial could not, in most cases, be served in time to comply with the 10 clear day requirement, and, unless the execution creditor consents, either leave for short service would have to be obtained or the action would have to be adjourned.

In *Haycock v. Sapphire Corundum Co.* (1903), 7 O.L.R. 21, an execution was registered 5 days before the date of trial. The execution was known to the Court, but no notice of trial was served on the execution creditor, nor did he appear at trial. The judgment, however, included him and dealt with his interest. Meredith C. J. stated: "It is the persons who are encumbrancers at the time fixed for the service of notice of trial, and those only, who are required to be served, service of notice of trial on them being the mode by which encumbrancers not already parties to the proceedings are brought in." Accordingly, the name of the execution creditor was stricken from the judgment. It will readily be seen that if a sale is taken of the premises under the Act, difficulty is bound to arise where an encumbrancer is on record and has not been dealt with by the Court. It is therefore prudent to have all interested persons before the Court in order that their interests may be dealt with in the judgment. An example of this situation is found in *Can. Foundry Co. v. Edmonton Portland Cement Co.,* [1919] 2 W.W.R. 310 (Alta.). The Court expressed the opinion that, since the certificate of action (*lis pendens* in Alberta) was registered, therefore the execution creditor was deemed to have notice of a pending action, and should have applied to be added as a party to the action.

§144 Unregistered Lien Claimants.

In Nova Scotia and Saskatchewan, it is not necessary for a lien claimant to register a claim for lien if, within the time limited by these Acts, an action is commenced by some other claimant and a certificate thereof is registered: N.S., sec. 24 and Sask., sec. 37(1). In all other provinces, if the lien claimant fails to register his lien within the required time, his lien ceases to exist: Ont., sec. 22(1); Nfld., sec. 24(1); Man., sec. 21; P.E.I., sec. 26; N.B., sec. 25; B.C., sec. 23(4); Alta., sec. 31.

In Nova Scotia if such an action is not commenced and a certificate therefore registered within the required time, the unregistered lien will cease to exist: N.S., sec. 25.

However, in Saskatchewan, section 37(1) provides that claims may be registered and actions commenced after the time limited for doing so has expired, and if so, the lien shall not be defeated except as against intervening parties becoming entitled to a lien or charge upon the land, whose claim, with respect to the land, is registered prior to the registration of the lien, or as against an owner in respect of payments made in good faith to a contractor after expiry of the holdback period and before registration of a lien or notice of the lien is given to him.

The Saskatchewan Court of Appeal, in a recent decision held that a lien filed more than 37 days after the last materials were supplied but before the owner was entitled to pay out the holdback under the Act was valid but that another lien, similarly late and filed after the owner became entitled to pay out the holdback, was invalid: *M.L. Plumbing & Heating Ltd. v. Smithson* (1977), 73 D.L.R. (3d) 481 (Sask. C.A.). However, where lien claimants did not register claims for lien until after the expiry of the statutory period during which an owner was required to retain holdback, the Court held that the owner was entitled to set off his claim for damages against the contractor against the holdback which was still in the owner's hands: *Rasmussens' Ltd. v. Melville Country Club,* [1977] 4 W.W.R. 382 (Sask.).

Unregistered lien claimants are not named in the statement of claim, but are to be served with notice of trial, and once so served, are deemed to be parties to the action: N.S., sec. 33(4). In Saskatchewan if a person commencing an action has knowledge of an unregistered lien claimant, he must join this claimant as a party defendant in the originating notice; Sask., sec. 47(1)(*c*). In Nova Scotia, an unregistered lien claimant so served must file his claim, in prescribed form, verified by affidavit: N.S., sec. 33(4). It is recommended practice that the unregistered lien claimant either register his lien, file his lien verified by affidavit, or, at the very least, give notice of his lien to the owner or other person primarily liable, to avoid any risk of losing his lien before trial, if the action upon which he is relying is dismissed or settled, or the property sold: see *Morton v. Grant,* [1956] O.W.N. 523 (C.A.); *Stinson v. Mackendrick* (1924), 55 O.L.R. 358 (C.A.); *Charters v. McCracken* (1916), 36 O.L.R. 260 (C.A.); *Cook v. Koldoffsky* (1916), 35 O.L.R. 555 (C.A.); *Richards v. Chamberlain* (1878), 25 Gr. 402; *Sterling Lbr. Co. v. Jones* (1916), 36 O.L.R. 153 (C.A.); *Cut-Rate Plate Glass Co. v. Solodinski* (1915), 34 O.L.R. 604 (C.A.); *Wanty v. Robins* (1888), 15 O.R.

474 (C.A.). Moreover, an unregistered lien claimant who has registered his lien, filed notice thereof verified by affidavit or sent written notice thereof, will be less likely to be prejudiced by the failure of a claimant commencing an action to enforce a lien, or by the failure of the claimant commencing the action to prove his lien at trial: *Baines v. Curley* (1916), 38 O.L.R. 301 (C.A.); *Ramsay v. Graham* (1912), 3 O.W.N. 972; *Ogilvie v. Cooke,* [1952] O.R. 862 (C.A.); *Howard v. Herod Const. Co.* (1932), 41 O.W.N. 198 (C.A.); *Del Frari v. Wright,* [1960] O.R. 430; *McPherson v. Gedge* (1883), 4 O.R. 246 (C.A.); *Crawford v. Hesselink* (1958), 15 D.L.R. (2d) 294 (Nfld.); *N. S. Sand & Gravel Ltd. v. Kidstone Estates Ltd.* (1973), 13 N.S.R. (2d) 431; *Silver v. R.R. Seeton Const. Ltd.* (1977), 74 D.L.R. (3d) 212, (N.S.).

In order to protect unregistered claimants respecting a settlement before trial or a consent to dismissal of the action, it was the former practice in Ontario (registration of the lien within the proper time now being mandatory under the amendments to the Ontario Mechanics' Lien Act) to require that an affidavit be filed stating that to the knowledge of the claimant having carriage of the action, there were no unregistered lien claimants other than those before the Court. However, there appeared to be no authority for this requirement.

§145 Commencement of Action.

In most of the provinces, a mechanics' lien action is commenced by the claimant filing a statement of claim in the appropriate Court office: Ont., sec. 29(2); Nfld., sec. 31(2); Man., sec. 30; N.S., sec. 33(2); N.B., sec. 34 and Alta., sec. 36(1). In Prince Edward Island and British Columbia, the action is commenced according to the ordinary procedure of the Court: P.E.I., sec. 34 and B.C., sec. 30.

In Saskatchewan actions are commenced by the issue of an originating notice; Sask. sec. 46(1). In an action to enforce a lien against a homestead leave of the Court must first be obtained; Sask. sec. 45(2). See *North Amer. Lbr. and Supply Co. v. Sworak* (1958), 27 W.W.R. 111 (Sask.) as to when leave will be granted.

The Acts of most provinces provide that a registered lien will also cease to exist unless an action is commenced to realize the lien and a certificate thereof is registered in the appropriate Registry or Land Titles Office, within the time limited by the Act, or unless within that time an action is commenced by any other person to enforce a lien on the same land: Ont., sec. 23; Nfld., sec. 25; Man., sec. 22; N.S., secs. 25(1), 26; N.B., sec. 27; B.C., sec. 27; Alta., sec. 32. See *Brousseau v. Muircrest Invts. Ltd.* (1977), 15 O.R. (2d) 145 at 155 (C.A.); *Silver v. R. R. Seeton Const. Ltd.* (1977), 74 D.L.R. (3d) 212 (N.S.). See also Chapter 7, Loss or Discharge of Lien, §80, *ante,* and Chapter 10, Jurisdiction, §119, *ante.*

Where no other action is commenced so as to protect him, and the lien claimant fails to commence his own action within the time limited his failure is more than just a procedural error which may be curable, it is a defect going to the very right to a lien and thus an application to extend the time for commencing the action will be dismissed: *Friedman v. Stanton,* [1966] 2 O.R. 59; *Resources Enrg. of Can. Ltd. v. Loch Lomond Shopping Centre Ltd.* (1969), 2 N.B.R. (2d) 629.

Where a Mechanics' Lien action was commenced before a personal action, the Court granted an application for an order staying the personal action, holding that the subsequent personal action was an abuse of the court process, distinguishing *Hamilton Bridge Works Co. v. Gen. Contracting Co.* (1909), 14 O.W.R. 646; *Rockwall Concrete Forming Ltd. v. Robintide Invt. Ltd.* (1977), 15 O.R. (2d) 422. But see *Standard Indust. Ltd. v. E-F Wood Specialties Inc.* (1977), 16 O.R. (2d) 398 where an ordinary action was commenced prior to a Mechanics' Lien action the Court after considering the decisions in the *Hamilton Bridge* and *Rockwall* cases, *supra,* dismissed the defendant's application to stay the ordinary action. See further §83 *ante.*

In Saskatchewan the registered owner or person claiming to be entitled to become the registered owner or a purchaser under agreement of sale may at any time after the registration of the lien require the registrar to notify the lien claimant by registered mail that unless the lien claimant commences action within thirty days from the date of mailing of the notice, and registers the required Certificate of Action, that the lien shall cease to exist. If the lien claimant fails to commence action and register his Certificate of Action within the prescribed period, the lien expires and the registrar must vacate the registration of the lien. A Judge may extend the time for instituting the action under proper circumstances; section 38(1). The British Columbia Act contains a similar provision except the time limit is twenty one days; B.C., secs. 26(1), 27. See *Young Elec. Ltd. v. Kristiansen* (1976), 1 B.C.L.R. 200. There is no discretion in the Court to extend the time: *Mike's Contracting Ltd. v. Dawson Lands Ltd.* (1977), 1 R.P.R. 353.

§146 Pleadings Generally.

The majority of the Acts contemplate only two pleadings in the action, namely, a statement of claim, and a statement of defence: Ont., secs. 29(2), (4), 38(1); Nfld., sec. 31(2), (4); Man., secs. 30, 32(1); N.S. sec. 33(2), (7); N.B., secs. 34, 36; Alta., secs. 36(1), 38(1). In British Columbia, Prince Edward Island and Saskatchewan, the pleadings follow the practice and procedure of the appropriate Court: B.C., sec. 30; P.E.I., sec. 34 and Sask., sec. 46(1).

The degree of technical formality of the pleadings in ordinary actions is not required in mechanics' lien actions. Meredith C.J., in *R. Bickerton &*

Co. v. Dakin (1891), 20 O.R. 695, stated that "it was never intended that the benefits of the Act should be frittered away by requiring the skill of a special pleader to secure them." See also *Barrington v. Martin* (1908), 16 O.L.R. 635 (C.A.); *Fitzgerald and Powell v. Apperley,* [1926] 2 W.W.R. 689 (Sask. C.A.). Moreover the Acts of Ontario (sec. 18(1)), and Newfoundland (sec. 20(1)), specifically provide that a substantial compliance with the provisions respecting the statement of claim and statement of defence is sufficient, and no lien is invalidated by reason of the failure to comply with the provisions unless prejudice is shown, and then only to the extent of the prejudice. Further, in Ontario, when an action in the Judicial District of York has been referred to the Master for trial pursuant to section 31(2), the Master may grant leave to amend any pleadings: sec. 31(4). Amendments under section 31(4) had been restricted to correction of palpable errors or matters of form; *Western Caissons Ltd. v. Toronto Transit Commn.,* [1966] 2 O.R. 528 at 534; *Scarborough Painting Ltd. v. Buckley* (1974), 4 O.R. (2d) 253. These cases have now been overruled and the Court has power to make amendments of substance; *Union Elec. Supply Co. v. Joice Sweanor Elec. Ltd.* (1974), 5 O.R. (2d) 457 (C.A.).

In Ontario, where the lienholder registered his claim for lien and certificate of action in the proper Registry Office, but filed his statement of claim in another County, the Court refused to accept the argument that no action was ever commenced at all by reason of his failure to file the statement of claim with the Court in the county in which the land was situate. The Court stated that the curative section, (sec. 18), in the Ontario Act could be used to remedy the defect: *Handley Lbr. Ltd. v. Ples,* [1971] 2 O.R. 628.

In *John C. Love Lbr. Co. v. Moore,* [1963] 1 O.R. 245 (C.A.), the Court allowed amendments to the statements of claim at trial stating: "The trial having proceeded fully upon the basis of claims personally upon the premises, we think justice demands and we so order, that the respondents and I mean all of the respondents be and they are at liberty to amend their statements of claim as they may be so advised in order to put it beyond all doubt that, as they made abundantly clear in the evidence at trial, they seek to establish liability upon the appellant by way of personal claim as a result of the promises or inducements made by him respectively to them": see also *Don Walker Co. v. Andrews,* [1963] 1 O.R. 358 at 361 (C.A.).

However, in Nova Scotia, leave to amend the plaintiff's statement of claim against an existing mortgagee defendant, which raised a new cause of action against the defendant, was refused as it was held to be barred by the limitation period: *Saltzman v. Eastside Holding & Brokerage Co.* (1971), 2 N.S.R. (2d) 265 (C.A.); *N.S. Sand & Gravel v. Kidstone Estates* (1973), 13 N.S.R. (2d) 431. On an interlocutory application to strike out a lien claimant's action, the owner alleged that the land description was deficient and the relief claimed was improper, and therefore the action not properly commenced. The Court however noted that the defects resulted in no prejudice to the applicant and accordingly amendments were permitted; *C.L. Francis & Co. v. Lunney* (1972), 6 N.B.R. (2d) 728. Where the plaintiff lien claimant moved at trial to amend its statement of claim to change the description of the land where one lot was mistakenly omitted from the legal description, the Court citing *Man. Bridge & Iron Works Ltd. v. Gillespie* (1914), 29 W.L.R. 394, ruled that the defendant owners would suffer no prejudice if the amendment was allowed and accordingly granted the application: *Walter F. Golding Const. Co. v. Bell* (1975), 13 N.B.R. (2d) 47. Similarly, notwithstanding the addition or substitution of a new cause of action, an amendment to the statement of claim was allowed as the new cause of action arose out of substantially the same facts as the original cause of action: *E.S. Martin Const. Ltd. v. Penhorn Mall Ltd.,* (1975), 12 N.S.R. (2d) 331, 62 D.L.R. (3d) 498 (C.A.). See further *Grannan Plumbing & Heating Ltd. v. Simpson Const. Ltd.* (1977), 17 N.B.R. (2d) 569 where the Court allowed amendments in order to permit determination of all questions arising in connection with the lien action.

Where the amount claimed in the statement of claim is too great, an amendment may be made at trial to reduce the amount: *Bradshaw v. Saucerman* (1913), 3 W.W.R. 761, affirming 4 D.L.R. 476 (Y.T. C.A.).

Although the Acts of the remaining provinces have curative sections, they apply to curing defects in claims for lien, and make no reference to pleadings: Man., sec. 17(1); N.S., sec. 20(1); P.E.I., sec. 22; N.B., sec. 22(1); Sask., sec. 33(1); B.C., sec. 22(5) and Alta., sec. 27. Nevertheless, it is submitted that the general principles outlined previously, respecting amendments to pleadings, apply equally to them because the Acts are to be liberally construed in respect of sections dealing with procedure: *Nobbs and Eastman v. C.P.R.* (1913), 6 W.W.R. 759 (Sask.); *R. Bickerton & Co. v. Dakin, supra; Clarke v. Williams,* [1939] 3 W.W.R. 481 (B.C.).

Recently, however, in British Columbia, where the lien claimant had commenced action in the wrong Court, the Court refused to transfer it to the right County Court and dismissed the action: *Tempo Bldg. Supplies Ltd. v. Weston Realty Projects Ltd.* (1973), 32 D.L.R. (3d) 643 (B.C. C.A.). Further, in this province it was held that a Mechanics' Lien action must be commenced in the County Court by Writ and not by Counter-Claim in an action commenced originally in the Small Claims Court: *Lachimia v. Kappert,* [1976] W.W.D. 141. See also Chapter 1, Introduction, §1, *ante,* and §§147, *post* and 135, *ante.*

It is not the practice to amend the claim for lien after the statement of claim has been amended, although in *Fairy and Stephenson v. Doner,* [1947] O.W.N. 217, the Court, after allowing a motion to add a party defendant, indicated that both the statement of claim and the claim for lien should be amended to include the added party. Where the amendment is sought in respect of parties to the action, see §135, *ante*.

§147   The Statement of Claim (Form 10).

There is no prescribed form set out in any of the Acts respecting the statement of claim as there is for the claim for lien. The name and address of the plaintiff and/or his solicitor is required to be endorsed on the statement of claim in some provinces: Man., sec. 31; N.B., sec. 35. In the remaining provinces reference should be made to the decision in *Crerar v. C.P.R.* (1903), 5 O.L.R. 383. The present practice in Ontario, however, is to endorse only the name and address of the plaintiff's solicitor on the statement of claim.

Careful consideration should be given to determining the style of cause in the action, having regard to the difficulty in which the lien claimant may find himself if he must apply for an order adding parties: see §135, *ante*.

In most provinces an action brought by one claimant is deemed to have been brought on behalf of all lien claimants; however, any number of lien claimants on the same land may join in the action: Ont., sec. 30; Nfld., sec. 31(7); Man., sec. 35; N.S., sec. 33(3); P.E.I., sec. 40; N.B., sec. 38; Sask., sec. 46(13). It is not necessary to make any lien claimants parties defendant in the action, but all lien claimants served with the notice of trial or the statement of claim, as the case may be, shall, for all purposes be deemed to be parties to the action: Ont., sec. 29(5); Nfld., sec. 31(5); Man., sec. 34; N.S., sec. 33(4); P.E.I., sec. 43; N.B., sec. 41; Alta., secs. 36(2), 37(2). Where, however, the lien claimant seeks a remedy against another claimant, it is recommended practice in Ontario to name that other lien claimant as a party defendant. Further, in Ontario there is no statutory requirement for a lien claimant, other than the plaintiff commencing the action, to prepare and file a statement of claim. Registered lien claimants already have their claim on record in the Registry Office, and must file a duplicate of the claim for lien, bearing the Registrar's certificate of registration before the trial of the action: sec. 19. It is generally accepted practice, however, if the lien claim is contested, for the Court to request a statement of claim from the particular lien claimant, and allow the defendant to file a statement of defence to the claim. The style of cause of the original plaintiff is usually continued.

The Court's attitude respecting amendments to the particulars pleaded in the statement of claim is more lenient than its attitude respecting amendments to the style of cause. A statement of claim that generally complies with the Act, and sets forth sufficient facts or particulars to disclose the issues to be tried, will be considered adequate, subject to any necessary amendments that may be made before or at trial: *Nelson v. Brewster* (1906), 3 W.L.R. 362 (Alta.); *Roberts v. McDonald* (1887), 15 O.R. 80; *Barrington v. Martin* (1908), 16 O.L.R. 635 (C.A.); *Fitzgerald and*

Powell v. Apperley, [1926] 2 W.W.R. 689 (Sask. C.A.), and see also §146, *ante.*

Where a statement of claim was signed by an articled clerk instead of a barrister or solicitor pursuant to Rule 4 of The Nova Scotia Rules of Practice, the Court held that this was a curable defect where there had been no prejudice to the other party: *Sharon Sales Ltd. v. South Shore Dev. Ltd.* (1971), 3 N.S.R. (2d) 186 (C.A.).

The plaintiff should specifically state in the statement of claim all relief asked for, including a declaration that he is entitled to a lien, and to an order for the sale of the premises in default of payment. If no prejudice has been shown, amendments to the prayer for relief may be made at or before trial: see *Lewis v. Armstrong Bros.* (1957), 18 D.L.R. (2d) 718 (N.B. C.A.), and §§135 and 146, *ante.* It was previously thought that since the various Acts restrict lien claims to the value of the work done, materials supplied or services performed, it would be improper to include in the statement of claim, claims other than for the value of such work, material and services. It was further suggested that damage claims by the lien claimant against the "owner" or other person primarily liable, not being the subject of a lien, could not therefore be claimed in an action to realize upon a lien. These views were questioned as a result of decisions which gave the lien claimant personal judgment for damages for delay over and above the amount found due for work done, materials supplied and services rendered: *Bermingham Const. Ltd. v. Moir Const. Co.,* [1959] O.R. 355 (C.A.); *Earle F. Wakefield Co. v. Oil City Petroleums (Leduc) Ltd.,* [1958] S.C.R. 361, reversing 22 W.W.R. 267; which was affirmed 29 W.W.R. 638 (P.C.), and *Maltby's Ltd. v. Can. Packers Ltd.,* [1947] O.W.N. 757. More recently, an application to strike out the defendant's counterclaim relating to its claim for damages for injury to its name, goodwill and reputation was dismissed on the ground that since there was a direct contractual relationship between the plaintiff lien claimant and the defendant, the matter in issue could more readily be determined in one action: *Aqua-Pond Indust. Ltd. v. Gould* (1974), 3 O.R. (2d) 439. In Ontario, it was held that a claim for damages for loss of tarpaulins rented to a defendant was not the proper subject matter of a Mechanics' Lien nor could the Court award personal judgment on such a claim under section 40 of the Act: *Alros Products Ltd. v. Dalecore Const. Ltd.* (1973), 2 O.R. (2d) 312 (C.A.). See also *A.J. (Archie) Goodale Ltd. v. Risidore Bros. Ltd.* (1975), 8 O.R. (2d) 427 (C.A.). Similarly, in *East Central Gas Co-op. Ltd. v. Henuset Ranches & Const. Ltd.* (1976), 1 Alta. L.R. (2d) 345, affirmed 4 Alta. L.R. (2d) 39 (C.A.), the Court held that damages for loss of prospective profits was not the proper subject matter of the lien pursuant to the Builders' Lien Act (Alberta). Where no work has actually been performed and the claim is for damages for breach of contract by cancellation, no lien lies: *Alspan Wrecking Ltd.*

v. Dineen Const. Ltd., [1972] S.C.R. 829.

See also Chapter 10, Jurisdiction, §127, *ante.*

The argument advanced in favour of allowing the lien claimant to claim for damages in his statement of claim, may be summarized as follows: Although the Acts restrict the lien to the value of the work done, material supplied and services rendered, there is no provision expressly prohibiting a claim for damages. On the contrary the Acts specifically empower the Judge or Officer trying the action to completely dispose of all the questions arising *inter partes* and also empower such Judge or Officer to award personal judgment: Ont., secs. 38(4), 40; Nfld., secs. 38(4), 40; Man., secs. 39, 43; N.S., secs. 34, 45; P.E.I., secs. 45(1), 49; N.B., secs. 43, 46; Sask., secs. 51(1), (2); B.C., secs. 30, 39; Alta., secs. 44, 45(1). Moreover, the argument that the rights (*i.e.* to discovery) a party would have, if the claim for damages were made in an ordinary action, are jeopardized due to the summary procedure of a mechanics' lien action, is not as forceful as in the past, having regard to the fact that most Acts have now expanded such rights: see Chapter 10, Jurisdiction, §120, *ante,* and §156, *post.* If therefore, the lien claimant wishes to include a claim for damages in his mechanics' lien action, he should, in the prayer for relief, differentiate between what amount he claims is lienable and what amount is not, and for which he seeks personal judgment only.

Where the sole purpose of a lien filed against an owner's land was to unlawfully force settlement of the contractor's claim an action for damages lies against the claimant: *Guilford Indust. Ltd. v. Hankinson Management Services Ltd.,* [1974] 1 W.W.R. 141 (B.C.). In this case, the defendant filed liens for outrageous sums for which there was no legal foundation encumbering the lands of the plaintiff for a long period of time and thereby preventing the sale of the land. The Court noted that the lien proceedings "were initiated for an unlawful purpose, namely, to obtain a settlement by means of legal 'blackmail'". The Court awarded the plaintiff general damages in the sum of $50,000 and exemplary damages in the sum of $10,000, citing *Rookes v. Barnard,* [1964] A.C. 1129, [1964] 1 All E.R. 367 at 410, where the Court stated "Where a defendant with a cynical disregard for a plaintiff's rights has caluculated that the money to be made out of his wrongdoing will probably exceed the damages at risk, it is necessary for the law to show that it cannot be broken with impunity".

§148 Affidavit Verifying the Statement of Claim.

The New Brunswick Act (sec. 34), is the only Act which provides that the statement of claim must be verified by affidavit. In *Resources Enrg. of Can. Ltd. v. Bathurst Shopping Centre Ltd.* (1969), 1 N.B.R. (2d) 924, the Court held that an affidavit verifying the statement of claim, which was irregular as to form, in that it was sworn before a Commissioner for taking oaths rather than a Notary Public, as required for affidavits sworn outside the province, was a nullity and, therefore, no action at law had been commenced. The Court therefore, refused an order extending the statutory period of 90 days for filing the statement of claim in order that a re-sworn affidavit of verification could be filed.

A similar provision to the New Brunswick Act was some time ago deleted from the Ontario Act, but the cases decided under the Ontario section may still be of some general application in New Brunswick. Absence of the affidavit verifying the statement of claim renders the claim a nullity, and also precludes the claimant from obtaining a personal judgment: *Lewis v. Armstrong Bros.* (1957), 18 D.L.R. (2d) 718 (N.B. C.A.). It has been held that the affidavit may be made by the plaintiff's agent or assignee, if such agent or assignee has knowledge of the facts set out in the statement of claim, and the affidavit so states: *Lemon v. Young* (1916), 10 O.W.N. 82 (C.A.). Where an affidavit verifying a claim for lien was made by the wife of the solicitor of the lien claimant who did not have personal knowledge of the facts deposed to, the lien claim was held to be a nullity: *Bazarin v. Pezim*, [1965] 1 O.R. 606. Formerly, in Ontario, the affidavit verifying the statement of claim could not be sworn by the claimant's own solicitor or it was a nullity, and would thereby nullify the statement of claim: *Lewis v. Armstrong Bros., supra; R. V. Demmings & Co. v. Caldwell Const. Co.* (1955), 4 D.L.R. (2d) 465 (N.B. C.A.); *McLean v. Leth*, [1950] 1 W.W.R. 536, affirming (*sub nom. Geo. D. McLean and Associates Ltd. v. Leth*) [1949] 4 D.L.R. 282 (B.C. C.A.); *Braden v. Brown*, [1917] 3 W.W.R. 906 (B.C. C.A.). The following cases may be of some further assistance on this subject: *Burchill v. Marino*, [1951] 2 D.L.R. 518 (N.B.); *Northey v. Wood* (1951), 4 W.W.R. 271 (B.C. C.A.); *W. J. Trick Co. v. Ont. Potteries Co.* (1923), 25 O.W.N. 369 (C.A.); *Bruce v. Nat. Trust Co.* (1913), 4 O.W.N. 1372; *Lemon v. Young, supra; Barrington v. Martin* (1908), 16 O.L.R. 635 (C.A.); *Martello v. Barnet* (1925), 57 O.L.R. 670 (C.A.); *Richardson v. Lohn* (1932) 46 B.C.R. 224; *Can. Sand etc. Co. v. Poole* (1907), 10 O.W.R. 1041. It was held in *Crerar v. C.P.R.* (1903), 5 O.L.R. 383, that the plaintiff's solicitor may, however, execute the affidavit as agent for the plaintiff. It was held in *Clarkson Const. Co. v. Shaw,* [1950] O.W.N. 196, that the question of the validity of the affidavit verifying the statement of claim should be dealt with at trial and not on an interlocutory motion. The Ontario Court has held that if a statement of claim on behalf of one plaintiff is against more than one property, only one affidavit is necessary: *Martello v. Barnet, supra*.

§149   Certificate of Action.

In Ontario, the action is commenced by filing the statement of claim in the proper Court Office. A certificate of the action thus commenced (in some jurisdictions called a certificate of *lis pendens*) is obtained from this office and the plaintiff then registers this certificate in the Registry Office in which the land involved is situate: secs. 22(2), 23(1). The Acts of the following provinces have the same provision respecting the registration of the certificate of action or *lis pendens:* Nfld., secs. 24(2), 25(1); Man., sec. 22; N.S., secs. 25(1), 26; N.B., sec. 27; B.C., secs. 26(1), 27; Alta., sec. 32, and Sask., secs. 37(1), 38(1); the Act of Prince Edward Island has no requirement that a certificate of action be obtained and registered.

Except in Saskatchewan, the failure to register a certificate of action within the time prescribed by the various Acts is fatal to the claimant's right to a lien: *Dunn v. Holbrook* (1899), 7 B.C.R. 503 (C.A.); *St. Clair Const. Co. v. Farrell* (1921), 49 O.L.R. 201 (C.A.); *McCoubrey v. Carver Const. Co.,* [1942] 3 W.W.R. 648 (B.C.); *Ogilvie v. Cooke,* [1952] O.R. 862 (C.A.); Sask., sec. 37(2). See further §145, Commencement of action.

The reasoning behind this appears to be that because the various Acts specifically require the registration of such a certificate within a specified time otherwise the lien even when registered is lost and ceases to exist, the complete failure to so register is more than a procedural error which the Courts have seen fit to cure, but goes rather to the very right of a lien and in the latter case the Courts will apply a strict interpretation to the Act: see *Constable v. Belvedere Holdings (1962) Ltd.* (1966), 58 W.W.R. 96 (Y.T. C.A.); *Friedman v. Stanton,* [1966] 2 O.R. 59; *Resources Enrg. of Can. Ltd. v. Bathurst Shopping Centre Ltd.* (1969), 1 N.B.R. (2d) 924; *Resources Enrg. of Can. Ltd. v. Loch Lomond Shopping Centre Ltd.* (1969), 2 N.B.R. (2d) 629 and Chapter 7, Loss or Discharge of Lien, §80, *ante,* and Chapter 10, Jurisdiction, §119, *ante.* However, in *Dom. Const. Co. (Niagara) Ltd. v. Branscombe,* [1970] 2 O.R. 523 (C.A), the Ontario Court of Appeal held that the claimant's lien was valid even though the certificate of action was registered after the required time, because funds were subsequently paid into Court pursuant to an order under section 25(4)(*a*) (presently section 25(2)(*a*)) of the Ontario Act. Under section 25(5) (presently 25(3)) where an order was made pursuant to section 25(4)(*a*), the lien did not cease to exist because a certificate of action had not been registered. As a result, section 25(5) was held to qualify the effect of non-compliance with section 23 respecting the registration of a certificate of action within 90 days after the last work is done or the last material is supplied. Section 25(3) has recently been amended to alleviate the problem raised in this case.

In British Columbia it was held to be unnecessary and improper to register a Certificate of *lis pendens* after payment into Court has been made under section 33(1): *Universal Supply Co. v. S. Radatske Const. Co.* (1973), 29 D.L.R. (3d) 251 (B.C. C.A.); *Re Van Horne Elec. Ltd.* (1977), 2 B.C.L.R. 71 (C.A.). A similar result was reached in Alberta: *Re Driden Indust. Ltd. and Sieber* (1974), 44 D.L.R. (3d) 629 (Alta. C.A.).

Where, however, the lien claimant commencing the action does obtain and register a certificate of the action, but that certificate, or the registration thereof, is in some way defective, the reported cases are in conflict. In *Curtis v. Richardson* (1909), 18 Man. R. 519, the Court held that the certificate must comply with the statutory form. Accordingly, a certificate, to the effect that some title or interest in the land was called in question, without any reference therein to a mechanics' lien, was not a sufficient compliance with the statute and was therefore invalid. However, negligence of the Registrar in the registration of a certificate of action will not prejudice the lien claimant: *Gorman, Clancey and Grindley v. Archibald* (1908), 1 Alta. L.R. 524; *Lawrie v. Rathbun* (1876), 38 U.C.Q.B. 255 (C.A.). Moreover, in a recent Ontario decision, the Court in *Peter Leitch Const. Ltd. v. Aquativity Ltd.*, [1971] 2 O.R. 666, held that where the Registrar refused to allow the claimant to register both a claim for lien and a certificate of his action against unpatented lands, but did allow same to be put on title by way of deposit, the action was properly commenced. The Court in this case relied upon the curative section (sec. 18) of the Ontario Act. The recent trend, at least in Ontario, is to rely upon the curative section of the Act respecting defects in form or registration of the certificate of action within the prescribed time. In this regard, it should be noted that the curative section of the Ontario and Newfoundland Acts is somewhat wider than those of other provinces: Ont., sec. 18; Nfld., sec. 20(1) and §146, *ante*. But see, in Alberta, *Summers' Agricultural Services Ltd. v. Vacation Properties Ltd.*, [1972] 2 W.W.R. 477.

In Ontario, it is not the practice to amend the certificate of action if an amendment is made to the statement of claim after the certificate of action is registered: *Fairy and Stephenson v. Doner*, [1947] O.W.N. 217; *Simac v. Waltman*, [1947] O.W.N. 264.

§150   Service of the Statement of Claim.

In Ontario, the statement of claim must be served within 30 days after it has been filed: sec. 29(3). The time for service may be extended by the Judge having jurisdiction, or, in the Judicial District of York, by the Master: sec. 29(3) (see Form 53). The Court stated in *Campbell v. Turner*, [1937] 1 W.W.R. 228 (Man. C.A.), and *Pease Heating Co. v. Bulmer* (1908), 12 O.W.R. 258, that the application must be made at the earliest opportunity, and an adequate reason must be given for inability to serve within the proper time. However, in *Orr v. Davie* (1892), 22 O.R. 430, Boyd C. declared, "I should think it almost a matter of course to extend the period unless the Master was satisfied that the proceeding ... was frivolous or an abuse of the process of the Court." A motion to dismiss a lien action on the ground that the statement of claim was not served within the month required by the former Ontario Act was dismissed where no prejudice was shown: *Moyer v.*

Martin, [1951] O.W.N. 395 (C.A.). See also Ont., sec. 18 and Nfld., sec. 20(1).

An order must be obtained for service of the statement of claim out of the jurisdiction: *Sakalo v. Tassotti,* [1963] 2 O.R. 537 (C.A.); *MacDonald v. Consol. Gold Mining Co.* (1901), 21 C.L.T. 482 (N.S.); *McIver v. Crown Point Mining Co.* (1900), 19 P.R. 335. As a statement of claim in a mechanics' lien action is analogous to a writ of summons in an ordinary action, the mode of service should follow as closely as possible the rules in connection with the latter: *Sakalo v. Tassotti, supra.* Personal service is mandatory unless an order for substitutional service is obtained: sec. 47 (see Form 52); *R. Bickerton & Co. v. Dakin* (1890), 20 O.R. 695; *Orr v. Davie, supra; Pearcy v. Foster* (1921), 51 O.L.R. 354.

The Acts of Newfoundland (secs. 31(3), 47), and Nova Scotia (sec. 33(6), are to the same effect as that of Ontario with respect to the time allowed for serving the Statement of Claim, except that the time limit in Nova Scotia is expressed to be within one month after filing the statement of claim.

The Acts of the remaining provinces do not specify the time for and the manner of serving the document that is required to commence action, and as a result, reference should be made to the relevant Court's rules of practice: Alta., sec. 50; B.C., sec. 30; Sask., sec. 59(2); P.E.I., sec. 34; Man., secs. 28, 57; N.B., sec. 61(1) and see *Anderson Mfg. Co. v. Boulay* (1969), 1 N.B.R. (2d) 717. It should be noted, however, that the Acts of New Brunswick and Prince Edward Island specifically allow service of such document upon the defendant whether he is within or without the jurisdiction: N.B., sec. 34; P.E.I., sec. 37(1).

§151 Statement of Defence.

In Ontario, the defendant is required to deliver his statement of defence within the same time as that prescribed for entering an appearance in the Supreme Court: sec. 29(4). Rule 35 of the Ontario Supreme Court Rules of Practice provides that where served within Ontario, a defendant shall appear within 10 days of being served, including the day of service. If the plaintiff obtains an order allowing service upon the defendant outside of Ontario, the order usually extends the time required for delivery of the statement of defence. Generally, to the same effect are: N.S., sec. 33(7); B.C., sec. 30; Alta., sec. 38(1), and Sask., sec. 47(2), (3) — 20 days. In Newfoundland, the time is 10 days: sec. 31(4) and in Manitoba and Prince Edward Island, the time is 16 days: Man., sec. 32(1); P.E.I., sec. 38. With the exception of Ontario, British Columbia, Nova Scotia, Alberta and Saskatchewan, the Acts of the remaining provinces specifically empower the Court to extend the time for delivery of the statement of defence: Nfld., sec. 31(4); Man., sec. 32(2); P.E.I., sec. 38; N.B., sec. 36(2). In those provinces which do not provide for such an extension, reference should be made to the relevant Rules of Practice: see Chapter 10, Jurisdiction, §120, *ante.*

In Ontario (sec. 38(3)), and Newfoundland (sec. 38(3)), any person who is served with a statement of claim, and who subsequently makes default in delivering a statement of defence, shall nevertheless be served with notice of trial, and is entitled to defend on such terms as to costs and otherwise as the Judge or Officer trying the action may deem just. The Court interpreted the Ontario section in *Ron-Dal Contractors Ltd. v. Ondrey* (1974), 3 O.R. (2d) 290 (C.A.), as allowing a defendant to set up not only a defence but to permit a counterclaim to be brought before the Court.

In a recent Manitoba case it was held that section 39(2) does not bring within the ambit of that province's Act all actions beyond the scope of the Act and particularly does not authorize the joining of a party as a defendant through a counterclaim in order to obtain a personal judgment against that party for what amounts to an allegation of tortious conduct based on negligent misrepresentation: *Western Caissons (Man.) Ltd. v. Trident Const. Ltd.* (1975), 54 D.L.R. (3d) 289 (Man.).

The Court in *Elliott v. Rowell* (1916), 11 O.W.N. 203, stated that: "The plaintiff must prove his claim in open Court and submit it to full investigation and to any contest which the lienholders and subsequent encumbrancers may choose to make against it." See also *Robertson v. Bullen* (1908), 13 O.W.R. 56. A default judgment signed after failure of the defendant to file a Statement of Defence at the "pre-trial" in Ontario was set aside as the Appellant Court held that the "pre-trial" hearing procedure was not a trial: *Kennedy Glass Ltd. v. Jeskay Const. Co.,* [1973] 3 O.R. 493 (Div.Ct.). However, the Acts of some provinces provide that judgment may be obtained for default in delivering a Statement of Defence: P.E.I., sec. 38(2); N.B., sec. 36(2); Man., sec. 32(1) and Alta., sec. 39(3) (after pre-trial). And see further Chapter 10, Jurisdiction, §133(*b*), *ante,* for a discussion of default judgments generally.

With the exception of Nova Scotia, none of the Acts make provision for a form for the statement of defence: see N.S., sec. 46 and Forms G and H of that province's Act. Thus, in other jurisdictions the format of the statement of defence is governed by the relevant Rules of Practice: see Chapter 10, Jurisdiction, §120, *ante.* As with the statement of claim, the technical rules of pleading in an ordinary action are not as stringently applied in mechanics' lien actions: see §146, *ante.* See also *Don Walker Co. v. Andrews,* [1963] 1 O.R. 358 (C.A.), where one of the grounds of appeal was that the trial Judge had allowed evidence to be adduced on behalf of the defendant owner to show payment by a promissory note given by the owner to the contractor who subsequently negotiated it to a supplier, although this was not pleaded. The Court of Appeal indicated that the owner was merely called upon to place before the Court all payments to or against the contractor, and then it was encumbent upon the Court to take accounts considering all relevant claims by either party whether or not such amounts had been pleaded in detail. If necessary, the Court was willing to direct an amendment, since no party had been prejudiced.

The owner may defend on any grounds available to him, and is not prejudiced by the conduct or lack of defence of his contractor as co-defendant: see *Haggerty v. Grant* (1892), 2 B.C.R. 173. In this case the plaintiff brought action against the contractor and owner. Judgment by default was given against the contractor. The Court permitted the validity of the lien, and the amount alleged to be owing, to be disputed by the defendant owner, notwithstanding that a judgment had already been given specifying an amount owing by the contractor to the subcontractor.

The validity of the lien may be attacked and the quantum not disputed. The most common defence of this nature is that the registration of the claim for lien or certificate of action is defective due to factors such as the expiry of the time limited by the Act, or the registration of the lien upon the wrong property. In New Brunswick, the Court of Appeal upheld the validity of a lien claim where the evidence at trial disclosed that the action had been commenced within the proper time although there was no proof that a Certificate of Action had been registered and the issue had not been raised at trial. The Court stated that if there had in fact been a failure to file the Certificate required by the Act, the failure to do so was a matter pending the action to be pleaded as a ground of defence under the New Brunswick Rules of Court: *Annett Chemicals Ltd. v. Moncton* (1971), 3 N.B.R. (2d) 698 (C.A.).

The lack of the required law stamps on the statement of claim will not affect its validity, and will not form the basis of a valid defence: *James Henderson & Sons v. Russell House Ltd.,* [1931] 1 W.W.R. 342 (B.C.). Less common defences of this nature are, that the work or service performed or material supplied is not the proper subject matter of a lien, or that there is no statutory "owner" upon whose estate or interest a lien could attach, or that the property in question is of such a nature as to be immune to the provisions of The Mechanics' Lien Act. A defence that "the plaintiff is not entitled to the lien asked for" was held to be an improper pleading as it was a conclusion of law: *Imperial Elevator Co. v. Welch* (1906), 16 Man. R. 136, and it was therefore ordered stricken from the statement of defence.

If no question of the validity of the lien is raised, the amount owing may be disputed and the defence of set-off is available to a defendant. Moreover, the defendant may counterclaim for damages he has occasioned. Pleas of inferior material, bad workmanship, or nonconformity to contract are proper constituents of the statement of defence and counterclaim.

In *Langlais v. Lavoie* (1975), 12 N.B.R. (2d) (C.A.), where the

363

defendant claimed a set-off for improper workmanship and failed to plead a counterclaim, even though the set-off was in excess of the plaintiff's claim, the defendant was held entitled only to judgment dismissing the plaintiff's action.

Damages have been allowed against plaintiffs for delay, non-completion and loss of use of moneys that would have been payable by the owner to the contractor but for the lien claimant's delay.

In Ontario a counterclaim for damages for injuries to the defendant's name, goodwill, and reputation, and damages suffered under a separate contract completely unrelated to that which formed the subject matter of the Mechanics' Lien Action were held to be valid pleas: *Aqua-Pond Indust. Ltd. v. Gould* (1974), 3 O.R. (2d) 439.

For a discussion of the principles respecting set-off, damages and counterclaim, see Chapter 4, Rights and Duties of the Owner, §§41, 42, 45 and 46, *ante;* Chapter 10, Jurisdiction, §§125 and 127, *ante,* and Chapter 3, The Lien Claimant, §29(*e*), *ante.*

With respect to the amending of the statement of defence, see §§135, 146 and 147, *ante.* See further *R. Bickerton & Co. v. Dakin* (1890), 20 O.R. 695; *Orr v. Davie* (1892), 22 O.R. 430; *Pearcy v. Foster* (1921), 51 O.L.R. 354; *Crawford v. Wojtyna,* [1953] O.W.N. 369; *Don Walker Co. v. Andrews, supra.*

In *Can. Lbr. Yards Ltd. v. Paulson,* [1922] 2 W.W.R. 465 (Sask.), the Saskatchewan Court held that only in exceptional cases should the Judge refuse to accept admissions deemed to be made in default of pleadings. In *Boucher v. Belle-Isle* (1913), 41 N.B.R. 509 (C.A.), the statement of defence denied the filing of the lien in time. At trial, the plaintiff did not prove that the filing was in time, but no objection was taken by the defendant. On appeal it was held that it was clearly the duty of the plaintiff to prove his whole case, a part of which was that the lien was properly in existence, and this was so, notwithstanding the absence of objection at trial. Under section 21(1) of the Ontario Act, it is a condition precedent to the continuance of the right of a claimant to a lien that the claim should be registered within 37 days after the completion or abandonment of the contract. If the performance of this condition precedent is intended to be contested, it must be distinctly specified in the pleadings of the defendant: *Hulshan v. Nickling,* [1957] O.W.N. 587 (C.A.). See also Ontario Rules of Practice, Rule 146, in this respect.

§152   The Reference.

The Acts of Ontario and Manitoba contain specific provisions in respect of referring the action or a question in the action to a judicial officer for trial or enquiry.

In Ontario, section 31(2) provides that in actions commenced in the

Judicial District of York (Toronto area) on motion after defence or defence to counterclaim has been delivered, or the time for delivery of same has expired, a Judge of the Supreme Court may refer the whole action to the Master for trial pursuant to section 72 of the Judicature Act or at trial may direct a reference to the Master pursuant to section 71 or 72 of the Judicature Act. Where the parties do not consent and the other conditions referred to in section 72 of the Judicature Act are not present the Mechanics' Lien Action in the Judicial District of York must be heard by a judge of the Supreme Court: *V.K. Mason Const. Ltd. v. Courtot Invts. Ltd.* (1975), 9 O.R. (2d) 325. In practice, however, lien actions in the Judicial District of York are usually tried by a Master: see *Orlando Masonry Contractors v. Dinardo,* [1971] 3 O.R. 774.

Section 32 then provides that a master to whom a reference for trial has been directed shall have all the jurisdiction, authority and power of the Supreme Court to try and completely dispose of the action. Where a counterclaim was related to questions arising out of a separate contract not related to the property in question in the Mechanics' Lien Action, the Court found that the Master would not have jurisdiction to dispose of the counterclaim and accordingly the matter was not referred to him: *Aqua-Pond Indust. Ltd. v. Gould* (1974), 3 O.R. (2d) 439.

In Manitoba, section 56 provides that in actions brought in the County Court of Winnipeg, a Judge of the Court may refer the action to the referee of the Court of Queen's Bench and after enquiries and accounts are made and taken by the referee, he embodies them in a report for which, upon adoption thereof, the Judge shall give judgment.

None of the other Acts have a similar provision.

§153 Representation.

In Ontario, any lienholder may be represented by an agent who is not a barrister and solicitor, where he claims an amount not exceeding $200.00: sec. 38(8). See also N.S., sec. 34(5).

§154 Interlocutory Proceedings.

The Ontario Act specifically provides for the following interlocutory proceedings:

(a) Where a certificate of action has been registered for 2 years or more and no appointment has been taken out for trial, any interested party on an *ex parte* motion may obtain an order vacating the certificate of action and discharging all liens dependent thereon: sec. 22(3). (See Form 84.)

(b) An order may be made allowing security for, or payment into Court of, the amount of the claim or claims for lien, and costs, thereupon vacating the lien or liens and certificate of action. The order may be made on any other proper ground and the Court has power to dismiss the action under this section: sec. 25(2). (See Forms 46, 47 and 48.)

Generally, lien claimants are entitled to have paid into Court the highest amount for which the owner could reasonably be foreseen to be liable: *Otis Elevator Co. v. Commonwealth Holiday Inns of Can. Ltd.,* [1972] 2 O.R. 536. The Court in this case added an amount of less than 10% for costs. In addition, the owner was given the option of paying the amount into Court or, alternatively, furnishing security by way of a bond, in accordance with the Guarantee Companies Securities Act, R.S.O. 1970, c. 196. In many cases the security allowed is a bond (see form 96) or a letter of credit (see form 97) approved by the Court. In Ontario see the Guarantee Companies Securities Act, R.S.O. 1970, c. 196 and R.R.O. 1970 Regulation 387 for the list of approved Guarantee Companies.

In a recent application by an owner to pay moneys into Court, where there were duplication of liens by the subcontractors and the general contractor, the Court ruled that the total security should be equal to the lien amount claimed by the general contractor plus a reasonable amount for costs: *Nation Drywall Contractors Ltd. v. All Round Properties Administration Ltd.* (1975), 10 O.R. (2d) 295. See also *Re Cloverlawn Invts. Ltd.* (1977), 7 A.C.W.S., 251.

In an originating application to allow security for or payment into Court and for an order that the registration of several liens be vacated, pursuant to the Mechanics' Lien Act of Nova Scotia (section 28(4)), the Court permitted the applicant to file a supplementary affidavit supplying the contract price and the amount paid to the contractor. Accordingly, the Court was prepared to grant the application upon satisfaction that the amount offered to be paid in as security would be the maximum amount payable by the owner on the contract price including extras, after deducting the amount already lawfully paid to the contractor and the amounts previously paid into Court as security: *Re Cloverlawn Invts. Ltd.,* (1977), 7 A.C.W.S. 251. However, a pleading by a defendant in a lien action of set-off and counterclaim will not be considered or applied in the reduction of the amount to be paid into Court: *Bristol Const. Co. v. D. K. Invts. Ltd.,* [1972] 4 W.W.R. 119 (B.C.).

In British Columbia the Court held that the Mechanics' Lien Act did not permit it to reduce the amount of the security already paid into Court: *E. A. Parker Devs. Ltd. v. Doric Devs. Ltd.,* [1977] 3 W.W.R. 191 (B.C.). See also *Re Pecco Cranes (Can.) Ltd.,* [1973] 3 O.R. 737.

In *Saccary v. Jackson* (1975), 11 N.S.R. (2d) 316 (C.A.) a Nova Scotia Court refused to dismiss the plaintiff's action under the "on any other proper ground", sub-section of the Act since there were questions of law involved which should be dealt with at the time of the trial when all the facts were before the Court.

(c) If a certificate of action has not been registered within the prescribed time, an *ex parte* order may be made vacating the registration of the claim for lien upon production of the certificate of search of the proper Registrar of deeds together with a certified copy of the registered claim for lien: sec. 25(5). (See Form 83 and *Armitage v. Beaver Lbr. Co.,* [1973] 1 O.R. 418.

(d) Where money has been paid into Court or a bond deposited, the Court may, upon such notice to the parties as it requires, order the money to be paid out of Court to the persons entitled thereto or the delivery up of the bond for cancellation, as the case may be: sec. 25(6). See *Bond Structural Steel (1965) Ltd. v. Cloverlawn Invts. Ltd.,* [1973] 3 O.R. 856, and *Carefree Design Enterprises Ltd. v. Nat. Trailer Convoy of Can. Ltd.,* [1976] W.W.D. 174 (B.C.).

(e) An order may be made requiring the "owner" or his agent, or the mortgagee or his agent, or the unpaid vendor or his agent, or the contractor or his agent, or the subcontractor or his agent, as the case may be, to produce and permit any lien claimant to inspect any contract or agreement, or mortgage, or agreement for sale, on the accounts, or any other relevant document upon such terms as to costs as may be deemed just: sec. 28(3). (See Form 85.)

(f) If the plaintiff fails to serve his statement of claim within one month after it is filed, he may obtain an order extending the time for service: sec. 29(3). (See Form 53.)

(g) A motion may be made for an order to speed the trial of the action: sec. 29(6). (See Form 37.)

(h) Outside the Judicial District of York, an order may be made directing the action to be tried by a Judge of the Supreme Court: sec. 31(1). (See Forms 23 and 24.)

(i) In the Judicial District of York, an order may be made referring the whole action, or a question arising therein, to the Master: sec. 31(2). (See Form 25.) See *V.K. Mason Const. Ltd. v. Courtot Invts. Ltd.* (1975), 9 O.R. (2d) 325.

(j) Where an order has been made referring the whole action to the Master for trial, any person brought into the proceedings subsequent to this order and served with notice of trial may obtain an order setting aside the judgment directing the reference: sec. 31(3). (See Forms 24 and 36.)

(k) Where an action is referred to the Master for trial, an order may be obtained granting leave to amend any pleading: sec. 31(4). (See Form 86.) *Union Elec. Supply Co. v. Joice Sweanor Elec. Ltd.* (1974), 5 O.R. (2d) 457 (C.A.).

(l) The Court may order the appointment of a receiver: sec. 34(1). (See Forms 27, 28 and 29.)

(m) The Court may order the appointment of a trustee: sec. 34(2). (See Forms 30, 31, 32, 33 and 34.)

(n) Where a trustee is appointed the Court may order that the property be offered for sale subject to any mortgage or encumbrance: sec. 34(3).

(o) Where a trustee is appointed, an order may be made for the completion of any mortgage, lease or sale, and for the vesting of the property in a purchaser and for possession, before the trial of the action: sec. 34(5), (6). (See Forms 32 and 78.)

(p) Where more than one action has been brought, an order may be made consolidating the actions and giving conduct of the consolidated action to any plaintiff: sec. 36. (See Form 51.)

(q) An order may be made giving carriage of proceedings to any lienholder: sec. 37.

(r) An application may be made to the Judge or Officer having jurisdiction to fix a date for trial: sec. 38(1). (See Forms 40 and 41.)

(s) The Judge or Officer having jurisdiction may order service of notice of trial in any manner he deems necessary: sec. 38(2).

(t) The Court may make an order for the preservation of any property pending the determination of the action or any appeal: sec. 35. (See Form 34.)

(u) An application may be made to the Court for directions as to pleadings, discovery, production or any matter relating to the action or reference including the cross-examination of a lien claimant or his agent or assignee on his affidavit verifying the claim: sec. 38(10). See *Kleenaire Equipment Ltd. v. Dennis Commercial Properties Ltd.,* [1970] 3 O.R. 776. (See Forms 50 and 57.) There is no jurisdiction to compel a deponent on an affidavit verifying a claim for lien to submit to cross-examination on the affidavit prior to the action being commenced or the reference being ordered: *Re Pecco Cranes (Can.) Ltd.,* [1973] 3 O.R. 737.

(v) After judgment the Court may make all necessary orders for the completion of the sale and for vesting of the property in a purchaser: sec. 39(2). (See Forms 68-81.)

(w) After judgment the Court may vary the form of judgment to meet the circumstances of the case: sec. 38(5).

(x) After trial, the Court may allow a lien claimant who did not prove his claim at trial to be let in to prove his claim: sec. 38(7). (See Form 54.)

(y) The Court may direct in what manner service of documents should be made: sec. 47.

(z) Where an architect, engineer or other person, neglects or refuses to issue and deliver a certificate upon which payments are to be made under a contract or subcontract, the Court may make an order that the work or materials to which the certificate would have related has been done or placed or furnished and any such order has the same force and effect as if the certificate had been issued and delivered by the architect, engineer or other person: sec. 11(4).

For those applications which are provided for in the Acts of the other provinces reference should be made to the Table of Concordant Sections, *post*.

The Ontario Act (sec. 46(2)), further provides that, with the exception of the foregoing, no interlocutory proceedings are permitted without an order of the Judge or Officer having jurisdiction, and then only upon proper proof that such proceedings are necessary. See also Nfld., sec. 46(2); Sask. sec. 58(2). In *Aqua-Pond Indust. Ltd. v. Gould* (1974), 3 O.R. (2d) 439, the Ontario Court granted consent pursuant to section 46(2) *pro tunc*.

In an early Ontario decision of *Robertson v. Bullen* (1908), 13 O.W.R. 56, it was stated that interlocutory motions are to be discouraged. The general propriety of this earlier statement is to be doubted in view of the nature of many of today's mechanics' lien actions. Moreover, the Ontario Act now provides that the ordinary Rules of Practice of the Court apply unless otherwise provided in the Act: Ont., sec. 46(4) and see also Chapter 10, Jurisdiction, §120, *ante*. Motions for a summary disposition of lien actions are discussed in §133, *ante*. Motions to amend pleadings and add parties have previously been referred to in this Chapter. A motion for particulars was refused in *Rowlin v. Rowlin* (1907), 9 O.W.R. 297, as the small amount of the claim did not warrant the expense of obtaining particulars. The basic object of the Act, to enforce liens at the least expense, having regard to the amount and nature of the lien, (Ont., sec. 46(1)), usually guides the Judge or Officer hearing interlocutory applications. See also *King v. Georgetown Floral Co.* (1904), 3 O.W.R. 587, and *V. K. Mason Const. Ltd. v. Courtot Invts. Ltd.* (1974), 6 O.R. (2d) 655. The Court stated in *Muttart Bldrs. Supplies Ltd. v. Hutton Const. (Brantford) Ltd.*, [1973] 2 O.R. 238 at 245 "Sometimes the informality and expediency which the Act directs, can result in added expense rather than savings". See also *Macon Drywall Systems Ltd. v. H. P. Hyatt Const. Ltd.* (1973), 17 C.B.R. (N.S.) 6 (Ont.).

There is no right of appeal in Ontario from an order made on an interlocutory motion in a mechanics' lien action: *R. v. Algoma Dist. Ct. Judge, Ex parte Consol. Denison Mines Ltd.*, [1958] O.W.N. 330; appeal quashed (*sub nom. Perini Ltd. v. Consol. Denison Mines Ltd.*) [1959] O.W.N. 119 (C.A.); *Moyer v. Martin*, [1951] O.W.N. 395 (C.A.); *Pearcy v. Foster* (1921), 51 O.L.R. 354; *Douglas Elec. Co. v. Tremaine* (1925), 28 O.W.N. 75; *McAuley v. Mansfield* (1922), 53 O.L.R. 68. See also *Yoles & Rotenberg Ltd. v. H. H. Robertson Co.* (1920), 18 O.W.N. 85; *Western Caissons Ltd. v. Toronto Transit Commn.*, [1966] 2 O.R. 528 at 534, affirming [1966] 2 O.R. 528 at 529; *Albern Mechanical Ltd. v. Newcon Const. Ltd.*, [1971] 1 O.R. 350; *Livingston & Sons Ltd. v. Anglehart*, [1958]

O.W.N. 197 (C.A.); *Bennett & Wright Contractors Ltd. v. H.E.P.C. Ont.,* [1972] 1 O.R. 20; *Macon Drywall Systems Ltd. v. H. P. Hyatt Const. Ltd.,* [1972] 3 O.R. 189, but see *Kleenaire Equipment Ltd. v. Dennis Commercial Properties Ltd., supra,* and §172, *post.*

It has been held that if the matter in appeal is from an Order and not a judgment or report that there is no right of appeal: *Jim-Mac Const. Ltd. v. Julann Devs. Ltd.,* Ont. Div. Ct., Holland J., September 17, 1974 (in the process of being reported).

§155   Security for Costs.

In *A. P. Green Fire Brick Co. v. Interprov. Steel Corpn. Ltd.* (1964), 48 W.W.R. 449 (Sask.), the defendant owner applied for security for costs against the plaintiff lien claimant. The defendant argued that such an application was permissible in a mechanics' lien action because section 46 of the Saskatchewan Act provided that such actions were to be tried in the District Court in the same manner as ordinary actions. The Court agreed with this contention, but refused the order on the following grounds: the lien action before the Court was a class action and thus the plaintiff was not *dominus litus;* the defendant having pleaded set-off and being required to prove same, at trial, was itself a plaintiff in the issues to be tried, and finally since the defendant had not held back the required percentage, he was a party to his own insecurity as to costs.

This decision raises significant questions as to whether such an application can be maintained in other provinces. The Act of Nova Scotia provides that an action to realize a lien is enforceable in the County Court according to the ordinary procedure of such Court, except to the extent varied by the Act: N.S., sec. 33. The following provinces have similar provisions: B.C., sec. 30; Man., secs. 28, 57; P.E.I., sec. 34; N.B., sec. 61(1). In Ontario, the action is enforced by action in the Supreme Court, and unless otherwise provided by the Act, the Rules of Practice and procedure of such Court are made applicable: Ont., secs. 29(1), 46(4). See to the same effect: Sask., sec. 59(2); Nfld., secs. 31(1), 46(4) and Alta., sec. 50. See also Chapter 10, Jurisdiction, §120, *ante.*

As a result, therefore, in each province the procedure and Rules of Practice of the relevant Court are made applicable to lien actions, and thus it would appear that an application for security for costs may be made. However, the object of all Mechanics' Lien Acts is to provide an inexpensive method to realize upon a lien, and thus proceedings should be of a summary nature: *e.g.,* Ont., sec. 46(1), (2). Whether this object of the Act will of itself hinder such an application is not as yet known, and until such time, as the Courts of the other provinces judicially determine the matter, in respect of the wording of that province's Act, the matter will remain in doubt. See *Caruso v. Campanile,* [1972] 1 O.R. 437; *Muttart Bldrs. Supplies Ltd. v.*

Hutton Const. (Brantford) Ltd., [1973] 2 O.R. 238, *Macon Drywall Systems Ltd. v. H. P. Hyatt Const. Ltd.* (1972), 17 C.B.R. (N.S.) 6 (Ont.), for an interpretation of the effect of section 46(4) of the Ontario Act. For a further discussion of this topic, see Chapter 10, Jurisdiction, §§120 and 126, *ante.*

§156 Productions, Particulars, and Examinations.

The rights and duties of the various parties to the action to examine and have examined before trial, contracts, accounts, mortgages or agreements for sale, have been fully discussed in §56, *ante.*

The Acts of Ontario, Newfoundland and Alberta specifically provide for applications respecting pleadings, productions, discovery, or generally any other matter relating to the action: Ont., sec. 38(10); Nfld., sec. 38(9); Alta., sec. 39(3). In Ontario, for example, the application is made to the Judge having jurisdiction or, in the County of York, the Master for directions. Moreover, both the Ontario and Newfoundland Acts specifically provide that an order may be made for the cross-examination of the deponent of the affidavit verifying the lien claim: Ont., sec. 38(10); Nfld., sec. 38(9). See also *Kleenaire Equipment Ltd. v. Dennis Commercial Properties Ltd.,* [1970] 3 O.R. 776, and *Re Pecco Cranes (Can.) Ltd.,* [1973] 3 O.R. 737. In those provinces whose Acts do not contain such specific provisions, reference should be made to the procedure and Rules of Practice of the relevant Court: see Chapter 10, Jurisdiction, §120, *ante.*

Particulars may be ordered if the Court deems it necessary having regard to the amount and nature of the claims in each particular case. In *Rowlin v. Rowlin* (1907), 9 O.W.R. 297, particulars were refused, as the amount involved in the action was very small. However, in *King v. Georgetown Floral Co.* (1904), 3 O.W.R. 587, particulars were ordered, as the Court held that in the circumstances of the case, this would be the least expensive way of proceeding, having regard to the amount and nature of the liens in question. An application for particulars of a Statement of Claim in an action commenced in the Judicial District of York should be heard by a Master and not by a Judge: *V.K. Mason Const. Ltd. v. Courtot Invts. Ltd.* (1974), 6 O.R. (2d) 655. See also Ont., sec. 46(1); Nfld., sec. 46(1) and Forms 57 and 87.

Examinations for discovery may be ordered if the circumstances warrant it: *Sanderson Pearcy & Co. v. Foster* (1923), 53 O.L.R. 519 (C.A.); *Turner Valley Supply Co. v. Scott,* [1940] 3 W.W.R. 529, reversing [1940] 2 W.W.R. 478 (Alta. C.A.); *Cobban Mfg. Co. v. Lake Simcoe Hotel Co.* (1903) 5 O.L.R. 447 (C.A.); *King v. Georgetown Floral Co., supra., Muttart Bldrs. Supplies Ltd. v. Hutton Const. (Brantford) Ltd., supra; Macon Drywall Systems Ltd. v. H.P. Hyatt Const. Ltd., supra.* See also §120, *ante.* In *Wade v. Tellier* (1909), 13 O.W.R. 1132, it was held that once the trial was

371

entered upon, the Judge or Officer presiding thereat is the proper person to make an order for discovery.

§157 Conduct, Consolidation and Carriage of Actions.

If more than one action is brought to realize liens in respect of the same land, consolidation of the actions may be ordered on the application of any party to any one of the actions or any other interested person, and conduct of the consolidated action may be given to any plaintiff: Ont., sec. 36; Nfld., sec. 36; Man., sec. 45; N.S., sec. 36; P.E.I., sec. 51; N.B., sec. 48; Sask., sec. 48; Alta., sec. 42. See also B.C., sec. 35, which is generally similar. See further *Del Frari v. Wright,* [1960] O.W.N. 103; *Marble Centre Ltd. v. Kennedy Const. Co.* (1972), 29 D.L.R. (3d) 64.

In British Columbia, by section 34, if more than one action is commenced in respect of the same contract, the owner or contractor must apply to have the actions consolidated, and, if he fails to do so, he must pay the costs of the additional actions or action, as the Judge may decide.

Any lienholder may apply for the carriage of the proceedings: Ont., sec. 37; Nfld., sec. 37; Man., sec. 46; N.S., sec. 37; P.E.I., sec. 52; N.B., sec. 49; Sask., sec. 48; Alta., sec. 39(3)(e). The word "carriage" in these sections, and the word "conduct" in the previous sections, have, in practice, been given the same meaning. It wold appear that "conduct" applies where two or more actions have been commenced, and that "carriage" applies where only one action has been instituted. It is to be noted that "conduct" may only be given to a plaintiff, while "carriage" may be given to any lienholder. This might indicate that a plaintiff may be awarded conduct of only the consolidated actions in the overall lien action, while a separate application for carriage of the entire proceedings might be made by any lien claimant. If the person having carriage of the proceedings is not properly prosecuting the action, then another lien claimant can apply to have carriage awarded to him. These sections have not, to date, been judicially interpreted.

Conduct or carriage is not necessarily given to the first claimant to commence an action, but the amount of the claim, the validity of the claim, and experience of counsel, as well as other factors, will be considered by the Court. It is not clear at what stage an application for conduct or carriage may be brought. A motion should be brought at the earliest stage after a second action is commenced for conduct and consolidation to avoid multiplicity of proceedings. Carriage of the proceedings should only be given to a lien claimant after an action is commenced.

It has been the practice, in respect of applications for both carriage and conduct of the action, to serve notice of motion on all lien claimants in the action who have registered claims, and on those of whose claims the Court has notice. The validity of this requirement has not been the subject of a reported judgment to date. Reference may be made to *Sheppard v. Davidovitch* (1916), 10 O.W.N. 159. See also §160, *post*.

Where a personal action and a lien action were commenced by different plaintiffs, the Alberta Court held in *Olsen & Johnson Co. v. McLeod* (1913), 13 D.L.R. 945 (Alta.), that the actions should not be consolidated. The judgment in a consolidated action is a judgment as to each claim, and the Court will make a finding as to each party: *Gabriele v. Jackson Mines Ltd.* (1906), 15 B.C.R. 373 (C.A.). See also *Sundberg v. Hansen* (1976), 5 A.C.W.S. 30. For the purposes of appeal, each claim is deemed to be severable: *Gabriele v. Jackson Mines Ltd., supra*.

In Manitoba a subcontractor registered a lien for repairs performed for a general contractor. Subsequently, the contractor commenced a separate action in the Court of Queen's Bench against a number of defendants including the subcontractor arising out of the question of responsibility for the repairs. The Mechanics' Lien action was consolidated with the Queen's Bench action and this action was allowed to proceed: *Foxboro Co. v. Trident Const. Ltd.,* [1975] W.W.D. 167 (Man. C.A.).

In Ontario a trial Judge in refusing to join third parties in a Mechanics' Lien action suggested the following solution in order to have all parties before the Court in order to avoid multiplicity of proceedings, "If an independent action were commenced against third parties by a defendant, it would seem to me that the desirability of that action being tried together with the Mechanics' lien action would constitute a proper and probably sufficient ground for such an application under s. 31(1) so that some of the alleged disadvantages of third party proceedings not being available under the Mechanics' Lien Act would thus be avoided": *Anchor Shoring Ltd. v. Halton Region Conservation Authority; Dufferin Materials and Const. Ltd. v. Halton Region Conservation Authority,* (1977), 15 O.R. (2d) 599 at 603.

§158 Appointment for Trial, and Notice of Trial.

The Acts of most provinces provide that the parties are to obtain an appointment for trial and serve notice of trial upon specified persons within the time limited by each Act.

In Ontario, for example, section 38(1) provides that either the plaintiff or a defendant named in the pleadings may, after the delivery of the statement of defence, where the plaintiff's claim is disputed, or after the time limited for defence in all other cases (except where the action is to be tried by a Supreme Court Judge under section 31(1)), apply *ex parte* to the Judge or Officer having jurisdiction to try the action to fix a trial date. The Judge or Officer shall then appoint the time and place of trial and the order signed by the Judge or Officer shall form part of the record of the proceedings: see Forms 40 and 41.

The party obtaining the appointment for trial must, at least 10 clear days before the trial date, serve notice of trial: sec. 38(2), (Form 42) upon the following parties:

(a) Solicitors for defendants who have appeared by solicitors, and upon defendants personally who have appeared on their own behalf or who have not appeared at all.

(b) All lienholders who have registered their claims as required by the Act, or of whose claims the party obtaining the appointment for trial has notice.

(c) All other persons having any charge, encumbrance or claim on the land subsequent in priority to the liens, who are not already parties: see *Haycock v. Sapphire Corundum Co.* (1903), 7 O.L.R. 21. Service upon persons in this group renders them parties to the action: *Metals Recovery Co. v. Molybdenum Products Co.* (1919), 46 O.L.R. 532 (C.A.).

In computing the period of "ten clear days," both the first and last days are excluded (Ontario Rules of Practice, Rule 175(2)). Service shall be personal unless otherwise directed by the Judge or Officer who has jurisdiction to try the action, and he may direct in his discretion in what manner the notice of trial may be served: sec. 38(2).

Failure to serve the notice of trial within 10 clear days is not an incurable defect: *Orr v. Davie* (1892), 22 O.R. 430. If the notice of trial is not served within the time prescribed, either leave to serve on short notice should be obtained, or the trial date should be extended. In Ontario, it is specifically provided that any person interested in the land and having been served with a statement of claim, notwithstanding that he has made default in delivering a statement of defence, must nevertheless be served with a notice of trial: sec. 38(3). See also §151, Statement of Defence, *ante*.

The usual practice after obtaining an appointment for trial is to search the title of the premises, and search for executions, and then to serve all necessary parties with the notice of trial. Following this, on the eleventh day before the trial, sub-searches are made to bring the abstract of title up to date and to ascertain if any further encumbrancers have appeared on title. A further execution certificate is also obtained at this time. If any further encumbrancers or execution creditors appear, these persons should be served immediately. The service cannot usually be effected within the 10 clear day period stipulated, but as has been previously discussed, this difficulty can usually be overcome: *Orr v. Davie, supra*. Notwithstanding that it was held in the early case of *Fraser v. Griffiths* (1902), 1 O.W.R. 141, that a purchaser subsequent to the registration of a certificate of action is bound by the judgment, it would be wise to serve notice of trial upon such subsequent purchaser.

The Act of Newfoundland is the same as that of Ontario with the exception that where a statement of defence is delivered, the application to fix a trial date must be on notice: Nfld., sec. 38. The Acts of Manitoba, Nova Scotia, New Brunswick and Prince Edward Island contain similar provisions; the latter two provinces requiring the application for a trial date to be on notice: Man., secs. 36, 37; N.S., secs. 34(1), 35; N.B., secs. 39, 40; and P.E.I., secs. 41, 42. In British Columbia and Saskatchewan the procedure is governed by the practice in ordinary actions: B.C., sec. 30; Sask. sec. 46(1). In Alberta, the plaintiff must, before setting the action down for trial, make application for a pre-trial and serve notice thereof upon all parties: sec. 39. Where a defence is filed and no order is made at the pre-trial hearing, any party may set the action down for trial: sec. 43.

§159   The Pre-Trial.

As previously stated in §158, *ante,* the Act of Alberta specifically provides for a pre-trial application. Section 39(1) provides that at any time after the expiry of the time limited for defence, the plaintiff may, and before setting the action down for trial must, make a pre-trial application. Upon receiving a date for the pre-trial, the plaintiff then serves notice thereof: sec. 39(2). The powers of the Court at the pre-trial are listed in section 39(3). If the Court does not dispose of the action at the pre-trial and does not appoint a date for trial, then provided a defence has been filed, any party may then set the action down for trial: sec. 43. None of the other Acts specifically provide for a pre-trial.

However, in Ontario, at least in the Judicial District of York, it has been the long standing practice to have a pre-trial hearing. In *B. A. Robinson Plumbing & Heating Ltd. v. Dunwoodco Ltd.,* [1968] 2 O.R. 826, the Court stated: "In the County of York, and so far as I have been informed, in the other counties as well, it has been found necessary, in view of the multiplicity of parties and issues, to devise some procedure whereby all of the lien claimants and the parties to the plaintiff's action can be brought together in order that the nature of the various claims and the issues may be ascertained, and, as frequently occurs, resolved. In the absence of unusual industry on the part of a lien claimant, it is normally at this pre-trial meeting that he first becomes aware of the extent of the proceedings in which he is involved." The hearing takes place on the return date of the notice of trial served pursuant to section 38(2), even though the notice of trial does not mention the pre-trial hearing. At the pre-trial many of the preliminary details of the action are ruled upon. For example, if more than one action has been commenced, an order is often made consolidating the actions and granting "conduct" to a plaintiff (sec. 36), or "carriage" of the action may be given to a lien claimant (sec. 37), as the case may be. An order to produce documents pursuant to section 28(3) may be made at this time. The question as to whether discoveries, particulars, or productions will be allowed is argued in many cases at this time. Admissions made by the parties that will reduce the length of the actual trial are often made and recorded. As the pre-trial is usually the first time the various parties have met together, it is often a fertile ground for the settlement of the action. It is a wise practice to prepare all aspects of a client's case carefully before attending at the pre-trial, and also to have one's client available in case settlement can be effected. If settlement is not reached, then the Court will at this time give a date for the trial of the action. A pre-trial hearing is, however, not a trial within the meaning of section 38(4) of the Mechanics' Lien Act: *Kennedy Glass Ltd. v. Jeskay Const. Ltd.,* [1973] 3 O.R. 493 (Div.Ct.).

A further notice of trial with the new date is not served unless ordered by the Court. The Court will not usually order a new notice of trial served upon parties who appear at the pretrial by solicitors, but only upon those who did not attend at the pre-trial, or those who, although attending, were not represented by solicitors. The Court usually does not require a further search of title to be made for new encumbrancers prior to the new date for trial or a new execution certificate to be filed, although it is submitted that it is prudent practice to do so.

§160　Proceeding to Trial Before a Supreme Court Judge in Ontario.

By far the majority of the lien actions tried, are tried by a Master in the Judicial District of York or a Local Judge (County Court Judge) of the Supreme Court in Counties outside of York. Only rarely is the action tried by a Supreme Court Judge at the regular sittings, pursuant to section 31(1), (2). But see *V. K. Mason Const. Ltd. v. Courtot Invts. Ltd.* (1975), 9 O.R. (2d) 325.

There are a number of reasons for this. The Supreme Court lists of actions are lengthy and thus the actual trial of the action could be delayed. The practice of having a Master or Local Judge try the action is now well established and it has been found to be well suited to lien actions. Moreover, even though the Ontario Act, by section 46(4), provides that the Rules of Practice of the Supreme Court are to govern the procedure, *except as varied by the Act,* many practical problems arise respecting procedure outlined in the Act as opposed to the procedure adopted by the Supreme Court in ordinary actions. For example, in the Judicial District of York, because of the lengthy Court lists, it is virtually impossible to obtain a specific trial date as contemplated by section 38(1). As a result, service of the notice of trial within 10 clear days is difficult — the only solution being to serve it 10 clear days before the date sittings commence. This may, however, affect the status of an execution creditor who files his execution on the day of the sittings, but the trial does not take place until 20 days into the sittings: see §143, *ante.*

Nevertheless, where the action is to be tried by a Supreme Court Judge, at the regular sittings, the practice of the Court generally, is to follow its rules rather than The Mechanics' Lien Act. It is also the practice of the Court to require the use of the forms provided in the Supreme Court Rules of Practice, rather than the forms used where the action is tried by a Master or Local Judge of the Supreme Court. Therefore, except for the fact that the action is commenced by a statement of claim, rather than a writ of summons, the action is the same as an ordinary Supreme Court action in respect of the practice, procedure and forms to be used.

§161 Payment into Court Before Trial.

In Ontario, there are four instances where money may be paid into Court before trial.

Firstly, where the owner wishes to discharge any registered lien and vacate any registered certificate of action, thus clearing the title, he may make application to pay money into Court or deposit security with the Court pursuant to section 25(2). The application is made to the Judge having jurisdiction, or in the Judicial District of York, to the Master, upon notice to the lienholders: see Form 47. The Judge or Master, on the return of the motion, may require the full amount of the lien claims, plus such costs as he may fix, to be paid into Court before the order will be granted, or such lesser sum or other security as in his discretion he shall decide upon: Forms 46 and 48.: *Nation Drywall Contractors Ltd. v. All Round Properties Administration Ltd.* (1975), 10 O.R. (2d) 295; *Re Cloverlawn Invts. Ltd.* (1977), 7 A.C.W.S., 251; *Otis Elevator Co. v. Commonwealth Holiday Inns of Can. Ltd.,* [1972] 2 O.R. 536. However, a pleading by a defendant in a lien action of set-off and counterclaim will not be considered or applied in the reduction of the amount to be paid into Court: *Bristol Const. Co. v. D. K. Invts. Ltd.* [1972] 4 W.W.R. 119 (B.C.).

The practice in Ontario has been to allow such applications *ex parte* where the payment into Court or security deposited is the full amount set out in the claim for lien plus 25% for costs.

In British Columbia, the Court held that it had no jurisdiction to subsequently reduce the security already posted: *E. A. Parker Devs. Ltd. v. Doric Devs. Ltd.,* [1977] 3 W.W.R. 191 (B.C.). In Ontario see *Re Pecco Cranes (Canada) Ltd.,* [1973] 3 O.R. 737. See also §154(*b*), *ante.*

The Court has no jurisdiction to vacate a lien registered under the Builders and Workers Act of Manitoba: *Phillips-Anderson Constructors Ltd. v. Tuxedo Estates Co.* (1977), 77 D.L.R. (3d) 473 (Man. C.A.).

A certificate of this order is obtained from the Registrar of the proper Court, and this certificate is then registered in the Registry Office, clearing the title of the property in question. The moneys so paid into Court under this section are in no way an admission of liability, and the lien claimants have no right at this stage to accept such sums or part thereof in payment of their claims. The moneys merely take the place of the property discharged as security for the lien: sec. 25(4). See also *Pedlar People Ltd. v. McMahon Plastering Co.* (1960), 33 W.W.R. 47 (Alta.); *Laguna Holdings Ltd. v. Plempe,* [1972] 1 W.W.R. 211 (B.C.); *Re Tri-Lateral Enterprises Ltd.* (1977), 74 D.L.R. (3d) 517 (Ont.); *Ocean Air Conditioning & Refrigeration Contractors Ltd. v. Dan; Re A & W Food Services of Can. Ltd. and Vancouver A & W Drive-Ins Ltd.,* [1976] 3 W.W.R. 131 (B.C.), and §23 and §89, *ante.* The moneys are only subject to the claims of those who, at the date of the application to pay the funds into Court, have:

(a)   a subsisting claim for lien, or

(b)   given notice of a claim for lien, pursuant to section 11(6) or section 14. See further in this respect, §23, *ante,* and *Ocean Air Conditioning and Refrigeration Contractors Ltd. v. Dan; Re A & W Food Services of Can. Ltd. and Vancouver A & W Drive-Ins Ltd., supra.*

Although section 25(4) of the Ontario Act provides that where money is paid into Court or security posted and the lien vacated, that the amount the Court finds due to the lien claimant is a first charge upon the money or security, this charge is limited to situations in which the sale of the owner's equity in the lands results in the realization of less than the owner's statutory liability. Where an owner paid into Court the statutory holdback amount required to discharge all liens, the Court held that all lien claimants should share this fund on a pro rata basis: *Bond Structural Steel (1965) Ltd. v. Cloverlawn Invts. Ltd.,* [1973] 3 O.R. 856. But see, *contra, Nor. Elec. Co. v. Frank Warkentin Elec. Ltd.* (1972), 27 D.L.R. (3d) 519 (Man. C.A.). and *Re Collavino Bros. Ltd.* (1977), 9 A.C.W.S. 351. As to the entitlement to any excess funds paid into Court under section 25(2) after the lien claimants have been satisfied; see *Re Tri-Lateral Enterprises Ltd.* (1977), 74 D.L.R. 517 (Ont.).

The following acts are generally to the same effect as Ontario. Nfld., sec. 27(2), (3), (4); Man., sec. 25(2); N.S., sec. 28(4); P.E.I., sec. 54(1), (2), (3), (4), (5); N.B., sec. 51(1), (2), (3), (4), (5); Sask., sec. 40(1), (2), (3), (4), (5); B.C., sec. 33(1), (2) and Alta., sec. 35(1), (2). See further Chapter 2, The Lienable Interest, §23, *ante.*

Secondly, when a trustee is appointed before trial with the power to sell the statutory "owner's" interest in the property in question in the lien action, the proceeds, upon such sale taking place, are then paid into Court and take the place of the estate or interest in the land upon which the liens are claimed (sec. 34(4)), to await the outcome of the trial. See further on this subject, Chapter 10, Jurisdiction, §130, *ante.*

Thirdly, the owner or person primarily liable to retain the required holdback, may pay the same into Court to discharge his statutory liability respecting the holdback: sec. 11(7). This sum is usually paid into Court with the statement of defence: Form 11. This is done *ex parte.* The purpose of payment into Court is merely to discharge his statutory holdback duty, and is not an admission of liability, nor a payment in satisfaction of any claim: *Brookfield Bros. Ltd. v. Shofer,* [1930] 2 D.L.R. 137, reversing [1929] 4 D.L.R. (2d) 491 (N.S. C.A.); *Cross and Grant v. Brooks* (1958), 13 D.L.R. (2d) 491 (B.C. C.A.). The payment into Court to discharge the statutory liability or, alternatively, the filing of a security bond and vacating of a lien by the owner does not thereafter permit the owner to be struck out as a defendant: *Dom. Bridge Co. v. Janin Const. Ltd.* (1973), 3 N & P.E.I.R. 418 (Nfld. C.A.). See also Alta., sec. 18; Nfld., sec. 13(7); B.C., sec. 21(4); Man. sec. 9(7); N.B., sec. 17; N.S., sec. 12(5); P.E.I., sec. 17; Sask., sec. 20(8), (9), and Chapter 4, Rights and Duties of the Owner, §46(c), and as to the question of costs, see Chapter 12, Practice After Trial, §167(d), *post.*

In *Kay v. Imperial Lbr. (Jasper Place) Ltd.* (1965), 51 W.W.R. 80 (Alta.) the Court stated that it was unnecessary for the owners to make payment into Court until the lien holders had proven their lien. But in the recent case of *Bre-Aar Excavating Ltd. v. D'Angela Const. (Ont.) Ltd.* (1976), 8 O.R. (2d) 598, the Court found the defendant dilatory in not paying the holdback into Court at the time the Statement of Defence was due.

The amount of the owner's holdback should be put in issue in the Statement of Defence, failing which the Court may award the entire amount paid into Court to the lien claimants: *Nelson Lbr. Co. v. Integrated Bldg. Corpn.,* [1976] 2 W.W.R. 538 (Alta. C.A.).

Where moneys are paid into Court by an owner to discharge his statutory liability, with the Court's sanction, no subsequent claim in another action lies against him: *L. W. Bennett Co. v. University of Western Ontario,* [1960] O.W.N. 561; affirmed [1962] O.R. 145.

If the lien action fails, the money paid into Court must be repaid to the owner or person who paid it. The sums cannot be retained in Court pending commencement of another action: *Nixon v. Sumner,* [1937] 4 D.L.R. 806 (B.C. C.A.). See however *Re Tri-Lateral Enterprises Ltd., supra.*

Fourthly, since section 46(4) of the Ontario Act makes the Rules of Practice of the Supreme Court applicable to mechanics' lien actions, except to the extent that these rules are varied by the Act, it would therefore appear that the defendant could make payment of an amount into Court in full satisfaction of the plaintiff's claim: Rule 306 *et. seq.* There may, however, be a problem in respect of a payment into Court of this type; that is, the Local Judge or Master before whom leave is requested for such a payment in, may be one and the same as the Local Judge or Master who is to try the action. See, however, *Caruso v. Campanile,* [1972] 1 O.R. 437. In respect of the remaining provinces, reference should be made to Chapter 10, Jurisdiction, §120, *ante,* and the relevant Rules of Practice of the appropriate Court.

§162   Fees on Registration of Lien and Commencement of Action.

In Ontario, a fee of $5.00 plus $1.00 for each additional parcel of land (where more than one parcel is described in the instrument), is payable for the registration of a claim for lien, assignment of lien, discharge of lien, order vacating a lien and certificate of action in any Registry Office. In the Land Titles Office, the fee is $5.00, plus $1.00 for each additional parcel described. For the fees in other provinces, reference should be made to the relevant Land Titles or Registry Acts and the regulations thereof.

The fee in Ontario respecting the commencement of an action payable by every plaintiff, every plaintiff by counterclaim and every lien claimant, including every person recovering a personal judgment is as follows:

(a) $5.00 on a claim or counterclaim not exceeding $500.00.

(b) $10.00 on a claim or counterclaim exceeding $500.00, but not exceeding $1,000.00.

(c) $10.00 on a claim or counterclaim exceeding $1,000.00, plus $1.00 for every $1,000.00 or a fraction thereof in excess of $1,000.00.

(d)   No fees are payable on a claim for wages only, and in no case shall the fee on a claim exceed $75.00, or on a counterclaim exceed $25.00.

The plaintiff who commences his action by filing his statement of claim pays the required fee at this time. The defendant who has a counterclaim pays his fee when the defence is filed. Lienholders who do not commence an action must, however, pay the prescribed fees before they may prove their liens at trial. A duplicate of the claim for lien must be filed on or before the trial of the action and it is at this time that the prescribed fee is paid: sec. 19.

The Acts of Alberta (sec. 53(*a*)), and British Columbia (sec. 51), also provide that no fees are payable on wage claims. In Nova Scotia, a plaintiff is required to pay a fee of $1.00 by law stamp when filing his statement of claim: sec. 41. In British Columbia, the fee payable in stamps by the plaintiff is $2.00 on every $100.00 or fraction thereof, of the amount of his claim up to $1,000.00.

12

Practice After Trial

§163 Judgment.

The powers given to the trial Judge or Officer respecting judgment have been previously referred to in Chapter 10, §121, *ante*. The Mechanics' Lien Acts generally provide for the complete disposition of the actions and questions arising therein, the adjustment of the rights and liabilities of all parties and the granting of all necessary relief: see *Dixon v. Ross* (1912), 46 N.S.R. 143 (C.A.); *Grannan Plumbing & Heating Ltd. v. Simpson Const. Ltd.* (1977), 17 N.B.R. (2d) 569.

In actions where the sub-trade lien claimants are claiming against the contractor under his direct contractual obligations to them, and against the statutory "owner" for the amount of the holdback he is required to retain, the judgment will provide:

(a) For a personal judgment against the contractor for the full amount of the allowed lien claims. See, however, *Noren Const. (Toronto) Ltd. v. Rosslyn Plaza Ltd.,* [1970] 2 O.R. 292 (C.A.).

(b) For the payment into Court within a specified time (usually 15 days), of the amount of holdback the owner is required to retain, and that, upon payment into Court, the liens shall be discharged and the certificate of action vacated;

(c) That, in default of the payment into Court of the required holdback, a sale shall be had of the owner's interest to satisfy the lien claims;

(d) That, if the sale of the owner's interest does not realize sufficient moneys to discharge the owner's holdback obligations to the lien claimants, then a personal judgment against the "persons primarily liable for such claim" is given for the deficiency. In the *Noren Const. (Toronto) Ltd. v. Rosslyn Plaza Ltd.* case, *supra,* the Court held that the primary debtor was the contractor and it would therefore appear from this case that the short fall is the responsibility of the contractor and not the "owner". See further §164.

(e) If the owner has paid the required amount of holdback into Court before trial, that payment out of Court of this sum be made to the claimants who have proved their liens, and a personal judgment given for the balance, if any, against the contractor;

(f) If the owner has paid an insufficient holdback into Court before trial, that payment out of Court of this sum to the lien claimants be made, and that the owner pay into Court the balance of the required holdback, the lienholders being given the above mentioned rights of sale of the owner's interest on default of payment into Court of such balance;

(g) If the contractor has a valid lien claim himself against the owner, that he be awarded judgment on this claim in the action in the same manner as any other lien claimant: Form 95 and in Ontario, Forms 7 and 8, R.R.O. 1970, Reg. 575, as amended by O. Reg. 849/75.

In situations where the statutory "owner" has contracted directly with the lien claimants, the judgment will provide for the following:

(a) a personal judgment for the amount of the allowed lien claims;

(b) failing payment, a sale of the owner's estate or interest;

(c) if the sale is insufficient to satisfy the claims, a personal judgment against the owner for any remaining deficiency after sale: see Form 95 and in Ontario, Forms 7 and 8, R.R.O. 1970, Reg. 575, as amended by O. Reg. 849/75.

§164 Personal Judgment.

In Alberta, British Columbia and New Brunswick, where a lien claimant fails to establish a "valid" lien he may nevertheless recover a personal judgment against any party to the action against whom he might recover such a judgment in an ordinary action: Alta., sec. 45(1); B.C., sec. 39; N.B., sec. 47. In Manitoba, Nova Scotia, Prince Edward Island and Saskatchewan a like provision exists except that the recovery of a personal judgment appears limited to cases where the action is one "on the contract" or "in contract": Man., sec. 43; N.S., sec. 45; P.E.I., sec. 49; Sask., sec. 53. As a result of amendments made in 1970 to the Acts of Ontario and Newfoundland the word "valid" does not appear in the corresponding section of these Acts: Ont., sec. 40, and Nfld., sec. 40. Therefore, in Ontario and Newfoundland, the following cases should be read in the light of these amendments.

In *Burgess v. Khoury (Albrechtsen's Claim)*, [1948] O.W.N. 789, it was stated that a personal judgment could only be awarded in a lien action "if it is proved that the claimant could have enforced a lien but for his failure to take the steps and follow the procedure prescribed in the Act". Since the lien claimant architect, in this case, had no right to a lien for preparing plans for a building that was not proceeded with, no personal judgment was given. In *Niagara Concrete Pipe Ltd. v. Charles R. Stewart Const. Co.*, [1956] O.W.N. 769, the Court held that, since no lien could arise respecting work done on a public highway, no personal judgment could be given. See also *Parsons Plumbing & Heating Co. v. Fletcher Invt. Ltd.* (1966), 55 W.W.R. 442 (Man. C.A.); *Bazarin v. Pezim*, [1965] 1 O.R. 606; *Constable v.*

Belvedere Holdings (1962) Ltd. (1966), 58 W.W.R. 96 (Y.T.C.A.): *Foreman v. McGowan,* [1931] O.R. 584 (C.A.); *Kendler v. Bernstock* (1915), 33 O.L.R. 351 (C.A.); *Robertson v. Bullen* (1908), 13 O.W.R. 56. In *Hectors Ltd. v. 26th Ave. Estates Ltd.* (1963), 39 D.L.R. (2d) 493 (Alta.), the argument that a lien claimant who establishes a valid lien should not be awarded personal judgment in addition to his right of sale, was rejected by the Court. The Court, however, refused to award personal judgment to one of the contractors for material not delivered to the site since no lien rights could arise under the Act for such material. However, in *Hubert v. Shinder,* [1952] O.W.N. 146 (C.A.), the Ontario Court of Appeal approved a personal judgment given to a lien claimant for work done on laundry machinery which the Court found was not the subject of a lien under the provisions of the Act. See also *Breeze v. Midland Ry.* (1879), 26 Gr. 225. The New Brunswick Court in *Burchill v. Marino,* [1951] 2 D.L.R. 518 (N.B.) and in *Warren Gen. Contracting Ltd. v. Robichaud* (1973), 6 N.B.R. (2d) 821 (C.A.) quoted with approval the statement of Sutherland J. in *Johnson & Carey Co. v. Can. Nor. Ry.* (1918), 44 O.L.R. 533 at 538, varying 43 O.L.R. 10 (C.A.), that "the significance to be attached to the word 'valid' in the expression 'valid lien' is, I think, this: a lien which could under the statute be found to exist in favour of a claimant by reason of the fact that he had performed work or service or furnished materials to be used in the making, constructing, erecting, *etc.* of any erection, building, railway, *etc.*, which could be legally the subject of a lien under the Act, and which, but for his failure to take steps and follow the procedure provided in the Act, would have been found to entitle him to a lien. In such case he can still be given the personal judgment mentioned in the section."

In *McMurray v. Parsons,* [1953] O.W.N. 414, where a lien claimant had failed to register a certificate of action and his lien had therefore ceased to exist, and no other lien claims depended upon his action, the Court, on a motion before trial, held that it had no jurisdiction to hear the action, and a personal judgment could not be given. It was further stated, however, that, once a trial is taken to determine if lien rights do exist, then the Court being seized of the action could grant a personal judgment. See also *Kendler v. Bernstock* (1915), 33 O.L.R. 351 (C.A.), and *Ogilvie v. Cooke,* [1952] O.R. 862 (C.A.). In *Taylor v. Taylor,* [1954] O.W.N. 575, a motion was made at the opening of trial for dismissal of the action on the grounds that the plaintiff's certificate of action had not been registered in time. This question being in dispute, the presiding officer heard the evidence, disallowed the claim for lien, but awarded the plaintiff personal judgment. He stated that, "unless it is patently demonstrable from the pleadings and the abstract that no lien exists, it is the duty of the Court to decide the matter on the evidence adduced, and that, having gone so far, the Court in its discretion may continue to hear the whole of the evidence and give judgment for a lien or a personal judgment or dismiss the action as the facts appear. ... This is not to say that in the circumstances of another case it would not be proper to hear evidence only on the issue of whether or not a lien existed, and finding that none did, to dismiss the action." In *Billinkoff's Ltd. v. Mid West Const. (1969) Ltd.,* [1973] 5 W.W.R. 26 (Man.), the lien claimant closed its case without his counsel having filed a certificate of search to identify the land charged with the lien as being the property of the defendant and without having filed a certified copy of its lien claim. The Court disallowed the lien but granted the claimant personal judgment. Note, however, that a motion before the trial Judge prior to entry of the judgment to re-open the case to permit the lien claimant to adduce further evidence for the purpose of establishing a lien was granted: [1974] 2 W.W.R. 100.

In *Geo. D. McLean & Associates Ltd. v. Leth,* [1949] 4 D.L.R. 282; affirmed (*sub nom. McLean v. Leth*) [1950] 1 W.W.R. 536 (B.C. C.A.), a motion was served before trial to dismiss the action on the grounds that the Court had no jurisdiction to entertain the action as there was no valid claim for lien. The Court of Appeal indicated that the proper procedure would have been to hear the evidence respecting both the claim for lien and the claim for a personal judgment, but in this case upheld the trial Judge when he dismissed the lien at the start of the trial and let the question of personal judgment stand for trial. See also *Burchill v. Marino, supra;* and *Northey v. Wood* (1951), 4 W.W.R. (N.S.) 271 (B.C. C.A.). The New Brunswick Court of Appeal, however, in *Lewis v. Armstrong Bros.* (1957), 18 D.L.R. (2d) 718 (N.B. C.A.), held that, since the affidavit verifying the statement of claim in the action was sworn by the plaintiff's solicitor, the claim was a nullity, and therefore no action was ever commenced, and there was no jurisdiction to hear the mechanics' lien action. As was stated by Jones J.: "The action to enforce the lien itself disappears, and as the right to a personal judgment is wholly dependent on an action having been commenced, there is no jurisdiction to give a personal judgment." But see *Geo. D. McLean & Associates Ltd. v. Leth, supra,* and *Burchill v. Marino, supra.*

Where at the opening of trial, the action having been dismissed as against the owners and there therefore being no lienable interest upon which the lien could attach, the Court refused to hold the trial merely for the purpose of giving personal judgment against a contractor. The Court stated:

"1. The Mechanics' Lien Act authorizes an abridged proceeding in an action to enforce a lien which may severely limit rights which the parties may have if the action were brought in the ordinary way, *e.g.,* right to discovery, unfettered right to interlocutory proceedings, right to jury trial, judgment on default, *etc.,* and this being the case, it smacks of an abuse of the process to bring an action in this form not to realize the lien but for personal judgment.

"2. An action under The Mechanics' Lien Act necessarily involves encumbering the title of the owner during the currency of the proceedings. Lien actions, brought merely for the purpose of allowing the plaintiff to recover personal judgment against a party other than the owner, ought to be discouraged where, as here, it is admitted that the lien against the land had expired before the action was brought.": *Sersanti v. Caprio*, [1970] 1 O.R. 173.

It was stated in the Ontario decision of *Bazarin v. Pezim*, [1965] 1 O.R. 606: "In my opinion subsection (3) of section 36 would not be available to every person entitled to register a claim for a lien but who did not. Otherwise any person having any claim in respect of any of the matters described in section 5 of the Act could, utilizing the procedure provided by The Mechanics' Lien Act, obtain a personal judgment regardless of the amount of his claim. Having regard to the function, purposes and object of the Act from its content as a whole it is my view there was no intention to make its machinery and procedure available for such purpose and that subsection (3) of section 36 does not permit it."

As was stated in *Sersanti v. Caprio, supra,* if none of the defendants in a mechanics' lien action are found to have any estate or interest in the land in question upon which the lien can attach, no personal judgment can be awarded. See also *Campbell-Bennett Ltd. v. Comstock Midwestern Ltd.,* [1954] S.C.R. 207, affirming 8 W.W.R. (N.S.) 683; *Pankka v. Butchart,* [1956] O.R. 837 (C.A.); *Bain v. Director, Veterans' Land Act,* [1947] O.W.N. 917; *Johnson & Carey Co. v. Can. Nor. Ry.* (1918), 44 O.L.R. 533, varying 43 O.L.R. 10 (C.A.); *Richvale Ready Mix Co. v. Belle Aire Const. Co.,* [1960] O.W.N. 230; *Seabord Const. Ltd. v. Central Realties Ltd.* (1977), 14 Nfld. & P.E.I.R. 135 (Nfld. C.A.). This general statement as it affects Ontario and Newfoundland would have to be modified following the amendments in 1970 of those provinces' Acts, at least if the action had proceeded to a point at trial where evidence was being taken on the question as to whether the claimant was entitled to a lien. It appears that at this stage the Court will allow a personal judgment even if the claimant was unable to establish a right to any lien as a result of none of the defendants being found to have an estate or interest in the land.

In *A.J. (Archie) Goodale Ltd. v. Risidore Bros. Ltd.,* (1975), 8 O.R. (2d) 427 (C.A.), it fell to the Court of Appeal to ascertain the meaning of section 40 of the Ontario Act. The Court held that section 40 was not limited to a situation where the lien claimant had established that he would have had a valid lien if he had taken the proper steps and followed the required procedure but that it was wide enough to include an action where the claim was one which was not legally the subject of a lien under the Act. In this case the plaintiff had sought a lien for the transportation of heavy machinery and its installation by bolting it in place. It was pointed out that the Court might well refuse to grant a personal judgment if the claim were one where it was clearly demonstrable from the pleadings that it would not be the subject of a lien.

A defendant in Manitoba attempted to reduce the personal judgment against it by arguing that since a County Court Judge heard the action, that personal judgment would have to be restricted to the maximum County Court jurisdiction of $2,000.00. The Court held that The Mechanics' Lien Act (sec. 43) entitled the claimant to personal judgment for *any amount found due* regardless of the monetary jurisdiction of the County Court. Moreover, The County Courts Act of Manitoba expressly excluded mechanics' lien actions from such limitation: *Parsons Plumbing & Heating Co. v. Fletcher Invt. Ltd.* (1966), 55 W.W.R. 442 (Man. C.A.).

In *Bermingham Const. Ltd. v. Moir Const. Co.,* [1959] O.R. 355 (C.A.), a personal judgment was allowed to a lien claimant for damages for delay. However, where a lien claimant sought a lien for damages for loss of and damage to tarpaulins and blankets rented to the defendant for use on a construction site, the Court held that no lien was available for such a claim for damages and further that a claim for damages, which could not be the subject matter of a claim for lien, could not result in a personal judgment under section 40 of the Ontario Act: *Alros Products Ltd. v. Dalecore Const. Ltd.* (1973), 2 O.R. (2d) 312 (C.A.). See further §127, *ante.*

There must be privity of contract between parties before a personal judgment may be awarded under this section of the Act: see *Western Caissons (Man.) Ltd. v. Trident Const. Ltd.* (1975), 54 D.L.R. (3d) 289 (Man.); *Nor. Elec. Co. v. Frank Warkentin Elec. Ltd.* (1972), 27 D.L.R. (3d) 519 (Man. C.A.); *D. Porter & Son v. MacLeod* (1951), 29 M.P.R. 83 (N.S.); *Re Mabou Coal Mine* (1909), 8 E.L.R. 299 (N.S.); and *Lewis v. Armstrong Bros., supra.* See further Chapter 4, Rights and Duties of the Owner, §47, *ante.*

In Ontario, by section 38(4), the trial judgment or report may direct payment forthwith by those found primarily liable to pay the lien claims, and execution may be issued forthwith in the case of these judgments. Where, however, after a trial of a mechanics' lien action in Ontario the Court found a general contractor personally liable to its sub-trades and also awarded the sub-trades a lien against the owner's land for the amount of the holdback, which in this case was in excess of the total amount of the sub-trades' claims, a request for immediate personal judgment against the general contractor was refused, the Court holding that this section of the Act was permissive and not mandatory; *Noren Const. (Toronto) Ltd. v. Rosslyn Plaza Ltd.,* [1970] 2 O.R. 292 (C.A.). See also *D. & M. Bldg. Supplies Ltd. v. Stravalis Holdings Ltd.* (1976), 13 O.R. (2d) 443; *Revelstoke Sawmill Co. v. Cabri Consol. S. Dist.,* [1924] 1 W.W.R. 282 (Sask. C.A.); and *A.W. Cassidy & Co. v. Hicks,* [1929] 2 D.L.R. 353 (Sask. C.A.). In view of these decisions, it may well be that lien claimants will now attempt to launch personal actions against the persons they contracted directly with, as well as a mechanics' lien action, rather than be unduly delayed in realizing a personal judgment. Such attempts to prosecute personal actions, however, are being met with applications to stay and the decisions on these applications to stay have gone both ways. In *Rockwall Concrete Forming Ltd. v. Robintide Invts. Ltd.* (1977), 15 O.R. (2d) 422 and *Kingston Road Lbr. Ltd. v. Lazarevich Bros. & Assoc. Ltd.* (1976), 3 A.C.W.S. 33, applications to stay were granted. The Court noted in the *Rockwall* case that the defendant had already paid into Court in the mechanics' lien action the total amount of the claim plus costs to vacate the lien claim and the Court inferred that it would be prejudicial to the defendant to have to pay money a second time should the plaintiff obtain judgment against the defendant in the personal action.

However, in *Standard Indust. Ltd. v. E-F Wood Specialties Inc.* (1977), 16 O.R. (2d) 398, the Court dismissed an application to stay the personal action. The court distinguished the *Rockwall* case by finding that in the case before it, no prejudice to the defendant could be shown by allowing the personal action to proceed which could not be compensated for in costs. See also *Hamilton Bridge Works Co. v. Gen. Contracting Co.* (1909), 14 O.W.R. 646, where a personal action was started before the mechanics' lien action and the Court refused to stay the personal action.

Accordingly, it is submitted that a most unsatisfactory state of affairs has developed and that unless there is some compelling reason for refusing an immediate personal judgment under section 38(4) of the Ontario Mechanics' Lien Act, immediate judgment should be given.

This section of the various Acts dealing with personal judgment must not be confused with those sections dealing with the sale by successful lien claimants of the statutory "owner's" interest. While there do not appear to be any reported Canadian decisions directly on point, it is submitted that where a sale is taken of the interest of an owner who cannot be fixed with a contractual liability to the claimant, and the sale does not realize sufficient proceeds to satisfy the owner's holdback liability, no personal judgment for the deficiency may issue against the owner. The benefit conferred by the charging section of the Act is not a lien upon or liability of the owner himself but is a lien "upon the estate or interest of the owner in the land": sec. 5(1) of the Ontario Act. If the owner's interest in the land has been exhausted, no further personal liability will attach. This view finds support in a number of American decisions which should be read in light of the specific provisions of the applicable mechanics' lien acts. See by way of example: *DiStephano v. Hall*, 32 Cal. Rptr. 770; *Neptume Gunite Co. v. Munroe Enterprises Inc.*, 40 Cal. Rptr. 367; *Rogers v. Whitson*, 39 Cal. Rptr. 849; *Roberts v. Security Bank*, 238 P. 673 and *Mitchell v. Flandro*, 506 P. (2d) 455.

§165 Interest.

Decisions of the Courts of the various provinces respecting the allowance of interest and as to the rate, in actions generally and in mechanics' lien actions in particular, have varied considerably.

In *Triangle Storage Ltd. v. Porter,* [1941] 3 W.W.R. 892 (B.C. C.A.), interest after judgment in favour of the successful lien claimant was not allowed as it was held that the contract did not provide for interest; it would not attach simply because payment had been improperly withheld, and The Mechanics' Lien Act did not permit it. The Court found that the declaration, that the claimant was entitled to a lien, was not a judgment debt within the provisions of the Dominion Interest Act and that in British Columbia a lien was limited to the amount "actually owing" which could not include interest. See, however, the dissent of McDonald J.A., following *Imperial Lbr. Co. v. Johnson,* [1923] 1 W.W.R. 920 (Alta. C.A.), and *Lbr. Mfrs.' Yards Ltd. v. Weisgerber,* [1925] 1 W.W.R. 1026 (Sask. C.A.), to the effect that interest is incidental to a claim for lien and ought to be added to the claim entirely apart from the Dominion Interest Act. See also *Re Northwest Elec. Ltd.,* [1973] 4 W.W.R. 232 (B.C.); *Dobbelsteyn Elec. Ltd. v. Whittaker Textiles (Marysville) Ltd.* (1976), 14 N.B.R. (2d) 584; *Brunswick Const. Ltée. v. Villa des Jardins Inc.* (1977), 17 N.B.R. (2d) 107 (C.A.); *Grannan Plumbing & Heating Ltd. v. Simpson Const. Ltd.* (1977), 17 N.B.R. (2d) 569; *Curran & Briggs Ltd. v. Ryder (No. 2)* (1977), 19 N.B.R. (2d) 337; and *Leisure Cedar Homes Const. Inc. v. Hranisauljewicz* (1976), 22 N.S.R. (2d) 372. The *Triangle Storage* case, *supra,* should now also be read in British Columbia in light of the Prejudgment Interest Act, 1974 (B.C.), c. 65 which, subject to certain exceptions, requires the Court to add to a pecuniary judgment an amount of interest calculated on the amount of the judgment at a rate the Court considers appropriate in the circumstances (but not less than the rate applicable in respect of interest on a judgment under the Dominion Interest Act). The interest is calculated from the date on which the cause of action arose. See *Coast Tractor & Equipment Ltd. v. McDonald's Hatcheries Ltd.,* [1977] 2 W.W.R. 479 (B.C.), where interest at the rate of 18% per annum was awarded under this Act.

Similar to the British Columbia legislation on prejudgment interest are the recent amendments to the Judicature Act of Ontario. The Judicature Amendment Act, 1977 (No. 2) (Ont.), c. 51, s. 3, repeals the former sections 38 and 39 and substitutes an entirely new section 38 which provides that a person who is entitled to a judgment for the payment of money is entitled to claim and to have included in the judgment an award of interest thereon at the "prime rate". The "prime rate" is defined as being the lowest rate of interest quoted by chartered banks to the most credit-worthy borrowers for prime business loans, as determined and published by the Bank of Canada.

Prejudgment interest under the Ontario amendments is calculated, where the judgment is given upon a liquidated claim, from the date the cause of the action arose to the date of judgment, and, where the judgment is given upon an unliquidated claim, from the date the person entitled to interest gave notice in writing of his claim to the person liable therefor to the date of judgment.

The Ontario amendments further provide, however, that the Judge has a discretion in respect of the whole or any part of the amount for which judgment is given and where he considers it just to do so in all the circumstances, to disallow interest under the new section 38, or to fix a rate higher or lower than the prime rate, or to allow interest under the new section for a period other than that provided in the section. Moreover, the section specifically prohibits an award of interest under the section where interest is payable by a right other than under the section, or on interest accruing under the section, or, except by consent of the judgment debtor, where the judgment is given on consent, among other grounds.

The section on prejudgment interest in Ontario applies to the payment of money under judgments delivered after the section came into force but limited to that period of time after the section came into force.

In *North Star Services Ltd. v. Indust. Mtge. & Finance Corpn. (1964)*, 48 W.W.R. 570 (B.C.), the Court distinguished the *Triangle Storage* case, *supra,* and held that interest could be added to the claim for lien from the time written demand was made therefor. The Court relied on section 30(2) of the British Columbia Mechanics' Lien Act to the effect that the Court may adjudge that the claimant is entitled to a lien "for the amount found to be due" and if a certain amount is found to be due, even though that amount includes interest, the lien should be for that amount. See also *Br. Pac. Properties Ltd. v. Minister of Highways* (1960), 20 D.L.R. (2d) 187 at 207 (B.C. C.A.); *McKinnon and McKillop v. Campbell River Lbr. Co.,* [1922] 2 W.W.R. 556; affirmed 64 S.C.R. 396; and *McGettigan v. Guardian Assur. Co.,* [1936] 3 W.W.R. 345 (B.C.). But see *A. B. Cushing Mills Ltd. v. Barker* (1952), 5 W.W.R. (N.S.) 170 (Alta.). It was stated by Anglin C.J.C. in *R. v. MacKay,* [1928] Ex. C.R. 149; reversed as to interest [1930] S.C.R. 130, that "where interest is allowed it is on the grounds of contract, express or implied, or by virtue of a statute. ... Interest is really asked for here as damages for detention of the compensation money pending the ascertainment of what is due. As such it cannot be recovered." In Ontario, it was held in *Hurst v. Downard* (1921), 50 O.L.R. 35 (C.A.), that, when by contract the lien claimant was to receive 50% of a mortgage to be arranged when the roof was completed on the building in question, and the mortgage was not arranged when the roof was completed, and the owner abandoned the project, interest could not be allowed on the amount of the plaintiff's lien claim. However, the plaintiff was allowed interest on 50% of the amount involved which could have been borrowed on the mortgage, a sum which the

Court held in equity was the interest bearing debt. On the other hand in *Toronto Ry. v. Toronto Corpn.,* [1906] A.C. 117, it was said that "in all cases where, in the opinion of the Court, the payment of a just debt has been improperly withheld, and it seems to be fair and equitable that the party in default should make compensation by payment of interest, it is encumbent upon the Court to allow interest for such time and at such rate as the Court may think right." The Court referred to a section of The Judicature Act corresponding to the [former] section 38 (R.S.O. 1970, c. 228), which stated: "Interest shall be payable in all cases in which it is now payable by law, or in which it has been usual for a jury to allow it". In *Lbr. Mfrs.' Yards Ltd. v. Weisgerber* [1925] 1 W.W.R. 1026 (C.A.) it was held that an owner who failed to pay for materials at the time the price was due was improperly withholding a just debt and, since it was just and reasonable in this case that he should pay compensation therefor, interest was allowed, calculated from the date when the claim should have been paid. See also *H. G. Winton Ltd. v. One Medical Place Ltd.,* [1968] 2 O.R. 384 (C.A.).

When a defendant agrees to pay a specified interest rate from the date payments are due, the Court is bound to follow the terms of such agreement: *Hectors Ltd. v. 26th Ave. Estates Ltd.* (1963), 39 D.L.R. (2d) 493 (Alta.); *Clarke v. Moore* (1908), 1 Alta. L.R. 50; *Imperial Lbr. Yards Ltd. v. Saxton,* [1921] 3 W.W.R. 524 (Sask. C.A.); *Security Lbr. Co. v. Thielens,* [1922] 3 W.W.R. 385 (Sask.); *Lbr. Mfrs.' Yards Ltd. v. Weisgerber, supra.*

In *Charlottetown Metal Products Ltd. v. Usen Fisheries Ltd.* (1973), 5 N. & P. E.I.R. 60 (P.E.I.), it was held, following the decision in *Stewart v. Crowell Bros. Co.* (1954), 35 M.P.R. 249 (N.S. C.A.), that an agreement to pay interest may be implied or may be inferred from trade usage or from a course of dealing between the parties. However, in the *Charlottetown Metal Products* case no implied agreement was established and the claim for interest was not allowed. See also *Ivan B. Crouse & Son Ltd. v. Cameron* (1974), 6 N.S.R. (2d) 612, affirmed as to interest 6 N.S.R. (2d) 590 (C.A.) and *Hawker Indust. Ltd. v. H.B. Nickerson & Sons Ltd.* (1970), 16 D.L.R. (3d) 459. In Manitoba, reference may also be made to the dissenting judgment in *Banfield, McFarlane, Evans Real Estate Ltd. v. Hoffer,* [1977] 4 W.W.R. 465 (Man. C.A.) where the decision in *Chambers v. Leech,* [1976] 4 W.W.R. 568 (Man. C.A.) was criticized. In the *Chambers* case, interest had been awarded on the basis that a just debt had been unreasonably withheld. After tracing the historical basis for awarding interest in Manitoba, the dissenting Judge in the *Banfield* case found that the basis for awarding interest in Manitoba did not extend to the equitable discretion of the Court as in Ontario [prior to The Judicature Amendment Act, 1977 (No. 2) (Ont.), c. 51] but was limited to cases where there was a contractual obligation to pay interest or an obligation to be implied from trade usage.

In *Evergreen Irrigation Ltd. v. Belgium Farms Ltd.* (1976), 3 A.R. 248, it was held that a notation on the plaintiff's invoices that interest at the rate of 1 1/2 per cent per month would be charged on overdue accounts did not create a contract by the defendant to pay interest. However, although the Court had a discretion to award compensation by way of interest under The Judicature Act, R.S.A. 1970, c. 193, s. 34(16), on the basis that payment of a just debt had been improperly withheld, the Court refused to award interest in the circumstances of this case, holding that there were issues which the defendant was entitled to have tried and for that reason it could not be said that payment had been arbitrarily withheld. In *Savioli & Morgan Co. v. Vroom Const. Ltd.* (1975), 10 O.R. (2d) 381, the plaintiff claimed moneys under a building contract together with interest. The defendant counter-claimed for backcharges in excess of the plaintiff's claim. The Court refused to exercise its discretion in favour of awarding interest. Each party was acting in good faith in advancing its claim. The wide disparity between the claim and counterclaim required detailed examination by way of evidence to ascertain what was owing by either party to the other. See also *Bausch & Lomb Optical Co. v. Maislin Tpt. Ltd.* (1975), 10 O.R. (2d) 533 where an interest award was refused, the Court holding that payment had not been unreasonably withheld where a serious question of foreign law required determination.

If no agreement to pay interest is found, and interest is allowed, various Courts have limited interest to the rate of 5%, either because they considered it a just rate in the circumstances or because they considered themselves bound by section 3 of the Interest Act, R.S.C. 1970, c. I-18: *Chambers v. Leech,* [1976] 4 W.W.R. 568 (Man. C.A.); *Chenier v. Madill; Mercier v. Plant & Anderson Ltd.* (1974), 2 O.R. (2d) 361; *Thomas Fuller Const. Co. (1958) v. Continental Ins. Co.,* [1973] 3 O.R. 202; *Popular Indust. Ltd. v. Frank Stollery Ltd.* (1973), 1 O.R. (2d) 372 (C.A.); *Gettle Bros. Const. Co. v. Alwinsal Potash Ltd.* (1969), 5 D.L.R. (3d) 719, affirmed 15 D.L.R. (3d) 128n (Sask. C.A.); *Fitzgerald and Powell v. Apperley,* [1926] 2 W.W.R. 689 (Sask. C.A.). The above cases, as they relate to interest awards, should now be read, however, in light of the decision of the Supreme Court of Canada in *Prince Albert Pulp Co. v. Foundation Co. of Can.,* [1977] 1 S.C.R. 200 [and should further be read in Ontario in light of The Judicature Amendment Act, 1977 (No. 2) (Ont.), c. 51.]

Where no rate of interest has been agreed upon but interest has been allowed, there has been a divergence of opinion as to the rate of interest and as to the time from which the interest will commence to run. In *Lbr. Mfrs.' Yards Ltd. v. Weisgerber, supra,* interest commenced from the date upon which the claim should have been paid. To the same effect is *Gustavson Internat. Drilling Co. v. B.P. Explorations Can. Ltd.* (1977), 3 A.R. 221 where interest was allowed at 10½%. In *Shona v. Arbus Invts. Ltd.* (1975), 11 O.R. (2d) 296, the Court, after considering the rate charged by the Bank of Canada, allowed interest at the rate of 8% from the date moneys were due to the plaintiff under an agreement. In *Sidan Invts. Ltd. v. W.B. Sullivan Const. Ltd.* (1974), 3 O.R. (2d) 121, in view of the general rise in interest rates and because the parties themselves, in their agreement, had recognized the commercial acceptability of the rate, interest was allowed at the rate of 8½% from the date of the defendant's default under an agreement with the plaintiff. In *Leslie R. Fairn & Associates v. Colchester Devs. Ltd.* (1976), 60 D.L.R. (3d) 681 (N.S. C.A.), the Court awarded interest at the rate of 8% by way of additional damages to compensate for interest expense incurred by the plaintiff in borrowing money to pay for the extra work occasioned by the negligence of the defendant architects. In *Ames v. Fry Mills-Spence Securities Ltd.* (1975), 10 O.R. (2d) 203, interest was allowed at 9% on the basis that the defendant had improperly withheld payment of a just debt to the plaintiff. The Court indicated, moreover, that it was entitled to take judicial notice that the bank rate of interest on loans to customers was between 11% and 13% at that time. In *Wood v. Guar. Co.* (1976), 10 O.R. (2d) 661, interest at the rate of 10% was awarded by way of damages against an insurer which failed to pay under an insurance policy, with the interest running from the date the moneys should have been paid under the policy. In *St. Vital Flooring Co. v. Inducon Const. of Can. Ltd.* (1975), 56 D.L.R. (3d) 601 (Man.), interest at the rate of 10% was awarded from the date that the first demand for payment had been made. In *Bre-Aar Excavating Ltd. v. D'Angela Const. (Ont.) Ltd.* (1975), 8 O.R. (2d) 598, the Court awarded interest at the court rate against an owner on the amount of the holdback from the date the statement of claim was served on the owner until the holdback was paid into court and on the amount which the owner was found liable to repay because of a breach of a section 2(3) trust from the date of service of the statement of claim until the date of judgment. In *Imperial Lbr. Co. v. Johnson,* [1923] 1 W.W.R. 920 (Alta. C.A.), and *Metallic Roofing Co. v. Jamieson* (1903), 2 O.W.R. 316, interest was allowed from the date of the commencement of the action. See also *Chambers v. Leech,* [1976] 4 W.W.R. 568 (Man. C.A.). In *Fitzgerald and Powell v. Apperley, supra,* interest was recovered from the time when the plaintiff first demanded interest in writing. Since there was no evidence of a demand prior to the writ being issued, interest was payable from the time the writ was served on the defendant. In *North Star Services Ltd. v. Indust. Mtge. & Finance Corpn.* (1964), 48 W.W.R. 570 (B.C.), interest was recovered from the date written demand therefor was made. It was held in Saskatchewan, where there was no agreement to pay interest and no demand until proceedings were commenced, that interest should be paid from the date of service of the statement of claim at 5%: *Gettle Bros. Const. Co. v. Alwinsal Potash of Can. Ltd., supra.* See also *Beaver Lbr. Co. v. Curry, supra.* In *Orlando Masonry Contractors v. Dinardo,* [1971] 3 O.R. 774, where interest was not claimed in the statement of claim, interest on the amount of the claims for lien established at trial was awarded pursuant to The Judicature Act, R.S.O. 1970, chapter 228. The interest was to run from the date of confirmation of the Master's report.

In the case of *Prince Albert Pulp Co. v. Foundation Co. of Can. Ltd.,* [1977] 1 S.C.R. 200 on appeal from the Saskatchewan Court of Appeal, interest was awarded at the plaintiff's borrowing rate from time to time on the amount found to be due to it on the basis that the defendant, in refusing to pay the plaintiff the costs of construction which it had incurred under a cost-plus contract, in essence compelled the plaintiff to finance part of the costs of construction at its own expense. The Court also held that it was not prevented from awarding interest at greater than 5% by section 3 of the Interest Act, R.S.C. 1970, c. I-18, which reads in part "... whenever any interest is payable by the agreement of parties or by law, and no rate is fixed by such agreement or by law, the rate of interest shall be five per cent per annum." The Court responded to the defendant's argument that section 3 limited the rate of interest to 5% by stating at 211: "It would appear ... that s. 3 is intended to apply where parties to an agreement have stipulated for the payment of interest, but no rate has been provided for, or where by law it is directed that interest be paid but no rate has been set. The *Toronto Railway* [*v. Toronto Corpn., supra*] case decided that a Court may allow interest where payment of a just debt has been improperly withheld, and it is fair and equitable that the debtor should make compensation by payment of interest, 'at such rate as the Court may think right'. Where a Court, in its judgment, has awarded interest on this principle, the rate which it fixes is payable by law and the rate is fixed by law. In such a case the section would not be applicable."

Interest cannot be added to the amount of a prior mortgage under the Act, which would result in the allowance to the mortgagee of priority for something more than an amount equal to the actual value of the land at the time the first lien arose: *Travis Lbr. Co. v. Cousineau, supra.* However, in the case of a subsequent mortgage, in computing priorities, interest may be added to the principal: *M. Sullivan & Son Ltd. v. Rideau Carlton Raceway Holdings Ltd.,* [1971] S.C.R. 2; *Godden Lbr. Co. v. Morrow,* [1962] O.W.N. 17; *A.B. Cushing Mills Ltd. v. Barker* (1952), 5 W.W.R. (N.S.) 170 (Alta.).

§166 Apportioning Judgment Against Property.

A claim for lien may be registered against a number of properties, and the Court has jurisdiction to equitably apportion, against the respective properties, the percentage of the total claim found to be due against each: Ont., sec. 17; Nfld., sec. 19; N.B., secs. 21(1), 50; P.E.I., secs. 21(1), 53 and Sask., sec. 32. The Act of Alberta, section 6, provides that where a lien attaches to an estate or interest in more than one lot respecting a separate improvement on each lot, the lien will not attach so as to make any one lot liable for more than the price of work done or materials supplied to the improvement for that lot, less a proportionate share of any money paid to the claimant respecting work done or materials supplied to improvements on all of the lots.

In Ontario (sec. 33), and Newfoundland (sec. 33), where an owner enters into an entire contract for the supply of material to be used in several buildings, the person supplying the material may ask to have his lien follow the form of the contract, and that it be for an entire sum upon all the buildings, but in case the owner has sold one or more of the buildings the Judge or Officer has jurisdiction equitably to apportion against the respective buildings the amount included in the claim for lien under the entire contract. The meaning of this section in the Ontario Act was reviewed in the case of *Accurate Kitchens & Woodworking Ltd. v. Coreydale Bldrs. Ltd.,* [1970] 3 O.R. 488. The Court stated:

"If the claimants having an entire lien are allowed to set it up as against each individual building, the other lien claimants will be prejudiced to the extent that the amount of the lien exceeds the value of the material of that lien claimant incorporated into the building. A lien claimant who supplies material for the construction of a building ought reasonably to expect that his lien will rank with the liens of all other material suppliers and workmen who provide materials and service for that building, *e.g.,* if he provides materials to the value of $5,000.00 for a house which when constructed will have cost $25,000.00 he might reasonably expect that he will get 20% of all moneys realized on the lien. But if someone who has supplied materials on five other houses as well is allowed to set up his lien claim for six houses against the moneys realized upon the lien on the one house the other lien claimants in respect of that building may be severely prejudiced by having their *pro rata* shares reduced.

"In my view it was to prevent this kind of injustice that the concluding words were added to section 32(2). I must confess that I find myself considerably troubled by the words 'equitably to apportion'. If there was no evidence as to the quantity of materials incorporated in any of the particular buildings one supposes that a straight division of the amount of the lien by the number of buildings would be the most equitable way to apportion the lien claim among the respective buildings. Since the concluding words are permissive, if any evidence were led as to the value of the materials incorporated in the individual buildings, the apportionment would be upon the basis of such evidence and not a matter of equitable apportionment at all." See also *Ont. Lime Assn. v. Grimwood* (1910), 22 O.L.R. 17; *Livingston v. Miller* (1863), 16 Abb. Pr. 371 at 378 (N.Y.); *Boake v. Guild,* [1932] O.R. 617; affirmed (*sub nom. Carrel v. Hart*) [1934] S.C.R. 10; *Alta.*

Lbr. Co. v. Yeats, [1950] 1 W.W.R. 397 (Alta.); *Polson v. Thomson* (1916), 10 W.W.R. 865 (Man. C.A.); *Enrg. & Plumbing Supplies (Vancouver) Ltd. v. Total Ad Devs. Ltd.* (1975), 59 D.L.R. (3d) 316 (B.C) and Chapter 3, The Lien Claimant, §39, *ante.*

§167 Costs.

(a) *Settlement Before Trial.*

None of the Acts of the various provinces makes provision for costs of the successful parties where settlement is made before trial and in such a circumstance the costs are negotiated among the parties.

In Ontario it has been the practice for many years to allow costs to successful lien claimants according to the following scale:

Guide to Schedule of Costs
Where Lien Filed — Preparation, Appearance
and no Actual Trial

Client's Claim	Costs
$ 100 to 200	$25.00
201 to 300	30.00
301 to 400	35.00
401 to 500	45.00
501 to 600	55.00
601 to 800	75.00
801 to 1,000	90.00
1,001 to 1,500	115.00
1,501 to 2,000	125.00
2,001 to 3,000	150.00
3,001 to 4,000	200.00
4,001 to 5,000	250.00
5,001 to 7,000	300.00
7,001 to 10,000	350.00
10,001 to 20,000	400.00

In all cases disbursements additional.

It is submitted that this scale of costs may now be out of date. The updated guide set out below, it is submitted, would be more appropriate, subject, however, to compliance with any legislation governing increases in costs.

Suggested Revised Guide to
Schedule of Costs Where Lien Filed —
Preparation, Appearance and no Actual Trial

Client's Claim	Costs
$ 100 to 200	$ 30.00
201 to 300	40.00
301 to 400	50.00
401 to 500	60.00
501 to 600	65.00
601 to 800	90.00
801 to 1,000	105.00
1,001 to 1,500	130.00
1,501 to 2,000	140.00
2,001 to 3,000	175.00
3,001 to 4,000	225.00
4,001 to 5,000	275.00
5,001 to 7,000	325.00
7,001 to 10,000	375.00
10,001 to 20,000	425.00
20,001 to 30,000	500.00
30,001 to 50,000	600.00
50,001 to 75,000	800.00

over 75,000 to be negotiated

In all cases disbursements additional.

Salvage Costs:

Additional sum for person having conduct of action covers statement of claim — registration of certificate of action — services — appointment for trial — services — abstract — certificates — preparation for trial with respect to holdback and with respect to propriety of other claims — judgment — distribution.

(b) *To the Plaintiff and Successful Claimants After Trial.*

In Ontario, costs of the action, exclusive of actual disbursements, awarded to the plaintiff and successful lienholders cannot exceed in the aggregate 25% of the total amounts found to have been actually due on the liens at the time they were registered. The costs are apportioned in such manner as the Judge or Officer trying the action may direct. In this apportionment he shall have regard to the actual services rendered by or on behalf of the parties respectively: Ont., sec. 45(2). See also P.E.I., sec. 58; N.S., sec. 40(1); Man., sec. 49; N.B., sec. 55(1); and Sask., sec. 56(2), which are generally to the same effect. See further *Winnipeg Supply & Fuel Co. v. Genevieve Mtge. Corpn.; Wiebe v. Dom. Bronze Ltd.,* [1972] 1 W.W.R. 651 (Man. C.A.) and *Baines v. Harman* (1927), 60 O.L.R. 223 (C.A.). The Ontario Act (sec. 45(2)), further provides that if a counterclaim is set up by a defendant, the amount and apportionment of costs is in the discretion of the Court, and it is presumably not governed by the 25% maximum. Reference may be had to the following authorities respecting costs of counterclaims: *Modern Cloak Co. v. Bruce Mfg. Co.* (1923), 53 O.L.R. 366 (C.A.); *Foster v. Viegel* (1889), 13 P.R. 133; *Frank v. Rowlandson* (1920), 48 O.L.R. 464 (C.A.); *Stark v. Batchelor* (1928), 63 O.L.R. 135 (C.A.).

In *Wallace v. Luton* (1955), 16 W.W.R. 653 (B.C.), the British Columbia Court of Appeal ordered a new trial of a mechanics' lien action, the costs of the first trial to be awarded on the basis of the success of the parties at the new trial. The plaintiff was awarded costs in the second trial, but the Court held that the 25% maximum prescribed by the Act covered both trials, and the plaintiff could not be awarded the maximum 25% for each trial. The British Columbia Court in *Burrard Const. Supplies Ltd. v. Burnaby S. Trustees* (1956), 20 W.W.R. 491 (B.C. C.A.), held that the trial Judge could refer the taxation of costs to the taxing officer, but that the taxing officer was restricted to the 25% maximum. See now, however, section 52 of the British Columbia Act. Similarly, in *Baines v. Harman, supra,* the Ontario Court of Appeal held that the trial Judge or Master could seek the assistance of the taxing officer but that his findings were not binding or conclusive on the Judge or Master, in whom the final discretion was vested.

In *Crawford v. Wojtyna,* [1953] O.W.N. 369, the plaintiff was successful on a motion for judgment at trial for failure of the defendant to deliver an amended statement of defence, and the Court held that the most the plaintiff could recover for costs, including all interlocutory applications, was 25% of the amount due on the lien.

It was held in *Ray Kennedy Const. Ltd. v. Moore Park Homes Ltd.* (1975), 10 O.R. (2d) 127 (Div. Ct.) that the allowance for "actual disbursements" under section 45(2) of the Ontario Act did not include fees paid by the successful lien claimant for preliminary investigative and field work and verbal reports on earth quantities by a professional engineer. By virtue of section 46(4) of the Act, the tariff of disbursements provided for in the Rules of Practice governed the extent of allowable disbursements. See also *Cobban Mfg. Co. v. Lake Simcoe Hotel Co.* (1903), 5 O.L.R. 447 (C.A.), where counsel fees paid by a solicitor to a counsel whom he had retained were not allowed as disbursements. The Manitoba Act, by section

51, specifically provides that counsel fees shall not be included as a disbursement, whereas in Prince Edward Island, by section 60, counsel fees are deemed to be a disbursement. Most of the Acts stipulate that where the least expensive course is not taken by a plaintiff, the costs allowed to him shall in no case exceed what would have been incurred if the least expensive course had been taken: see Ont., sec. 45(4); B.C., sec. 54; Man., sec. 52; N.B., sec. 57; N.S., sec. 40(3); P.E.I., sec. 61; and Sask., sec. 56(4). See also *Hill-Clark-Francis Ltd. v. Lanthier,* [1958] O.W.N. 233; *A. B. Cushing Mills Ltd. v. Barker* (1952), 5 W.W.R. (N.S.) 170 (Alta.). In *Humphreys v. Cleave* (1904), 15 Man. R. 23 (C.A.), it was held that the trial Judge had exclusive jurisdiction to decide what the "least expensive course" would have been, and therefore the taxing officer before whom the costs were taxed was not a proper person to decide that issue.

In *Foster v. Brocklebank* (1915), 8 W.W.R. 464 (Alta.), where a plaintiff commenced an action against a railway company as "owner", although a school board was the actual owner, costs were awarded to the defendant railway company against the plaintiff, but were added to the plaintiff's claim against the school board. In Ontario, sub-trades succeeded in their claims for lien against a general contractor and the general contractor succeeded in its claim against the owner. The Court granted a "bullock" order against the owner: *Noren Const. (Toronto) Ltd. v. Rosslyn Plaza Ltd.,* [1970] 2 O.R. 292 (C.A.). In Saskatchewan, the Court held on the facts, that the costs of the lien claimant sub-trades against the contractor be paid out of the amount found due between the owner and the contractor, and the costs of the contractor against the owner were ordered paid by the owner. *Gettle Bros. Const. Co. v. Alwinsal Potash of Can. Ltd.* (1969), 5 D.L.R. (3d) 719; affirmed 15 D.L.R. (3d) 128n (Sask. C.A.). A premature action was brought in *Crown Art Stained Glass Co. v. Cooper* (1910), 1 O.W.N. 1047, and costs were awarded against the plaintiff. See also *Dodge Mfg. Co. v. Hortop Milling Co.* (1909), 14 O.W.R. 3. In *Fairy and Stephenson v. Doner,* [1947] O.W.N. 217, costs of a motion to add a party defendant after the action had been commenced were awarded against the plaintiff. Where more than one action was brought the person bringing the subsequent action was not entitled to costs of this subsequent action under the relevant Saskatchewan legislation of the day: *St. Pierre v. Rekert* (1915), 23 D.L.R. 592 (Sask. C.A.).

Where success was divided in a mechanics' lien action, the Court allowed the lien claimant only 50% of its costs: *H. G. Winton Ltd. v. One Medical Place Ltd.,* [1968] 2 O.R. 384 (C.A.). See also *Winnipeg Supply & Fuel Co. v. Genevieve Mtge. Corpn.; Wiebe v. Dom. Bronze Ltd.,* [1972] 1 W.W.R. 651 (Man. C.A.).

Where a plaintiff failed to establish a lien at trial, but secured a personal judgment, the Court held that no costs could be awarded to the plaintiff, as costs were limited by the Act to 25% of the lien, and where there was no lien established, there could be no order for the payment of costs: *D. Faga Const. Co. v. Havenbrook Const. Co.,* [1968] 2 O.R. 800. But see *Taylor v. Taylor,* [1954] O.W.N. 575 where costs were awarded even though no lien was established. In *Cooper Plastering Co. v. Burnaby Bd. of S. Trustees* (1962), 39 W.W.R. 361 (B.C. C.A.), the Court held that costs provided for under section 52 of that province's Act related only to costs of an action to enforce a lien and not to costs in respect of a personal judgment. Costs of the latter fall to be determined under the province's County Court Act. In *Warren Gen. Contracting Ltd. v. Robichaud* (1973), 6 N.B.R. (2d) 821 (C.A.), the plaintiff failed to establish a valid lien at trial but was awarded a personal judgment. The plaintiff was also awarded costs of the action except any costs relating to the plaintiff's claim for lien.

(c) Against the Plaintiff and Other Claimants After Trial

In Ontario, where costs are awarded against the plaintiff or other lien claimants, these costs shall not exceed 25% of the claim of the plaintiff and the other claimants, exclusive of actual disbursements. These costs again are to be apportioned in the trial Judge or Officer's discretion: Ont., sec. 45(3); P.E.I., sec. 59; N.S., sec. 40(2); Man., sec. 50; N.B., sec. 56; Sask., sec. 56(3). A lien claimant against whom costs are assessed is only liable to pay the amount of costs entailed in the contesting of his particular claim: *Can. Bank of Commerce v. Crane Ltd.* (1956), 39 M.P.R. 133 (N.S. C.A.).

In *Bodnar v. Hazet Holdings Ltd.* (1975), 11 O.R. (2d) 414 a lien claimant commenced an action for work done and the owner counterclaimed, in part, for defective work. The Master found that portions of the work were defective and set off the amount of the defective work against the amount otherwise owing to the plaintiff. Costs were awarded to the plaintiff in the action but the counterclaim was dismissed without costs. On a motion before the same Master for leave to appeal the denial of costs on the counterclaim, the Master granted leave determining that he had erred and should have allowed a separate set of costs of the counterclaim to the defendant.

In *Standard Indust. Ltd. v. E-F Wood Specialties Inc.* (1977), 16 O.R. (2d) 398, it was held that a lien claimant who commences and simultaneously prosecutes both a mechanics' lien action and a personal action in respect of the same debt in circumstances where such a course of action cannot be practically justified may be penalized in costs in either or both actions.

The Court may order that the costs of successful parties be paid out of the holdback moneys in Court before the amounts of the lien claims are paid: *Travis Lbr. Co. v. Cousineau; Beaver Lbr. Co. v. Cousineau,* [1956] O.W.N. 585 (C.A.); *A. B. Cushing Mills Ltd. v. Barker* (1952), 5 W.W.R.

170 (Alta.); *Wesner Drilling Co. v. Tremblay* (1909), 18 O.L.R. 439 (C.A.). However, in *B.A. Robinson Plumbing & Heating Ltd. v. Dunwoodco Ltd.,* [1968] 2 O.R. 826, the Court, while finding that it had jurisdiction to order either that the costs be paid first or that they be pro-rated with the claims, held that the proper method of distribution where there was a deficiency was to order both the claims and costs to be pro-rated. See also *Can. Bank of Commerce v. Crane Ltd.* (1956), 39 M.P.R. 133 (N.S. C.A.).

It has been held that a solicitor's lien for costs takes priority over lien claimants, trust beneficiaries under the Act, assignments of accounts, and Crown liens, on the theory that the solicitor has recovered or preserved property: see Ontario Rules of Practice, Rule 696; *Re Cirone, Sabato and Priori (Con-Form Const. Co.)* (1966), 9 C.B.R. (N.S.) 231 (Ont.); *L.&D. Cartage & Dev. Co. v. Sterling Const. Co.,* [1963] 2 O.R. 420; *Babiak v. Assiniboine S. D. No. 2* (1966), 55 W.W.R. 309 (Man.); *Nor. Elec. v. Frank Warkenkin Elec. Ltd.* (1972), 27 D.L.R. (3d) 519 (Man. C.A.). Where, however, the mechanics' lien of a subcontractor exceeded the lien of the contractor, and accordingly upon the distribution of a fund in Court, the Court directed that the amount of the subcontractor's lien be paid to the subcontractor and awarded a judgment to the subcontractor against the contractor for the deficiency, no property of the contractor was recovered or preserved entitling the contractor's solicitor to a solicitor's lien on the fund in Court: *Mandatori v. Pyrid Const. Ltd.,* [1969] 1 O.R. 431 (Ont. C.A.).

The parties to the action may agree as to the disposition of costs and, while this does not oust the discretion of the Court in awarding costs, the agreement, if clear on its face, should be the governing factor in the award: *Can. Bank of Commerce v. Crane Ltd., supra.*

(d) Costs and the Owner.

The payment of costs, or receipt of costs, by the owner who has paid into Court the correct amount of holdback after being served with a statement of claim in a mechanics' lien action, is in some doubt, if the reported cases are reviewed. The practice in Ontario has been to award no costs in cases where the owner has paid in the required holdback, and this sum has been accepted by all parties, and the owner has been relieved of further liability. In *Hall v. Hogg* (1890), 14 P.R. 45, the Court stated that the owner should pay into Court the amount admitted to be due less his costs, which costs should be taxed as though he were a stakeholder watching the case. In *Anglin & Co. v. Simmons,* [1933] O.W.N. 136 (C.A.), when sufficient holdback was paid into Court the Court awarded the lien claimants' costs up to the time of payment in. No costs were awarded after this date. See also *Sanderson Pearcy & Co. v. Foster* (1923), 53 O.L.R. 519 (C.A.). In *Kilcup v. Lloydminster* (1961), 36 W.W.R. 558 (Sask. C.A.), the owner paid sufficient holdback into Court and was awarded its costs of the action and appeal fixed at $50.00.

When insufficient holdback is paid in by the owner, he is only liable for the costs of the issue as to the correct amount of the holdback: *Western Tractor & Equipment Co. v. Milestone School Unit No. 12* (1960), 33 W.W.R. 249 (Sask. C.A.). See also *Union Elec. Supply Co. v. Gillin Enrg. & Const. Ltd.,* [1971] 3 O.R. 125.

In Alberta (sec. 54), and British Columbia (sec. 38), where proceedings have arisen from the failure of the owner or contractor to fulfill the terms of his contract or to comply with the provisions of the Act, the Court may order the owner and contractor or either of them to pay all the costs of the proceedings and order a final judgment against them in default of those costs. In *Cooper Plastering Co. v. Burnaby Bd. of S. Trustees, supra,* the Court held that this section was in the nature of a penalty.

(e) *Interlocutory Applications.*

The Acts provide that, unless otherwise provided therein, all costs of and incidental to all applications and orders are in the discretion of the Judge or Officer: Ont., sec. 45(1); Sask., sec. 56(6); P.E.I., sec. 62; N.S., sec. 40(5); N.B., sec. 58(1); Man., sec. 53 and B.C., sec. 56.

In 1925 an Ontario Court held, in *Sanderson Pearcy & Co. v. Foster, supra,* per Mowat J., that "the luxury of obtaining discovery must, if desired, be paid for by the examining party". See also *Turner Valley Supply Co. v. Scott,* [1940] 3 W.W.R. 529; [1941] 2 W.W.R. 140 (Alta. C.A.). It is submitted that, when dealing with modern building contracts, examinations for discovery and other interlocutory proceedings will often be essential. The basic idea of a summary procedure in mechanics' lien actions expounded in reported decisions from the inception of the Act, and set out in the Act itself, is today in many instances most impractical. Actions are now taken by giant building concerns one against the other, in litigation where even the sub-trades' contracts may frequently run into the millions of dollars. The size and nature of the various claims in the lien action should be regarded carefully, and it is submitted that full discoveries and other interlocutory proceedings should be taken in actions where necessary, without any restrictions such as were imposed in *Sanderson Pearcy & Co. v. Foster, supra.* See comments to this effort in *Macon Drywall Systems Ltd. v. H. P. Hyatt Const. Ltd.,* [1972] 3 O.R. 189 and in *Muttart Bldrs.' Supplies Ltd. v. Hutton Const. (Brantford) Ltd.,* [1973] 2 O.R. 238. See also *V.K. Mason Const. Ltd. v. Courtot Invts. Ltd.* (1974), 6 O.R. (2d) 655.

In Ontario where a lien is discharged or vacated under section 25, or where judgment is given in favour of or against a claim for lien, in addition to the costs of the action, the Court may allow a reasonable amount for the costs of drawing and registering the claim for lien or vacating the registration of the lien. This does not apply where the claimant fails to establish a valid lien: sec. 45(5). Similar provisions are contained in the Acts of the majority of the provinces: Nfld., sec. 45(2); B.C., sec. 55; Man., sec. 54; N.B., sec. 59; N.S., sec. 40(4); P.E.I., sec. 63 and Sask., sec. 56(5). But see *Warren Gen. Contracting Ltd. v. Robichaud* (1973), 6 N.B.R. (2d) 821 (C.A.).

(f) Salvage Costs.

As previously stated specific provisions are made in a majority of the Acts for the fixing of the amount and the apportionment of the costs of the parties, having regard to the actual work and service rendered by the parties (Ont., sec. 45), as usually there are more than two parties to the action, and, in the majority of cases, more than one lien claimant. In practice one of the lien claimants is given carriage of the action and the major burden of proceeding with the mechanical steps of getting the action on for trial, the conduct of the trial, preparation of the formal judgment, and distributing the moneys found due under the judgment, falls on this person. Accordingly, this claimant is entitled to a far greater share of the costs than any of the other parties. Costs in these circumstances are known as salvage costs. "The term 'salvage costs' as used in this context denotes those additional costs over and above the costs fairly referable to the realization of the plaintiff's claim the results of which benefit all of the lienholders equally.": *B. A. Robinson Plumbing & Heating Ltd. v. Dunwoodco Ltd.,* [1968] 2 O.R. 826. The Court in this case reviewed in detail the grounds for allowing salvage costs and stated:

"A mechanics' lien action, while it is a class action, *i.e.,* is brought on behalf of all lien claimants, differs from other class actions in that not only is a fund recovered in which all lien claimants are entitled to share but the individual lien claims are resolved as well so that the distribution of the fund is also determined. While there are questions as to which the lien claimants are in the same interest, *e.g.,* the amount of the holdback and/or the amount properly owing by the owner to the person or persons through whom the individual lien claimants claim, there are also questions as to which the lien claimants are adverse to one another, *e.g.,* the right of any other lien claimant to share in the holdback when the total lien claims exceed the holdback.

"It is, one supposes, in recognition of the difficulties inherent in such actions that the Judge or Officer who tries the action is given such wide powers as those granted to him by section 42.

"In the County of York, and, so far as I have been informed, in the other counties as well, it has been found necessary, in view of the multiplicity of parties and issues, to devise some procedure whereby all of the lien claimants and the parties to the plaintiff's action can be brought together in order that the nature of the various claims and the issues may be ascertained, and, as frequently occurs, resolved. In the absence of unusual industry on the part of a lien claimant, it is normally at this pre-trial meeting that he first becomes aware of the extent of the proceedings in which he is involved.

"There are two courses open to the plaintiff. He may adopt the view that his function is only to get all the parties before the Court at the pre-trial hearing, in which case it is usually found to be desirable to appoint some group from among the lien claimants to review the various lien claims, the question of the owner's liability, *etc.,* and make recommendations to the lien claimants when the matter is again brought on. In such a situation it is usual to recompense the solicitors who constitute the committee by an award of 'salvage costs'. Counsel for the plaintiff in this case has adopted the alternative mode of proceeding, *i.e.,* before the trial he has thoroughly canvassed the lien claimants, reached conclusions as to the probable validity of their claims and by reason thereof, all the various lien claims have been resolved. In addition, he has conducted inquiries and interviewed witnesses on the question of the holdback and by virtue thereof an agreement has been reached between all parties as to the amount thereof. He is asking for salvage costs ... and having regard to the complexity of the issues, the number of claimants and the time spent by him in the resolution of these claims, I fix the salvage costs at the amount requested."

See also *Hill-Clark-Francis Ltd. v. Lanthier,* [1958] O.W.N. 233; *Baines v. Harman* (1927), 60 O.L.R. 223 (C.A.); *Bre-Aar Excavating Ltd. v. D'Angela Const. (Ont.) Ltd.* (1975), 8 O.R. (2d) 598; and *Curran & Briggs Ltd. v. Ryder (No. 2)* (1977), 19 N.B.R. (2d) 337.

In the *B.A. Robinson Plumbing & Heating* case, *supra,* the court also held that the salvage costs should be paid out of the fund before the claims and costs of the lien claimants.

(g) *Costs of Sale.*

In the majority of the jurisdictions, only actual disbursements are awarded to the party carrying out the sale of the premises under the Act: see Sask., sec. 51(5); *Security Lbr. Co. v. Leibrand,* [1923] 2 W.W.R. 216 (Sask. C.A.); P.E.I., sec. 47(1); N.S., sec. 34(6); Man., sec. 41(1); N.B., sec. 45(1). In Ontario, by section 39(1), in Newfoundland, by section 39(1) and in Alberta, by section 47(3) and (4), fees and disbursements are allowed to a person carrying out the sale. In *Monarch Lbr. Co. v. Wall,* [1923] 3 W.W.R. 1117 (Sask.), the Saskatchewan Court held that costs respecting the obtaining of an order confirming the sale proceedings were allowable. The costs and disbursements of a sale under the above sections do not come within the 25% maximum rule respecting costs of the trial of the action.

(h) *Costs of Appeal.*

In Ontario the costs of an appeal are not governed by subsections (2) and (3) of section 45, but, subject to any order of the Divisional Court, are based upon the scale of costs allowed in County Court appeals where the amount involved is within the proper competence of the County Court, and, where it exceeds that amount, upon the Supreme Court scale: Ont., sec. 43(5). The Acts of the other provinces where the 25% maximum allowance is in effect do not contain similar provisions to the above mentioned provision in Ontario. It would seem, however, that the cost of an appeal would not fall within the 25% rule in these provinces: see *Gearing v. Robinson* (1900), 19 P.R. 192; *Wallace v. Luton* (1955), 16 W.W.R. 653 (B.C.).

No costs of the appeal were allowed to an appellant who might have appeared at trial, but who allowed judgment to go against him and then prosecuted a successful appeal: *Conmee v. North Amer. Ry. Contracting Co.* (1889), 13 P.R. 433. See also *Metals Recovery Co. v. Molybdenum Products Co.* (1919), 46 O.L.R. 532 (C.A.). See also §172, *infra,* respecting costs on appeal. In *Standard Prestressed Structures Ltd. v. Bank of Montreal,* [1968] 2 O.R. 281, where the amount of liens proved against a trust fund was reduced on appeal, the costs of the lien claimants were also reduced. The successful appellant was awarded its costs of appeal out of the trust fund.

§168 Claims Not Proved at Trial.

In the majority of the provinces a lienholder who has not proved his claim at trial may subsequently apply to the Judge or Officer before whom the trial was taken to be let in to prove his claim. The application must be made before distribution of the amount realized in the action for the satisfaction of the lien claims. Strict terms as to costs are usually imposed if the application is granted: see Ont., sec. 38(7); Nfld., sec. 38(7); Alta., sec. 51; Sask., sec. 49; P.E.I., sec. 50; N.S., sec. 34(4); Man., sec. 44. If the claim is allowed the judgment is thereupon amended to include the new claim. These sections only pertain to claimants not before the Court at trial and do not include any lien claimants who have been served with a notice of trial and whose claims have been dismissed because they have not attended at the trial. Nor do they apply to any unregistered lienholders in the applicable provinces who have given the required notice of their lien to the proper parties, deposited a copy of the notice verified by affidavit with the Court, and have been subsequently unable to prove a lien at trial. The motion to prove a claim after trial must be supported by affidavit evidence to explain the failure to prove the lien at trial. The only valid explanation would seem to be the claimant's lack of knowledge of the trial proceedings, and it is submitted that it would be difficult even on this ground to justify the admission of the claimant to the action at this stage. The notice of motion must be served on all parties to the action, except unsuccessful lien claimants: Form 54. To allow a claimant to prove his claim after trial in many cases creates great prejudice, as in reality it will create a whole new trial, all the parties being obliged to re-attend and, if necessary, to contest the new claimant's claim. If the claim is allowed, the judgment which is, in many cases, lengthy and mathematically complex, will have to be re-drawn and approved again by all parties. The costs involved in this procedure, in many cases, outweigh any possible gain the lien claimant might receive.

§169 Judicial Sale.

The ultimate remedy given to lien claimants by the Acts is the right to sell the interest of the statutory "owner" according to the procedure set out therein, and this gives a very distinct advantage to lien claimants over claimants in ordinary actions. In Ontario, section 38(6) provides that the Judge or Officer may order the owner's estate sold and may direct the sale to take place at any time (usually 15 days) after judgment or confirmation of the report, allowing a reasonable time for advertising the sale. The Acts of the other provinces are generally to the same effect: see Nfld., sec. 38(6); Alta., sec. 45(2), (3); B.C., sec. 30(2); Man., sec. 40(1); N.B., sec. 44(1); N.S., sec. 34(2); P.E.I., sec. 46(1) and Sask., sec. 51(3). With the exception of Ontario and Newfoundland, all of the Acts provide that the Court may order the removal and sale of materials: Alta., sec. 45(4); B.C., sec. 30(2); Man., sec. 40(2); N.B., sec. 44(2); N.S., sec. 34(3); P.E.I., sec. 46(2) and Sask., sec. 51(4). In addition the Acts of Alberta (sec. 48), and British Columbia (sec. 30(2)), provide that the Court may order the building removed and sold and the proceeds applied in satisfaction of the liens. In Prince Edward Island (sec. 46(2)), the power of sale by the Court also extends to personal property. There is no authority to sell a mortgage under the powers contained in the Act (*Cut-Rate Plate Glass Co. v. Solodinski* (1915), 34 O.L.R. 604 (C.A.)), unless the mortgagee falls within the definition of "owner".

The Acts of all the provinces except British Columbia, provide that where a sale takes place, the proceeds are to be paid into Court to the credit of the action and are to await the Court's direction as to distribution: Ont., sec. 39(1); Nfld., sec. 39(1); Alta., secs. 46, 47; Man., sec. 41(1); N.B., sec. 45(1); N.S., sec. 34(6); P.E.I., sec. 47(1) and Sask., sec. 51(5). The Acts, however, differ in their treatment of costs and disbursements of the sale: see §167, *ante.*

In Ontario, section 39(1) provides that where an amount sufficient to satisfy the judgment and costs is not realized from the sale, the Judge or Officer certifies the amount of the deficiency and the names of the persons who are entitled to recover the deficiency, showing the amount which each is entitled to recover, and the persons liable to pay the same, allowing credit for any payments already made, and the persons entitled may enforce payment of the amounts found due by execution or otherwise. Having regard to the differences in the Acts respecting costs and disbursements, as previously indicated, all of the Acts of the other provinces, with the exception of British Columbia, have similar provisions respecting deficiency upon the sale: Nfld., sec. 39(1); Alta., secs. 46(2), 49; Man., secs. 41(1), 42; N.B., secs. 45(1), 46; N.S., sec. 34(6); P.E.I., secs. 47(1), 48 and Sask., sec. 51(5). See further §164, *ante*.

The Judge or Officer may make all necessary orders for completion of the sale and for vesting the property in the purchaser: Ont., sec. 39(2). With the exception of Nova Scotia, which requires that all proper parties join in the conveyance to the purchaser, the Acts of the remaining provinces are generally to the same effect: Nfld., sec. 39(2); Alta., sec. 45(3)(*c*); B.C., sec. 30(2); Man., sec. 41(2); N.B., sec. 45(2); P.E.I., sec. 47(2); and Sask., sec. 51(3). A purchaser in a sale under the Act only acquires the title of the person whose interest is sold, and therefore any liability for taxes or other prior claims against the land must be paid or assumed by the purchaser: *Wesner Drilling Co. v. Tremblay* (1909), 18 O.L.R. 439 (C.A.).

Where a judgment and vesting order were improperly granted by the presiding Judge in a mechanics' lien action and some years later the judgment and order were attacked in a collateral proceeding it was held that the judgment and order must be treated as valid unless reversed on appeal in the original mechanics' lien action: *Marchand v. Hynes* (1977), 3 R.P.R. 1 (N.S. C.A.).

§170 Procedure on Sale in Ontario.

As previously stated, at the expiry of the time for payment of the lien claims as provided for in the judgment (usually 15 days), the plaintiff may proceed to enforce his right to a sale. In actions tried by a Supreme Court Judge, the sale proceedings and report on sale will usually be referred to the Local Master, or the Master in the Judicial District of York. In actions outside the Judicial District of York which are ordinarily tried by the local Supreme Court Judge (County Court Judge), he is in the majority of the Counties also the Local Master. In the Judicial District of York the action is almost invariably referred to the Master for trial and disposition under section 31(2)(*a*). But see *V.K. Mason Const. Ltd. v. Courtot Invts. Ltd.* (1975), 9 O.R. (2d) 325. Therefore, unless the action is tried by a Supreme Court Judge, or by the County Court Judge sitting as Local Judge of the Supreme Court in Counties in which the County Judge is not also the Local Master, the same Judge or Officer tries the action, gives judgment, orders the sale, carries out the sale, reports on the sale, and orders distribution of the proceeds of the sale when the same has been completed. In the following outline of the procedure on sale the functions of the Local Master will be those of the trial Judge or Officer in the proper circumstances.

The plaintiff makes an *ex parte* application to the trial Judge for an order for sale pursuant to judgment. The application is supported by an affidavit of the plaintiff or his solicitor as to the non-payment of the amount found due to the lien claimants by the owner (Form 68), and a certificate of the accountant of the Supreme Court that no payment into Court has been made: Form 67. The trial Judge then makes an order for sale pursuant to judgment and usually orders that the sale proceedings be taken under the direction and supervision of the Local Master of the Supreme Court: Form 69.

The order directing a sale pursuant to judgment, as well as the original judgment, are produced to the Local Master who will then proceed to carry out the sale. An appointment is obtained for settling the form of advertisement and conditions of sale. The plaintiff serves notice of the appointment to settle the form of the advertisement and the conditions of sale on all parties except unsuccessful lien claimants: Form 70. The sale may, in the Local Master's discretion, be by tender, by public sale (conducted either by the Local Master or by an auctioneer), or by private sale, or partly by one mode and partly by another. See also the Ontario Rules of Practice, Rules 441 *et seq.* and Ont., sec. 46(4). On the return of the appointment, the Local Master will settle the form of procedure for the sale and will approve the drafts of the form of advertisement, if any, and the conditions of sale. The form of advertisement will generally follow Form 71, and the conditions of sale, Form 73. The time and place of sale are also fixed. The plaintiff should at this time produce at least one written valuation of the property: Form 75. All parties attending on the application may present argument on valuation and method of procedure on the sale, for the consideration of the Local Master: *Norwich Union Life Ins. Society v. Oke,* [1933] O.W.N. 673. The amount of a reserve bid, if any, will be fixed, but will not be disclosed by the Local Master. Directions for advertisement of the sale in newspapers or by posting in the vicinity of the property may be given. If the sale is ordered by an auctioneer, an affidavit of his fitness to act should be produced to the Local Master (Form 76), unless the auctioneer is well known to the Court. A consent to act should also be obtained from the proposed auctioneer and filed with the Court. The sale by auction will usually carry a reserve bid and, if so, the Local Master furnishes the auctioneer with a sealed reserve bid: Form 74. Generally, all parties may bid except the party having conduct of the sale, or other persons in a fiduciary position. In *Baron v. Baron* (1967), 61 W.W.R. 496 (Man.), the Master fixed a reserve bid and gave it to the auctioneer in a sealed envelope without specific instructions as to its disclosure. When the bidding closed, the auctioneer announced the reserve bid and called for further bids; one was received at the reserve price and the property sold. The Court refused to vitiate the sale, holding that under these circumstances, there being no fraud or *mala fides* the auctioneer was warranted in dealing with the property in such manner as seemed to him best to secure the highest price. On a judicial sale, the Court is not bound to order the sale to the highest bidder. The interest of the lien creditors rather than those of the respective purchasers must be considered and the offer of a known purchaser in a strong financial position is preferable to that of an undisclosed principal: *Hector's Ltd. v. 26th Ave. Estates Ltd.* (1963), 43 W.W.R. 85 (Alta.).

A purchaser of the property draws an offer to purchase and submits it to the plaintiff's solicitor. If the offer is acceptable, approval of the offer is then obtained by the plaintiff's solicitor from the Local Master. When this approval is obtained, the plaintiff's solicitor executes the offer to purchase on behalf of the plaintiff as vendor, and the purchaser advances the required deposit to the plaintiff's solicitor, who thereupon pays this sum into Court. If the sale is by auction, the auctioneer will prepare an affidavit setting out the results of the sale: Form 77.

When the sale has been completed according to the conditions of sale and the proceeds paid into Court, the Local Master will make a report on the sale. A certificate of the accountant of the Supreme Court showing payment in full of the purchase price must be filed (Form 66), together with an affidavit of advertisement when ordered (Form 72), and of the auctioneer (Form 77), where applicable. The report will direct to whom the moneys are to be paid and may add to the costs of the person conducting the action his actual fees and disbursements in connection with the sale: Ont., sec. 39(1). In *A. B. Cushing Mills Ltd. v. Barker* (1952), 5 W.W.R. (N.S.) 170, the Alberta Court held that the "proceeds of sale" referred to in the Act meant the amount realized after deducting the necessary expenses of the sale; and therefore, where the order for sale directed that the sale should be subject to a certain rate of commission payable to the selling agent, this amount was deducted from the sale price, and the balance held to be the proceeds of sale.

The lack of reported decisions respecting the procedure on sale in Ontario was discussed in the case of *MacPherson v. Laurence,* [1956] O.W.N. 79. The Court stated that no definite or actual procedure was laid down in the Act, and that "all sales seem now to be conducted in accordance with the Rules of Practice respecting sales in the Master's office or by a procedure closely analogous thereto": see Ont., sec. 46(4).

If no appeal is taken from the Local Master's report and by lapse of time it is confirmed, an application is then made to the trial Judge to distribute the proceeds of sale that are in Court: Form 80. The order on sale of property after judgment is only a collateral matter in the nature of a step in carrying out the original judgment, and therefore is an interlocutory proceeding and no appeal lies. See further §172, *post; Livingston & Sons Ltd. v. Anglehart,* [1958] O.W.N. 197 (C.A.). An order may then be made vesting in the purchaser whatever title the statutory "owner" possessed: Ont., sec. 39(2). See also Form 78. This order will also vest the interest of all parties before the Court in the action who are found to be subsequent in priority to lien claims, and will vest the interest of all lien claimants.

The accountant of the Supreme Court upon production of the order on distribution, the report on sale and the Judgment, will thereupon pay the moneys out of Court to those entitled. Where the judgment or subsequent report on distribution directs costs to be paid out of Court, the solicitors for the parties awarded costs are entitled to have the cheques drawn in their favour upon filing an affidavit of non-payment of their costs: Form 65. See also Rule 738, Ontario Rules of Practice. In practice the judgment or report on distribution, if no objection is taken, will dispense with the filing of the affidavit of non-payment of the solicitor's costs, or the judgment will provide for payment of costs directly to the solicitors. See Chapter 8, Priorities, for priorities on distribution of proceeds. See also Rules of Practice, Rules 735, 736 and 738, respecting payment of moneys out of Court, applicable to mechanics' lien proceedings.

§171 Stated Case.

In Ontario if, in the course of proceedings commenced to enforce a lien, a question of law arises, the Judge or Officer trying the case may, at the request of any party, state the question in the form of a stated case to be heard by the Divisional Court: *Re Ellwood Robinson Ltd. and Ohio Dev. Co.* (1975), 7 O.R. (2d) 556. Notice of the hearing must be served by the applicant upon all parties concerned: sec. 42(1). See also Form 60. The Judge or Officer stating the case will give directions for service of notice of the hearing. It was held in *Moyer v. Martin,* [1951] O.W.N. 395 (C.A.), that the power of stating a case pursuant to section 42(1) was reserved exclusively to the Judge or Officer trying the case, and therefore there was no jurisdiction to state a case arising out of an interlocutory application. A stated case must set out the facts material for the determination of the question raised: sec. 42(2); *Kahn v. Wacket,* [1957] O.W.N. 557 (C.A.); *Union Elec. Supply Co. v. Joice Sweanor Elec. Ltd.* (1974), 5 O.R. (2d) 457 (C.A.); Form 59. All papers necessary for the hearing of the appeal must be transmitted to the Registrar of the Supreme Court: sec. 42(2). The Act of Newfoundland contains similar provisions respecting a stated case: see Nfld., sec. 42(1), (2). In those provinces whose Acts do not contain a similar statutory provision, reference should be made to the case of *Nanaimo Contractors Ltd. v. Patterson* (1964), 48 W.W.R. 600 (B.C. C.A.), which was an appeal by way of a stated case from a judgment of the trial Judge on a point of law heard, upon the consent of the parties, as a preliminary issue before trial.

§172 Appeals.

In Prince Edward Island (sec. 57), Nova Scotia (sec. 38), Manitoba (sec. 48(1)), and New Brunswick (secs. 53, 54), in actions in which the total claims of the plaintiff and all lien claimants do not exceed $100.00, there is no right of appeal. In Alberta (sec. 52) and Saskatchewan (sec. 55) the sum is $200.00 provided, however, that in Saskatchewan an appeal where less than $200.00 is involved may be allowed upon leave of a judge of the Court of Appeal. In British Columbia (sec. 36(1)), an appeal may be taken to the same extent as provided for other actions in the County Court. A right of appeal is allowed in Ontario (sec. 43(1)), and Newfoundland (sec. 44), only to each individual claimant who obtains a judgment of over $200.00 in the action. In Nova Scotia (sec. 38), Prince Edward Island (sec. 56), and New Brunswick (sec. 53), where the amount recovered prohibits the right of appeal, an application for a new trial may be made to the trial Judge within 14 days after judgment is pronounced. In *Gabriele v. Jackson Mines Ltd.* (1906), 15 B.C.R. 373 (C.A.), it was held that each individual claimant must have recovered more than $250.00 before a right of appeal lay; but see the present British Columbia section 36(1) regarding that province's present rules respecting appeals.

As the various provinces provide different tribunals before which a mechanics' lien action may be brought, the Appellate Court also varies with the respective jurisdictions. For example, in Ontario an appeal lies to the Divisional Court and thereafter, with leave, to the Court of Appeal: The Mechanics' Lien Act, sec. 43(1); the Judicature Act, R.S.O. 1970, c. 228, as amended, secs. 17 and 29. The Acts of Saskatchewan (sec. 55), New Brunswick (sec. 54) and Manitoba (sec. 48) provide for an appeal to the Court of Appeal. In Alberta (sec. 52(1)) and Nova Scotia (sec. 39) an appeal lies to the appellate division of the Supreme Court; in Newfoundland (sec. 43), and Prince Edward Island (sec. 57), to the Supreme Court. Certain provinces will not permit a further right of appeal to a higher Court after the first appellate tribunal has made its decision: N.S., sec. 39; N.B., sec. 54(1). British Columbia (sec. 36(2)), makes specific reference to appeals to the Supreme Court of Canada. In Manitoba and Ontario an appeal lies to the Supreme Court of Canada: see *Day v. Crown Grain Co.* (1907), 39 S.C.R. 258, reversing 16 Man. R. 366, which reversed 2 W.L.R. 142; affirmed [1908] A.C. 504; *Carrel v. Hart,* [1934] S.C.R. 10, affirming *(sub nom. Boake v. Guild),* [1932] O.R. 617, subject now to the obtaining of leave.

There is no right of appeal in Ontario from an interlocutory order made in a mechanics' lien action: *Western Caissons Ltd. v. Toronto Transit Commn.,* [1966] 2 O.R. 528 at 534, affirming [1966] 2 O.R. 528 at 529; *Albern Mechanical Ltd. v. Newcon Const. Ltd.,* [1971] 1 O.R. 350; *Livingston & Sons Ltd. v. Anglehart,* [1958] O.W.N. 197 (C.A.); *R. v.*

Algoma Dist. Ct. Judge; Ex parte Consol. Denison Mines Ltd., [1958] O.W.N. 330; appeal quashed *(sub nom. Perini Ltd. v. Consol. Denison Mines Ltd.)* [1959] O.W.N. 119 (C.A.); *Moyer v. Martin,* [1951] O.W.N. 395 (C.A.); *Pearcy v. Foster* (1921), 51 O.L.R. 354; *Douglas Elec. Co. v. Tremaine* (1925), 28 O.W.N. 75; *McAuley v. Mansfield* (1922), 53 O.L.R. 68; *Bennett & Wright Contractors Ltd. v. H.E.P.C. Ont.,* [1972] 1 O.R. 20; *Macon Drywall Systems Ltd. v. H.P. Hyatt Const. Ltd.,* [1972] 3 O.R. 189. It has been held that if the matter in appeal is from an order and not a judgment or report that there is no right of appeal: *Jim-Mac Const. Ltd. v. Julann Devs. Ltd.,* Ont. Div. Ct., Holland J., September 17, 1974 *(in the process of being reported).*

In an action outside of the Judicial District of York, section 31(1) provides that the matter shall be tried by the Local Judge of the Supreme Court (*i.e.,* High Court) in the county or district in which the action was commenced. Section 118 of The Judicature Act provides that, except in the Judicial District of York, every Judge of a County Court is a Local Judge of the High Court (i.e., Supreme Court) and has the like powers and authority. An appeal from a decision of a Local Judge of the High Court would lie to the Divisional Court and thereafter, with leave, to the Court of Appeal: The Judicature Act, secs. 17 and 29; The Mechanics' Lien Act, sec. 43(1). Section 31(1) of The Mechanics' Lien Act, Ontario, further provides that upon application of any party, the Court may direct the action be tried by a Judge of the Supreme Court instead of a Local Judge of the Supreme Court. In these circumstances, an appeal lies to the Divisional Court and therafter, with leave, to the Court of Appeal.

An appeal from a Local Master's report on distribution of the proceeds of a sale of the statutory "owner's" interest lies to a Judge in Court: *Travis Lbr. Co. v. Cousineau,* [1956] O.W.N. 585 (C.A.). See also *Wesner Drilling Co. v. Tremblay* (1909), 18 O.L.R. 439 (C.A.); *Kennedy v. Haddow* (1890), 19 O.R. 240.

In an action commenced in the Judicial District of York, section 31(2) of The Mechanics' Lien Act, Ontario, provides that it shall be tried by a Judge of the Supreme Court, in which case an appeal would lie to the Divisional Court. However, section 31(2)(*a*) and (*b*) further provides that a Judge of the Supreme Court may refer the whole of the action or a question in the action to the Master for trial. Where a question in the action is referred to the Master by a Supreme Court Judge trying the action pursuant to section 71 or 72 of The Judicature Act, an appeal would appear to lie to a Judge in Court according to the Rules of Practice: sec. 43(2) of The Mechanics' Lien Act and Rule 513 of the Rules of Practice. Where the entire action is referred to the master pursuant to section 72 of The Judicature Act, an appeal lies in a like manner and to the same extent as from the decision of a Judge trying the action in the Supreme Court without a jury: sec. 43(3), (4); that is to the

Divisional Court and thereafter, with leave to the Court of Appeal: secs. 17 and 29, The Judicature Act. The notice of appeal in these circumstances must be served within 15 days of service of the notice of filing the Master's report: sec. 43(3).

Appeals have been allowed respecting orders adding parties defendant: *R. V. Demmings & Co. v. Caldwell Const. Co.* (1955), 4 D.L.R. (2d) 465 (N.B. C.A.); *Dorrell v. Campbell* (1916), 10 W.W.R. 492 (B.C. C.A.). However, in *Saltzman v. Eastside Holding & Brokerage Co.* (1970), 2 N.S.R. (2d) 265 (C.A.), where the plaintiff sought to amend his statement of claim after the time for commencing the action had passed, not by adding new defendants but by alleging that certain mortgagees already parties defendant were "owners" within the meaning of the Act, the application was dismissed as an attempt to assert a new cause of action after expiry of the limitation period.

Mr. Justice Hodgins in *Baines v. Harman* (1927), 60 O.L.R. 223 (C.A.), expressed doubts if an appeal would lie respecting the question of costs alone. He further stated that the Court's power on appeal to vary an award of costs should be limited to seeing that the statutory maximum was properly observed. See also *Jamieson v. Hagar* (1919), 17 O.W.N. 104. However, where the Judge had no jurisdiction to make the order as to costs, an appeal from the order will lie without leave: *Rockwell Devs. Ltd. v. Newtonbrook Plaza Ltd.,* [1972] 3 O.R. 199 (C.A.); *Ray Kennedy Const. Ltd. v. Moore Park Homes Ltd.* (1975), 10 O.R. (2d) 127 (Div. Ct.).

Generally, the time limited for appeal is governed by the ordinary rules of Court in force in each of the provinces. In Ontario as previously mentioned, in the Judicial District of York, where an action has been referred to the Master for trial, the Act specifically provides that the time for appeal expires 15 days after the date of service of notice of filing the Master's report: sec. 43(3). The time for appeal may in certain circumstances be extended by the Court: *Howe v. Kaministiqua Pulp & Paper Co.* (1923), 52 O.L.R. 43. It was held in *Wallace v. Bath* (1904), 7 O.L.R. 542, that the date of pronouncing the judgment was the date upon which the time for appeal commenced to run.

The Ontario Act (sec. 43(5)), provides that the costs of an appeal shall not be governed by the 25% maximum allowance provided for by sections 45(2) and 45(3) of the Act. The costs of the appeal are in the discretion of the Appeal Court, but if no specific order is made then they shall be on the County Court scale where the amount involved is within the proper competence of the County Court, and where it exceeds this amount, on the Supreme Court scale. The Acts of the other provinces where the 25% maximum allowance is in effect do not contain similar provisions to the above mentioned provision in Ontario. It would seem, however, that the costs of an appeal would not fall within the 25% rule in these provinces: see

Gearing v. Robinson (1900), 19 P.R. 192; *Wallace v. Luton* (1955), 16 W.W.R. 653 (B.C.).

An Appellate Court is reluctant to interfere with a finding of fact made by a trial Judge, but if convinced that there has been a substantial error it must give effect to its own opinion: *Piggott Lbr. Co. v. Bersch* (1926), 30 O.W.N. 8 (C.A.). See also *Whaley v. Linnenbank* (1915), 90 O.W.N. 211; reversed 36 O.L.R. 361 (C.A.).

In *Ryder v. Garner*, [1955] O.W.N. 9 (C.A.), the Ontario Court of Appeal upon fresh evidence being found allowed the matter to be referred back to the Master for trial on the new evidence. A reference back to the Master to perfect his reference pursuant to directions contained in the reasons for judgment of the Court of Appeal was taken in the case of *H. G. Winton Ltd. v. One Medical Place Ltd.*, [1968] 2 O.R. 384 (C.A.). See also *Alkok v. Grymek*, [1968] S.C.R. 452.

13

Liens on Chattels

§173 Rights Given by The Mechanics' Lien Act.

While not specifically creating liens on chattels, several of the Mechanics' Lien Acts provide a mode of realizing such a lien through the sale of the chattel during the lienholders' possession of it: see Ont., sec. 48; B.C., sec. 42; N.S., sec. 44. This was pointed out in *Evans v. Martin*, [1950] 1 W.W.R. 1 (B.C. C.A.), where the Court held that The Mechanics' Lien Act did not of itself confer any possessory lien for the cost of repairs to a chattel on a garage keeper since he enjoyed this right by virtue of the common law so long as he retained possession. See also *Alta. Drilling & Dev. Co. v. Lethbridge Iron Works Co.*, [1947] 1 W.W.R. 983 (Alta.). The lien may also arise by virtue of statute, as for example under the provincial Conditional Sales Acts, Bills of Sale and Chattel Mortgages Acts, and the Civil Code of Quebec which provides, by article 441, that whoever is bound to give back a moveable object upon which he has made improvements or additions, for which he is entitled to be reimbursed, may retain it until he has been paid. See also in this connection *Ex parte Willoughby* (1881), 16 Ch.D. 604; *Belleau v. Pitou* (1887), 13 Q.L.R. 337; *Sterling Securities Corpn. v. Hicks Motor Co.*, [1928] 2 W.W.R. 74 (Sask. C.A.); *R. Angus (Alta.) Ltd. v. Union Tractor Ltd.* (1967), 61 W.W.R. 603 (Alta.).

The Mechanics' Lien Act gives the right of sale to a person who has bestowed money or skill and materials upon a chattel in the alteration or improvement of it, or who has increased its value in such a manner as to become entitled to a lien upon the chattel for the amount or value of the money or skill and materials which he has bestowed on the chattel. The Act gives him, in addition to any other remedies which he may have, and so long as the lien exists, but not afterwards, the right to sell the chattel by auction if the amount to which he is entitled remains unpaid for a period of 3 months after he became entitled to payment. This right to sell the chattel did not exist at common law and the sale must accordingly take place strictly in accordance with the provisions of the Act: *Schultz v. Reddick* (1878), 43 U.C.Q.B. 155.

Notice must be given to the owner of the lienholder's intention to sell, by advertisement in a newspaper having general circulation in the municipality in which the work was done (Form 82), setting forth the name of the persons indebted to the claimant, the amount of the debt, a description of the chattel, the time and the place of the sale and the name of the auctioneer. In Newfoundland the advertisement must also be published in *The Newfoundland Gazette*: Nfld., sec. 48(1). In Saskatchewan, if there is no newspaper published in the locality in which the work was done, or within ten miles of that place, then not less than five notices of the sale must be posted in the most public places within that locality for one month: Sask., sec. 60(2). In Ontario, Newfoundland and Nova Scotia, one week's notice of the sale must be given by advertisement. In British Columbia, two week's notice is given and in Saskatchewan, one month. The claimant must also, except in British Columbia, leave a similar notice in writing at the last known place of residence, if any, of the owner. It would appear that this requirement is dispensed with in Nova Scotia if the owner is not a resident of the county in which the work was done, and in Ontario, if he is not a resident of the municipality in which it was done. In Saskatchewan the notice may also be sent to the owner by registered letter, if his address is known, or left at his residence: Sask., sec. 60(2).

In British Columbia, sections 43 to 50 of The Mechanics' Lien Act provide a procedure for asserting and realizing on a lien for the cost of repairs to a motor vehicle or aircraft after possession of the vehicle or aircraft has been delivered up to the owner. As will be seen, in other jurisdictions the delivery up of possession of the chattel on which the lien is claimed will usually terminate the lien automatically, and this would also be true in British Columbia of a lien on a chattel other than a motor vehicle or an aircraft. In order to maintain the lien on the motor vehicle or aircraft the garage keeper must, before surrendering possession to the owner, obtain an acknowledgment of the owner's indebtedness in writing. He must further file an affidavit of lien in the office of the Registrar-General at Victoria, within 15 days following delivery up of possession to the owner: sec. 43. Once the affidavit of claim of lien is filed, the lien continues for a further 180 days from the date of filing but will cease to exist at the end of that time unless, in the meantime, the motor vehicle or the aircraft has been seized and returned to the garage keeper: sec. 47. See also: The Garagemen's Lien Act, R.S.A. 1970, c. 155 as amended; The Garagemen's Liens Ordinance, R.O.N.W.T. 1974, c. G-2; The Garage Keepers Act, R.S.M. 1970, c. G10; and the Garage Keepers Act, 1970 (Sask.), c. 25, which contain similar provisions with respect to liens on motor vehicles, and, in the case of the Alberta and Manitoba Acts, with respect to liens for the repair of farm vehicles.

Where work was performed on a British Columbia motor vehicle in Alberta and the motor vehicle was returned to British Columbia, the British

Columbia Court held the Alberta garage man could have no lien in British Columbia for work done in Alberta: *Internat. Harvester Co. v. Can. Kenworth Ltd.* (1962), 40 W.W.R. 126 (B.C.). It was held in *Trudeau Automotive v. Stevens,* [1975] W.W.D. 185 (B.C.), where the defendant had signed a work order before the plaintiff commenced work on the defendant's motor vehicle which stated: "An express mechanic's lien is hereby acknowledged on above car or truck to secure the amount of repairs thereto", that such an acknowledgment did not constitute the "acknowledgment of indebtedness" required under section 43 of the British Columbia Mechanics' Lien Act in order to preserve the lien after possession of the vehicle had been surrendered to the defendant. The Court pointed out: that a work order, which is simply a request to do work, cannot be said to be "an invoice or other statement of account", within the meaning of section 43; that the work order must specify, at the very least, that a certain sum of money is due and owing; and that such an acknowledgment on the work order is of no assistance to the lien claimant since no lien exists until the garage keeper has actually bestowed money, skill or materials upon the vehicle. It was held in *Palm Dairies Ltd. v. United Diesel Injection Ltd.,* [1975] W.W.D. 117 (Alta.), where the Court was considering the effect of a similar section in the Alberta Garagemen's Lien Act, that this section presupposes that the garageman had possession of a motor vehicle when he obtains the required "acknowledgment of indebtedness". In that case, the lien claimant carried out repairs to an engine but the whole vehicle was never on his premises. The engine was released to the owner upon the owner giving the usual "acknowledgment of indebtedness", a lien was filed and subsequently a vehicle containing the engine was seized under the lien. The Court held that no right of lien arose in these circumstances since the Act only applies to motor vehicles and the engine, which was all the lien claimant ever had in his possession, could not be considered to be a "motor vehicle" within the meaning of the Act.

All of the Acts provide that the lien claimant shall apply the proceeds of the sale of the chattel as follows: firstly, in payment of the amount which is due to him; secondly, in payment of the costs of advertising and of the sale; and the balance of the proceeds must be turned over to the person entitled thereto upon application being made to the lien claimant accordingly: *e.g.,* Ont., sec. 48(2); Sask., sec. 60(3); Nfld., sec. 48(2). The British Columbia Act (sec. 42), further provides that a notice in writing of the result of the sale is to be left at or mailed to the address of the owner at his last known place of abode or business. The delivery of such a notice would appear to be prudent, even in jurisdictions where it is not required, in order that the owner may be appraised immediately of the amount of the sale price and the charges and expenses deducted from it. Accordingly, if any dispute arises, the evidence of the auctioneer as to the facts will be freshly and readily available.

§174 The Creation of the Lien.

The lien is created by the common law (and generally by statute) as a result of the workman or artisan having repaired, added to or otherwise improved a chattel or moveable object, and it gives to the workman or artisan the right to retain the chattel until his account has been paid: *Sterling Securities Corpn. v. Hicks Motor Co.,* [1928] 2 W.W.R. 74 (Sask. C.A.); *Royal A. Vaillancourt Co. v. Trans Can. Credit Corpn.,* [1963] 1 O.R. 411 (C.A.). The lien extends to the cost of both labour and materials, and the owner of the article has no right to reclaim or repossess it until both have been paid for. The right to retain the article is similar to the right of retention given under a contract of pawning or pledging. It is only under a contract of pawning or pledging that the common law gives the lienholder the right to realize on the security. The right to realize on the security in other circumstances is given by statutes such as The Mechanics' Lien Act: Ont., sec. 48.

The common law recognizes two classes of liens, the general and the particular lien. The general lien is founded either upon custom or specific contract and is a lien upon any personal property for a general debt or account due to the person claiming it. It operates as a form of floating charge upon any of the personal property of the person who owes the account which is in the hands of the lien claimant. A general lien may be exercised by a banker or a lawyer, for example, upon all of the client's or customer's papers in his hands and he is not bound to give them up until payment of the owner's indebtedness has been made to him. The actual papers or securities retained by the claimant may not have any connection with the account for which he claims payment but so long as they are in his possession, he has the right to retain them under his general lien: see *Blackburn v. Macdonald* (1857), 6 U.C.C.P. 380 (C.A.); *Bock v. Gorissen* (1860), 45 E.R. 689 (C.A.).

In contrast, the particular lien attaches only to the actual property of the debtor upon which the labour and materials have been expended and attaches only so long as the article remains in the lien claimant's possession. This lien is the lien of an artisan which arises upon his bestowing skill, labour or money upon personal property with the express or implied authority of the owner: see *Blackburn v. Macdonald, supra; Scarfe v. Morgan* (1838), 150 E.R. 1430; *Cassils & Co., v. Holden Wood Bleaching Co.* (1914), 84 L.J.K.B. 834 (C.A.); *Sterling Securities Corpn. v. Hicks Motor Co., supra; Hutchison v. Hawker Siddeley Can. Ltd.* (1972), 32 D.L.R. (3d) 759 (N.S.). In *Cassils v. Holden, supra,* it was held that the claimant, although in possession of the goods and having expended labour and materials on them, was not entitled to a particular lien since he was unable to establish a custom of the trade or the implied authority of the owner permitting him to retain the goods in default of payment for his services.

The cases of *Castellain v. Thompson* (1862), 143 E.R. 41, and *Chase v. Westmore* (1816), 105 E.R. 1016, create some confusion in the common law on the question as to whether or not the chattel must be enhanced in value by the lien claimant in order for him to be entitled to assert a lien. Where the lien is given by statute, however, it can only arise if the specific provisions of the statute are complied with. It was held in *Therrien v. Royal Bank* (1941), 79 Que. S.C. 366, that article 441 of the Civil Code of Quebec will not be construed as creating a lien where a transformation in the chattel does not amount to an improvement upon or an addition to the moveable object. See also in this connection *Belleau v. Pitou* (1887), 13 Q.L.R. 337. In *Allied Equipment Rentals Ltd. v. Pfob & Diro Machine & Steel Co.* (1964), 48 W.W.R. 125 (Alta.), it was held that, under the Alberta Possessory Liens Act, it must be shown that any money spent by the person claiming the lien enhanced the value of the chattel, and that the work had been done on, or the materials had been added directly to, the chattel.

The lien, or privilege of retention of the chattel, given by the common law or by statute will only entitle the claimant to retain possession of it. It will not have the effect of transferring ownership of the chattel to the lien claimant, and he can only realize on his lien by complying with the provisions of statutes such as The Mechanics' Lien Act: Ont., sec. 48; *Alta. Drilling & Dev. Co. v. Lethbridge Iron Works Co.*, [1947] 1 W.W.R. 983 (Alta.).

The Civil Code of Quebec contains a number of articles providing for liens in favour of specific persons. For example, article 1994a gives a lien to persons engaged in the fishing industry; article 1994c provides for a lien in favour of persons engaged in the lumber industry; and article 1994d gives a lien to workmen who have performed services for circuses, theatres and other exhibitions. Article 2006 gives certain specific privileges to servants and employees.

§175 Possession of the Chattel.

The right to the particular lien is predicated upon possession of the chattel and if the claimant surrenders possession of it, he will lose his lien: *Crabtree v. Griffith* (1863), 22 U.C.Q.B. 573 (C.A.); *Hackett v. Coghill* (1903), 2 O.W.R. 1077; affirmed 3 O.W.R. 827 (C.A.); *Evans v. Martin,* [1950] 1 W.W.R. 1 (B.C. C.A.); *Kendal v. Fitzgerald* (1862), 21 U.C.Q.B. 585 (C.A.); *Royal A. Vaillancourt Co. v. Trans Can. Credit Corpn.,* [1963] 1 O.R. 411 (C.A.); *Wilson v. Doyon,* [1964] Que. S.C. 93; *Perron v. Fortin* (1924), 30 R.L.N.S. 398; *Wishnevitski v. Allan Motors Ltd.* (1955), 15 W.W.R. 421 (Sask.); *Hutchison v. Hawker Siddeley Can. Ltd.* (1972), 32

D.L.R. (3d) 759 (N.S.). Even if the claimant subsequently regains possession of the chattel after having voluntarily surrendered possession of it, the lien will not be revived: *Reilly v. McIllmurray* (1898), 29 O.R. 167 (C.A.); *Hackett v. Coghill, supra; Katzman v. Mannie* (1919), 46 O.L.R. 121; varied 48 O.L.R. 551 (C.A.); *Colonial Finance Corpn. v. Bourgoin* (1933), 71 Que. S.C. 157; *Can. Gas Power & Launches Ltd. v. Schofield* (1910), 15 O.W.R. 847. However, the claimant may maintain a lien for any work which is done on the chattel after he regains possession: *Can. Gas Power & Launches Ltd. v. Schofield, supra; Colonial Finance Corpn. v. Bourgoin, supra; Hackett v. Coghill, supra.* If the claimant delivers up part of the goods on which he had a lien, he will lose his lien with respect to the goods delivered but will retain his lien on goods which are still in his possession, although his lien will be limited to the amount of his account with respect to the goods retained: *Kendal v. Fitzgerald, supra; Steeves v. Cowie* (1903), 40 N.S.R. 401 (C.A.). In *Hutchison v. Hawker Siddeley Can. Ltd., supra,* it was held that a workman who performs work on a ship loses his lien when he relinquishes possession of the ship and he is not entitled to a lien on the ship's lifeboats, of which he retains possession, if no work has been done on the lifeboats themselves. It was held in *Re Rauf* (1974), 5 O.R. (2d) 31, that a lien on two mares for stallion service fees extended to the two foals born of the mares while they were in the possession of the claimant.

The claimant must have acquired possession of the chattel lawfully, and a lien cannot be enforced on a chattel which came into the claimant's possession through a thief: *Lortie v. Bedard* (1921), 60 Que. S.C. 299; *Katzman v. Mannie* (1919), 46 O.L.R. 121; varied 48 O.L.R. 551 (C.A.). Similarly, the claimant will not be deprived of his lien if he loses possession of the chattel by reason of fraud, violence or theft: *Security Loan Co. v. Hewlett* (1951), 3 W.W.R. (N.S.) 370 (Man. C.A.); *Crabtree v. Griffith, supra.* It was held in a Quebec case that the onus is on the lien claimant to establish that he has not lost possession of the chattel at any time after the work had been done: *Therrien v. Royal Bank* (1941), 79 Que. S.C. 366. It was held in *Chew v. Traders Bank* (1909), 19 O.L.R. 74 (C.A.), that if the chattel was destroyed by fire while in the possession of the lien claimant, the lien would be lost. It was further held in that case that the lien claimant would have no lien on the proceeds of a fire insurance policy placed by the owner. It was held in *Allied Equipment Rentals Ltd. v. Pfob & Diro Machine & Steel Co.* (1964), 48 W.W.R. 125 (Alta.), that a lien could not be enforced on equipment for work done on it without the true owner's knowledge on the instructions of a person to whom the owner had merely lent the equipment so that he could have it measured.

While the possession of the chattel by the lien claimant may be either actual or constructive, it must be continuous, and the lien claimant must have a right to the continuous possession of it. Accordingly, as was held in *Crabtree v. Griffith* (1863), 22 U.C.Q.B. 573 (C.A.), and *Dixon v. Dalby* (1853), 11 U.C.Q.B. 79 (C.A.), a livery stable keeper has no lien for the board of a horse where the owner has the right to use the horse whenever he wishes. However, in *Roberts v. Bank of Toronto* (1894), 21 O.A.R. 629, affirming 25 O.R. 194, the Court indicated that a restricted and limited possession of the chattel might be enough to support a lien and held that there was no necessity that the claimant be the owner or tenant of the lands on which the goods were situated. See also in this connection, *Byers v. McMillan* (1887), 15 S.C.R. 194, reversing 4 Man. R. 76, which reversed 3 Man. R. 361; *Webber v. Cogswell* (1877), 2 S.C.R. 15, affirming 11 N.S.R. 47; *McKenzie v. Mattinson* (1902), 40 N.S.R. 346; *Ex parte Willoughby* (1881), 16 Ch. D. 604; *Smith v. Hayward* (1924), 51 N.B.R. 369; *Automobile & Supply Co. v. Hands Ltd.* (1913), 28 O.L.R. 585; *Re Capital Tobacco Co.; Ex parte Plant Ltd.* (1925), 29 O.W.N. 137; *Hayward v. G.T.R.* (1872), 32 U.C.Q.B. 392 (C.A.); *R. Angus (Alta.) Ltd. v. Alta. Tractor Parts Ltd.* (1964), 44 D.L.R. (2d) 337 (Alta. C.A.).

While the lien will normally be lost if the claimant voluntarily surrenders possession of the chattel to the owner, it has been held that a conditional surrender of the chattel during the course of the repairs will not have this effect: see *Albermarle Supply Co. v. Hind & Co.,* [1928] 1 K.B. 307 (C.A.); *Traders Finance Corpn. v. Bond Motor Sales,* [1954] O.W.N. 785 (C.A.); *J. H. Early Motor Co. v. Siekawitch,* [1931] 3 W.W.R. 521 (Sask. C.A.), and *Indust. Accept. Corpn. v. Tompkins Contracting Ltd.* (1967), 60 W.W.R. 546 (B.C.). In each of these cases, however, there was an express understanding between the owner and the garage man that the motor vehicle was to be returned to the garage when it was not being used and the owner acknowledged the garage man's right to possession. In *Wilson v. Doyon,* [1964] Que. S.C. 93, where the garage man released the automobile to the owner on receipt of a cheque, (which was subsequently returned N.S.F.), for part of his account on the owner's undertaking, (never honoured), to pay the balance of the account in one month's time, the garage man subsequently regained possession of the vehicle when it was brought back for further repairs, which were paid for by the owner's insurers. It was held that the lien had been lost when the garage man voluntarily surrendered possession of the automobile and it could not be revived by his regaining possession of it later. The Court indicated, however, that the result would have been otherwise if the cheque which was given and not honoured had been for the full amount of the account.

It has been held on several occasions that the lienholder is not entitled to assert a lien for the cost of storing the chattels while he retains possession of them, and this is so even though he pays a third party to store them: see *Winchester v. Busby* (1889), 16 S.C.R. 336, affirming 27 N.B.R. 231;

Katzman v. Mannie (1919), 46 O.L.R. 121; varied 48 O.L.R. 551 (C.A.); *Can. Gas Power & Launches Ltd. v. Schofield* (1910), 15 O.W.R. 847; *Can. Steel & Wire Co. v. Ferguson Bros.* (1915), 8 W.W.R. 416, reversing 7 W.W.R. 557 (Man. C.A.); *Heriteau v. W. D. Morris Realty Ltd. (Capital Storage Co.),* [1943] O.R. 724. It was held in *Security Loan Co. v. Hewlett* (1951), 3 W.W.R. (N.S.) 370 (Man. C.A.), that the lienholder was not entitled to a lien for the cost of regaining possession of the chattel.

See also in this connection §173, *ante,* with regard to the provisions of the British Columbia Mechanics' Lien Act, and of the Acts of various other provinces which are cited in that article, which permit a garage-keeper to retain his lien for the cost of repairs to certain vehicles, even though he has delivered up possession of the same to his customer, provided he follows the appropriate procedures before doing so. In general, he must first obtain an "acknowledgment of indebtedness" from the customer and must then file a claim for lien in the appropriate government office within the prescribed number of days after surrendering possession of the vehicle.

§176　Loss of the Lien.

As was shown in the previous article, the loss of possession of the chattel will result in the loss of the lien except in very limited circumstances. In addition, as pointed out by Draper C.J. in *Dempsey v. Carson* (1862), 11 U.C.C.P. 462 (C.A.), "it [a lien] is neither a *jus in re* nor *jus ad rem,* and it may be waived by any act or agreement between the parties by which the right is given up". If the provisions of the agreement between the owner and the person asserting the lien are inconsistent with the existence of a lien, the right to a lien will be taken to have been waived. This is also true if the conduct of the parties is inconsistent with the existence of the lien: *Jorgenson v. Sitar,* [1937] 2 W.W.R. 251 (Man. C.A.); *Can. Credit Men's Trust Assn. v. Heinke* (1957), 23 W.W.R. 305 (B.C.); *Re Leith* (1866), 16 E.R. 276 (P.C.); *Ritchie v. Grundy* (1891), 7 Man. R. 532; *Re Taylor, Stileman and Underwood,* [1891] 1 Ch. 590, 597 (C.A.); *Re Rauf* (1974), 5 O.R. (2d) 31.

The taking of security or the giving of credit for payment by the lienholder does not, of itself, destroy the lien unless the security taken is inconsistent with its existence in which event it will be discharged. In *Re King* (1924), 26 O.W.N. 392, 424, it was held that the giving of a lien note by the debtor to the lienholder was inconsistent with the lien and operated as a discharge of it. In *Renald v. Walker* (1858), 8 U.C.C.P. 37 (C.A.), it was held that the taking of a bill of exchange payable at a future date by the lienholder amounted to an abandonment of his lien. It was further held that the insolvency of the owner of the goods before the bill of exchange fell due would not revive the lien. It was held in *Dempsey v. Carson* (1862), 11 U.C.C.P. 462 (C.A.), where a new agreement waiving a present right of payment was entered into after the lien came into existence, and there had been an acceptance of security and part performance of the residue of the agreement, that this amounted to a waiver of the lien although it did not amount to an accord and satisfaction of the original debt.

It has been held that if the lienholder recovers a judgment for the price of his work, issues execution, and has the chattel upon which he claims his lien seized under his execution, he will lose his lien since he has voluntarily parted with possession of it: *Rumely v. The Vera M.,* [1923] 1 W.W.R. 253 (B.C.); *Re Coumbe, Cockburn & Campbell* (1877), 24 Gr. 519. It was held in *Edborg v. Imperial Timber etc. Co.* (1914), 6 W.W.R. 180 (B.C.), however, that the lien will not ordinarily be destroyed by the mere obtaining of judgment for the debt. It was held in *Ryan v. McNeil* (1974), 51 D.L.R. (3d) 151 (P.E.I.), that one who takes in a horse for boarding and training has a lien for his reasonable charges. It was held further than when the owner demands the return of the horse and refuses to pay the owner's charges, the claimant is entitled to refuse to deliver the horse, but he must then take prompt steps to mitigate his damages by realizing on the lien.

The statement was made in *Hearn v. Eastern Motors Ltd.* (1924), 56 N.S.R. 463 (C.A.), by Harris C. J. that, "The law is well settled that where a person has a lien but bases his refusal to surrender the property upon some right independent of or inconsistent with the lien, he is held to have waived his lien and cannot afterwards set it up". See also in this connection *Barbeau v. Piggott* (1907), 9 O.W.R. 234; affirmed 10 O.W.R. 715 (C.A.), and *Llado v. Morgan* (1874), 23 U.C.C.P. 517 (C.A.), to the same effect. It was held in the latter case, however, that a person having a valid lien for storage who refused to deliver the chattels up to the owner since he also claimed a lien on other grounds, which subsequently proved untenable, did not thereby dispense with a tender of the sum properly due him, nor did his act amount to a conversion unless the evidence clearly showed that such a tender would be useless since it would be refused.

As was pointed out in *McBride v. Bailey* (1857), 6 U.C.C.P. 9, 523 (C.A.), by Richards J., "when a party having an undoubted lien claims that lien and something more, he does not necessarily waive his lien, nor waive a tender of the sum for which he claims this lien, unless he in effect intimates to the party, that there is no necessity of his tendering the amount of an acknowledged lien, as he will hold the property for the amount claimed". Accordingly, the mere fact that the lien claimant claims an amount in excess of that for which he actually has a claim for lien does not dispense with or waive tender of the amount of the acknowledged lien. However, as was held in *Willis v. Sweet* (1888), 20 N.S.R. 449 (C.A.), a tender of the amount for which the lien claimant is entitled to a lien will discharge the lien and entitle the owner to possession of the chattel, and such possession may be recovered by legal process without the necessity of payment into Court of the amount of the lien. See also in this connection *Kendal v. Fitzgerald* (1862), 21 U.C.Q.B. 585 (C.A.); *Winchester v. Busby* (1889), 16 S.C.R. 336, affirming 21 N.B.R. 231; *Prov. Ins. Co. v. Maitland* (1858), 7 U.C.C.P. 426 (C.A.); *Nevius v. Schofield* (1881), 21 N.B.R. 124 (C.A.).

§177 The Lien Claimant, the Chattel Mortgagee and the Unpaid Vendor.

Where chattels such as motor vehicles are sold under conditional sale, or hire-purchase agreements under which the title to the vehicle is reserved to the vendor until full payment of the purchase price has been made, it cannot be said that repairs or improvements to the motor vehicle have been authorized by the owner if the purchaser or hirer subsequently has work done on the chattel. However, the Courts have tended to regard the purchaser as being in the same position as a bailee of the motor vehicle who has been given possession of it under such terms as either oblige him to keep it in repair or entitle him to use it in such a way as to require it to be repaired in order that it may be used. The purchaser is accordingly held to have the implied authority of the owner to subject it to the ordinary lien of the repairer: *Commercial Finance Corpn. v. Stratford* (1920), 47 O.L.R. 392; *Can. Gas Power & Launches Ltd. v. Schofield* (1910), 15 O.W.R. 847; *Gurevitch v. Melchior* (1921), 29 B.C.R. 394 (C.A.); *J. H. Early Motor Co. v. Siekawitch*, [1931] 3 W.W.R. 521 (Sask. C.A.); *Gen. Securities Ltd. v. Bretts Ltd.* (1956), 19 W.W.R. 385 (B.C.); *Universal Sales Ltd. v. McCallum* (1956), 3 D.L.R. (2d) 150 (N.B.); *Security Loan Co. v. Hewlett* (1951), 3 W.W.R. (N.S.) 370 (Man. C.A.); *Calmar's Garage v. Eric's Late Model Cars Ltd.* (1956), 19 W.W.R. 382 (Alta.); *Green v. All Motors*, [1917] 1 K.B. 625 (C.A.); *Keene v. Thomas*, [1905] 1 K.B. 136; *Vernon Finance Ltd. v. Brandt* (1959), 22 D.L.R. (2d) 231 (B.C.). As was pointed out in *Vernon Finance Ltd. v. Brandt, supra,* most conditional sale agreements contain a clause requiring the purchaser to take proper care of the vehicle, and this alone ought to give the conditional purchaser the owner's authority to effect repairs and subject the vehicle to a lien therefor. It was also held in that case that the garage man's lien for repairs effected on the motor vehicle at the request of the conditional purchaser was not cut down or limited by the further stipulation in the contract between the buyer and the seller by which the purchaser undertook to keep the motor vehicle free from liens and encumbrances. The following decisions are to the same effect: *Universal Sales Ltd. v. McCallum, supra; Commercial Finance Corpn. v. Stratford, supra; Alliance Finance Co. & Standard Motors Ltd. v. Simons,* [1928] 3 W.W.R. 621 (B.C. C.A.); *Gen. Securities Ltd. v. Bretts Ltd., supra.*

In *Weir v. Doc Landa Trailer Repairs Ltd.* (1964), 49 W.W.R. 359 (Sask. C.A.), a trailer had been repaired on the instructions of one who had leased it under an agreement which contained an option to purchase. The repairer's right to assert a lien for the repairs was upheld against the owner on the ground that the option to purchase was only consistent with the lessee's duty to have the trailer repaired if it were damaged. The Court found that the right and duty of the lessee of the trailer to have it repaired was an implied term of the contract of hiring, and that having it repaired was an act reasonably incidental to the use of the trailer by him. A chattel mortgagor also has the implied authority of the owner to authorize repairs to a chattel which is in his legal possession and to thereby subject the chattel to the lien of the repairer: *Royal A. Vaillancourt Co. v. Trans Can. Credit Corpn.,* [1963] 1 O.R. 411 (C.A.).

§178 Release of Chattel by Lien Claimant on Owner Posting Security.

In Ontario where an owner seeks to recover possession of his chattel and the defendant lienholder does not dispute the owner's title, but claims to retain the property by virtue of his lien, the Court may order that the plaintiff owner pay into Court the amount of money in respect of which the lien is claimed and such further sum, if any, for interest and costs as the Court directs, and that upon payment into Court being made, the property claimed be given up to the owner: Ontario Rules of Practice, Rule 371. The owner is not required to pay into Court storage charges while his chattel is held under the lien: *Otaco Ltd. v. Salem Enrg. (Can.) Ltd.,* [1944] O.W.N. 449. The amount to be paid into Court for security for costs is the full amount of the estimated costs of the action together with interest up to the anticipated date of the disposition of the action: *Ness Bros. Ltd. v. Barrie Airways Ltd.,* [1963] 2 O.R. 109.

14

The Law of Construction Privileges in Quebec*

This Chapter is now in its fourth edition. Extensive litigation has taken place since the last date of publication (third edition, 1972) and a considerable number of new cases involving problems relating to the law of construction privileges have been added to an already rich series of judicial decisions.

The Chapter contains a statement of the main principles, rules and problems related to the law of construction privileges in Quebec (those of the workman, the supplier of materials, the builder and the architect: arts. 2013 *et seq.* of the Civil Code, hereafter referred to as C.C.). The relevant articles of the Civil Code have been reproduced in the Appendix, §193, *post.* As well, numerous references to materials are provided in the footnotes for further study.

The reader will note that the whole matter of security upon property, both moveable and immoveable (personal and real) is under scrutiny by the Office de revision du Code civil. The final report and proposed legislation will include revised provisions of the law of privileges.

The reader is advised to relate each paragraph to the others as he reads, since many provisions of the law are applicable to more than one area of construction privileges — identical or related comments have not been repeated when this is the case. This remark is especially applicable to §§182, 183 and 184, *post.*

§179 Introduction to the Laws of Construction Privileges in Quebec.

Under the law of Quebec, the general rule of the *patrimoine* is that the whole of a person's property is liable for the fulfilment of his obligations except such property as is specially declared to be exempt from seizure: C.C.

---

* This Chapter was included in the second edition under the title "Mechanics' Liens in Quebec"; it had been rewritten from the first edition by Dean John W. Durnford, and from the second edition by Yves A. Caron. For the present edition, the Chapter has been revised, modified, up-dated and augmented by Leonard W. Flanz of the Quebec Bar.

art. 1980. Articles 552 and 553 of the Code of Civil Procedure (C.C.P.) list certain essentials of life which the law declares exempt from seizure. As well, donors and testators may stipulate that their gifts and legacies shall be so exempted as constituting alimentary provision, although they may be seized by creditors subsequent to the gift with the permission of a Judge and to the extent that he determines. These, however, are merely exceptions to the rule that a creditor may cause to be seized and brought to sale all and any of his debtor's property, under the "common pledge" concept: C.C. art. 1981.

Another general principle of Quebec law is that where a debtor's assets are insufficient, when realized, to satisfy all his debts, his creditors will share in the proceeds ratably, *i.e.*, they will all be treated as being on the same footing, regardless of the respective dates on which the various debts were incurred. The important exception to this rule is that creditors will not be treated as ranking equally where there are among them legal causes of preference (C.C. art. 1981), the legal causes of preference being privileges and hypothecs: C.C. art. 1982.

A privilege is a right which a creditor has of being preferred to other creditors according to the origin of his claim: C.C. art. 1983. What this means is that certain categories of debts are declared privileged by the law by reason of their special nature rather than because of the personality of the creditor. Thus funeral expenses are privileged because of the desirability of the dead being buried rather than because of a desire on the part of the legislator to favour the undertaker over creditors.

A privilege exists only where the law confers it (C.C. arts. 1981, 1983); unlike the hypothec, it cannot be stipulated in any private agreement, but rather results from the effect given by the law to that agreement. Unless the debt appears in the list of claims declared privileged by the Civil Code, it will only rank as an ordinary debt. There are exceptions to this rule which do not concern us here (*e.g.*, under the Quebec Succession Duties Act, R.S.Q. 1964, ch. 70, government claims for succession duties are also privileged), but even these are not true exceptions, since they too are privileges conferred by law (in this case by specific Acts). From this it will be realized that a privilege is an exceptional right, which principle is frequently reiterated in the cases relating to contested privileged claims. The application of this principle will result in the loss of a privilege where the requirements of the Civil Code have not all been complied with: *e.g.*, C.C. art. 2013e. Yet, perhaps because of an unconscious sympathy on the part of the Judges for the creditor who has made the construction of a building possible through his labour and materials, there are instances where the Courts have relented somewhat in the application of this rigorous rule.[1]

---

1   The best example of this underlying reasoning can be seen in *1366 Dorchester Street West Inc. v. Val Royal Bldg. Materials Ltd.*, [1965] R.L. 353 at 361: "The law's intention

The effect of a privilege is to give the privileged creditor a right of preference over other creditors in the proceeds from the sale of property. Both the Civil Code and the Code of Civil Procedure regulate the enforcement and execution of privileges and the order of priority for the payment of privileged claims: C.C. arts. 2009 *et seq.,* and C.C.P. arts 660 *et seq.* The privilege is indivisible by nature, thus it will remain valid to secure the whole debt and will affect the property in its entirety as long as some part of the debt remains outstanding. What is more, it covers all the operations of the person who benefits from it after its creation, up to an amount equal to the value added to the property.[2] The right given to the privileged creditor is a "real right accessory", as opposed to a "real right principal" (the best example of which is ownership). A privilege gives no right of ownership in the property, nor any right to any dismemberment (*e.g.,* personal *servitude,* such as *usufruct*) in that property. Its character is to secure the claim of a creditor with respect to one particular thing (thus it is a real right), as a result of a situation which by law is said to be "privileged". Thus a distinction is made between the privileged right which is executory against the immoveable (*i.e.* against the owner), and the debt itself, with respect to which recourse may be had against the principal debtor.[3] It is an accessorial right since it exists for the repayment of the principal debt or obligation, and remains only insofar as the principal debt continues to exist.[4] Once the principal debt is somehow extinguished, the privilege ceases to exist.[5]

§180 Privileges upon Immoveable Property.

Quebec law divides all property into the two categories: moveables and immoveables: C.C. art. 374. Lands and buildings fall into the latter: C.C. art. 376. Hence in the study of the Quebec equivalent of mechanics' liens, the Civil Code privileges on moveables (C.C. arts. 1993-2008) are of no interest.

In most cases, the validity of a privilege upon immoveable property depends upon the registration by the creditor of his contract or of a notice,

---

was to give a privilege to the persons, who by their brains or labour or materials, contributed to the erection of a building, subject only to compliance with some simple rules and which privilege would extend only to the increased value given the building and which building would otherwise remain the common pledge of all creditors ... It seems to the Court that, sometimes, the Courts have forgotten the words of 2013 ['The workmen ... have a privilege and a right of preference over all the other creditors on the immoveable ...'] and the fact that the workmen *etc.* have usually benefited the mass of creditors — by creation of an asset, while benefiting themselves preferentially only to the extent of the additional value."

2   See *Nineteenhundred Tower Ltd. v. Cassiani,* [1967] Que. Q.B. 787; affirmed [1967] S.C.R. vi.
3   *La Rivière Inc. v. Can. Surety Co.,* [1973] Que. C.A. 151.
4   *Brassard v. Abandonato,* [1957] Que. S.C. 45.
5   See §191, *post,* on extinction.

which results in full existence, conservation and opposability of the privilege as against third parties. The privilege upon immoveable property, being a real right, carries with it the right to "follow" the property into whose hands it may be, and gives a right of preference on the proceeds resulting from the sale of such property.

For the privilege to be valid, the immoveable against which the privilege is to be registered must be susceptible of seizure and judicial sale, since the privilege can only be exercised on the proceeds of such a sale. Subject to some exceptions, property belonging to the Crown may not be seized, the reason being that the Crown is presumed to be solvent and therefore able to pay all of its debts without the necessity of preference.

Generally speaking, property that is part of the public domain is regarded as not being an object of commerce under C.C. article 1059, and therefore as exempt from seizure, irrespective of whether such property is for the use of the public or for the private use of the State.[6] Such property may include airports and public buildings. On the other hand, some properties belonging to a government or a public corporation, such as a School Board, have been held to be susceptible of seizure and therefore susceptible of being the object of a construction privilege. Recent cases have distinguished certain properties that are not part of the public domain, such as schools[7] and municipal buildings[8].

6　See *Richard Lasalle Const. Ltée v. Comcepts Ltd.* [1973] Que. C.A. 944, where the Court held that the theory of "dualité domaniale" has no application in Quebec Civil law vis-à-vis Crown property and that the expression "public domain" encompasses all assets of the state, without distinction; also, in the recent case of *Commn. Scolaire Chomedy de Laval v. Société d'Habitation du Québec,* Prov. Ct. (Montreal) no. 500-02-037896-763, Laurier J., October 17, 1977, (unreported) it was held that the property of the Quebec Housing Corporation, an agent of the Crown, could not be seized in execution of a privileged right.

7　*Kredl Inc. v. Tétrault Frères Ltée,* [1967] Que. S.C. 285; *Laminated Structures Ltd. v. Lemieux & Frères Inc.,* [1967] Que. S.C. 355. School properties are said to be excluded from the public domain, and therefore subject to seizure and execution, by virtue of The Education Act. In the case of *Héroux et Allard Const. Inc. v. Collège d'Enseignement General et Professionnel de Victoriaville,* [1976] Que. S.C. 1753, it was held that the property of the C.E.G.E.P. could be seized in execution and hence could be the object of a privilege inasmuch as the Loi des collèges d'enseignement général et professionnel (1966/67 (Que.), c. 71) in virtue of which the C.E.G.E.P. was established allowed the C.E.G.E.P. to hypothecate its property, which in turn rendered such immoveable subject to seizure.

8　See *Montréal v. Hill-Clark-Francis (Que.) Ltd.,* [1968] Que. Q.B. 211 (C.A.), in which a distinction was made between such municipal buildings or assets as are part of the public domain, *e.g.,* an aqueduct, and such properties or machinery and equipment that are merely incidental to the administration of the public domain and which can form part of the private domain of the municipality; also, *Stanton Pipes (Can.) Ltd. v. Sylvain,* [1966] Que. Q.B. 860 (C.A.), in which it was held that an aqueduct was part of a public domain and therefore not susceptible of seizure; also, *Calor Ltd. v. Kwiat,* [1975]

The current rule is that where a municipality or other public corporation uses its properties for a non-public purpose, such as putting it up for lease to private business, then such properties are subject to privileged rights.[9]

There have been further difficulties with respect to the type of property that may be subject to a construction privilege: *e.g.,* the Civil Code uses the word "building" and it has not always been easy to determine what in fact constitutes a building. The Quebec Superior Court has held that work related to the construction of a parking lot surrounding a motel would by itself give occasion to the creation of a privilege.[10]

Recently, the Quebec Superior Court confirmed that a privilege may exist on an immoveable by nature (in this instance, an inflatable geodesic dome tennis court) independently of the land on which the structure is situated. The Court applied article 415 C.C. which recognizes that buildings, construction, works, etc. may belong to a third party, while article 376 C.C. provides that lands and buildings are immoveable by their nature.[11]

§181 Construction Privileges Equivalent to Mechanics' Liens.

The term "mechanics' liens" is unknown to Quebec law, but its equivalent is to be found amongst the provisions of the Civil Code concerning privileges on immoveables. The Code deals with these privileges in C.C. articles 2009 to 2015. Article 2009 lists those claims which carry a privilege on immoveables. In addition to such items as funeral expenses and seigniorial dues, the list includes: "The claim of the workman, supplier of materials, builder and architect, subject to the provisions of articles 2013 and following."

C.C. article 2013 reads as follows: "The workman, supplier of materials, builder and architect have a privilege and a right of preference over all other creditors on the immoveable, but only upon the additional value given to such immoveable by the work done or by the materials."

Two salient points are to be noted in this article. The first is that it is

---

Que. C.A. 858, where the Court held that a municipal incinerator held by the City for the general usage of the Public, was not an object of commerce, formed part of the public domain and, accordingly, could not be the object of a privilege.

9   Such would be the case where a corporation owned a ball park, for example, which would be leased to various clubs, whether such clubs were the property of the city or not. On this question, see B. Reis, The Applicability of the Contractor's Privilege to Public Property (1971), 31 R. du B. 321.

10   *Verdun Indust. Bldg. Corpn. v. Regent Equipment & Paving Corpn.,* [1968] Que. S.C. 506. See also 185, *post.*

11   *Héroux et Allard Const. Inc. v. Collège d'Enseignement Général et Professional de Victoriaville,* [1976] Que. S.C. 1753.

concerned with a privilege which only applies to the particular property to which the work and materials have been contributed and not to the debtor's property as a whole. The second point is that the privilege exists only to the extent of the additional value resulting from the work or materials.[12] Should the proceeds realized on the judicial sale of the property (following the obtaining of a judgment) be insufficient to pay all the privileged claims, it becomes necessary to establish the additional value given by the work and/or materials to the property against which the privileged creditors who supplied them may exercise their privileges. The valuation is done by the Prothonotary in order to determine the value of the immoveables or parts of immoveables in relation to the value of the whole, and the proportion attributable to each creditor in the amount to be distributed: C.C.P. arts. 721, 722; C.C. art. 2013*b*. As between themselves, this particular group of creditors rank in the following order of preference: the workman, the supplier of materials, the builder, and the architect: C.C. art. 2013*c*

Recently, the Quebec Court of Appeal, in a concurrent finding, held that each creditor should be collocated by the Prothonotary for his share as regards the additional value given to the immoveable by all of work and materials and not as regards solely the additional value he himself has given. The Court thus adopted the theory expounded by Giroux instead of that of Marler.[13]

An example will illustrate the foregoing. An owner engages two contractors to make improvements to his house. He pays neither of them. The first contractor has paid his own workmen and suppliers of material, the second has not. As privileged claims lie in favour of workmen, suppliers of materials and builders only as regards the additional value arising from their own work, the first contractor, having paid his workmen and suppliers, will be paid by preference over all the other creditors out of the amount allotted to his improvement. As to the second contractor, because his workmen and suppliers of materials have not been paid, their privileged claims will rank as regards the amount allotted to his improvement in the order established by C.C. article 2013*c, i.e.,* the workmen will rank first, the suppliers of materials second, and the second contractor (builder) third.[14]

As a corollary to these rules, it will be appreciated that while the

---

12   *Ethier v. Duguay,* [1961] Que. P.R. 399; *Gadbois & Colle v. Stinson-Reeb Bldrs. Supply Co.,* [1929] S.C.R. 587 at 594, 11 C.B.R. 40, [1929] 4 D.L.R. 1035; *Re Legault; G.A. Grier & Sons v. Lamarre* (1939), 67 Que. K.B. 356, 21 C.B.R. 195 (C.A.); Marler, The Law of Real Property, p. 354; Giroux, Le Privilège Ouvrier (1933), pp. 390, 407.

13   See *Duval & Gilbert Inc. v. Réjean Lapierre Inc.,* [1974] Que. C.A. 483; Giroux, Le Privilège Ouvrier (1933), pp. 393 *et seq.; contra:* Marler, The Law of Real Property, pp. 362-363, 377-378; *Pipon v. Goldstein,* (1940) 46 R.L.N.S. 431; Demers Traité de Droit Civil du Québec, XIV, pp. 168-169.

14   Marler, The Law of Real Property, pp. 377-378.

workman will rank before the supplier of materials and the latter before the builder and so forth, if the amount owing to them is more than the additional value that the work and materials have given the property, the workman will not have a privileged claim for his entire wages at the expense of those ranking after him, and so on down the line. Each will suffer a proportionate reduction (*pari passu*). Thus if the additional value is less than their claims by 10%, a reduction will be made to that extent from each of these creditors' privileged claims.[15]

It will be appreciated that the foregoing remarks apply only to privileges (real right in the property). While the creditor may find the privileged portion of his claim reduced, this will not affect his personal recourse for the full amount against his debtor, though of course the usefulness of this recourse may be destroyed by the debtor's insolvency.

§182 The Privilege of the Workman.

(a) *Subject and Object of the Workman's Privilege.*[16]

C.C. article 2013*a* defines the workman as including "the artisan, the laborer and generally everyone who makes his living by manual labor". This will not include a person who supplies a bulldozer, pays the cost of running it and operates it himself.[17] The determinate feature in qualifying one's efforts as giving rise to a workman's privilege is the nature of the work performed rather than the mode of payment. Thus, *e.g.,* where a person qualifies as a builder or contractor, he is entitled to a privilege as such, notwithstanding that he is to be paid on an hourly basis, as is a workman.[18]

The workman's privilege covers arrears of wages up to 20 days for work done on an immoveable property and exists whether he is engaged by the owner of the property himself, or by a contractor: C.C. art. 2013*d*. The privilege does not include the expenses of board and lodging, of transportation or the use of scaffolding.[19] Nor will it avail in favour of a workman who does not work on the actual immoveable itself: thus where a supplier of materials was engaged to supply stone for the erection of a church, the workmen hired by the contractors to cut the stone in a quarry

---

15 Marler, The Law of Real Property, pp. 362-363; Oscar Désautels, Etude sur la loi des privilèges (1927-28), 30 R. du N. 144 at 154-156.

16 For recent articles dealing with the Workman's Privilege, see: Le Privilège ouvrier, ses bénéficiaires, son objet, ses formalités, (1975) C.P. du N. pp. 65-102, Jacques Auger; Le Privilège de l'ouvrier, du fournisseur de matériaux, du constructeur et de l'architecte: la fin des travaux, (1975) C.P. du N. pp. 103-130, Serge Binette; Les Effets des Privilèges de l'art. 2013 C.C., (1975) C.P. du N. pp. 131-182, Paul Yvan Marquis.

17 *Cleroux v. Lefebvre-Dubois,* [1953] Que. S.C. 116.

18 *NC-RA Holdings Ltd. v. Falardeau,* [1965] R.L. 347.

19 *Lalancette v. Porcheron,* [1946] Que. P.R. 101; see footnotes 19 and 32, *post.*

were held by the Court of Appeal not to have a privilege on the church property.[20]

(b)   Formalities and Judicial Suit.

No formality is necessary to secure the workman's privilege,[21] *i.e.,* no notice need be given to the owner of the property affected, and it need not be registered against the property in the registry office (the land titles office): C.C. art. 2013*d.* However, the workman must sue his debtor within 30 days after the end of the work[22] on pain of the extinction of his privilege, and the owner of the property as well as the Registrar must be called into the action, the latter being required to make note of the suit in the index of immoveables: C.C. art. 2013*d.*[23]

As a protection to the owner of the property, C.C. article 2013*d* entitles him to retain out of the contract price an amount sufficient to pay the privileged claims,[24] the article providing for the fixing of the amount by the architect or engineer appointed by agreement of the parties, or failing their agreement, by a Judge of the Superior Court. Moreover, C.C. article 2013*d* also stipulates that the builder may not demand payment of the contract price before giving the owner a statement of all amounts due by him for labour and materials.

While the owner of the property may protect himself by retaining certain amounts in order to pay the privileged creditors,[25] it may happen that a privilege is registered against the property which the owner is prepared to contest. In this situation, there is no provision which comes to the aid of the owner, for nothing in the Code provides for relief of the owner with respect to this property, and it would normally mean that the privilege would remain registered against the property until the parties have settled their claims.[26]

---

20   *Bernier v. Foucault et Syndics de la Paroisse du Précieux-Sang* (1941), 70 Que. K.B. 315 (C.A.); see §182(*b*), *post,* for a discussion on whether other work than "construction" may give occasion to a workman's privilege.

21   This privilege thus differs from that of the supplier (§183, *post*), builder and architect: §184, *post.*

22   This slippery term (end of the work) is discussed in full in §185, *post.*

23   As to which Court (superior v. provincial) is competent to hear the workman's action, see C.P.P. arts. 31, 32 and 34; see also *Place Victoria St-Jacques Co. v. Potvin,* [1969] Que. Q.B. 1133 (C.A.).

24   Note the similar provision in C.C. art. 2013*c* in respect of the privilege of the supplier of materials; §182, *post.*

25   See *Marleau v. Jack Elliott Const. Ltd.,* [1975] Que. S.C. 824.

26   In *Gagnon v. Desruisseaux,* [1967] Que. P.R. 162, it has been held that the owner of the property may deposit money as security to obtain the discharge of a privilege at the Prothonotary's office. It will then enable the owner to dispose of his property or to effect it otherwise without having to worry about the privilege which is secured by the deposit of such an amount of money. The rationale of the Court was that it was not within the

§183 The Privilege of the Supplier of Materials.

(a) Subject and Object of the Supplier's Privilege.

"The supplier of materials has a privilege on the immoveable in the construction of which the materials supplied to the proprietor or builder have been used, or for the construction of which they have been specially prepared": C.C. art. 2013e. According to C.C. article 2013a the supplier of materials includes not only those who supply raw materials, but suppliers of every manufactured object which enters into any construction as well.[27] While this privilege exists even as regards materials that have been specially prepared, it has been held that the same must at least have been delivered to the owner or builder,[28] unless such delivery has been rendered impossible by reason of some fault on the part of the owner or builder. For the privilege to exist with respect to materials supplied, such materials must have become immoveables by nature and not merely immoveable by destination: this interpretation is based on the second paragraph of C.C. article 2013a. Otherwise, the supplier of materials which have simply been attached by destination could revendicate and remove them from the property. Only what is an "integral part" of the construction is the object of the privilege.[29] One must also refer to the law of sale of goods and to the notion of immoveable by destination, where the party must be owner of both the immoveable and the goods or fixtures.

The Court has made a distinction between the French and English versions of C.C. article 2013e, since the French version talks about materials

---

intention of the Code to restrict the rights of a registered owner if he takes the proper means of guaranteeing the claims of his creditors, however contested.

However, more recent cases do not accept this principle; see *Universal Stone Inc. v. Dame Rovira,* [1973] Que. C.A. 1089; also *Cleroux v. Adler,* [1952] Que. Q.B. 524, and *J. Dawe Forming (Quebec) Ltd. v. Grunco Const. Ltd.,* [1975] Que. S.C. 1034.

27 It will not include one who agrees to finance the contractor who will do the actual construction; *Kirouac v. Rigler,* [1949] Que. S.C. 219.

28 In *Vachon & Fils Ltée v. Beach Const. Co.,* [1961] Que. S.C. 320, doors and windows had been specially prepared and were in fact incorporated into the building. However, the supplier of materials had registered his privilege before making delivery, and this registration was held to be premature; but it should be noted that the owner of the property, having been notified of the privileged claim, had retained the required amount out of the contract price (being entitled to do so by C.C. art. 2013e) and was prepared at all times to pay the supplier, and when sued tendered the money into Court. Consequently, in this instance the supplier of materials was paid, though he was ordered to pay the costs of the action as regards the owner.

29 In *Terreau & Racine Ltée v. Hôtel Loretteville Inc.,* [1965] Que. S.C. 313, tiles, sinks and electrical systems were immoveable by nature while other materials such as electrical fixtures were not. Thus only the former were subject to the supplier's privilege. See Giroux, Le Privilège Ouvrier, (1933), p. 78, n. 68; also, *A. St-Germain et Fils Inc. v. Corpn. Hôpital des Monts Inc.,* [1976] Que. S.C. 125; and *Les Const. Fernand Binette Inc. v. Marine Indust. Ltd.,* [1976] Que. S.C. 289.

as they "entrent" in the building, whereas the word "used" appears in the English text. Modern construction techniques involve a number of materials that are actually used in the construction of a building but are not incorporated in the finished product, such as the forms used for pouring concrete, which are at a later stage removed and retained by the builder.

The Supreme Court of Canada, in a recent decision[29a], now appears to have settled this issue. A supplier of materials had supplied lumber to a builder who in constructing a building used the lumber for forms for the pouring of concrete. The Court, in setting aside the judgments of the Quebec Superior Court and of the Quebec Court of Appeal, decided that the supplier was entitled to a privilege for the price of lumber. The Supreme Court of Canada interpreted articles 2013, 2013a and 2013e C.C. and stated that the lumber was "used in the construction of an immoveable even though the lumber was not incorporated into the immoveable". The Court stated that the principle intended by the legislator, and stated in article 2013 C.C., is that those persons whose labour or materials have conferred additional value on an immoveable benefit from a right of preference in that immoveable. The question of incorporation, as opposed to mere delivery, had previously been stressed by the Court in other cases.[30]

The Quebec Court of Appeal has held that the privilege encompasses not only the capital of the debt, but in certain instances, applying article 2124 C.C., to the interest as well, although the Court refused to extend the real right to cover the disguised indemnity quae service charge of 15%.[31]

Once it is determined in which situations the supplier will be entitled to a privilege, and for which materials, we must examine what the supplier must do in order to conserve his privilege.

(b) Registration of Notice of Privilege.

Where the supplier of materials deals directly with the owner, his privilege is conserved only if there is registered, before the expiration of 30 days after the end of the work, a notice drawn up in the form of an affidavit containing the names, surnames and domiciles of the creditor and debtor, a description of the property affected, and a statement of his claim specifying the nature and the price of the materials supplied: C.C. arts. 2013e and 2103.

29a *Lumberland Inc. v. Nineteen Hundred Tower Ltd.* [1977] 1 S.C.R. 581, [1977] 1 Que. S.C. 581, 10 N.R. 393.

30 In *Pagé v. Beach Const. Co.,* [1953] Que. S.C. 284, the Court compared the French and English versions of C.C. art. 2013e and concluded that the materials had to be incorporated in the building for there to be a privilege, provided that they had been especially prepared for its construction.

31 *J.-H. Genest v. Cafor Internat. Holdings Ltd.,* [1974] Que. C.A. 481; see also re interest, *Guay v. Strato Const. Inc.,* [1974] C.S. 594, where the Court applied article 720 C.C.P. as well as article 2124 C.C.

The same requirement exists where the supplier of materials is dealing with a builder instead of the owner of the property: C.C. art. 2013*e*. There have been some difficulties in establishing who is the owner, or the true owner, of the property. For example, there are cases in which the owner of a piece of land incorporates a subsidiary corporation for the purposes of acquiring and administering certain immoveable properties. Although this subsidiary is a fully owned and controlled corporation, it constitutes a separate entity, and if the notice is given by the supplier of materials to the parent company, it could be argued that such a notice was not valid as against the subsidiary, which was in fact the "legal" owner of the property. It has been held, however, that in such cases the parent company should be held to be, for all intents and purposes, the real proprietor under the terms of C.C. article 2013*e*. The Courts have stressed that this article does not require notice to be given to the "registered" proprietor but only to the proprietor.[32] There has also been some difficulty experienced when the work is done or the materials supplied for one project but where the owner is erecting several constructions on different lots, at one time (*e.g.*, a single project for several homes). It would seem to be sufficient that the notice to the owner must contain a desription of each property sought to be affected by a privilege with a clear indication of the additional value claimed for the work or materials for *each* of such immoveables. Thus, where the project entails several lots and several constructions, while it is not necessary to register a separate and individual notice for every lot, and every home, it would not be sufficient to register a single notice without specifying the work, materials and additional value given to each. It would also be important to determine sufficiency, whether the supplier, builder, etc. was engaged pursuant to a single contract for the project as a whole or, rather, on a one contract per home basis.[33]

(c)   *Notice to the Owner of the Property.*

Where the supplier of materials is contracting with a builder instead of

---

32   *Air-Care Ltd. v. Blais*, [1964] Que. S.C. 241. The question of who should be the addressee of the notice (*e.g.* proprietor v. registered owner) was raised with some acuity in *Fréchette Inc. v. Hôtel Motel Sept-Iles Ltée*, [1971] Que. C.A. 630, and the Court of Appeal decided in favour of the registered owner; the facts of the case involved a promise of sale which was subsequently annulled. See comments on this case by Y. Caron (1972), 74 R. du N. 487.

33   See *Gadbois & Colle v. Stimson Reeb Bldrs. Supply Co.*, [1929] S.C.R. 587; *Munn & Shea Ltd. v. Hogue Ltée*, [1928] S.C.R. 398; *Crane Supply Co. v. Gérald Robitaille*, [1975] Que. S.C. 380; *Heller-Natofin Ltd. v. Webster & Sons Ltd.*, Que. S.C. (Montreal) no. 18-000151-73, Rothman J. March 19, 1973 (unreported); *Mirlaw Invts. Ltd. v. C.C. Const. Inc.*, Que. S.C. (Montreal) no. 05-01470-72 Lesage J., August 23, 1973 (unreported); Giroux, Le Privilège Ouvrier, pp. 322-324; *Fernando St-Hilaire Ltée v. Montmartre Const. Ltd.*, [1975] Que. S.C. 823.

with the owner of the property, there is the additional requirement that he give notice to the owner, in writing,[34] of his contract with the builder for the delivery of materials (C.C. art. 2013e), and his privilege will subsist only as regards those materials delivered after the giving of the notice. This means the notice must be given before the delivery of the materials. It has also been held that the privilege will not extend to cover materials prepared prior to the notice to the owner and delivered subsequent thereto.[35] This notice is therefore crucial and judgments on privilege actions taken by suppliers of materials have often hinged on whether the notice given was sufficient.

The supplier of materials has the burden of proving that the notice has been given. In the *Saint-Michel Lbr. Ltd.* case,[36] the notice was sent by registered letter dated February 22, 1955. The post office records having been destroyed before the trial, the Court accepted the owner's evidence that neither he nor his wife was at home to open the door to the postman as both were working, and his categoric statement that he did not receive the postman's notification until March 2 or 3 that a registered letter was being held for him at the post office, and that he only picked up the letter the following day, resulting in the notice being received too late to conserve the supplier's privilege. It will be seen from this that the supplier must not only establish that notice was sent but that it was also received.[37] In another case, where the owner was a corporation, notice given to its president was held to be sufficient, as he had signed the construction contract and was actively engaged in supervising the work.[38]

---

34   The necessity of writing was held to be a condition of the privilege; the mere general knowledge by the proprietor that materials have been supplied to the contractor is not sufficient to be regarded as equivalent to the written notice required by the law: *Pierre Brault Inc.* v. *L.P. Tremblay & Frères Ltée*, [1965] Que. S.C. 392. See footnote 30 *post*, and related text, and *Roy* v. *J.E.C. Giroux Ltée*, [1969] Que. Q.B. 201 (C.A.). See also: *Matériaux Gatineau Inc.* v. *Jasmin*, [1973] Que. S.C. 289, where the Court again confirmed that the notice must be in writing, and, further, that parole evidence to establish verbal notice to the owner is inadmissible, the claim of the supplier being a civil, and not a commercial matter: and *Jarjour* v. *Dupont*, [1973] Que. S.C. 329.

35   *Gamma Indust. Inc.* v. *La Corpn. Scolaire Régionale de Champlain*, [1975] Que. S.C. 821.

36   *Saint-Michel Lbr. Ltd.* v. *Granger*, [1958] Que. S.C. 396. It has been held that the failure of a supplier of materials to give notice could not support an application for cancellation of the registration of a privilege where the applicant, though he was the owner of the property when the materials were delivered, was not registered as such at that time. Since his contract of purchase was not registered, it could not be used to oppose the supplier's claim: *Le "Citoyen"* v. *Allied Bldg. Supply (Ottawa) Ltd.*, [1964] Que. S.C. 63; see C.C.P. arts. 805 and 806.

37   This was so held in *Dorval* v. *Plante*, [1951] Que. S.C. 359.

38   *Cantin Fils. Ltée* v. *Tremblay*, [1954] Que. Q.B. 673n (C.A.).

A letter sent by the supplier to the owner's architect has been held to be not in conformity with the requirements of article 2013e C.C.[39]

The notice given to a lessee of the property by a supplier of materials is not valid as it does not meet the requirements of C.C. article 2013e.[40] On the other hand, the notice given to an emphyteutic lessee would appear to be valid, since C.C. article 569 declares that the lessee "enjoys all the rights attached to the quality of a proprietor" and that "emphyteusis carries with it alienation". The notice given to the registered owner immediately prior to his granting an emphyteutic lease is binding on the lessee.[41]

As a corollary, the Quebec Court of Appeal has held that the termination of the emphyteutic lease by application of the resolutory clause may carry with it the right to ask for the radiation of privileges created after the registration of the lease but not those privileges born, or created, prior thereto.[42]

As to the contents of these notices, while C.C. article 2013e gives the owner of the property the right to retain from the contract price with the builder, an amount sufficient to meet the privileged claims of the supplier of materials (unless the builder furnishes a duly signed discharge or renunciation), the notice which the supplier must give to the owner need not mention the price of the materials nor indicate to the owner the amount which he should retain from the contract price.[43] In *Marmette v. Menuiserie du Nouveau Québec,*[44] it was held that the notice given by the supplier of materials under C.C. articles 2013e and 2103 was not sufficiently detailed: the notice did not state any date of delivery and stated only generally that materials that had been supplied were "des matériaux de construction, plus particulièrement des portes et des châssis", without reference to any other materials that had been delivered for the construction of a series of houses. The Court thought that this notice did not leave the trustee in bankruptcy with sufficient information for the identification of the claim and for the making up of their decision as to whether they were going to pay the bills or oppose the claim, especially in view of the fact that the notice indicated that there had been only one sale and delivery and one transaction generally.

---

39 *L'Assur. Vie Desjardins v. Les Boiseries Plessis Ltée,* [1971] Que. C.A. 680; see also footnote 84 on page 448.

40 *Grondin v. Daoust-Sansoucy,* [1971] Que. C.A. 64.

41 *Duskes v. Concreters Ready Mix Ltd.,* [1970] Que. C.A. 922; see *Gauthier v. B. & M. Fortin Inc.,* [1971] Que. C.A. 11.

42 [1975] Que. C.A. 202.

43 *Laminated Structures Ltd. v. Lemieux & Frères Inc.,* [1967] Que. S.C. 355 at 357-358; *Papillon v. Bérubé,* [1964] Que. K.B. 310 (C.A.); *Morissette v. Pichette,* [1955] Que. S.C. 231; *Faille v. Lefrançois* (1927), 33 R.L.N.S. 100; Demers, Traité de Droit Civil du Québec, XIV, p. 186. *Contra: Millen & Frère Ltée v. René* (1940), 78 Que. S.C. 534.

44 [1966] Que. S.C. 115.

The Court of Appeal has held that insofar as the notice given under article 2013e enables the owner of the property to establish whether the privilege is that of a supplier of materials (nature of the claim), whether the materials are identifiable and whether they are incorporated in the immoveable property, and finally to establish whether the price claimed for the materials is the effective price of such materials, then the notice is sufficient and should be regarded as valid. For the Court, it was a question of fact to determine whether the notice met those requirements or not, and it stressed that there was no need for special formalism in this case, as long as the notice was sufficient to determine the nature of the claim, the nature of the materials and the fact of their incorporation in a specified immoveable. The necessity of registration is a conservatory measure; it is not the formalities that confer the privilege, but the law. The formalities are only to provisionally maintain the privilege, while awaiting for the supplier to exercise it.[45]

The use of modern techniques such as photostatic reproduction of documents will now permit the registration of a complete file of invoices and other documents. It would seem, however, in the light of the above case, that the Courts will not require this formality, provided that the notice contains sufficient information for the proprietor to discern what materials are being referred to by the supplier. It has been held as well, that the notice need not be signed.[46] Where a supplier delivered materials in instalments over an approximate 2 month period, and immediately following each delivery mailed an account to the builder and a copy of it to the owner, this was held to be insufficient notice to conserve the supplier's privilege against the owner's property as regards the materials delivered after the first delivery, the supplier's signature to the documents again being considered unnecessary.[47]

---

45 *Roy v. J.E.C. Giroux Ltée,* [1969] Que. Q.B. 201 at 204-207 (C.A.). In *Duskes v. Concreters Ready Mix Ltd.,* [1970] Que. C.A. 922 at 928, the Court of Appeal has suggested that a mere indication of a global amount was not strict compliance with the terms of C.C. art. 2013e and 2013f, but there were other grounds on which to decide that case. One would hope that the *Roy v. Giroux* case will be applied in the future.

46 In *Mott Co. v. Associated Textile of Can.* (1934), 57 Que. K.B. 300 (C.A.), the supplier of materials, being doubtful of the builder's solvency, obtained a request from the latter, signed by him and addressed to the owner of the property, instructing him to pay the supplier's account directly. The supplier took this document to the owner who refused to be bound by it. Subsequently the builder went bankrupt and the supplier registered a privilege against the property. The Court held that the document, which had not originally been intended as a notice, complied sufficiently with the Code's notice provisions even though it had not been signed by the supplier, as it conveyed to the owner the information required by the article, namely that the supplier had contracted with the builder to furnish materials. See also *Morissette v. Pichette, post,* at p. 233.

47 *Darabaner v. Pruneau Ltée,* [1960] Que. Q.B. 1042 (C.A.). In *Morissette v. Pichette,* [1955] Que. S.C. 231, the privilege of the supplier of materials was held to affect all the

It has also been held that the knowledge which the owner has of a cession of priority of hypothec signed by the supplier is not sufficient to constitute notice as required by article 2013e C.C., the Court stating the object and purpose of the cession of priority of hypothec was not to notify the owner of the supply of materials.[48]

(d) *Judicial Suit.*

Once the proper notices have been given, the supplier must sue his debtor (being the owner: see footnote 110, *post,* and related text, or a separate builder, as the case may be), within 3 months after the end of the work on pain of the extinction of his privilege. The Registrar must be called into the case so that the action will be registered against the property (in the registry or land titles office); and where the debtor who is sued is a builder, the owner must also be called into the case: C.C. art. 2013e.

The action of the supplier of materials must be a distinct one brought under the provisions of C.C. article 2013e. A petition under the Winding-Up Act does not constitute a valid exercise of the right of action provided for the Civil Code, as was held in *Pierre L'Heureux Inc. v. Doric Const. Ltée.*[49]

(e) *Right of Revendication.*

C.C. article 2013e gives the supplier of materials an additional right. Where the owner or builder is insolvent or fails to pay at the periods agreed upon, the supplier may revendicate (*i.e.,* obtain the repossession of) the materials which he has supplied but which have not yet been incorporated into the building. This right of revendication is not subject to the requirements affecting the privilege of the supplier of materials (such as the giving of notice and the registration of the claim); nor is it subject to the conditions imposed by C.C. article 1999 in favour of the ordinary unpaid vendor.[50]

§184 The Builder's and Architect's Privilege.

(a) *Builder's Privilege.*

A builder is defined by C.C. article 2013a as including "both contractor

---

materials delivered, the owner at the time of each delivery having been given a copy of the bill and having signed it, the owner also having indicated where the materials should be put.

48 *L'Office Municipal d'Habitation de Drummondville v. Béton Drummond Ltée,* [1975] Que. S.C. 571.

49 [1964] Que. S.C. 570. This case dealt with the privilege of a sub-contractor and on action under C.C. art. 2013f, but the same reasoning would apply to C.C. art. 2013e.

50 *J. H. Lebeuf Ltée v. Les Curé et Marguilliers de l'Oeuvre et Fabrique de la Paroisse de St. Augustin* (1922), 33 Que. K.B. 565 (C.A.). C.C. arts. 1998 and 1999 have been reproduced in the Appendix, §192, at the end of this Chapter.

and subcontractor". It will not include a person who agrees to finance the contractor who will do the actual construction.[51]

It would appear that the builder must have the requisite licence to carry on his trade, failing which he lacks the capacity to register a valid privilege for his work.[52] In the case of *Enterpreneurs Gén. G.V.L. Inc. v. G. Lacaille Excavation Inc.,* the builder executed excavation works and supplied concrete. The Court, confirming that the articles of the Code with respect to privileges must be restrictively interpreted, determined that the provisions of The Building Contractors Vocational Qualifications Act[53] were of public order and, since the builder in this case failed to obtain the specified licence from the Board established by the Act, the privilege was struck down.

(b) Architect's (and Engineer's?) Privilege.

As far as architects are concerned, only those who comply with the provisions of The Architect's Act are permitted to practise as such, and thus benefit from the architect's privilege.[54]

Since the basis of a privilege is the additional value given to the immoveable, it has been held that the immoveable must be constructed in accordance with the plans of the architect, failing which the privilege will not attach.[55] In the *L.T. Investments Inc. v. Schrier* case, one architect had prepared a set of plans for a building and, subsequently, a second architect submitted another set of plans according to which the building was ultimately erected. The Court denied to the first architect the right of privilege.

It has also been held that a landscape architect, although entitled to the title of "Architect", is not entitled to register a privilege.[56] The Judge noted that although the legislator has provided, in article 12 of the Architect's Act,[57] that "landscape-architect" is a legal title and that such a person does not commit an illegal practice in contravention of the Architect's Act by the use of such title, nevertheless the legislator did not see fit to add "landscape-architect" to the list of persons enumerated in 2013 C.C. However, see also the case comment on this holding by M. Tancelin[58] where this judgment is questioned and where the author suggests that since the Association of

---

51 *Kirouac v. Rigler,* [1949] Que. S.C. 219.
52 *Entrepreneurs Gén. G.V.L. Inc. v. G. Lacaille Excavation Inc.,* Que. S.C. (Montreal), no. 500-05-002826-780, Mackay J., February 18, 1978 (unreported).
53 (1975) R.S.Q. 53.
54 R.S.Q. 1964, c. 261, s. 12.
55 *L.T. Invts. Inc. v. Schrier,* [1973] Que. S.C. 784.
56 *B-7 Const. Inc. v. Atelier d'Urbanisme Larouche et Robert Inc.,* [1972] Que. S.C. 394.
57 R.S.Q. 1964 261; re-en. 1973 (Que.), c. 59, s. 15.
58 Tancelin, Privilège de l'Architecte, Architecte Paysagiste, Urbaniste Conseil — Interprétation, (1971) 12 C. de D. 683.

Architects was only created after the drafting of 2013 C.C., the interpretation by the judiciary of the word "architect" in 2013 C.C. should not be limited to members of the association; the author further suggests that it would be preferable for the judiciary to resolve litigation with solutions adapted to contemporary society rather than strict adherence to the reading of legal texts. Nevertheless, this case comment seems to overlook the basic point raised by the trial judge that only the legislator has the right and the power to change the law.

The traditionally strict interpretation of the articles of the Civil Code dealing with privileges did not accept that the word "architect" could mean anything but "architect". This question has been revived in the Courts, and one Judge has been prepared to include "engineer" within the meaning of "architect" in C.C. article 2013. Whereas the strict interpretation rule was said to limit the effect of C.C. article 2013 to architects alone,[59] it was decided in *Fraser-Brace Enrg. v. Chassé, Tremblay & Associés*[60] that the historical background of these professions, their involvement in the construction business and the jurisprudential developments in the law of lease and hire with respect to construction contracts[61] justified the inclusion of engineers within the scope of C.C. article 2013. The basic argument being that if one is to hold the engineer responsible for the loss resulting from a defect in construction, on the same basis as the architect,[62] it would be just and fair to afford him a privilege to secure the payment of his fee, on the same basis as the architect.[63] From that point of view, the reasoning is faultless, especially since it is pointed out that the engineer should benefit from the same rights as the architect under C.C. article 2013, not because the two words are assimilable, but because the two professions never were the object of a distinction having regard to the interpretation of the law of construction. The codifiers intended to extend the responsibility of defects to all those who today exercise one or the other of these professions, and it is the co-ordinated reunion of their participation which allows the complete realization of the work.[64]

Traditionalists remain doubtful because of the "strict" interpretation rule:[65] this rule being to the effect that each privilege deprives the unsecured

---

59 See *Matos v. H. Brummer Const. Co.*, [1969] Que. S.C. 67, where the engineer was denied a privilege.

60 [1970] Que. S.C. 342.

61 C.C. art. 1688; see *Can. Elec. Light Co. v. Pringle* (1920), 29 Que. K.B. 26 at 28-30, cited in [1970] Que. S.C. 342, at 344.

62 Under the provisions of C.C. art. 1688.

63 Under the provisions of C.C. art. 2013.

64 *Fraser-Brace Engineering v. Chassé, Tremblay & Associés*, [1970] Que. S.C. 342, at 344-345.

65 See comment by P.Y. Marquis, in (1971) 31 R. du B. 342, *re* the *Fraser-Brace* case, *ante*.

creditor of a chance of participating in the assets of the debtor. But in view of the limitations put on the exercise of privileges and namely of the "value-added" requirement, the broader interpretation of C.C. article 2013 is not shocking. Indeed, it has long been desired by all concerned and it may be just as well that a new way of justifying the change has been found. A recent judgment of the Quebec Court of Appeal has again reviewed the capacity of the engineer to register a privilege and has decided (in a 2-1 decision) that the engineer is entitled to avail himself of the architect's privilege created by Article 2013 C.C.[66] This, of course, raises the question of the desirability of the architect's privilege in the first place, an advantage that is not available in other jurisdictions.[67]

(c)   Registration of Notice of Privilege.

Both the builder's and the architect's privileges are similarly dealt with in C.C. article 2013f. Each has a privilege on the immoveable for the work he has done as such, provided that within 30 days after the end of the work a statement of claim is registered against the property and notice of the registration is given to the owner within the same delay. As a result of the case of *Air-Care Ltd. v. Blais*,[68] the rule may be established that if a person (owner) works on his own building, there is no need to give himself a notice of the work. Such a rule would extend to cases where the owner is the same person but acting through different corporations or agencies.[69] On the other hand, where the original owner has subsequently granted an emphyteutic lease, the notice of C.C. article 2013f by the subcontractor has now to be given to the lessee, who has all the powers of the owner under C.C. article 569.[70]

When there is a condition in the contract that the work has to be completed by the builder and delivered upon completion, the latter may not demand the execution of the obligation of the owner before the work is completed; similarly, it will not be possible for the builder to claim a privilege before completion.[71]

The form of the notice required by C.C. article 2031f to be given to the owner by the contractor is regulated in C.C. article 2103. This notice must be in the form of an affidavit sworn to before one of the persons mentioned in C.C. article 2103. The question of the validity of notices received before a

---

66   *Wolofsky v. Aetna Casualty and Surety Co.*, [1976] Que. C.A. 102; *contra:* see *Wolofsky v. Carrière Du Pont Ltée*, [1972] Que. S.C. 836.
67   A question which is being studied by the Office de revision du Code civil. See the comment of M. Tancelin, (1970) 11 C. de D. 597, re the *Fraser-Brace* case, *ante.*
68   [1964] Que. S.C. 241.
69   See *ibid.,* at 249-250.
70   *Duskes v. Concreters Ready Mix Ltd.,* [1970] Que. C.A. 922, at 927.
71   *Marmette v. Deschênes,* [1966] Que. S.C. 1.

notary but without the attestation of two witnesses was raised in *P.E. Elec. Inc. v. Auguste Lessard Const. Ltée*[72] and the Court held that where the requirements of C.C. article 2013*f* and 2103 were met, there was no need to add extra formalism. This decision confirms a constant notarial practice.

The Quebec Court of Appeal has recently held that where the builder's contract entails both the supply of materials as well as the execution of works and manpower, the privilege is that of a builder and the law does not require in such circumstances that the builder divide his privilege and exercise the former (*i.e.* as supplier) according to 2013*e* C.C., and the latter (*i.e.* as builder) according to 2013*f* C.C.[72a] . The Court also distinguished articles 2013*e* and 2013*f* C.C. with respect to the notice requirements, holding that whereas the former requires of the supplier a detailed recitation of the account and materials furnished, no such requirement exists with respect to the builder pursuant to 2013*f* C.C. which specifies only "... a statement of his claim".

(d) Judicial Suit.

A second requirement to conserve the builder's or architect's privilege is that an action must be taken against the owner within 6 months after the end of the work on pain of the extinction of the privilege, and the Registrar must be called into the case so that he may register the action against the property: C.C. art. 2013*f*. It has been held that the action brought under C.C. article 2013*f* must be a distinct one and that a petition under The Winding-Up Act would not qualify as such.[73]

(e) Notice by the Subcontractor to the Owner of the Property.

Where all or part of the work has been done by subcontract, the subcontractor also has a privilege on the property for work done by him subsequent to his having notified the owner of the existence of the subcontract, provided he gives the notice described above and takes the action within 6 months of the end of the work: C.C. art. 2013*f*. This notice must be given by all subcontractors. Thus the subcontractor's privilege, like that of the supplier of materials is dependent on his having given prior notice to the owner. There is, however, one marked difference in the notice requirements. While C.C. article 2013*e* states that the notice to be given by the supplier of materials must be in writing, C.C. article 2013*f* does not specify any particular form as regards the subcontractor's notice, so that a verbal notice is valid. The problem with a verbal notice, however, lies in the difficulty of proof. Under the ordinary rules of evidence, written proof is

72 [1971] Que. S.C. 290; see comment in (1971) 73 R. du N. 367.
72a *Hershorn v. Miro Const. Inc.,* [1973] Que. C.A. 1022.
73 *Pierre L'Heureux Inc. v. Doric Const. Ltée,* [1964] Que. S.C. 570; see footnote 49, *ante.*

required unless the matter to be proved falls into one of the exceptional categories where proof by testimony is permitted. C.C. article 1233 sets forth the instances where testimonial evidence is allowed:

"1233. Proof may be made by testimony:

1. Of all facts concerning commercial matters;

2. In all matters in which the principal sum of money or value in question does not exceed five hundred dollars.

. . .

7. In cases in which there is a commemcement of proof in writing."

The second category needs no comment.

As to the first category, Quebec law envisages contracts of a commercial nature as well as those of a civil nature, so that if the work being done is by virtue of the former type of contract, the giving of the notice may be proved by testimony. However, contracts relating to immoveable property are generally considered to be civil in nature,[74] and it is only under exceptional circumstances that they can be commercial. One instance where a contract affecting an immoveable will be treated as a commercial matter as against the owner (it must be commercial for the party against whom proof is to be made by testimony) is where this owner is a merchant who engages a contractor to enlarge his store for the purpose of furthering his business.[75]

If the contract is civil in nature for the owner, the subcontractor cannot use testimonial evidence to prove the notification to the owner unless the other exception avails in his favour, *i.e.,* unless there is a commencement of proof in writing. In what cases can there be said to be a commencement of proof in writing? This expression has been defined by Rinfret J. as connoting "a writing emanating from the party against whom it is to be used which tends to render probable the existence of the fact which is desired to be proved."[76] Thus where there is a writing emanating from the other party (it is not essential that it be actually signed by the other party), which tends to render probable the fact to be proved, then recourse to testimony is allowed. C.C.P. article 319 also permits the evidence of the other party to be used as a commencement of proof in writing. Thus where the other party's evidence is contradictory and improbable, or he is evasive or hesitant or pretends loss of memory as regards facts that should be well known to him, so that it is evident he is trying to hide the truth, then his evidence will

---

74   Perrault, Traité de Droit Commercial, Vol. I, p. 327.

75   *Blais v. Paradis* (1932), 54 Que. K.B. 495 (C.A.).

76   *Johnston v. Buckland,* [1937] S.C.R. 86 at 103, [1937] 2 D.L.R. 433; see also André Nadeau, Le Commencement de Preuve par écrit, (1957), 17 R. du B. 489.

constitute a commencement of proof in writing which will allow testimony to be used by his adversary.

The foregoing rules of evidence seem, on the whole, to have been uniformly applied by the Courts to the problem of how the subcontractor is to prove that he has notified the owner of his subcontract where he did not do so in writing.[77] It has been held at least once, however, that testimonial evidence of the notice to the owner could not be accepted unless there was a commencement of proof in writing.[78]

As to testimonial proof of delivery of a written notice, it has been held that when the notice by the subcontractor has been given by way of delivering to the owner of the building a copy of the agreement between the general contractor and the subcontractor at the time it was signed, the proof of such delivery will be allowed by way of testimonial evidence. When the owner of the property receives such a copy of the contract, he is notified of the subcontract within the meaning of C.C article 2013*f.*[79]

While the notice need not be in writing, it is nonetheless essential that it be given; mere knowledge of the existence of a sub-contract on the part of the owner will not suffice.[80] It has been held that even where the owner was aware of the existence of the sub-contract, spoke with the president of the supplier company before the construction work commenced, saw the supplier's trucks circulating around the building being constructed and, further, saw the cession of priority of hypothec signed by the supplier, in the absence of *actual notice,* verbal or written, the privilege of the sub-contractor cannot avail.[81]

---

77   The following are reported judgments on the question, but it will be appreciated that they do not all consider all the principles of evidence involved: *Richman v. Seni Const. Co.* (1929), 67 Que. S.C. 400, 35 R. de Jur. 193; *Billet v. Loranger,* [1945] Que. S.C. 160; *Bélisle v. Riendeau,* [1950] Que. S.C. 39, 52 R. du N. 452; *Renaud v. Roussel,* [1961] Que. P.R. 384.

78   *Norio v. Better Homes Bldrs. Ltd.,* [1960] Que. S.C. 224. See N.H. Salomon, Meredith Memorial Lectures, McGill University, 1969, pp. 33-34.

79   *Ouellet v. Hamel,* [1963] Que. Q.B. 64 (C.A.).

80   *Compagnie de Carrelages de Qué. Ltée v. Darabaner,* [1959] Que. Q.B. 861 (C.A.); *Demontigny v. Gen. Const. Inc.,* [1970] Que. S.C. 459; *Poirier v. Rimont Const. Ltée,* [1958] Que. S.C. 617; *A. Blondin Ltée v. Morin,* [1943] Que. K.B. 701 (C.A.); *Concrete Column Clamps Ltd. v. Québec,* [1940] S.C.R. 522 at 528, [1940] 4 D.L.R. 421 at 424; see also the borderline decision of *Blouin v. Martineau* (1923), 63 Que. S.C. 73. *Contra: Commn. des Ecoles Catholiques de Montréal v. Can. Iron Works Co.* (1935), 58 Que. K.B. 565 (C.A.). It was held that the knowledge which the owner had of the subcontract in this particular case was sufficient without the subcontractor having given notice. However, the facts were special: there was a stipulation in the principal contract that all subcontracts had to be approved by the owner and it had so approved in writing both the subcontractor and the terms of the subcontract. The two dissenting Judges were of the opinion that notice was still required to be given despite these special circumstances. (This judgment is summarized in 38 R. du N. 44).

81   *Plombelec Inc. v. Angers et Parent Inc.,* [1975] Que. S.C. 360.

In another case, written tenders were submitted to and opened in the presence of the owner; the lowest tender (that of the sub-contractor seeking the enforcement of the privilege in the case at bar) was accepted by a representative of the owner. While the Court of Appeal found that the owner had knowledge of the sub-contract, nevertheless, it held that actual notice had to be given (and was not); the Court stated that such notice was required not for the purpose of divulging the contract to the owner but rather to alert the owner of the sub-contractor's intention to avail itself of its privileged rights.[82]

It takes more than an informal discussion between the subcontractor and the owner to be valid as a notice under C.C. article 2013*f*. The notice must actually be given to the owner or to someone having his authority to receive it,[83] and in particular the architect lacks such authority.[84] The question whether the notice is given to the owner or to a person who acts for the owner or is his representative has been discussed earlier.[85] In another case, the Court decided that a notice had been validly given to a person who was owner of a building and land and who had dealt with the main contractor in the construction of a new building, but who nevertheless alleged that the proprietor of the new building was not he but a business operated in the building by his wife. He knew that the work was being done on the new building on his land by the contractor and by the subcontractor, and the Court of Appeal thought that there was no reason to distinguish between the two parties in this case and held that the notice had been validly given.[86] In a case where the subcontractor had not properly given a notice to the owner of the land, but simply tried to refer to such a notice in the affidavit given for requiring the registration of the privilege, the Court held that if this was to be regarded as a notice at all, it would have to be invalid because it had been given after the execution of the sub-contract and therefore did not meet the requirements of C.C. article 2013*f*.[87]

The reason for the notice requirement is simple: when the owner has received notice of the subcontract, he can retain and hold back some of the money from the general contractor until there is some evidence that the claims of the subcontractors have been satisfied and that he is in no danger

---

82 *La Banque Provinciale du Can. v. Adélard Laberge Ltée*, [1973] Que. C.A. 1115.
83 *Be-vi Invt. Corpn. v. Cescutti, post; Compagnie de Carrelages de Qué. Ltée v. Darabaner, ante; Poirier v. Rimont Const. Ltée, ante.*
84 *Hamelin v. J.B. Laplante Inc.*, [1958] Que. Q.B. 395 (C.A.); *Sharpe v. Budd* (1907), 17 Que. K.B. 17 (C.A.).
85 See *Air-Care Ltd. v. Blais*, [1964] Que. S.C. 241; *James H. Wilson Ltd. v. Spécialités de Cuisine Inc.*, [1963] Que. Q.B. 21 (C.A.); *Duskes v. Concreters Ready Mix Ltd.*, [1970] Que. C.A. 922 at 927.
86 *Wallcrete of Can. Ltd. v. Mednick*, [1968] Que. Q.B. 182 (C.A.).
87 *Gravel v. Diana Const. Ltée*, [1961] Que. S.C. 476.

of being forced to pay the price a second time or of losing his property should a privilege be registered against it. On the other hand, the owner cannot exercise the right to hold back the amount of money necessary to pay the subcontractors until and unless he has been properly notified of the subcontract.[88]

In contrast to the stand taken by the Courts in relation to the privilege of the supplier of materials, it has been held that the notice must indicate the nature of the subcontract and the price for which it is being carried out, to enable the owner to ascertain the amount he should retain for his protection from the contract price.[89] The contrast is made greater by the provision in C.C. article 2013*f* of a procedure to fix a suitable amount to be retained by the owner out of the contract price to meet the sub-contractor's claim, whereas there is no equivalent provision in C.C. article 2013*e* as regards the claim of the supplier of materials, so that the owner may not know what sum to retain.

On the other hand, it may not always be possible to indicate the price or amount for which the contract is concluded, especially where the operation is carried out on a cost-plus basis, for example. There may be other circumstances under which the total amount of the contract cannot be determined in advance. In fact, C.C. article 2013*f* provides that where such a notice is given, the proprietor is entitled to retain amounts sufficient to satisfy the claims of subcontractors: this would seem to shift the burden on the latter to specify the amount which could be retained. More recently, the Courts have been more lenient with respect to the contents of notices, stating that no sacramental forms are required.[90] The Court has also rejected as pure formalism a plea that a privilege was null because it was described, in the notice of registration, as a "supplier's privilege" when it was really a "sub-contractor's privilege", if the memorandum registered and the accompanying documents clearly revealed the true nature of the privilege.[91]

Finally, where the notice in question has not been given, who may raise this objection? In a case where a general contractor wanted to contest the validity of a subcontractor's privilege, he argued that the subcontractor had not given sufficient notice to the proprietor of his intention to avail himself of the privilege upon the immoveable. It was held that the general contractor had no legal interest to raise the question whether the subcontractor's notice was sufficient, since the notice is not a matter of public order, and therefore

---

88 In *Be-vi Invt. Corpn. v. Cescutti*, [1966] Que. S.C. 65, it was decided that a privilege was invalid because the reasons had not been properly given, and therefore the owner was not entitled to retain some of the money.

89 *Hamelin v. Perron* (1941), 79 Que. S.C. 418; *Renaud v. Roussel*, [1961] Que. P.R. 384; Demers, Traité de Droit Civil du Québec, XIV, p. 191.

90 *Voltec Ltée v. La Caisse Populaire de Québec*, [1971] Que. S.C. 149.

91 *Sofinec Inc. v. Amico Inc.*, [1969] Que. Q.B. 941.

cannot be raised by any other but the owner. If the owner does not invoke a lack of notice to him by a sub-contractor in an action on a privilege, this right cannot be exercised by a contractor.[92] Even where the sub-contractor has signed a valid renunciation of privilege, and notwithstanding registers a privilege, it has been held that the general contractor, having no legal interest *in res,* lacks the quality to seek the radiation of the privilege.[93]

However, a very recent judgment of the Court of Appeal holds that the builder does have sufficient legal interest to seek (in this instance by way of motion pursuant to article 805 C.C.P.) the radiation of the sub-contractor's privilege in that: (a) as long as the privilege of the sub-contractor remains registered against the property, the owner has the right to withhold sufficient funds in accordance with article 2013*f* C.C., and (b) the renunciation to privilege signed by the sub-contractor constituted a stipulation pour autrui.[94]

§185 The Importance and Difficulty of Fixing the Date of the "End of the Work".

(a) *Introduction to this Problem.*

The delays for registration of the privileges and the taking of action on them run from the date of the "end of the work". The importance of the fixing of this date is self-evident: a privilege that is registered more than 30 days after the end of the work is lost, and a duly registered privilege that is not sued on within the specified delays which also run from the date of the end of the work, is extinguished.

In a straightforward case, where a building is erected without interruption from start to finish, and there remains nothing more to be done, it is easy to ascertain the date of the end of the work. Not all buildings, however, are so erected, especially where financial difficulties are experienced on the part of the owner or the builder. These difficulties may cause those involved in the construction to wish to protect themselves by exercising their privileged rights, while at the same time resulting in the date of the end of the work becoming difficult to determine. The Courts have therefore had the hapless task of attempting to fix the date of the end of the

---

92   *James H. Wilson Ltd. v. Specialités de Cuisine Inc.,* [1963] Que. Q.B. 21 (C.A.).

93   *J.-H. Dupuis Ltée v. Ubald Blouin & Fils Ltée,* [1972] Que. S.C. 605. Note however that the judgment is concerned primarily with the general contractor's right to proceed via article 805 C.C.P. in a summary petition, and leaves open, implicitly, the legal recourse via a writ of summons.

94   *Pisapia Const. Inc. v. St-Fabien Indust. Inc.,* Que. C.A. no. 09-596-75, October 19, 1977 (unreported). Similarly, in the case of *Laurent Gagnon Inc. v. Can. Financial Co.,* Que. S.C. no. 200-05-005543-777, George Pelletier J., January 27, 1978 (unreported), the Court held that the contractor/builder has sufficient legal interest to lodge a motion to radiate a sub-contractor's privilege.

work in the individual instances submitted to them. They have not received much help from the definition of the "end of the work" given in C.C. article 2013*a* because of its generality: "The words 'end of the work' means the date at which the construction is ready for the use for which it is intended." In fact, it has been stated that the Legislature purposely gave only a very general definition of this term so as to leave the fixing of the actual date to the discretion of the Courts.[95] The latter, faced with having to apply the general definition to various combinations of situations, have now evolved certain principles to guide them. These principles are relatively simple in themselves but may not always be easy to apply to any particular set of facts.[96]

Some of the fact situations that the Courts have been faced with, and their treatment of the same, will now be examined.

(b)   The Occupation of the Building by the Owner or Tenant.

In view of the wording of the definition to the effect that the "end of the work" is when the construction is ready for the use for which it is intended, it might at first sight appear logical to conclude that the occupation of the premises by the owner or tenants constitutes conclusive evidence that the end of the work has occurred. This, however, is not so. The Courts have recognized the fact that premises are often occupied before they have been completed. Consequently the delays within which privileged claims must be exercised will not run from the date of occupation if the end of the work has not yet been reached.[97]

This rule has been confirmed in *Corpn. de Crédit Adanac v. Turcotte*[98] which involved the construction of a new building and the subsequent operation of a *dation en paiement* clause where the creditor claimed that a

---

95   *Billet v. Loranger,* [1945] Que. S.C. 160.

96   There is an excellent article by Walter S. Johnson, Q.C. entitled The "End of the Work" (1951), 11 R. du B. 245, but it must be borne in mind that a number of important judgments have been reported since the writing of the article. There is also a discussion by Giroux in Le Privilège Ouvrier (1933), pp. 298 *et seq.*

97   Marler, The Law of Real Property, p. 357; Demers, Traité de Droit Civil du Québec, XIV, p. 174; Johnson, The "End of the Work", *ante,* pp. 247 *et seq.;* Giroux, Le Privilège Ouvrier, p. 300; *Banque Jacques-Cartier v. Picard* (1900), 18 Que. S.C. 502; *Quintal v. Bénard* (1901), 20 Que. S.C. 199; *Letellier de Saint-Just v. Blanchette* (1910), 21 Que. K.B. 1 (C.A.); *Brunswick Balke Collender Co. v. Racette* (1915), 49 Que. S.C. 50 (Ct. of Rev.); *J.L. Vachon & Fils Ltée v. Corbeil* (1929), 35 R.L.N.S. 453; *Commn. des Ecoles Catholiques de Montréal v. Can. Iron Works Co.* (1935), 58 Que. K.B. 565 at 570 *et seq.* (C.A.); *Kirallah v. Gagnon* (1936), 61 Que. K.B. 264 (C.A.); *La Perrelle Lumber Co. v. Langlois* (1938), 77 Que. S.C. 1; *Jubinville v. Dagenais,* [1942] Que. S.C. 475; *Asconi Bldg. Corpn. v. Creswell-Pomeroy Ltd.,* [1942] Que. K.B. 718 at 720 and 722 (C.A.).

98   [1966] Que. Q.B. 768 (C.A.). The rule has been maintained in subsequent decisions; see *Laporte v. Gagnon,* [1971] Que. C.A. 1.

privilege could not be opposed to him. The Court held that the fact that the owner occupied the building before the end of the work was to be regarded as irrelevant in determining the date of the end of the work.

(c) *What will Constitute Sufficient Work Remaining to be done to Establish that the "End of the Work" has not yet been Reached?*

Uncertainty in the law is at the best of times unhealthy. It is doubly so in situations like those in which privileged creditors such as the builder find themselves; conservation of their privileges depend on the correct computation of delays starting from the "end of the work". It is no doubt with a view to solving this problem and to inserting an element of certainty into the matter, that the Courts have frequently repeated a strong statement in their judgments to the effect that the end of the work is only arrived at once all the work has been accomplished, and that so long as work remains to be done, the end of the work has not occurred.[99] An examination of these judgments discloses, however, that in most of these cases the Courts were faced with situations where either quite important work remained to be done or where the remaining work formed an integral part of the work contracted for. Many examples may be cited: in *Corpn. de Crédit Adanac v. Turcotte*,[100] where, on the date on which the end of the work is alleged to have occurred, the storm windows, the fixtures for the garage door, the storm door and the fire insulation were missing and the chimney was incomplete, the Court held that the "end of the work" means the time when the immoveable is ready for the use for which it is intended, including the integral execution of the contract.[101] This appears to be the prevailing rule

---

99   *Banque Jacques-Cartier v. Picard, ante; Quintal v. Bénard, ante; Letellier de Saint-Just v. Blanchette, ante; Brunswick Balke Collender Co. v. Racette, ante; Blouin v. Martineau* (1923), 63 Que. S.C. 73; *J.L. Vachon & Fils Ltée v. Corbeil, ante; Commn. des Ecoles Catholiques de Montréal v. Can. Iron Works Co., ante,* at pp. 570 *et seq.; Kirallah v. Gagnon, ante,* especially at pp. 272-273. See (1967), 13 McGill Law Journal, pp. 179-180 for a short review of unreported cases; *Corpn. de Crédit Adanac v. Turcotte* [1966] Que. Q.B. 768 (C.A.); *Armoires de Cuisine de Montréal Ltée v. Maiorno,* [1969] R.L. 129.

100 [1966] Que. Q.B. 768 (C.A.).

101 *Laporte v. Gagnon, ante.* In *Duskes v. Concreters Ready Mix Ltd.,* [1970] Que. C.A. 922, a sidewalk remained to be completed (the privilege was declared null on other grounds). In *Letellier de Saint-Just v. Blanchette, ante,* the carpentry work had not been completed; in *Brunswick Balke Collender Co. v. Racette, ante,* the only parts of the hotel that had been completed were the bar and the dining room — the bedroom floors had not been finished; in *Blouin v. Martineau, ante,* while the bulk of the plastering had been done, plaintiff's plastering contract called for him to do more plastering work once carpentry repairs of a nature to damage the plaster were finished; in *Commn. des Ecoles Catholiques de Montréal v. Can. Iron Works Co., ante,* a relatively small amount of work remained to be done (as listed on p. 571), but this work formed an integral part of what had been stipulated in the contract; in *Kirallah v. Gagnon, ante,* the house was far

for the moment, and indeed one that substantially conforms with the word and spirit of paragraph 4 of C.C. article 2013*a*. Where, in a very recent case, the Court stated that some parts of the work had been foreseen in the plans and were a part of the integral execution of a project, then, as minimal as they were they entered into account to determine the end of the work. In other cases, the Courts did not postpone the date of the end of the work. Thus in *Desbiens v. Vilandré*,[102] all the work had been completed by the end of April, 1921, save for the installation of a double door which apparently the contractor overlooked and which he only put on at the end of March, 1922. The privilege which was registered within 30 days of this latter date was held to be too late: the work had been accepted, the contractor had removed his tools and unused materials and the owner had given a note in payment of the work, all in March or April, 1921. The double door was only installed and the privilege registered once the note had been unpaid and the property had been retroceded by the owner to his vendor. In *Paquin v. Beauchamp*,[103] the Court took quite a strict view of the builder's privilege. There remained to be done the installation and painting of two or three pantry window frames and the painting of a banister. The Court pointed out that the contractor had previously withdrawn his men, that three out of four lodgings were occupied and the place was ready for occupancy, and that the work under the contract was practically finished. In other words, the end of the work had occurred before these details had been attended to. In *Schulte United Properties v. Germain*,[104] the additional work consisted of repairing, for $2.30, a basin which leaked (the leak was an accidental event that might have occurred at any time and could not affect the completion date of the work which had been undertaken), and the installation of ventilating apparatus and of a pump in the furnace room. It was held that the

---

from completed. See *Armoires de Cuisine de Montréal Ltée v. Maiorno*, [1969] R.L. 129, and also *Standard Elec. Co. v. Protestant Bd. of School Commrs. of Montreal*, Superior Court, Montreal, No. 691463, July 3, 1968, in which Batshaw J. studied the recent decisions and held that when as many as close to 500 items remain incomplete, missing or defective in the building for a total amount of $45,000, this was not to be held trivial in the construction and therefore the privilege would be held to be valid because the end of the work has not been reached. But see *contra: Forcillo v. Sirois*, [1966] Que. S.C. 96. See also *Chauffage Laurentien v. J. Aimé Perron Ltée*, [1975] R.L. 374, where minor exterior work had yet to be completed and the Court held that the end of the work had not been achieved.

102 (1922), 61 Que. S.C. 124. In *Ménard v. Indri*, [1970] Que. C.A. 1172, the Court of Appeal accepted the preponderance of the proof against the registrant of a privilege where the construction had been terminated and inhabited and some subsequent repairs were made: the registration was tardy, having taken place more than 30 days after the end of the work.
103 (1931), 69 Que. S.C. 139.
104 (1932), 53 Que. K.B. 386 (C.A.); see also, *Bélair v. Pichette*, [1963] Que. Q.B. 575n (C.A.).

installation in question had not formed part of the work the contractor had undertaken, and so the privilege, registered within 30 days thereafter was too late, the work contracted for having been completed some time previously. The additional work had consisted of unforeseen incidentals, the owner thinking that a ventilator would be unnecessary, and the pump being merely a replacement for a previously existing one. In *Alppi v. Hamel*,[105] the plaintiff had supplied materials to a contractor who had built a block of flats. After the building was completed by the contractor in accordance with the contract and the plans, the owner decided to make a bedroom for himself out of the space in the attic above the premises destined to be leased and proceeded to have this done. It was held that the supplier of materials lost his privilege by not registering it within the 30 day period after the completion of the building, the additional work not having postponed the completion of the building for the purpose for which it had been designed. In *Leo Perrault Ltée v. Easterbrook*,[106] after the house had been completed, it was purchased by a man who was a cabinet maker by trade. On his own, he decided to make a coal bin for the house, because of a threatened shortage of oil which caused him to decide to burn coal. He also installed some storm sashes, made two chests of drawers and put in two extra cupboards and did extra work outside the house itself. These were held to be in the nature of additions or improvements and did not postpone the date of the end of the work, not being necessary for the completion of the building. In *Riedl v. Gauthier*,[107] a letter sent by the contractor to the owner to the effect that the work was completed was held to be sufficient to establish the date of the end of the work, as there was no other evidence to the contrary.

(d)   *The Effect of the Suspension or Abandonment of the Work.*

It will be recalled that the date given in C.C. article 2013*a* for the "end of the work" is "the date which the construction is ready for the use for which it is intended". Suppose the work is abandoned before the building is completed. From what date will the delays to register privileges start to run? It is particularly important to know because abandonment of the work generally occurs as a result of the owner or contractor running out of funds, thus leaving in doubt the question whether the work already done will be paid for and thus creating a situation wherein the builder, supplier or architect will want to register his privilege against the property if he can. The Courts have solved this problem by holding that the end of the work occurs when the same is abandoned,[108] and that this is not affected by a later completion

---

105 (1938), 66 Que. K.B. 448 (C.A.).
106 [1943] Que. S.C. 79.
107 [1963] Que. P.R. 359.
108 See *Leo Perrault Ltée v. Brault*, [1957] Que. Q.B. 827 (C.A.); *Rochon v. Garneau* (1934), 73 Que. S.C. 5; *Blais v. Blais*, [1958] Que. S.C. 715; *Dorval v. Plante*, [1951] Que. S.C.

of the building by a subsequent owner.[109] Thus, a letter sent by the owner to the contractor ordering him to interrupt the construction and abandon the work is sufficient to establish the end of the work for what has been done prior to that date. A distinction has been made between the definitive abandonment and mere suspension. In the event of a suspension, the delays for the exercise of the privilege run only from the date of the final completion.[110] Moreover, the bankruptcy of the owner will not of itself constitute evidence of an abandonment, as the owner may be hoping to reach a compromise with his creditors, or the trustee may continue the construction in his place and stead.[111] The problem here therefore, is to determine whether in fact the owner has merely suspended operations or completely abandoned them.

In one case work was suspended in order to wait for warmer temperatures to complete the work, and the construction was occupied in the meantime. This was held to be a mere suspension of the work, and since the parties intended to and in fact did complete the work according to plan, the end of the work took place upon final completion.[112]

In another case, the defendant/owner was building a motel and restaurant; during the month of December, 1970, work proceeded. About the middle of that month, the defendant disappeared, or at least ceased to show up at the job-site. Various tradesmen, not being paid, left the site and were advised by the bank manager that no funds would be available for them. There was no further communication between the trades people and the defendant, while the painting, plumbing and electrical work remained

359; see also *Cook v. Archibald* (1919), 29 Que. K.B. 364, 57 D.L.R. 256; affirmed on different grounds *(sub nom. Archibald v. Maher)* 61 S.C.R. 465, 57 D.L.R. 603. However, see the remarks made in *Leo Perrault Ltée v. Brault, supra,* concerning the reasoning of the Supreme Court, and see also Johnson, The "End of the Work" (1951), 11 R. du B. 245 at 256-257. See also the borderline decision of *Billet v. Loranger,* [1945] Que. S.C. 160. See the discussion by Giroux, Le Privilege Ouvrier (1933), pp. 309 *et seq.* See also: *Mont-Royal Concrete Floor Ltd. v. Beauharnois Holding Ltd.,* [1975] Que. S.C. 146.

109 *Leo Perrault Ltée v. Brault, ante.*

110 See *Re Leblanc,* [1960] Que. Q.B. 661 (C.A.); *Provost v. Dinardo,* [1946] Que. S.C. 477; *Jubinville v. Dagenais,* [1942] Que. S.C. 475; *La Perrelle Lumber Co. v. Langlois* (1938), 77 Que. S.C. 1; *Kirallah v. Gagnon* (1936), 61 Que. K.B. 264 (C.A.); see also the borderline decision of *J. L. Vachon & Fils Ltée v. Corbeil* (1929), 35 R.L.N.S. 453. See also: *Beaudet v. Les Placements Amsyl Inc.,* [1975] Que. S.C. 155.

111 See *Re Leblanc, ante; Re Legault* (1939), 67 Que. K.B. 345 (C.A.); *Chauffage Laurentien v. J. Aimé Perron Ltée,* [1975] R.L. 374; and see also Johnson, The "End of the Work", *ante,* at pp. 257-258. *Contra:* Demers, Traité de Droit Civil du Québec, XIV, p. 175. On the question of suspension and abandonment of the work, see P.G. Jobin, L'interruption des travaux de construction, (1966-67), 8 Les Cahiers de Droit 287.

112 *Laporte v. Gagnon,* [1971] Que. C.A. 1; see also *Duskes v. Concreters Ready Mix Ltd.,* [1970] Que. C.A. 922.

unfinished. The situation remained static until the date of the Sheriff's sale in July 1971. Yet, the Court found that defendant had at no time manifested his intention to suspend or abandon the work and did nothing to lead the tradesmen to believe that his intention was to abandon the work. Accordingly, and citing the Appeal Court case of *Leblanc Boulais v. Grenier,*[113] the Court held that the work could not be considered to be abandoned as at the Sheriff's sale in July, 1971.[114]

In a very recent case, minor work, including the placing of gravel near the garage entrance, and the caulking of the windows at the rear of the house and the concrete finishing of the walls, all of an approximate cost of approximately $300.00 had been suspended in January, because of weather and because of a bankruptcy. The Court of Appeal, in reversing the lower Court, stated that to determine the date of the end of the work (within the meaning of Article 2013*a* C.C.), it is necessary to establish the moment when all work, as provided for in the plans and specifications, is finished, including, in reaching such determination, any work which may have been suspended pending more favourable weather. The Court of Appeal further confirmed that while abandonment of the work may constitute the end of the work, what is contemplated thereby is the definitive abandonment of same by the owner.[115]

(e)   Does the "End of the Work" Occur Only on the Completion of the Whole Building, or following Each Stage of the Construction?

Where the owner of the buiding is only having certain work done, and stops at the end of that work, it is evident that when this work has been carried out, the "end of the work" has been reached.[116] But where construction is carried through the various stages necessary to completion of the building as a whole, is there an "end of the work" when the foundations have been laid, another when the steel work has been put up and so forth? It was so held in *Vezio v. Lessard,*[117] where a workman engaged in the construction of the foundations lost his privilege because the Court decided that the end of the work had occurred when the foundations had been finished and consequently the workman had sued too late. While other decisions have shown similar tendencies,[118] the better opinion seems

---

113 *Re Leblanc; Boulais v. Grenier,* [1960] Que. Q.B. 661.

114 *Moynan v. Major,* [1975] Que. P.R. 253.

115 *Archambault De Ste-Rose Ltée v. André Hétu,* [1977] Que. C.A. 186.

116 See *Dorval v. Plante,* [1951] Que. S.C. 359, though perhaps some of the remarks in the judgment go further than warranted.

117 (1926), 64 Que. S.C. 298; see a criticism of this judgment by Oscar Desautels in Etude sur la loi des Privilèges, (1927-28), 30 R. du N. 144 at 151 *et seq.;* see *Forcillo v. Sirois,* [1966] Que. S.C. 96.

118 See in particular *Asconi Bldg. Corpn. v. Creswell-Pomeroy Ltd.,* [1942] Que. K.B. 718

to be that the "end of the work" takes place only when the whole building has been erected.[119] Recent cases confirm this view.[120]

In recent years, there have been a number of construction projects involving large buildings such as shopping centres where some of the construction is left incomplete in order for the tenants themselves to be able to complete the construction and final design of the space that they will occupy, according to their own individual needs. Furthermore, it may happen in a number of cases that the building will be entirely finished in some of its parts while other areas will remain under construction or will be left unfinished until they are rented. A number of questions may arise with respect to partly completed and partly uncompleted buildings, particularly with respect to deficiencies that may develop after the building has been completed in some part, which may be defined, according to the specifications of the contractor, as uncompleted work. These problems will have to be raised in the process of determining whether the end of the work has arrived with respect to some of the areas but not with respect to others. In view of the fact that the end of the work has generally been defined in terms of the use for which the building was intended, the Courts will have to resort to the contracts between the parties in order to establish the moment of the end of the work. This is not likely to be an easy task, and we must await future decisions in this area.[121]

§186 Are the Privileges Limited to Construction?

It has been held that a workman engaged in the levelling of a vacant lot and in the placing of sod thereon will not have a privilege, no construction being involved.[122] Similarly, a supplier of materials will have no privilege for furnishing gravel for the levelling of ground around a building being erected.[123] On the other hand, it has been held more recently that work done for the construction of a parking lot surrounding a building is to be regarded as part of a construction which gave additional value to the property, and

---

(C.A.), and the criticism of same by Walter Johnson in The "End of the Work", (1951), 11 R. du B. 245 at 253-255.

119 See *Raymond v. Tremblay*, [1955] Que. P.R. 399 and authorities therein mentioned; *Picard v. Rome*, [1959] Que. S.C. 23 and the comment on the same together with a review of the authorities by Hubert Senecal (1959-60), 6 McGill Law Journal 131; Giroux, Le Privilège Ouvrier, (1933), pp. 299-300. *Contra:* Demers, Traité de Droit Civil du Québec, XIV, p. 174.

120 See *Corpn. de Crédit Adanac v. Turcotte*, [1966] Que. Q.B. 768 (C.A.); *Kredl Inc. v. Tétrault Frères Ltée*, [1967] Que. S.C. 285; but see *Forcillo v. Sirois*, [1966] Que. S.C. 96. See also: *Fernando St. Hilaire Ltée v. Montmartre Const. Inc.*, [1975] Que. S.C. 823.

121 See N.H. Salomon, Meredith Memorial Lectures, McGill University, 1969, p. 43.

122 *Boileau v. Terreault* (1934), 73 Que. S.C. 129.

123 See *Robert v. Bouliane*, [1956] R.L. 446; see also Demers, Traité de Droit Civil du Québec, XIV, pp. 157, 172.

therefore justified the creation of a privilege in favour of the contractor.[124] Again, where a lumber dealer claimed a privilege in virtue of building materials supplied, it was alleged that his privilege had been registered after the 30 day delay following the end of the work. He was allowed to prove that, in the contract for the building of this house, one clause provided that "lawns extending over the entire lot to be completed, sodded ..." and that this clause was to be read as being included in the general conditions of the contract. The Court held that since the levelling and sodding of the lawns had to be completed, the end of the work did not take place until this was done and therefore the supplier of building materials was allowed to register his privilege since he was still within the prescribed delay.[125]

It would therefore result that where a whole construction operation is the object of the contract, then the more marginal portions of the contracts, such as levelling the grounds, paving the driveways, sodding the lawn and making the sidewalks would be included in the "construction" and, provided they fulfil the other requirements of the law with respect to the validity of their privileges, the creditors of such claims (workmen, suppliers, subcontractors) will have as much of a privilege as the bricklayers or plumbing contractors. Where similar work (paving, levelling) is carried out independently outside the general construction, there have been doubts as to whether privileges arise from such work. In fact, this question is linked to the more difficult problem of determining whether repairs and alteration work to buildings will give rise to privileges.

The main difficulty here lies in the terms of the Civil Code itself. Whereas Mechanics' Lien Acts provide for a more complete definition of what constitutes work, the Code uses the word "construction" without qualification, although it does not specifically exclude the possibility of repairs or alterations. In fact, what would happen in the case of the demolition of a house in order to make a garden? Is this a "construction"?

Among the requirements for the existence of a privilege, we find the necessity of an added value to the property as a result of the construction: this does not necessarily result from repairs. In other circumstances, repairs may add to the value of the property without there really being a "construction" going on. One could argue that from a strict point of view, the owner and the other creditors should not benefit from the lack of privilege of the repairman, and that it is only fair to recognize his privilege. On the other hand, where retroactive *dation en paiement* is concerned, the

---

124 *Verdun Indust. Bldg. Corpn. v. Regent Equipment & Paving Corpn.,* [1968] Que. S.C. 506.

125 See *Goodfellow v. Martel,* Superior Court, Montreal, No. C-140,883, January 17, 1936, commented on in (1967), 13 McGill Law Journal 179. But see *Gosselin v. Houle,* [1963] Que. S.C. 143 in which it was decided that the levelling work around a motel was not sufficient to create a privilege of contractor under C.C. art. 2013f.

unjust enrichment and unfair advantage arguments do not seem very strong.

Where real construction takes place, there is no doubt now that all those (enumerated in C.C. article 2013) who participate in any manner in the construction are held to have a privilege. Where repairs are concerned, legal writers have conducted a few exercises in soul-searching to find solutions to this problem, some of which may finally prevail.

Some Judges were reticent to the idea that repairs could give rise to a privilege.[126] Others expressed their doubts as to whether repairs were included in construction, their opinion being somehow influenced by the fact that under these specific issues the repairs had not added to the value of the property.[127]

The leading case in favour of a privilege resulting from repair-work is that of *Masson v. Solomon,*[128] where a majority of the Court of Appeal confirmed the judgment of the Superior Court. This is being held as a rather weak decision,[129] but since it is the only major one available and since it eventually maintains the privilege of the person who participated in repair works, it would seem to retain some validity. One of the supporting arguments comes from the Old (*i.e.,* pre-1866) Law, which afforded a privilege for work done in the "building, re-building, or repair of buildings ...", and which is said to have been kept in the single word "construction" used in C.C. article 2013; this is being challenged, however, owing to the subsequent amendments to the Civil Code. Since the present C.C. article 2013 was revised in 1916, references to the Old Law are not admissible.

But the main reason for the judgment was that C.C. article 2013 confers a privilege on persons who "by the work done or by the materials" supplied have contributed an additional value to the property, and that it was therefore irrelevant to *quaere* whether the work or the materials had been applied to the erection of a new building or the repair of an old one, since there was no distinction in the Code. One of the Judges saw in this particular case a mere work of repair and decoration of deteriorated surfaces (and consequently dissented) where another thought that this constituted

---

126 In *Rochon v. Garneau* (1934), 73 Que. S.C. 5, maintenance, plastering work and decoration were not sufficient to qualify as "construction".

127 *Hudon v. Olitsky,* [1945] Que. S.C. 201. See also *Bellefeuille v. Bellefeuille,* [1953] R.L. 170, where it was held that painting did not give rise to a privilege, not being construction; and see also Giroux, Le Privilège Ouvrier, (1933), pp. 84-85, 113-116.

128 (1935), 73 Que. S.C. 196; affirmed (1937), 62 Que. K.B. 50. Comment on this case by H. Turgeon (1936-37), 39 R. du N. 381. See the cases cited in *Masson v. Solomon; Desbiens v. Vilandré,* (1923) 61 Que. S.C. 124 at 125, in which it was said that "constructor" included a building contractor as well as a repairing contractor; *Riordon Co. v. John W. Danforth Co.* (1923), 4 C.B.R. 248.

129 See J.W. Durnford, The Articles of the Civil Code on the Privileges of the Builder: some of the Problems they Pose and Suggested Amendments thereto, (1962) 8 McGill Law Journal 176, at 183; H. Turgeon, *loc. cit.* (1936-37) 39 R. du N. 381.

renovation to the point of reconstruction (and thus agreed to the existence of a privilege). The judgment of the majority remains valid, however, and this decision has been followed in more than one other case.[130]

It may be stated that the *Masson* case, *supra,* provides a sufficient basis for further decisions in the same line and that the privilege of a repair contractor would be maintained provided there was an additional value to the property as a result of the work. In the case of old buildings being renovated, the value-added element becomes a pure question of fact.[131] Partial construction would qualify for the privilege under the same condition.

§187 The Sale of the Property before the Privilege is Registered.

The sale (by the owner) of the property on which the work has been or is being done will not affect the privileges in question, provided, of course, that registration and the initiation of action are done within the delays allowed.[132] This will even apply in favour of a supplier of materials where the materials are only delivered and incorporated into the house after the registration of the sale by the owner-builder to the third party.[133]

The Court of Appeal has, however, introduced a distinction with respect to the sale of the property and the payment of the privileged claim. In

---

130 *Sirois v. Novis*, [1943] R.L. 418. See also *Lachance v. McMahan*, [1974] Que. S.C. 644, where the work was for the replacement of three windows and a double door as well as the recovering of the aluminum on the building. Citing *Masson v. Solomon*, the Judge held that the text of article 2013 C.C. does not distinguish between a new construction or renovation and repair work, the essential factor being whether any plus value had been given to the building.

In another case the work comprised repairs and touch-up work in empty apartments in a building of approximately 100 units. The Court held that there was no additional value given by such work and the privilege was denied; *Mallon v. Thoo Mao Tham*, [1975] C.P. 174.

In a more recent case the Court rejected a privilege for maintenance, repairs and improvements brought to a factory but stated that in certain instances (*e.g.* the re-starting of an abandoned plant requiring major renovations without which the operations could not be re-commenced, or without which it could not attain the function and use for which it was destined) repairs, renovations and improvements could form the basis of a privileged claim. This case also contains an exhaustive list and partial review of the doctrine and jurisprudence on repairs; *Gagnon v. Temisply Inc.*, [1976] Que. S.C. 1748. See other cases to the contrary, footnote 107, p. 454.

131 See Demers, Traité de Droit Civil du Québec, Vol. XIV, pp. 167-168.

132 C.C. art. 2083; *Munn & Shea Ltd. v. Hogue Ltée*, [1928] S.C.R. 398, [1928] 4 D.L.R. 1; *Kirallah v. Gagnon* (1936), 61 Que. K.B. 264 (C.A.); *Picard v. Rome*, [1959] Que. S.C. 23; Marler, The Law of Real Property, p. 359; Johnson, The "End of the Work", (1951), 11 R. du B. 245, at 260-261.

133 *Page v. Beach Const. Co.*, [1953] Que. S.C. 284.

a case[134] where the owner who had ordered materials from a supplier subsequently sold the property to a third party, it was held that an action taken by the supplier of materials against the subsequent owner of the property was valid for the purposes of maintaining the privileged claim in existence in compliance with the provisions of C.C. article 2013e, and was therefore sufficient for the purpose of securing the claim by privilege as against the property. The Court took the view that the word "debtor" in C.C. article 2013e included not only the actual debtor, *i.e.,* the person who has ordered the materials, but also the proprietor (the subsequent buyer, in this case) of the immoveable which was subject to the privilege, and who, in that capacity, became the debtor responsible for the debt. Pratte J. dissented from this decision arguing that the debtor of the debt incurred for the supply of materials was the person who had ordered them and not the owner of the property at the time of the action. If one takes the view that the action for privilege and, for that matter, the privilege itself are based on the motion of value added, the decision of the majority in this case is a valid one, since it is to be expected that the price paid by the new owner of the property reflects in some way the work being done and therefore the price of materials supplied. One could then consider the new owner of the property as the transferee of the rights and obligations of the first owner for the purposes of whatever rights and duties that were attached to the immoveable. Even if the previous owner was not sued personally with respect to the debt for the supply of materials, it would seem clear that, since the debt is related to the immoveable, and since the privilege, being a real right, is to be exercised on the proceeds from the immoveable, it is only normal to extend the meaning of "debtor" in C.C. article 2013e to include not only the person who had ordered the materials or made the subcontract, but also the subsequent owner of the property. This being the case, the subsequent owner of the property would not be regarded only as "the debtor of the privilege" but also as "the debtor of the debt" without it being possible to distinguish between those two capacities. The privileged right is a charge on the property involved in the contract and exists by virtue of the claim against the person

134 *City Properties Ltd. v. Rock Utilities Ltd.,* [1967] Que. Q.B. 195 (C.A.). See also the rather interesting case of *Saillant Inc. v. Plombelec Inc.,* [1975] Que. S.C. 1224, where at the time that the supplier commenced the work, A was the registered owner of the property, at the date of registration of the privilege, B was the registered owner, at institution of legal proceedings C was the registered owner, while pendente lite, D became the registered owner in exercise of the *dation en paiement* clause. D sought the radiation of the privilege alleging that at the time of institution of the suit, the supplier had sued A (the original owner) but had failed to implead B (the owner at the time of the suit). The Court held that while article 2013e C.C. specifies that the suit must be commenced within three months of the end of the work, the article does not require the impleading of the owner within such period (an appeal has been lodged to the Quebec Court of Appeal and is now pending).

who has made the contract. When the original owner sells the property, it is then logical to suppose that he also transfers his rights and obligations with respect to such property to the subsequent owner. Therefore, not only the privilege but also the debt could be enforced against the new owner with respect to the property, notwithstanding the position of the persons involved in the contract of the supply of materials.[135]

§188 The Menace of the Resolutory Clause in Deeds of Sale and of the "Dation en Paiement" Clause in Deeds of Hypothecary Loans.

One fact is not disputed: the privileges of the builder *et al.* will rank before that of the unpaid vendor: C.C. art. 2009. Another is rarely disputed: these privileges will also rank before an ordinary hypothec (mortgage). The reasoning for this is usually based on the provisions of C.C. article 2130 as well as on the other provisions of the title on privileges and hypothecs. The very nature and purpose of the privilege[136] makes it an obvious rule. Indeed, the "privilege" as introduced in C.C. article 1982 and following is meant as a "real right" which affects the property of the debtor, either specifically or generally, as the case may be. This is particularly evident in the Chapter entitled "Of the Effect of Privileges and Hypothecs with Regard to the Debtor or Other Holder" and in C.C. article 2053 and following, concerning the rights of privileged and hypothecary creditors. The privilege is therefore different from the "preference" that exists under other Acts, such as the Bankruptcy Act, for example; the privilege is more like the lien known in the Common Law jurisdictions. Whereas a preference means the right of a creditor to be paid before other creditors, assuming that they all had unsecured claims, the privilege works as a real right, insuring a preference of payment to the privileged creditor out of the proceeds from the assets that are subject to this privilege. In other words, where there remains a balance of

---

135 See *contra,* N.H. Salomon, Meredith Memorial Lectures, McGill University, 1969, at pp. 41-42.

136 C.C. art. 2013; Marler, The Law of Real Property, pp. 342, 376, 377; Giroux, Le Privilège Ouvrier, pp. 34, 37, 46, 407-408; Philippe Demers J., Des Privilèges et des Hypothèques, Journées du Droit Civil Français, p. 527; J.W. Durnford, The Articles of the Civil Code on the Privileges of the Builder: some of the problems they pose and suggested amendments thereto, (1962), 8 McGill Law Journal 176; Oscar Desautels, Etude sur la loi des privilèges (1927-28), 30 R. du N. 144 at 145; *La Perrelle Lumber Co. v. Langlois* (1938), 77 Que. S.C. 1 (where the hypothec was registered on May 2, the end of the work occurred on July 16 and the privilege was registered on August 6); *Supertest Petroleum Corpn. v. Jacques-Cartier Automobiles Inc.,* [1960] Que. S.C. 329; affirmed [1963] Que. Q.B. 336 (C.A.). See the comments by Roger Comtois, (1960-61), 63 R. du N. 109, and Alberta Mayrand, (1963), 23 R. du B. 413. This case involved the claims of the Crown in the right of the Province of Quebec with respect to sales and corporation taxes; those claims were said to rank as privileged debts, ahead of a conventional hypothec even though registered after it.

price in a sale (which is secured by a privilege: C.C. arts. 2009 and 2014), or where there is a hypothec securing a loan, and the judicial sale of the property does not realize sufficient proceeds to pay all of the preferred creditors, the builder *et al.* will be paid first, that is, according to their rank under C.C. articles 2009 and 2013*c*, subject always, of course, to their claims being limited to the additional value which their work and materials have given to the property: C.C. art. 2013.[137]

Despite the favoured position of the privileges of the builder and others, their privileges are exposed to the threat of being extinguished by either the resolutory clause in a deed of sale or the *dation en paiement* clause in a deed of loan. Where the vendor of a property sells it with only part of the price being paid in cash, there remains a balance of price. The payment of the latter by the purchaser is frequently secured not only by the vendor's privilege conferred by law, as well as a hypothec created in the deed, but also by a resolutory clause, which stipulates that in the event of default on the part of the purchaser with respect to the payments, the vendor may elect to dissolve the sale and regain title to the property, free of all privileges with which the property may have been encumbered. It has been held by the Supreme Court of Canada (affirming judgments of the Quebec Superior and Appeal Court) that even though the creditor of the resolutory clause right participates in the carrying out of the construction work, and encourages the general contractor to continue such work and personally guarantees payment of the promissory note in favour of the general contractor, this does not constitute a tacit renunciation of the seller's right to have the privilege struck out.[138] The *dation en paiement* (giving in payment) clause in deeds of hypothecary loans is along similar lines — should the borrower default with respect to the payments, the lender has the right to give notice to the borrower to the effect that he elects to become owner of the property retroactive to the date of the loan, free of whatever privileges are registered against the property subsequent to the deed of loan. As a result, the purchaser or the borrower may have construction work carried out on the property, run out of funds, and the builder *et al.* who though they were fully secured by their privileges provided for by law, may suddenly wake up to find that the owner's vendor or hypothecary creditor has exercised his

---

137 See *Boiteau Inc. v. Benoit Dumais Ltée.*, [1975] Que. S.C. 1030.

138 *Stendel v. Moidel*, [1977] 2 S.C.R. 256; see also: *Meco Elec. (1960) Inc. v. Lawrence*, [1977] 2 S.C.R. 264, where the facts were similar to those of *Stendel v. Moidel (supra)*, with the distinction that instead of a promissory note, the seller had written a letter to the privileged creditor undertaking jointly and severally with the debtor to repay the sum represented by the privilege. The Supreme Court of Canada upheld the cancellation of the privilege and affirmed the finding by the Appeal Court that there was no evidence of a tacit renunciation by the seller of the ordinary effects of cancellation of the sale, namely the annihilation of all privileges caused to encumber the immoveable by the purchaser.

resolutory or *dation en paiement* clause, thereby wiping out the privileges and leaving the builder *et al.* without a recourse because of the insolvency of the person for whom the work was done and the materials supplied.

Not all are agreed that such clauses are valid or even desirable insofar as they destroy the privileges of the builder *et al.*,[139] but the fact remains that they have been enforced in a number of reported judgments.[140]

Several cases involving new constructions, hypothecs and *dation en paiement* clauses have been decided in the Courts in recent years. A perfect example of the operation of a resolutory clause in the above manner, may be

---

139 Marler, The Law of Real Property, pp. 365-366; Demers, Traité de Droit Civil du Québec, XIV, pp. 157-158, 169, 185, 189, 237; Faribault, Traité de Droit Civil du Québec, XI, pp. 345-346, 525; Bergeron, De la clause dite "dation en paiement" dans les contrats de prêts hypothécaires, (1960), 4 Cahiers de Droit 5. Reference should also be made to Challies J., The Doctrine of Unjustified Enrichment in the Law of the Province of Quebec, 2nd ed., pp. 104-108, and to André Morel, L'évolution de la doctrine de l'enrichissement sans cause, pp. 104-107.

140 As to resolutory clauses, see *Latour v. L'Heureux* (1899), 16 Que. S.C. 485 (Ct. of Rev.); *Provost v. Paquin* (1913), 44 Que. S.C. 511 (Ct. of Rev.); *Vachon v. Deschénes* (1935), 59 Que. K.B. 193 (C.A.); *Lanthier v. Rink* (1939), 78 Que. S.C. 70. *Contra: Dussault v. Grenier* (1934), 72 Que. S.C. 138; but see the critical comment by Henri Turgeon (1934-35), 37 R. du N. 540; *Lamoureux v. Robert* (1935), 41 R. de Jur. 29; *Barbeau v. Robitaille* (1926), 41 Que. K.B. 536 at 542 (C.A.). See also the general cases of *Krukowsky v. Paré* (1937), 63 Que. K.B. 126 (C.A.); *Pilon v. Amiot* (1939), 42 Que. P.R. 340; *Perras v. Godin,* [1956] Que. Q.B. 871 (C.A.); *Sharpe v. Purity Flour Mills Ltd.,* [1959] Que. Q.B. 633 (C.A.); *Dansereau v. Boissy,* [1955] Que. S.C. 385; *Charbonneau v. Doucet,* [1958] R.L. 186; *Fortier v. Roy,* [1957] Que. Q.B. 664 (C.A.); *Val Morin Mountain Lodge Inc. v. Laperle,* [1961] Que. Q.B. 410, affirming [1964] R.L. 29 (C.A.), and comment thereon by Roger Comtois (1961), 21 R. du B. 530. See also *Stendel v. Moidel,* [1977] 2 S.C.R. 256.

As to the *dation en paiement* clauses, see *G.A. Brown Inc. v. Allan,* [1953] Que. S.C. 349; *Dumberry v. Moquin,* [1959] Que. S.C. 184, and see the comment by Roger Comtois (1959-60), 62 R. du N. 165. See also the general cases of *Plouffe & Cie. v. Aubin* (1930), 50 Que. K.B. 280 (C.A.); *Goldsmith v. Montreal Motor Tpt. Co.* (1934), 72 Que. S.C. 277; *Décarie v. Décarie* (1921), 60 Que. S.C. 143; *Re Michelin* (1958), 37 C.B.R. 101 (Que.), and see the comment thereon by Roger Comtois (1958-59), 61 R. du N. 224; *Re Beauchâtel Const. Inc.,* [1961] Que. S.C. 145; *Re Ireland,* [1962] Que. S.C. 95; *Goulet v. Coco Island Inc.,* [1961] Que. S.C. 402; *Côté and La Caisse Populaire de Montmorency v. Sternlieb,* [1958] S.C.R. 121; *Thibeault v. Lafaille,* [1951] Que. S.C. 188; *Caisse Populaire de Scott v. Guillemette,* [1962] Que. Q.B. 293 (C.A.); *Alarie v. Crédit Mauricien Inc.,* [1956] Que. Q.B. 693 (C.A.); *Bissonnette v. Compagnie de Finance Laval,* [1963] Que. Q.B. 391 (C.A.); *Beaver Hall Invt. Ltd. v. Ravary Bldrs. Supply Co.,* [1963] Que. S.C. 388; Armand Lavallée, Validité et effet de la clause de dation en paiement dans un acte de prêt hypothécaire, (1963), 23 R. du B. 291; *Chartrand v. Desrochers,* [1962] Que. S.C. 465; comment by Roger Comtois (1964), 66 R. du N. 248, re *Bissonnette v. Compagnie de Finance Laval, supra; Hamel v. R & R Enterprises Ltd.,* [1964] Que. Q.B. 361 (C.A.); see generally: Michel Pourcelet, De la clause résolutoire à la clause de dation en paiement dans les ventes immobilières, (1964), 66 R. du N. 285, and comments by Yves Caron, (1966), 68 R. du N. 500.

seen in a 1965 Court of Appeal case. In *Larin v. Brière*,[141] an immoveable was subject to a contract of sale including a resolutory clause with retroactive effect. The Court held that when the resolutory clause was executed, the vendor had a right to the cancellation of privileges which had been created as a result of construction contracts made between the purchaser and workmen and suppliers of materials. As well, it was held that the resolution of the contract, whether judicial or contractual, operates in such a way as to put the parties in the same position as they were before the contract. The privileges were therefore not valid, since the buyer was thus deemed never to have been the owner of the immoveable in question.

The above rule has been maintained to the extent that the privilege will not be opposable against a hypothecary creditor who has registered his deed of loan before the construction has started — he is able to enforce the *dation en paiement* clause in the event of a default on the loan.[142] This situation, however, has been distinguished from the situation where the hypothecary loan has not been registered before the construction has started and the supplies of materials made, but has been registered before the work has ended. In this situation, it has been held that the privilege comes into existence at the time the workmen start the execution of their obligations and start doing the work or delivering materials to be incorporated in the building, though at that time, no formality is required by law for the creation of the privilege. It is the duty of the hypothecary creditor to see that his deed of loan is registered before the work even starts. In the present situation, the effect of the resolutory clause will not affect the privilege which validly existed before the registration of the deed of loan.[143] The decision in *Louis Belle-Isle Lbr. Inc. v. Craft Finance Corpn.*[144] confirmed this rule. This case involved a supplier of materials who started to make supplies before the deed of loan was concluded but terminated those supplies after the deed of loan had been registered. The Court held that the rules in C.C. articles 2013, 2013*e* and 2103 must be read together. The preference given to the supplier of materials over subsequent creditors is maintained from the beginning, if all the required formalities are subsequently followed. When the supplier of materials started his deliveries, he was dealing with the owner of the property, and his privilege was valid

---

141 [1965] Que. Q.B. 800 (C.A.); comment by Y. Caron, in (1966), 68 R. du N. 500.
142 See *C.E. Marchand v. Montmartre Const. Inc.*, [1974] Que. S.C. 447; and *Assistance Loan and Finance Corpn. v. Bourassa*, [1972] Que. C.A. 631, where the Court of Appeal stated that the burden of proof rested on the builder or supplier to prove that his privilege was created prior to the registration of the deed of loan.
143 *Nineteenhundred Tower Ltd. v. Cassiani*, [1967] Que. Q.B. 787, affirmed [1967] S.C.R. vi. See also: *Beaudet v. Les Placements Amsyl Inc.*, [1975] Que. S.C. 155.
144 [1966] Que. Q.B. 135; affirmed [1966] S.C.R. 661, followed in *Sofinec Inc. v. Amico Inc.*, [1969] Que. Q.B. 941.

from that time, although some of the materials may have been delivered at a later date.[145] In this context, the date of the beginning of the work is equally important as that of the end of the work, and the supplier or subcontractor should take all necessary steps to assure himself of the ownership of the property and of its hypothecary status at that moment, in view of preserving his privilege.

It has been held that the date of "birth" of the privilege is the time that the creditor commenced execution of the work and not the date that the contract for same was signed, the rationale being that the basis of the privilege is the additional value given to the immoveable and that such additional value does not occur unless and until the work is actually commenced pursuant to the contract.[146] Where a contract provided for the supply and installation of elevators the Court stated that the privilege was created as soon as the creditor commenced the execution of his obligations, and subsisted as long as he remained prepared to complete the execution thereof and until incorporation to the immoveable.[147] In a recent case one judge of the Court of Appeal (the only one of a 3-judge bench who pronounced on this issue, albeit an *obiter dictum*) stated that the privilege is created at the moment that the creditor commences to execute his obligations pursuant to the contract and that this may occur even prior to incorporation of the materials to the physical structure and hence prior to the plus value actually having been given to the building.[148]

Where, pursuant to a contract to supply windows and doors to a building then under construction, the supplier commenced work on his own premises, prior to the registration of a deed of loan (containing a *dation en paiement* clause) but delivered and installed the windows subsequent thereto, the Court held that the privileged right was "born" the moment the supplier commenced work (*i.e.,* at his own plant) while delivery and/or incorporation to the building are merely a continuation of the execution of his obligations flowing from the contract.[149]

From the decisions outlined above, we may draw some conclusions as to the advisability of the creditor's checking with the registry office at different times, as the effect of the execution of a *dation en paiement* or resolutory clause, which was registered at the time of the supplying of materials or execution of the work, would seem to be the extinction of the creditor's privilege. While it would not be practical in every instance to

---

145 See the recent case on point of *L. Drolet & Fils Inc. v. Desrochers,* Que. S.C. (Arthabaska), no. 05-000113-77, Lacourcière J., December 15, 1977.

146 *Assistance Loan and Finance Corpn. v. Bourassa,* [1972] Que. C.A. 631.

147 *Ascenseurs Leclerc Ltée v. Sinotal Inc.,* [1975] Que. S.C. 1027.

148 *Caisse de Dépôt et de Placement du Québec v. Armor Ascenseur Québec Ltd.,* [1975] Que. C.A. 202.

149 *Roger Landry Ltée v. Place St-Gabriel Inc.,* [1973] Que. S.C. 12.

conduct an examination of the relevant deeds in the registry office before supplying work or materials, where large amounts are involved this would be advisable. Once the creditor checks with the registry office at the time of his contract to ascertain the fact that he is actually dealing with the owner of the property, there is no obligation for him, once the deliveries have started, to recheck with the registry office to see whether the owner's title has been modified or transferrred. The effect of a subsequent *dation en paiement* clause will not affect the supplier whose privilege has been created before its registration, provided that that privilege has been preserved by the fulfilment of the required formalities (*e.g.,* notice, registration and action). It follows as well from these cases, that the registration of the privilege, when required (C.C. art. 2103), will not "create" the privilege, but rather will simply confirm and preserve its existence. The privilege comes into being once the work or supplies have started, provided that value is added (C.C. art. 2013) to the property by such work or supplies. The privilege does not have to be registered from the beginning, as indeed the Civil Code provides for its registration after the end of the work.

Thus the decisions of the Courts recognize that both a privilege and a *dation en paiement* clause have a retroactive effect (in the case of a privilege, to the date of the beginning of the work; in the case of a *dation en paiement,* the date of registration), it would seem that there may be only one way of giving the workers, contractors and suppliers of materials due protection for the additional value given by them to the property, where the property is held subject to a *dation en paiement* or a resolutory clause registered before the work or supplies began. If the hypothecary creditor with a *dation en paiement* clause, or for that matter, the vendor with a resolutory clause, is to be held, upon the default of the debtor, retroactively owner of the property, the workman or supplier of materials may be entitled to treat him, as one of the "owners" of the property. *Pendente conditione,* the registered owner of the property is deemed to be owner subject to a resolutory clause, while the lender or the vendor with resolution, is deemed to be owner subject to a suspensive condition. The person who is dealing with the apparent owner, but who realizes that there is a resolutory clause or a *dation en paiement* clause registered against the property, would therefore be wise not only to give notice to the apparent owner but also to the beneficiary of such clauses who may well become the owner (retroactively) after the execution of the clause. The lender of money who exercises the resolutory or *dation en paiement* clause will be deemed to have been the absolute owner of the property from the date of the registration of his deed. By the giving of the above described double notice, he would have been given notice of the contract for work, supplies of materials or construction, following a contract between the supplier or constructor and the apparent owner, and if, after receiving notice of such a contract he does not oppose the execution of that contract (which he is unlikely to do since in most cases the loan that he has made is for the purpose of construction or repairs), it could be argued that he will have had due notice of the contract in his capacity as deemed owner of the property and the privilege will remain valid despite the exercise of the resolutory clause. Under the present situation, there is no other way of protecting the suppliers of materials and workmen for the work done on properties which are subject to such rigorous clauses.

This reasoning appears to have been accepted in some recent decisions of the Quebec Superior Court but the issue does not yet appear to have been dealt with by the Court of Appeal. Where the hypothecary creditor had paid a part of the supplier's claim and had performed certain proprietary acts, the Court refused to strike down the privilege, holding that the word "proprietor" in 2013e C.C., sub-paragraph 4, must be liberally interpreted so as to include the hypothecary creditor who exercises the resolutory clause.[150]

However, it could also be argued that privileges, being exceptional, must be restrictively interpreted and thus "proprietor" in article 2013e and f C.C. refers only to the registered owner. Support for this position could be taken from the definition of proprietor given by Giroux:[151] "Le propriétaire de l'article 2013, c'est la personne ou ses successeurs qui cause l'amélioration d'un immeuble sur lequel elle a des droits réels principaux et saisissables, celle qui donne le contrat d'entreprise. ... C'est bien là ce qu'envisage le legislateur, puisqu'il se réfère au propriétaire comme à la personne tenue de payer le coût de l'entreprise, c'est-à-dire à la personne qui cause l'amélioration de l'immeuble. Ce propriétaire est le propriétaire de l'immeuble de l'article 2013 ... et engage, suivant les conditions posées par la loi, ce bien comme sûreté des créances dues à ceux qui contribuent à l'amélioration de son immeuble, c'est-à-dire aux divers créanciers de l'article 2013." And Giroux further states:[152] "La dénonciation, l'avis d'enregistrement du privilège signifiés à son propriétaire qui n'a pas causé l'amélioration de l'immeuble ... ne peuvent assurer au créancier de l'article 2013 un privilège sur la propriété de ce propriétaire; ces procédures ne sont que conservatoires

---

150 *Simcard Ltée v. Liberato Spensiere Ltée,* Que. S.C. (Montreal) no. 05-002303-756, Monet J., January 12, 1978 (unreported). See also the case of *Heller-Natofin Ltd. v. Quincaillerie Quemont Hdwe. Inc.,* Que. S.C. (Montreal) no. 500-09-000007-765, Dugas J., December 18, 1975 (unreported), where the Court stated that the lender who receives notice of the contract, and later exercises the *dation en paiement* clause, receives such notice in its retroactive capacity of "proprietor" within the meaning of article 2013e and f C.C. But see also *contra: Roy Marchand Indust. Ltée v. Liberato Spensieri Ltée,* Que. S.C. (Montreal) no. 500-05-001086-758 Beauregard J., June 27, 1977 (unreported). For comments on this issue see: Yves Caron, (1966) 68 R. du N. 500.

151 Giroux, Le Privilège Ouvrier, p. 201, #195.

152 Giroux, Le Privilège Ouvrier, p. 203, #197(3).

et ne peuvent préserver un droit qu'en autant qu'il existe; et le privilège ... ne peut affecter une telle propriété."

It should also be recalled that whereas the owner/builder has the right to retain sufficient funds from the contract price to pay the privileged claims, the articles of the Code contain no such provision with respect to the seller with a resolutory clause or a lender with a *dation en paiement* clause. Thus the lender who disburses the entire proceeds of the loan, subsequently receives a "notice" under 2013*e* or *f*, and thereafter, due to a default by his borrower, exercises the *dation en paiement* clause, would not have retained any funds for such privileged claim. Moreover, if the concept of retroactive ownership is extended, as suggested in the *Simcard v. Spensieri* and *Heller-Natofin v. Quincaillerie Quemont* cases, *supra,* could it also be argued that the lender now having become owner retroactively, in exercise of the *dation en paiement* clause, is responsible for the damages suffered by a third party while the borrower was still owner, pursuant to article 1055 C.C.? It is submitted that this latter jurisprudence has exposed the seller and/or lender with a resolutory clause to a legal position and responsibility not intended by the legislator.

The matter of *dation en paiement* has of course been affected by the introduction in 1964 of C.C. articles 1040*a et seq.* (unconscionable transactions), requiring the creditor to give 60 days' notice to his debtor before exercising the *dation en paiement* clause. Where the debtor is bankrupt, and the Trustee had not registered his appointment against the property, it has been held that the notice must be given to the bankrupt debtor and not to the Trustee in bankruptcy.[153] C.C. article 1040*b* provides that the debtor or another interested party may remedy the default at any time before final judgment or voluntary assignment. Thus, a privileged creditor, as any other hypothecary creditor,[154] will be entitled to repay the amount due on behalf of the debtor who has defaulted on the loan and is about to lose his property as a result of the *dation en paiement* clause. Having thus paid the hypothecary creditor who had priority over him, the creditor may then proceed to execute his own privileged claim in accordance with the provisions of the law.

§189 The Danger to Privileges Where the Property is Held Under a Promise of Sale.

It may happen that the person for whom the construction is being done is merely holding the property under a promise of sale, and a supplier of materials, thinking that this individual is the owner of the property, fails to

---

153 In *Re J.W. Kilgour & Bro. Ltd. and Dionne,* Que. S.C. (Bankruptcy), no. 11-000251-773, Greenberg J., October 26, 1977.
154 *Côté v. Sternlieb,* [1958] S.C.R. 121.

give the notice required by the law to be delivered to the owner,[155] where the supplier is not dealing with the owner (C.C. art. 2013e), thus losing his privilege. This is not the place to enter into a discussion of the old and controversial question whether, under Quebec law, a promise of sale is equivalent to a sale; suffice it to say that judgments have been rendered denying the existence of privileges because the title to the property was not vested in the promisee.[156] On the other hand, the privilege has sometimes been maintained where the promisee has been put into possession of the property in such a way as to constitute him its owner,[157] or where the construction has been done with the consent or tolerance of the owner.[158]

Where the owner of an immoveable has promised to sell his property to a building contractor who has accepted his promise, the sale is valid as between the two parties and, for the purposes of validating a privilege, the latter must be regarded as the owner, although his title has not yet been registered. In this situation, the vendor cannot oppose a privilege on the grounds that a proper notice had not been given to him.[159] There will, however, be no privilege in any circumstance where the workman or contractor have been employed by a tenant as opposed to the owner or the possessor of the property. The law does not provide for any form of privilege resulting from such work on an immoveable property: C.C. art. 2013d.[160]

§190 Renunciation and Waivers.

In many deeds of hypothec, the hypothecary creditor requires, as a condition of the loan, that the contractor, subcontractors and suppliers of

---

155 See *Nineteenhundred Tower Ltd.* v. *Cassiani,* [1967] Que. Q.B. 787 at 794; affirmed [1967] S.C.R. vi.

156 *Leo Perrault Ltée* v. *Blouin,* [1959] Que. Q.B. 764 (C.A.); *Page* v. *Beach Const. Co.,* [1960] Que. S.C. 244; *Compagnie Jos. Lefrançois* v. *H. Bergeron Ltée* (1931), 37 R.L.N.S. 1; *Marquis Ltée* v. *Rousseau* (1932), 70 Que. S.C. 529; *Gadbois* v. *Denovan* (1917), 52 Que. S.C. 81 (Ct. of Rev.); *Kalmanovitch* v. *Frank* (1917), 52 Que. S.C. 171 (Ct. of Rev.); *W. Rutherford & Sons Co.* v. *Racicot* (1909), 19 Que. K.B. 428 (C.A.); see also *Metivier* v. *Wand* (1898), 13 Que. S.C. 445, where, while it was held that a privilege would be valid if the person who was holding the property under a promise of sale were treated as its owner, the privilege was nonetheless declared void as the promisee had violated the terms of the promise of sale, thereby nullifying it.

157 Under C.C. art. 1478; see *Marmette* v. *Deschênes,* [1966] Que. S.C. 1.

158 *Gage Invt. Inc.* v. *Ménard* (1931), 50 Que. K.B. 315 (C.A.), and see the comments on it by Rivard J. in *Vachon* v. *Deschênes* (1935), 59 Que. K.B. 193 at 200-201 (C.A.), and by Choquette J. in *Leo Perrault Ltée* v. *Blouin,* [1959] Que. Q.B. 764 at 769 (C.A.); *Chartrand* v. *Chagnon* (1935), 74 Que. S.C. 52; *Barbeau* v. *Robitaille* (1926), 41 Que. K.B. 536 (C.A.); *Sylvain* v. *Vachon,* [1957] Que. S.C. 233; *Lavoie* v. *Desrosiers* (1914), 46 Que. S.C. 89 (Ct. of Rev.); see also Marler, The Law of Real Property, p. 365, and Demers, Traité de Droit Civil du Québec, pp. 169, 185.

159 *Germain* v. *R. Duchêsne & Fils Ltée,* [1966] Que. S.C. 298.

160 *Pépin* v. *Racine,* [1972] Que. P.R. 29.

materials renounce or waive in advance the privilege to which they may be entitled as a result of their work or supplies. One may question whether such a renunciation or waiver is valid on the grounds that a privilege may be a matter of public policy. However, it may also be argued that a privilege, though created by law, is a matter of private right, which may be waived. It has been held that there is no privilege where an unconditional and absolute renunciation or simple waiver has been given in advance, and the Courts will enforce the contractual agreement.[161] In many cases, however, the contract is not an absolute renunciation but a simple waiver of priority in favour of the hypothecary creditor. This case has been distinguished from the case where there is not only a grant of priority with respect to the hypothec but also a full grant of priority with respect to a *dation en paiement* clause (the Courts holding that a separate grant of priority is needed for each).

It has been found that in some cases the hypothecary creditor finds less advantage in exercising a *dation en paiement* clause which will give him the ownership of a property, but would at the same time extinguish the debt, and therefore, both his personal and real recourses as a hypothecary creditor (as a consequence, he will not be allowed to sue his debtor for payment of money outstanding). Where the property is not worth taking in payment for the debt, the hypothecary creditor would instead enjoy a priority over the privileged creditors so as to be paid before them out of the proceeds of the sale of the property. Mr. N. H. Salomon[162] has suggested a way out of the dilemma of a privileged creditor who has ceded priority to another creditor. He suggests that the renunciation or waiver of priority is equivalent to a *stipulation pour autrui* under C.C. article 1029. Since in most cases the waiver of priority of the privilege is not given directly to the creditor, but to the contractor or to the owner of the property, it would follow that, if the creditor has not accepted this stipulation under C.C. article 1029, the stipulation could not be enforced by him because it has not been so accepted. This may not be the best solution to the problem, but, as Mr. Salomon pointed out, it probably is the only one that is available to annul the renunciation or waiver of priority.

The waiver consented to by the privileged creditor may take many forms: it may be a mere renunciation of the privilege, which would extinguish his total right of preference,[163] although the question of public policy might be raised here, or it may be a cession of right or of preference in

---

161 *Martin & Frère Ltée v. H. Brummer Const. Co.,* [1961] Que. Q.B. 537 (C.A.).

162 Meredith Memorial Lectures, McGill University, 1969, p. 39.

163 *Assistance Loan and Finance Corpn. v. Bourassa,* [1972] Que. C.A. 631, where the Court of Appeal confirmed the validity of such a renunciation; see also: *Weiss v. Silverman,* (1919) 58 S.C.R. 363, and *Bargain City Ltd. v. Georges Bellemare et Fils Ltée,* [1964] Que. Q.B. 628. See however, the rather interesting decision in *Chauffage Laurentien v. J. Aimé Perron Ltée,* [1975] R.L. 374, where the Court refused to uphold

favour of another party.[164] As is the rule in other areas of the law of security on property, such cessions would simply equal an exchange of ranks between the parties to the cession. Where, however, the transferee or beneficiary of the waiver can also exercise a retroactive right of *dation en paiement,* the transferor may well be left without an object on which to exercise his preference. Through the angle of the law of mandate, the Court of Appeal has endeavoured to interpret strictly a waiver of privilege or cession of priority. Where a person has been authorized to consent to a waiver of priority in favour of a hypothecary creditor, there is no implicit authority or consent to cede priority in favour of the same person with respect to the exercise of a *dation en paiement* right which would simply erase the privilege through its retroactive effect.[165]

§191 Extinction of Privileges.

Construction privileges are extinguished where the beneficiary of the privilege does not take the necessary steps for its enforcement: registration of a notice where applicable (C.C. arts. 2013*e*, 2013*f*) and the bringing of an action within the prescribed periods (30 days in the case of a workman (C.C. art. 2013*d*), 3 months in the case of a supplier of materials (C.C. art. 2013*e*) or 6 months in the case of a builder or architect (C.C. art. 2013*f*)). The action is taken against the debtor,[166] and the Registrar must be called into the case in order to give him notice of the action and to cause him to note the same in the index of immoveables. Where the person sued is a builder, the owner must also be called into the case: C.C. art. 2013*e*.

Since the requirements prescribed in C.C. articles 2013 and following are very strict with respect to the validity of a construction privilege, the consequence of the failure to comply with the same, results in the extinction of the privilege.

C.C. article 2081 enumerates the legal causes of extinction of privileges as: total loss of the thing subject to the privilege; determination or legal extinction of the conditional right of the grantor; confusion of the qualities of debtor and creditor, subject to revival upon eviction; express or tacit remission of the privilege; complete extinction of the privileged debt; as a result of a sheriff's sale, forced licitation or similar sale; confirmation of title

---

the renunciation to privilege on the rationale that the document contained an implicit obligation that the defendant/owner would fulfill its obligations vis-à-vis the various creditors.

164 *Heller-Natofin Ltd. v. Plomberie & Chauffage Bouchard & Frères Ltée.,* [1975] Que. S.C. 537.

165 *London Life Ins. Co. v. Benoit,* (1939), 66 Que. K.B. 483 (C.A.); *Dallaire & Fils Ltée v. La Société d'Entreprise de Crédit Inc.,* [1970] Que. C.A. 497.

166 The owner, (see footnote 134, *ante,* and related text) or a separate builder, as the case may be.

under the Code of Civil Procedure; prescription; or by legal extinction of the right after 30 years following registration, as provided under C.C. article 2081a. Upon extinction, the privilege is no longer valid, and the law provides for the cancellation of registration: C.C.P. arts. 805-807.[167]

The same rules apply where the registration has been made illegally, irregularly or on the strength of a void title. On the other hand, the privilege of a person enumerated in C.C. article 2013 may be invalid for lack of fulfilment of prescribed formalities, but the personal and other real recourses of the creditor remain available for the execution of his claim.[168]

Since the privilege exists by virtue of the declaration of the law, and not as a product of a contractual arrangement, where the circumstances required by the law are not met (*e.g.,* where there is no value added to the property), there is no privilege. One may not speak of an imperfect privilege: if the requirements are met, there is a privilege, if not, there is none.

§192 Some Procedural Aspects Relating to the Law of Construction Privileges.

(*a*)   *The institution of proceedings seeking the cancellation of the registration of a privilege.*

Article 110 of the Code of Procedure states:

110. Unless otherwise provided, every action is instituted by a writ of summons in the name of the Sovereign.

Article 805 of the Code of Procedure, found in Chapter Five of the Code, under the heading "CANCELLATION OF REGISTRATION OF PRIVILEGES AND HYPOTHECS AND JUDICIAL RECOGNITION OF THE RIGHT OF OWNERSHIP ACQUIRED BY PRESCRIPTION" states:

805. When a registration has been made illegally, irregularly or on the faith of a void title, or when the registered right has been annulled, rescinded or extinguished by prescription or otherwise, a judge of the

---

167 See: *M.F. Dev. Inc. v. Megiddo Realty Corpn.,* [1966] Que. S.C. 386; *Fari Inc. v. Jacques S. Guillion & Associés Ltée,* [1966] Que. S.C. 526: *1366 Dorchester St. West Inc. v. Val Royal Bldg. Materials Ltd.,* [1965] R.L. 353; *Riedl v. Gauthier,* [1963] Que. P.R. 359; *Pierre L'Heureux Inc. v. Doric Const. Ltée,* [1964] Que. S.C. 570; *Meco Elec. (1960) Inc. v. Redbrooke Estates Ltd.,* [1968] Que. Q.B. 741 (C.A.). Most of these cases deal with problems already discussed, and mainly the end of the work, the suspension or interruption of the work and the validity of notices. *Note:* old C.C.P. art. 1088a was renumbered as C.C.P. art. 805 in the new C.C.P. of 1965.

168 Such as his personal contract rights against those with whom he has entered into contracts and his rights against the surety, real or personal: *Demontigny v. Gen. Const.,* [1970] Que. S.C. 459.

district in which the immoveable is situated may, on motion, order that it be cancelled.

The motion must be served in the manner prescribed by the judge, unless he dispenses with service, and it may be contested in accordance with the ordinary rules. The judge may require such proof as he considers necessary.

Where the owner, or another person having a legal interest, seeks the cancellation of the registration of a privilege, the question arises as to whether such cancellation should be obtained by the issue of a writ of summons and declaration, in an ordinary action, or rather whether the more summary and expeditious procedure of a Petition to Radiate pursuant to article 805 C.C.P. can be the procedural vehicle.

This procedural issue is not a new one in that article 805 C.C.P. contains essentially the same provision as article 1088 of the "old" Code of Procedure.

In determining which recourse is the appropriate one, the Courts have tended to confirm the distinction between the debt itself, on the one hand, and the privileged right, on the other hand, which, as we have already seen, is the real right accessory to the debt itself.

It would seem that where the sole issue before the Court is the validity of the privilege itself, and there is no contestation or dispute relating to the merits of the debt itself, the proper recourse would be a Petition in virtue of article 805 C.C.P.

Conversely, where the matter before the Court deals with the merits of the principal debt itself, or, together with the right to the privilege, the proper recourse would appear to be an ordinary action (*i.e.* by way of a writ of summons and declaration in the ordinary course).

Where the cancellation of the registration of the privilege was sought on the grounds that the privilege was illegal and irregularly registered in that the privileged creditor had signed a renunciation of privilege and, in addition, had registered a notice of privilege against several lots and several buildings globally, without distinguishing the additional value given to each, the Court held that the article 805 C.C.P. recourse was appropriate.[169]

In another case, the architect whose plans were not used for the construction, had registered a privilege. The owner sought the cancellation of such registration by way of article 805 C.C.P. The Court held that a Motion to Radiate, pursuant to article 805 C.C.P. may be employed whenever the Court is able to radiate the privilege without touching upon the claim upon which it is based; conversely, whenever the Court must, at

---

169 *Heller-Natofin Ltd. v. Plomberie & Chauffage Bouchard & Frères Inc.,* [1975] Que. S.C. 537.

the same time, necessarily decide the value of the privileged claim, only an action commenced by writ of summons may be employed.[170]

Where the privilege is ill-founded on its very face, the summary recourse will be available. Thus, where the privileged creditor, in the notice of privilege, did not allege that the notice had been registered within thirty days of the end of the work, and, in his action, did not allege that proceedings had been instituted to conserve the privilege within three or six months of the end of the work, the Court held that the summary recourse was the appropriate procedure.[171]

It has also been held that since article 805 C.C.P. provides that the Motion to Radiate may be contested in accordance with the ordinary rules, the mere fact of a contestation to the Petition will not divest the Court of jurisdiction *ratione materia*. The Court, in comparing the old article 1088*a* C.C.P. to the present article 805 C.C.P., noted the new inclusion in the present article which specifically provides for the contestation of the Petition to Radiate; the Court stated that the purpose of articles 805 *et seq.* C.C.P. was to facilitate and accelerate the procedure by which the owner could clear the title to the property. Moreover, the Court declared that where the proceedings seeking the cancellation of the privilege were but an accessory to the principal demand, recourse must be had to an ordinary action.[172]

Where the cancellation of the registration of the privilege was sought on the ground of remission by the creditor of the claim, the Court held that the proper recourse was by way of an ordinary action since the Court found that to dispose of the litige it would be necessary to decide upon the merits of the claim.[173]

In another case it has been held that recourse by way of Petition in virtue of article 805 C.C.P. is available only when the title or registered right challenged has previously been judicially recognized as null, rescinded or extinguished by prescription or otherwise.[174]

(b) *The simultaneous co-existence of the action in declaration of privilege and the petition seeking cancellation of the privilege: the exception of lis pendens.*

There have been numerous instances where the privileged creditor has

170 *L.T. Invts. Inc. v. Schrier*, [1973] Que. S.C. 784.
171 *Perreault v. Val-Mar Swimming Pools Ltd.*, [1971] Que. S.C. 539.
172 *Société Namur Inc. v. Nor-Mix Ltée*, [1967] Que. S.C. 452.
173 *Gauvin v. Lemieux*, [1970] Que. S.C. 244.
174 *Litvack v. Alric Dev. Corpn.*, [1973] Que. S.C. 947; see also: *S.R.G.D. Inc. v. La Société Gaudreau Cie*, [1975] Que. S.C. 827; *Wilfrid Bédard Inc. v. Assistance Loan and Finance Corpn.*, [1966] Que. Q.B. 113; *Sofinec Inc. v. Amico Inc.*, [1969] Que. Q.B. 941; *Laurent Gagnon Inc. v. Can. Financial Co.*, Que. S.C. no. 200-05-005543-777, Pelletier J., January 27, 1978 (unreported); *Dame Deslandes v. Touchette*, [1955] Que. Q.B. 851.

instituted proceedings in the ordinary course against his principal debtor and has impleaded, as *mis-en-cause* (and correctly so), the owner of the property; concurrently, the owner (or the hypothecary creditor having been declared owner in virtue of the resolutory or *dation en paiement* clause) seeks the cancellation of the privilege, by way of Petition in virtue of article 805 C.C.P., and this prior to judgment being rendered on the first action; accordingly, the issue of litispendance has been raised before the Courts.

In the matter of *Simcard Ltd. v. Vincenzo Lattanzio*[175], the Court noted that neither the Code of Civil Procedure nor the Civil Code defined litispendance although, relying on a constant stream of jurisprudence and doctrine, it confirmed that the elements comprising, and the rules applied, in matters of *lis pendens* are the same that are to be applied in *res judicata,* as set forth in article 1241 C.C., which states:

> The authority of a final judgment (*res judicata*) is a presumption *juris et de jure;* it applies only to that which has been the object of the judgment, and when the demand is founded on the same cause, is between the same parties acting in the same qualities, and is for the same thing as in the action adjudged upon.

In the *Simcard v. Lattanzio* case (*supra*), Lattanzio had instituted proceedings against Spensieri, as owner of an immoveable upon which Lattanzio had registered a privilege as contractor; the action had been instituted by way of writ of summons and declaration in the ordinary course.

Meanwhile, Simcard had instituted legal proceedings against Spensieri under another record number seeking title to the property by way of *dation en paiement,* and, in the same action, seeking the radiation of all privileges registered against the immoveable and, in this latter action, accordingly, Simcard had impleaded Lattanzio as *mis-en-cause.*

Simcard sought to intervene in the action lodged by Lattanzio against Spensieri and in the conclusions of its intervention sought the striking down of the privilege. Lattanzio opposed the reception of the intervention, invoking litispendance. In the first instance, the Judge dismissed the intervention; the Appeal Court confirmed this judgment finding identity of parties, of object and of cause and hence that there was litispendance.

In another case, the privileged creditor had instituted legal proceedings (by way of ordinary action) against the principal debtor and had impleaded the owner as *mis-en-cause;* the owner then lodged a Petition seeking the cancellation of the privilege, pursuant to article 805 C.C.P., before the action on privilege had been disposed of. The Court found that the Motion to Radiate the Privilege could not co-exist with the action on privilege.[176]

---

175 *Simcard Ltd. v. Lattanzio,* [1976] Que. C.A. 248.
176 *J. Dawe Forming (Que.) Ltd. v. Grunco Const. Ltd.,* [1975] Que. S.C. 1034; see also:

Where the Motion to Radiate pursuant to article 805 C.C.P. was served prior to the service of the action in the ordinary course, it was held that the institution of legal proceedings by way of the Petition were commenced prior and, therefore, the preliminary motion to dismiss the petition, invoking litispendance, was dismissed.[177]

(c) Right to intervene in Court proceedings by a secured creditor.

Suppose the unpaid seller or lender has not instituted proceedings against his debtor but the immoveable, secured by resolutory or *dation en paiement* clause, is sought to be affected by a privilege and brought to Sheriff sale so that the privileged creditor would be paid by preference in accordance with his rank, out of the proceeds of such sale.

We have already seen that on a Sheriff sale, the privilege will outrank the hypothec of the unpaid vendor, or of the lender, while the exercise of the resolutory or *dation en paiement* clause, if registered prior to the birth of the privilege, will take priority over the privileges.

Hence, it is of course in the interest of the unpaid seller or lender to so act as to best protect his rights.

In a series of cases involving Caisse de Dépôt et de Placement du Quebec and Armor Ascenseur Québec Limitée[178] the facts giving rise to the litigation were as follows:

At the beginning of October 1970, Beauharnois Holding Ltd. contracted with Armor Ascenseur Quebec Ltée for the supply and installation of elevators in a building to be constructed by Beauharnois; on October 14, 1970, Armor purchased the materials for the purpose of the contract. On October 16, 1970, Beauharnois entered into an emphyteutic lease, containing a *dation en paiement* clause, with Caisse de Dépôt et de Placement du Québec. On March 29, 1972, Armor registered a notice of privilege; on May 1, 1972, Armor sued on the privilege (without impleading Caisse de Dépôt), and on July 17, 1972, caused the property to be seized by the Sheriff pursuant to a judgment rendered in its favour declaring the privilege valid.

On August 17, 1972, Beauharnois having defaulted to fulfill its obligations in favour of Caisse de Dépôt, the latter obtained judgment

Partitions G.F. Inc. v. Scalia Bros. Corpn., Que. S.C. (Montreal), no. 500-05-022358-772, Deslandes J., December 5, 1977 (unreported); *Poulin v. Gabail Const. Inc.,* Prov. Ct. (Montreal), no. 500-02-027999-775, Lande J., September 27, 1977 (unreported).
177 *Les Restaurants S.T.C. Inc. v. Les Entreprises Dimo Ltée,* [1977] Que. S.C. 219.
178 *Caisse de Dépôt et de Placement du Québec v. Armor Ascenseur Québec Ltd.,* [1975] Que. C.A. 202; *Caisse de Dépôt et de Placement du Quebec v. Armor Ascenseur Québec Ltée,* Que. C.A. no. 09-000315-754, March 29, 1976 (unreported); *Armor Ascenseur Québec Ltée v. Caisse de Dépôt et de Placement du Québec,* Que. C.A. no. 09-000385-757, March 29, 1976 (unreported).

cancelling the emphyteutic lease and, on March 14, 1972, Caisse de Dépôt obtained a second judgment which declared it absolute owner of the immoveable in question in execution of the *dation en paiement* clause contained in the emphyteutic lease; both judgments reserved to Caisse de Dépôt the right to ask for the radiation of all charges and encumbrances registered subsequent to October 16, 1970, being the date of the signature of the emphyteutic lease.

In the meantime, Caisse de Dépôt had lodged a tierce opposition to the judgment obtained by Armor on July 17, 1972, but the Court of Appeal, confirming the dismissal of the tierce opposition, held that the tierce opposition was not the right recourse (Caisse de Dépôt not having been declared owner at the time of such proceeding) and that the proper proceeding would have been an action to radiate the privilege.

Caisse de Dépôt then lodged an action seeking the radiation of the privilege and was met by a contestation of such motion on the grounds of chose jugée; the contestation was maintained in the Court of first instance but reversed in appeal, the Court finding, *inter alia,* that a new element had been introduced in that Caisse de Dépôt had now been declared owner of the immoveable in question by way of *dation en paiement.*

In the meantime, and notwithstanding the appeal by Caisse de Dépôt to the Court of Appeal from the judgment of the Court of first instance maintaining the exception to dismiss by Armor to the action in radiation of privilege lodged by Caisse de Dépôt. Armor had given instructions to the Sheriff to proceed with the Sheriff sale of the immoveable in execution of the judgment rendered in its favour declaring its privilege valid. To prevent the sale from taking place, Caisse de Dépôt, invoking article 673 C.C.P., requested, and obtained in first instance, a sursis of the execution on the grounds that without the sursis its real rights with respect to the immoveable would be seriously and irreparably prejudiced and compromised.

The Appeal Court maintained the Court of first instance and stated that the real rights of Armor were totally protected and would remain so until such time as judgment was rendered on the action in radiation of the privilege. The Court of Appeal further stated that unless the sursis of execution was maintained, the Sheriff sale would take place, pending the action in radiation of the very same privilege, which would in effect preclude Caisse de Dépôt from obtaining a judgment therein.

It would seem, particularly from the notes of Mr. Justice Mayrand in [1975] Que. C.A. 202, at page 203, that as long as the *dation en paiement* clause creditor has not obtained judgment thereon, he cannot intervene in the legal proceedings instituted by the privileged creditor and that such intervention at such stage of the proceedings would probably be held to be premature.

A similar finding issued in another case, where the Court dismissed an opposition to the seizure of an immoveable property taken by a chirographic creditor; the opposant, the Caisse Populaire, was a hypothecary lender and the deed of loan contained a *dation en paiement* clause; its borrower, the defendant in the case, defaulted and, at the time of the seizure by plaintiff of the immoveable, the Caisse Populaire had given the 60-day notice prescribed by article 1040 C.C., the delay for which notice was to expire on August 9, 1976, while the Sheriff sale of the immoveable had been fixed for August 2, 1976. The Court stated that as long as the delay of the 60 days had not expired and the Caisse Populaire had not obtained title to the property either by way of judgment or by voluntary *dation en paiement,* opposant's legal position was no different from that of any hypothecary creditor and the hypothecated immoveable remained in the patrimony of the debtor and, accordingly, the Court dismissed the opposition.[179]

If this is so, perhaps the only recourse available to the unpaid vendor, or to the lender, who wishes to exercise the resolutory clause or the *dation en paiement* clause, would be to obtain a judgment by way of *dation en paiement* (after service and registration of the 60-day notice provided for in article 1048 C.C.), and, pending the obtaining of such judgment, in order to block the Sheriff sale, such creditor would be obliged to seek sursis of execution in accordance with article 673 C.C.P. There are two cases where such procedure was adopted by the hypothecary creditor, exercising the *dation en paiement* clause, and sanctioned by the Court.[180]

In the case of *Compagnie Miron Ltée v. Jeandur Const.*[181], the Court refused to receive an intervention lodged by a hypothecary creditor to an action in declaration of privilege holding that in the circumstances before the Court, the hypothecary creditor did not have the "probable interest" specified in article 212, C.C.P.

On the other hand, in another case the Court came to the opposite conclusion, found that the hypothecary creditor had sufficient interest to intervene, and received the intervention.[182]

---

179 *Gravel Photograveur Inc. v. Zicat,* [1976] Que. S.C. 1143.

180 *Adelard Laberge Ltée v. Les Hôtels Bolduc & Associés Inc.,* Que. S.C. No. 200-05-002589-757, Jacques J., June 1, 1977 (unreported); and *Vibrek Inc. v. Les Hôtels Bolduc & Associés Inc.,* Que. S.C. no. 200-05-003097-750, Jacques, J., June 8, 1977 (unreported).

181 *Compagnie Miron Ltée v. Jeandur Const. Inc.,* Que. S.C. (Montreal) no. 500-05-008611-772, Melançon J., October 19, 1977 (unreported).

182 *Otto Zinner Carpets Inc. v. Richelieu Indust. Leasehold Inc.* Que. S.C. (Montreal) no. 500-05-016028-779, Jasmin J., October 26, 1977 (unreported). A similar judgment was rendered in the matter of *Iverbille Lbr. Inc. v. Joe's Steak House (Old Montreal) Ltd.,* Que. S.C. (Montreal) no. 500-05-022645-756, Beauregard J., June 14, 1976 (unreported).

In view of the provisions of article 1040*b* C.C., which provides that the debtor or any other interested person (*i.e.* a privileged creditor, etc.) may remedy the omission or default mentioned in the 60-day notice at any time before judgment, it is submitted that the lender, prior to obtaining judgment by way of *dation en paiement,* may not intervene in a pending proceeding by a privileged creditor and may not oppose a judgment obtained by a privileged creditor. Nevertheless, in order to prevent the inferior ranking of the hypothec and the possibility that the funds realized on a Sheriff sale would be insufficient to pay the hypothecary claim, it would seem that the appropriate recourse would be a motion in sursis of execution directed against the judgment obtained by the privileged creditor, coupled with an action by the hypothecary creditor by way of *dation en paiement.*

(d) *The effect of the bankruptcy of the principal debtor.*

The action in declaration of privilege is in essence a recourse by a creditor seeking a personal right vis-à-vis the principal debtor and a real right vis-à-vis the owner's immoveable.

Where the principal debtor has become bankrupt, it has been held that because of the two distinct recourses, namely the personal right recourse and the real right recourse, the privileged creditor may pursue the personal right avenue only upon being authorized to do so by the Bankruptcy Court pursuant to section 49(1) of the Bankruptcy Act (R.S.C. 1970, c. B-3) but, even without such permission, may institute or continue an action for the real right.[183]

§193 Appendix.

Relevant Articles of the Quebec Civil Code.

1695.   Architects, builders and other workmen, have a privilege upon the buildings, or other works constructed by them, for the payment of their work and materials, subject to the rules contained in the title **Of Privileges and Hypothecs,** and the title **Of Registration of Real Rights.**

2009.   The privileged claims upon immoveables, are hereinafter enumerated and rank in the following order:
1. Law costs and the expenses incurred for the common interest of the creditors;
2. Funeral expenses, such as declared in article 2002, when the proceeds of the moveable property have proved insufficient to pay them;

---

183 See: *Eugène Falardeau Ltée v. L'Office Municipal d'Habitation de Québec* [1976] Que. C.A. 244; *Centre Olympia de Repentigny Inc. v. La Cie Repentigny Elec. Inc.,* [1977] Que. C.A. 188; *B. & R. Gauthier Inc. v. Albert Verroeulst,* [1976] Que. S.C. 131.

3. The expenses of the last illness, such as declared in article 2003, and subject to the same restriction as funeral expenses;
4. The expenses of tilling and sowing;
5. Assessments and rates;
6. Seignorial dues;
7. The claim of the workman, supplier of materials, builder and architect, subject to the provisions of articles 2013 and following;
8. The claim of the vendor;
9. Servants' wages, and those of employees of railway companies engaged in manual labour, under the same restriction as funeral expenses.

2013. The workman, supplier of materials, builder and architect have a privilege and a right of preference over all the other creditors on the immoveable, but only upon the additional value given to such immoveable by the work done or by the materials.

2013a. The word "workman" includes the artisan, the laborer and generally every one who makes his living by manual labor.

The words "supplier of materials" include the supplier not only of raw materials but also of every manufactured object which enters into any construction.

The word "builder" includes both contractor and subcontractor.

The words "end of the work" mean the date at which the construction is ready for the use for which it is intended.

2013b. In case the proceeds are insufficient to pay all the claims, the additional value given to the property is established by a relative valuation made by the Prothonotary in accordance with articles 721 and 722 and the Code of Civil Procedure.

2013c. Such privileges rank as follows:
1. The workman;
2. The supplier of materials;
3. The builder;
4. The architect.

2013d. The workman has a privilege, by reason of the work he has done on an immoveable, for arrears up to twenty days, whether he was engaged by the proprietor or by a contractor. No formality is necessary to secure this privilege.

Such privilege shall subsist for thirty days after the end of the work, and need not be registered. But the privilege is extinguished on failure of the workman to sue his debtor within such delay, and to bring the proprietor into the case, as well as the registrar of the division in which the property is situated in order to give notice of such privilege to the latter, who must make note of the suit in the index of immoveables.

During the whole period and up to the end of the work, the proprietor is entitled to retain, on the contract price, an amount sufficient to pay the privileged claims. Any amount fixed by the sworn certificate of the architect or engineer in charge of the work shall be deemed sufficient, and, failing such architect or engineer, a like certificate may be given by a licensed architect or a duly qualified engineer of this province, who may be agreed upon by the interested parties, or failing such agreement appointed by a judge of the Superior Court.

The builder may not exact any payment on the contract price before he furnishes to the proprietor a statement under his signature, of all amounts due by him for labor and materials.

Several workmen may join in one action, the costs of which shall be those of a personal action for the amount claimed.

2013e.   The supplier of materials has a privilege on the immoveable in the construction of which the materials supplied to the proprietor or builder have been used, or for the construction of which they have been specially prepared.

However, in the case where the supplier of materials contracts with the proprietor himself, such privilege is conserved only by registration, before the expiration of thirty days after the end of the work, of a notice containing:
   1. The names, surname and domicile of the creditor and of the debtor;
   2. The description of the immoveable affected by the privilege;
   3. A statement of the claim specifying the nature and price of the materials supplied to the proprietor or specially prepared to be supplied to him.

In the case where the supplier of materials contracts with the builder, he must notify the proprietor of the immoveable in writing that he has made a contract with the builder for delivery of materials. His privilege is conserved for all the materials supplied after such notice provided he registers, within thirty days after the end of the work, a notice similar to that mentioned in the preceding paragraph.

In order to meet the privileged claims of the supplier of materials the proprietor of the immoveable is entitled to retain on the contract price an amount sufficient to pay them, until the builder has handed to him either a discharge or a renunciation of their privileges, signed by them.

Such privilege is extinguished on failure of the supplier of materials to sue his debtor within three months after the end of the work and to call the registrar into the case, in order to have him make an entry of the action in the index of immoveables. In the case where the action is directed against the builder, he must also call the proprietor into the case.

The supplier of materials is also entitled, in the case of the insolvency of the proprietor or builder, or in case of failure to make payment at the periods agreed upon, to revendicate the materials he has supplied, but which have not yet been incorporated into the building.

The registration of these notices is effected by deposit.

2013*f*. The builder or the architect, has a privilege on the immoveable for the work he has done as such, provided that before the expiration of thirty days after the end of the work, he registers at the registry office of the division in which the property is situated, a statement of his claim. Notice of such registration must be given, within the same delay, to the proprietor.

Such privilege is extinguished after six months following the date of the end of the work, unless the creditor takes an action against the proprietor to preserve it. In such action the registrar must be called into the case, in order to give him notice of such action, and to cause him to note the same in his index of immoveables.

In the case where the builder has had the work done, either wholly or in part, by subcontract, if the subcontractor has notified the proprietor of his contract, such subcontractor shall have a privilege upon the immoveable for all work done after such notification provided that before the expiration of thirty days after the end of the work he registers a statement of his claim. Such privilege is subject to the same formalities as that of the builder or architect, in so far as concerns its creation and extinction. The proprietor, in case the subcontractor has notified him of his subcontract, is entitled to retain, on the contract price, an amount sufficient to meet the privileged claim of the subcontractor; and any amount fixed by a certificate given in compliance with the formalities contained in article 2013*d*, shall be deemed sufficient.

The registration of these statements is effected by deposit.

2015. With regard to immoveables, privileges produce no effect among creditors, unless they are made public in the manner determined in the title **Of Registration of Real Rights,** saving the exceptions there mentioned.

2083. All real rights subject to be registered take effect from the moment of their registration against creditors whose rights have been registered subsequently or not at all. If however a delay be allowed for the registration of a title and it be registered within such delay, such title takes effect even against subsequent creditors who have obtained priority of registration.

2094. Privileged claims not registered take effect as regards other unregistered claims, according to their rank or their date, and are preferred to simple chirographic claims; saving the exceptions contained in articles 2090 and 2091.

2103. The privilege of every person, except the workmen mentioned in article 2012, is created and preserved by the registration within the proper delay at the registry office of the division in which the immoveable is situated, of a notice, drawn up in the form of an affidavit of the creditor or his representative sworn to before a justice of the peace, a commissioner of the Superior Court or a notary, setting forth the name, occupation and residence of the creditor, the nature and amount of his claim, and the cadastral number of the immoveable so affected.

This notice is registered by deposit. It must be presented in duplicate at the registry office. One duplicate remains there and the other, bearing a certificate of registration, is delivered to the person who presented it.

After the expiration of six months from the date of registration of any privileged claim, or from the date of the end of the work, whichever be the latest, without an action having been taken to preserve it, any interested party may cause the registrar to radiate such claim by filing with him a written application to that effect, supported by affidavit of the expiry of such delay, and served on the privileged creditor or his representative not later than eight days prior to such filing.

In the event of an action having been taken, the Registrar is bound to radiate the registration of the claim upon the filing with him of a judgment dismissing the action or other order of the Court ordering him so to do, or of a certificate from the Prothonotary establishing that the action has been discontinued.

These last two articles are those referred to in footnote 50, *ante.*

1998.   The unpaid vendor of a thing has two privileged rights:
1. A right to revendicate;
2. A right to preference upon its price.

In the case of insolvent traders these rights must be exercised within thirty days after the delivery.

1999.   The right to revendicate is subject to four conditions:
1. The sale must not have been made on credit;
2. The thing must still be entire and in the same condition;
3. The thing must not have passed into the hands of a third party who has paid for it;
4. It must be exercised within eight days after the delivery; saving the provision concerning insolvent traders contained in the last preceding article.

TABLE OF FORMS

1. Claim for lien for work or service.
2. Claim for lien for wages.
2A. Claim for lien for wages by several claimants.
3. Claim for lien for materials.
4. Affidavit verifying claim.
5. Notice of claim for lien against holdback for work done on, or materials supplied to, a street or public work.
5A. Notice of claim for lien against holdback for wages earned while working on street or public work.
5B. Notice of claim for lien against holdback for wages earned by several claimants while working on street or public work.
6. Notice of lien.
7. Assignment of lien.
8. Discharge of lien.
9. Certificate of action.
10. Statement of claim.
11. Statement of defence and counterclaim.
12. Affidavit proving claim of lienholder in foreclosure proceedings.
13. Notice of application for advice and direction of Court as to distribution of a section 2 trust fund.
14. Affidavit of trustee in support of application for directions as to distribution of section 2 trust fund.
15. Order directing reference to Registrar in bankruptcy as to persons entitled to section 2 trust fund.
16. Order of Registrar directing method of ascertaining section 2 claimants.
17. Notice to creditors who may have claims against a section 2 trust fund.
18. Proof of claim against a section 2 trust fund.
19. Trustee's report on claims against section 2 trust fund.
20. Order fixing date of hearing of disputed section 2 claims.
21. Notice to be sent to section 2 claimant whose claim is disputed.
22. Registrar's report on distribution of section 2 trust fund.
23. Affidavit for use on motion for order directing trial by a Supreme Court Judge.
24. Order directing trial of action by Supreme Court Judge.
25. Judgment directing a reference for trial to the Master at Toronto.
26. Judgment directing a reference for trial to the Master at Toronto made by trial Judge.
27. Consent of receiver to act.
28. Application for appointment of receiver.
29. Order appointing receiver.
30. Consent of trustee to act.
31. Application for appointment of trustee.

FORMS

FORM 1
Claim for Lien for Work or Service
THE MECHANICS' LIEN ACT
Claim for Lien

JOHN DOE, of 80 Richmond Street West, Toronto 1, Ontario, under The Mechanics' Lien Act, R.S.O. 1970, chapter 267, claims a Lien upon the Estate of JOHN JONES and EDITH JONES, 9 George Street, Toronto 12, Ontario in the undermentioned land in respect of the following work (or service or materials), that is to say: Painting the exterior of the building erected on the lands hereinafter described. The work or service was completed on the 10th day of June, 1971 (or the work or service is to be completed on or before the   day of   , 19   ) and the name and address of the person for whom the work was done or service performed is QUICKSILVER CONSTRUCTION LIMITED, 10 John Street, Toronto 10, Ontario.

The amount claimed as due (or to become due) is the sum of $1,000.00.

The following is a description of the land to be charged:

[*Here set out a concise description of the land to be charged sufficient for the purpose of registration.*]

[*Where credit has been given insert:* The work was done (or services were performed) on credit, and the period of credit agreed to expired (or will expire) on the 10th day of September, 1971.]

DATED at Toronto this 12th day of July, 1971.

....
Signature of Claimant

(See Form 1 in the regulations made under the Ontario Act, R.R.O. 1970, Reg. 575.)

FORM 2
Claim for Lien for Wages
THE MECHANICS' LIEN ACT
Claim for Lien for Wages

JOHN DOE, of 80 Richmond Street West, Toronto 1, Ontario, under The Mechanics' Lien Act, R.S.O. 1970, chapter 267, claims a Lien upon the Estate of SAMUEL SMITH and EDITH SMITH, of 9 George Street, Toronto 12, Ontario, in the undermentioned land in respect of work performed (or to be performed) thereon while in the employment of

QUICKSILVER CONSTRUCTION LIMITED, of 10 John Street, Toronto, Ontario, on or before the 1st day of June, 1971.

The amount claimed as due is $500.00 for 20 days' wages.

The following is a description of the land to be charged:

[*Here set out a concise description of the land to be charged sufficient for the purpose of registration.*]

DATED at Toronto, this 30th day of June, 1971.

....
Signature of Claimant

(See Form 2 in the regulations made under the Ontario Act, R.R.O. 1970, Reg. 575.)

FORM 2A

Claim for Lien for Wages by Several Claimants
THE MECHANICS' LIEN ACT
Claim for Lien for Wages by Several Claimants

The following persons claim a Lien under The Mechanics' Lien Act, R.S.O. 1970, chapter 267, upon the Estate of JOHN JONES and EDITH JONES, of 9 George Street, Toronto 12, Ontario, in the undermentioned land in respect of wages for labour performed (or to be performed) thereon while in the employment of QUICKSILVER CONSTRUCTION LIMITED, of 10 John Street, Toronto, Ontario:

> JOHN DOE, of 80 Richmond Street West, Toronto 1, Ontario, $100.00 for 5 days' wages for work done on or before the 30th day of May, 1971.

> ROBERT ROE, of 11 Williams Street, Toronto 8, Ontario, $150.00 for 10 days' wages for work done on or before the 2nd day of June, 1971.

> WILLIAM COE, of 10 Rogers Street, Toronto 3, Ontario, $125.00 for 8 days' wages for work done on or before the 3rd day of June, 1971.

The following is the description of the land to be charged:

[*Here set out a concise description of the land to be charged sufficient for the purpose of registration.*]

DATED at Toronto, this 30th day of June, 1971.

(Signatures of the Several Claimants)

(See Form 3 in the regulations made under the Ontario Act, R.R.O. 1970, Reg. 575.)

FORM 3

Claim for Lien for Materials
THE MECHANICS' LIEN ACT
Claim for Lien for Materials

JOHN DOE, of 80 Richmond Street West, Toronto 1, Ontario, under The Mechanics' Lien Act, R.S.O. 1970, chapter 267, claims a Lien upon the Estate of JOHN SMITH and MARY

SMITH, both of 9 George Street, Toronto 12, Ontario, in the undermentioned land in respect of the following materials, that is to say, concrete blocks.

The last material was furnished on the 1st day of June, 1971 (or the material is to be furnished on or before the 15th day of July, 1971) and the name and address of the person for whom the material was furnished is QUICKSILVER CONSTRUCTION LIMITED, of 10 John Street, Toronto, Ontario.

The amount claimed as due (or to become due) is the sum of $1,000.00.

The following is the description of the land to be charged:

[*Here set out a concise description of the land to be charged sufficient for the purpose of registration.*]

[*Where credit has been given insert:* The materials were furnished on credit, and the period of credit agreed to expired (or will expire) on the   day of   , 19 .]

DATED at Toronto, this 30th day of June, 1971.

....
Signature of Claimant

(See Form 1 in the regulations made under the Ontario Act, R.R.O. 1970, Reg. 575.)

FORM 4
Affidavit Verifying Claim
THE MECHANICS' LIEN ACT
Affidavit Verifying Claim

I, JOHN DOE, named in the above (or annexed) claim, make oath: That the facts contained therein are true. (Or WE, JOHN DOE, ROBERT ROE, and WILLIAM COE, named in the above (or annexed) claim, make oath and each for himself makes oath that the facts contained therein, so far as they relate to him, are true.)

(Where the Affidavit is made by an agent or assignee a clause must be added to the following effect:

I have full knowledge of the facts set forth in the above (or annexed) claim.)

SWORN before me at Toronto, in the Municipality of Metropolitan Toronto, this 30th day of June, 1971.   }

or

The said John Doe and Robert Roe were SEVERALLY SWORN before me at Toronto, in the Municipality of Metropolitan Toronto, this 30th day of June, 1971.   }

A Commissioner for taking Affidavits, etc.

(See Form 4 in the regulations made under the Ontario Act, R.R.O. 1970, Reg. 575.)

FORM 5

FORM 5
Notice of Claim Against Holdback for Work Done on, or Materials Supplied to, a Street or Public Work
THE MECHANICS' LIEN ACT
Notice of Claim

JOHN WORKMAN, of 80 Richmond Street West, in the City of Toronto, in the Municipality of Metropolitan Toronto, hereby gives notice under subsection 5a of section 11 and under section 21a of The Mechanics' Lien Act of a claim in respect of work done (or materials placed or furnished) for Quicksilver Sewer and Water Main Services Limited of 10 John Street, Toronto, Ontario, in respect of a public work (or a municipal public street or highway) located at [*here give the address or a description of the location of the land*].

The following is a short description of the nature of the work done or to be done or service performed or to be performed or materials placed or furnished or to be placed or furnished:

The work (or service) was completed (or the last material was placed or furnished) on the 5th day of November, 1971, (or the work or service is to be completed or the material is to be placed or furnished on the   day of   19   .) The amount claimed as due (or to become due) is the sum of $1,000.00. [*Where credit has been given insert:*] The work was done (or services were performed, or materials were placed or furnished) on credit and the period of credit agreed to will expire on the 5th day of December, 1971.

DATED at Toronto, this 12th day of November, 1971

....
Signature of Claimant

Note: While this Form may be used as notice under subsection 5a of section 11 of the Ontario Act, it will only be effective where the owner, contractor or subcontractor whom it is intended to bind is given notice.

(See Form 1a in the regulations made under the Ontario Act, R.R.O. 1970, Reg. 575, as amended by O. Reg. 849/75.)

FORM 5A
Notice of Claim for Lien Against Holdback for Wages Earned While Working on Street or Public Work
THE MECHANICS' LIEN ACT
Notice of Claim for Lien for Wages

JOHN DOE, of 80 Richmond Street West, Toronto, Ontario (if claimant is a personal representative or assignee, set out the facts) hereby gives notice under subsection 5a of section 11 and under section 21a of The Mechanics' Lien Act of a claim for lien for work done or to be done on or in respect of the undermentioned public work (or municipal public street or highway) while the employment of Quicksilver Sewer and Water Main Services Limited of 10 John Street, Toronto, Ontario.

The work was done on or before the 4th day of June, 1978.

The amount claimed as due is the sum of $500.00 for 10 days wages.

The subject public work (or municipal public street or highway) is located at the west side of

492

Yonge Street between Front and Queen Streets in the City of Toronto, in the Municipality of Metropolitan Toronto.

DATED at Toronto, this 7th day of July, 1978.

....
Signature of Claimant

Note: While this Form may be used as notice under subsection 5a of section 11 of the Ontario Act, it will only be effective where the owner, contractor or subcontractor, whom it is intended to bind, is given notice.

(See Form 2a in the regulations made under the Ontario Act, R.R.O. 1970, Reg. 575, as amended by O. Reg. 849/75.)

FORM 5B

Notice of claim for Lien Against Holdback for Wages Earned
by Several Claimants While Working On Street Or Public Work

THE MECHANICS' LIEN ACT

Notice of Claim for Lien for Wages by Several Claimants

The following persons hereby give notice under subsection 5a of section 11 and under section 21a of The Mechanics' Lien Act of a claim for lien for work done on or in respect of the undermentioned public work (or municipal public street or highway) while in the employment of Quicksilver Sewer and Water Main Services Limited, 10 John Street, Toronto, Ontario.

JOHN DOE of 80 Richmond Street, Toronto, Ontario, $600.00 for 12 days wages for work done on or before the 4th day of June, 1978.

ROBERT COE of 11 William Street, Toronto, Ontario, $500.00 for 10 days wages for work done on or before the 2nd day of June, 1978.

WILLIAM COE of 10 Rodgers Road, Toronto, Ontario, $700.00 for 20 days wages for work done on or before the 5th day of June, 1978.

The subject public work (or municipal public street or highway) is located at The Parliament Buildings, Queen's Park, Toronto, Ontario.

DATED at Toronto, this 8th day of July, 1978.

....
(Signature of Claimant)

....
(Signature of Claimant)

....
(Signature of Claimant)

Note: While this Form may be used as notice under subsection 5a of section 11 of the Ontario Act, it will only be effective where the owner, contractor or subcontractor, whom it is intended to bind, is given notice.

(See Form 3a in the regulations made under the Ontario Act, R.R.O. 1970, Reg. 575, as amended by O. Reg. 849/75.)

FORM 6
Notice of Lien

TAKE NOTICE that JOHN DOE, of 80 Richmond Street West, Toronto 1, Ontario, claims to be entitled to a lien under The Mechanics' Lien Act, R.S.O. 1970, chapter 267, upon the Estate of JOHN SMITH and MARY SMITH, of 9 George Street, in the City of Toronto, in the Municipality of Metropolitan Toronto, in the following lands:

[*Here set out a concise description of the land to be charged sufficient for the purpose of registration.*]

The said lien is in respect of the supply of concrete blocks which materials were furnished (or were to be furnished) for QUICKSILVER CONSTRUCTION LIMITED, of 10 John Street, in the City of Toronto, Municipality of Metropolitan Toronto, and were delivered (or are to be delivered) by the said JOHN DOE upon the said property on or before the 1st day of June, 1971.

The amount claimed as due (or to become due) is the sum of $1,000.00.

DATED at Toronto this 15th day of June, 1971.

John Doe,
80 Richmond Street West,
Toronto, Ontario.
Per:

....
Signature of Claimant or his
Solicitor or Agent

FORM 7
Assignment of Lien

THIS ASSIGNMENT made in duplicate this 10th day of June, 1971.

BETWEEN: JOHN DOE, of the City of
Toronto, in the Municipality
of Metropolitan Toronto, Building
Contractor,
hereinafter called The Assignor,

— and —

WILLIAM COE, of the City of
Toronto, in the Municipality of
Metropolitan Toronto, Building
Contractor,
hereinafter called The Assignee.

WITNESSETH that in consideration of the payment of the sum of Five Hundred Dollars ($500.00) of lawful money of Canada by the Assignee to the Assignor, the receipt of which is hereby acknowledged by the Assignor, the Assignor doth hereby assign and release to the Assignee all his right, title and interest in and to a certain lien under The Mechanics' Lien Act, R.S.O. 1970, chapter 267, a claim for which is dated the 1st day of June, 1971, and which was registered on the 2nd day of June, 1971, in the Registry Office for the Registry Division of Toronto as number 12345 M.L.

There is presently owing upon the said lien the sum of $600.00.

SIGNED, SEALED AND DELIVERED
in the presence of

Witness   "John Doe" (Seal)

[*An Affidavit of execution must be attached to this document if it is to be registered.*]

FORM 8

Discharge of Lien

IN THE MATTER OF
THE MECHANICS' LIEN ACT,
R.S.O. 1970, Chapter 267

I, JOHN DOE, of the City of Toronto, in the Municipality of Metropolitan Toronto, in the Province of Ontario, do hereby acknowledge to have received from **QUICKSILVER CONSTRUCTION LIMITED** the sum of One Thousand Dollars ($1,000.00) in full discharge of my Mechanics' Lien as a subcontractor upon the following land and premises:

[*Here set out a concise description of the land to be charged sufficient for the purpose of registration.*]

which Mechanics' Lien bears date the 10th day of April, A.D. 1971, and was registered in the Registry Office for the City of Toronto, on the 11th day of April, A.D. 1971 at 7 minutes past 3:00 o'clock in the afternoon as No. 12345 M.L. and which said Mechanics' Lien has not been assigned.

DATED this 1st day of June, 1971.

Witness: "John Doe"

Harry Smith

[An Affidavit of execution must be attached to this document if it is to be registered, but see section 25(1)(b) regarding Limited Companies.]

FORM 9

Certificate of Action

CERTIFICATE OF ACTION ON MECHANICS' LIEN
IN THE SUPREME COURT OF ONTARIO
IN THE MATTER OF
THE MECHANICS' LIEN ACT,
R.S.O. 1970, Chapter 267

BETWEEN:

JOHN DOE

Plaintiff,

— and —

495

FORM 9

JOHN SMITH and QUICKSILVER
CONSTRUCTION LIMITED
Defendants.

This is to certify that an action has been commenced in the said Court to enforce a claim for lien for $825.00 against certain land being: [*the description of the land contained in the Plaintiff's Statement of Claim is inserted here.*]

This Certificate is given for the purpose of registration pursuant to the Statute in that behalf.

(Court Seal)
        Given under my hand and the Seal
        of the said Court at Brampton
        this 10th day of July, A.D. 1978
        being an officer duly authorized
        to give this certificate

        Local Registrar, S.C.O.

FORM 10

Statement of Claim

IN THE SUPREME COURT OF ONTARIO
IN THE MATTER OF
THE MECHANICS' LIEN ACT,
R.S.O. 1970, Chapter 267

BETWEEN:

JOHN DOE
Plaintiff,

— and —

JOHN SMITH, MARY SMITH, QUICKSILVER CONSTRUCTION
LIMITED and ACE MORTGAGE COMPANY LIMITED
Defendants.

STATEMENT OF CLAIM

1. The Plaintiff is an electrician residing at the City of Toronto, in the Municipality of Metropolitan Toronto.

2. The Defendant, Mary Smith, is the registered owner of the lands and premises described in the claim for lien hereinafter set forth. The Defendant, John Smith, is the husband of the said Defendant, Mary Smith.

3. The Defendant, Quicksilver Construction Limited, is a body corporate incorporated under the laws of the Province of Ontario, having its head office at the City of Toronto, in the Municipality of Metropolitan Toronto, where it carries on business as a building contractor.

4. The Defendant, Ace Mortgage Company Limited, is a body corporate, incorporated under the laws of the Province of Ontario, having its head office at the City of Toronto, in the Municipality of Metropolitan Toronto, where it carries on business as a mortgage company.

5. On or about the 10th day of February, 1971, the Plaintiff entered into a contract in writing with the Defendant, Quicksilver Construction Limited, which contract the Plaintiff craves leave to produce and refer to at the trial of this action whereby the Plaintiff agreed to do all the electrical work and supply all the electrical materials in connection with the wiring of a home being erected on the lands and premises described in the claim for lien hereinafter

496

set forth by the said Defendant, Quicksilver Construction Limited. The price or sum agreed upon in the said contract for doing the said work and supplying the said materials was $1,000.00.

6. On or about the 1st day of February, 1971, the Defendant, Quicksilver Construction Limited, entered into a contract in writing with the Defendant, John Smith, to erect a home in accordance with plans and specifications supplied by Black & Black, Architects, on the lands and premises described in the claim for lien hereinafter set forth, owned by the Defendant, Mary Smith. The price or sum agreed upon in the said contract was $50,000.00.

7. The Plaintiff has completed his work and supplied the material he was required to supply under his said contract with the Defendant, Quicksilver Construction Limited. During the course of the work, the Plaintiff was requested by the said Defendant, Quicksilver Construction Limited, to supply and install three exterior electrical outlets as an extra to the said contract at an agreed upon price of $25.00 which exterior outlets have been supplied and installed by the Plaintiff.

8. The Plaintiff has received from the Defendant, Quicksilver Construction Limited, on account of its indebtedness to the Plaintiff under the said contract, the sum of $200.00 and accordingly there is presently due and owing to the Plaintiff by the said Defendant the sums of $800.00 upon the said contract and $25.00 for the said extras.

9. The Plaintiff performed his last work upon the said premises on or about the 5th day of August, 1971, and an invoice for the work done and materials supplied under the contract and as an extra to it was mailed to the said Defendant, Quicksilver Construction Limited, on or about the 10th day of August, 1971.

10. There was no agreement between the Plaintiff and the Defendants or any of them that the Plaintiff would not be entitled to a lien upon the lands and premises described in the claim for lien hereinafter set forth for the work done and the materials supplied.

11. By reason of performing the said work and supplying the said materials as hereinbefore set out, the Plaintiff became and is entitled to a lien upon the estate or interest of the Defendants, Mary Smith, John Smith and Ace Mortgage Company Limited, in the lands and premises more particularly described in the claim for lien hereinafter set forth in the sum of $825.00 together with interest on the said sum and the costs of this action pursuant to the provisions of The Mechanics' Lien Act.

12. On the 10th day of September, 1971, the Plaintiff, in pursuance of the said Act, caused to be registered in the Registry Office for the Registry Division of Toronto, a Claim for Lien which is in the words and figures as follows:

JOHN DOE, of 80 Richmond Street West, Toronto 1, Ontario, under The Mechanics' Lien Act, R.S.O. 1970, chapter 267, claims a Lien upon the Estate of JOHN SMITH and MARY SMITH, of 9 George Street, Toronto 12, Ontario, in the undermentioned land in respect of the following work, service or materials, that is to say: Supplying electrical work and materials. The work was completed on the 5th day of August, 1971, and the name and address of the person for whom the work was done or service performed is QUICKSILVER CONSTRUCTION LIMITED, 10 John Street, Toronto 10, Ontario. The amount claimed as due (or to become due) is the sum of $825.00. The following is the description of the land to be charged: [*Here set out the description of the land contained in the Claim for Lien*].

DATED at Toronto, this 10th day of September, 1971.

"JOHN DOE"

....

which claim is verified by the Affidavit of John Doe as claimant and is sworn before a Commissioner for taking Affidavits in the Province of Ontario as required by the said Statute.

13. The lands referred to in the second paragraph of this Statement of Claim and which are more particularly described in the said claim for lien hereinbefore set forth are the lands occupied by the said Defendants, Mary Smith and John Smith, and are the lands for which the Plaintiff furnished the materials and the labour hereinbefore set forth.

14. The Plaintiff alleges that the work done and materials supplied by him pursuant to the said contract between the said Defendant and the Defendant, Quicksilver Construction Limited, were furnished with the privity and consent of the said Defendant, John Smith, pursuant to the provisions of section 6 of The Mechanics' Lien Act, and accordingly that the estate and interest of the said Defendant, Mary Smith, is subject to the Plaintiff's lien in accordance with that section.

15. The Plaintiff alleges, as the fact is, that the Defendant, Ace Mortgage Company Limited, became the mortgagee of the lands and premises hereinbefore described by virtue of a certain indenture of mortgage dated the 10th day of December, 1970, which was registered in the Registry Office for the Registry Division of Toronto on the 11th day of December, 1971, as Number 54321 E.P.

16. The Plaintiff further alleges that the said mortgage was fully advanced to the Defendants, John Smith and Mary Smith, on the 11th day of December, 1970, in the amount of $25,000.00 which said advance was, at the date upon which the first lien arose in relation to the said lands and premises, in excess of the actual value of the said lands and premises.

17. The Plaintiff therefore claims priority over the said mortgage of the Defendant, Ace Mortgage Company Limited, to the extent that the said advance of $25,000.00 exceeded the actual value of the said lands and premises at the time the first lien arose.

18. The Plaintiff therefore claims:
   (a) Payment of the sum of $825.00 by the Defendants or any of them;
   (b) Payment of interest on the sum of $825.00 at the rate of   % per annum from the 10th day of August, 1971 to the date of Judgment herein by the Defendants or any of them;
   (c) Payment of its costs of this action by the Defendants or any of them;
   (d) That in default of payment of the said sum of $825.00 and interest and costs by the Defendants or any of them, all the estate and interest of the said Defendant, Mary Smith, in the said lands hereinbefore set out may be sold and the proceeds applied in and towards payment of the Plaintiff's costs, claim and interest pursuant to The Mechanics' Lien Act;
   (e) Priority over the mortgage of the Defendant, Ace Mortgage Company Limited, to the extent that the advance of $25,000.00 made by the said Defendant exceeded the actual value of the lands and premises hereinbefore described at the time that the first lien arose on the said lands;
   (f) For the purposes aforesaid and for all other purposes, that all proper directions be given, inquiries made and accounts taken;
   (g) Such further and other relief as the nature of this case may require.

The Plaintiff proposes that this action be tried at the City of Toronto, in the Municipality of Metropolitan Toronto.

DELIVERED at Toronto, this 2nd day of November, 1971, by BLANK & BLANK, 1 Bay Street, Toronto, Ontario, Solicitors for the Plaintiff.

FORM 11

Statement of Defence and Counterclaim

IN THE SUPREME COURT OF ONTARIO
IN THE MATTER OF
THE MECHANICS' LIEN ACT,
R.S.O. 1970, Chapter 267

BETWEEN:

JOHN DOE

Plaintiff,

— and —

JOHN SMITH, MARY SMITH, QUICKSILVER CONSTRUCTION
LIMITED and ACE MORTGAGE COMPANY LIMITED

Defendants.

STATEMENT OF DEFENCE AND COUNTERCLAIM

1. The Defendants, John Smith and Mary Smith, admit the allegations contained in Paragraphs 1, 2, 3 and 4 of the Statement of Claim herein, but save as hereinafter expressly admitted, deny all other allegations contained in the said Statement of Claim and put the Plaintiff to the strict proof thereof.

2. The said Defendants, John Smith and Mary Smith, admit that the Defendant, John Smith, entered into a contract in writing with the Defendant, Quicksilver Construction Limited, dated the 1st day of February, 1971, as alleged in the Statement of Claim, which contract the said Defendants crave leave to refer to at the trial of this action and allege, and the fact is, that the said contract provided that the completion of the said contract, evidenced by a final certificate of the architects, Messrs. Black & Black, should be a condition precedent to the payment to the said Defendant, Quicksilver Construction Limited, of the contract price.

(3. [*In the alternative.*] The Defendants, John Smith and Mary Smith, allege, as the fact is, that the Plaintiff had completed 98% of the work to be done by him under his contract with the Defendant, Quicksilver Construction Limited, on or before the 30th day of July, 1971 at which time the said Defendants occupied the building being erected under their aforementioned contract with Quicksilver Construction and commenced to use the said building for the purpose for which it was intended to be used. The said Defendants accordingly allege that the plaintiff is not entitled to a lien on the lands and premises owned by the said Defendant Mary Smith pursuant to the provisions of sections 1(1)(*a*), 1(3) and 22(1) of The Mechanics' Lien Act.)

3. The Defendants, John Smith and Mary Smith, allege, and the fact is, that the said Defendant, Quicksilver Construction Limited, has not completed the said contract nor have the said architects, Messrs. Black & Black, issued a final certificate of completion of the said contract.

4. The Defendants, John Smith and Mary Smith, allege, and the fact is, that it was an implied condition of the said contract between the Plaintiff and the said Defendant, Quicksilver Construction Limited, that the Plaintiff would perform the electrical work set out in the said contract in a good, proper and workmanlike manner and that the material supplied by the Plaintiff should be of good quality and suitable for the purposes for which it was intended. The said Defendants further allege that part of the work done by the plaintiff was done negligently, carelessly and unskilfully and that some of the material supplied by the Plaintiff was not of good quality and in particular that cover plates of the wrong colour were

installed in the master bedroom. The said Defendants, John Smith and Mary Smith, complain particularly of the manner in which the door chimes were installed by the Plaintiff inasmuch as the wires have not been connected to the buttons at the doors of the premises.

5.   The Defendants, John Smith and Mary Smith, further allege that neither of them instructed the Plaintiff or the Defendant, Quicksilver Construction Limited, to install exterior electrical outlets on the premises and allege that they are accordingly not indebted to the Plaintiff for the supply and installation of the same.

6.   The Defendants, John Smith and Mary Smith, allege, and the fact is, that the Plaintiff performed his last work and supplied his last materials on the premises more than 37 days prior to the date on which the Plaintiff's claim for lien was registered, having done his last work or supplied his last material under the said contract on the 30th day of July, 1971, and accordingly the said Defendants allege that the Plaintiff is not entitled to a lien on the lands and premises owned by the said Defendant, Mary Smith, pursuant to section 22(1) of The Mechanics' Lien Act.

7.   The said Defendants, John Smith and Mary Smith, further allege, and the fact is, that the Plaintiff has failed to comply with the provisions of section 23(1) of The Mechanics' Lien Act, in that he failed to commence an action to enforce his alleged lien or to register a certificate of action in the proper Registry Office within 90 days after he performed his last work or supplied his last materials under his contract with the said Defendant, Quicksilver Construction Limited.

8.   The Defendants, John Smith and Mary Smith, allege, and the fact is, that the value of the work completed by the Defendant, Quicksilver Construction Limited, at the time that the said Defendant abandoned its contract with the said Defendants, John Smith and Mary Smith, amounted to $4,000.00, and that the liability of the said Defendants to all subcontractors calculated in accordance with subsection 1 of section 11 of The Mechanics' Lien Act is in the sum of $600.00 which said sum the said Defendants paid into Court on the 4th day of November, 1971, pursuant to the provisions of subsection 7 of the said section 11.

9.   The said Defendants, John Smith and Mary Smith, therefore allege that they are not indebted to the Plaintiff in the sum of $825.00 as claimed by him and that the Plaintiff is not entitled to a lien upon the lands and premises described in his Statement of Claim.

10.   The said Defendants, John Smith and Mary Smith, therefore pray that this action be dismissed with costs.

COUNTERCLAIM

11.   By way of Counterclaim, the Defendant, John Smith, repeats the allegations contained in his Statement of Defence and claims the sum of $500.00 for damages against the Plaintiff for faulty and defective workmanship.

12.   The Defendants, John Smith and Mary Smith, therefore claim:

    (a) Damages in the sum of $500.00;

    (b) Their costs of this action and counterclaim;

    (c) Such further and other relief as this Court deems just.

DELIVERED at Toronto this 5th day of November, 1971, by WHITE & WHITE, 2 Bay Street, Toronto, Ontario, Solicitors for the Defendants, John Smith and Mary Smith.

FORM 12

Affidavit Proving Claim of Lienholder in Foreclosure Proceedings
(Court and Style)

AFFIDAVIT

I, JOHN DOE, of the City of Toronto, in the Municipality of Metropolitan Toronto, Electrician, make oath and say:

1. THAT I did on the 5th day of August, 1971, cause a claim for a mechanics' lien to be registered against the lands and premises in question in this action for the sum of $800.00.

2. THAT I have not obtained a Judgment with respect to the said lien but that I claim my lien is a valid lien and I did on the 2nd day of November, 1971, cause an action to be commenced in this Court to realise the said lien in which the appointment for trial has been given for the 3rd day of December, 1971.

SWORN BEFORE ME at the City of Toronto, in the Municipality of Metropolitan Toronto, this 20th day of November, A.D. 1971.

"John Doe"

A Commissioner, etc.

FORM 13

Notice of Application for Advice and Direction of Court as to Distribution of a Section 2 Trust Fund

IN THE SUPREME COURT OF ONTARIO
IN BANKRUPTCY

IN THE MATTER OF THE BANKRUPTCY OF QUICKSILVER CONSTRUCTION LIMITED with head office at the City of Toronto, in the Province of Ontario

TAKE NOTICE that a motion will be made on behalf of L. W. Haldain, the Trustee of the Estate of Quicksilver Construction Limited, a bankrupt, before The Honourable Mr. Justice Black in Chambers, at the Court House, 361 University Avenue, Toronto, on Thursday, the 10th day of September, 1971, at the hour of 11:00 o'clock in the forenoon or so soon thereafter as the motion can be heard for directions in respect of the distribution of $95,000.00 received by the Trustee in Bankruptcy of Quicksilver Construction Limited in respect of work done by the bankrupt for John Smith, Fidel Corporation and Brackett Limited and if this Honourable Court sees fit, directing a reference to the Registrar of this Court to determine the persons entitled to share in the said funds, appointing John Black to represent the interests of The Canada Wide Bank on the said reference and giving power to the Registrar to appoint such other persons as he sees fit to represent the various parties interested in the said funds and to fix the compensation of the Trustee for administering the said funds, and for such further and other Order as this Court may see fit.

AND TAKE NOTICE that upon and in support of such motion will be read the Affidavit of

L. W. Haldain, filed, and such further and other material as Counsel may advise and the Court permit.

DATED at Toronto, this 4th day of September, 1971.

WHITE & WHITE
2 Bay Street,
Toronto, Ontario.
Solicitors for the Trustee.

FORM 14

Affidavit of Trustee in Support of Application for Directions as to Distribution of Section 2 Trust Fund

IN THE SUPREME COURT OF ONTARIO
IN BANKRUPTCY
IN THE MATTER OF THE BANKRUPTCY OF QUICKSILVER CONSTRUCTION LIMITED, with head office in the City of Toronto, in the Province of Ontario.

AFFIDAVIT

I, L. W. HALDAIN, of the City of Toronto, in the Municipality of Metropolitan Toronto, Chartered Accountant, make oath and say as follows:

1. THAT on the 1st day of May, 1971, Quicksilver Construction Limited made an Assignment in Bankruptcy and I was named Trustee in the said assignment.

2. THAT on the 25th day of May, 1971, my appointment as Trustee in Bankruptcy of the Estate of Quicksilver Construction Limited was confirmed at the first meeting of the creditors of the said bankrupt company.

3. THAT since the 1st day of May, 1970, I have been actively engaged in connection with the administration of the bankrupt estate and have personal knowledge of the facts deposed to in this affidavit.

4. THAT the said Quicksilver Construction Limited prior to its bankruptcy had entered into a number of construction contracts under which moneys remained payable to Quicksilver Construction Limited at the date of its bankruptcy.

5. THAT Quicksilver Construction Limited had contracts with John Smith, Fidel Corporation and Brackett Limited on which I have received payment in full of all moneys owing to Quicksilver Construction Limited for work done by it on these projects as follows:

John Smith—re erection of home in Newmarket	$10,000.00
Fidel Corporation—re addition to sugar refinery	65,000.00
Brackett Limited—re swimming pool	20,000.00

6. THAT while I anticipate that further moneys will be received by me on other construction contracts entered into by Quicksilver Construction Limited, I have now received the majority of the money payable to the said Quicksilver Construction Limited on such construction contracts and I believe that it is in the best interests of those persons who may be entitled to share in a distribution of the said proceeds of the said construction contracts that the moneys presently in my hands be distributed in accordance with the Order of this Court in the usual manner at this time.

7. THAT I have been informed by my solicitors that the said funds received by me as

aforesaid are trust funds pursuant to the provisions of section 2 of The Mechanics' Lien Act, R.S.O. 1970, chapter 267.

8. THAT in order to properly ascertain the persons entitled to the said funds, I desire that the matter should be referred to the Registrar of this Court to ascertain whether the amounts in question are trust funds pursuant to section 2 of The Mechanics' Lien Act, R.S.O. 1970, chapter 267, and if so, who are the proper parties to share in the said funds.

9. THAT The Canada Wide Bank holds an assignment of Book Debts of the said Quicksilver Construction Limited and it accordingly has an interest in the question of whether or not the said funds are trust funds within the meaning of section 2 of The Mechanics' Lien Act, R.S.O. 1970, chapter 267, and if so, whether there will be any surplus funds available after the claims of the beneficiaries of the said trust funds have been satisfied, which surplus may be applied on its said assignment.

SWORN BEFORE ME at the City of
Toronto, in the Municipality of Metropoli-
tan Toronto, this 3rd day of September,
A.D. 1971.

"L. W. Haldain"

A Commissioner, etc.

FORM 15

**Order Directing Reference to Registrar in Bankruptcy as to Persons
Entitled to Section 2 Trust Fund**

IN THE SUPREME COURT OF ONTARIO
IN BANKRUPTCY

THE HONOURABLE MR.   THURSDAY, THE 10TH DAY
JUSTICE BLACK   OF SEPTEMBER, A.D. 1971

IN THE MATTER OF THE BANKRUPTCY OF QUICKSILVER
CONSTRUCTION LIMITED, of the City of Toronto, in the Province of
Ontario.

UPON THE APPLICATION of L. W. Haldain, Trustee of the Estate of Quicksilver Construction Limited, a Bankrupt, upon reading the Affidavit of L. W. Haldain, filed, and upon hearing Counsel for the applicant and Counsel appearing on behalf of The Canada Wide Bank and Counsel on behalf of the ordinary creditors of the bankrupt estate:

1. IT IS ORDERED AND ADJUDGED that the determination of the persons who supplied materials and services to Quicksilver Construction Limited in respect of the following contracts and the amount to which such persons are entitled to be paid out of the funds received by the Trustee from the said contracts and the interests of any other persons in the said funds be referred to the Registrar of this Honourable Court:

John Smith—re erection of home in Newmarket	$10,000.00
Fidel Corporation—re addition to sugar refinery	65,000.00
Brackett Limited—re swimming pool	20,000.00

2. AND IT IS FURTHER ORDERED that D. E. Beard be and he is hereby appointed to represent the interests of all ordinary creditors of the Bankrupt Estate who did not supply material and services with respect to the said contracts and to represent the interests of such creditors on the said reference before the Registrar.

3. AND IT IS FURTHER ORDERED that R. M. Lowd be and he is hereby appointed to

represent the interests of The Canada Wide Bank on the said reference before the Registrar.

4.   AND IT IS FURTHER ORDERED that the Registrar shall have the power to appoint such other persons as he sees fit to represent the various parties interested in the said funds.

5.   AND IT IS FURTHER ORDERED that the Registrar shall determine the commission to be paid to the Trustee for his care, pain, trouble, and time expended in and about administering, arranging, settling and distributing the said funds and in connection with this reference which commission shall be in addition to any compensation he may be entitled to as Trustee of the Bankrupt Estate and shall be payable out of the said funds forthwith after confirmation of the Registrar's Report.

6.   AND IT IS FURTHER ORDERED that the costs of this reference shall be in the discretion of the Registrar and shall be paid out of the said funds forthwith after the confirmation of the Report of the Registrar.

7.   AND IT IS FURTHER ORDERED that the costs of all parties appearing on this application shall be paid out of the said funds forthwith after taxation thereof, the costs of the Trustee to be taxed as between solicitor and client.

8.   AND IT IS FURTHER ORDERED AND ADJUDGED that the persons who supplied materials and services to Quicksilver Construction Limited in respect of the contracts set forth in the Affidavit of L. W. Haldain, filed on this application, as well as such other persons who may be found to have an interest in the funds received by the said Trustee, be paid out of the said funds, the respective amounts found due to them in accordance with the Report of the Registrar forthwith after confirmation of the said Report of the Registrar.

....
Registrar

_____

FORM 16

Order of Registrar Directing Method of Ascertaining Section 2 Claimants

IN THE SUPREME COURT OF ONTARIO
IN BANKRUPTCY

THE REGISTRAR   THURSDAY, THE 17TH DAY
OF SEPTEMBER, 1971

IN THE MATTER OF THE BANKRUPTCY OF QUICKSILVER CONSTRUCTION LIMITED, of the City of Toronto, in the Province of Ontario.

UPON THE APPLICATION of L. W. Haldain, Trustee of the Estate of Quicksilver Construction Limited, a Bankrupt, upon hearing read the Order of The Honourable Mr. Justice Black dated the 10th day of September, 1971, and upon hearing Counsel for the Trustee, Counsel appointed for The Canada Wide Bank and Counsel appointed to represent the interests of all ordinary creditors who did not supply material and services with respect to the contracts involved in this application:

1.   IT IS ORDERED that all creditors who have proved claims with the Trustee of the Estate of Quicksilver Construction Limited, a Bankrupt or of whose claims the said Trustee has notice, be sent notice by prepaid registered mail in the terms contained in the paper writing marked "A" annexed hereto on or before the 30th day of September, 1971, to file claims in respect of the said funds involved in this application not later than the 15th day of October, 1971, which claims shall be filed in the form contained in the paper writing marked "B" annexed hereto, otherwise they shall be excluded from all benefit in the said funds unless otherwise ordered by this Court.

2.   AND IT IS FURTHER ORDERED that subsequent to the 15th day of October, 1971, the Trustee shall prepare and file with the Court a report in respect of all claims received by him indicating which claims are, in his opinion, proper to be admitted to share in the said funds and which claims are, in his opinion, not proper claims.

3.   AND IT IS FURTHER ORDERED that the Trustee shall apply for further directions in respect of this matter after the filing of his report.

....
Registrar

(The paper writing marked "A" referred to in the above Order is Form 17).

(The paper writing marked "B" which is referred to in the above Order is Form 18).

FORM 17

Notice to Creditors Who May Have Claims Against a Section 2 Trust Fund

To The Creditors of Quicksilver Construction Limited

The undersigned is the Trustee of Quicksilver Construction Limited, a Bankrupt. At the date of the bankruptcy of Quicksilver Construction Limited, it was a party to certain construction contracts under which moneys were payable to it. Certain of these moneys have been paid to the Trustee, the details of which are as follows:

Persons with whom the Bankrupt had contract	Project	Amount received by the Trustee
John Smith	erection of home in Newmarket	$10,000.00
Fidel Corporation	addition to sugar refinery	65,000.00
Brackett Limited	swimming pool	20,000.00

If you supplied materials and/or services to the Bankrupt in respect of these contracts, would you please complete the Declaration which is enclosed and attach it to your account showing full particulars of the materials and/or services supplied. After you have had the statutory declaration sworn, would you please return it to the undersigned at the address shown below. Please do not show your account with respect to other materials and/or services which you may have rendered to Quicksilver Construction Limited and for which you have not received payment.

The purpose of asking you to file the said Declaration is to determine whether or not you have a claim under section 2 of The Mechanics' Lien Act, R.S.O. 1970, chapter 267, and if you do, the extent of such claim.

Please co-operate by returning your claim form promptly. Your claim is to be filed on or before the 15th day of October, 1971.

TAKE NOTICE that pursuant to the Order of the Court, if you do not file your claim within the time hereinbefore fixed you will be preemptorily excluded from participating in the said funds.

AND FURTHER TAKE NOTICE that the balance of the said funds remaining after payment of such claims as are found to be valid under section 2 of The Mechanics' Lien Act,

R.S.O. 1970, chapter 267, are claimed by The Canada Wide Bank under a general assignment of book debts.

L. W. Haldain,
3 Bay Street,
Toronto, Ontario.
Trustee in Bankruptcy.

THIS IS THE PAPER WRITING MARKED "A" REFERRED TO IN
THE ANNEXED ORDER

....
Registrar

FORM 18

Proof of Claim Against a Section 2 Trust Fund

IN THE MATTER OF THE BANKRUPTCY OF
QUICKSILVER CONSTRUCTION LIMITED

I, JOHN DOE, residing at the City of Toronto, in the County of York, in the Province of Ontario, do solemnly declare and say:

1.   THAT I am a credior (or the   of the undermentioned creditor) of the said Quicksilver Construction Limited and have knowledge of all the circumstances connected with the debt hereinafter referred to.

2.   THAT the said Quicksilver Construction Limited was at the date of the Bankruptcy, namely the   day of   , 19   , and still is justly and truly indebted to me (or the firm name, if applicable) for materials and services supplied on the following contract or contracts: [*specify the particular contract or contracts on which material and services were supplied, the amounts owing and in detail the amount of material and services supplied to each contract*].

AND I MAKE this solemn declaration conscientiously believing it to be true and knowing that it is of the same force and effect as if made under oath and by virtue of The Canada Evidence Act.

DECLARED BEFORE ME at the City of
Toronto, in the Province of Ontario, this
       day of   , 19   .

....

A Commissioner, etc.

Signature of Creditor or
Declarant

THIS IS THE PAPER WRITING MARKED "B"
REFERRED TO IN THE ANNEXED ORDER

....
Registrar

FORM 19

Trustee's Report on Claims Against Section 2 Trust Fund
IN THE SUPREME COURT OF ONTARIO
IN BANKRUPTCY

IN THE MATTER OF THE BANKRUPTCY OF QUICKSILVER CONSTRUCTION LIMITED, of the City of Toronto, in the Province of Ontario.

Pursuant to the Order of the Registrar, dated the 17th day of September, 1971, I, L. W. Haldain, Trustee of the Estate of Quicksilver Construction Limited, a Bankrupt, hereby report to the Court that the following claims have been received by me pursuant to the notice sent to creditors as provided in the said Order. The Trustee further reports that he has indicated after the name of the claimant whether or not the claim is proper to be admitted to share in the said funds and the reasons for disallowing claims which are not proper to share in the said funds.

Claimant	Claims Received	Claims Admitted	Claims Disputed	Comment
John Smith				
John Electric Limited	500.00	500.00		
W.C. Plumbing Supplies	200.00		200.00	Insufficient reference to contract
Fidel Corporation				
John Smith Company	150.00		150.00	No evidence submitted
John Doe Limited	480.00	480.00		
Brackett Limited				
John's Electric	600.00	600.00		
W.C. Plumbing Supplies Limited	800.00		800.00	No reference to contract
Great West Lumber Company	600.00		600.00	Withdrawn at the request of lien claimant

All of which is Respectfully Submitted.

DATED this 1st day of November, 1971.

L. W. HALDAIN,
3 Bay Street,
Toronto, Ontario.
Trustee in Bankruptcy.

FORM 20
Order Fixing Date of Hearing of Disputed Section 2 Claims
IN THE SUPREME COURT OF ONTARIO
IN BANKRUPTCY

THE REGISTRAR }   THURSDAY, THE 9TH DAY
OF NOVEMBER, A.D. 1971

IN THE MATTER OF THE BANKRUPTCY OF QUICKSILVER CONSTRUCTION LIMITED, of the City of Toronto, in the Province of Ontario.

UPON THE APPLICATION of L. W. Haldain, Trustee of the Estate of Quicksilver Construction Limited, a Bankrupt, for further directions, and upon reading the Affidavit of Service of the Notices referred to in paragraph 1 of the Order of the Registrar dated the 17th day of September, 1971, and the Report of the Trustee prepared pursuant to paragraph 2 of the Order of the Registrar, dated the 17th day of September, 1971, filed, and upon hearing Counsel for the Trustee and Counsel appointed to represent the interests of The Canada Wide Bank and Counsel appointed to represent the interests of all ordinary creditors who did not supply material and services with respect to the contracts involved in this application:

1. IT IS ORDERED that all creditors whose claims are disputed in the Report of the Trustee shall be sent notice by prepared registered mail in the terms contained in the paper writing marked "A" annexed hereto on or before the 19th day of November, 1971.

2. AND IT IS FURTHER ORDERED that the Trustee shall apply for further directions in respect of this matter after the hearing of the above claims.

....

Registrar

(Form 21 is the paper writing marked "A" referred to in the above Order.)

FORM 21
Notice to be Sent to Section 2 Claimant Whose Claim is Disputed
IN THE SUPREME COURT OF ONTARIO
IN BANKRUPTCY

IN THE MATTER OF THE BANKRUPTCY OF QUICKSILVER CONSTRUCTION LIMITED, of the City of Toronto, in the Province of Ontario.

By an Order of this Court bearing date the 10th day of September, 1971, it was ordered that it be referred to the Registrar of this Court to ascertain what amount, if any, of the sums of money received by the Trustee in Bankruptcy of Quicksilver Construction Limited in respect of the contracts referred to in the said Order were trust funds for the benefit of the persons who supplied materials and services with respect to the said contracts and to determine the names of such persons and the amounts to which they were respectively entitled to be paid out of the said funds.

TAKE NOTICE that pursuant to the said Order the Registrar in Bankruptcy has fixed Wednesday, the 29th day of November, 1971 at the hour of 11:00 o'clock in the forenoon at his Chambers, 145 Queen Street West, Toronto, to consider the claim filed by you in respect of the said funds. Unless you then and there appear, you will be forever barred and you will be peremptorily excluded from participating in the said funds. On the day fixed you are not to bring your witnesses, but are to attend for the purpose of receiving further directions in respect of the trial of your claim.

Your claim has been disputed on the following grounds: (*the materials supplied by you were not supplied to the projects mentioned in the Notice—or such other grounds as may be applicable*).

THIS NOTICE does not affect your claim to rank as an unsecured creditor or against other funds of the bankrupt estate which will be considered in due course.

DATED at Toronto, this 18th day of November, 1971.

L. W. HALDAIN,
3 Bay Street,
Toronto, Ontario.
Trustee in Bankruptcy

(This is the paper writing marked "A" referred to in the annexed Order.)

....

Registrar

FORM 22

Registrar's Report on Distribution of Section 2 Trust Fund

IN THE SUPREME COURT OF ONTARIO
IN BANKRUPTCY

IN THE MATTER OF THE BANKRUPTCY OF QUICKSILVER CONSTRUCTION LIMITED, of the City of Toronto, in the Province of Ontario.

REPORT OF THE REGISTRAR
Friday, the 8th day of December, 1971

Pursuant to the reference directed by the Order of the Honourable Mr. Justice Black dated the 10th day of September, 1971, I proceeded to ascertain, what amounts, if any, of the funds received by the Trustee in Bankruptcy in respect of construction contracts performed for various parties by the bankrupt, prior to its bankruptcy, were trust funds, and what persons who supplied materials and services with respect to the said contracts were entitled to share in the said funds.

I was attended by Counsel appointed by the said Order to represent the interests of all ordinary creditors who did not supply materials and services with respect to the contracts involved in this matter, by Counsel appointed by the said Order to represent the interest of The Canada Wide Bank and by Counsel for the Trustee, and I directed that the Trustee should send notice by prepaid registered mail to all creditors who had proved claims with the Trustee of the Estate of Quicksilver Construction Limited, a Bankrupt, requesting that they file claims in respect of the said funds in a form approved by me. After mailing the said notices, I received a report from the Trustee in respect of the claims received by him, which report indicated the claims which were in the opinion of the Trustee, proper to share in the trust fund and the claims which in the opinion of the Trustee should be disputed.

Upon receipt of the Trustee's Report, I directed that all creditors whose claims were disputed by the Trustee should be sent notice in a form approved by me requiring them to attend on a fixed day for the purpose of receiving further directions in respect of the trial of their claims.

On the day fixed, the only creditors whose claims were disputed who appeared before me

509

were W.C. Plumbing Supplies Limited and John Smith Company, both of whom elected to withdraw their claims and I accordingly disallowed the claims of W.C. Plumbing Supplies Limited and John Smith Company as well as the claims of all other creditors whose claims were disputed by the Trustee. I further decided which claims were proper to rank against the funds involved in this application.

I then directed that the costs of the various parties on the reference be fixed at the following amounts:

White & White, representing the Trustee $1,294.50
D. E. Beard, representing all ordinary creditors who did
    not supply materials and services with respect to the
    contracts involved in the application $1,200.00
R. M. Lowd, representing The Canada Wide Bank .... $ 300.00

The total sum of the funds involved in the application amounted to $95,000.00. I find that L. W. Haldain, Trustee, is entitled to receive a commission of 7½% of the said amount plus disbursements as compensation for his care, pain, trouble and time expended in and about administering, arranging, settling and distributing the amount to which the claimants under section 2 of The Mechanics' Lien Act, R.S.O. 1970, chapter 267, are entitled, which compensation shall be payable out of the amount to be distributed to the said claimants. This compensation is in addition to any compensation which the Trustee will be entitled to receive as Trustee of the Bankrupt Estate.

Attached to this Report and marked Schedule "A" is a detailed list of the contracts involved in this application and of the proposed distribution of the funds and the proper persons to share in the amount available for distribution in the amounts shown opposite their names in the said Schedule.

Attached to this Report and marked Schedule "B" is a list of those persons who submitted claims to the Trustee against the said funds, but whose claims have been disallowed.

Pursuant to the Order of the Honourable Mr. Justice Black, dated the 10th day of September, 1971, I direct that forthwith upon confirmation of this Report the Trustee shall distribute the relevant funds in accordance with the fundings of this Report as follows:

(a) To Messrs. White & White, representing the Trustee the sum of $1,294,50.
(b) To D. E. Beard, representing all ordinary creditors who did not supply material and services with respect to the contracts involved in the application the sum of $1,200.00.
(c) To R. M. Lowd, representing The Canada Wide Bank the sum of $300.00.
(d) To the persons entitled to share in the various funds available for distribution, the amount shown opposite their respective names in Schedule "A" attached hereto.
(e) To The Canada Wide Bank, the balance of the said funds together with accrued interest, if any.

All of which having been proven to my satisfaction by proper and sufficient evidence, I humbly certify.

....
Registrar

[*Annex as schedule "A" to the report a list of the various contracts involved and set out under each contract the names of the persons whose claims have been proved valid together with the amounts to which they are entitled. Set out the amount available for distribution with respect to each contract, the amount of the dividend and the exact amount which each valid claimant will receive on the distribution. Annex as Schedule "B" a list of those whose claims were disallowed, together with the amounts of such disallowed claims.*]

FORM 23

**Affidavit for Use on Motion for Order Directing Trial
by a Supreme Court Judge**

IN THE SUPREME COURT OF ONTARIO
IN THE MATTER OF
THE MECHANICS' LIEN ACT,
R.S.O. 1970, Chapter 267

BETWEEN:

JOHN DOE

Plaintiff,

— and —

MARY SMITH and QUICKSILVER
CONSTRUCTION LIMITED

Defendants.

AFFIDAVIT

I, JOHN DOE, of the City of Hamilton, in the Regional Municipality of Hamilton-Wentworth, Electrician, make oath and say as follows:

1.   THAT I am the Plaintiff in this action and as such have knowledge of the matters hereinafter deposed to.

2.   THAT my claim in this action is for the sum of $35,000.00 an amount in excess of the ordinary monetary jurisdiction of the County Court.

3.   THAT I am informed by my solicitor that the Statement of Claim and Statement of Defence in this action disclose that many complicated questions of law will have to be decided at the trial of this action and that the Plaintiff and Defendant are almost entirely agreed as to the state of the accounts between the parties so that very few questions, if any, will arise at the trial with respect to the taking of accounts.

4.   That in view of the complicated questions of law to be determined and the large amount of my claim, it is desired that an Order be made pursuant to the provisions of subsection 1 of section 31 of The Mechanics' Lien Act, directing that this action be tried by a Judge of the Supreme Court at the regular sittings of the Court for the trial of actions in the Judicial District of Hamilton-Wentworth.

SWORN BEFORE ME at the City of
Hamilton, in the Regional Municipality of
Hamilton-Wentworth this   day of
         19 .

"John Doe"

   A Commissioner, etc.

FORM 24

Order Directing Trial of Action by Supreme Court Judge

IN THE SUPREME COURT OF ONTARIO
IN THE MATTER OF
THE MECHANICS' LIEN ACT,
R.S.O. 1970, Chapter 267

HIS HONOUR JUDGE BLACK   }   FRIDAY, THE 10TH DAY
LOCAL JUDGE   OF JUNE, A.D. 1971

BETWEEN:

JOHN DOE

Plaintiff,

— and —

MARY SMITH and QUICKSILVER
CONSTRUCTION LIMITED

Defendants.

UPON THE APPLICATION of the Plaintiff and upon reading the Affidavit of John Doe and the pleadings herein, filed, and upon hearing what was said by Counsel for the Plaintiff and for the Defendants:

1. IT IS ORDERED that this action be and the same shall be tried before a Judge of the Supreme Court at the regular sittings of this Court for the trial of actions without a jury to be held at the City of Hamilton, in the Judicial District of Hamilton-Wentworth.

2. AND IT IS FURTHER ORDERED that the costs of this application shall be costs in the cause (or as the case may be).

....

Registrar

FORM 25

Judgment Directing a Reference for Trial to the Master at Toronto

IN THE SUPREME COURT OF ONTARIO
IN THE MATTER OF
THE MECHANICS' LIEN ACT,
R.S.O. 1970, Chapter 267

THE HONOURABLE   }   FRIDAY, THE 10TH DAY
MR. JUSTICE BLACK   OF JUNE, 1971

BETWEEN:

JOHN DOE

Plaintiff,

— and —

QUICKSILVER CONSTRUCTION LIMITED
and JOHN SMITH

Defendants.

UPON THE APPLICATION of the Plaintiff made pursuant to the provisions of subsection

2 of section 31 of The Mechanics' Lien Act, in the presence of Counsel for the Plaintiff and the Defendants, and upon reading the pleadings in this action and upon hearing what was alleged by Counsel aforesaid (and the parties by their Counsel consenting thereto, or as the case may be):

1.   THIS COURT DOTH ORDER AND ADJUDGE that this action be and the same is referred to the Master at Toronto for trial.

2.   AND THIS COURT DOTH FURTHER ORDER AND ADJUDGE that the parties do recover the respective amounts found due by the Master from the parties found liable by the Master forthwith after confirmation of the Report of the Master.

3.   AND THIS COURT DOTH FURTHER ORDER AND ADJUDGE that the Master do determine all questions arising in this action and on the said reference, and that the findings of the Master respecting the matters so referred be effective on confirmation of the Master's Report.

4.   AND THIS COURT DOTH FURTHER ORDER that the Master do determine the question of costs in this action and of the Reference, and that the costs be taxed and paid as the Master shall direct.

JUDGMENT SIGNED the   day of   , 19   .

....
Assistant Registrar, S.C.O.

(See Form 5 in The Regulations made under the Ontario Act, R.R.O. 1970, Reg. 575.)

———

FORM 26

Judgment Directing a Reference for Trial to the Master at Toronto
Made by Trial Judge

IN THE SUPREME COURT OF ONTARIO
IN THE MATTER OF
THE MECHANICS' LIEN ACT,
R.S.O. 1970, Chapter 267

THE HONOURABLE   ⎫   day, the   day
MR. JUSTICE BLACK   ⎬   of   , 19   .
BETWEEN: ⎭

JOHN DOE

Plaintiff,

— and —

QUICKSILVER CONSTRUCTION LIMITED
and JOHN SMITH

Defendants.

THIS ACTION coming on for trial this day at the sittings holden at Toronto for trial of actions without a jury, in the presence of Counsel for all parties, upon hearing read the pleadings herein and what was alleged by Counsel aforesaid and it appearing that the question in dispute in this action consists wholly or partly of matters of account:

1.   THIS COURT DOTH ORDER AND ADJUDGE that this action be and the same is referred to the Master at Toronto for trial.

2.   AND THIS COURT DOTH FURTHER ORDER AND ADJUDGE that the parties do recover the respective amounts found due by the Master from the parties found liable by the Master forthwith after confirmation of the Report of the Master.

3.   AND THIS COURT DOTH FURTHER ORDER AND ADJUDGE that the Master do determine all questions arising in this action and on the said Reference and that the findings of the Master respecting the matters so referred be effective on confirmation of the Master's Report.

4.   AND THIS COURT DOTH FURTHER ORDER that the Master do determine the question of costs in this action and of the Reference and that the costs be taxed and paid as the Master shall direct.

JUDGMENT SIGNED the   day of   , 1971.

....

Assistant Registrar, S.C.O.

FORM 27

Consent of Receiver to Act
(Court and Style of Cause)

CONSENT

The Quality Trust Company hereby consents to an Order appointing it the Receiver of the rents and profits of the property upon which the lien or liens are filed in this action.

This Consent is given by The Quality Trust Company at the request of Black and White, Solicitors for the Plaintiff herein, and on condition that the appointment of the Company as Receiver, if made, will be pursuant to the provisions contained in The Mechanics' Lien Act, R.S.O. 1970, chapter 267, and amendments thereto, and particularly in connection with subsection 1 of section 34 thereof.

DATED at Toronto, this 1st day of October, 1971.

The Quality Trust Company

(Seal)

FORM 28

Application for Appointment of Receiver
(Court and Style of Cause)

NOTICE OF MOTION

TAKE NOTICE that an application will be made on behalf of the Plaintiff before the presiding Judge in Chambers of this Honourable Court, at Osgoode Hall, in the City of Toronto, on Tuesday, the 15th day of October, 1971 at 11:00 o'clock in the forenoon or so soon thereafter as the motion can be heard for an Order pursuant to subsection 1 of section 34 of The Mechanics' Lien Act, R.S.O. 1970, chapter 267, appointing The Quality Trust Company receiver of the rents and profits of the property upon which the liens in this action have been filed.

AND TAKE NOTICE that upon and in support of such motion will be read the Affidavit of

John Doe and the Consent of The Quality Trust Company, filed, and such further and other material as Counsel may advise and the Court permit.

DATED at Toronto, this 4th day of October, 1971.

> BLACK AND WHITE,
> 1 Bay Street,
> Toronto, Ontario,
> Solicitors for the Plaintiff.

TO: etc.

FORM 29

Order Appointing Receiver

IN THE SUPREME COURT OF ONTARIO
IN THE MATTER OF
THE MECHANICS' LIEN ACT,
R.S.O. 1970, Chapter 267

THE HONOURABLE MR. JUSTICE BLACK IN CHAMBERS	TUESDAY, THE 15TH DAY OF OCTOBER, 1971

(Style of Cause)

UPON THE APPLICLATION of John Doe, the Plaintiff herein, for an Order appointing a Receiver of the rents and profits of the property upon which the liens in this action have been filed pursuant to subsection 1 of section 34 of The Mechanics' Lien Act, and upon hearing read the pleadings and proceedings herein, the Consent of the Quality Trust Company and the Affidavit of John Doe, filed, and upon hearing Counsel for the Plaintiff and for the Defendants, and for Hardwood Flooring Limited and Plaster Ceiling Limited, lien claimants:

1. IT IS ORDERED that The Quality Trust Company be and it is hereby appointed Receiver of the rents and profits of the property against which the liens have been filed in this action, known as Lot 500, Plan 7000, Etobicoke.

2. AND IT IS FURTHER ORDERED that the said The Quality Trust Company deposit with this Court security in the sum of Ten Thousand Dollars ($10,000.00).

....
Assistant Registrar, S.C.O.

FORM 30

Consent of Trustee to Act
(Court and Style of Cause)

CONSENT

The Quality Trust Company hereby consents to an Order appointing it Trustee with power to manage the property upon which the lien or liens in this action are filed, such management to be under the supervision and direction of this Honourable Court with power when so directed by this Honourable Court to mortgage, lease or sell the said property and/ or to complete or partially complete the said premises and in the event that mortgage moneys are advanced to it as Trustee pursuant to such power, such money to take priority over all liens existing at the date of its appointment as Trustee. In the alternative, The Quality Trust Company consents to its appointment as Trustee as aforesaid if the application for the appointment of the Trustee is referred by the presiding Judge in Chambers to the Judge or Officer having jurisdiction to try the action.

This Consent is given by The Quality Trust Company at the request of Black and White, Solicitors for the Plaintiff herein, and on condition that the appointment of the company as Trustee, if made, will be pursuant to the provisions contained in The Mechanics' Lien Act, R.S.O. 1970, chapter 267, and in particular subsections 2 and 3 of section 34 thereof.

DATED at Toronto, this 1st day of October, 1971.

The Quality Trust Company

(Seal)

FORM 31

Application for Appointment of Trustee

IN THE SUPREME COURT OF ONTARIO
IN THE MATTER OF
THE MECHANICS' LIEN ACT,
R.S.O. 1970, Chapter 267

(Style of Cause)

TAKE NOTICE that an application will be made on behalf of the Plaintiff before the presiding Judge in Chambers of this Honourable Court, at Osgoode Hall, in the City of Toronto, on Tuesday, the 15th day of October, 1971, at 11:00 o'clock in the forenoon or so soon thereafter as the application can be heard for an Order pursuant to the provisions of subsection 2 of section 34 of The Mechanics' Lien Act, and amendments thereto appointing The Quality Trust Company as Trustee with power to manage, mortgage, lease and sell the property upon which the liens in this action are filed, such management and sale to be under the supervision and direction of this Honourable Court and with power to complete or partially complete the premises, and in the event that mortgage moneys are advanced to the said Trustee to be appointed as the result of such power, such moneys to take priority over all liens existing as of the date of its appointment, and for such further or other Order as this Honourable Court may deem just.

AND TAKE NOTICE that upon and in support of such motion will be read the Affidavit of John Doe, the Statement of Claim herein, the Consent of The Quality Trust Company, and such further and other material as Counsel may advise and the Court permit.

DATED at Toronto, this 4th day of October, 1971.

BLACK AND WHITE,
1 Bay Street,
Toronto, Ontario.
Solicitors for the Applicant.

TO: etc.

FORM 32

Order Appointing a Trustee

IN THE SUPREME COURT OF ONTARIO

IN THE MATTER OF

THE MECHANICS' LIEN ACT,

R.S.O. 1970, Chapter 267

THE HONOURABLE MR. JUSTICE ⎱ TUESDAY, THE 15TH DAY
BLACK, IN CHAMBERS ⎰ OF OCTOBER, A.D. 1971

(Style of Cause)

UPON THE APPLICATION of the plaintiff for an Order appointing The Quality Trust Company Trustee of the lands and premises upon which the liens in this action are filed pursuant to subsection 2 of section 34 of The Mechanics' Lien Act, and amendments thereto and upon reading the Affidavit of John Doe, the Consent of The Quality Trust Company, and the Statement of Claim, filed, and upon hearing Counsel for the Applicant, Counsel for the Defendants and Counsel for Hardwood Flooring Limited and Plaster Ceiling Limited, lien claimants, no one appearing for Dry Wall Limited, a lien claimant, although duly served with Notice of this application:

1.   IT IS ORDERED that The Quality Trust Company be and it is hereby appointed Trustee of the property upon which the liens in this action are filed with power to manage, mortgage, lease and sell the said property and to complete or partially complete the said property under the supervision and direction of the Court.

2.   AND IT IS FURTHER ORDERED that it is referred to the Master (*or the Judge, as the case may be*) to supervise and direct the management, mortgaging, leasing, sale or completion of the said property as may be most expedient or advisable in the interests of all parties pursuant to the provisions contained in subsections 2 and 3 of section 34 of The Mechanics' Lien Act, and to deal with and dispose of the costs of this application and reference.

....

Assistant Registrar, S.C.O.

FORM 33

Affidavit in Support of Application to Appoint a Trustee

(Court and Style of Cause)

AFFIDAVIT

I, JOHN DOE, of the City of Toronto, in the Municipality of Metropolitan Toronto, Electrician, make oath and say:

1.   THAT I am the Plaintiff in this action and as such have knowledge of the matters herein deposed to.

2.   THAT I did on or about the 10th day of August, 1971, cause a claim for mechanics' lien for the sum of $1,000.00 and costs of $50.00 to be registered against the lands and premises more particularly described in the Statement of Claim herein, and subsequently on or about the 20th day of September, 1971, I did cause a certificate of action to be registered on the title to the lands and premises described in the Statement of Claim herein.

517

3. THAT I am informed by my solicitors, Black & White, that there are several liens registered against the said property.

4. THAT I am further informed by my solicitors, Black & White, and verily believe that two contracts of sale have been entered into by the Defendants for the sale of Lots 10 and 11, being part of the lands and premises described in the Statement of Claim herein, and attached to this my Affidavit are true copies of the said Offers to Purchase being marked Exhibit "A" to this my Affidavit.

5. THAT I have attended on the said lands and premises described in the Statement of Claim herein and have determined that while the homes situated on Lots 10, 11, 12 and 13 are substantially completed they are not being cared for and it is my opinion that they ought to be completed and sold or leased as quickly as possible so as to obtain the best possible purchase price for the same or alternatively to lease the same so as to protect them from deterioration due to vandalism and the action of the elements.

6. THAT I am of the opinion that it is in the interest of all parties to this action that a Trustee be appointed to manage, complete and sell the aforementioned premises in order that the aforementioned sales be not lost due to the delay occasioned through the conduct of this action, and in order that the properties upon which Offers to Purchase have not been received may be sold or leased before they are damaged by the elements or by vandalism.

SWORN BEFORE ME at the City of Toronto, in the Municipality of Metropolitan Toronto, this 1st day of October, A.D. 1971.

        "John Doe"

    A Commissioner, etc.

FORM 34

Order Appointing a Trustee to Preserve the Property

IN THE SUPREME COURT OF ONTARIO
IN THE MATTER OF
THE MECHANICS' LIEN ACT,
R.S.O. 1970, Chapter 267

HIS HONOUR JUDGE
BLACK, IN CHAMBERS

        TUESDAY, THE 15TH DAY
        OF NOVEMBER, 1971

(Style of Cause)

UPON THE APPLICATION of the Plaintiff for an Order appointing The Quality Trust Company Trustee of the property upon which the liens in this action are filed pursuant to section 35 of The Mechanics' Lien Act, and amendments thereto, and upon reading the Affidavit of John Doe, the Consent of The Quality Trust Company and the pleadings herein, filed, and upon hearing what was said by Counsel for the Plaintiff and Counsel for the Defendant:

1. IT IS ORDERED that The Quality Trust Company be and it is hereby appointed Trustee of the property upon which the liens in this action are filed, with power to manage and preserve the said property pending the determination of this action and any appeal.

2. AND IT IS FURTHER ORDERED that the said Trustee may appoint and pay a

FORM 36

caretaker for the said property and do all necessary acts to protect and preserve the said property.

3. AND IT IS FURTHER ORDERED that the said Trustee is not at this time required to deposit any security with this Court (*or is required to deposit security in the sum of five thousand dollars, or as the case may be*).

FORM 35

Application to Set Aside Judgment Directing a Reference to the Master for Trial

(Court and Style of Cause)

TAKE NOTICE that an application will be made on behalf of John Smith, a lien claimant, before the presiding Judge in Chambers of this Honourable Court, at Osgoode Hall, in the City of Toronto, on Friday, the 18th day of November, 1971, at 11:00 o'clock in the forenoon or so soon thereafter as the application can be heard for an Order setting aside the Judgment of the Honourable Mr. Justice Black dated the 15th day of October, 1971, referring this action to the Master at Toronto for trial pursuant to the provisions of subsection 2 of section 31 of The Mechanics' Lien Act, R.S.O. 1970, chapter 267.

AND TAKE NOTICE that upon and in support of such motion will be read the Affidavit of John Smith, the pleadings herein, filed, and such further and other material as Counsel may advise and the Court permit.

DATED at Toronto, this 11th day of November, 1971.

I. M. WISE,
5 Bay Street,
Toronto, Ontario.
Solicitor for the Applicant.

TO: etc.

FORM 36

Order Setting Aside Judgment Directing a Reference to The Master

IN THE SUPREME COURT OF ONTARIO
IN THE MATTER OF
THE MECHANICS' LIEN ACT,
R.S.O. 1970, Chapter 267

THE HONOURABLE MR. JUSTICE   FRIDAY, THE 18TH DAY
LAW IN CHAMBERS   OF NOVEMBER, 1971

(Style of Cause)

UPON THE APPLICATION of John Smith, a lien claimant, made pursuant to the provisions of subsection 3 of section 31 of The Mechanics' Lien Act, in the presence of Counsel for the Plaintiff, for the Defendants and for Hardwood Flooring Limited and Plaster Ceiling Limited, lien claimants, upon reading the Affidavit of John Smith and the pleadings in this action, filed, and upon hearing what was alleged by Counsel aforesaid:

1. IT IS ORDERED that the Order of The Honourable Mr. Justice Black dated the 15th day of October, 1971 referring this action to the Master at Toronto for trial pursuant to

519

section 69 of The Judicature Act, R.S.O. 1970, chapter 228, be and the same is hereby set aside.

2. AND IT IS FURTHER ORDERED that this action shall be tried by a Judge of the Supreme Court of Ontario at the regular sittings of this Court for the trial of actions without a jury at Toronto.

....
Assistant Registrar, S.C.O.

FORM 37

Notice of Application to Speed the Trial of the Action

(Court and Style of Cause)

TAKE NOTICE that an application will be made on behalf of John Doe, a lien claimant in this action, before the presiding Judge in Chambers, at Osgoode Hall, in the City of Toronto, on Friday, the 10th day of November, 1971, at the hour of 11:00 o'clock in the forenoon or so soon thereafter as the application can be heard for an Order pursuant to subsection 6 of section 29 of The Mechanics' Lien Act, R.S.O. 1970, chapter 267, to speed the trial of this action.

AND TAKE NOTICE that upon and in support of such application will be read the pleadings and proceedings herein, the Affidavit of John Doe, filed, and such further and other material as Counsel may advise and the Court permit.

DATED at Toronto, this 5th day of November, 1971.

BLACK AND WHITE,
1 Bay Street,
Toronto, Ontario.
Solicitors for the Applicant.

TO: etc.

FORM 38

Notice of Motion by Wage Earner for Speedy Judgment

(Court and Style of Cause)

TAKE NOTICE that an application will be made on behalf of John Doe, before the presiding Judge in Chambers of this Honourable Court, at Osgoode Hall, in the City of Toronto, on Friday, the 10th day of November, 1971, at the hour of 11:00 o'clock in the forenoon or so soon thereafter as the application can be heard for an Order pursuant to subsection 2 of section 15 of The Mechanics' Lien Act, R.S.O. 1970, chapter 267, giving Judgment on the claim for lien of the said John Doe against the lands and premises owned by John Smith described as follows:

[*Here set out a concise description of the property.*]

AND TAKE NOTICE that upon and in support of such application will be read the Abstract of Title, the Affidavit of the said John Doe, and the claim for lien of the said John

Doe, filed, and such further and other material as Counsel may advise and the Court permit.

DATED at Toronto, this 5th day of November, 1971.

> BLACK AND WHITE,
> 1 Bay Street,
> Toronto, Ontario.
> Solicitors for the Applicant.

TO: etc.

FORM 39

Particulars of Wage Earner's Claim to be Filed in Support of
Application for Speedy Judgment

(Court and Style of Cause)

I, JOHN DOE, of the City of Toronto, in the Municipality of Metropolitan Toronto, Labourer, make oath and say as follows:

1. THAT I claim to be entitled to a lien upon the property of John Smith, of 10 George Street, in the City of Toronto and Municipality of Metropolitan Toronto, which property is known as the whole of Lot 500, according to a Plan registered in the Registry Office for the Registry Division of the City of Toronto as Number 1000.

2. THAT I was engaged by the said John Smith to excavate a swimming pool on the said premises by hand at a wage of $10.00 per day, commencing on the 1st day of August, 1971.

3. THAT I commenced to excavate the said swimming pool on the said lands on the 1st day of August, 1971, and worked continuously in digging the said excavation until Friday, the 24th day of August, 1971, a period of 25 days.

4. THAT I have received no moneys on account of the said work performed by me and the said John Smith is accordingly indebted to me in the sum of $250.00.

5. THAT on the 20th day of September, 1971, I caused to be filed in the Registry Office for the Registry Division of the City of Toronto, a claim for lien for the said sum of $250.00 plus $25.00 for costs.

6. THAT it is desired that an Order be made in this action pursuant to the provisions of subsection 2 of section 15 of The Mechanics' Lien Act, R.S.O. 1970, chapter 267, granting Judgment to me for the amount of my said claim for lien and costs.

SWORN BEFORE ME at the City of Toronto, in the Municipality of Metropolitan Toronto, this 4th day of November, A.D. 1971.	"John Doe"

A Commissioners, etc.

FORM 40

Master's Order Appointing Time and Place of Trial

(Court and Style of Cause)

UPON THE APPLICATION of the Plaintiff made pursuant to the provisions of subsection 1 of section 38 of The Mechanics' Lien Act, R.S.O. 1970, chapter 267, and upon reading the

FORM 40

Judgment of Reference herein, dated the 29th day of April, 1971, filed, and upon hearing what was said by Counsel for the Plaintiff:

1. IT IS ORDERED that the trial of this action shall take place at 145 Queen Street West, in the City of Toronto, in the Municipality of Metropolitan Toronto, on Wednesday, the 10th day of June, 1971 at 10:30 o'clock in the forenoon.

....

Master

FORM 41

Judge's Order Appointing Time and Place of Trial

(Court and Style of Cause)

UPON THE APPLICATION of the Plaintiff made pursuant to the provisions of subsection 1 of section 38 of The Mechanics' Lien Act, R.S.O. 1970, chapter 267, upon reading the pleadings herein, filed, and upon hearing what was said by Counsel for the Plaintiff:

1. THIS COURT DOTH ORDER that the trial of this action shall take place at the Court House in the City of Kingston in the County of Frontenac, on Wednesday, the 10th day of June, 1971 at the hour of 10:30 o'clock in the forenoon.

DATED at Kingston, this 4th day of May, 1971.

....

Local Judge

FORM 42

Notice of Trial

(Court and Style of Cause)

NOTICE OF TRIAL

TAKE NOTICE that pursuant to the Order of His Honour Judge E. W. White, dated the 10th day of October, 1971, this action will be tried at the Court House, in the Town of Brampton in the County of Peel, on Tuesday, the 5th day of November, 1971 at the hour of 10:30 o'clock in the forenoon, by His Honour Judge E. W. White and at such time and place the said Local Judge will proceed to try the action and all questions as provided by The Mechanics' Lien Act.

AND FURTHER TAKE NOTICE that if you do not appear at the trial and defend the action or prove your claim, if any, the proceedings will be taken in your absence and you may be deprived of all benefit of the proceedings and your rights disposed of in your absence.

AND FURTHER TAKE NOTICE that all parties and lien claimants shall bring with them on the day herein set for trial, all mortgages, contracts, agreements, orders, cheques, notes, delivery slips, time books, books of account, diaries, duplicate original liens and any other books or papers necessary to prove liens or defences. If any person fails to comply with these directions, the costs of the day may be given against him in the event that an adjournment is necessary for the production of any of the above-mentioned documentary evidence.

THIS IS a Mechanics' Lien action brought by the above-named Plaintiff against the above-named Defendants to enforce a mechanics' lien against the following lands:

[*Here set out a description of the lands.*]

THIS NOTICE is served by Black and White, 1 Bay Street, Toronto, Ontario, Solicitors for the Plaintiff.

DATED at Toronto this 12th day of October, 1971.

(See Form 6 in The Regulations made under the Ontario Act, R.R.O. 1970, Reg. 575.)

FORM 42A
Notice of Trial Where Claim Pertains to Holdback for Work
Done on Street or Public Work

(Court and Style of Cause)

NOTICE OF TRIAL

TAKE NOTICE that, pursuant to the Order of His Honour Judge E. W. White dated the 4th day of May, 1978 this action will be tried at the Court House in the City of Brampton, in the Regional Municipality of Peel on Tuesday, the 15th day of June, 1978 at the hour of 10:30 o'clock in the forenoon by His Honour Judge E.W. White and at such time and place the said Local Judge will proceed to try the action and all questions as provided by The Mechanics' Lien Act.

AND FURTHER TAKE NOTICE that if you do not appear at the trial and defend the action or prove your claim, if any, the proceedings will be taken in your absence and you may be deprived of all benefit of the proceedings and your rights disposed of in your absence.

AND FURTHER TAKE NOTICE that all parties and lien claimants shall bring with them on the day herein set for trial all mortgages, contracts, agreements, orders, cheques, notes, delivery slips, time-books, books of account, diaries, and any other books or papers necessary to prove liens or defences. If any person fails to comply with these directions, the costs of the day may be given against him in the event that an adjournment is necessary for the production of any of the above-mentioned documentary evidence.

This is a Mechanics' Lien action, brought by the above-named plaintiffs, against the above-named defendants, to enforce a mechanics' lien against the amounts required to be retained by section 11 of the Act in connection with the work done on the following lands: [*here set out description of lands or otherwise identify work*].

This notice is served by Black and White, 1 Bay Street, Toronto, Ontario, Solicitors for the plaintiff.

DATED at Toronto, this 10th day of May, 1978.

TO: The above-named defendant

(See Form 6*a* in the regulations made under the Ontario Act, R.R.O. 1970, Reg. 575, as amended by O. Reg. 849/75.)

FORM 43

Consent of Trustee to Order Permitting Claimant to Proceed
Against Bankrupt Contractor

IN THE SUPREME COURT OF ONTARIO

IN BANKRUPTCY

IN THE MATTER OF THE BANKRUPTCY OF QUICKSILVER CON-
STRUCTION LIMITED, of the City of Toronto, in the Province of Ontario:

AND IN THE MATTER OF THE APPLICATION OF JOHN DOE.

I, L. W. HALDAIN, Trustee in Bankruptcy of the Estate of Quicksilver Construction
Limited, hereby Consent to an Order being made as follows:

1. Giving leave to John Doe to commence and prosecute an action in the Supreme Court of
Ontario under The Mechanics' Lien Act, R.S.O. 1970, chapter 267, against the Trustee of the
property of the said Quicksilver Construction Limited to enforce its lien against the property
hereinafter described and being in the City of Toronto, in the Municipality of Metropolitan
Toronto, and being composed of:

[*Here set out a concise description of the property.*]

2. Providing that the said John Doe's right to prosecute his action under The Mechanics'
Lien Act pursuant to such Order shall be for the purpose only of establishing in that action
the amount for which he is entitled to prove in the Bankruptcy of Quicksilver Construction
Limited after realization under his lien.

3. Extending the time for filing a declaration under subsection 1 of section 99 of the
Bankruptcy Act, R.S.C. 1970, chapter B-3, until after the expiration of 30 days from the
completion of the sale of the aforesaid lands pursuant to the Judgment of the Court
adjudicating upon the applicant's claim for lien for whatever amount may be found owing
thereunder as against the said Trustee and co-defendant.

4. Extending the time for filing any claim which the said John Doe may have as an
unsecured creditor after realization under his lien as required by section 97, subsection 1 of
the Bankruptcy Act until it shall have been ascertained what amount the said John Doe shall
receive under his lien.

5. Authorizing all other persons who may be entitled to enforce mechanics' liens against the
within mentioned property to take such proceedings as may be necessary to protect their
rights thereunder and the provisions of sections 2, 3, and 4 of this Consent shall apply to all
such lienholders in the bankruptcy proceedings.

DATED at Toronto, this 10th day of October, 1971.

"L. W. HALDAIN"
Trustee of the Estate of
Quicksilver Construction
Witness: Limited in Bankruptcy.

FORM 44
Order Permitting Claimant to Proceed Against Bankrupt Contractor
IN THE SUPREME COURT OF ONTARIO
IN BANKRUPTCY

THE REGISTRAR   MONDAY, THE 12TH DAY
                                                       OF OCTOBER, 1971.

IN THE MATTER OF THE BANKRUPTCY OF QUICKSILVER CON-
STRUCTION LIMITED, of the City of Toronto, in the Province of Ontario:

AND IN THE MATTER OF THE APPLICATION OF JOHN DOE.

UPON THE APPLICATION of Counsel for leave to commence and prosecute the claim for lien of John Doe and the claims of other lienholders against the property hereinafter described and upon reading the Consent of L. W. Haldain, the Trustee in Bankruptcy of the Estate of Quicksilver Construction Limited, filed, and upon hearing what was alleged by Counsel for the said John Doe:

1.   IT IS ORDERED that the applicant be and he is hereby authorized to commence and prosecute an action in the Supreme Court of Ontario under The Mechanics' Lien Act, R.S.O. 1970, chapter 267, against the Trustee of the property of the said Quicksilver Construction Limited to enforce his lien against the property hereinafter described and being in the City of Toronto, in the Municipality of Metropolitan Toronto, and being composed of:

[*Here set out a concise description of the property.*]

2.   AND IT IS FURTHER ORDERED that the applicant's right to prosecute his action under The Mechanics' Lien Act pursuant to this Order shall be for the purpose only of establishing in that action the amount for which he is entitled to prove in the bankruptcy of Quicksilver Construction Limited after realization under his lien.

3.   AND IT IS FURTHER ORDERED that the time for filing a declaration under subsection 1 of section 99 of the Bankruptcy Act, R.S.C. 1970, chapter B-3, be extended until after the expiration of 30 days from the completion of the sale of the aforesaid lands pursuant to the Judgment of the Court adjudicating upon the applicant's claim for lien for whatever amount may be found owing thereunder as against the said Trustee and co-defendant.

4.   AND IT IS FURTHER ORDERED that the time for filing any claim which the said John Doe may have as an unsecured creditor after realization under his lien as required by section 97, subsection 1 of the Bankruptcy Act be and the same is hereby extended until it shall have been ascertained what amount the said John Doe shall receive under his lien.

5.   AND IT IS FURTHER ORDERED that all other persons who may be entitled to enforce mechanics' liens against the within mentioned property be and they are hereby authorized to take such proceedings as may be necessary to protect their rights thereunder and that the provisions of sections 2, 3, and 4 of this Order shall apply to all such lienholders in the bankruptcy proceedings.

....
                                                       Registrar

525

FORM 45

Consent to Order Discharging Liens and Dismissing Action

(Court and Style of Cause)

CONSENT

We hereby consent to an Order being made in this action as follows:

(a) Discharging the claim for lien of John Doe, dated the 1st day of June, 1971, and registered on the 1st day of June, 1971 as Number 52 M.L. in the Registry Office for the Registry Division of Toronto against the title to the lands described in the Statement of Claim in this action.

(b) Discharging the claim for lien of John Smith, dated the 3rd day of June, 1971 and registered on the 4th day of June, 1971 as Number 56, in the Registry Office for the Registry Division of Toronto against the title of the lands described in the Statement of Claim in this action.

(c) Vacating the certificate of this action dated the 25th day of July, 1971 and registered on the 25th day of July, 1971 as Number 74 E.D., in the Registry Office for the Registry Division of Toronto against the title to the lands described in the Statement of Claim in this action.

(d) Dismissing this action without costs.

DATED at Toronto, this 1st day of August, 1971.

> BLACK AND WHITE,
> Solicitors for the Plaintiff,
> John Doe.

Witness: JOHN SMITH.

> LAWLESS & LAWLESS,
> Solicitors for the Defendants.

FORM 46

Order Discharging Liens and Dismissing Action

IN THE SUPREME COURT OF ONTARIO
IN THE MATTER OF
THE MECHANICS' LIEN ACT,
R.S.O. 1970, Chapter 267

H. G. WHITE   FRIDAY, THE 5TH DAY
MASTER   OF AUGUST, 1971.

(Style of Cause—if more than one action, all styles of cause)

(Preamble)

1. IT IS ORDERED that each of the following claims for lien registered in the Registry Office for the Registry Division of Toronto against the title to the lands described in Schedule "A" hereto, be and the same are hereby discharged:

Registration Number	Date of Claim	Date of Registration	Claimant
56 M.L.	June 1, 1971	June 1, 1971	John Smith
52 M.L.	June 3, 1971	June 4, 1971	John Doe

2. AND IT IS FURTHER ORDERED that the following certificates of the above-

mentioned actions respectively registered in the said Registry Office for the Registry Division of Toronto against the title to the lands described in Schedule "A" hereto, be and the same are hereby vacated:

(a) Certificate of Action commenced by J. Doe Limited, dated the 4th day of July, 1971 and registered on the 4th day of July, 1971 as Number 60 M.L.

(b) Certificate of Action commenced by John Smith, dated the 15th day of July, 1971 and registered on the 15th day of July, 1971 as Number 74 M.L.

3. AND IT IS FURTHER ORDERED that these actions be and the same are hereby dismissed without costs.

....

Master

[Annex Schedule "A" to Order which sets out a description of the lands sufficient for the purpose of registration.]

FORM 47

**Application for Order Vacating Liens on Furnishing Security
or on Payment into Court**

(Court and Style of Cause)

TAKE NOTICE that an application will be made on behalf of the Defendant, John Smith, the owner of certain property against which a Lien has been registered by you before H. G. White, Master, in his Chambers at Osgoode Hall, in the City of Toronto, on the 24th day of September, 1971, at the hour of 10:00 o'clock in the forenoon or so soon thereafter as the application may be heard, for an Order pursuant to subsection 2 of section 25 of The Mechanics' Lien Act, R.S.O. 1970, chapter 267, vacating the registration of the said lien upon the posting of such security or the payment into Court of such moneys as the said Master may direct.

AND TAKE NOTICE that upon and in support of such application will be read the Affidavit of John Smith, the Abstract of Title, filed, and such further or other material as Counsel may advise and the Court permit.

DATED at Toronto, this 18th day of September, 1971.

BLACK AND WHITE,
1 Bay Street,
Toronto, Ontario,
Solicitors for the Defendant,
John Smith.

TO: the registered lien claimant
or his solicitor.

FORM 48
Order Discharging Liens on Payment into Court or Furnishing Security
IN THE SUPREME COURT OF ONTARIO
IN THE MATTER OF
THE MECHANICS' LIEN ACT,
R.S.O. 1970, Chapter 267

H. G. WHITE	FRIDAY, THE 24TH DAY
MASTER	OF SEPTEMBER, 1971.

(Style of Cause)

UPON THE APPLICATION of John Smith for an Order vacating the registration of a claim for lien and the certificate of this action pursuant to the provisions of subsection 2 of section 25 of The Mechanics' Lien Act, and upon reading the Affidavit of John Smith and the Abstract of Title, filed, and upon hearing what was alleged by Counsel on behalf of the Applicant and Counsel for the Plaintiff, and upon the Applicant paying into Court to the credit of this action the sum of $1,000.00 together with costs in the sum of $250.00:

1.   IT IS ORDERED that the registration of the claim for lien of John Electric dated the 4th day of July, 1971 and registered in the Registry Office for the Registry Division of Toronto on the 5th day of July, 1971 as Number 53 M.L., against the lands referred to in Schedule 1 hereto be and the same is hereby vacated.

2.   AND IT IS FURTHER ORDERED that the Certificate of this Action dated the 25th day of August, 1971 and registered in the Registry Office for the Registry Division of Toronto on the 25th day of August, 1971 as Number 65 M.L., against the lands referred to in the said Schedule 1 hereto, be and the same is hereby vacated.

....
Master

[*Attach schedule 1 setting out a description of the property sufficient for the purpose of registration.*]

FORM 49
Affidavit of Search as to Liens
(Court and Style of Cause)
AFFIDAVIT

I, JOHN SMITH, of the City of Toronto, in the Municipality of Toronto, Solicitor, make oath and say:

1.   THAT I am a member of the law firm of Black and White, solicitors for the Defendant in this action, and as such have knowledge of the matters hereinafter deposed to.

2.   THAT on the 23rd day of September, 1971, I did make a search in the Registry Office for the Registry Division of Toronto of the title to the lands and premises described in the Statement of Claim in this action.

3.   THAT my said search of title disclosed that a Claim for Lien by the Plaintiff in this action dated the 4th day of July, 1971 was registered against the title to the said lands on the 5th day of July, 1971 as instrument number 54 M.L.

4.   THAT my said search of title further disclosed that a Certificate of this action dated the

25th day of August, 1971 was registered in the said Registry Office on the 25th day of August, 1971 as instrument number 65 M.L. against the title to the said lands.

5.   THAT there are no other Claims for Lien or Certificates of Action registered against the said lands (*or as the case may be*).

6.   (*And in jurisdictions where applicable*) THAT to the best of my knowledge and belief, there are no unregistered Claims for Lien against the said lands either for work done or materials supplied or arising in any manner whatsoever.

SWORN BEFORE ME at the City of
Toronto, in the Municipality of Metropolitan Toronto, this 23rd day of September,
1971.

"John Smith"

 A Commissioner, etc.

FORM 50

Order Permitting Discovery

IN THE SUPREME COURT OF ONTARIO
IN THE MATTER OF
THE MECHANICS' LIEN ACT,
R.S.O. 1970, Chapter 267

THE HONOURABLE MR. JUSTICE BLACK IN CHAMBERS	FRIDAY, THE 15TH DAY OF NOVEMBER, 1971.

(Style of Cause)

(Preamble)

1.   IT IS ORDERED that each party (or as the case may be) shall be at liberty to examine the other for discovery in this action within fifteen days following the date of this Order in accordance with the Rules of Practice and procedure of this Court.

2.   AND IT IS FURTHER ORDERED that the costs of this application shall be costs in the cause (or as the case may be).

....
Judge

FORM 51

Order Consolidating Actions

IN THE SUPREME COURT OF ONTARIO
IN THE MATTER OF
THE MECHANICS' LIEN ACT,
R.S.O. 1970, Chapter 267

H. G. WHITE MASTER	FRIDAY, THE 15TH DAY OF NOVEMBER, 1971.

(All styles of cause)

(Preamble)

1.   IT IS ORDERED that all of the above entitled actions be and the same are hereby

consolidated into one action and shall henceforth be carried on as one action under the following style of cause: [*set out one style of cause*].

2.   AND IT IS FURTHER ORDERED that the Plaintiff, John Doe, shall have the conduct of the consolidated action.

3.   AND IT IS FURTHER ORDERED that the costs of this application shall be to the Plaintiff in the cause (or as the case may be).

....
Master

_____

FORM 52

Order for Substitutional Service

(Court and Style of Cause)

UPON THE APPLICATION of the Plaintiff and upon reading the Affidavit of Albert Smith, filed, and upon hearing what was said by Counsel for the Plaintiff:

1.   IT IS ORDERED that service of the Statement of Claim in this action by mailing the same together with a copy of this Order to John Jones at 2 George Street, in the City of Toronto, in the Municipality of Metropolitan Toronto, by prepaid registered mail shall be good and sufficient service of the said Statement of Claim and Order on the said Defendant, John Jones.

(*Or alternatively*: 1. IT IS ORDERED that service of the Statement of Claim in this action by leaving the same together with a copy of this Order with an adult person residing at 2 George Street, in the City of Toronto, in the Municipality of Metropolitan Toronto, shall be good and sufficient service of the said Statement of Claim and Order on the said Defendant, John Jones.)

....
Master

_____

FORM 53

Order Extending Time for Service of Statement of Claim

(Court and Style of Cause)

UPON THE APPLICATION of the Plaintiff and upon reading the Affidavit of John Black, filed, and upon hearing what was said by Counsel for the Plaintiff:

1.   IT IS HEREBY ORDERED that the time limited for service of the Statement of Claim in the within action be and the same is hereby extended to the 15th day of November, 1971.

....
Judge or Master

_____

FORM 54

Notice of Application to Prove Claims for Lien After Trial

(Court and Style of Cause)

TAKE NOTICE that an application will be made on behalf of John Doe, a lien claimant herein, to H. G. White, Master, at his Chambers at 145 Queen Street West, in the City of Toronto, in the Municipality of Metropolitan Toronto, on Tuesday, the 20th day of October, 1971, at 10:00 o'clock in the forenoon to prove the claim for lien of the said lien claimant pursuant to subsection 7 of section 38 of The Mechanics' Lien Act, R.S.O. 1970, chapter 267.

DATED at Toronto, this 4th day of October, 1971.

TO: etc.

FORM 55

Demand for Information Under Section 28

(Court and Style of Cause)

NOTICE TO PRODUCE

TAKE NOTICE that pursuant to subsection 1 of section 28 (or subsection 2 of section 28), of The Mechanics' Lien Act, R.S.O. 1970, chapter 267, I demand that you produce for my inspection within two days from the date hereof your contract or agreement with Quicksilver Construction Limited, Contractor, in respect of which work, service or material is or is to be performed or furnished or placed in relation to the construction of a dwelling house on Lot 2, according to a Plan registered in the Registry Office of the Registry Division of Toronto as Number 1000. If the contract or agreement is not in writing then I demand that you inform me of the terms thereof. (*If the demand is made under section* 28(2) *adapt form to particulars required of mortgagee or unpaid vendor.*)

ALSO I demand that within the same time you inform me of, or produce a statement of, the state of the accounts between you and the said Quicksilver Construction Limited (or a mortgage statement).

I claim to be the holder of a lien on the said land upon the Estate or interest of John Smith and Mary Smith in the said Lot 2, Plan 1000.

DATED at Toronto this 4th day of November, 1971.

TO: The owner (or mortgagee, as the case may be).

FORM 56

Notice to Produce

(Court and Style of Cause)

TAKE NOTICE that you are hereby required to produce and show to the Court at the trial of this action all books, papers, letters, copies of letters and other writings and documents in your custody, possession or power containing any entry, memorandum or minute relating to the matters in question in this action and particularly the following:

(1) All cheques given by you in payment or satisfaction of all accounts for work done

and materials supplied in the erection of the house premises in the Statement of Claim herein mentioned;

(2) All purchase orders issued by you in connection with the purchase of any materials or labour used in the erection of the said house and premises;

(3) (such other information as may be required).

DATED at Toronto this 4th day of November, 1971.

TO: etc.

FORM 57

Notice of Application for Particulars

(Court and Style of Cause)

TAKE NOTICE that by special leave of H. G. White, Master, an application will be made on behalf of the Plaintiff herein before H. G. White, Master, of the Supreme Court of Ontario, at 145 Queen Street West, in the City of Toronto, in the Municipality of Metropolitan Toronto, on Tuesday, the 8th day of December, 1971, at 10:00 o'clock in the forenoon or so soon thereafter as the motion may be heard for an Order that the Defendants do furnish the Plaintiff the following particulars in writing of the matters alleged in the Statement of Defence in this action and that unless such particulars are delivered in four days, the Statement of Defence in this action is to be stricken out:

(a) The part of the work done negligently, carelessly or unskilfully, referred to in paragraph 4 of the Statement of Defence;

(b) The manner in which the materials referred to in paragraph 5 of the Statement of Defence proved to be unsatisfactory for the purposes for which they were intended to be used;

(c) (such other particulars as may be required).

AND TAKE NOTICE that upon and in support of such application will be read the Statement of Defence herein, filed, the Demand for Particulars served on the solicitors for the Defendants on the 8th day of November, 1971, and the Affidavit of John Doe, filed.

DATED at Toronto this 1st day of December, 1971.

BLACK AND WHITE,
1 Bay Street,
Toronto, Ontario,
Solicitors for the Plaintiff.

TO: etc.

FORM 58

Notice of Application for Order Permitting Inspection of Premises

(Court and Style of Cause)

TAKE NOTICE that an application will be made on behalf of the Plaintiff before H. G. White, Esquire, Master, of the Supreme Court of Ontario, at 145 Queen Street West in the City of Toronto, in the Municipality of Metropolitan Toronto at the opening of the trial of this action (or as the case may be) on Monday, the 8th day of December, 1971, at 10:30 o'clock in the forenoon or so soon thereafter as the motion can be heard for an Order permitting James Brown, a qualified building contractor, to inspect the lands and premises in question in this action for the purpose of giving evidence at the trial of the action and also for an Order permitting the Plaintiff to inspect the lands and premises in question in this action or for such further or other Order as the nature of the case may require.

AND TAKE NOTICE that upon and in support of such application will be heard the evidence of the Plaintiff adduced viva voce (or as the case may be) and such further and other evidence or material as Counsel may advise and the Court permit.

DATED at Toronto this 21st day of November, 1971.

BLACK AND WHITE,
1 Bay Street,
Toronto, Ontario,
Solicitors for the Plaintiff.

TO: etc.

FORM 59

Form of Stated Case

IN THE SUPREME COURT OF ONTARIO

BETWEEN:

JOHN DOE

Plaintiff,

— and —

JOHN SMITH and MARY SMITH and
QUICKSILVER CONSTRUCTION LIMITED

Defendants.

STATEMENT OF CASE FOR THE COURT OF APPEAL

At the request of the Plaintiff, a case is hereby stated for the opinion of the Court pursuant to section 42 of the Mechanics' Lien Act, 1968-69 (Ont.), chapter 65.

1.   The Plaintiff registered a lien against the lands of the Defendants on the 30th day of April, 1970 and filed a Statement of Claim on the 12th day of May, 1970 and registered a Certificate of this action thereunder on the 13th day of May, 1970.

2.   The within action was referred to me pursuant to Judgment of Reference dated the 25th day of May, 1970.

3.   The Plaintiff in his Statement of Claim claims to be entitled to a lien on the Estate and interest of the Defendants, John Smith and Mary Smith, for rental of a bulldozer complete with operator at an hourly rate, to the Defendant, Quicksilver Construction Limited, which company was engaged by the said Defendants, John Smith and Mary Smith, to erect a building on the lands and premises described in the Statement of Claim herein.

4.   The Plaintiff performed his last work and service on the 21st day of April, 1970.

5.   At the commencement of the trial of this action, the Defendant, Quicksilver Construction Limited, pursuant to Notice of Motion dated the 12th day of June, 1970, moved before me to dismiss the action of the Plaintiff on the ground that the Plaintiff was not entitled to claim a lien for the rental of a bulldozer as set out in the Statement of Claim upon the lands in question in this action, and I granted the Motion on the following grounds:

"Subsection 5 of Section 5 of the Mechanics' Lien Act, 1968-69 (Ont.), chapter 65, not having been proclaimed in force until the 1st day of May, 1970, the Plaintiff was not

FORM 59

entitled to a claim for lien for rental of a bulldozer and operator having completed his last work and registered a claim for lien prior to the date upon which the aforesaid section was proclaimed in force. No costs."

6. Was I right in my decision as set forth in paragraph 5 hereof?

"H. G. White"

....

Master

The 15th day of June, 1970.

FORM 60

Notice of Hearing of Stated Case

IN THE SUPREME COURT OF ONTARIO
IN THE MATTER OF
THE MECHANICS' LIEN ACT,
R.S.O. 1970, Chapter 267

BETWEEN:

JOHN DOE

Plaintiff,

— and —

JOHN SMITH and MARY SMITH and
QUICKSILVER CONSTRUCTION LIMITED

Defendants.

TAKE NOTICE of the hearing at the May sittings of the Court of Appeal of the within case stated by H. G. White, Master, at the Supreme Court of Ontario.

DATED at Toronto, Ontario, this 1st day of March, 1971.

LAW & LAW,
4 Bay Street,
Toronto, Ontario,
Solicitors for the Defendant,
Quicksilver Construction Limited.

TO: etc.

FORM 61

Notice to Landlord of Contract With Tenant

TAKE NOTICE that pursuant to subsection 1 of section 7 of The Mechanics' Lien Act, R.S.O. 1970, chapter 267, I hereby give you notice that I have entered into a contract with John Doe, Contractor, of the City of Toronto, in the Municipality of Metropolitan Toronto, to supply and furnish the following materials:

all electrical equipment and materials necessary to install a complete electrical service in the said premises.

to property known as 1 Bay Street, in the city of Toronto, in the Municipality of

Metropolitan Toronto.

DATED at Toronto this 1st day of December, 1971.

> JAMES BROWN,
> 10 Bay Street,
> Toronto, Ontario.

TO: etc.

FORM 62

Notice From Landlord Declining Responsibility

TAKE NOTICE that I will not be responsible for the materials (or work, or service) which in your notice to me, dated the 1st day of December, 1971, you stated you have contracted to supply and furnish (or perform) to (or, upon or in respect of) the property known as 1 Bay Street, Toronto, nor for any other materials, work or service which you may supply or furnish to, or perform upon or in respect of the said property, nor for the payment or satisfaction of any claim which you may have in relation to the supplying or furnishing or performing of any materials, work or services to, upon or in respect of the said property.

DATED at Toronto, this 12th day of December, 1971.

> JAMES SMITH,
> 700 Albert Street,
> Toronto, Ontario.

TO: etc.

FORM 63

Notice of Payment to Lien Claimant Under Section 12

(Court and Style of Cause)

TAKE NOTICE that pursuant to section 12 of The Mechanics' Lien Act, R.S.O. 1970, chapter 267, I hereby give you notice that on the 8th day of December, 1971, I paid to the John Doe Electric Company, the sum of $500.00 which payment will be applied by me on my contract with you dated the 4th day of July, 1971.

DATED at Toronto this 10th day of December, 1971.

> "JAMES SMITH"

TO: etc.

FORM 64

Notice of Payment into Court

TAKE NOTICE that John Doe, of the Borough of North York, in the Municipality of Metropolitan Toronto, against whose Estate in Lot 5, Plan 5000, registered in the Registry Office for the Registry District of Toronto Boroughs and York South liens had been registered, has paid into Court to the credit of this action the sum of $1,000.00 in accordance with section [*here insert number of section or relevant rule under which moneys paid in.*]

DATED at Toronto this 8th day of December, 1971.

TO: etc.

FORM 65

Affidavit as to Non-payment of Solicitors' Costs

(Court and Style of Cause)

I, JAMES BLACK, of the City of Toronto, in the Municipality of Metropolitan Toronto, Solicitor, make oath and say:

1.   THAT I am the solicitor for John Doe, one of the lienholders in this action, and as such have personal knowledge of the matters herein deposed to.

2.   THAT pursuant to the Report of H. G. White, Master, herein, the costs of the said John Doe were fixed at the sum of $100.00.

3.   THAT pursuant to the said Report of the said H. G. White, Master, it was ordered that the money paid into Court to the credit of this action be paid out and among the moneys so directed to be paid out was the said sum of $100.00 for costs to me.

4.   THAT I am entitled to receive the said costs not having been paid my costs or any part thereof and the said costs in the amount of $100.00, payment of which is sought, are justly due to me.

SWORN BEFORE ME at the City of Toronto, in the Municipality of Metropolitan Toronto, this 10th day of November, 1971.

    A Commissioner, etc.

"James Black"

FORM 66

Accountant's Certificate as to Money in Court

SUPREME COURT OF ONTARIO
Office of the Accountant
Toronto

Jones v. Smith, #8000

I CERTIFY there is in Court to the credit of the above action the sum of Five Thousand Dollars ($5,000.00), including interest to the 30th of September, 1980 (*or as the case may be*).

....
Accountant

23rd February, 1981.

FORM 67

Accountant's Certificate as to Non-payment into Court

SUPREME COURT OF ONTARIO
Office of the Accountant
Toronto

CENTENNIAL WINDOW WASHERS LIMITED

Plaintiffs,

— and —

536

TORONTO-DOMINION CENTRE LTD.

Defendants.

I certify that no money has been paid into Court to the credit of the above action.

....
Accountant

1st February, 1961.

FORM 68

Affidavit as to Non-payment of Judgment

(Court and Style of Cause)

AFFIDAVIT

I, JOHN DOE, of the City of Toronto, in the Municipality of Metropolitan Toronto, electrician, make oath and say:

1.   THAT I am the Plaintiff in this action and as such have full knowledge of the matters hereinafter deposed to.

2.   THAT on the 8th day of December, 1971, I recovered a Judgment with respect to a claim for lien against the lands and premises described in the Statement of Claim herein for the sum of $2,000.00 and for costs the sum of $125.00, making together the sum of $2,125.00, a true copy of which Judgment is annexed hereto and marked Exhibit "A" to this my Affidavit.

3.   THAT I speaking positively for myself and to the best of my knowledge and belief as to other persons lastly say that I have not nor hath nor have any other person or persons by my Order or for my use received the said sum of $2,125.00 or any part thereof nor any security or satisfaction whatsoever therefor save and except the said lien and Judgment thereon (or as the case may be).

SWORN BEFORE ME at the City of
Toronto, in the Municipality of Metropolitan Toronto, this 4th day of December,
1971.

"John Doe"

   A Commissioner, etc.

FORM 69

Order for Sale

IN THE SUPREME COURT OF ONTARIO
IN THE MATTER OF
THE MECHANICS' LIEN ACT,
R.S.O. 1970, Chapter 267

H. G. WHITE,
MASTER

FRIDAY, THE 8TH DAY
OF DECEMBER, 1971.

(Style of Cause)

UPON THE APPLICATION of the Plaintiff and upon reading the Affidavit of John Doe and the Certificate of the Accountant of the Supreme Court of Ontario, filed, and upon hearing what was said by the solicitor for the Plaintiff:

1.   IT IS ORDERED that the lands and premises described in the Statement of Claim

537

herein mentioned or a competent part thereof be forthwith sold in pursuance of and in manner directed by the Judgment in this action with the approbation of the Master of this Court at Toronto.

....

Master

FORM 70

Notice of Appointment to Settle Conditions of Sale

(Court and Style of Cause)

TAKE NOTICE that H. G. White, Esquire, Master, has appointed the hour of 10:00 o'clock in the forenoon, on Thursday, the 20th day of December, 1971, in his Chambers at 145 Queen Street West, in the City of Toronto, in the Municipality of Metropolitan Toronto, to settle the form of the advertisement and the conditions for sale of the lands against which a lien is filed in this action and to make all necessary arrangements for the said sale.

DATED at Toronto this 10th day of December, 1971.

BLACK AND WHITE,
1 Bay Street,
Toronto, Ontario,
Solicitors for the Plaintiff.

TO: etc.

FORM 71

Form of Advertisement of Sale

Judicial Sale of 1 George Street, Toronto

IN THE SUPREME COURT OF ONTARIO
IN THE MATTER OF
THE MECHANICS' LIEN ACT,
R.S.O. 1970, Chapter 267

(Style of Cause)

PURSUANT to the judgment and order for sale made in this cause there will be offered for sale by sealed tender delivered to H. G. White, Master of the Supreme Court of Ontario at Room 205, 145 Queen Street West, Toronto, on or before the 4th day of December, 1971, the lands and premises known as No. 1 George Street, in the City of Toronto.

The property will be offered for sale subject to a reserve bid fixed by the Court and subject to three mortgages [*Here set out particulars of the mortgages*]. The purchaser shall pay down to the Vendor's solicitor on the day of sale 10% of the purchase money and shall pay the balance of the purchase money into Court without interest within 30 days after the date of sale. Adjustments to be made as of date of closing at which time vacant possession (or as the case may be) will be given. The purchaser shall search the title at his own expense. The vendor shall not be bound to produce any abstract of title or any deeds or evidence of title other than those in his possession or control. In all other respects the conditions of sale are the standing conditions of sale settled by the undersigned.

On the premises is said to be erected a three storey solid brick dwelling house. Further

538

particulars and conditions of sale may be had from Black and White, Solicitors, 1 Bay Street, Toronto.

DATED at Toronto this 4th day of November, 1971.

....

Master

FORM 72

Affidavit as to Publication of Advertisement

(Court and Style of Cause)

I, JAMES BLACK, of the City of Toronto, in the Municipality of Metropolitan Toronto, Solicitor, make oath and say:

1. THAT a true copy of the advertisement now produced and shown to me marked as Exhibit "A" to this my affidavit was published in the issues of The Toronto Daily Moon published in the City of Toronto, on the 10th day of November, 1971, and on the 17th day of November, 1971 and on the 24th day of November, 1971.

2. THAT I have examined copies of the said newspaper published on each of the said three days.

SWORN BEFORE ME at the City of
Toronto, in the Municipality of Metropoli-
tan Toronto, this 28th day of November,   }   "James Black"
1971.

    A Commissioner, etc.

FORM 73

Conditions of Sale

CONDITIONS OF SALE

1. No person shall advance less than fifty dollars at any bidding under one thousand dollars nor less than one hundred dollars at any bidding over one thousand dollars and no person shall retract his bidding.

2. The highest bidder shall be the purchaser, and if any dispute arises as to the best or highest bidder, the property will be put up at a former bidding.

3. The parties to the action are at liberty to bid with the exception of the vendors, trustees, agents and other persons in a fiduciary situation.

4. The purchaser shall at the time of the sale pay down a deposit equal to 10% of his purchase money to the vendor or his solicitor and shall pay the remainder of the purchase money into Court to the credit of this action within fifteen days after the day of sale without interest. And upon such payment the purchaser shall be entitled to a conveyance or vesting order and to be let into possession. The purchaser at the time of sale is to sign an agreement for the completion of the purchase.

5. The purchaser shall have the conveyance prepared at his own expense and tender the same for execution, or may, in the alternative, apply for a vesting order.

6. If the purchaser shall fail to comply with the conditions aforesaid or any of them, the

deposit and all other payments made thereon shall be forfeited and the premises may be resold and the deficiency, if any, by such resale, together with all charges attending the same, or occasioned by the defaulter, are to be made good by the defaulter.

7.   The property will be offered for sale subject to a reserved bid fixed by the Master (or Judge) of the Supreme Court of Ontario (or as the case may be).

8.   The vendor shall not be required to furnish any abstract of title and shall produce only such deeds, copies of deeds or evidence of title or such other evidences of title as are in his possession or control.

9.   The purchaser shall be allowed ten days from the date of sale to investigate the title which he shall do at his own expense, and if within that time he shall furnish in writing the vendor with any objection to the title which the vendor shall be unable or unwilling to remove, the vendor may by notice in writing to the purchaser's solicitor rescind the sale, in which case the vendor shall not be liable for any compensation, costs, damages or expenses incurred by the purchaser. If within the said ten days the purchaser shall not have furnished any objection to title as aforesaid he shall be deemed to have accepted the same.

10.   The sale to be closed within fifteen days from said date of sale with adjustments as of date of closing, at which time vacant possession is to be given to the purchaser (or as the case may be).

DATED at Toronto this 4th day of November, 1971.

"H. G. White"

....

Master

Approved

I hereby agree to purchase the lands and premises as set out in the annexed advertisement for sale, this day sold to me by public auction in accordance with the terms of the said advertisement and the above conditions for the sum of twenty-five thousand dollars.

....

Purchaser

FORM 74

Reserve Bid

(Court and Style of Cause)

The Reserve Bid fixed by the Master to which the property in this action is to be subject, is as follows:

$25,000.00

In the event there is no bid equal to or greater than the Reserve Bid, the said property is to be declared not sold.

DATED at Toronto this 4th day of November, 1971.

TO: Ace & Company, Auctioneers.

"H. G. White"

....

Master

FORM 75

Affidavit of Valuator

(Court and Style of Cause)

I, GEORGE PRICE, of the City of Toronto, in the Municipality of Metropolitan Toronto, Real Estate Agent and Valuator, make oath and say:

1.   That I have been for a number of years past engaged in valuing real estate, and have carried on such business in the City of Toronto and have had considerable experience in the valuation and sale of house property (or such other qualifications as the deponent may have), and on the 25th day of October, 1971, I carefully examined the property known as 1 George Street in the City of Toronto, being composed of the whole of lot 500 according to plan 5000 filed in the Registry Office for the Registry Division of Toronto and having a frontage of 60 feet on the east side of George Street, by a depth of about 200 feet, more or less, in order to form an opinion as to the value thereof and the amount which the said premises ought to realize on a sale thereof pursuant to the order for sale in this action.

2.   On the said property there is erected a 10 suite, three storey, solid brick apartment building about five years old, all of which suites are rented under leasing agreements in writing having a minimum of two years yet to run [*describe the lands and premises in detail*].

3.   I have in the paper writing contained in the envelope now produced and shown to me marked Exhibit "A" to this my affidavit set forth the full value of the said premises and the amount which in my judgment and belief should be fixed as the reserve bid on the lands and premises on the said sale.

SWORN BEFORE ME at the City of
Toronto, in the Municipality of Metropoli-
tan Toronto, this 4th day of December, 1971.   "G. Price"

   A Commissioner, etc.

FORM 76

Affidavit as to Fitness of Auctioneer

(Court and Style of Cause)

I, JOHN DOE, of the City of Toronto, in the Municipality of Metropolitan Toronto, electrician, make oath and say as follows:

1.   That I have for the last ten years known and been well acquainted with George Price, Auctioneer and land and estate agent, and during all that time he has carried on business as an auctioneer and real estate agent at the City of Toronto, in the Municipality of Metropolitan Toronto.

2.   That I have on several occasions employed the said George Price as an auctioneer and land valuator and I am acquainted with several persons who are also in the habit of employing him in those capacities and he has invariably given satisfaction to me, and I am informed that he has given satisfaction to such other persons.

3.   That the said George Price is a person of respectability and integrity and is of considerable ability as an auctioneer and real estate agent, and in my judgment he is a fit and

541

proper person to be employed to sell the lands and premises in question in this action which are situated at the City of Toronto, in the Municipality of Metropolitan Toronto.

SWORN BEFORE ME at the City of Toronto, in the Municipality of Metropolitan Toronto, this 10th day of November, 1971.	"John Doe"

    A Commissioner, etc.

FORM 77

Affidavit of Auctioneer

(Court and Style of Cause)

AFFIDAVIT

I, GEORGE PRICE, of the City of Toronto, in the Municipality of Metropolitan Toronto, Auctioneer, appointed by H. G. White, Master of this Court to sell the lands and premises comprised in the particulars hereinafter referred to, make oath and say:

1.   That I did, in accordance with the appointment of the said Master at the time and place and subject to the conditions specified in the advertisement and conditions of sale hereunder annexed and marked respectively Exhibits "A" and "B" to this my affidavit, offer for sale by public auction the lands and premises described in the said advertisement.

2.   That the highest bid made for the said property was the sum of thirty thousand dollars and the said bid was made on behalf of John Doe whereupon he was declared by me to be and did become the purchaser as appears by the signed contract appearing at the end of the said Conditions of Sale.

3.   The only other bidders at the said sale were John Smith and Mary Brown both of the Borough of North York, in the Municipality of Metropolitan Toronto.

4.   The said sale was conducted by me in a fair, open and proper manner according to the best of my skill and judgment.

SWORN BEFORE ME at the City of Toronto, in the Municipality of Metropolitan Toronto, this 4th day of December, 1971.	"George Price"

    A Commissioner, etc.

FORM 78

Vesting Order

IN THE SUPREME COURT OF ONTARIO
IN THE MATTER OF
THE MECHANICS' LIEN ACT,
R.S.O. 1970, Chapter 267

H. G. WHITE, MASTER	FRIDAY, THE 29TH DAY OF DECEMBER, 1971.

(Style of Cause)

Upon the application of the Plaintiff pursuant to the order of H. G. White, Esq., Master, dated the 4th day of November, 1971, directing that the lands and premises described in the Statement of Claim herein be forthwith sold in pursuance of and in the manner directed by the judgment in this action upon reading the Offer to Purchase the said property submitted by John Smith and approved by me the Statement of Adjustments submitted by the solicitor for the Plaintiff and upon hearing what was said by counsel for the applicant (or as the case may be):

1. It is ordered that the following lands and premises, namely [*Here set out a concise description of the property sufficient for the purpose of registration*] be and the same are hereby vested in the said John Smith, his heirs, executors, successors and assigns, for all the estate, right, title and interest of ... [*Here set forth each party or persons whose estate or interest in the lands is vested in the purchaser*] therein and thereto.

2. And it is further ordered that the Registrar of Deeds for the Registry Division of Toronto is directed to enter John Smith as Owner in fee simple of the said lands and premises free of all of the above claims.

"H. G. White"

....
Master

FORM 79

Report on Sale

(Court and Style of Cause)

Tuesday, the 4th day of January, 1972.

PURSUANT to the judgment herein dated the 10th day of August, 1971, I have, under the provisions of The Mechanics' Lien Act, R.S.O. 1970, chapter 267, and the general Rules of Court, in the presence of the solicitors for the plaintiff and for the defendant settled an advertisement and particulars and conditions of sale, for the sale of the lands referred to in the said judgment, and such advertisement having been duly published in the issues of The Toronto Moon, published in the City of Toronto, in the Municipality of Metropolitan Toronto, on the 14th day of November, 1971 and the 21st day of November, 1971 and copies of such advertisement having also been posted up in the vicinity of the said lands, as directed by me; the said lands were offered for sale by public auction according to the said advertisement on the 15th day of December, 1971, by Mr. George Price, auctioneer, appointed for that purpose, and on the evidence adduced before me, I find that such sale was conducted in a fair, open and proper manner, when John Smith of the City of Toronto, in the Municipality of Metropolitan Toronto, was declared the highest bidder for and became the purchaser of the same, at the price or sum of thirty thousand dollars payable as follows: 10% thereof at the time of sale, and the balance to be paid into Court within fifteen days thereafter. The whole purchase price or sum of thirty thousand dollars has been paid into Court to the credit of this action.

"H. G. White"

....
Master

FORM 80
Report Distributing Proceeds of Sale
(Court and Style of Cause)

Wednesday, the 20th day of January, 1972.

PURSUANT to the judgment herein dated the 10th day of August, 1971, and pursuant to the provisions of The Mechanics' Lien Act, R.S.O. 1970, chapter 267, and the general Rules of Court, in the presence of the solicitors for the plaintiff and for the defendant, I settled an advertisement and particulars and conditions of sale, for the sale of the lands referred to in the said judgment, and on the 15th day of December, 1971, proceeded to sell the said lands and premises by public auction as set out in the Report on Sale dated the 4th day of January, 1971, under which report John Smith became the purchaser of the said lands and premises. The said report has been confirmed in accordance with the provisions of Rule 512 of the Consolidated Rules of Practice and the sale duly completed and the proceeds of the said sale amounting to thirty thousand dollars have been paid into Court.

By the said Judgment the following parties are entitled to the sums of money set opposite their respective names: [*Here set out names of persons entitled to the moneys and the amounts to which they are respectively entitled*].

I have set out in schedule "A" of this report how the money in Court is to be dealt with and I direct that the sums set out therein be paid out to the persons shown in the said schedule.

"H. G. White"
....
Master

FORM 81
Order for Payment out of Court
IN THE SUPREME COURT OF ONTARIO
IN THE MATTER OF
THE MECHANICS' LIEN ACT,
R.S.O. 1970, Chapter 267

THE HONOURABLE ⎫ TUESDAY, THE 5TH DAY
MR. JUSTICE GREEN ⎬ OF DECEMBER, 1971
IN CHAMBERS ⎭

(Style of Cause)

UPON the application of the plaintiff and upon hearing read the Report of H. G. White, Esq., Master, dated the 20th day of November, 1971:

1. IT IS ORDERED that the moneys paid into Court to the credit of this action be paid out in accordance with the directions contained in the said Report.

....
Assistant Registrar, S.C.O.

FORM 82
Advertisement of Sale of Chattel
TAKE NOTICE that George Brown, of the City of Toronto, in the Municipality of

544

Metropolitan Toronto, is indebted to John Smith of the said City in the sum of Four Hundred Dollars for mechanical work and improvements made upon a 1968 Pontiac sedan and in that the said John Smith has remained unpaid for more than three months, pursuant to section 48 of The Mechanics' Lien Act, R.S.O. 1970, chapter 267, a sale of the said automobile will be had by public auction on the 15th day of December, 1971, at the hour of 1:00 o'clock in the afternoon at the auction rooms of George Price, 5 George Street, in the City of Toronto, to be conducted by George Price, auctioneer.

The sale is subject to a reserve bid of Four Hundred and Thirty-five Dollars.

DATED at Toronto, this 4th day of December, 1971.

> George Brown,
> 5 George Street
> Toronto, Ontario.

FORM 83

Certificate of Registrar

IN THE SUPREME COURT OF ONTARIO
IN THE MATTER OF
THE MECHANICS' LIEN ACT,
R.S.O. 1970, Chapter 267

AND IN THE MATTER OF The Title to Lot 500 Plan 5000

I, GEORGE BROWN, Deputy Registrar of the Registry Office for the Registry Division of Toronto, do hereby certify that the claim for lien dated the 1st day of May, 1971, was registered on the 2nd day of May, 1971, in the said registry Office as number 12345 M. L. against certain lands and premises therein described as being all of lot 500 according to plan 5000 registered in the said Registry Office.

DATED at Toronto this 20th day of June, 1971.

> "George Brown"
> ....
> Deputy Registrar

....
Witness
[*Attach Affidavit of Execution*]

FORM 84

Affidavit of Search for Use on Application to Vacate Liens and
Certificates Under Section 22(3)

(Court and Style of Cause)

I, JOHN DOE, of the City of Toronto, in the Municipality of Metropolitan Toronto, Solicitor, make oath and say:

1. That I am a member of the law firm of Black and White, Solicitors for the Defendant George Brown, the owner of the lands and premises described in the schedule attached to this my affidavit and marked as Exhibit "A".

2. That a Claim for Lien dated the 1st day of May, 1969, was registered against the said

lands by John Smith in the Registry Office for the Registry Division of Toronto on the 2nd day of May, 1969, as number 12345 M.L.

3. That subsequently a Certificate of this Action was registered in the said Registry Office on the 5th day of July, 1969, as number 23456 M.L. against the said lands.

4. That no notice of the trial of this action has been served on my said firm, and that I am informed by the Defendant George Brown, and verily believe that no such notice of trial has been served upon him or brought to his attention.

5. That I did on the 20th day of July, 1971, make a search in the Registry Office for the Registry Division of Toronto, of the said lands and found that no Claim for Lien or Certificate of Action other than those mentioned above had been registered against the said lands.

6. That I have made a search at Central Office of the file in this action, in order to ascertain if an Order has been made appointing the time and place for the trial of this action and so far as appears from the said file, no such Order has been taken out.

SWORN BEFORE ME at the City of Toronto, in the Municipality of Metropolitan Toronto, this 21st day of July, 1971.

"John Doe"

....
A Commissioner, etc.

FORM 85

Order for Inspection of Documents Made Under Section 28(3)

IN THE SUPREME COURT OF ONTARIO
IN THE MATTER OF
THE MECHANICS' LIEN ACT,
R.S.O. 1970, Chapter 267

H. G. WHITE
MASTER

TUESDAY, THE 7TH DAY
OF DECEMBER, 1971.

(Style of Cause)

UPON the application of the Plaintiff for an Order pursuant to the provisions of subsection 3 of section 28 of The Mechanics' Lien Act, upon reading the Plaintiff's demand for particulars and upon hearing what was said by counsel for the Plaintiff and for the Defendant John Smith:

1. It is ordered that the Defendant John Smith produce to the Plaintiff for his inspection the contract between the said Defendant and the Defendant Quicksilver Construction Limited within five days.

2. It is further ordered that the cost of this application shall be costs to the Plaintiff as against the said Defendant John Smith in any event of the cause (or as the case may be).

"H. G. White"

....
Master

FORM 86

Order of Master Permitting Amendment of Pleading

IN THE SUPREME COURT OF ONTARIO

IN THE MATTER OF

THE MECHANICS' LIEN ACT,

R.S.O. 1970, Chapter 267

(Style of Cause)

(Preamble)

1.   It is ordered that the Plaintiff be at liberty to amend the twelfth paragraph in his Statement of Claim by substituting the words "the sum of twelve thousand dollars" in the second line thereof for the words "eleven thousand dollars".

2.   It is further ordered that the cost of this application shall be costs in the cause (or as the case may be).

"H. G. White"

....

Master

FORM 87

Demand for Particulars

(Court and Style of Cause)

DEMAND FOR PARTICULARS

The Defendant demands that the Plaintiff do within 10 days of the date hereof furnish the Defendant with the following particulars of the Plaintiff's Statement of Claim:

(a) Details of the work alleged to have been ordered by the Defendant as an extra to the contract referred to in paragraph five thereof.

(b) (as the case may be).

DATED at Toronto this 5th day of October, 1971.

BLACK AND WHITE,
1 George Street,
Toronto, Ontario.
Solicitors for the Defendant.

FORM 88

Notice of Trial — Before Supreme Court Judge

(Court and Style of Cause)

NOTICE OF TRIAL

TAKE NOTICE that this action has been set down for trial at the sittings at Hamilton, commencing on the 8th day of September, 1971 (or, if action is to be tried at the Toronto non-jury sittings — TAKE NOTICE that this action has been set down on the 4th day of September, 1971 for trial at the Toronto non-jury sittings —).

AND FURTHER TAKE NOTICE that if you do not appear at the trial and defend the

547

action or prove your claim, if any, the proceedings will be taken in your absence and you may be deprived of all benefit of the proceedings and your rights disposed of in your absence.

AND FURTHER TAKE NOTICE that all parties and lien claimants shall bring with them on the day herein set for trial all mortgages, contracts, agreements, orders, cheques, notes, delivery slips, time books, books of account, diaries, duplicate original liens and any other books or papers necessary to prove liens or defences. If any person fails to comply with these directions the costs of the day may be given against him in the event that an adjournment is necessary for the production of any of the above-mentioned documentary evidence.

THIS IS a mechanics' lien action brought by the above-named plaintiffs against the above-named defendants to enforce a mechanics' lien against the following lands: [*Here set out a concise description of the lands contained in the Statement of Claim*].

THIS NOTICE is served by Black and White, 1 Bay Street, Toronto, Ontario, Solicitors for the Plaintiff.

DATED at Toronto, this 15th day of August, 1971.

FORM 89

Notice to Claimant of Amount Admitted to be Owing

(Court and Style of Cause)

NOTICE

TAKE NOTICE that the Defendant has paid into Court the sum of $5,000.00 pursuant to section 25(2) of The Mechanics' Lien Act, R.S.O. 1970, chapter 267.

AND FURTHER TAKE NOTICE that of the sum of $5,000.00 so paid into court, the Defendant offers, subject to the approval of this Court, the sum of $2,000.00 in full satisfaction of the claimant's claim in the action herein.

DATED at Toronto, this 20th day of November, 1971.

FORM 90

Notice of Acceptance of Amount Admitted to be Owing

(Court and Style of Cause)

NOTICE

TAKE NOTICE that the Plaintiff John Doe, (or the claimant), accepts the sum of $2,000.00 in full satisfaction of its claim herein, out of the sum of $5,000.00 paid into Court by the Defendant pursuant to section 25(2) of The Mechanics' Lien Act, R.S.O. 1970, chapter 267, conditional upon the Defendant obtaining a direction of this Court for the payment out of Court of this sum to the Plaintiff.

DATED at Toronto, this 25th day of November, 1971.

FORM 91

Order for Payment out of Court of Amount Accepted in Satisfaction

IN THE SUPREME COURT OF ONTARIO
IN THE MATTER OF
THE MECHANICS' LIEN ACT,
R.S.O. 1970, Chapter 267

H. G. WHITE,
MASTER

FRIDAY, THE 30TH DAY
OF NOVEMBER, 1971.

(Style of Cause)

UPON the application of the Plaintiff, upon reading the Notice of Offer of Payment of the amount owing by the Defendant to the Plaintiff John Doe (or lien claimant), the Notice of Acceptance of the same by the Plaintiff (or lien claimant), and upon hearing what was said by Counsel for the Plaintiff:

1.   IT IS ORDERED that the sum of Two Thousand Dollars accepted by the Plaintiff in full satisfaction of his claim herein be paid out of Court to the Plaintiff (or lien claimant) forthwith.

2.   AND IT IS FURTHER ORDERED that the Defendant do pay to the Plaintiff (or lien claimant), his costs of this action to date forthwith after taxation thereof (or as the case may be).

"H. G. WHITE"

....

Master

FORM 92

Master's Report (Ordinary Action)

IN THE SUPREME COURT OF ONTARIO
IN THE MATTER OF
THE MECHANICS' LIEN ACT,
R.S.O. 1970, Chapter 267

H. G. WHITE,
MASTER

MONDAY, THE 8TH DAY
OF DECEMBER, A.D. 1971

(Style of Cause)

PURSUANT to the Judgment of Reference herein dated the 5th day of October, 1971 and it appearing that the following persons have been duly served with Notice of Trial herein (*set out names of all persons served with Notice of Trial*) I was attended by Counsel for the Plaintiff and for [*Here set out proper names of persons represented by Counsel*] no one appearing for John Smith although duly notified as aforesaid (or as the case may be) and upon hearing the evidence adduced and what was alleged by Counsel for the Plaintiff and for George Brown and Quicksilver Construction Limited and the Defendant (or, and by Mary Smith appearing in person, as the case may be):

1.   I FIND that the Plaintiff and the several persons mentioned in Schedule 1 hereto are respectively entitled to a lien under The Mechanics' Lien Act upon the land described in Schedule 2 hereto for the amounts set opposite their respective names in the second, third and fourth columns of Schedule 1, and the persons primarily liable for the claims respectively are set forth in the fifth column of Schedule 1.

549

2.   (AND I FIND that the several persons mentioned in Schedule 3 hereto are also entitled to some lien, charge or encumbrance upon the land for the amounts set opposite their respective names in the fourth column of Schedule 3, according to the facts).

3.   AND I DIRECT that upon the Defendant John Smith (the owner) paying into Court to the credit of this action the sum of Forty Thousand Dollars [*gross amount of liens in Schedule 1 for which the owner is liable*] on or before the 23rd day of December, 1971 next, that the liens in Schedule 1 mentioned be and the same are hereby discharged and the money so paid into court is to be paid out in payment of the claims of the lienholders.

4.   In case the Defendant (*owner*) makes default in payment of the money into Court, I direct that the land be sold with the approbation of the Master of this Court at Toronto and that the purchase money be paid into Court to the credit of this action.

5.   AND I DIRECT that the purchase money be applied in or towards payment of the several claims mentioned in Schedule(s) 1 (and 3) as the Master shall direct with subsequent interest and subsequent costs to be computed and taxed by the Master.

6.   AND I DIRECT that in case the purchase money is insufficient to pay in full the claims of the several persons mentioned in Schedule 1, the persons primarily liable for such claim as shown in Schedule 1 do pay to the persons to whom they are respectively primarily liable the amount remaining due to such persons forthwith after the same shall have been ascertained by the Master.

7.   (AND I FIND AND DECLARE that Jack Johnson and William Brown have not proved any lien under The Mechanics' Lien Act, and that they are not entitled to any such lien, and I direct that the claims of liens registered by them against the land mentioned in Schedule 2 be and the same are hereby discharged, according to the facts.)

"H. G. White"
....
Master

[*The Schedules referred to in the Report are the same as those attached to the ordinary judgment which appears as Form 95.*]

(See Form 8 in the regulations made under the Ontario Act, R.R.O. 1970, Reg. 575.)

FORM 92A

Master's Report Where Claim Relates to Work on Street or Public Work

IN THE SUPREME COURT OF ONTARIO
IN THE MATTER OF
THE MECHANICS' LIEN ACT,
R.S.O. 1970, Chapter 267

H. G. WHITE,	}	MONDAY, THE 5TH DAY
MASTER		OF DECEMBER, A.D. 1977

(Style of Cause)

Pursuant to the judgment of reference herein dated the 5th day of October, 1977 and it appearing that the following persons have been duly served with notice of trial herein [*set out names of all persons served with notice of trial*] I was attended by counsel for the plaintiff and for [*here set out proper names of persons represented by counsel*] no one appearing for John Smith although duly notified as aforesaid (or as the case may be) and upon hearing the evidence adduced and what was alleged by counsel for the plaintiff and for George Brown and Quicksilver Construction Limited and the defendant (or and by Mary Smith appearing in person),

1.   I find and declare that amount required to be retained by the defendant, the Town of Goodwill (the owner) under section 11 of The Mechanics' Lien Act is the sum of $5,000.00.

2.   I find and declare that the plaintiff and the several persons mentioned in Column 1 of Schedule 1 hereto are respectively entitled to a lien under The Mechanics' Lien Act which lien is a charge on the amount required to be retained by section 11 of the Act for the amounts set opposite their respective names in columns 2, 3 and 4 of Schedule 1 and the person primarily liable is set forth in Column 6 of Schedule 1.

3.   And I direct that upon the defendant, the Town of Goodwill (the owner) paying into Court to the credit of this action the sum of $5,000.00 (gross amount of liens in Schedule 1 for which the owner is liable) on or before the 28th day of December next, that the liens mentioned in Schedule 1 be and the same are hereby discharged and the money so paid into Court is to be paid out to the plaintiff and the several persons mentioned in Column 1 of Schedule 1 in accordance with Column 5 of Schedule 1.

4.   And I direct that in case the amounts required to be retained by section 11 of The Mechanics' Lien Act are insufficient to pay in full the claims of the several persons mentioned in Schedule 1, the persons primarily liable for such claim as shown in Column 6 of Schedule 1 do pay to the persons to whom they are respectively primarily liable the amount remaining due to such persons forthwith after the same has been ascertained.

5.   And I find and declare that Jack Johnson and William Brown have not proved any lien under The Mechanics' Lien Act, and that they are not entitled to any such lien.

"H. G. White"

....

Master S.C.O.

(See Form 9 in the regulations made under the Ontario Act, R.R.O. 1970, Reg. 575 as amended by O. Reg. 849/75.)

Schedule 1

Names of lienholders entitled to mechanics' liens	Amount of debt and interest (if any)	Costs	Total	Prorated Share	Persons Primarily Liable

....

(signature of officer)

551

FORM 93
Judgment
(Two actions commenced—money paid into Court)
IN THE SUPREME COURT OF ONTARIO
IN THE MATTER OF
THE MECHANICS' LIEN ACT,
R.S.O. 1970, Chapter 267

HIS HONOUR JUDGE BLACK	FRIDAY, THE 8TH DAY
LOCAL JUDGE	OF DECEMBER, 1971

BETWEEN:

JOHN DOE

Plaintiff,

— and —

MARY SMITH, and
QUICKSILVER CONSTRUCTION LIMITED

Defendants,

AND BETWEEN:

ROBERT ROE

Plaintiff,

— and —

MARY SMITH, and
QUICKSILVER CONSTRUCTION LIMITED

Defendants.

These actions coming on for trial before His Honour Judge Black, Local Judge of this Court, at the Court House, in the Town of Brampton, in the County of Peel, upon opening of the matter and it appearing that the following persons have been duly served with Notice of Trial herein, the Defendants, MARY SMITH and QUICKSILVER CONSTRUCTION LIMITED, and SAM WHITE, R. W. LOWD, QUICKSET PLASTERING LIMITED, ROY SMITH, and T. URWIN, lien claimants, and all such persons (or as the case may be) appearing at the trial (or, and the following persons not having appeared, setting out the names of non-appearing persons); and it appearing that actions had been commenced by JOHN DOE and ROBERT ROE and it appearing that the Defendant, MARY SMITH has paid into Court to the credit of this action the sum of $5,000.00 in full satisfaction of her statutory liability as owner of the lands and premises against which the claims for lien in this action have been filed, and that all persons at the trial had consented thereto by their Counsel; and upon hearing the evidence adduced and what was alleged by Counsel for the Plaintiff and for the other lien claimants and for the Defendants (or, and by QUICKSILVER CONSTRUCTION LIMITED appearing in person):

1. THIS COURT DOTH ORDER AND ADJUDGE that these actions be consolidated, the Plaintiff, JOHN DOE, to have carriage of the consolidated actions.

2. THIS COURT DOTH DECLARE that the Plaintiff and the several persons mentioned in the First Schedule hereto are respectively entitled to a lien under The Mechanics' Lien Act upon the land described in the Second Schedule hereto for the amounts set opposite their respective names in the 2nd, 3rd and 4th columns of the said First Schedule and the persons primarily liable for the said claims respectively are set forth in the 5th column of the said Schedule.

3. AND THIS COURT DOTH FURTHER DECLARE that ROY SMITH and R. URWIN have not proved any lien under The Mechanics' Lien Act, and that they are not

552

entitled to any such lien, and This Court Doth Order and Adjudge that the claims for liens registered by them against the land mentioned in the Second Schedule be and the same are hereby discharged.

4.   AND THIS COURT DOTH FURTHER ORDER AND ADJUDGE that each of the persons mentioned in the 1st column of the said First Schedule hereto do recover from the Defendant, QUICKSILVER CONSTRUCTION LIMITED, the amount set opposite the name of such person in the 9th column of the said Schedule such amount being the amount set opposite the name of such person in the 4th column of the said Schedule less the amount or amounts hereinafter ordered to be paid out of Court to such person.

5.   AND THIS COURT DOTH FURTHER DECLARE that the several persons mentioned in the 1st column of the said First Schedule are respectively entitled to a charge under The Mechanics' Lien Act, upon the sum of $5,000.00 paid into Court to the credit of this action by the Defendant, MARY SMITH, for the amounts set opposite their names in the 6th, 7th and 8th columns of the said Schedule and that the Defendant, MARY SMITH, is not liable for the payment of any further sum.

6.   AND THIS COURT DOTH FURTHER ORDER AND ADJUDGE that the said sum so paid into court be paid out of Court as follows:

   (a) To the solicitors for the Plaintiff, JOE DOE, as salvage costs, $300.00;
   (b) To the claimants mentioned in column 1 of the First Schedule hereto the amounts set opposite their respective names in the 6th column of the said First Schedule;
   (c) To their solicitors on record as set out in column 1 of the said First Schedule hereto the amounts set opposite their respective names in the 7th column of the said First Schedule.

7.   AND THIS COURT DOTH FURTHER ORDER that Affidavits of Non-Payment of Solicitors' Costs be and the same are hereby dispensed with.

8.   AND THIS COURT DOTH FURTHER ORDER AND ADJUDGE that these actions be and the same are hereby dismissed as against the Defendant, MARY SMITH, without costs.

9.   AND THIS COURT DOTH FURTHER ORDER AND ADJUDGE that the following Claims for Lien registered in the Registry Office for the Registry Division of Peel against the lands and premises described in the Second Schedule hereto be and the same are hereby discharged:

Claimant	Date	Date of Reg'n.	Reg'n. No.
John Doe	May 4, 1971	May 4, 1971	25486
Robert Roe	May 10, 1971	May 11, 1971	25498
Sam White	May 10, 1971	May 11, 1971	25504
R. W. Lowd	May 12, 1971	May 14, 1971	25509
Quickset Plastering Ltd.	May 20, 1971	May 21, 1971	25536

10.   AND THIS COURT DOTH FURTHER ORDER AND ADJUDGE that the following Certificates of Action registered in the Registry Office for the Registry Division of Peel against the lands and premises described in the Second Schedule hereto be and the same are hereby vacated.

Claimant	Date	Date of Reg'n.	Reg'n. No.
John Doe	July 6, 1971	July 6, 1971	25642
Robert Roe	July 21, 1971	July 22, 1971	25704

JUDGMENT SIGNED this 14th day of December, 1971.

....
Judge

SCHEDULE 1

(1) Lien Claimants and their Solicitors	(2) Amount of Debt	(3) Costs	(4) Total	(5) Name of Primary Debtor	(6) Pro Rata Share of moneys in Court	(7) Costs	(8) Total to be paid out of Court	(9) Balance Due (Col. 4 less Col. 8)
John Doe — White, White & Black	$3,500.00	$225.00	$3,725.00	Quicksilver Construction Ltd.	$1,240.85	$225.00	$1,465.85	$2,259.15
Robert Roe — P. T. Jones	1,500.00	150.00	1,650.00	"	531.85	150.00	681.85	968.15
Sam White — D. B. Sennett	4,000.00	200.00	4,200.00	"	1,418.00	200.00	1,618.00	2,582.00
R. W. Lowd — F. H. Fort	700.00	75.00	775.00	"	248.45	75.00	323.45	451.55
Quickset Plastering Ltd. — J. L. Lawless	1,300.00	150.00	1,450.00	"	460.85	150.00	610.85	839.15
	11,000.00	800.00	11,800.00		3,900.00	800.00	4,700.00	7,100.00

Distribution = 35.45%

....
Judge

SCHEDULE 2

Amount in Court	11,000.00
Salvage Costs	5,000.00
Total Costs to Lien Claimants	300.00
Balance for Distribution	800.00
Claims to rank on balance for distribution	3,900.00
	11,000.00

....
Judge

The lands in question in this matter are (set out a description sufficient for registration purposes).

_____

FORM 94

Judgment

(Contractor Bankrupt—Money paid into Court)

IN THE SUPREME COURT OF ONTARIO

IN THE MATTER OF

THE MECHANICS' LIEN ACT,

R.S.O. 1970, Chapter 267

HIS HONOUR JUDGE BLACK	FRIDAY, THE 8TH DAY
LOCAL JUDGE	OF DECEMBER, 1971

(Style of Cause)

This action coming on for trial before His Honour Judge Black, Local Judge of this Court, at the Court House, in the Town of Brampton, in the County of Peel, upon opening of the matter and it appearing that the following persons have been duly served with Notice of Trial herein, the Defendants, Mary Smith and L. W. Haldain, Trustee of the Estate of Quicksilver Construction Limited, a Bankrupt, Robert Roe, Sam White, R. W. Lowd, Quickset Plastering Limited, Roy Smith and T. Urwin, lien claimants, and all such persons (or as the case may be) appearing at the trial (or, and the following persons not having appeared, setting out the names of non-appearing persons); and it appearing that the Defendant, Mary Smith, has paid into Court to the credit of this action the sum of $5,000.00 in full satisfaction of her statutory liability as owner of the lands and premises against which the claims for lien in this action have been filed, and that all persons at the trial had consented thereto by their Counsel; and upon hearing the evidence adduced and what was alleged by counsel for the Plaintiff and for the other lien claimants and for the Defendants (or, and by Robert Roe appearing in person as the case may be):

1. THIS COURT DOTH DECLARE that the Plaintiff and the several persons mentioned in the First Schedule hereto are respectively entitled to a lien under The Mechanics' Lien Act upon the land described in the Second Schedule hereto for the amounts set opposite their respective names in the 2nd, 3rd and 4th columns of the said First Schedule, and the person primarily liable for the said claims is the Estate of Quicksilver Construction Limited, in Bankruptcy.

2. AND THIS COURT DOTH FURTHER DECLARE that Roy Smith and T. Urwin have not proved any lien under The Mechanics' Lien Act, and that they are not entitled to any such lien, and THIS COURT DOTH ORDER AND ADJUDGE that the Claims for Lien registered by them against the land mentioned in the Second Schedule hereto be and the same are hereby discharged.

3. AND THIS COURT DOTH ORDER that the claimants mentioned in column 1 of the said First Schedule hereto are entitled to rank as unsecured creditors against the Estate of Quicksilver Construction Limited, a Bankrupt, for the amounts set opposite their respective names in column 9 of the said First Schedule hereto.

4. AND THIS COURT DOTH FURTHER DECLARE that the several persons mentioned in the 1st column of the said First Schedule are respectively entitled to a charge under The Mechanics' Lien Act, upon the sum of $5,000.00 paid into Court to the credit of this action by the Defendant, Mary Smith, for the amounts set opposite their respective names in the 6th, 7th and 8th columns of the said First Schedule and that the Defendant, Mary Smith, is not liable for the payment of any further sum.

5. AND THIS COURT DOTH FURTHER ORDER AND ADJUDGE that the said sum so paid into Court be paid out of Court as follows:

(a) To the solicitors for the Plaintiff, John Doe, as salvage costs, $300.00;

(b) To the claimants mentioned in column 1 of the First Schedule hereto the amounts set opposite their respective names in the 6th column of the said First Schedule;

(c) To their solicitors on record as set out in column 1 of the said First Schedule hereto, the amount set opposite their respective names in the 7th column of the said First Schedule hereto.

6. AND THIS COURT DOTH FURTHER ORDER that Affidavits of Non-Payment of Solicitors' Costs be and the same are hereby dispensed with.

7. AND THIS COURT DOTH FURTHER ORDER AND ADJUDGE that this action be and the same is hereby dismissed as against the Defendant, Mary Smith, without costs.

8. AND THIS COURT DOTH FURTHER ORDER AND ADJUDGE that the following Claims for Lien registered in the Registry Office for the Registry Division of Peel against the lands and premises described in the Second Schedule hereto be and the same are hereby discharged:

Claimant	Date	Date of Reg'n.	Reg'n. No.
John Doe	May 4, 1971	May 4, 1971	25486
Robert Roe	May 10, 1971	May 11, 1971	25498
Sam White	May 10, 1971	May 11, 1971	25504
R. W. Lowd	May 12, 1971	May 14, 1971	25509
Quickset Plastering Ltd.	May 20, 1971	May 21, 1971	25536

9. AND THIS COURT DOTH FURTHER ORDER AND ADJUDGE that the registration of the Certificate of this Action dated the 22nd day of July, 1971 and registered on the 23rd day of July, 1971 in the Registry Office for the Registry Division of Peel as instrument number 25724 against the title to the lands and premises described in the Second Schedule hereto be and the same is hereby vacated.

JUDGMENT SIGNED this 14th day of December, 1971.

....
Judge

SCHEDULE 1

(1) Lien Claimants and their Solicitors		(2) Amount of Debt	(3) Costs	(4) Total	(5) Name of Primary Debtor	(6) Pro Rata Share of moneys in Court	(7) Costs	(8) Total to be paid out of Court	(9) Balance Due (Col. 4 less Col. 8)
John Doe	White, White & Black	$3,500.00	$225.00	$3,725.00	Estate of Quicksilver Construction Ltd.	$1,240.85	$225.00	$1,465.85	$2,259.15
Robert Roe	P. T. Jones	1,500.00	150.00	1,650.00	"	531.85	150.00	681.85	968.15
Sam White	D. B. Sennett	4,000.00	200.00	4,200.00	"	1,418.00	200.00	1,618.00	2,582.00
R. W. Lowd	F. H. Fort	700.00	75.00	775.00	"	248.45	75.00	323.45	451.55
Quickset Plastering Ltd.	J. L. Lawless	1,300.00	150.00	1,450.00	"	460.85	150.00	610.85	839.15
		11,000.00	800.00	11,800.00		3,900.00	800.00	4,700.00	7,100.00

Distribution = 35.45%

SCHEDULE 2

Amount in Court	11,000.00
Salvage Costs	5,000.00
Total Costs to Lien Claimants	300.00
Balance for Distribution	800.00
Claims to rank on balance for distribution	3,900.00

The lands in question in this matter are (set out a description sufficient for registration purposes).

....
Judge

....
Judge

_____

557

FORM 95
Judgment
(Owner ordered work and no money paid into Court)

HIS HONOUR JUDGE BLACK   FRIDAY, THE 8TH DAY
LOCAL JUDGE   OF DECEMBER, 1971

(Style of Cause)

These actions coming on for trial before His Honour Judge Black, Local Judge of this Court, at the Court House, in the Town of Brampton, in the County of Peel, upon opening of the matter and it appearing that the following persons have been duly served with Notice of Trial herein, the Defendant, Mary Smith, and Norman Owens and Paul Quick, lien claimants, and Roy Smith and T. Urwin, execution creditors, and all such persons appearing at the trial (or, and the following persons not having appeared, setting out the names of non-appearing persons), upon hearing the evidence adduced and what was alleged by Counsel for the Plaintiff, for the Defendant and for the lien claimants and execution creditors aforesaid (or, and by Roy Smith appearing in person):

1. THIS COURT DOTH DECLARE that the several persons mentioned in Schedule 1 hereto are respectively entitled to a lien under The Mechanics' Lien Act, R.S.O. 1970, chapter 267, upon the land described in Schedule 2 hereto for the amounts set opposite their respective names in the 2nd, 3rd and 4th columns of Schedule 1 and the persons primarily liable for the said claims respectively are set forth in the 5th column of Schedule 1.

2. AND THIS COURT DOTH FURTHER DECLARE that the several persons mentioned in Schedule 3 hereto are also entitled to some lien, charge or encumbrance upon such land as execution creditors of the Defendant for the amounts set opposite their respective names in the 4th column of the said Schedule 3.

3. AND THIS COURT DOTH FURTHER ORDER AND ADJUDGE that upon the Defendant, Mary Smith, paying into Court to the credit of this action the sum of $2,600.00 on or before the 23rd day of December next, that the liens mentioned in Schedule 1 be and the same are hereby discharged and the money so paid into Court is to be paid out in payment of the claims of the lienholders.

4. In case the said Defendant, Mary Smith, shall make default in payment of the said Money into Court, THIS COURT DOTH ORDER AND ADJUDGE that such land be sold with the approbation of the Master of this Court at Brampton, and that the purchase money be paid into Court to the credit of this action.

5. AND THIS COURT DOTH FURTHER ORDER AND ADJUDGE that such purchase money be applied in or towards payment of the several claims mentioned in Schedules 1 and 3 as the Master shall direct, with subsequent interest and subsequent costs to be computed and taxed by the Master.

6. AND THIS COURT DOTH FURTHER ORDER AND ADJUDGE that in case such purchase money shall be insufficient to pay in full the claims of the several persons mentioned in Schedule 1, the person primarily liable for such claim, as shown in Schedule 1 do pay to the persons to whom she is respectively primarily liable the amount remaining due to such persons forthwith after the same has been ascertained by the Master.

....
                                         Judge

FORM 95

SCHEDULE 1

(1)	(2)	(3)	(4)	(5)
Name of Lienholders entitled to Mechanics' Liens	Amount of Debt and interest if any	Costs	Total	Name of Primary Debtor
John Doe	$ 750.00	$150.00	$ 950.00	Mary Smith
Norman Owens	1,100.00	200.00	1,300.00	Mary Smith
Paul Quick	350.00	50.00	350.00	Mary Smith
	$2,200.00	$400.00	$2,600.00	

....
Judge

———————

SCHEDULE 2

The lands in question in this matter are (here set out concise description sufficient for registration).

....
Judge

———————

SCHEDULE 3

(1)	(2)	(3)	(4)
Names of persons entitled to encumbrances other than Mechanics' Liens	Amount of debt and interest, if any	Costs	Total
Roy Smith	$200.00	$25.00	$225.00
T. Urwin	205.00	20.00	225.00
	$405.00	$45.00	$450.00

....
Judge

(See Form 7 in the regulations made under the Ontario Act, R.R.O. 1970, Reg. 575.).

———————

FORM 95A

Judgment Where Claim Relates to Work on Street Or Public Work

HIS HONOUR JUDGE BLACK

LOCAL JUDGE

}

FRIDAY, THE 8TH DAY

OF DECEMBER, A.D. 1977

(Style of Cause)

This action coming on for trial before His Honour Judge Black, Local Judge of this Court, at the Court House, in the City of Brampton, in the Regional Municipality of Peel, upon opening of the matter and it appearing that the following persons have been duly served with notice of trial herein (set out names of all persons served with notice of trial) and all such persons (or as the case may be) appearing at the trial (or, and the following persons not having appeared set out names of non-appearing persons) and upon hearing the evidence adduced and what was alleged by counsel for the plaintiff and for C.D. and E.F. and the defendant (or and by A.B. appearing in person).

1. THIS COURT DOTH DECLARE that amount required to be retained by the defendant A.B. (the owner) under section 11 of The Mechanics' Lien Act is the sum of $5,000.00.

2. THIS COURT DOTH FURTHER DECLARE that the plaintiff and the several persons mentioned in Column 1 of Schedule 1 hereto are respectively entitled to a lien under The Mechanics' Lien Act which lien is a charge on the amount required to be retained by section 11 of the Act for the amounts set opposite their respective names in columns 2, 3 and 4 of the said Schedule 1 and the person primarily liable is set forth in Column 6 of Schedule 1.

3. AND THIS COURT DOTH FURTHER ORDER AND ADJUDGE that upon the defendant A.B. (the owner) paying into Court to the credit of this action the sum of $5,000.00 (gross amount of liens in Schedule 1 for which the owner is liable) on or before the 28th day of December next, that the liens mentioned in Schedule 1 be and the same are hereby discharged and the money so paid into Court is to be paid out to the plaintiff and the several persons mentioned in Column 1 of Schedule 1 in accordance with Column 5 of Schedule 1.

4. AND THIS COURT DOTH FURTHER ORDER AND ADJUDGE that in case the amounts required to be retained by section 11 of The Mechanics' Lien Act are insufficient to pay in full the claims of the several persons mentioned in Schedule 1, the persons primarily liable for such claim as shown in Column 6 of Schedule 1 do pay to the persons to whom they are respectively primarily liable the amount remaining due to such persons forthwith after the same has been ascertained.

5. AND THIS COURT DOTH DECLARE that (here set out names of those who did not prove liens) have not proved any lien under The Mechanics' Lien Act, and that they are not entitled to any such lien.

"J. S. Black"

....

Local Judge

(The schedule referred to in the Judgment is the same as that which is attached to the Master's Report for this type of action, *i.e.* Form 92A.)

(See Form 7*a* in the regulations made under the Ontario Act, R.R.O. 1970, Reg. 575, as amended by O. Reg. 849/75.)

FORM 96

Bond posted as Security Under Section 25(2)

LIEN BOND

NO.   AMOUNT:

KNOW ALL MEN BY THESE PRESENTS that we SMITH CONSTRUCTION (hereinafter called the Principal) and the BOZO INSURANCE COMPANY (hereinafter called the Surety), are jointly and severally bound unto the ACCOUNTANT OF THE SUPREME COURT OF ONTARIO (hereinafter called the Obligee) his successors in office and assigns in the sum of ONE HUNDRED THOUSAND DOLLARS ($100,000.00) of good and lawful money of Canada, for which payment well and truly to be made we bind ourselves and each of us for the whole, our and each of our successors and assigns, firmly by these presents.

THE CONDITION of this obligation is such that this bond stands in lieu of and in place of all and singular that certain parcel or tract of land situate, lying and being in (Insert legal description of land) against which the following claims for a Mechanics' Lien have been registered in the Registry Office for the Registry Division:

Date of Reg'n.	Claimant	Instrument No.
March 26, 1969	Watson	552818
March 10, 1969	Brown	553648
March 13, 1969	Jones	552996

To the intent and condition that if the said SMITH CONSTRUCTION shall pay or cause to be paid into the Supreme Court of Ontario as may be directed or provided by the Judgment in any action in the said Court any amount or amounts not exceeding in the aggregate ONE HUNDRED THOUSAND DOLLARS ($100,00.00) including costs for which the said Watson, Brown and Jones or any person who had on the date of the application in respect of which this bond is filed with the said Court, a subsisting claim for lien or given notice of his claim under subsection 6 of section 11 or section 14 of The Mechanics' Lien Act shall by the said Judgment be found to be entitled to a lien upon all or any of the said lands or to a charge under The Mechanics' Lien Act upon the security furnished by this Bond, then this obligation to be void and of no effect or else to remain in full force and virtue subject to further order of the said Court.

PROVIDED that the amount for which Watson, Brown and Jones shall by the said Judgment be found entitled to a lien upon all or any of the said lands or to a charge under The Mechanics' Lien Act upon the security furnished by this Bond, shall be a first charge upon the said security furnished by this Bond.

PROVIDED that in no event shall the Surety be liable for a greater sum that the penalty of this Bond and any payments under this Bond shall reduce the Surety's liability by the amount of such payments.

IN WITNESS WHEREOF these Presents have been executed by the Principal under its hand and seal and by the Surety by its seal and by the signature of its Attorney this   day of   , 1972.

....
Smith Construction

....
Bozo Insurance Company

FORM 97

Letter of Credit Posted as Security Under Section 25(2)
LETTER OF CREDIT

NO.   AMOUNT:

KNOW ALL MEN by these presents that we, Smith Construction (hereinafter called the Principal) and the Bank of Bozo (hereinafter called the Surety) are jointly and severally bound unto THE ACCOUNTANT OF THE SUPREME COURT OF ONTARIO (hereinafter called the Obligee) his successors in office and assigns, in the sum of ONE HUNDRED THOUSAND DOLLARS ($100,000.00) of good and lawful money of Canada for which payment well and truly to be made we bind ourselves and each of us for the whole, our and each of our successors and assigns, firmly by these presents.

THE CONDITION OF THIS OBLIGATION is such that this letter of credit stands in lieu of and in place of all and singular that certain parcel or tract of land situate, lying and being in (insert legal description of land) against which the following claims for a Mechanics' Lien have been registered in the (insert description of proper Registry Office or Land Titles Office):

Date of Registration	Claimant	Instrument No.
March 26, 1978	Watson	552818
March 10, 1978	Brown	553648
March 13, 1978	Jones	552996

To the intent and condition that if the said SMITH CONSTRUCTION shall pay or cause to be paid into the Supreme Court of Ontario as may be directed or provided by the Judgment in any action in the said court any amount or amounts not exceeding in the aggregate ONE HUNDRED THOUSAND DOLLARS ($100,000.00) including costs for which the said Watson, Brown and Jones or any person who had on the date of the application in respect of which this letter of credit is filed with the said court, a subsisting claim for lien or given notice of his claim under subsection 6 of section 11 or section 14 of The Mechanics' Lien Act shall by the said Judgment be found to be entitled to a lien upon all or any of the said lands or to a charge under the Mechanics' Lien Act upon the security furnished by this Letter of Credit, then this obligation to be void and of no effect, or else to remain in full force and virtue subject to further order of the said Court.

PROVIDED that the amount for which Watson, Brown and Jones shall by the said Judgment be found entitled to a lien upon all or any of the said Lands or to a charge under The Mechanics' Lien Act upon the security furnished by this Letter of Credit, shall be a first charge upon the said security furnished by this Letter of Credit.

PROVIDED that in no event shall the Surety be liable for a greater sum that the penalty of this Letter of Credit and any payments under this Letter of Credit shall reduce the Surety's liability by the amount of such payments.

IN WITNESS WHEREOF these Presents have been executed by the Principal and Surety under the signatures and seals of the proper signing officers this   day of   , 1978.

....
Smith Construction Limited

....
The Bank of Bozo

TABLE OF CONCORDANT SECTIONS

Ont.	Subject Matter	*Alta.	B.C.	Man.	N.B.	Nfld.	N.S.	P.E.I.	Sask.
S. 1(1)	Interpretation								
	(a) Completion of the Contract	2(1)(a)	2	–	–	2(1)(a)	–	1(a)	2(1)(a)
	(b) Contractor	2(1)(b)	2	2(a)	–	2(1)(b)	1(a)	1(b)	2(1)(b)
	(ba) Crown							–	–
	(bb) Estate or interest in land								
	(c) Materials	–	2	2(c)	–	2(1)(g)	1(c)	–	2(1)(g)
	(d) Owner	2(1)(g)	2	2(d)	–	2(1)(i)	1(d)	1(j)	2(1)(h)
	(da) Public Work								
	(e) Registrar	2(1)(i)	2	2(f)	–	2(1)(k)	1(e)	1(n)	2(1)(i)
	(f) Registry Office	–	2	2(g)	–	2(1)(l)	1(l)	1(l)	–
	(g) Subcontractor	2(1)(j)	2	2(h)	–	2(1)(m)	1(f)	1(o)	2(1)(n)
	(h) Wages	2(1)(k)	2	2(i)	–	2(1)(n)	1(g)	1(p)	2(1)(o)
	(i) Workman					2(1)(o)		cf 1(g)	2(1)(e)
S. 1(2)	Work includes service	2(1)(l)	2		–	2(1)(e)		1(q)	2(1)(p)
(3)	Contract deemed substantially performed	2(2)				2(2)			2(2)
(4)	Idem, where work incomplete	2(3)				2(3)			2(3)
S. 1a(1)	Application of Act to Crown								
(2)	Application of sec. 7 of Proceedings against Crown Act								
S. 2(1)	Contract price a trust fund		3(1)	**3 B.W.A.	3(1)				3(1)
(2)	Saving		3(3)		3(3)				3(2)
(3)	Trust fund in hands of owners								3(3)
S. 2(4)	Mortgage advances, etc. a trust fund								3(4)
(5)	Saving								
(6)	Protection for money lenders								3(6)
(7)	Offence and penalty		3(2)		3(2)				6(1)
S. 3	Limit of time re: claim to trust moneys								8(2)
S. 4(1)	Agreement by wage earners waiving application of Act to be void	cf 3	10(1)		6(1)	4(1)	3(1)	5	cf 11
(2)	Exception as to certain employees		10(1)		5	4(2)	3(2)		–
(3)	Effect upon third party of agreement waiving lien		9	3	5	5	4	4	cf 11

* The Alberta Act is known as "The Builders Lien Act".
** B.W.A. = "The Builders and Workers Act" of Manitoba

TABLE OF CONCORDANT SECTIONS

Ont.	Subject Matter	Alta.	B.C.	Man.	N.B.	Nfld.	N.S.	P.E.I.	Sask.
s. 5(1)	General right to a lien	4(1), 7(1)	5	4(1), 5(1)	4(1), (5)	7(1)	5, 7(1)	2, 3(4)	12(1),14(1),17(1)
(2)	Streets or highways and Crown public works exempt except for holdback	7(2)	—	—	4(6)	cf 6(1)	—	3(5)	14(2)
(3)	Lien attaches where materials incorporated into building	—	—	—	—	7(2)	—	—	—
(4)	Interpretation of term "agent"	—	—	—	—	7(3)	—	—	2(1)(m)
(5)	Lien for rented equipment	4(4)	—	—	—	8	—	—	—
s. 6	When husband's interest liable for work done or materials furnished on land of married woman	cf 11	11	—	11	—	6	11	16
s. 7(1)	Where estate charged is leasehold	12(1)	cf 14	cf 5(2)	12(1)	9(1)	7(2)	12(1)	cf 17(2)
(2)	Forfeiture or cancellation of lease, effect on lienholder	12(2)	—	cf 5(3)	12(2)	9(2)	cf 7(3)	12(2)	—
(3)	Prior mortgages	cf 9(2)	cf 7(1)	cf 4(2)	cf 9(2)	9(3)	cf 8	9(4)	cf 15
(4)	When first lien arose	8	12	—	8	9(4)	—	8	—
(5)	Future advances	—	—	—	—	9(5)	—	—	—
(6)	Registered agreement for sale and purchase of land has same priority as mortgage	9(4)	7(3)	cf 11(2)	cf 9(4)	9(6)	cf 14(2)	cf 9(5)	26(2)
s. 8	Application of insurance	13	16	6	13	10	9	13	cf 4
s. 9	Limit of owner's liability	cf 15(1) (5)	cf 6	7	4(2)	11	10	3(1)	18(1)
s. 10	Limit of lien when claimed by other than contractor	cf 15(5.1),(5.2)	—	8	4(3)	12	11	3(2)	18(2)
s. 11(1)	Holdback	15(1)-(3), (5.1), (5.2)	21(1)	9(1)	15(1), (2)	13(1)	12(1)	15(1), (2)	19(1), (3)
(2)	Reduction in amount retained when architect's certificate given	16(1), (2)	—	9(3)	15(4)	13(2)	—	—	20(1)
(3)	Idem, subcontract deemed complete as of date of certificate	16(5)	—	9(4)	15(5)	13(3)	—	—	20(6)
(4)	Court order in lieu of certificate	16(4)	—	—	15(6)	13(4)	12(3)	15(4)	20(2)-(5)
(5)	Lien a charge on holdback	15(4)	21(2)	9(5)	—	13(5)	—	—	19(2)
(5a)	Charge on further amounts retained in case of notice re Crown or municipality	cf 15(6)	cf 21(3)	—	—	—	—	—	—
s. 11(6)	Payments made in good faith without notice of lien	18	21(4)	9(6)	15(7)	13(6)	12(4)	15(5)	20(7)
(7)	Payment of percentage and discharge of liens	—	21(5)	9(7)	17	13(7)	12(5)	17	20(8), (9)
(8)	Amendment of contracts to conform to section	—	21(6)	9(8)	15(8)	13(8)	cf 15(4)	15(6)	19(5)
(9)	Where percentage not to be applied	15(7)	—	cf 12(4)	15(9)	13(9)	—	—	—
s. 12	Payments made directly by owner to persons entitled to lien	cf 20	—	10	18	14	13	18	22
s. 13	Right of subcontractor to file lien if main contract not complete	41(1), cf 41(2)	—	—	19	15	—	19	23
s. 14(1)	Priority of lien	cf 9(1)-(3)	cf 12, 7(1)-(3)	11(1)	9(1)-(3)	16(1)	14(1)	cf 9(1)-(3)	25(1),(2), 26(1)
(2)	Priority among lienholders	cf 47(3), (5)	40	11(3)	10(1)	16(2)	14(3)	10(1)	26(3)
(3)	Mortgage given to person entitled to lien void as against lienholders	—	10(3)	—	7(2)	16(3)	—	7(2)	26(4)
s. 15(1)	Priority of liens for wages	10(1)	cf 7(4)	12(1)	10(2), (3)	17(1)	15(1)	10(2)	28(1)
(2)	Enforcing lien to such case by motion for speedy judgment	—	—	12(3)	—	17(2)	15(3)	—	cf 41(1)
(3)	Calculating percentage when contract not fulfilled	—	—	—	—	17(3)	—	—	28(2), (3)
(4)	Devices and payments made to defeat priority of workman null and void	10(2)	10(2)	12(5)	6(2), 7(1)	17(4)	15(5)	6, 7(1)	28(4), 27

Ont.	Subject Matter	Alta.	B.C.	Man.	N.B.	Nfld.	N.S.	P.E.I.	Sask.
S. 16(1)	Registration of claim for lien and its contents	25(1), (2)	cf 24(2)-(3) / cf 22(1)-(3)	14, 15	20(1), (2) (5)	18(1)	17, 18(1)	20(1), (2), (5)	30(1), (2)
(2)	Verification of claim by affidavit	25(5), (6), cf (7) / 25(4)	cf 22(4)	15(2)	20(3), (4)	18(2)	18(2)	20(3), (4)	30(3), (4)
(3)	Description of lands where lien registered against railway	—	—	—	20(7)	18(3)	18(3)	20(7)	—
S. 17(1)	What may be included in claim	—	—	16	21	19(1)	19	21	32(1)
(2)	Apportionment of claims against respective properties	—	—	—	50	19(2)	—	53	32(2)
S. 18(1)	Substantial compliance sufficient re: registration and contents of claim (curative section)	27(1), (2)	22(5)	17(1)	22(1)	20(1)	20(1)	22(1)	33(1)
(2)	Registration necessary	27(3)	—	17(2)	22(2)	20(2)	20(2)	22(2)	33(2)
S. 19	Duplicate of claim for lien to be filed on or before trial	—	24(1)	—	23(2)	21	cf 33(5)	23(2)	—
S. 20	Status of lienholder (deemed a purchaser pro tanto)	—	—	19	26	22	22	27	34(2)
S. 21(1)	Limit of time for registration by contractor or subcontractor	30(1)	23(1)	20(1)	24(4)	23(1)	23(1)	25(4)	36(1)
(2)	By materials supplier	30(2)	23(2)	20(2)	24(3)	23(2)	23(2)	25(3)	36(2)
(3)	For services	30(3)	cf 23(3)	20(3)	24(2)	23(3)	23(3)	25(2)	36(3)
(4)	For wages	30(4)	23(3)	20(4)	24(1)	23(4)	23(4)	25(1)	36(3)
S. 21a(1)	S.S. 16, 17, 19 and 20 do not apply to Crown and municipal contracts	—	—	—	—	—	—	—	—
(2)	Notice of claim to holdback	—	—	—	—	cf 23(5)	—	—	—
(3)	Service on municipality	—	—	—	—	cf 23(5)	—	—	—
(4)	Service on Crown	—	—	—	—	—	—	—	—
(5)	Time for service of notice	—	—	—	—	23(5)	—	—	—
(6)	Method of service of notice	—	—	—	—	—	—	—	—
(7)	Contents of notice	—	—	—	—	—	—	—	—
(8)	Verification of notice	—	—	—	—	—	—	—	—
S. 22(1)	Expiry of liens for which claim not registered	31	23(4)	21	25	24(1)	cf 24	26	cf 37
(2)	Certificate of action to be registered upon commencement of action	32(1)(b)	cf 26(1)	cf 22	cf 27	24(2)	cf 25(1)	—	cf 37
(3)	Vacating certificate of action, where action not proceeded with	33(2)	—	—	—	24(4)	—	—	—
(4)	Section not applicable to Crown and municipal contracts	—	—	—	—	cf 25(3)	—	—	—
S. 22a	Time for claiming liens against Crown and municipalities	—	—	—	—	—	—	—	—
S. 23(1)	When lien to cease if registered and not proceeded upon	32	27	22	27	25(1)	25(1), 26	28	cf 38(1)
S. 23a	Expiration of liens against Crown and municipalities	—	—	—	—	cf 25(2)	—	—	—
S. 24	Assignment or death of lien claimant	21	29	24(1), (2)	29	26	27	30	29
S. 25(1)	Discharge of lien by registration of receipt	cf 34(1)(a) / cf 34(2)(a)	cf 28	25(1)	30(1), (2)	27(1)	28(1)	31(1), (2)	39
(2)	Security or payment into Court and vacating lien and certificate of action	35(1)	33(1)	25(2), (3)	51(1), (2)	27(2)	28(4)	54(1), (2)	40(1), (2)
(3)	Effect of order under subs. 2, cl. (a) or (b) (no need to register certificate of action)	—	—	—	—	27(3)	—	—	cf 40(3)

Ont.	Subject Matter	Alta.	B.C.	Man.	N.B.	Nfld.	N.S.	P.E.I.	Sask.
(4)	Money paid into Court takes place of land	35(2)	—	—	51(3), (4)	27(4)	—	54(3), (4)	40(3), (4)
(5)	When notice of application to vacate not requisite	—	—	—	30(4)	27(5)	28(5)	29(5)	—
(6)	Payment of money out of Court	—	—	—	—	27(6)	—	—	40(5)
(7)	Form of Order vacating liens and certificates to be registered	—	cf 33(2)	cf 23(6)	—	27(7)	—	cf 54(5)	—
S. 26(1)	Effect generally of taking security or extending time for payment	22(1)	41	26(1)	31(1)	28(1)	29(1)	32(1)	42(1)
(2)	When period of credit not expired, lienholder must be holder of bill or note at time of proving claim	22(2)	cf 41	cf 26(2)	cf 31(2)	28(2)	29(2)	cf 32(2)	42(2)
(3)	Time for bringing action not extended where bill or note negotiated	—	—	—	—	28(3)	29(3)	—	—
(4)	Time for bringing action by person who gave time for payment not extended	—	41	26(3)	31(3)	28(4)	29(4)	32(3)	—
S. 27	Proving claim in action by another lien holder before period of credit has expired	23	41	26(4)	31(3)	29	30	32(4)	43
S. 28(1)	Lienholder's right to have production of contract or agreement	24(1), (2)	17	27(1)	32(1), (2)	—	31(1)	33(1), (2)	44(1), (3), (4)
(2)	Lienholder's right to have statement of mortgage or unpaid vendor	24(3), (4)	—	—	32(3), (4)	30(1)	—	33(3), (4)	44(1), (3), (4)
(3)	Obtaining order for production of contract, agreement or statement from Court	24(5)	—	27(2)	52	cf 30(2)	31(2)	55	44(6)
S. 29(1)	How lien claim enforceable	36(1)	cf 30(1)	cf 28	cf 33(1)	31(1)	cf 33(1)	cf 34, 1(c)	cf 46(1)-(9),2(1)(c)
(2)	Filing statement of claim	36(1)	cf 30(1)	30	cf 34	31(2)	33(2)	cf 35	cf 46(11)
(3)	Service of statement of claim	cf 37	cf 30(1)	cf 28, 32(1)	cf 34	31(3)	33(6)	cf 37(1)	cf 46(12)
(4)	Delivery of statement of defence	38	cf 30(1)	cf 32(1),(2)	cf 36(1)-(3)	31(4)	33(7)	cf 38(1),(2), 39	cf 47(2),(3)
(5)	Unnecessary to make lien claimants parties defendant, as all lien claimants served with notice of trial deemed parties	cf 36(2), 37(2)	—	—	—	31(5)	—	—	—
(6)	Motion to speed trial	—	—	34	41	31(6)	33(4)	43	—
S. 30	Lienholders joining in action	—	—	35	38	31(7)	33(3)	40	46(13)
S. 31(1)	Tribunal and place of trial	cf 2(1)(c)	cf 2, 30(1)	2(b), 28, 29	cf 1, 33	2(1)(d), (f), 31(1), 32	cf 33(1)	cf 1(c), (f), 34	cf 2(1)(c), 46(1)-(9)
(2)	Idem, in York County reference to Master	—	—	56	—	—	—	—	—
(3)	Application to set aside judgment directing a reference to Master	—	—	—	—	—	—	—	—
(4)	Power of Master to amend pleadings on reference	—	—	—	—	—	—	—	—
S. 32	Powers of Local Judges, etc. to dispose of action	cf 44	cf 30(1), (3)	cf 39(2)	cf 43(1)	cf 51	—	—	cf 46(5), (10)
S. 33	Where contract covers several buildings	—	—	—	cf 50	33	—	cf 53	—
S. 34(1)	Power to appoint receiver of rents and profits	40(1)	—	—	—	34(1)	—	—	50(1)
(2)	Power to direct sale and appoint trustee	40(2), (3)	—	—	—	34(2)	—	—	50(3)
(3)	Property may be offered for sale by trustee subject to mortgage	40(4)	—	—	—	34(3)	—	—	50(4)
(4)	Proceeds to be paid into Court	40(5)	—	—	—	34(4)	—	—	50(5)
(5)	Orders for completion of sale	40(6)	—	—	—	34(5)	—	—	50(6)
(6)	Vesting of title	cf 40(7)	—	—	—	cf 34(6)	—	—	50(7)
S. 35	Order for preservation of property	cf 48	—	—	—	35	—	—	—

Ont.	Subject Matter	Alta.	B.C.	Man.	N.B.	Nfld.	N.S.	P.E.I.	Sask.
S. 36	Consolidation of actions	42	cf 34, 35	45	48	36	36	51	cf 48
S. 37	Transferring carriage of proceedings	cf 39(3)(e)	—	46	49	37	37	52	cf 48
S. 38(1)	Appointing day for trial	cf 39, 43	—	36	39	38(1)	34(1)	cf 41	—
(2)	Notice of trial and service of	cf 39(2)	—	37	40	38(2)	35	42	cf 46(1)
(3)	Idem, where no defence filed, must still serve defendant with notice of trial	—	—	—	—	38(3)	—	—	—
(4)	Trial and judgment	44	cf 30, 39	39(1), (2) cf 42, 56(1)	43(1),(2), cf 46	38(4)	34(1), cf 42	45(1),(2), cf 48	51(1), (2)
(5)	Power to vary form of judgment					38(5)			
(6)	Sale	45(2), (3)	cf 30(2)	40(1)	44(1)	38(6)	34(2)	46(1)	51(3)
(7)	Letting in lienholders who have not proved their claims at trial	51(1), (2)	—	44	—	38(7)	34(4)	50	49
(8)	Right of lienholders to representation	—	—	—	—	—	cf 34(5)	—	—
(9)	Trial of action by different Judge	cf 39(3), 38(6)	—	—	—	38(8)	—	—	—
(10)	Application for directions as to pleadings etc.	—	—	—	—	38(9)	—	—	—
S. 39(1)	Report where sale is had	46(1), (2)	cf 40	41(1)	45(1)	39(1)	34(6)	47(1)	51(5)
(2)	Completion of sale	45(3)(c)	cf 30(2)	41(2)	45(2)	39(2)	—	47(2)	51(3)
S. 40	Where lien not established — personal judgment	45(1)	cf 39	43	47	40	cf 45	49	cf 53
S. 41	Right of lienholder's whose claims not payable to share in proceeds					41			
S. 42(1)	Stated case					42(1), (3)			
(2)	Transmission of papers re: stated case					42(2)			
S. 43(1)	Judgment to be final if for $200.00 or less (otherwise appeal lies to Court of Appeal)	52(1), (2)	cf 36(1)	47, 48(1), (2)	cf 53, cf 54(1),(2)	43, 44	cf 38, cf 39	cf 56, cf 57	cf 55
(2)	Appeal from reference								
(3)	Confirmation of Master's report			cf 56					
(4)	Appeal from judgment or report								
(5)	Costs of appeal								
S. 44	Fees payable in lien actions	cf 53	cf 51			cf 50(1)	cf 41		
S. 45(1)	Costs not otherwise provided for are discretionary	cf 54	56	53	58(1), (2)	cf 45(1)	40(5)	62	56(6)
(2)	Limit of costs to plaintiffs	cf 55	cf 52	49	55(1)	—	40(1)	58	56(2)
(3)	Limit of costs against plaintiffs	—	cf 53	50	56	—	40(2)	59	56(3)
(4)	Costs where least expensive course not taken	—	54	52	57	—	40(3)	61	56(4)
(5)	Costs of drawing and registering and vacating registration of lien	—	55	54	59	45(2)	40(4)	63	56(5)
S. 46(1)	Procedure to enforce liens to be of summary nature	36(6)	—	—	—	46(1)	—	—	58(1)
(2)	Interlocutory proceedings — when allowed	cf 39(3)(f)	—	—	61(2)	46(2)	—	—	58(2)
(3)	Assistance of experts	—	—	—	—	46(3)	—	—	59(1)
(4)	Rules of Practice of Supreme Court apply unless otherwise provided	50	cf 30(1)	28,57	61(1)	46(4)	cf 33(1)	34	cf 59(2)
S. 47	Service of documents (except statement of claim and notice of trial) by registered mail	—	—	—	—	47	—	—	—
S. 48(1)	Right of mechanics entitled to lien on chattel to sell chattel	—	42	—	—	48(1)	44(1)	—	60(1)(2)

Ont. — Subject Matter	Alta.	B.C.	Man.	N.B.	Nfld.	N.S.	P.E.I.	Sask.
(2) Application of proceeds of sale of chattel	—	42	—	—	48(2)	44(2)	—	60(3)
S. 49 Forms, posting of notices and offices of Crown for service to be prescribed by regulation	55	—	cf 58	cf 62	cf 50(1)	cf 46	—	—

PROVISIONS NOT CONTAINED IN ONTARIO ACT

Interpretation Section:

Subject Matter	Alta.	B.C.	Man.	N.B.	Nfld.	N.S.	P.E.I.	Sask.
Aircraft	—	2	—	—	—	—	—	—
Claimant	—	2	—	—	—	—	—	—
Corporation	2(1)(c)	2	—	—	2(1)(c)	—	1(c)	2(1)(c)
Court	—	2	—	—	2(1)(d)	—	—	—
Garage-keeper	—	2	—	—	—	—	1(d)	2(1)(d)
Highway	2(1)(d)	2	—	—	—	—	1(e)	2(1)(c)
Improvement	—	2	2(b)	—	2(1)(f)	—	1(f)	2(1)(e)
Judge	2(1)(e)	—	—	—	—	—	1(g)	2(1)(f)
Labourer	—	—	—	—	—	—	—	—
Land	—	—	—	—	—	1(b)	1(h)	—
Lien	—	—	—	—	—	—	—	—
Lienholder	2(1)(f)	2	—	—	—	—	—	—
Materialman	—	2	—	—	—	—	—	—
Motor vehicle	—	2	—	—	—	—	—	—
Municipality	—	—	—	—	—	—	1(i)	2(1)(i)
Municipal Authority	—	—	—	—	2(1)(h)	—	—	—
Person	—	2	2(e)	—	2(1)(j)	—	1(k)	2(1)(k)
Prescribed	2(1)(h)	—	—	—	—	—	—	—
Prothonotary	—	—	—	—	—	—	1(m)	—
Registrar General	—	—	—	—	—	—	—	—
Registered	—	2	—	—	—	—	—	—
Registry	—	—	—	—	2(1)(l)	—	—	2(1)(l)
Statutory period	—	—	—	—	—	—	—	2(1)(m)
Services	—	—	—	—	—	—	—	—
Work	2(1)(2)	2	—	—	—	—	1(q)	2(1)(p)
Trust fund where consideration of contract not money	—	—	—	—	—	—	—	3(5)
Proceeds of Fire Insurance a trust fund	—	—	—	—	—	—	—	4
Lien on trust fund and its priority	—	cf 19	—	—	—	—	—	5(1)
Trust fund to be distributed from time to time on pro rata basis	—	—	—	—	—	—	—	5(2)
Owner, contractor etc. deemed to have notice of lien on trust fund	—	—	—	—	—	—	—	5(3)

TABLE OF CONCORDANT SECTIONS

Subject Matter	Alta.	B.C.	Man.	N.B.	Nfld.	N.S.	P.E.I.	Sask.
No prosecution re improper use of trust fund without consent of Attorney General	—	—	—	—	—	—	—	6(2)
May apply to Judge to settle dispute over trust money	—	—	—	—	—	—	—	7
Action to assert claims for trust money may be by originating notice	—	—	—	—	—	—	—	8(1)
Judge may extend time for commencing action with respect to trust money	—	—	—	—	—	—	—	8(3)
No appeal from Order made under sec. 8(3)	—	—	—	—	—	—	—	9
Proceedings to settle dispute under sec. 7 considered an action	—	—	—	—	—	—	—	10
Waiver by anyone prohibited	3	—	—	—	—	—	—	11
Exception of streets and highways (cf Ont., sec. 5(2))	5(1)	4	—	2	cf 6(1), 6A	2	—	—
Definition of "street", "road" or "highway"	5(2)	2	—	cf 1	6(2)	—	cf 1(d)	—
Exception of irrigation district	5(2)	—	—	—	—	—	—	—
No lien for less than $20.00	26(3)	8	4(1)	cf 4(4)	—	—	cf 3(3)	cf 30(5)
Person having a lien on mine or well also has lien on fixtures etc.	—	—	—	—	—	—	—	12(4)
Where lien is in respect of recovery of mineral, it attaches only to the mineral and not the surface land	4(2)	—	—	—	—	—	—	—
Idem, lien attaches to minerals even if severed from land	4(3)	—	—	—	—	—	—	12(2)
Lien attaches and takes effect from registration as against subsequent purchasers, mortgagees etc.	—	—	—	—	—	8	—	12(3)
Owner deemed to have authorized work if done with his knowledge	—	14	—	—	—	—	—	—
Owner's liability for works on premise held under option	—	15	—	—	—	—	—	—
Limitation of lien attaching to estates in more than one lot, etc.	6	—	—	—	—	—	—	—
Lien in respect of condominium property	—	—	—	—	—	—	—	13
Provisions as to leasehold inapplicable in respect of lien re: minerals	12(3)	—	—	—	—	—	—	—
Removal of material prohibited	14(1)	20	13(1)	14(1)	—	16(1)	14(1)	14(3)
Charge or lien on materials in favour of material supplier	14(2)	—	13(3)	14(2)	—	16(2)	14(2)	14(4)
Court order to prevent removal of material	—	—	13(1)	—	—	—	—	14(3)
Idem, costs on application	—	—	13(2)	—	—	—	—	—
Retention of percentage (holdback) where contract price exceeds $15,000.00	15(8)	—	9(2)	15(3)	—	12(2)	15(3)	cf 19(4)
Underestimating value of work when calculating percentage to be retained	—	—	—	—	—	—	—	—
On receiving notice, owner to retain amount owing to lienholder as well as holdback	—	—	—	16(1)	—	—	16(1)	—
Amount so retained as above constitutes fund separate from holdback for person	—	—	—	—	—	—	—	—

Subject Matter	Alta.	B.C.	Man.	N.B.	Nfld.	N.S.	P.E.I.	Sask.
giving notice	—	—	—	16(2)	—	—	16(2)	—
Amount retained to be distributed among lienholders giving notice pro rata	—	—	—	16(3)	—	—	16(3)	—
Payment under this section not to disentitle lienholder to claim any balance out of holdback	—	—	—	16(4)	—	—	16(4)	—
Payment of amount of retainer under this section, plus holdback, so as to discharge liens	—	—	—	17	—	—	17	—
Holdback plus amount payable on contract less payments made in good faith prior to registration of lien, constitute lien fund	15(1)	—	—	—	—	—	—	—
"Lien Fund" not liable for more than holdback plus any additional sum owing to contractor or subcontractor where lien claimed by person other than contractor	15(5.1)	—	—	—	—	—	—	—
"Lien Fund" not liable for more than holdback plus any additional sum owing to contractor or subcontractor where more than one claim arising from work done for same contractor or subcontractor	15(5.2)	—	—	—	—	—	—	—
Definition of term "Supervisor"	16(1)	—	—	—	—	—	—	—
Written demand for certificate of completion: re release of holdback	16(3)	—	—	—	—	—	—	20(2)-(4)
Court may make completion order where contract not under supervision of supervisor	16(6)	—	—	—	—	—	—	21
Mortgagee may retain holdback and if so, deemed compliance by owner	17	—	—	—	—	—	—	—
Application to pay Lien Fund into Court if lien registered	18(2)	—	—	—	—	—	—	—
Idem, notice of application	18(3)	—	—	—	—	—	—	—
Payment operates as discharge of owner	18(4)	—	—	—	—	—	—	—
Powers of Court on application to pay into Court	18(5)	—	—	—	—	—	—	—
Payment of holdback in money although contract not payable in money	19(1)	—	—	—	—	—	—	24(1), (2)
Idem, Judge may fix the "money's worth"	19(2)	—	—	—	—	—	—	24(3)
Registration of notice of change of address for service	28(1)	—	—	20(6)	—	—	20(6)	—
Entry of change of address by Registrar	28(2)	—	—	cf 20(6)	—	—	cf 20(6)	31
Not necessary to set out name of owner of oil or gas well in claim	25(3)	—	—	—	—	—	—	cf 31
Affidavit verifying lien claim may be made as to facts of which deponent is informed	25(7)	22(4)	—	—	—	—	—	—
Registrar to be supplied with forms of claim for lien and affidavit	26(1)	22(3)	—	—	—	—	—	—
Registrar to decide if his office one in which lien should be registered	26(2)	22(3)	—	—	—	—	—	—
Registration of lien on minerals held directly from Crown and application of provisions of Act thereto	26(5)	—	—	—	—	cf 32(4)	—	—
Liability for wrongful registration of claim for lien	29	—	—	—	—	—	—	cf 35(1)

Subject Matter	Alta.	B.C.	Man.	N.B.	Nfld.	N.S.	P.E.I.	Sask.
Time for registration of claim for lien not extended by completion of work not done or improperly done	30(5)	—	—	—	—	—	—	—
Certificate of lis pendens granted to any lienholder who is a party to action	32(2)	—	—	—	—	—	—	—
Idem, any such lienholder may register same	32(3)	—	—	—	—	—	—	—
Cancellation of registration of certificate of lis pendens by registrar	32(4)	—	cf 23(6)	cf 28	—	—	—	—
Upon registration of certificate — liens continue to exist until action concluded	33(1)	—	—	—	—	—	—	—
Cancellation of lien by Registrar upon proof lien no longer exists	34(1)(b) 34(2)(b)	—	—	—	—	—	—	—
Cancellation of lien and certificate of Registrar upon Court order or certificate of Court Clerk	34(3)	cf 28	cf 23(6)	cf 28	—	—	cf 29(4)	cf 38(2)
Parties to be named as defendants by lienholder who is not the contractor	36(3)	—	—	—	—	—	—	—
Idem, by lienholder who is the contractor	36(4)	—	—	—	—	—	—	—
Definition of "prior registered encumbrance"	36(5)	—	—	—	—	—	—	—
Persons to be served with statement of claim	37(1)	—	—	—	—	—	—	cf 47(1), (2)
All persons served with statement of claim deemed parties	37(2)	—	—	—	—	—	—	—
Not required to file defence if not named as a defendant	38(2)	—	—	—	—	—	—	—
Notice to lienholder to prove lien, after service of statement of claim	38(3)	—	—	—	—	—	—	—
Time for filing affidavit of particulars proving lien	38(4)	—	—	—	—	—	—	47(2)
Loss of lien for failure to so file affidavit	38(5)	—	—	—	—	—	—	cf 47(4)
Examination of lienholder on affidavit proving claim	38(6)	—	—	—	—	—	—	—
Application for pre-trial hearing	39(1)	—	—	—	—	—	—	—
Notice of such application	39(2)	—	—	—	—	—	—	—
Powers of Court upon hearing of pre-trial application	39(3)	—	—	—	—	—	—	—
Proceeds of receivership to be paid into Court	40(5)	—	—	—	—	—	—	50(2)
No receiver or trustee to be appointed with respect to homestead	—	—	—	—	—	—	—	50(8)
Entering action for trial where defence filed and no order made at pre-trial hearing	43	—	—	—	—	—	—	—
Trial Judge may direct sale and removal of materials	45(4)	cf 30(2)	40(2)	44(2)	—	34(3)	46(2)	51(4)
Court order for sale subject to prior encumbrances or at upset price	47(1)	cf 7(1)	—	—	—	—	—	—
Moneys realized from sale, receivership, trusteeship or insurance proceeds to be paid into Court	47(2)	—	—	—	—	—	—	—

Subject Matter	Alta.	B.C.	Man.	N.B.	Nfld.	N.S.	P.E.I.	Sask.
Order of distribution of moneys paid into Court	47(3)	40	—	—	—	—	—	—
Idem, where sold at upset price	47(4)	—	—	—	—	—	—	—
Amount in excess of 6 weeks' wages owing to labourer to be deducted from his employer's share of such distribution	47(6)	—	—	—	—	—	—	—
Court may order removal and sale of structure	48(1)	cf 30(2)	—	—	—	—	—	—
How excess of proceeds of sale of structure to be applied	48(2)	—	—	—	—	—	—	—
Judgment under Act enforceable as a judgment of the Court	49	—	cf 42	—	—	—	—	—
No fees payable by a labourer or for filing order record, judgment etc.	53	cf 51	—	—	—	—	—	—
Payment of costs by owner or contractor where proceedings arise because of their failure to comply with Act or terms of contract	54	38	—	—	—	—	—	—
Rules and tariff of costs may be prescribed by Lt.-Governor in Council	55	—	—	55(2)	cf 50(1)	—	—	—
Mortgagee subrogated to rights and priority of the lien upon payment of lien claim	9(3)	7(2)	—	—	—	—	—	—
Workman's lien on mine or mineral claim has priority over all encumbrances	—	7(4)	—	—	—	cf 32(2)	—	—
Filing affidavit of lien deemed notice to all persons	—	13	—	—	—	—	—	—
Owner may demand particulars of contract or agreement, etc. from contractor or subcontractor	24(1)	18	—	cf 32(5)	—	—	cf 33(5)	cf 44(2)-(4)
Lienholder may demand production of contracts by contractor or subcontractor	—	—	—	—	—	—	—	cf 44(1)(c)
Liability of contractor and subcontractor to lienholder if fail to produce contracts	24(2)	—	—	cf 32(6)	—	—	cf 33(6)	cf 44(4)
Owner and contractor may withhold payments under contracts if information not supplied	—	—	—	—	—	—	—	44(5)
No appeal from Court order directing production of contract, books etc.	—	—	—	—	—	—	—	44(7)
Assignment by contractor or counterclaim against him not to defeat lien or trust	—	19	—	—	—	—	—	cf 25(2)
Affidavit of lien valid if sworn before solicitor, etc.	—	22(2)	—	—	cf 49(4)	—	—	—
No affidavit to be adjudged insufficient for not filing in proper Registry Office	—	22(3)	—	—	—	—	—	—
Procedure to file claim for lien	—	24(1), (2)	cf 14(1)-(4)	cf 23(1), (2)	—	—	—	—
Procedure for registration respecting Crown lands	—	—	14(6)	—	—	—	—	—
Procedure to file claim for lien under Mineral Act or Placer Mining Act	—	25(1)	cf 14(5)	—	—	—	—	—
Action to be commenced within one year	—	26(1)	—	—	—	—	—	—
Action to be commenced within two years	—	—	22	—	—	—	—	—
Owner or other person may send notice to lienholder to commence action within specified time or his lien will cease to exist	—	26(2)	23(1)-(4), cf 23(5)	—	—	—	cf 29(1)-(3)	38(1)

Subject Matter	Alta.	B.C.	Man.	N.B.	Nfld.	N.S.	P.E.I.	Sask.
Such notice deemed to be given and received in ordinary course of mails	—	26(3)	—	—	—	—	—	—
Not necessary to set out copy of claim for lien in plaint (statement of claim)	—	31	—	—	—	—	—	—
Production of claim for lien bearing Registry Office stamp is sufficient proof of filing	—	32	—	—	—	—	—	—
If action dismissed lien remains in force until appeals disposed of	—	36(2)	—	—	—	—	—	—
Purchaser of leasehold interest at sale under Act is deemed an assignee of lease	—	37	—	—	—	—	—	52
Lien in respect of motor vehicle or aircraft	—	43	—	—	—	—	—	—
Affidavit of lien in respect of motor vehicle or aircraft	—	44	—	—	—	—	—	—
Fee for filing lien in respect of motor vehicle or aircraft	—	45	—	—	—	—	—	—
Duty of Registrar-General of Motor Vehicles	—	46	—	—	—	—	—	—
Duration of lien in respect of motor vehicle or aircraft	—	47	—	—	—	—	—	—
Priority as between charge and lien on motor vehicle or aircraft	—	48	—	—	—	—	—	—
Enforcement of lien in respect of motor vehicle or aircraft	—	49	—	—	—	—	—	—
Garage-keeper's power of sale	—	50	—	—	—	—	—	—
Microfilm of documents authorized	—	57	—	—	—	—	—	—
Where estate charged is leasehold owner liable if his consent endorsed on claim of lien	—	—	5(2)	—	—	7(2)	—	17(2)
Wage-earner entitled to enforce lien where contract not fulfilled	—	—	12(2)	—	—	15(2)	—	28(2)
Fee for registration of claim for lien	—	cf 51	14(7), 18(2) 24(3), (4)	cf 23(1)	—	cf 21	23(3)	cf 34(1)
Assignee may register lien or assignment of lien	—	—	29	33(2)	—	—	—	—
Transferring lien action to another Court	—	—	—	—	32(2)	—	—	cf 46(2)-(8)
Statement of claim to contain address of plaintiff's solicitor and office where defence to be filed	—	—	31	cf 35	—	—	cf 36	—
Statement of claim to be verified by Affidavit	—	—	—	34	—	—	—	—
Plaintiff may sign interlocutory judgment if defence not filed in time	cf 39(3)(a)	—	32(1)	36(2)	—	—	38(2)	47(4)
Upon registration lien arises and takes effect from commencement of work or service, etc.	—	—	4(2)	—	—	—	—	—
Defendant may get leave to defend	cf 39(3)(a)	—	32(2)	36(3)	—	—	39	—
Statement of defence to contain address for service of defendant or his solicitor	—	—	33	37	—	—	—	—
Lienholders not parties to action to file statement with Court after served with notice of trial	—	—	38	42	—	cf 33(5)	44	—
Deficiency after sale recoverable by usual process of the Court	—	—	42	cf 46	—	42	48	cf 51(5)
Trial Judge may grant new trial where no appeal because total claims less than $100.	—	—	47	53	—	38	56	—

Subject Matter	Alta.	B.C.	Man.	N.B.	Nfld.	N.S.	P.E.I.	Sask.
Counsel fees not deemed disbursements in fixing costs	—	—	51	—	—	—	60	—
Counsel fees shall be deemed disbursements	—	—	—	—	—	—	—	—
No fees on payments into or out of Court	—	—	55	60	—	—	64	—
Costs of applications and orders not otherwise provided for are in discretion of Judge	—	—	—	—	—	—	—	56(6)
Trial by referee in Winnipeg	—	—	56	—	—	—	—	—
Judge may permit amendments so as to remove prejudice created by failure to comply with Act	—	—	—	22(3)	—	—	22(3)	—
If claim settled before action, owner liable to lienholder for cost of registering lien	—	—	—	23(3)	—	—	—	—
Time for registering lien against oil or gas wells and pipelines	—	—	—	—	—	—	—	36(1)(c), 36(2)(c)
Time for registering lien where contract under supervision of architect	—	—	—	24(5)	—	23(5)	25(5)	36(4)
Discharge of lien to acknowledge amount paid	—	—	—	30(2)	—	cf 28(1)	31(2)	—
Registrar to index discharge in Mechanics' Lien Index, etc.	—	—	—	30(3)	—	cf 28(2)	31(3), 24	—
Lienholder may demand particulars of contractor	cf 24(1)	cf 18	—	32(5), (6)	—	—	33(5), (6)	—
Sale under judgment to be by Sheriff	—	—	—	44(1)	—	—	—	—
Sheriff's remuneration on sale	—	—	—	44(3)	—	—	—	—
Order vacating liens to be filed forthwith	—	—	—	51(5)	—	—	54(5)	—
Scale of costs where action transferred to another Court	—	—	—	58(2)	—	—	—	46(6)
Recording of registration of claim for lien	26(4)	cf 24(3), 25(2)	18(1)	23(1), (2)	18(4)	21	23(1), (2), 24	34(1)
Registration of two copies of claim for lien where part of land under Real Property Act and part is not	—	—	14(2)	—	—	—	—	—
Method and effect of registering two copies of lien	—	—	14(3)	—	—	—	—	—
Minister of Justice charged with administration of the Act	—	—	—	—	3	—	—	—
Certificate of action to be granted by Court Clerk	—	—	—	—	24(3)	—	—	—
Discharge of lien may be signed by officer of corporation without corporate seal if verified by affidavit	—	—	—	—	27(1)(b)	cf 28(1)	cf 31(1)	—
Particulars of certificate of action to be recorded on registration	—	—	—	—	27(8)	—	—	—
Particulars of orders discharging liens and vacating certificates of action to be recorded on registration	—	—	—	—	29(9)	—	cf 24	—
Court to make all necessary orders to enable trustees appointed under Act to carry out powers given to them under Act	—	—	—	—	34(7)	—	—	—
Persons before whom an affidavit may be taken	—	—	—	—	49(1)	—	—	—
Idem, where affidavits taken outside of province	—	—	—	—	49(2)	—	—	—

Subject Matter	Alta.	B.C.	Man.	N.B.	Nfld.	N.S.	P.E.I.	Sask.
Certain seals and signatures accepted without proof	—	—	—	—	49(3)	—	—	—
Solicitor for any party may take affidavit	—	—	—	—	49(4)	—	—	—
Regulations which may be made by Lt.-Governor in Council	—	—	—	cf 62	50(1)	—	—	—
Publication of regulations and effect thereof	—	—	—	—	50(2)	—	—	—
Disposition of fees collected by Registrars	—	—	—	—	50(3)	—	—	—
Jurisdiction of District Courts	—	—	—	—	51	—	—	cf 46(1)
Form prescribed for certificate vacating lien	—	—	—	—	—	43	—	—
Expiry of unregistered lien	—	—	—	—	—	24	—	37(1)
Registered lien expires unless re-registered within 6 months where period of credit, not expired and no action commenced	—	—	25(1)	—	—	25(2)	—	—
Fee for registration of discharge of lien	—	—	—	—	—	28(3)	31(3)	—
Liens on mining properties, leases and licences	—	—	—	—	—	32(1)	—	—
Such lien has priority over all other liens, mortgages, etc.	—	—	—	—	—	32(2)	—	—
Not necessary to describe property or lease in claim	—	—	—	—	—	32(3)	—	—
Place of registration of such lien	—	—	—	—	—	32(4)	—	—
Proceedings may be taken within 6 months	—	—	—	—	—	32(5)	—	—
Definition of expression "mine"	—	—	—	—	—	32(6)	—	—
Papers may be served by any literate person	—	cf 51	—	—	—	33(8)	—	—
Every statement of claim accompanied by fee of $1.00 paid by law stamp	—	—	—	—	—	41	—	—
Writ to direct filing of statement of defence	—	—	—	—	—	—	36	—
Defendant may enter appearrance within time limited for defence	—	—	—	—	—	—	37(2)	—
General interpretation of the Act	—	—	—	—	—	—	65	—
Act does not apply to Crown as defined in Public Works Creditors Payment Act, 1973	—	—	—	—	—	—	—	2(4)
Assignments of contract moneys by contractors and subcontractors invalid as against liens	—	—	—	—	—	—	—	25(2)
Notice of claim for lien on mine to be sent by Registrar to owner	—	—	—	—	—	—	—	35(2)
All such lien claims discharged upon surrender of lease, permit, etc. re: mine, mineral, oil or gas well	—	—	—	—	—	—	—	35(3)
Notice of reinstatement	—	—	—	—	—	—	—	35(4)
Subsections (3), (4) are retroactive	—	—	—	—	—	—	—	35(5)

Subject Matter	Alta.	B.C.	Man.	N.B.	Nfld.	N.S.	P.E.I.	Sask.
Failure to register claim not to defeat lien except as against intervening parties etc.	—	—	—	—	—	—	—	37(2)
Application to Judge for summary determination of disputes	—	—	—	—	—	—	—	41(1)
Appeal of summary determination lies to Court of Appeal	—	—	—	—	—	—	—	41(2)
Leave to commence actions against homesteads and practice in such actions including appeals								45
Idem: Sec. 45 does not apply to actions where lienholder has been given a notice under Sec. 38(1)	—	—	—	—	—	—	—	45(18)
Action to be brought at judicial centre nearest where owner resides or carries on business or where contract performed	—	—	—	—	—	—	—	46(9)
Defendant may claim set-off or may counterclaim for anything arising in same transaction including damages	—	—	—	—	—	—	—	46(10)
Proceedings to be commenced by originating notice	—	—	—	—	—	—	—	46(11)
Unless otherwise ordered shall not be less than 30 days between date of last service and hearing	—	—	—	—	—	—	—	46(12)
Persons to be named as Defendants in originating notice	—	—	—	—	—	—	—	47(1)
All defendants to file detailed particulars of claims or disputes and serve copies on plaintiff	—	—	—	—	—	—	—	47(2), (3)
Claimant who fails to appear loses his claim	—	—	—	—	—	—	—	47(4)
Limit of costs where amount found due to lienholder not more than $200.00	—	—	—	—	—	—	—	57
Court may extend time for registering documents or taking proceedings subject to rights of third parties	—	—	—	—	—	—	—	—
Queen's Bench practice to be adopted in certain cases	—	—	57	—	—	—	—	54
Forms in schedule or similar to be used	—	—	58	—	—	46	—	cf 59(2)
Form of, and method of service of notice of lien to mortgagee or unpaid vendor	—	—	—	9(3)	—	—	—	—
Supreme Court may direct notice of hearing of a stated case be given to interested persons	—	—	—	—	42(3)	—	—	—

THE MECHANICS' LIEN ACT
R.S.O. 1970, Chapter 267
As Amended 1975, Chapter 43

Interpretation

1.—(1) In this Act,

    (a) "completion of the contract" means substantial performance, not necessarily total performance, of the contract;

    (b) "contractor" means a person contracting with or employed directly by the owner or his agent for the doing of work or the placing or furnishing of materials for any of the purposes mentioned in this Act;

    (ba) "Crown" includes Crown agencies to which *The Crown Agency Act* applies; 1975, c. 43, s. 1, *enacted.*

    (bb) "estate or interest in land" includes a statutory right given or reserved to the Crown to enter any lands or premises of any person or public authority for the purpose of doing any work, construction, repair or maintenance in, upon, through, over or under any such lands or premises; 1975, c. 43, s. 1. *enacted.*

    (c) "materials" includes every kind of movable property;

    (d) "owner" includes any person and corporation, including the Crown, a municipal corporation and a railway company, having any estate or interest in the land upon which or in respect of which work is done or materials are placed or furnished, at whose request, and

        (i) upon whose credit, or

        (ii) on whose behalf, or

        (iii) with whose privity or consent, or

        (iv) for whose direct benefit,

    work is done or materials are placed or furnished and all persons claiming under him or it whose rights are acquired after the work in respect of which the lien is claimed is commenced or the materials placed or furnished have been commenced to be placed or furnished; 1975, c. 43, s. 1, *amended.*

    (da) "public work" means the property of the Crown and includes land in which the Crown has an estate or interest, and also includes all works and properties acquired, constructed, extended, enlarged, repaired, equipped or improved at the expense of the Crown, or for the acquisition, construction, repairing, equipping, extending, enlarging or improving of which any public money is appropriated by the Legislature, but not any work for which money is appropriated as a subsidy only; 1975, c. 43, s. 1, *enacted.*

    (e) "registrar" includes a master of titles;

    (f) "registry office" includes a land titles office;

    (g) "subcontractor" means a person not contracting with or employed directly by the owner or his agent for any of the purposes mentioned in this Act, but contracting

with or employed by a contractor or, under him, by another subcontractor;

(h) "wages" means the money earned by a workman for work done by time or as piece work, and includes all monetary supplementary benefits, whether by statute, contract or collective bargaining agreement;

(i) "workman" means a person employed for wages in any kind of labour, whether employed under a contract of service or not.

Work includes service

(2) In this Act, the expression "the doing of work" includes the performance of a service, and corresponding expressions have corresponding meanings.

Substantial performance

(3) For the purposes of this Act, a contract shall be deemed to be substantially performed,

(a) when the work or a substantial part thereof is ready for use or is being used for the purpose intended; and

(b) when the work to be done under the contract is capable of completion or correction at a cost of not more than,

(i)   3 per cent of the first $250,000 of the contract price,

(ii) 2 per cent of the next $250,000 of the contract price, and

(iii) 1 per cent of the balance of the contract price.

Idem

(4) For the purpose of this Act, where the work or a substantial part thereof is ready for use or is being used for the purpose intended and where the work cannot be completed expeditiously for reasons beyond the control of the contractor, the value of the work to be completed shall be deducted from the contract price in determining substantial performance.

Application of Act

1a.—(1) Subject to subsection 2 of section 5, this Act binds the Crown but does not apply in respect of work under a contract as defined in *The Ministry of Transportation and Communications Creditors Payment Act, 1975* and to which that act applies. 1975, c. 43, s. 2, *enacted.*

Application of R.S.O. 1970, c. 365, s. 7

(2) Section 7 of *The Proceedings Against the Crown Act* does not apply in respect of proceedings against the Crown under this Act. 1975, c. 43, s. 2, *enacted.*

GENERAL

Trust funds in hands of contractors

2.—(1) All sums received by a builder, contractor or subcontractor on account of the contract price constitute a trust fund in his hands for the benefit of the owner, builder, contractor, subcontractor, Workmen's Compensation Board, workmen, and persons who have supplied materials on account of the contract or have rented equipment to be used on the contract site, and the builder, contractor or subcontractor, as the case may be, is the trustee of all such sums so received by him and he shall not appropriate or convert any part thereof to his own use or to any use not authorized by the trust until all workmen and all persons who have supplied materials on the contract or who have rented equipment to be used on the contract site and all subcontractors are paid for work done or materials supplied on the contract and the Workmen's Compensation Board is paid any assessment with respect thereto.

Exception

(2) Notwithstanding subsection 1, where a builder, contractor or subcontractor has paid in whole or in part for any materials supplied on account of the contract or for any rented equipment or has paid any workman who has performed any work or any subcontractor who has placed or furnished any materials in respect of the contract, the retention by such builder, contractor or subcontractor of a sum equal to the sum so paid by him shall be deemed not to be an appropriation or conversion thereof to his own use or to any use not authorized by the trust.

Trust funds in hands of owners

(3) Where a sum becomes payable under a contract to a contractor by an owner on the certificate of a person authorized under the contract to make such a certificate, an amount equal to the sum so certified that is in the owner's hands or received by him at any time thereafter shall, until paid to the contractor, constitute a trust fund in the owner's hands for the benefit of the contractor, subcontractor, Workmen's Compensation Board, workmen, and persons who have supplied materials on account of the contract or who have rented equipment to be used on the contract site, and the owner shall not appropriate or convert any part thereof to his own use or to any use not authorized by the trust until all workmen and all persons who have supplied materials on the contract or who have rented equipment to be used on the contract site and all contractors and subconstractors are paid for work done or materials supplied on the contract and the Workmen's Compensation Board is paid any assessment with respect thereto.

Advances on mortgage, etc., a trust fund

(4) All sums received by an owner, other than the Crown, a municipality as defined in *The Department of Municipal Affairs Act* or a metropolitan or regional municipality or a local board thereof, which are to be used in the financing, including the purchase price of the land and the payment of prior encumbrances, of a building, structure or work, constitute, subject to the payment of the purchase price of the land and prior encumbrances, a trust fund in the hands of the owner for the benefit of the persons mentioned in subsection 1, and, until the claims of all such persons have been paid, the owner shall not appropriate or convert any part thereof to his own use or to any use not authorized by the trust. 1975, c. 43, s. 3, *amended.*

Exception

(5) Notwithstanding subsection 4, where an owner has himself paid in whole or in part for any work done, for any materials placed or furnished or for any rented equipment, the retention by him from any moneys received from the lender under subsection 4 of the sum equal to the sum so paid by him shall be deemed not to be an appropriation or conversion thereof to his own use or to any use not authorized by the trust.

Protection for money lenders

(6) Notwithstanding anything in this section, where money is lent to a person upon whom a trust is imposed by this section and is used by him to pay in whole or in part for any work

done, for any materials placed or furnished or for any rented equipment, trust moneys may be applied to discharge the loan to the extent that the lender's money was so used by the trustee, and any sum so applied shall be deemed not to be an appropriation or conversion to the trustee's own use or to any use not authorized by the trust.

Offence and penalty

(7) Every person upon whom a trust is imposed by this section who knowingly appropriates or converts any part of any trust moneys referred to in subsection 1, 3 or 4 to his own use or to any use not authorized by the trust is guilty of an offence and on summary conviction is liable to a fine of not more than $5,000 or to imprisonment for a term of not more than two years, or to both, and every director or officer of a corporation who knowingly assents to or acquiesces in any such offence by the corporation is guilty of such offence, in addition to the corporation, and on summary conviction is liable to a fine of not more than $5,000 or to imprisonment for a term of not more than two years, or to both.

Limit of time for asserting claims to trust moneys

3. No action to assert any claim to trust moneys referred to in section 2 shall be commenced against a lender of money to a person upon whom a trust is imposed by that section except,

    (a) in the case of a claim by a contractor or subcontractor in cases not provided for in clauses *b, c* and *d,* within nine months after the completion or abandonment of the contract or subcontract;

    (b) in the case of a claim for materials, within nine months after the placing or furnishing of the last material;

    (c) in the case of a claim for services, within nine months after the completion of the service; or

    (d) in the case of a claim for wages, within nine months after the last work was done for which the claim is made.

Agreements waiving application of Act are void

4.—(1) Every agreement, oral or written, express or implied, on the part of any workman that this Act does not apply to him or that the remedies provided by it are not available for his benefit is void.

Exception

(2) Subsection 1 does not apply,

    (a) to a manager, officer or foreman; or

    (b) to any person whose wages are more than $50 a day.

Effect upon third party of agreement waiving lien

(3) No agreement deprives any person otherwise entitled to a lien under this Act, who is not a party to the agreement, of the benefit of the lien, but it attaches, notwithstanding such agreement.

CREATION OF LIENS

General right to a lien

5.—(1) Unless he signs an express agreement to the contrary and in that case subject to section 4, any person who does any work upon or in respect of, or places or furnishes any materials to be used in, the making, constructing, erecting, fitting, altering, improving or repairing of any land, building, structure or works or the appurtenances to any of them for any owner, contractor or subcontractor by virtue thereof has a lien for the price of the work or materials upon the estate or interest of the owner in the land, building, structure or works and appurtenances and the land occupied thereby or enjoyed therewith, or upon or in respect of which the work is done, or upon which the materials are placed or furnished to be used, limited, however, in amount to the sum justly due to the person entitled to the lien and to the sum justly owing, except as herein provided, by the owner, and the placing or furnishing of the materials to be used upon the land or such other place in the immediate vicinity of the land designated by the owner or his agent is good and sufficient delivery for the purpose of this Act, but delivery on the designated land does not make such land subject to a lien.

Where lien against Crown or municipality

(2) Where the land or premises upon or in respect of which any work is done or materials are placed or furnished is,

(a) a public street or highway owned by a municipality; or

(b) a public work,

the lien given by subsection 1 does not in any event attach to such land or premises but shall instead constitute a charge on amounts directed to be retained by section 11, and the provisions of this Act shall be construed, *mutatis mutandis,* to have effect without requiring the registration or enforcement of a lien or a claim for lien against such land or premises. 1975, c. 43, s. 4, *re-enacted.*

Lien attaches where materials incorporated into building

(3) The lien given by subsection 1 attaches as therein set out where the materials delivered to be used are incorporated into the land, building, structure or works, notwithstanding that the materials may not have been delivered in strict accordance with subsection 1.

Interpretation

(4) In subsection 1, "agent" includes the contractor or subcontractor for whom the materials are placed or furnished, unless the person placing or furnishing the materials has had actual notice from the owner to the contrary.

Lien for rented equipment

(5) A person who rents equipment to an owner, contractor or subcontractor for use on a contract site shall be deemed for the purposes of this Act to have performed a service for which he has a lien for the price of the rental of the equipment used on the contract site, limited, however, in amount to the sum justly owed and due to the person entitled to the lien from the owner, builder, contractor or subcontractor in respect of the rental of the equipment.

When husband's interest liable for work done or materials furnished on land of spouse

6. Where work is done or materials are placed or furnished to be used upon or in respect of the land of a married woman, or in which she has an interest or an inchoate right of dower, with the privity or consent of her husband, he shall be presumed conclusively to be acting as her agent as well as for himself for the purposes of this Act unless before doing the work or placing or furnishing the materials the person doing the work or placing or furnishing the materials has had actual notice to the contrary.

Where estate charged is leasehold

7.—(1) Where the estate or interest upon which the lien attaches is leasehold, the fee simple is also subject to the lien if the person doing the work or placing or furnishing the materials gives notice in writing, by personal service, to the owner in fee simple or his agent of the work to be done or materials to be placed or furnished unless the owner in fee simple or his agent within fifteen days thereafter gives notice in writing, by personal service, to such person that he will not be responsible therefore.

Forfeiture or cancellation of lease, effect of on lienholder

(2) No forfeiture or attempted forfeiture of the lease on the part of the landlord, or cancellation or attempted cancellation of the lease except for non-payment of rent, deprives any person otherwise entitled to a lien of the benefit of the lien, but the person entitled to the lien may pay any rent accruing after he becomes so entitled, and the amount so paid may be added to his claim.

Prior mortgages

(3) Where the land and premises upon or in respect of which any work is done or materials are placed or furnished are encumbered by a mortgage or other charge that was registered in the proper registry office before any lien under this Act arose, the mortgage or other charge has priority over all liens under this Act to the extent of the actual value of the land and premises at the time the first lien arose, such value to be ascertained by the judge or officer having jurisdiction to try an action under this Act.

When first lien arose

(4) The time at which the first lien arose shall be deemed to be the time at which the first work was done or the first materials placed or furnished, irrespective of whether a claim for lien in respect thereof is registered or enforced and whether or not such lien is before the court.

Future advances

(5) Any mortgage existing as a valid security, notwithstanding that it is a prior mortgage within the meaning of subsection 3, may also secure future advances, subject to subsection 1 of section 14.

Registered agreement for sale and purchase of land has same priority as mortgage

(6) A registered agreement for the sale and purchase of land and any moneys *bona fide* secured or payable thereunder has the same priority over a lien as is provided for a mortgage and mortgage moneys in subsections 3 and 5, and for the purposes of this Act the seller shall be deemed to be a mortgagee, and any moneys *bona fide* secured and payable under such agreement shall be deemed to be mortgage moneys *bona fide* secured or advanced.

Application of insurance

8. Where any of the property upon which a lien attaches is wholly or partly destroyed by fire, any money received by reason of any insurance thereon by an owner or prior mortgagee

or chargee shall take the place of the property so destroyed and is, after satisfying any prior mortgage or charge in the manner and to the extent set out in subsection 3 of section 7, subject to the claims of all persons for liens to the same extent as if the money had been realized by a sale of the property in an action to enforce the lien.

Limit of amount of owner's liability

9. Save as herein otherwise provided, the lien does not attach so as to make the owner liable for a greater sum than the sum payable by the owner to the contractor.

Limit of lien when claimed by other than contractor

10. Save as herein otherwise provided, where the lien is claimed by any person other than the contractor, the amount that may be claimed in respect thereof is limited to the amount owing to the contractor or subcontractor or other person for whom the work has been done or the materials were placed or furnished.

Holdback

11.—(1) In all cases, the person primarily liable upon a contract under or by virtue of which a lien may arise shall, as the work is done or the materials are furnished under the contract, retain for a period of thirty-seven days after the completion or abandonment of the work done or to be done under the contract 15 per cent of the value of the work and materials actually done, placed or furnished, as mentioned in section 5, irrespective of whether the contract or subcontract provides for partial payments or payment on completion of the work, and the value shall be calculated upon evidence given in that regard on the basis of the contract price or, if there is no specific contract price, on the basis of the actual value of the work or materials.

Reduction in amount retained

(2) Where a contract is under the supervision of an architect, engineer or other person upon whose certificate payments are to be made and thirty-seven days have elapsed after a certificate issued by that architect, engineer or other person to the effect that the subcontract has been completed to his satisfaction has been given to the person primarily liable upon that contract and to the person who became a subcontractor by a subcontract made directly under that contract, the amount to be retained by the person primarily liable upon that contract shall be reduced by 15 per cent of the subcontract price or, if there is no specific subcontract price, by 15 per cent of the actual value of the work done or materials placed or furnished under the subcontract, but this subsection does not operate if and so long as any lien derived under that subcontract is preserved by anything done under this Act.

Idem

(3) Where a certificate issued by an architect, engineer or other person to the effect that a subcontract by which a subcontractor became a subcontractor has been completed to the satisfaction of that architect, engineer or other person has been given to that subcontractor, then, for the purposes of subsections 1, 2 and 3 of section 21, section 23 and section 23a, that subcontract and any materials placed or furnished or to be placed or furnished thereunder and any work done or to be done thereunder shall, so far as concerns any lien thereunder of that subcontractor, be deemed to have been completed or placed or furnished not later than the time at which the certificate was so given. 1975, c. 43, s. 5, *amended.*

Court order in lieu of certificate

(4) Where an architect, engineer or other person neglects or refuses to issue and deliver a certificate upon which payments are to be made under a contract or subcontract, the judge or officer having jurisdiction to try an action under this Act, upon application and upon being satisfied that the certificate should have been issued and delivered may, upon such terms and conditions as to costs and otherwise as he deems just, make an order that the work or materials to which the certificate would have related has been done or placed or furnished, as the case may be, and any such order has the same force and effect as if the certificate had been issued and delivered by the architect, engineer or other person.

Charge on holdback

(5) The lien is a charge upon the amount directed to be retained by this section in favour of lien claimants whose liens are derived under persons to whom the moneys so required to be retained are respectively payable. 1975, c. 43, s. 5, *re-enacted.*

Charge on further amounts payable in case of Crown or municipality

(5a) Where the lien does not attach to the land by virtue of subsection 2 of section 5, and a person claiming a lien gives to the owner, or a contractor or subcontractor notice in writing of the lien, the owner, contractor or subcontractor so notified shall retain out of amounts payable to the contractor or subcontractor under whom the lien is derived an amount equal to the amount claimed in the notice. 1975, c. 43, s. 5, *re-enacted.*

Payments made in good faith without notice of lien

(6) All payments up to 85 per cent as fixed by subsection 1 and payments permitted as a result of the operation of subsections 2 and 3 made in good faith by an owner to a contractor, or by a contractor to a subcontractor, or by one subcontractor to another subcontractor, before notice in writing of the lien given by the person claiming the lien to the owner, contractor or subcontractor, as the case may be, operate as a discharge *pro tanto* of the lien.

Payment of percentage and discharge of liens

(7) Payment of the percentage required to be retained under this section may be validly made so as to discharge all claims in respect of such percentage after the expiration of the period of thirty-seven days mentioned in subsection 1 unless in the meantime the appropriate steps have been taken to preserve the lien as provided by sections 22 and 23, or 22a and 23a, as the case may be, in which case the owner may pay the percentage into court in the proceedings, and such payment constitutes valid payment in discharge of the owner to the amount thereof. 1975, c. 43, s. 5, *amended.*

Amendment of contracts

(8) Every contract shall be deemed to be amended in so far as is necessary to be in conformity with this section.

Where percentage not to be applied

(9) Where the contractor or subcontractor makes default in completing his contract, the percentage required to be retained shall not, as against any lien claimant who by virtue of subsection 5 has a charge thereupon, be applied by the owner, contractor or subcontractor to the completion of the contract or for any other purpose nor to the payment of damages for

the non-completion of the contract by the contactor or subcontractor nor in payment or satisfaction of any claim against the contractor or subcontractor.

Payments made directly by owner to persons entitled to lien

12. If an owner, contractor or subcontractor makes a payment to any person entitled to a lien under section 5 for or on account of any debt, justly due to him for work done or for materials placed or furnished to be used as therein mentioned, for which he is not primarily liable, and within three days afterwards gives written notice of the payment to the person primarily liable, or his agent, the payment shall be deemed to be a payment on his contract generally to the contractor or subcontractor primarily liable but not so as to affect the percentage to be retained by the owner as provided by section 11. 1975, c. 43, s. 6, *amended.*

Rights of subcontractor

13. Every subcontractor is entitled to enforce his lien notwithstanding the non-completion or abandonment of the contract by any contractor or subcontractor under whom he claims.

Priority of lien

14.—(1) The lien has priority over all judgments, executions, assignments, attachments, garnishments and receiving orders recovered, issued or made after the lien arises, and over all payments or advances made on account of any conveyance or mortgage after notice in writing of the lien has been given to the person making such payments or after registration of a claim for the lien as hereinafter provided, and, in the absence of such notice in writing or the registration of a claim for lien, all such payments or advances have priority over any such lien.

Priority among lienholders

(2) Except where it is otherwise provided by this Act, no person entitled to a lien on any property or money is entitled to any priority or preference over another person of the same class entitled to a lien on such property or money, and each class of lienholders ranks *pari passu* for their several amounts, and the proceeds of any sale shall be distributed among them *pro rata* according to their several classes and rights.

Mortgage given to person entitled to lien void as against lienholders

(3) Any conveyance, mortgage or charge of or on land given to any person entitled to a lien thereon under this Act in payment of or as security for any such claim, whether given before or after such lien claim has arisen, shall, as against other parties entitled to liens under this Act, on any such land be deemed to be fraudulent and void.

PRIORITY OF WAGES

Priority of liens for wages

15.—(1) Every workman whose lien is for wages has priority to the extent of thirty days wages over all other liens derived through the same contractor or subcontractor to the extent of and on the 15 per cent directed to be retained by section 11 to which the contractor or subcontractor through whom the lien is derived is entitled, and all such workmen rank thereon *pari passu.*

Enforcing lien in such cases

(2) Every workman is entitled to enforce a lien in respect of any contract or subcontract

that has not been completed and, notwithstanding anything to the contrary in this Act, may serve a notice of motion on the proper persons, returnable in four days after service thereof before the judge or officer having jurisdiction to try an action under this Act, that the applicant will on the return of the motion ask for judgment on his claim for lien, registered particulars of which shall accompany the notice of motion duly verified by affidavit.

Calculating percentage when contract not fulfilled

(3) If the contract has not been completed when the lien is claimed by a workman, the percentage shall be calculated on the value of the work done or materials placed or furnished by the contractor or subcontractor by whom the workman is employed, having regard to the contract price, if any.

Devices to defeat priority of workmen

(4) Every device by an owner, contractor or subcontractor to defeat the priority given to a workman for his wages and every payment made for the purpose of defeating or impairing a lien are void.

REGISTRATION

Registration of claim for lien

16.—(1) A claim for a lien may be registered in the proper registry office and shall set out,

    (*a*) the name and an address for service of the person claiming the lien and of the owner or of the person whom the person claiming the lien, or his agent, believes to be the owner of the land, and of the person for whom the work was or is to be done, or the materials were or are to be placed or furnished, and the time within which the same was or was to be done or placed or furnished;

    (*b*) a short description of the work done or to be done, or the materials placed or furnished or to be placed or furnished;

    (*c*) the sum claimed as due or to become due;

    (*d*) a description of the land as required by *The Land Titles Act* or *The Registry Act* and the regulations thereunder, as the case may be; and

    (*e*) the date of expiry of the period of credit if credit has been given.

Verification of claim

(2) The claim shall be verified in duplicate by the affidavit of the person claiming the lien, or of his agent or assignee who has a personal knowledge of the matters required to be verified, and the affidavit of the agent or assignee shall state that he has such knowledge.

Lien against railway

(3) When it is desired to register a claim for lien against a railway, it is sufficient description of the land of the railway company to describe it as the land of the railway company, and every such claim shall be registered in the general register in the office for the registry division within which the lien is claimed to have arisen.

What may be included in claim

17.—(1) A claim for lien may include claims against any number of properties, and any number of persons claiming liens upon the same property may unite therein, but, where more

586

than one lien is included in one claim, each claim for lien shall be verified by affidavit as provided in section 16.

Apportionment of claims

(2) The judge or officer trying the action has jurisdiction equitably to apportion against the respective properties the amounts included in any claim or claims under subsection 1.

Informality

18.—(1) Substantial compliance with sections 16, 17, 21a, and 29 is sufficient and no claim for lien is invalidated by reason of failure to comply with any of the requirements of such sections unless, in the opinion of the judge or officer trying the action, the owner, contractor or sub-contractor, mortgagee or other person is prejudiced thereby, and then only to the extent to which he is thereby prejudiced. 1975, c. 43, s. 7, *amended.*

Registration necessary

(2) Nothing in this section dispenses with the requirement of registration of the claim for lien.

Duplicate to be filed

19. A duplicate of the claim for lien, bearing the registrar's certificate of registration, shall be filed on or before the trial of the action, where the action is to be tried in the Judical District of York, in the office of the master of the Supreme Court, or, where the action is to be tried elsewhere, in the office of the clerk of the county or district court of the county or district in which the action is to be tried.

Status of lien claimant

20. Where a claim is so registered, the person entitled to a lien shall be deemed to be a purchaser *pro tanto* and a purchaser within the provisions of *The Registry Act* and *The Land Titles Act,* but, except as herein otherwise provided, those Acts do not apply to any lien arising under this Act.

Limit of time for registration

21.—(1) A claim for lien by a contractor or subcontractor in cases not otherwise provided for may be registered before or during the performance of the contract or of the subcontract or within thirty-seven days after the completion or abandonment of the contract or of the subcontract, as the case may be.

Materials

(2) A claim for lien for materials may be registered before or during the placing or furnishing thereof, or within thirty-seven days after the placing or furnishing of the last material so placed or furnished.

Services

(3) A claim for lien for services may be registered at any time during the performance of the service or within thirty-seven days after the completion of the service.

Wages

(4) A claim for lien for wages may be regsitered at any time during the doing of the work for which the wages are claimed or within thirty-seven days after the last work was done for which the lien is claimed.

[(5) **Notice of claim to hold back,** *repealed* 1975, c. 43, s. 8. See 21*a*(2), below.]

Crown and municipal contracts

21a.—(1) Without limiting the generality of subsection 2 of section 5, where the lien does not attach to the land by virtue of subsection 2 of section 5, sections 16, 17, 19 and 20 do not apply. 1975, c. 43, s. 9, *enacted.*

Notice of claim to hold back

(2) Where the lien does not attach to the land by virtue of subsection 2 of section 5, any person who is claiming a lien shall give notice thereof in writing to the owner in the manner hereafter provided. 1975, c. 43, s. 9, *enacted.*

Service on municipality

(3) Where the claim is in respect of a public street or highway owned by a municipality, the notice required to be given to the owner by subsection 2 shall be given to the clerk of the municipality. 1975, c. 43, s. 9, *enacted.*

Service on Crown

(4) Where the claim is in respect of a public work, the notice required by subsection 2 to be given to the owner shall be given to the Ministry or Crown agency for whom the work is done or the materials are placed or furnished, or to such office as is prescribed by the regulations. 1975, c. 43, s. 9, *enacted.*

Time for service

(5) The notice required by subsection 2 shall be given within the time allowed for registration under section 21. 1975, c. 43, s. 9, *enacted.*

Method of service

(6) The notice required by subsection 2 may be served personally, or it may be sent by registered mail, in which case the date of mailing shall be deemed to be the date on which the notice was given. 1975, c. 43, s. 9, *enacted.*

Contents of notice

(7) The notice required shall set out,
　　(*a*) the name and address of the person making the claim and of the person for whom the work was done or the materials were placed or furnished, and the time within which the same was done or placed or furnished;
　　(*b*) a short desription of the work done or the materials placed or furnished;

(c) the sum claimed as due;

(d) the address or a description of the location of the land;

(e) the date of expiry of the period of credit if credit has been given. 1975, c. 43, s. 9, *enacted.*

Verification

(8) The matters set out in the notice shall be verified by the affidavit of the person claiming the lien, or his agent or assignee who has a personal knowledge of the matters, and the affidavit of the agent or assignee shall state that he has such knowledge. 1975, c. 43, s. 9, *enacted.*

EXPIRY AND DISCHARGE

Expiry of liens

22.—(1) Every lien for which a claim is not registered ceases to exist on the expiration of the time limited in section 21 for the registration thereof.

Registration of certificate of action

(2) Upon an action under this Act being commenced, a certificate thereof shall be registered in the registry office in which the claim for lien is registered.

Vacating orders

(3) Where a certificate of action has been registered for two years or more in the registry office and no appointment has been taken out for the trial of the action, the judge or, in the Judicial District of York, the master, may, upon the application *ex parte* of any interested person, make an order vacating the certificate of action and discharging all liens depending thereon.

Not applicable to Crown and municipal contracts

(4) This section does not apply to liens which, by virtue of subsection 2 of section 5, do not attach to the land. 1975, c. 43, s. 10, *enacted.*

Time for claiming liens against Crown and municipalities

22a. Where the lien does not attach to the land by virtue of subsection 2 of section 5, every lien for which notice has not been given as required by section 21a ceases to exist at the expiration of the time limited in section 21a for giving notice of claim thereof. 1975, c. 43, s. 11, *enacted.*

When lien to cease if registered and not proceeded upon

23.—(1) Every lien for which a claim is registered ceases to exist on the expiration of ninety days after the work has been completed or the materials have been placed or furnished, or after the expiry of the period of credit, where such period is mentioned in the registered claim for lien, unless in the meantime an action is commenced to realize the claim or in which a subsisting claim may be realized, and a certificate is registered as provided by section 22.

[(2) **Expiration of claim** and (3) **Idem,** *repealed* 1975, c. 43, s. 12.]

589

Expiration of liens against Crown and municipalities

23a. Every lien which by virtue of subsection 2 of section 5 does not attach to the land ceases to exist on the expiration of ninety days after,

   (a) the work has been completed or abandoned;

   (b) the materials have been placed or furnished; or

   (c) the expiry of the period of credit, where such period is mentioned in the notice referred to in section 21a,

unless in the meantime an action under this Act is commenced to realize the claim or in which a subsisting claim may be realized. 1975, c. 43, s. 13, *enacted.*

Assignment or death of lien claimant

24. The rights of a lien claimant may be assigned by an instrument in writing and, if not assigned, upon his death pass to his personal representative.

Discharge of lien

25.—(1) A claim for lien may be discharged by the registration of a receipt acknowledging payment,

   (a) where made by a lien claimant that is not a corporation, signed by the lien claimant or his agent duly authorized in writing and verified by affidavit; or

   (b) where made by a lien claimant that is a corporation sealed with its corporate seal.

Security or payment into court and vacating lien and certificate of action

(2) Upon application, the judge or, in the Judicial District of York, the master, may, at any time,

   (a) allow security for or payment into court of the amount of the claim of the lien claimant and the amount of the claims of any other subsisting lien claimants together with such costs as he may fix, and thereupon order that the registration of the claim for lien or liens and the registration of the certificate of action, if any, be vacated;

   (b) upon any other proper ground, order that the registration of the claim for lien or liens and the registration of the certificate of action, if any, be vacated; or

   (c) upon proper grounds, dismiss the action.

Effect of order under subs. 2, cl. a or b

(3) Notwithstanding sections 22 and 23, where an order to vacate the registration of a lien is made under clause *a* or *b* of subsection 2, the lien does not cease to exist for the reason that no certificate of action is registered.

Money paid into court

(4) Any money so paid into court, or any bond or other security for securing the like amount and satisfactory to the judge or officer, takes the place of the property discharged and is subject to the claims of every person who has at the time of the application a subsisting claim for lien or given notice of the claim under subsection 6 of section 11 or section 14 to the same extent as if the money, bond or other security was realized by a sale of the property in an action to enforce the lien, but such amount as the judge or officer finds to be owing to the person whose lien has been so vacated is a first charge upon the money, bond or other security.

Where notice of application to vacate not requisite

(5) Where the certificate required by section 22 or 23 has not been registered within the prescribed time and an application is made to vacate the registration of a claim for lien after the time for registration of the certificate, the order vacating the lien may be made *ex parte* upon production of a cetificate of search under *The Land Titles Act* or of a registrar's abstract under *The Registry Act,* as the case may be, together with a certified copy of the registered claim for lien.

Payment of money out of court

(6) Where money has been paid into court or a bond deposited in court pursuant to an order under subsection 2, the judge or, in the Judicial District of York, the master, may, upon such notice to the parties as he may require, order the money to be paid out to the persons entitled thereto or the delivery up of the bond for cancellation, as the case may be.

Registration number

(7) An order discharging a claim for lien or vacating a certificate of action shall be registered by registering the order or a certificate thereof, under the seal of the court, that includes a description of the land as required by *The Land Titles Act* or *The Registry Act* and the regulations thereunder, as the case may be, and a reference to the registration number of every registered claim for lien and certificate of action affected thereby.

EFFECT OF TAKING SECURITY OR EXTENDING TIME

Effect generally

26.—(1) The taking of any security for, or the acceptance of any promissory note or bill of exchange for, or the taking of any acknowledgment of the claim, or the giving of time for the payment thereof, or the taking of any proceedings for the recovery, or the recovery of a personal judgment for the claim, does not merge, waive, pay, satisfy, prejudice or destroy the lien unless the lien claimant agrees in writing that it has that effect.

Where period of credit not expired

(2) Where any such promissory note or bill of exchange has been negotiated, the lien claimant does not thereby lose his right to claim for lien if, at the time of bringing his action to enforce it or where an action is brought by another lien claimant, he is, at the time of proving his claim in the action, the holder of such promissory note or bill of exchange.

Time for bringing action not extended

(3) Nothing in subsection 2 extends the time limited by this Act for bringing an action to enforce a claim for lien.

Time for bringing action by person who gave time for payment

(4) A person who has extended the time for payment of a claim for which he has a claim for lien in order to obtain the benefit of this section shall commence an action to enforce the claim within the time prescribed by this Act and shall register a certificate as required by sections 22 and 23, but no further proceedings shall be taken in the action until the expiration of such extension of time.

Proving claim in action by another person

27. Where the period of credit in respect of a claim has not expired or there has been an extension of time for payment of the claim, the lien claimant may nevertheless, if an action is commenced by any other person to enforce a claim for lien against the same property, prove and obtain payment of his claim in the action as if the period of credit or the extended time had expired.

LIEN CLAIMANT'S RIGHTS TO INFORMATION

Production of contract or agreement

28.—(1) Any lien claimant may in writing at any time demand of the owner or his agent the production, for inspection, of the contract or agreement with the contractor for or in respect of which the work was or is to be done or the materials were or are to be placed or furnished, if the contract or agreement is in writing or, if not in writing, the terms of the contract or agreement and the state of the accounts between the owner and the contractor, and, if the owner or his agent does not, at the time of the demand or within a reasonable time thereafter, produce the contract or agreement if in writing or, if not in writing, does not inform the person making the demand of the terms of the contract or agreement and the amount due and unpaid upon the contract or agreement or if he knowingly falsely states the terms of the contract or agreement or the amount due or unpaid thereon and if the person claiming the lien sustains loss by reason of the refusal or neglect or false statement, the owner is liable to him for the amount of the loss in an action therefor or in any action for the enforcement of a lien under this Act, and subsection 4 of section 38 applies.

Statement of mortgagee or unpaid vendor

(2) Any lien claimant may in writing at any time demand of a mortgagee or unpaid vendor or his agent the terms of any mortgage on the land or of any agreement for the purchase of the land in respect of which the work was or is to be done or the materials were or are to be placed or furnished and a statement showing the amount advanced on the mortgage or the amount owing on the agreement, as the case may be, and, if the mortgagee or vendor or his agent fails to inform the lien claimant at the time of the demand or within a reasonable time thereafter of the terms of the mortgage or agreement and the amount advanced or owing thereon or if he knowingly falsely states the terms of the mortgage or agreement and the amount owing thereon and the lien claimant sustains loss by the refusal or neglect or misstatement, the mortgagee or vendor is liable to him for the amount of the loss in an action therefor or in any action for the enforcement of a lien under this Act, and subsection 4 of section 38 applies.

Production of contract or agreement

(3) The judge or, in the Judicial District of York, the master, may, on a summary application at any time before or after an action is commenced for the enforcement of the claim for lien, make an order requiring the owner or his agent or the mortgagee or his agent or the unpaid vendor or his agent or the contractor or his agent or the subcontractor or his agent, as the case may be, to produce and permit any lien claimant to inspect any such contract or agreement or mortgage or agreement for sale or the accounts or any other relevant document upon such terms as to costs as the judge or master considers just.

ACTIONS

How claim enforceable

29.—(1) A claim for lien is enforceable in an action in the Supreme Court.

Statement of claim, filing of

(2) An action under this section shall be commenced by filing a statement of claim in the office of the local registrar of the Supreme Court in the county or district in which the land or part thereof is situate.

Idem, service

(3) The statement of claim shall be served within thirty days after it is filed, but the judge having jurisdiction to try the action or, in the Judicial District of York, the master, may extend the time for service.

Statement of defence

(4) The time for delivering the statement of defence in the action shall be the same as for entering an appearance in an action in the Supreme Court.

Parties

(5) It is not necessary to make any lien claimants parties defendant to the action, but all lien claimants served with the notice of trial shall for all purposes be deemed to be parties to the action.

Motion to speed trial

(6) After the commencement of the action, any lien claimant or other person interested may apply to the judge having jurisdiction to try the action, or in the Judicial District of York, a judge of the Supreme Court, to speed the trial of the action.

Lien claimants joining in action

30. Any number of lien claimants claiming liens on the same land may join in an action, and an action brought by a lien claimant shall be deemed to be brought on behalf of himself and all other lien claimants.

Tribunal and place of trial

31.—(1) Except in the Judicial District of York, the action shall be tried by the local judge of the Supreme Court in the county or district in which the action was commenced, but, upon the application of any party or other interested person made according to the practice of the Supreme Court and upon notice, the court may direct that the action be tried by a judge of the Supreme Court at the regular sittings of the court for the trial of actions in the county or district in which the action was commenced.

Idem, York

(2) In the Judicial District of York, the action shall be tried by a judge of the Supreme Court, but,
  (a) on motion after defence or defence to counterclaim, if any, has been delivered or

the time for such delivery has expired, a judge of the Supreme Court may refer the whole action to the master for trial pursuant to section 72 of *The Judicature Act;* or

    (b) at the trial, a judge of the Supreme Court may direct a reference to the master pursuant to section 71 or 72 of *The Judicature Act.*

Application to set aside judgment directing a reference

(3) Where on motion the whole action is referred to the master for trial, any person brought into the proceedings subsequent thereto and served with a notice of trial may apply to a judge of the Supreme Court to set aside the judgment directing the reference within seven days after service of notice of trial and, if such person fails to make such application, he is bound by such judgment as if he were originally a party thereto.

Amendment of pleadings on reference

(4) Where the action is referred to the master for trial, he may grant leave to amend any pleading.

Powers of local judges S.C.O., etc.

32. The local judges of the Supreme Court and the master to whom a reference for trial has been directed, in addition to their ordinary powers, have all the jurisdiction, powers and authority of the Supreme Court to try and completely dispose of the action and questions arising therein and all questions of set-off and counterclaim arising under the building contract or out of the work done or materials furnished to the property in question.

Where contract covers several buildings

33. Where an owner enters into an entire contract for the supply of materials to be used in several buildings, the person supplying the materials may ask to have his lien follow the form of the contract and that it be for an entire sum upon all the buildings, but, in case the owner has sold one or more of the buildings, the judge or officer trying the action has jurisdiction equitably to apportion against the respective buildings the amount included in the claim for lien under the entire contract.

Power to appoint a receiver of rents and profits

34.—(1) At any time after the delivery of the statement of claim, the judge having jurisdiction to try the action or, in the Judicial District of York, a judge of the Supreme Court, may, on the application of any lien claimant, mortgagee or other person interested, appoint a receiver of the rents and profits of the property against which the claim for lien is registered upon such terms and upon the giving of such security or without security as the judge considers just.

Power to direct sale and appoint trustee

(2) Any lien claimant, mortgagee or other person interested may make an application to the judge having jurisdiction to try the action or, in the Judicial District of York, a judge of the Supreme Court, at any time before or after judgment, who may hear *viva voce* or affidavit evidence or both and appoint, upon such terms and upon the giving of such security or without security as the judge considers just, a trustee or trustees with power to manage, mortgage, lease and sell, or manage, mortgage, lease or sell, the property against which the claim for lien is registered, and the exercise of such powers shall be under the supervision and

direction of the court, and with power, when so directed by the court, to complete or partially complete the property, and, in the event that mortgage moneys are advanced to the trustee or trustees as the result of any of the powers conferred upon him or them under this subsection, such moneys take priority over every claim of lien existing as of the date of appointment.

Property offered for sale

(3) Any property directed to be sold under subsection 2 may be offered for sale subject to any mortgage or other charge or encumbrance if the judge so directs.

Proceeds to be paid into court

(4) The proceeds of any sale made by a trustee or trustees under subsection 2 shall be paid into court and are subject to the claims of all lien claimants, mortgagees or other persons interested in the property so sold as their respective rights are determined, and, in so far as applicable, section 39 applies.

Orders for completion of sale

(5) The judge shall make all necessary orders for the completion of any mortgage, lease or sale authorized to be made under subsection 2.

Vesting of title

(6) Any vesting order made of property sold by a trustee or trustees appointed under subsection 2 vests the title of the property free from all claims for liens, encumbrances and interests of any kind including dower, except in cases where sale is made subject to any mortgage, charge, encumbrance or interest as hereinbefore provided, but nothing in this section or elsewhere in this Act shall be deemed to extinguish the right to dower, if any, of any married woman or the right to have the value of her dower ascertained and deducted from the proceeds of the sale so paid into court.

Order for preservation of property

35. At any time after delivery of the statement of claim and before judgment, or after judgment and pending the hearing and determination of any appeal, any lien claimant, mortgagee or other interested person may make an application to the judge having jurisdiction to try the action or who tried the action, as the case may be, or, in the Judicial District of York, a judge of the Supreme Court, who may hear *viva voce* or affidavit evidence or both and make an order for the preservation of any property pending the determination of the action and any appeal.

Consolidation of actions

36. Where more actions than one are brought to realize liens in respect of the same land, the judge or officer having jurisdiction to try the action may, on the application of any party to any one of the actions or on the application of any other person interested, consolidate all such actions into one action and award the conduct of the consolidated action to any plaintiff as the judge or officer considers just.

Transferring carriage of proceedings

37. Any lien claimant entitled to the benefit of an action may at any time apply to the judge or officer having jurisdiction to try the action for the carriage of the proceedings, and the judge or officer may make an order awarding such lien claimant the carriage of the proceedings.

Appointing day for trial

38.—(1) After the delivery of the statement of defence where the plaintiff's claim is disputed, or after the time for delivery of defence in all other cases, either party may apply *ex parte* to a judge or officer having jurisdiction to try the action to fix a day for the trial thereof, and the judge or officer shall appoint the time and place of trial, and the order, signed by the judge or officer, shall form part of the record of the proceedings.

Notice of trial and service

(2) The party obtaining an appointment for the trial shall, at least ten clear days before the day appointed, serve notice of trial upon the solicitors for the defendants who appear by solicitors and upon the defendants who appear in person, and upon all the lienholders who have registered their claims as required by this Act or of whose claims he has notice, and upon all other persons having any charge, encumbrance or claim on the land subsequent in priority to the lien, who are not parties, and such service shall be personal unless otherwise directed by the judge or officer who may direct in what manner the notice of trial is to be served.

Idem

(3) Where any person interested in the land has been served with a statement of claim and makes default in delivering a statement of defence, he shall nevertheless be served with notice of trial and is entitled to defend on such terms as to costs and otherwise as the judge or officer having jurisdiction to try the action considers just.

Trial

(4) The judge, or where a reference for trial is directed, the master,
   (a) shall try the action, including any set-off and counterclaim, and all questions that arise therein or that are necessary to be tried in order to completely dispose of the action and to adjust the rights and liabilities of the persons appearing before him or upon whom notice of trial has been served;
   (b) shall take all accounts, make all inquiries, give all directions and do all other things necessary to finally dispose of the action and of all matters, questions and accounts arising therein or at the trial, and to adjust the rights and liabilities of and give all necessary relief to all parties to the action and all persons who have been served with the notice of trial; and
   (c) shall enbody the results of the trial,
      (i)   in the case of a judge, in a judgment, and
      (ii) in the case of a master, in a report,
   which judgment or report may direct payment forthwith by the person or persons primarily liable to pay the amount of the claims and costs as ascertained by the judgment or report, and execution may be issued therefor forthwith in the case of a judgment and after confirmation thereof, in the case of a report.

Power to vary form of judgment

(5) The form of the judgment or report may be varied by the judge or officer in order to meet the circumstances of the case so as to afford to any party to the proceedings any right or remedy in the judgment or report to which he may be entitled.

Sale

(6) The judge or officer may order that the estate or interest charged with the lien be sold, and may direct the sale to take place at any time after judgment or confirmation of the report, allowing, however, a reasonable time for advertising the sale.

Letting in lien claimants

(7) A lien claimant who did not prove his claim at the trial, on application to the judge or officer before whom the action or reference was tried, may be let in to prove his claim, on such terms as to costs and otherwise as are deemed just, at any time before the amount realized in the action for the satisfaction of liens has been distributed, and, where his claim is allowed, the judgment or report shall be amended so as to include his claim.

Right of lien claimants to representation

(8) Any lien claimant for an amount not exceeding $200 may be represented by an agent who is not a barrister and solicitor.

Action may be tried by any judge

(9) An action or reference under this Act may be tried by any judge or officer having jurisdiction to try the action or reference notwithstanding that the time and place for the trial or reference thereof were appointed and fixed by another judge or officer.

Applications for directions

(10) Any party to an action under this Act or any other interested person may at any time and from time to time apply to the judge having jurisdiction to try the action or, in the Judicial District of York, the master, for directions as to pleadings, discovery, production or any other matter relating to the action or reference, including the cross-examination of a lien claimant or his agent or assignee on his affidavit verifying the claim.

Report where sale is had

39.—(1) Where a sale is had, the moneys arising therefrom shall be paid into court to the credit of the action, and the judge or officer before whom the action was tried shall direct to whom the moneys in court shall be paid and may add to the claim of the person conducting the action his fees and actual disbursements incurred in connection with the sale, and, where sufficient to satisfy the judgment and costs is not realized from the sale, he shall certify the amount of the deficiency and the names of the persons who are entitled to recover the same, showing the amount that each is entitled to recover and the persons adjudged to pay the same, giving credit for payments made, if any, under subsection 4 of section 38, and the persons so entitled may enforce payment of the amounts so found to be due by execution or otherwise.

Completion of sale

(2) The judge or officer before whom the action was tried may make all necessary orders for the completion of the sale and for vesting the property in the purchaser.

Where lien not established

40. Where a lien claimant fails to establish a lien, he may nevertheless recover a personal judgment against any party to the action for such sum as may appear to be due to him and which he might recover in an action against such party.

Right of lienholders whose claims are not payable to share in proceeds

41. Where property subject to a lien is sold in an action to enforce a lien, every lienholder is entitled to share in the proceeds of the sale in respect of the amount then owing to him, although the same or part thereof was not payable at the time of the commencement of the action or is not then presently payable.

STATED CASE

Stated case

42.—(1) If in the course of proceedings to enforce a lien a question of law arises, the judge or officer trying the case may, at the request of any party, state the question in the form of a stated case for the opinion of the Court of Appeal, and the stated case shall thereupon be set down to be heard before the Court of Appeal and notice of hearing shall be served by the party setting down upon all parties concerned.

Transmission of papers

(2) The stated case shall set forth the facts material for the determination of the question raised, and all papers necessary for the hearing of the stated case by the Court of Appeal shall be transmitted to the registrar of the Supreme Court.

APPEAL

Appeal

43.—(1) Except where the amount of a judgment or report made on a reference for trial in respect of a claim or counterclaim is $200 or less, an appeal lies from any judgment or report under this Act to the Court of Appeal.

Appeal from reference

(2) Where a question is referred to the master for inquiry and report under subsection 2 of section 31, an appeal lies in the manner prescribed by the rules of court.

Confirmation of master's report

(3) Where an action is referred to the master for trial under subsection 2 of section 31, the report shall be filed and shall be deemed to be confirmed at the expiration of fifteen days from the date of service of notice of filing the same, unless notice of appeal is served within that time.

Appeal from judgment or report

(4) An appeal from a judgment or report made on a reference for trial lies in like manner and to the same extent as from the decision of a judge trying an action in the Supreme Court without a jury.

Costs of appeal

(5) The costs of an appeal shall not be governed by subsections 2 and 3 of section 45 but, subject to any order of the Court of Appeal, shall be upon the scale of costs allowed in county

court appeals where the amount involved is within the proper competence of the county court, and, where it exceeds that amount, upon the Supreme Court scale.

FEES AND COSTS

Fee

44. The fee payable by every plaintiff, every plaintiff by counterclaim and every lien claimant, including every person recovering a personal judgment, in any action to realize a lien under this Act is,

(a) $5 on a claim or counterclaim not exceeding $500;

(b) $10 on a claim or counterclaim exceeding $500 but not exceeding $1,000;

(c) $10 on a claim or counterclaim exceeding $1,000, plus $1 for every $1,000 or fraction thereof in excess of $1,000,

but no fee is payable on a claim for wages only, and in no case shall the fee on a claim exceed $75 or on a counterclaim exceed $25.

Costs not otherwise provided for

45.—(1) Subject to sections 2, 3, 4 and 5, any order as to costs in an action under this Act is in the discretion of the judge or officer who tries the action.

Limit of costs to plaintiffs

(2) The costs of the action, exclusive of actual disbursements, awarded to the plaintiffs and successful lienholders, shall not exceed in the aggregate 25 per cent of the total amount found to have been actually due on the liens at the time of the registration thereof, and shall be apportioned and borne in such proportion as the judge or officer who tries the action may direct, but in making the apportionment he shall have regard to the actual services rendered by or on behalf of the parties respectively, provided that, where a counterclaim is set up by a defendant, the amount and apportionment of the costs in respect thereof are in the discretion of the judge or officer who tries the action.

Limit of costs against plaintiffs

(3) Where costs are awarded against the plaintiff or other persons claiming liens, they shall not exceed, except in the case of a counterclaim, 25 per cent of the claim of the plaintiff and the other claimants, besides actual disbursements, and shall be apportioned and borne as the judge or officer who tries the action may direct.

Costs where least expensive course not taken

(4) Where the least expensive course is not taken by a plaintiff, the costs allowed to him shall in no case exceed what would have been incurred if the least expensive course had been taken.

Cost of drawing and registering and vacating registration of lien

(5) Where a lien is discharged or vacated under section 25 or where judgment is given in favour of or against a claim for a lien, in addition to the costs of the action, the judge or officer who tries the action may allow a reasonable amount for the costs of drawing and registering the claim for lien or of vacating the registration thereof, but this does not apply where the claimant fails to establish a valid lien.

RULES OF PRACTICE

Rules of practice

46.—(1) The object of this Act being to enforce liens at the least expense, the procedure shall be as far as possible of a summary character, having regard to the amount and nature of the liens in question.

Interlocutory proceedings

(2) Except where otherwise provided by this Act, no interlocutory proceedings shall be permitted without the consent of the judge having jurisdiction to try the action or, in the Judicial District of York, the master, and then only upon proper proof that such proceedings are necessary.

Assistance of experts

(3) The judge or officer having jurisdiction to try the action may obtain the assistance of any merchant, accountant, actuary, building contractor, architect, engineer or person in such way as he deems fit, the better to enable him to determine any matter of fact in question, and may fix the remuneration of any such person and direct payment thereof by any of the parties.

Rules of practice

(4) Unless otherwise provided in this Act, the Rules of Practice and Procedure of the Supreme Court apply to proceedings under this Act.

SERVICE OF DOCUMENTS

Service of documents

47. Except where otherwise directed by the judge having jurisdiction to try the action or, in the Judicial District of York, the master, all documents relating to an action under this Act, other than statements of claim and notices of trial, are sufficiently served upon the intended recipient if sent by registered mail addressed to the intended recipient at his address for service.

LIENS ON CHATTELS

Right of chattel lienholder to sell chattel

48.—(1) Every person who has bestowed money, skill or materials upon any chattel or thing in the alteration of improvement of its properties or for the purpose of imparting an additional value to it, so as thereby to be entitled to a lien upon the chattel or thing for the amount or value of the money or skill and material bestowed, has, while the lien exists but not afterwards, in case the amount to which he is entitled remains unpaid for three months after it ought to have been paid, the right, in addition to any other remedy to which he may be entitled, to sell by auction the chattel or thing on giving one week's notice by advertisement in a newspaper having general circulation in the municipality in which the work was done, setting forth the name of the person indebted, the amount of the debt, a description of the chattel or thing to be sold, the time and place of sale, and the name of the auctioneer, and leaving a like notice in writing at the last known place of residence, if any, of the owner, if he is a resident of the municipality.

Application of proceeds

(2) Such person shall apply the proceeds of the sale in payment of the amount due to him and the costs of advertising and sale and shall upon application pay over any surplus to the person entitled thereto.

Regulations

49. The Lieutenant Governor in Council may make regulations,

    (a) prescribing forms and providing for their use;

    (b) providing for and requiring the posting of notices on building sites;

    (c) prescribing the appropriate offices of the Crown to which notice of a claim for lien must be sent. 1975, c. 43, s. 14, *re-enacted.*

REGULATIONS
UNDER THE MECHANICS' LIEN ACT
R.R.O. 1970, Regulation 575
As Amended by O.Reg. 849/75

1.—(1) Every claim for lien under subsection 1 of section 16 of the Act shall be in Form 1, 2 or 3.

(1*a*) Every notice of claim for lien under section 21*a* of the Act shall be in Form 1*a*, 2*a* or 3*a*, as the case may be. O. Reg. 849/75, s. 1 (1).

(2) The affidavit verifying the lien required by subsection 2 of section 16 or by subsection 8 of section 21*a* of the Act shall be in Form 4. O. Reg. 849/75, s. 1(2).

(3) Where a reference for trial is directed under subsection 2 of section 31 of the Act the Judgment shall be in form 5.

(4) Service of a notice in Form 1*a*, 2*a* or 3*a*, as the case may be, may be used as notice under subsection 5*a* of section 11 of the Act. O. Reg. 849/75, s. 1(3).

(5) Every notice of trial served under susection 2 of section 38 of the Act shall be in Form 6 or 6*a*, as the case may be. O. Reg. 849/75, s. 1(3).

(6) After the trial, the results thereof shall be embodied,
    (a) in the case of a Judge, in a judgment in Form 7 or 7*a*, as the case may be; and
    (b) in the case of a Master, in a Report in Form 8 or 9, as the case may be. O. Reg. 849/75, s. 1(3).

2. Every contractor on a public work shall display and keep d'splayed in a conspicuous place on the site of the work the following notice:

> This project is a public work. Any person who places or furnishes any materials, or does any work on or in respect of this project may be protected by *The Mechanics' Lien Act*. Notices of claim for lien must be sent to the following address: (here set out the name and address of the appropriate office of the Crown to which notice of a claim for lien must be sent, as provided by section 3 of this Regulation). O. Reg. 849/75, s. 2, *part*.

3. The appropriate office of the Crown to which notice of a claim for lien in respect of a public work must be sent is as follows:

1. Where the contract is with a Ministry of the Crown, the office of the Director of Legal Services of that Ministry.
2. Where the contract is with the Ontario Housing Corporation, the office of the Director of Legal Services of the Ministry of Housing.
3. Where the contract is with a college of applied arts and technology, the office of the president of the college.
4. Where the contract is with any other office of the Crown, the chief executive officer of the office. O. Reg. 849/75, s. 2, *part.*

FORM 1

THE MECHANICS' LIEN ACT

CLAIM FOR LIEN

A.B. (name of claimant) of (here state address for service of claimant), (if claimant is a personal representative or assignee set out the facts) under *The Mechanics' Lien Act* claims a lien upon the estate of (here state the name and address of the owner of the land upon which the lien is claimed) in the undermentioned land in respect of the following work (or service or materials) that is to say (here give a short description of the nature of the work done or to be done or service performed or to be performed or materials furnished or to be furnished and for which the lien is claimed).

The work or service was completed or the last material was furnished on the .... day of ...., 19 ....., or the work or service is to be completed or the material is to be furnished on or before the .... day of ...., 19 ....., and the name and address of the person for whom the work was done or service performed or material furnished is ....

The amount claimed as due (or to become due) is the sum of $...............

The following is the description of the land to be charged (here set out a concise description of the land to be charged sufficient for the purpose of registration).

(Where credit has been given, insert): The work was done (or services were performed or materials were furnished) on credit, and the period of credit agreed to expired (or will expire) on the .... day of ...., 19.....

Dated at ...., this .... day of ...., 19 .....

....
(signature of claimant)

O. Reg. 162/70, Form 1.

FORM 1a

THE MECHANICS' LIEN ACT

NOTICE OF CLAIM

A.B. (name of claimant) of (here state address for service of claimant) (if claimant is a personal representative or assignee set out the facts) hereby gives notice under sub-section 5a of section 11 and under section 21a of *The Mechanics' Lien Act* of a claim for a lien in respect of work done (or materials placed or furnished) for (here state name and address of person for whom the work was done or the materials were placed or furnished) in respect of a public work (or a municipal public street or highway) located at (here give the address or a description of the location of the land).

The following is a short description of the nature of the work done or to be done or service performed or to be performed or materials placed or furnished or to be placed or furnished:

The work (or service) was completed (or the last material was placed or furnished) on the .... day of ...., 19 ....., or the work or service is to be completed or the material is to be placed or furnished on the .... day of ...., 19 .....

The amount claimed as due (or to become due) is the sum of $............... (Where credit has been given, insert:) The work was done (or services were performed, or materials were placed or furnished) on credit, and the period of credit agreed to expired (or will expire) on the .... day of ...., 19 .....

Dated at .... this .... day of ...., 19.....

....
(signature of claimant)

NOTE: While this Form may be used as notice under subsection 5a of section 11 of the Act, it will only be effective where the owner, contractor or subcontractor, whom it is intended to bind, is given notice, O. Reg. 849/75, s. 3, *part.*

FORM 2

THE MECHANICS' LIEN ACT

CLAIM FOR LIEN FOR WAGES

A.B. (name of claimant) of (here state address for service of claimant), (if claimant is a personal representative or assignee set out the facts) under *The Mechanics' Lien Act,* claims a lien upon the estate of (here state the name and address of the owner of the land upon which the lien is claimed), in the undermentioned land in respect of work performed (or to be performed) thereon while in the employment of (here state the name and address of the person upon whose request the work was or is to be performed) on or before the .... day of ...., 19.....

The amount claimed as due is $............... for .... days wages.

The following is the description of the land to be charged (here set out a concise description

605

FORM 2

of the land to be charged sufficient for the purpose of registration).

Dated at ...., this .... day of ...., 19.....

....

(signature of claimant)

O. Reg. 162/70, Form 2.

FORM 2a

THE MECHANICS' LIEN ACT

NOTICE OF CLAIM FOR LIEN FOR WAGES

A.B. (name of claimant) of (here state address for service of claimant) (if claimant is a personal representative or assignee, set out the facts) hereby gives notice under sub-section 5*a* of section 11 and under section 21*a* of *The Mechanics' Lien Act* of a claim for lien for work done or to be done on or in respect of the undermentioned public work (or municipal public street or highway) while in the employment of (here set out the name and address of the person at whose request the work was done or is to be done).

The work was done on or before the .... day of ...., 19.....

The amount claimed as due is the sum of $............... for .... days wages.

The subject public work (or municipal street or highway) is located at (here give the address or a description of the location of the land upon or in respect of which the work was done).

Dated at .... this .... day of ...., 19.....

....

(signature of claimant)

NOTE: While this Form may be used as notice under subsection 5*a* of section 11 of the Act, it will only be effective where the owner, contractor or subcontractor, whom it is intended to bind, is given notice, O. Reg. 849/75, s. 3, part.

FORM 3

THE MECHANICS' LIEN ACT

CLAIM FOR LIEN FOR WAGES BY SEVERAL CLAIMANTS

The following persons claim a lien under *The Mechanics' Lien Act,* upon the estate of (here state the name and address of the owner of the land upon which the lien is claimed) in the undermentioned land in respect of wages for labour performed (or to be performed) thereon while in the employment of (here state name and address or names and address of employers of the several persons claiming the lien).

A.B. of (address for service) $............... for .... days wages for work done on or before the .... day of ...., 19.....

C.D. of (address for service) $............... for .... days wages for work done on or before the .... day of ...., 19.....

E.F. of (address for service) $............... for .... days wages for work done on or before the .... day of ...., 19.....

The following is the description of the land to be charged (here set out a concise description of the land to be charged sufficient for the purpose of registration).

Dated at ...., this .... day of ...., 19.....

(signatures of several claimants):

O. Reg. 162/70, Form 3.

FORM 3a

THE MECHANICS' LIEN ACT

NOTICE OF CLAIM FOR LIEN FOR WAGES BY SEVERAL CLAIMANTS

The following persons hereby give notice under subsection 5a of section 11 and under section 21a of *The Mechanics' Lien Act* of a claim for lien for work done on or in respect of the undermentioned public work (or municipal public street or highway) while in the employment of (here state the name and address or names and addresses of the employers of the several persons claiming the lien):

A.B. of (address for service), $............... for .... days wages for work done on or before the .... day of ...., 19.....

C.D. of (address for service), $............... for .... days wages for work done on or before the .... day of ...., 19.....

E.F. of (address for service), $............... for .... days wages for work done on or before the .... day of ...., 19.....

The subject public work (or municipal public street or highway) is located at (here give the address or a description of the location of the land or premises upon or in respect of which the work was done).

Dated at ...., this .... day of ...., 19.....

....

(signature of claimant)

....

(signature of claimant)

....

(signature of claimant)

NOTE: While this Form may be used as notice under subsection 5a of section 11 of the Act, it will only be effective where the owner, contractor or subcontractor, whom it is intended to bind, is given notice. O. Reg. 849/75, s. 3, *part.*

FORM 4

THE MECHANICS' LIEN ACT

AFFIDAVIT VERIFYING CLAIM

I, A.B., named in the above (or annexed) claim, make oath that the facts contained therein are true.

or, We, A.B. and C.D., named in the above (or annexed) claim, make oath and each for himself makes oath that the facts contained therein, so far as they relate to him, are true.

Where the affidavit is made by an agent or assignee a clause must be added to the following effect: — I have full knowledge of the facts set forth in the above (or annexed) claim.

Sworn before me at ...., in the .... of ...., this .... day of ...., 19 .....

Or, The said A.B. and C.D. were severally sworn before me at ...., in the .... of ...., this .... day of ...., 19 .....

O. Reg. 162/70, Form 4.

FORM 5

THE MECHANICS' LIEN ACT

JUDGMENT DIRECTING A REFERENCE FOR TRIAL

(Style of Cause)

Upon the application of the plaintiff made pursuant to the provisions of subsection 2 of section 31 of *The Mechanics' Lien Act,* in the presence of counsel for the plaintiff and the defendants, and upon reading the pleadings in this action and upon hearing what was alleged by counsel aforesaid, (and the parties by their counsel consenting thereto, or as the case may be).

1. THIS COURT DOTH ORDER AND ADJUDGE that this action be and the same is referred to the Master at Toronto for trial.

2. AND THIS COURT DOTH FURTHER ORDER AND ADJUDGE that the parties do recover the respective amounts found due by the Master from the parties found liable by the Master forthwith after comfirmation of the report of the Master.

3. AND THIS COURT DOTH FURTHER ORDER AND ADJUDGE that the Master do determine all questions arising in this action and on the reference, and that the findings of the Master respecting the matters so referred be effective upon the confirmation of the Master's report.

4. AND THIS COURT DOTH FURTHER ORDER that the Master do determine the question of costs in this action and of the reference, and that the costs be taxed and paid as the Master shall direct.

O. Reg. 162/70, Form 5.

FORM 6

THE MECHANICS' LIEN ACT

NOTICE OF TRIAL

(Style of Cause)

TAKE NOTICE that, pursuant to the Order of .... dated the .... day of ...., 19....., this action will be tried at the .... in the .... of ...., in the County (or District) of .... on the .... day of .... by .... and at such time and place the .... will proceed to try the action and all questions as provided by *The Mechanics' Lien Act*.

AND FURTHER TAKE NOTICE that if you do not appear at the trial and defend the action or prove your claim, if any, the proceedings will be taken in your absence and you may be deprived of all benefit of the proceedings and your rights disposed of in your absence.

AND FURTHER TAKE NOTICE that all parties and lien claimants shall bring with them on the day herein set for trial all mortgages, contracts, agreements, orders, cheques, notes, delivery slips, timebooks, books of account, diaries, duplicate original liens, and any other books or papers necessary to prove liens or defences. If any person fails to comply with these directions, the costs of the day may be given against him in the event that an adjournment is necessary for the production of any of the above-mentioned documentary evidence.

This is a Mechanics' Lien action brought by the above-named plaintiffs against the above-named defendants to enforce a Mechanics' Lien against the following lands: (set out description of lands).

This notice is served by, etc.

Dated .... , 19.....

To ....

O. Reg. 162/70, Form 6.

FORM 6a

THE MECHANICS' LIEN ACT

NOTICE OF TRIAL

(Style of Cause)

TAKE NOTICE that, pursuant to the Order of .... dated the .... day of ...., 19....., this action will be tried at the .... in the ..9........... of ...., in the County (or District) of .... on the .... day of .... by .... and at such time and place the .... will proceed to try the action and all questions as provided by *The Mechanics' Lien Act*.

AND FURTHER TAKE NOTICE that if you do not appear at the trial and defend the action or prove your claim, if any, the proceedings will be taken in your absence and you may be deprived of all benefit of the proceedings and your rights disposed of in your absence.

AND FURTHER TAKE NOTICE that all parties and lien claimants shall bring with them on the day herein set for trial all mortgages, contracts, agreements, orders, cheques, notes, delivery slips, time-books, books of account, diaries, and any other books or papers necessary to prove liens or defences. If any person fails to comply with these directions, the

609

costs of the day may be given against him in the event that an adjournment is necessary for the production of any of the above-mentioned documentary evidence.

This is a Mechanics' Lien action, brought by the above-named plaintiffs, against the above-named defendants, to enforce a mechanics' lien against the amounts required to be retained by section 11 of the Act in connection with the work done on the following lands (set out description of lands or otherwise identify work).

This notice is served by. etc.

Dated: .... , 19.....

To: ....

O. Reg. 849/75, s. 3, *part.*

FORM 7

THE MECHANICS' LIEN ACT

JUDGMENT

(Style of Cause)

This action coming on for trial before .... at .... upon opening of the matter and it appearing that the following persons have been duly served with notice of trial herein (set out names of all persons served with notice of trial) and all such persons (or as the case may be) appearing at the trial (or and the following persons not having appeared set out names of non-appearing persons) and upon hearing the evidence adduced and what was alleged by counsel for the plaintiff and for C.D. and E.F. and the defendant (or and by A.B. appearing in person).

1. THIS COURT DOTH DECLARE that the plaintiff and the several persons mentioned in Schedule 1 hereto are respectively entitled to a lien under *The Mechanics' Lien Act* upon the land described in Schedule 2 hereto for the amounts set opposite their respective names in the 2nd, 3rd and 4th columns of Schedule 1, and the persons primarily liable for the claims respectively are set forth in the 5th column of Schedule 1.

2. (AND THIS COURT DOTH FURTHER DECLARE that the several persons mentioned in Schedule 3 hereto are also entitled to some lien, charge or encumbrance upon such land for the amounts set opposite their respective names in the 4th column of Schedule 3, according to the facts.)

3. AND THIS COURT DOTH FURTHER ORDER AND ADJUDGE that upon the defendant (A.B., the owner) paying into Court to the credit of this action the sum of .... (gross amount of liens in Schedule 1 for which the owner is liable) on or before the .... day of .... next, that the liens mentioned in Schedule 1 be and the same are hereby discharged and the money so paid into Court is to be paid out in payment of the claims of the lienholders.

4. In case the defendant (owner) makes default in payment of the money into Court this Court doth order and adjudge that such land be sold with the approbation of the Master of this Court at .... and that the purchase money be paid into Court to the credit of this Action.

5. AND THIS COURT DOTH ORDER AND ADJUDGE that such purchase money be applied in or towards payment of the several claims mentioned in Schedule(s) 1 (and 3) as the Master shall direct, with subsequent interest and subsequent costs to be computed and taxed by the Master.

6. AND THIS COURT DOTH FURTHER ORDER AND ADJUDGE that in case such purchase money is insufficient to pay in full the claims of the several persons mentioned in Schedule 1, the persons primarily liable for such claim as shown in Schedule 1 do pay to the persons to whom they are respectively primarily liable the amount remaining due to such persons forthwith after the same has been ascertained by the Master.

7. (AND THIS COURT DOTH DECLARE that .... have not proved any lien under *The Mechanics' Lien Act,* and that they are not entitled to any such lien, and this Court doth order and adjudge that the claims of liens registered by them against the land mentioned in Schedule 2 be and the same are hereby discharged, according to the fact.)

SCHEDULE 1

Names of lien-holders entitled to mechanics' liens	Amount of debt and interest (if any)	Costs	Total	Names of primary debtors

....
(Signature of Officer)

SCHEDULE 2

The lands in question in this matter are (Set out a description sufficient for registration purposes).

....
(Signature of Officer)

SCHEDULE 3

Names of persons entitled to encumbrances other than mechanics' liens	Amount of debt and interest (if any)	Costs	Total

....
(Signature of Officer)

O. Reg. 162/70, Form 7.

FORM 7a
THE MECHANICS' LIEN ACT

JUDGMENT
(Style of Cause)

This action coming on for trial before .... at .... upon opening of the matter and it appearing that the following persons have been duly served with notice of trial herein (set out names of all persons served with notice of trial) and all such persons (or as the case may be) appearing at the trial (or, and the following persons not having appeared set out names of non-appearing persons) and upon hearing the evidence adduced and what was alleged by counsel for the plaintiff and for C.D. and E.F. and the defendant (or and by A.B. appearing in person).

1. THIS COURT DOTH DECLARE that amount required to be retained by the defendant A.B. (the owner) under section 11 of *The Mechanics' Lien Act* is the sum of $............................

2. THIS COURT DOTH FURTHER DECLARE that the plaintiff and the several persons mentioned in Column 1 of Schedule 1 hereto are respectively entitled to a lien under *The Mechanics' Lien Act* which lien is a charge on the amount required to be retained by section 11 of the Act for the amounts set opposite their respective names in columns 2, 3 and 4 of the said Schedule 1 and the person primarily liable is set forth in Column 6 of Schedule 1.

3. AND THIS COURT DOTH FURTHER ORDER AND ADJUDGE that upon the defendant A.B. (the owner) paying into Court to the credit of this action the sum of $............................ (gross amount of liens in Schedule 1 for which the owner is liable) on or before the .... day of .... next, that the liens mentioned in Schedule 1 be and the same are hereby discharged and the money so paid into Court is to be paid out to the plaintiff and the several persons mentioned in Column 1 of Schedule 1 in accordance with Column 5 of Schedule 1.

4. AND THIS COURT DOTH FURTHER ORDER AND ADJUDGE that in case the amounts required to be retained by section 11 of *The Mechanics' Lien Act* are insufficient to pay in full the claims of the several persons mentioned in Schedule 1, the persons primarily liable for such claim as shown in Column 6 of Schedule 1 do pay to the persons to whom they are respectively primarily liable the amount remaining due to such persons forthwith after the same has been ascertained.

5. AND THIS COURT DOTH DECLARE that .... have not proved any lien under *The Mechanics' Lien,* and that they are not entitled to any such lien.

O. Reg. 849/75, s. 3, *part.*

FORM 8
THE MECHANICS' LIEN ACT

REPORT
(Style of Cause)

Pursuant to the judgment of reference herein dated .... and it appearing that the following persons have been duly served with notice of trial herein (set out names of all persons served with notice of trial) I was attended by counsel for the plaintiff and for .... no one appearing for .... although duly notified as aforesaid (or as the case may be) and upon hearing the evidence adduced and what was alleged by counsel for the plaintiff and for C.D. and E.F. and the defendant (or and by A.B. appearing in person).

1. I find that the plaintiff and the several persons mentioned in Schedule 1 hereto are respectively entitled to a lien under *The Mechanics' Lien Act* upon the land described in Schedule 2 hereto for the amounts set opposite their respective names in the second, third and fourth columns of Schedule 1, and the persons primarily liable for the claims respectively are set forth in the fifth column of Schedule 1.

2. (And I find that the several persons mentioned in Schedule 3 hereto are also entitled to some lien, charge or encumbrance upon the land for the amounts set opposite their respective names in the fourth column of Schedule 3, according to the facts.)

3. And I direct that upon the defendant (A.B. the owner) paying into Court to the credit of this action the sum of $.................... (gross amount of liens in Schedule 1 for which the owner is liable) on or before the .... day of .... next, that the liens in Schedule 1 mentioned be and the same are hereby discharged and the money so paid into court is to be paid out in payment of the claims of the lienholders.

4. In case the defendant (owner) makes default in payment of the money into Court, I direct that the land be sold with the approbation of the Master of this Court at .... and that the purchase money be paid into Court to the credit of this action.

5. And I direct that the purchase money be applied in or towards payment of the several claims mentioned in Schedule(s) 1 (and 3) as the Master shall direct with subsequent interest and subsequent costs to be computed and taxed by the Master.

6. And I direct that in case the purchase money is insufficient to pay in full the claims of the several persons mentioned in Schedule 1, the persons primarily liable for such claim as shown in Schedule 1 do pay to the persons to whom they are respectively primarily liable the amount remaining due to such persons forthwith after the same shall have been ascertained by the Master.

7. (And I find and declare that .... have not proved any lien under *The Mechanics' Lien Act* and that they are not entitled to any such lien, and I direct that the claims of liens registered by them against the land mentioned in Schedule 2 be and the same are hereby discharged, according to the fact.)

SCHEDULE 1

Names of lien-holders entitled to mechanics' liens	Amount of debt and interest (if any)	Costs	Total	Names of primary debtors

....
(Signature of Officer)

613

FORM 8

SCHEDULE 2

The lands in question in this matter are (Set out a description sufficient for registration purposes).

....
(Signature of Officer)

SCHEDULE 3

Names of persons entitled to encumbrances other than mechanics' liens	Amount of debt and interest (if any)	Costs	Total

....
(Signature of Officer)

O. Reg. 162/70, Form 8.

FORM 9

THE MECHANICS' LIEN ACT

REPORT

(Style of Cause)

Pursuant to the judgment of reference herein dated .... and it appearing that the following persons have been duly served with notice of trial herein (set out names of all persons served with notice of trial) I was attended by counsel for the plaintiff and for .... no one appearing for .... although duly notified as aforesaid (or as the case may be) and upon hearing the evidence adduced and what was alleged by counsel for the plaintiff and for C.D. and E.F. and the defendant (or and by A.B. appearing in person).

1. I find and declare that amount required to be retained by the defendant A.B. (the owner) under section 11 of *The Mechanics' Lien Act* is the sum of $............................

2. I find and declare that the plaintiff and the several persons mentioned in Column 1 of Schedule 1 hereto are respectively entitled to a lien under *The Mechanics' Lien Act* which lien is a charge on the amount required to be retained by section 11 of the Act for the amounts set opposite their respective names in columns 2, 3 and 4 of Schedule 1 and the person primarily liable is set forth in Column 6 of Schedule 1.

3. And I direct that upon the defendant A.B. (the owner) paying into Court to the credit of this action the sum of $................................... (gross amount of liens in Schedule 1 for which the owner is liable on or before the .... day of .... next, that the liens mentioned in Schedule 1 be and the same are hereby discharged and the money so paid into

614

Court is to be paid out to the plaintiff and the several persons mentioned in Column 1 of Schedule 1 in accordance with Column 5 of Schedule 1.

4. And I direct that in case the amounts required to be retained by section 11 of *The Mechanics' Lien Act* are insufficient to pay in full the claims of the several persons mentioned in Schedule 1, the persons primarily liable for such claim as shown in Column 6 of Schedule 1 do pay to the persons to whom they are respectively primarily liable the amount remaining due to such persons forthwith after the same has been ascertained.

5. And I find and declare that .... have not proved any lien under *The Mechanics' Lien Act,* and that they are not entitled to any such lien.

SCHEDULE 1

Names of lienholders entitled to mechanics' liens	Amount of debt and interest (if any)	Costs	Total	Prorated Share	Persons Primarily Liable

....
(Signature of Officer)

O. Reg. 849/75, s. 3, *part.*

615

GENERAL INDEX

618

623

625

INDEX OF FORMS